Beyond Nature and Culture

Beyond Nature and Culture

PHILIPPE DESCOLA

Translated by Janet Lloyd

Foreword by Marshall Sahlins

The University of Chicago Press
Chicago and London

The University of Chicago Press, Chicago 60637
The University of Chicago Press, Ltd., London
© 2013 by The University of Chicago
All rights reserved. Published 2013.
Paperback edition 2014.
Printed in the United States of America

21 20 19 18 17 16 15 14   3 4 5 6 7

ISBN-13: 978-0-226-14445-0 (cloth)
ISBN-13: 978-0-226-21236-4 (paper)
ISBN-13: 978-0-226-14500-6 (e-book)
DOI: 10.7208/chicago/9780226145006.001.0001

Originally published as Philippe Descola, *Par-delà nature et culture* (Paris: Éditions
Gallimard, 2005). © Éditions Gallimard, Paris, 2005.
Cet ouvrage a bénéficié du soutien des Programmes d'aide à la publication de
l' Institut Français.
This work, published as part of a program of aid for publication, received support
from the French Institute.
This work, published as part of a program providing publication assistance, received
financial support from the French Ministry of Foreign Affairs, the Cultural Services
of the French Embassy in the United States, and FACE (French American Cultural
Exchange).
Ouvrage publié avec le soutien du Centre national du livre, ministère français chargé
de la culture.
This work is published with support from the National Center of the Book, French
Ministry of Culture.

Library of Congress Cataloging-in-Publication Data

Descola, Philippe, author.
  [Par-delà nature et culture. English]
  Beyond nature and culture / Philippe Descola ; translated by Janet Lloyd.
      pages cm
  "Originally published as Philippe Descola, Par-delà nature et culture (Paris:
Éditions Gallimard, 2005). © Éditions Gallimard, Paris, 2005"—title page verso.
  Includes bibliographical references and index.
  ISBN 978-0-226-14445-0 (cloth : alkaline paper) 1. Philosophy of nature.
2. Human ecology. I. Lloyd, Janet (Translator), translator. II. Title.
  BD581.D3813 2013
  304.2—dc23

                            2012036975

♾ This paper meets the requirements of ANSI/NISO Z39.48-1992 (Permanence
of Paper).

For Léonore and Emmanuel

Contents

v   An Ecology of Relations

Foreword

Just when many thought anthropology was losing its focus, parallel to the disruptive effects of global capitalism on the cultural integrity of the peoples it traditionally studied, along came this remarkable work by Philippe Descola offering a novel theoretical armature of ontological dimensions and universal proportions for knowing the varieties of the human condition. It had seemed that Claude Lévi-Strauss, the founder of Professor Descola's chair at the Collège de France, was the last of the Big-Time Thinkers of the discipline, the likes of the long gone and increasingly forgotten anthropological forebears such as E. B. Tylor, Lewis Henry Morgan, James Frazer, A. R. Radcliffe-Brown, Ruth Benedict, and A. L. Kroeber. These were scholars of wide ethnographic knowledge who could rise to the famous challenge of *sapere aude* by proposing comparative generalizations of large geographic scale and corresponding intellectual ambition. All that seemed history until *Beyond Nature and Culture*, whose title, by its intention of relativizing and transcending the fundamental Western opposition of nature and culture, already announced the scope of the author's project. Indeed Professor Descola marshals not only an all-continent ethnography but a broad philosophical erudition in which, since we of the West are also one of the Others, the likes of Plato, Aristotle, Leibniz, Spinoza, or Foucault sometimes appear in the capacity of natives rather than scholarly interlocutors. In the French homeland of the Enlightenment, however, this grand intellectual synthesis may not seem as extraordinary and unanticipated as it does on the North American scene upon which it now appears.

It is necessary to summarily set that scene in order to appreciate the innovative import of Professor Descola's work. The large increase in the number of North American anthropologists since the 1950s has been matched by their

interest in increasingly varied and arcane cultural singularities. Just so, in the
last couple of years juried articles have appeared in prestigious American
anthropological journals on the gourmandization of hummus in Israel, the
biopolitics of the US war on fat, pyramid schemes in postsocialist Albania,
spatiality in Brazilian hip-hop and community radio, the occupy movement
in Žižek's hometown, and new uses of the honeybee. We have also learned
from studies of faith and authority in a Jordanian high school, deception and
intimacy in Greek psychiatry, campus sustainable food projects, the response
of religious Israeli women to the 2006 Lebanese war, local brands of pig farming in North Carolina, and postsocialist migration and slow coffee in northwest Chicago. (As I listened to an anthropological lecture recently on customs
officers in Ghana, the thought flashed across my mind that we used to study
customs in Ghana.) It is as if anthropology had reverted to the ontology that
Professor Descola calls "analogical" and of which Europe in the Middle Ages
and the Renaissance was a prime site. It was a world of minimal differences
among the plenitude of existing things, human and nonhuman, whose potentially chaotic fragmentation could be reduced by powerful hierarchical
principles such as the Great Chain of Being, but whose diversity lent itself
to ad hoc discoveries of resemblance and difference between phenomena of
disparate character and register. Using walnuts to cure migraines on the sup-
position that the similarity between the former and the human brain amounts
to a signature left by God at the moment of the creation seems as closely
motivated as the current functionalist attributions of diverse anthropological
minutiae to such totalized circumstances as hegemonic power or neoliberal
capitalism. Still, the cultural flotsam left in the wake of the postmodern deconstruction could hardly find any other explication than the global domination of capitalism, as this was the only "totalized narrative" that somehow
escaped the antistructural terror. Otherwise, the critique of essentialized categories and relations in favor of such popular notions as contested discourses
and permeable boundaries made indeterminacy the preferred conclusion of
cultural investigation. Certain politico-academic tendencies, moreover, abet-
ted the epistemological anarchy, both from the right and the left: neoliber-
alism, with its privileging of individualism and its hostility toward collective order in general; and the various emancipatory movements contending
against racism, gender inequality, homophobia, and third-world oppression,
for which the dominant structures were justifiably the enemy. In sum, we are
passing through an antistructural age.

   Beyond Nature and Culture offers a radical change in the current anthropological trajectory—a paradigm shift, if you will—that would overcome the
present analytical disarray by what amounts to a planetary table of the onto-

logical elements and the compounds they produce. (The chemical metaphor is the author's own preference.) The project is a comparative anthropology of ontology. Four basic ontological regimes of wide distribution—animism, totemism, analogism, and naturalism—are developed from an investigation of the identities and differences between humans and other beings and things in matters of their physical makeup and subjective or mental capacities. Each of these major ontologies is associated with specific ways of forming social collectives and characteristic moralities, as well as distinctive modes of knowing what there is. Further, the major ontological configurations are cross-cut by several types of relationship—exchange, predation, production, and so on—that are variously compatible or incompatible with them. Such is the general architecture. To thus state it, however, only betrays the richness of the text, which is marked by carefully described and analyzed ethnographic demonstrations, including much from the author's own fieldwork among the Achuar of Amazonia. Nor can this bare description convey the fertile promise of Professor Descola's project. Since the original appearance of the book, for example, he mounted a presentation of the four regimes in the form of visual images in an impressive installation at the Musée du quai Branly (Paris). Yet perhaps something of the innovative character of *Beyond Nature and Culture* can be expressed here by following the implications of Professor Descola's denial of the universal relevance of our own sense of nature and its supposed antithesis to culture, which he dates rather to the seventeenth-century triumph of naturalism in the West. What, for instance, could our notion of the "supernatural" mean for peoples who have no such sense of a "natural" realm composed of mindless, nonhuman realia subject only to their own laws? In effect, Professor Descola stakes out the neo-Copernican claim that other people's worlds do not revolve around ours.

Instead, the good anthropology revolves around theirs. For this, however, something more is entailed than the rectification of names. Consider the theoretical consequences of the luminous pages that Professor Descola devotes to our notion of "production" by comparison to peoples whose animist worlds are populated by plants, animals, and others things (or rather, subjects) with souls, consciousness, language, and culture just like their own—in other words, persons like themselves. By our naturalistic sense of things, production is, as he says, a "heroic model of creation" involving the imposition of form upon inert matter by an autonomous subject, whether god or mortal, who commands the process by a preestablished plan and purpose. This scheme of action is a combination of an ingrained individualism and a naturalistic materialism. It rests on two interdependent premises: "the preponderance of an individualized intentional agent as the cause of the coming-to-be of beings and things, and the radical difference between the ontological status of the creator and that of whatever he produces." Moreover, it is not only Marxists among us who theorize production as the major determining condition of social order and the dynamic force of historical change. Nor do we confine the idea to economic matters or relations to nature since we also "produce" children, art, knowledge, institutions, and more. But for the Achuar of Amazonia, plants are the children of the women who nurture them, and animals are the brothers-in-law of the men who hunt them. Here hunting is a social relationship where by means of reciprocating, cajoling, beguiling, nurturing, seducing, respecting, promising, or otherwise negotiating, the hunter induces the animal cum affinal-other to provide for his people's existence. In this regard of obtaining life from the outside, hunting is indeed like marriage, and all the more so since only the flesh of the animal is obtained by the hunter, even as the latter's respectful treatment preserves the soul of the brother-in-law animal, allowing him to give birth to another of the species. (Then again, is not gaining a wife and children like hunting, since often in Amazonia they are acquired by raiding other groups?) Such is the anthropological fertility issuing from thought that is not restricted to material productivity. Although Professor Descola's large comparative scheme, on the model of the great old-timers, might seem to some a case of the owl of Minerva taking wing at dusk, a strong argument can be made that it is rather Chanteclair, *le coq gaulois*, heralding forth a new anthropological dawn.

A word too about Janet Lloyd's excellent translation. It not only manages to make clear Professor Descola's sometimes complex thought, it also by some magic preserves his elegant Gallic voice in a stylish English prose.

Marshall Sahlins

Preface

Anyone who took careful note of the everyday animals we see living among us would find them doing things just as astonishing as the examples we gather from far-off times and places. Nature is One and constant in her course.

MONTAIGNE, "An Apology for Raymond Sebond"

Not so very long ago one could delight in the curiosities of the world without making any distinction between the information obtained from observing animals and that which the mores of antiquity or the customs of distant lands presented. "Nature was one" and reigned everywhere, distributing equally among humans and nonhumans a multitude of technical skills, ways of life, and modes of reasoning. Among the educated at least, that age came to an end a few decades after Montaigne's death, when nature ceased to be a unifying arrangement of things, however disparate, and became a domain of objects that were subject to autonomous laws that formed a background against which the arbitrariness of human activities could exert its many-faceted fascination. A new cosmology had emerged, a prodigious collective invention that provided an unprecedented framework for the development of scientific thought and that we, at the beginning of the twenty-first century, continue, in a rather offhand way, to protect. The price to be paid for that simplification included one aspect that it has been possible to overlook, given that we have not been made to account for it: while the Moderns were discovering the lazy propensity of barbaric and savage peoples to judge everything according to their own particular norms, they were masking their own ethnocentricity behind a rational approach to knowledge, the errors of which at that time escaped notice. It was claimed that everywhere and in every age, an unchanging mute and impersonal nature established its grip, a nature that human beings strove to interpret more or less plausibly and from which they endeavored to profit, with varying degrees of success. Their widely diverse conventions and customs could now make sense only if they were related to natural regularities that were more or less well understood by those affected by them. It was decreed, but with exemplary discretion, that our way of dividing up beings and things was a norm to which there were no exceptions. Carrying forward the work of philosophy, of whose predominance it was perhaps somewhat envious, the fledgling discipline of anthropology ratified the reduction of the multitude of existing things to two heterogeneous orders of reality and, on the strength of a plethora of facts gathered from every latitude, even bestowed upon that reduction the guarantee of universality that it still lacked. Almost without noticing, anthropology committed itself to this way of proceeding, such was the fascination exerted by the shimmering vision of "cultural diversity," the listing and study of which now provided it with its raison d'être. The profusion of institutions and modes of thought was rendered less formidable and its contingency more bearable if one took the view that all these practices—the logic of which was sometimes so hard to discover—constituted so many singular responses to a universal challenge: namely, that of disciplining and profiting from the biophysical potentialities offered by bodies and their environment. The present book was prompted by a sense of dissatisfaction with this state of affairs and a desire to remedy it by proposing an alternative approach to the relations between nature and society.

For such an undertaking, the circumstances are now favorable—for the vast construction with two superimposed levels that we have taken for granted for the past few centuries is now proving somewhat uncomfortable. Once the representatives of revealed religion had been ejected from the salons of polite society, the natural and life sciences set the tone on the subject of what can be known about the world. However, a number of tactless deserters are discovering, concealed behind the hangings and paneling, the hidden mechanisms that have been making it possible to seize upon the phenomena of the physical world, sift through them, and pronounce authoritatively upon them. If one imagines that to discuss culture one has to move to an upper floor, one might say that the staircase, always tricky to negotiate because it is so steep, has become so rickety that few are prepared to climb it in order to announce to the peoples of the world the material basis of their collective existence; nor are they foolhardy enough to descend it in order to present the scholars below with the contradictions presented by the social body. One might imagine different cultures occupying the multitude of little rooms from which various bizarre beliefs are seeping down to the ground floor: fragments of Eastern philosophy, remnants of hermetic Gnosticism, or multifaceted New Age systems, none of them very serious but liable, here or there, to weaken the barriers that have been constructed to separate humans from nonhumans—barriers that were believed to be better protected. As for the researchers sent out to the four corners of the planet in order to describe houses with more primitive designs than our own, who for a long time strove to itemize them according to the statutory plan that was familiar to them: they are now bringing back all kinds of information of a more unexpected nature. They tell us that some houses have no upper floors and in these nature and culture cohabit without difficulty in a single room; other houses do appear to have several stories, but these have strangely allotted functions, in such a way that science may bed down with superstition, political power may be inspired by canons of what is beautiful, and macrocosms and microcosms are in intimate dialogue. They even tell us that there are peoples with no houses at all, nor any stables or gardens, who feel scant inclination to cultivate a clearing to accommodate Being or to settle on an explicit plan to domesticate whatever is natural within them and around them. The two-story edifice of dualism, built to last by the great architects of the classical age, is, to be sure, still solid, for it is subject to constant restoration inspired by well-tried know-how. However, its structural faults are becoming increasingly apparent to those who do not take up residence there in a mechanical fashion and to those who would prefer to find lodgings that can accommodate peoples who are accustomed to different kinds of dwellings.

Nevertheless, the pages that follow will not provide any architectural plan for a new communal house that would be more accommodating to nonmodern cosmologies and better adapted to the circulation of facts and values. Yet it is reasonable to wager that the time is not far off when such a conceptual construction will begin to rise from the ground, even if it is as yet unclear who will take charge of the building site. For although it is commonly said, these days, that worlds are constructed, it is not known who are their architects and we still have very little idea about what materials are used in building them. In any case, such a building site would have to be the responsibility of any inhabitants of the current house who find themselves too cramped there, rather than of any discipline in particular, anthropology included.[1] As I see it, anthropology's mission is to attempt, alongside other sciences but using its own methods, to render intelligible the way in which organisms of a particular kind find a place in the world, acquire a stable representation of it, and contribute to its transformation by forging with it and between one another links either constant or occasional and of a remarkable but not infinite diversity. Before constructing a new charter for the future in gestation, we need first to map out those links, understand their nature more clearly, establish their modes of compatibility and incompatibility, and examine how they take shape in their patently distinctive ways of being in the world. If such an undertaking is to be successful, anthropology must shed its essential dualism and become fully monistic, not in the quasi-religious sense of the term promulgated by Haeckel and subsequently taken over by certain environmental philosophies, nor, of course, with a view to reducing the plurality of existing entities to a unity of substance, finality, and truth, as certain nineteenth-century philosophers attempted to do. Rather, our object must be to make it clear that the project of understanding the relations that human beings establish between one another and with nonhumans cannot be based upon a cosmology and an ontology that are as closely bound as ours are to one particular context. To this end, we need first to show that the opposition between nature and culture is not as universal as it is claimed to be. Not only does it make no sense to anyone except the Moderns, but moreover it appeared only at a late date in the course of the development of Western thought itself, in which its consequences made a singularly forceful impact on the manner in which anthropology has envisaged both its object and its methods.

Part I of this book will be devoted to this preliminary clarification. But it is not enough simply to underline the historical contingency and misleading effects of that opposition. It is also important to integrate it into a new analytic field within which modern naturalism, far from constituting the yardstick by which cultures distant in both time and space are judged, is but one of the possible expressions of the more general schemas that govern the objectivization of the world and of others. The task that I have set myself in the present work is to specify the nature of those schemas, elucidate the rules that govern their composition, and work out a typology of their organization.

In prioritizing a combinatory analysis of the modes of relations between existing entities, I found myself obliged to defer any study of their evolution: this was a choice of method rather than an ad hoc one. Quite apart from the fact that by trying to combine the evolutionary and the analytic tasks I would have far exceeded the reasonable dimensions of the present work, I am convinced that the origin of a system cannot be analyzed until its specific structure has been brought to light. That was a way of proceeding upon which Marx conferred legitimacy when he examined the genesis of forms of capitalist production and famously summed it up as follows: "The anatomy of the human being is the key to the anatomy of the ape."[2] In opposition to historicism and the naive faith that it places in explanations based on antecedent causes, we should emphatically remind ourselves that only knowledge of the structure of any phenomenon can make it possible to inquire relevantly into its origins. For Marx, a critical theory of the categories of political economy had necessarily to precede any inquiry into the order of appearance of the phenomena that those categories set out to distinguish. In just the same way, a genealogy of the constitutive elements of different ways of relating to the world and to others would be impossible to establish before first identifying the stable forms in which those elements are combined. Such an approach is not unhistorical. It remains faithful to Marc Bloch's recommendation to pay full attention to retrospective history: in other words, to concentrate first on the present the better to interpret the past.[3] Admittedly, what I mean by the "present" in what follows will often be ad hoc and diverse. Because of the diversity of the materials used, the unevenness of the sources available, and the need to refer to societies in a past state, the "present" will be more of an ethnographic present than a contemporary one: a kind of snapshot focused on a collectivity at one particular moment in its development, when it presented an exemplary paradigm for comparison: in other words, an "ideal type."

No doubt some will reckon that the project of setting to work on a monistic anthropology is extravagantly ambitious, given the great difficulties to be overcome and the profusion of materials to be considered. But readers should regard this book as, literally, an essay, in the sense of an attempt, a way of ascertaining that such a procedure is not only possible but also better suited for its purpose than procedures tried out in the past. As will by now be understood, my purpose is to find a way of envisaging the bases and consequences of otherness that will, it is hoped, be fully respectful of the diversity of forms in which things and the way they are used appear to our eyes. For it is time for anthropology to do justice to the generous movement that caused it to bloom by casting upon the world a more ingenuous eye, or at least one free of the dualist veil, which the evolution of industrialized societies has partly rendered outmoded and which has been the cause of many distortions in our apprehension of cosmologies very different from our own. These were reputed to be enigmatic and therefore deserving of scholarly attention, given that, in them, the demarcations between human beings and "natural objects" seemed blurred or even nonexistent. That was a logical scandal that had to be brought to an end. But what was scarcely noticed was the fact that that frontier was hardly any clearer among ourselves, despite all the epistemological apparatus mobilized to ensure that it was impermeable. Fortunately, that situation is changing, and it is now hard to act as if nonhumans are not everywhere at the very heart of social life, whether they take the form of a monkey with which one communicates in one's laboratory, the soul of a yam that visits the dreams of its cultivator, an electronic adversary to be beaten at chess, or an ox that is treated as the substitute for a person in some ceremonial rite. We must draw the consequences from all this. An analysis of the interactions between the world's inhabitants can no longer be limited to the sector made up of the institutions that govern the lives of human beings, as if all that is decreed to be external to these is nothing more than a disorderly conglomeration of objects lacking meaning or utility. Many so-called primitive societies invite us to overstep that demarcation line—societies that have never imagined that the frontiers of humanity extended no farther than the human race and that have no hesitation in inviting into their shared social life even the most humble of plants and the most insignificant of animals. Anthropology is thus faced with a daunting challenge: either to disappear as an exhausted form of humanism or else to transform itself by rethinking its domain and its tools in such a way as to include in its object far more than the *anthropos*: that is to say, the entire collective of beings that is linked to him but is at present relegated to the position of a merely peripheral role; or, to put that in more conventional terms, the anthropology of culture must be accompanied by an anthropology of nature that is open to that part of themselves and the world that human beings actualize and by means of which they objectivize themselves.

Acknowledgments

In an adventure such as the one that has resulted in this book, an author incurs so many debts that it is not possible to give all those to whom one has become obliged their rightful due. At the risk of seeming ungrateful, I have therefore chosen to be parsimonious with my thanks. As readers will note, the Achuar Indians initially propelled me on this journey that has led me to question earlier certainties. Other peoples, in Amazonia or elsewhere, would no doubt have done the same, but it was while living with the Achuar that my questions took shape, and my gratitude goes to them for that wake-up call. Although Claude Lévi-Strauss's influence on me took many forms, he stands alongside the Achuar because it was he who directed the ethnological thesis that I devoted to them, and it was his work that introduced me to the questions that I would raise in connection with them. If I have disagreed in this book with the details of some of his analyses, it was, I hope, the better to remain faithful to the spirit of his method and to the mission of anthropology as he himself defined it. Without his inspiration and example, none of what I have done would have been possible. It is now almost ten years since I began discussing the ideas and hypotheses put forward in these pages with Anne Christine Taylor, Eduardo Viveiros de Castro, and Bruno Latour, recasting them in the light of their knowledgeable remarks and filling them out with increased substance and assurance, thanks to all that I borrowed from their texts and our conversations. My debt to them is considerable but not burdensome, so generous are they in belittling it. In the case of Tim Ingold, I have profited not so much from our discussions but rather from the profound intuitions that fill his publications and the relevant criticisms that they contain of some of my own propositions. If I, in turn, have sometimes criticized him in these pages, that is because our points of view are sometimes so close that the detail of what separates us comes to acquire a decisive importance. My colleagues and friends in the research group that I direct at the Labora-toire d'anthropologie sociale in the Collège de France have listened to and discussed my oral presentations of several parts of the book. They include Michael Houseman, Frédéric Joulian, Dimitri Karadimas, Gérard Lenclud, Marika Moisseeff, France-Marie Renard-Casevitz, Carlo Severi, Alexandre Surallés, Wiktor Stoczkowski, and Noëllie Vialles. I thank them all for their remarks and comments and ask them to forgive me if I have not always taken them into account. Before becoming the subject of my teaching at the Col-lège de France from 2002 to 2004, the themes developed in this book were in part tackled in the course of my seminars at the École des hautes études en sciences sociales and also in various teaching courses at foreign universities, notably in Chicago, Rio de Janeiro, Buenos Aires, Louvain, and the London School of Economics. In all these places, my listeners' questions and their requests for clarification greatly helped me to formulate my ideas better and render them fit to be expressed publicly. Finally, I should like in particular to thank Bruno Latour and Anne Christine Taylor, who read my manuscript and whose judicious remarks enabled me to make it more legible.

PART ONE

Trompe l'Oeil Nature

Any attempt to demonstrate that nature exists would be absurd; for, manifestly, there are many natural beings.

ARISTOTLE, *Physics* 193A3–4

Vi que não há Natureza
Que Natureza não existe,
Que há montes, vales, planícies,
Que há árvores, flores, ervas,
Que há rios e pedras,
Mas que não há um todoa que isso pertença,
Que um conjunto real e verdadeiro
E uma doença das nossas ideias.

A Natureza é partes sem um todo
Isto é talvez o tal mistério de que falam.

I saw that there was no Nature,
That Nature does not exist,
That there are mountains, valleys, plains,
That there are trees, flowers, grasses,
That there are streams and stones,
But that there's not a whole to which this belongs,
That a real and true ensemble
Is a disease of our ideas.

Nature is parts without a whole.
This perhaps is that mystery they speak of.

Fernando Pessoa, *Poemas de Alberto Caeiro*

Configurations of Continuity

It was in the lower reaches of the Kapawi, a silt-laden river in upper Amazonia, that I began to question how self-evident the notion of nature is. Yet
nothing in particular distinguished Chumpi's house from other habitat sites
that I had earlier visited in this region of the borderlands between Ecuador
and Peru. As was the Achuar custom, the dwelling roofed by palms was set
in the middle of a clearing mostly covered by manioc plants and bordered
on one side by the rushing river. A few steps across the garden brought one
to the edge of the forest, a dark wall of tall trees encircling the paler border of banana trees. The Kapawi was the only way out from this horizonless
circular space. It was a tortuous and interminable route and it had taken a
daylong journey to reach Chumpi's house from a similar clearing inhabited
by his closest neighbors. In between lay tens of thousands of hectares of trees,
moss, and bracken, dozens of millions of flies, ants, and mosquitoes, herds of
peccaries, troops of monkeys, macaws and toucans, and maybe a jaguar or
two: in short a vast nonhuman proliferation of forms and beings left to live
independently according to their own laws of cohabitation. Around midaft-
ernoon, Chumpi's wife, Metekash, was bitten by a snake as she emptied the
kitchen waste into the undergrowth overlooking the river. Dashing toward
us, her eyes wide with pain and terror, she shrieked, "A lancehead [the name
of this snake], a lancehead! I'm dead, I'm dead!" The whole household took
up the cry, "A lancehead, a lancehead! It has killed her, killed her!" I injected
Metekash with a serum and she went to rest in a small confinement hut of
the kind customarily erected in such circumstances. Such an accident was
not uncommon in this region, especially in the course of tree felling, and the
Achuar were resigned, with a kind of fatalism, to the possibility of a mortal

outcome. All the same, it was, apparently, unusual for a lancehead snake to venture so close to a house.

Chumpi seemed as distressed as his wife. Seated on his sculpted wooden stool, his face furious and upset, he was muttering in a monologue in which I eventually became involved. No, Metekash's snakebite did not result purely from chance; it was vengeance sent by Jurijri, one of the "mothers of game" who watch over the destinies of the forest animals. After a long period when his only means of hunting had been a blowpipe, my host, by dint of bartering, had eventually managed to lay his hands on a shotgun, and using this shotgun, he had, on the previous day, effected a massacre of woolly monkeys. No doubt dazzled by the power of his weapon, he had fired at random into the group, killing three or four animals and wounding several more. He had brought home only three monkeys, leaving one mortally wounded, lodged in the bifurcation of a large branch. Some of the fleeing monkeys, peppered by shot, were now suffering helplessly or might already have expired before being able to consult their monkey-shaman. By killing, almost wantonly, more animals than were necessary to provide for his family and by not bothering about the fate of those that he had wounded, Chumpi had transgressed the hunters' ethic and had broken the implicit agreement that linked the Achuar people with the spirits that protected game. Prompt reprisals had duly followed.

Endeavoring, somewhat clumsily, to dissipate the guilt that was troubling my host, I pointed out that the harpy eagle and the jaguar have no qualms about killing monkeys, that life depends on hunting, and that, in the forest, every creature ends up as food for another. But, clearly, I had not understood at all.

> Woolly monkeys, toucans, howler monkeys—all the creatures that we kill in order to eat—are persons, just as we are. The jaguar is likewise a person, but is a solitary killer that respects nothing. We, the "complete persons," must respect those that we kill in the forest, for they are, as it were, our relatives by marriage. They live together among their own relatives; nothing they do is by chance; they talk among themselves; they listen to what we say; they intermarry in a proper fashion. In vendettas, we too kill relatives by marriage, but they are still relatives. They too can wish to kill us. Likewise with woolly monkeys: we kill them for food, but they are still relatives.

The innermost convictions that an anthropologist forges regarding the nature of social life and the human condition often result from a very particular ethnographic experience acquired while living among a few thousand individuals who have managed to instill in him doubts so deep concerning what he had previously taken for granted that his entire energy is then devoted to analyzing them in a systematic fashion. That is what happened in my own case when, as time passed and after many conversations with the Achuar, the ways in which they were related to natural beings gradually became clearer.[1] These Indians living on both sides of the frontier between Ecuador and Peru differ little from the other tribes that make up the Jivaro group, to whom they are linked through both their language and their culture, when they declare that most plants and animals possess a soul (*wakan*) similar to that of humans. This constitutes a faculty that classifies them as "persons" (*aents*) in that it provides them with a reflexive awareness and intentionality that enable them to experience emotions and exchange messages with both their peers and also members of other species, including humans. This extralinguistic communication is made possible by the recognized ability of a *wakan* soundlessly to convey thoughts and desires to the soul of another being, thereby modifying the latter's state of mind and behavior, sometimes without it realizing this. For this purpose humans have at their disposal a vast collection of magic incantations (*anent*) by means of which they are able, from a distance, to affect not only their fellows but also plants, animals, spirits, and even certain artifacts. Conjugal harmony, good relations with relatives and neighbors, successful hunting, the making of fine pottery and effective curare (a hunting poison), a garden filled with a wide variety of thriving plants: all these things depend on the relationships that the Achuar have managed to establish with many different interlocutors, both human and nonhuman—relations that ensure that these others are well disposed to them, thanks to the power of their *anent*.

For the Achuar, technical know-how is indissociable from an ability to create an intersubjective ambience in which regulated relations between one person and another flourish: relations between a hunter, animals, and the spirits that are the masters of hunted game; between the women, the garden plants, and the mythical figure that engendered the cultivated species in the first place and continues to the present day to ensure their vitality. Far from being no more than prosaic food-producing places, the forest and the cultivated plots constitute theaters of a subtle sociability within which, day after day, humans engage in cajoling beings distinguishable from humans only by their different physical aspects and their lack of language. However, the forms of this sociability differ depending on whether it is directed toward plants or toward animals. The women, who are the mistresses of the gardens to which they devote much of their time, address their cultivated plants as though they are children that need to be guided with a firm hand toward maturity. This mothering relationship is explicitly modeled on the guardianship that Nunkui, the spirit of the gardens, provides for the plants that she herself initially created. Meanwhile, the men, for their part, regard an animal that they hunt as a brother-in-law. This is an unstable and tricky relationship that demands mutual respect and circumspection. Political coalitions are in general based upon alliances with relatives by marriage, but these are also the most immediate enemies in vendettas. Blood relatives and relatives by marriage constitute the two mutually exclusive categories that govern the social classification of the Achuar and determine their relationships with one another; and the opposition between the two is reproduced in the conduct prescribed toward nonhumans. For the women, their plants are blood relatives; for the men, animals are relatives by marriage: the natural beings thus become real social partners.

But in these circumstances, is the description of "natural beings" any more than a linguistic convenience? Is there any place for nature in a cosmology that confers most of the attributes of human beings upon animals and plants? Can one speak of the appropriation or transformation of natural resources when the very activities favoring subsistence are regarded as one form of a multiplicity of individual pairings with humanized elements in the biosphere? Can one even describe as a "wild space" this forest that is barely touched by the Achuar, yet that they regard as an immense garden that is carefully cultivated by some spirit? A thousand leagues distant from Verlaine's "fierce and taciturn god," here nature is no transcendent element nor simply an object that needs to be socialized. Rather, it is a subject in a social relationship. It is an extension of the world of the homestead, and in truth it is domesticated even in its most inaccessible reaches.

The Achuar certainly draw distinctions between the entities by which the world is peopled. But the hierarchy of animate and inanimate objects that results is not based upon the degrees of perfection of the beings in question or upon the differences in their appearance or any progressive accumulation of their respective intrinsic properties. Rather, it is based upon the variations in the modes of communication that are made possible by an apprehension of perceived qualities that are unequally distributed. In that the category of "persons" includes spirits, plants, and animals, all of which are endowed with a soul, this cosmology does not discriminate between human beings and nonhuman beings. All that it does is create a hierarchical order according to the levels of the exchange of information that is reputed to be possible. The Achuar themselves obviously occupy the peak of this pyramid: they see one another and communicate in the same language. Dialogue is also possible with members of the other Jivaro tribes that surround them and whose dialects are more or less mutually intelligible, although it should be recognized that misunderstandings—either fortuitous or deliberate—do occur. With Spanish-speaking whites, as with neighboring peoples speaking the Quichua language, and also with ethnologists, the Achuar do meet and communicate, provided a common language exists. But mastery of that language is in many cases imperfect on the part of the interlocutors whose maternal language it is not; and this introduces the possibility of a semantic discordance that places in some doubt any correspondence between the faculties of the two parties that would set them both on the same level of reality. The further one moves away from the domain of "complete persons" (*penke aents*), who are defined principally by their linguistic aptitude, the more distinctions become emphasized. For instance, humans recognize plants and animals that, if they possess a soul, are themselves capable of recognizing humans. But although the Achuar can speak to them, thanks to their *anent* incantations, they do not immediately receive a response, for this can be communicated only through dreams. The same applies to spirits and certain mythological heroes. These are attentive to what is said to them, but in general they are invisible in their original form and so can be fully engaged with only in the course of dreams or hallucinogenic trances.

"Persons" able to communicate are also arranged in a hierarchy according to the degree of perfection of the social norms that govern the various communities to which they belong. Some nonhumans are very close to the Achuar because they are reputed to respect matrimonial rules identical to their own. Such is the case of the Tsunki river spirits and a number of species of game (e.g., woolly monkeys, toucans) and cultivated plants (e.g., manioc, groundnuts). On the other hand, there are some animals that enjoy sexual promiscuity and so constantly reject the principle of exogamy: howler monkeys and dogs, for example. The lowest level of social integration is occupied by solitary creatures: Iwianch spirits, who embody the souls of the dead and roam through the forest alone, and also the great predators, such as jaguars and anacondas. Yet, however distant they may seem from the laws of ordinary civility, all these solitary beings are the associates of shamans, who use them to spread misfortune or to oppose their own enemies. Although they are positioned on the boundaries of communal life, these harmful beings are not considered wild, because the masters whom they serve are included in society.

Does this mean that the Achuar would not recognize any entity as natural within their own ambience? Not exactly. The great social continuum that includes both humans and nonhumans is not entirely inclusive, for some elements in the environment communicate with no one, since they do not possess souls of their own. Most insects and fish, grasses, mosses, and brackens, and pebbles and rivers thus remain outside the social sphere and outside the network of intersubjectivity. In their mechanical and generic existence they perhaps correspond to what we call "nature." But does that justify our continuing to use this notion to designate a segment of the world that, for the Achuar, is incomparably more restricted than what we understand by that word? In modern thought, furthermore, "nature" only has meaning when set in opposition to human works, whether one chooses to call these "culture," "society," or "history," to use the language of philosophy and the social sciences, or "anthropized space," "technical mediation," or "*oikumene*," to use a more specialized terminology. A cosmology in which most plants and animals share all or some of the faculties, behavior, and moral codes ordinarily attributed to human beings is in no sense covered by the criteria of any such opposition.

Do the Achuar perhaps constitute an exceptional case, one of the picturesque anomalies that ethnography occasionally discovers in some remote corner of the planet?[2] Have I, out of a lack of perspicacity or a desire to be original, not been able or not wished to see the actual way in which they treat that dichotomy between nature and society? Just a few hundred kilometers to the north, in the Amazonian forest of eastern Colombia, the Makuna Indians present an even more radical version of a theory according to which the world is resolutely nondualist.[3]

Like the Achuar, the Makuna classify human beings, plants, and animals as "people" (*masa*) whose main attributes—mortality, social and ceremonial life, intentionality, and knowledge—are in every way identical. Within this community, distinctions among living beings are based on the particular characteristics that mythical origins, diets, and modes of reproduction confer upon each class of beings. They are not based on the greater or lesser proximity of those classes to the pinnacle of achievement that the Makuna would exemplify. The interaction between animals and human beings is likewise conceived as a relation of affinity, although this is slightly different from the Achuar model, given that among the Makuna a hunter regards his prey as a potential marriage partner rather than as a brother-in-law. However, the Makuna ontological classifications are far more flexible than those of the Achuar, by reason of a faculty of metamorphosis that is attributed to all: humans can become animals, animals can change into humans, and animals of one species can change into animals of another species. Their taxonomic grasp of reality is thus always contextual and relative, for the permanent swapping of appearances makes it impossible to attribute stable identities to the environment's living components.

The sociability that the Makuna ascribe to nonhumans is thus richer and more complex than that recognized by the Achuar. Just like the Indians themselves, animals live in communities, in "longhouses" that tradition situates at the heart of certain rapids or inside hills that are precisely mapped. They cultivate manioc gardens, move about in canoes, and, led by their chiefs, perform rituals every bit as elaborate as those of the Makuna themselves. The visible form of animals is really just a disguise. When they get home, they shed their appearance and deck themselves in ceremonial feathers and ornaments, thus ostensibly becoming the "people" that they have never ceased to be even as they swam in the rivers or roamed through the forest. This knowledge that the Makuna have relating to the double life led by animals is part of the teaching dispensed by their shamans, who are the cosmic mediators to whom society delegates the care of relations between the various communities of living beings. However, the premises upon which this knowledge is based are shared by one and all. Although they are, in part, esoteric, they nevertheless structure the conception of their environment that all the nonshamans share, and they dictate the manner in which the Makuna interact with that environment.

Many cosmologies analogous to those of the Achuar and the Makuna have been reported from the forest regions of the lowlands of South America.[4] Despite clearly detectable differences in their internal organization, all these cosmologies, without exception, draw no clear ontological distinctions between, on the one hand, humans and, on the other, numerous animal and plant species. Most of the entities that people the world are interconnected in a vast continuum inspired by unitary principles and governed by an identical regime of sociability. Relations between humans and nonhumans in fact appear to be no different from the relations that obtain between one human community and another. They are partly defined by the utilitarian constraints of subsistence, but they adopt different forms that are peculiar to each of the tribes and thereby serve to differentiate them. The Yukuna, a group speaking an Arawak language who are adjacent to the Makuna of Colombian Amazonia, provides a good illustration.[5] Like their neighbors who speak a Tukano language, the Yukuna have developed preferential associations with particular species of animals and particular varieties of the cultivated plants that provide them with their main foodstuffs. The mythical origin of the Yukuna and, in the case of the animals, the houses that these share are all situated within the limits of the Yukuna tribal territory. To the shamans falls the task of supervising the ritual regeneration of these species—species that are, in contrast, prohibited for the Tukano tribes that surround the Yukuna. Each tribal group is thus responsible for protecting the specific populations of the plants and animals that provide its nourishment. And this division of tasks helps to define local identities and systems of interethnic relations of the various tribal groups, for these vary according to their links with different nonhumans.

If the sociability of humans and that of animals and plants are so intimately connected in Amazonia, that is because their respective forms of collective organization stem from a common model that is quite flexible and that makes it possible to describe interactions between nonhumans by using the named categories that structure relations between humans or that represent some relations between humans on the model of symbiotic relations between other species. In the latter case, which is rarer, the relationship is not designated or described explicitly, since its characteristics are reputed to be familiar to everyone, thanks to their generally shared botanical and zoological knowledge. Among the Secoya, for example, dead Indians are thought to perceive the living in two different forms: they see men as oropendola birds and women as Amazon parrots.[6] This dichotomy, which organizes the social and symbolic construction of sexual identities, is based upon the ethological and morphological characteristics peculiar to the two species; and the classificatory function of those characteristics thus becomes clear, since the differences in the appearance and behavior of nonhumans are used to emphasize the anatomical and physiological differences between human men and women. Conversely, the Yagua of Peruvian Amazonia have elaborated a system for classifying plants and animals that is based on the relations between species, according to how they are defined by various degrees of consanguinity, friendship, or hostility.[7] The use of social categories to define relations of proximity, symbiosis, or competition between natural species is particularly interesting here in that it largely extends to include the plant kingdom. Thus, big trees maintain a hostile relationship: they provoke one another in fratricidal duels to see which will be the first to give way. Hostile relations likewise prevail between bitter manioc and sweet manioc, with the former seeking to contaminate the latter with its toxicity. Palm trees, on the other hand, maintain more pacific relations of an avuncular or cousinhood type, depending on the degree of resemblance between the species. The Yagua—like the Aguaruna Jivaros[8]—interpret morphological resemblances between wild plants and cultivated ones as indicating a kinship relationship, although they do not claim, on that account, that the similarity indicates that the two species share a common ancestor.

The diversity of the classificatory indicators used by Amerindians to account for the relations between organisms shows just how flexible boundaries are in the taxonomy of living beings. For the characteristics attributed to the entities that people the cosmos depend not so much on a prior definition of their essence but rather on the positions that they occupy in relation to one another by reason of the needs of their metabolism and, in particular, their diet. The identities of human beings, both living and dead, and of plants, animals, and spirits are altogether relational and are therefore subject to mutations and metamorphoses depending on the point of view adopted. In many cases it is said that an individual of one species apprehends the members of other species in accordance with his own criteria, so that, in normal conditions, a hunter will not realize that his animal-prey sees itself as a human being, or that it sees the hunter as a jaguar. Similarly, a jaguar regards the blood that it drinks as manioc beer, while the monkey-spider that the cacique bird thinks it is hunting is, to a man, nothing but a grasshopper, and the tapirs that a snake considers as its preferred prey are really human beings.[9] It is thanks to the ongoing swapping of appearances engendered by these shifting perspectives that animals in all good faith consider themselves endowed with the same cultural attributes as human beings. To them, their crests are feathered crowns, their pelts are clothing, their beaks are spears, and their claws are knives. The roundabout of perceptions in Amazonian cosmologies engenders an ontology that is sometimes labeled "perspectivism,"[10] which denies a privileged point of view from on high to human beings and holds that multiple experiences of the world can cohabit without contradiction. In contrast to modern dualism, which deploys a multiplicity of cultural differences against a background of an unchanging nature, Amerindian thought envisages the entire cosmos as being animated by a single cultural regime that becomes diversified, if not by heterogeneous natures, at least by all the different ways in which living beings apprehend one another. The common referent for all the entities that live in the world is thus not Man as a species but humanity as a condition.

Might the apparent inability to objectivize nature of many Amazonian peoples be a consequence of the properties of their environment? Ecologists certainly define a tropical forest as a "generalized" ecosystem that is characterized by an extremely wide diversity of animal and plant species, with small numbers of each that are very widely dispersed. Thus, out of roughly fifty thousand species of vascular plants present in Amazonia, fewer that twenty or so grow spontaneously in groups together, and where they do, that is in many cases an accidental result of human interference.[11] Immersed as they are in a monstrous plurality of life-forms that are seldom to be found all together in homogeneous groups, possibly the forest Indians gave up the idea of embracing as a whole the disparate conglomeration of entities that constantly clamor for the attention of their senses. Forced to settle for a mirage of diversity, they perhaps found no way of dissociating themselves from nature because they could not discern its profound unity, which was obscured by the multiplicity of its singular manifestations.

A rather enigmatic remark made by Claude Lévi-Strauss may indicate an interpretation of this type. He suggested that the tropical forest may be the

only environment that might allow one to attribute idiosyncratic characteristics to each member of a species.[12] Differentiating each individual as a particular type (Lévi-Strauss calls this a "mono-individual") is certainly something that *Homo sapiens* is adept at doing, by reason of his ability to develop
whatever personalities are acceptable to social life. However, the extreme
profusion of animal and plant species could equally encourage this process of
singularization. It was perhaps inevitable that, in an ambience as diversified
as the Amazonian forest, people's perception of relations between individuals
that are apparently all different should take precedence over the construction
of stable and mutually exclusive macrocategories.

Gerardo Reichel-Dolmatoff also suggests an interpretation based on the
peculiarities of the environment when he defends the idea that the cosmology of the Desana Indians of Colombian Amazonia constitutes a kind of descriptive model of the processes of ecological adaptation, formulated in terms
comparable to those of a modern systemic analysis.[13] According to Reichel-
Dolmatoff, the Desana conceive of the world in the manner of a homeostatic
system in which the quantity of energy expended, that is, the "output," is directly linked to the quantity of energy received, the "input." The biosphere's
provision of energy comes from two main sources. The first source is the sexual energy of individuals, which is regularly repressed by ad hoc prohibitions.
This energy returns directly to the global capital of energy that irrigates all the
biotic components of the system. The second source is the state of health and
well-being of humans, which results from a strictly controlled diet and engenders the energy necessary for all the nonbiotic elements of the cosmos (e.g., it
makes the movement of the celestial bodies possible). Each individual is thus
conscious of constituting but one element in a complex network of interactions that take place within not only the social sphere but also the entirety
of a universe that tends toward stability: in other words, a universe whose
resources and limits are finite. This imposes upon every individual ethical
responsibilities, in particular that of not upsetting the general equilibrium
of this fragile system and never using energy without rapidly restoring it by
means of various kinds of ritual operations.

But the principal role in this quest for a perfect homeostasis falls to the
shaman. In the first place, he intervenes constantly in human subsistence activities to ensure that they do not imperil the reproduction of nonhumans.
The shaman will thus personally check the quantity and degree of concentration of the plant poison prepared for fishing in a particular segment of the
river, or he will rule upon how many individual animals may be killed when
a herd of peccaries is located. Furthermore, the rituals that accompany such
hunts for food will present "occasions . . . for stocktaking, for weighing costs

and benefits, and for the eventual redistribution of resources." In these circumstances, the shaman's "book-keeping shows the general system of inputs and outputs."[14]

Such a transposition turns the shaman into a seemingly knowledgeable manager of an ecosystem, and the whole collection of religious beliefs and rituals into a kind of practical treatise on ecology; and its validity seems questionable. A shaman's conscious application of a kind of estimated optimization of the rare means available may correspond well enough to certain neo-Darwinian models that are applied in human ecology. However, that is not easy to reconcile with the fact that the Desana, like their neighbors, the Makuna, ascribe to animals and plants most of the attributes that they recognize themselves to possess. It is hard to see how those social partners of human beings could suddenly, in particular circumstances, lose their status as persons and be treated as no more than accounting units to be distributed on either side of a balance sheet of energy. There can be no doubt that the Amerindians of Amazonia possess a remarkable empirical understanding of the complex interrelations between the organisms within their environment and that they use that knowledge in their survival strategies. Nor can there be any doubt that they make use of social relations, in particular kinship, to define a whole range of interrelations between nonhuman organisms. However, it seems unlikely that these characteristics stem from their adaptation to a particular ecosystem that, thanks to its intrinsic properties, somehow provides an analogical model that makes it possible to work out how the world is organized.

The principal argument against such an interpretation lies in the existence of very similar cosmologies that have been elaborated by peoples living in a completely different environment, more than six thousand kilometers to the north of Amazonia. Unlike the Indians of the South American tropical forest, the Indians of the subarctic region of Canada exploit a remarkably uniform ecosystem. From the Labrador peninsula all the way to Alaska, the great northern forest spreads a continuous cloak of conifers in which the typical silhouette of the black spruce predominates, barely interrupted here and there by a few groves of alders, willows, silver birches, and balsam poplars. The animals are hardly more varied: the main groups of mammals are the following: herbivores (elk and caribou), rodents (beavers, hares, porcupines, muskrats), and carnivores (wolves, brown bears, lynxes, and wolverines). To these may be added twenty or so common species of birds and about a dozen of fish: far fewer than the approximately three thousand species to be found in the rivers of Amazonia. Many of these animals, such as caribou, geese, and sturgeons, are migratory and may disappear from some places for several years, eventually reappearing in such quantities that it seems as if the entire species has temporarily come together. In short, the characteristics of the northern forest are the exact opposite of those of the Amazonian forest, for the former "specialized" ecosystem includes few species, each of which is, however, represented by a great number of individuals. Yet despite the ostensible homogeneity of their ecological environment—and also despite their impotence in the face of the famines regularly engendered by such a harsh climate—the subarctic peoples do not appear to regard their environment as a domain of reality that is clearly distinct from the principles and values that govern human social life. In the Far North, as in South America, nature is not opposed to culture but is an extension of it and enriches it in a cosmos in which everything is organized according to the criteria of human beings.[15]

In the first place, many features of the landscape are attributed a personality of their own. Rivers, lakes, mountains, thunder, the prevailing winds, ice jams, and the dawn are all identified by a spirit that discreetly animates them. They are so many hypostases reputed to be attentive to the words and actions of humans. But it is above all in their conceptions of the animal world that the Indians of the northern Canadian forest most resemble those of Amazonia. Despite differences in language and ethnic affiliations, the same complex of beliefs and rites everywhere governs the hunter's relationship with his prey. As in Amazonia, most animals are regarded as persons with a soul, and this confers upon them attributes in every way identical to those of humans, such as reflexive consciousness, intentionality, an affective life, and respect for ethical principles. Cree groups are particularly explicit in this domain. According to them, the social life of animals resembles that of humans and is sustained by the same sources: solidarity, friendship, deference toward elders, and, in their case, the invisible spirits who preside over the migrations of game, manage the dispersion of animals, and are responsible for their regeneration. The only way in which animals differ from humans is thus in their appearance; and this is simply an illusion of the senses, for the distinctive corporeal forms that they usually adopt are merely disguises designed to fool the Indians. When animals visit humans in their dreams, they reveal themselves as they really are, that is, in their human form. Likewise, when their spirits express themselves publicly in the course of the ritual known as "the shaking lodge," they speak in the native Indian languages.[16] As for the extremely common myths that portray the union of an animal with a man or a woman, these simply confirm the common identity of the natures of animals and humans. It is said that such a union would be impossible were it not for the fact that the tender feelings of the human partner made it possible for him or her to perceive the true form of the desired one beneath its animal finery.

It would be mistaken to regard this humanization of animals as mere intellectual playfulness, a kind of metaphorical language relevant only within the circumstances surrounding the performance of rites or the recounting of myths. Even when speaking in altogether prosaic terms of tracking, killing, and eating game, the Indians unambiguously convey the idea that hunting is a mode of social interaction with entities that are well aware of the conventions that regulate it.[17] Here, as in most societies in which hunting plays an important part, it is by showing one's respect for the animals that one ensures their connivance. It is important to avoid waste, to kill cleanly and without causing undue suffering, to treat the bones and remains with dignity, and never to indulge in boasting or even to refer too clearly to the fate that awaits one's prey. Expressions referring to hunting seldom mention its ultimate end, the kill. Just as the Achuar of Amazonia speak vaguely of "going off into the forest," of "walking the dogs," or of "blowing the birds" (when it is a matter of blowpipe hunting), so too the Montagnais Indians say that they are "going to search" when they mean to hunt with a rifle or "going to see" when they mean to check on their traps.[18] Likewise, in Amazonia, it is customary for a young hunter who kills an animal of a particular species for the first time to treat it according to a particular ritual. Among the Achuar, for example, the young man declines to eat the game that he has brought home, for the still fragile relationship established with this new species would be irrevocably shattered if he did not show such restraint, and his prey's fellows would in future conceal themselves at his approach. Among the Ojibwa of Ontario, the same principle appears to dictate the behavior of a novice hunter: in this case, although he will eat his catch in the company of his fellow hunters, he does so only in the course of a ceremonial meal that ends with a kind of funerary ritual that disposes of the animal's remains.[19]

A hunter's relationship with animals may take other forms over and above these marks of consideration: seduction, for example, in which the prey is seen as a lover, or magic coercion that annihilates the animal's willpower and forces it to approach the hunter. But the most common of such relationships and the one that best emphasizes the parity between humans and animals is the bond of friendship that the hunter establishes over time with one particular member of the species. This forest friend is regarded as a companion who will serve as an intermediary among his fellow creatures, who, without balking, will then expose themselves within the range of a shot. No doubt it does involve a minor act of treachery on the intermediary's part, but this is of no consequence to his fellows, as the hunter's victim will soon be reincarnated in an animal of the same species, provided its remains have received the prescribed ritual treatment. For whatever the strategies employed to incite an animal to expose itself to a hunter, when the prey delivers itself up to the one who will consume it, it is always out of a feeling of generosity. The animal is moved by the compassion that it feels for the sufferings of humans, creatures that are vulnerable to famine, who depend upon itself for their survival. Far from being nothing more than an episodic technical manipulation of the autonomous natural environment, here hunting involves a continuous dialogue during which, as Tim Ingold observes, "both human and animal persons are constituted with their particular identities and purposes."[20]

Further north still, in the regions almost devoid of life except for the peoples who speak an Eskimo language and who have learned how to live there, an identical perception of the relationship of humans to the environment appears to prevail.[21] Humans, animals, and spirits all coexist there; and the reason that humans can feed on the animals, thanks to the benevolence of the spirits, is that the game offers itself to those who truly desire it, as is the case among the Cree. Inuit hunting rites and birth rites indicate that souls and flesh, which are so rare and so precious, circulate ceaselessly between different components of the biosphere, defined by their relative positions, not by an essence given for all eternity. Game is necessary for the production of humans—as a foodstuff, of course, but also because the souls of harpooned seals are reborn in human children; and, in just the same way, humans are necessary for the production of certain animals: the remains of the dead are left out for predators; afterbirths are offered to seals, and the souls of the dead sometimes return to the spirit in charge of marine game. As the shaman Ivaluardjuk confided to Karl Rasmussen, "the greatest peril of life lies in the fact that human food consists entirely of souls."[22] If animals are indeed persons, eating them is a form of cannibalism that is attenuated only slightly by the ongoing exchange of substances and spiritual principles between the principal actors in the world. This kind of dilemma is not faced solely by the inhabitants of the Far North. Many Amerindian cultures find themselves faced with the same problem: how can I take the life of another who is endowed with the same attributes as myself without compromising the links of connivance that I have managed to establish with the community of that creature's fellows? That is a difficult question that our humanist tradition has not prepared us to tackle in those particular terms; and it is one to which I shall be returning later in this work.

From the luxuriant forests of Amazonia to the glacial spaces of the Canadian Arctic, certain peoples thus envisage their insertion into the environment in a manner altogether different from our own. They regard themselves, not as social collectives managing their relations with the ecosystem, but rather as simple components of a vaster whole within which no real discrimination is really established between humans and nonhumans. Of course, differences do exist between all these cosmological arrangements: thus, by reason of the low number of species living in the most northern latitudes, the network of interrelations between the entities inhabiting this biosphere is not as rich and complex for the Amerindians of the North as it is for those of the South. But the structures of those networks are in every way analogous, as are the properties ascribed to their various elements; and this would seem to negate the idea that the symbolic ecology of the Amazonian Indians might result from their local adaptation to a more diverse environment.

So is this a purely American peculiarity? Ethnology and archaeology repeatedly show that in the past Indian America formed part of an original cultural whole the unity of which can still be glimpsed behind the effects of fragmentation brought about by colonial history. Clear evidence for this is provided by myths, with all their variations, which rest upon a homogeneous semantic substratum of which it is hard to believe that it does not proceed from a common conception of the world, forged in the course of thousands of years of movements of peoples and ideas. We know very little about this pre-Columbian history, which stretches much further back than used to be believed. So modern ethnology can provide little more than disparate chronicles of those "Middle Ages which lacked a Rome," as Lévi-Strauss has put it:[23] mere traces of an age-old shared basis, elements of which are combined in many diverse ways. Could it be that a particular way of representing the relations between humans and nonhumans results from that very ancient syncretism that, even today, still works its way to the surface in a pan-American schema?

Attractive though it may seem, the hypothesis of American exceptionality does not stand up to examination. One has only to cross the Bering Strait, in the direction opposite to that taken by the migrations that brought the ancestors of present-day Amerindian populations all the way from eastern Siberia to Alaska, to see that the hunting peoples of the taiga formulate their relations with the environment in a very similar manner.[24] Among the Tunkus, the Samoyeds, the Xant, and the Mansi, the whole forest is believed to be animated by a spirit. This usually takes the form of a large member of the Cervidae family but it may also manifest itself in many other incarnations. Trees too may possess souls of their own or may constitute plant doubles of certain humans, which is why it is forbidden to fell young trees. In the Buryat language the spirit of the woods is known as "Rich-Forest" and it may take two forms. One is positive, provides game for humans, and wards off their sicknesses. The other, often presented as the son or brother-in-law of the former, in contrast disseminates misfortune and death and spends its time hunting down human souls and devouring them. The ambivalence of Rich-Forest (which is equally characteristic of the configurations of "masters of game" among Amerindians) forces humans to take multiple precautions in their relations with the wild animals for which this double figure acts as a guardian.

The animals themselves all possess souls, identical in principle to those of humans—that is to say, a principle of life that is relatively autonomous vis-à-vis its material body. This makes it possible for a hunted animal's spirit to wander about, especially after its death, in order to ascertain from its fellows that it will, if necessary, be avenged. The animals' social organization resembles that of humans: the solidarity between members of the same species is assimilated to the supportive duties of members of the same clan, while the relations between species are described in the same way as the relations between different tribes are. Among the furry animals, certain individuals exercise control over their companions and are recognized as their "masters." Because they are bigger and more beautiful, it is they who best embody the characteristic features of the species that they represent and so are the species' preferred interlocutors with human hunters who request them to concede a few of their fellows as hunted prey. Such prototype figures are also present in indigenous America.[25] Their existence establishes a hierarchy in each animal community, as if it were necessary for there to be an intermediary between the master-spirits and the underlings—an intermediary of identical status to that of the human hunter—so that negotiations can unfold on an equal footing.

The relations that Siberian peoples entertain with the animal world vary according to the partners involved. Hunting for large cervids—in particular wild reindeer and elk—implies an alliance with the Spirit of the Forest, who is represented as a provider of women. By copulating, in his dreams, with this Spirit's daughter, the hunter consummates this alliance and wins the right to receive benefits from his father-in-law. Symbolic though it may seem, this link through marriage is reputed not to be totally imaginary. Because of the ability to travel during sleep that is attributed to souls, union with the daughters of the Spirit of the Forest at least takes on the air of a relationship between two persons. And, given that it is important not to arouse the jealousy of Rich-Forest's young ladies, men abstain from all sexual relations with their human wives before setting out on a hunting trip. To encourage generosity on the part of the father-in-law or other spirits who provide game, in the evening, in their invisible presence, the long stories that they love are told, while the smoke rising from the pipes of the hunters is agreeable to their impalpable nostrils.

Marriage alliances with animals other than cervids do not work, so it is necessary to take all kinds of precautions so as not to alienate them definitively. Cunning is one ploy: for example, one loudly proclaims that a member of another tribe is responsible for the death of an animal that one has oneself killed or, better still, to preserve his anonymity, the hunter wears a mask. As in America, hunters show moderation in their catch, conceal their intentions, take care not to name their quarry, and use euphemisms to refer to the kill. Such subterfuges are imperative in order to deter the hunted animals or their representatives from taking revenge. Proper treatment of a consumed animal's remains is just as important as in the Canadian subarctic, and for similar reasons: life continues so long as the bones subsist, so by placing the animal's intact skeleton, its skull, and in some cases its genital organs on little constructions in the forest, one is assured that its soul will return to the common stock of its species and will thereby produce the birth of another individual. To the extent that the bodily envelope is no more than an appearance, a transitory clothing that can be reconstituted from the framework of bones, the hunter does not destroy the hunted animal but simply appropriates its flesh in order to eat it. Furthermore, before being deposited in the forest, the animal's skull will have been taken to the hunter's home and installed in a place of honor. In the presence of relatives and neighbors who are invited for the ceremony, a party is organized in honor of the animal's soul. The celebration is punctuated by ceremonial thanks to the animal's soul, and it is encouraged to return among its fellows in order to persuade them too to visit the human beings.

For the exchange to be truly equitable, however, it is necessary to restore to the animals whatever has been taken from them, namely their meat. There are two ways of doing this. As among the Inuit, the human dead are exposed on a platform far from human habitation, so that predators may eat their remains. But a more direct way of feeding the animals is to take in the offspring of wild species and tend to their needs. Among Mongol peoples, these household animals are known as *ongon*, a name that is also given to figurines, generally representations of animals, which are said to act as intermediaries with the Forest Spirit and persuade it to allow good hunting. These effigies are kept close to the hearth and have to be treated in a considerate fashion, cheered by jokes and, above all, regularly fed. So they are smeared with fat and blood, and scraps of meat are placed in the cavities representing their mouths or in other purpose-built pockets. By feeding the various kinds of *ongon*, the hunters win their favor and at the same time discharge their debt to the animals that they hunt. As for the latter, through their domesticated emissaries they can rest assured, day after day, that the humans are punctiliously fulfilling their obligations.

In Siberia, as in America, then, many peoples seem resistant to the idea of a clear separation between their physical environment and their social environment. For them, these two domains that we normally distinguish are facets that are hardly contrasted within a continuum of interactions between human and nonhuman persons. So what? you might say. Are not America and eastern Asia part of one and the same cultural cluster? Did not the peoples who crossed the Bering Strait in the Pleistocene already bring with them a whole array of ideas and techniques that have no doubt been developed and enriched by subsequent waves of migration? It is not surprising that traces of it are to be found here and there between Siberia and the Tierra del Fuego.

The theory that certain material and ideological features of Amerindian cultures were diffused from Asia is by no means new. And to some extent, it is well founded. As early as the beginning of the twentieth century, research carried out by the Jesup expedition established the existence of a veritable North Pacific civilization. Archaeological evidence testifies to its unity, a product of several thousand years of migrating populations and intense exchanges in a vast region centered on the Bering Strait and extending from the south coast of the Okhotsk Sea all the way to Vancouver Island.[26] There is no reason why institutions and beliefs forged in the northern Pacific melting pot should not have spread well to the south of present-day Canada, in particular the feature most readily associated with eastern Siberia, namely shamanism.

We should remember that the term *çaman* comes from the Tungus language and that the first descriptions of shamanistic trances were provided as early as the seventeenth century by Russians who had traveled in eastern Siberia.[27] Ethnology, which took over this term in the early decades of the twentieth century, has tended to unify within a single descriptive category a whole collection of features originally identified in Siberia but reputed to be present in the "primitive religions" of other regions of the world, in particular America. The theory is that a shaman is a mediator between human beings and spirits with whom he can, at will, enter into contact by means of a voyage of the soul (in a trance or a dream) that enables him to mobilize their help in such a way as to prevent or ease the misfortunes of humans. Some authors have represented shamanism as a veritable conception of the world, a singular system for interpreting events that is based on an alliance between humans and deities;[28] or they have believed it to express the symbolism of a relationship with nature that is characteristic of hunting peoples.[29] If we adopt such a view, it becomes possible, on the basis of a common shamanistic inheritance, to explain many troubling similarities in the ways that Amerindians and Siberians conceive of their relations with the environment. Attributing souls to plants and animals, establishing relations with spirit mediators, exchanging food and identities with nonhumans: all such behavior is thus, in the end, regarded as manifesting a more general system of interpreting misfortune and remedying it that is centered upon the personality of an individual reputed to possess particular powers. This system is said to have originated in northern Asia, then spread into both North and South America with the arrival of immigrants from Siberia, thereby engendering cosmologies that are, seemingly, very similar.

This diffusionist hypothesis, upheld in particular by Mircea Eliade, implies a number of presuppositions, some of them contradictory.[30] To represent shamanism as a form of archaic religion defined by a few typical features (the presence of individuals who have mastered the techniques of ecstasy and can communicate with the supernatural beings that delegate them their powers) presupposes that one ascribes to the person and actions of the shaman an exaggerated role in the establishment of the way in which a society tries to give meaning to the world. It is as though one proclaimed the unity of Brahmanism, Greek religion, and Christianity on the grounds that a priest plays the central role, for he is the instrument of the liturgical mediation with the divine that is marked by a real or symbolic sacrifice. But, in Indian America at least, the part that shamans play in the management of relations with the various entities that inhabit the cosmos may be altogether negligible. Both in the subarctic region and in many Amazonian societies, relations between humans and nonhumans are mostly personal ones that are maintained and consolidated in the course of the existence of each and every member of the society. The bonds of connivance between individuals are frequently beyond the control of ritual specialists, whose tasks, where they exist, are in many cases limited to treating physical illnesses. It is therefore rash to affirm that a dominant conception of the world is the product of a religious system centered on one particular institution, namely shamanism, the effects of which may be restricted to a quite limited sector of social life. The diffusionist thesis furthermore implies, *a contrario*, that the cosmological configuration usually associated with shamanism ought to become blurred and then disappear the farther away one gets from the geographical zone where it originated—unless, of course, one considers that each and every form of deliberate mediation with supernatural entities stems from shamanism. But that would be an absurd position that would make shamanism the ancient basis of all religions and at the same time a totally empty concept given that, by encompassing too many different phenomena, it would be unable to define any of them in a meaningful fashion.

To protect ourselves against the attraction of a more reasonable diffusionism—that is, one that would not extend to the entire planet—we must distance ourselves from the idea of a hypothetical source of hypothetical shamanistic civilizations. So let us move more than six thousand kilometers to the south of eastern Siberia, crossing Mongolia, China, and Indochina, to reach the humid tropical forest of the Malay Peninsula. It is inhabited by a collection of ethnic groups speaking Môn-Khmer languages. The Malaysians refer to them as the Orong Asli ("the aboriginal peoples"). They live by hunting (with blowpipes) and gathering and the slash-and-burn cultivation of domesticated plants originating from tropical America, such as manioc and sweet potatoes. They inevitably put any Amerindian specialist in mind of many familiar features: the same techniques involving an extensive use of natural resources, the same dispersed habitat, the same fluid social organization. But it is above all in their representations of their relations with plants and animals that the Orong Asli present striking resemblances with the peoples we have examined above. As an example, let me take the Chewong, a small ethnic group in the hinterland of Pahang Province, whose symbolic ecology is known to us thanks to the research of Signe Howell.[31]

Chewong society is not limited to the 260 individuals of which it is composed, for it extends far beyond the ontological frontiers of humanity to encompass a myriad of spirits, plants, animals, and objects that are reputed to possess the same attributes as the Chewong themselves and that the Chewong describe collectively as "our people" (*bi he*). Despite their different appearances, all the entities within this forest cosmos mingle together in an intimate and egalitarian community that, as a whole, stands in opposition to the threatening and incomprehensible world outside, which is inhabited by "different people" (*bi masign*): Malaysians, Chinese, Westerners, and other aboriginal peoples. Within this saturated intimacy of social life, the beings that share the same immediate environment perceive themselves as complementary and interdependent. The ethical responsibility for ensuring that things run smoothly is assumed collectively as the function of each individual's actions—for allegiance to a moral code characterizes the conduct of all those that possess a reflexive consciousness (*ruwai*), whether they be human or nonhuman. For the Chewong, the reason certain plants and certain animals are "people" (*beri*) is partly because they are endowed with the same cognitive and moral capacities as themselves and partly because in certain circumstances their bodies may appear identical to the bodies of humans. *Ruwai* constitutes the true essence of a person and its principle of individuation, for the body is nothing but clothing that can be temporarily put aside, particularly during dreams. However, when the *ruwai* goes wandering, it does so in the form of a physical embodiment without which it could not be seen or recognized by other *ruwai*. While the *ruwai* of humans may be embodied in the form of a reduced model of a real body, a kind of homunculus, the *ruwai* of plants and animals, in contrast, takes the form of a human body rather than the "clothing" of its own species. Furthermore, while the *ruwai* of a human is unable to inhabit the body of another human, it may, on occasion, take on the appearance of a plant or an animal. Not only do distinctions between the natural, the supernatural, and the human have no meaning for the Chewong, but even the possibility of dividing reality into separate stable categories becomes illusory since one can never be sure of the identity of the person, whether human or nonhuman, that is masked by the "clothing" of another species.

There is, however, one attribute of beings that endures whatever changes they undergo and that, without their realizing it, distinguishes them by dividing them into homogeneous groups. Each class of persons endowed with a *ruwai* is believed to perceive the world in its own particular manner, by virtue of the particular characteristics of its faculty of sight. For example, it often happens that a Chewong in the forest falls into a trap that some spirit has laid to capture wild pigs. But as his eyes are "hot," unlike those of the spirits, which are "cold," he will not realize what has happened to him, except to the extent that his body feels the painful consequences of his fall. Nevertheless, humans are not particularly disadvantaged, for illusion cuts both ways: one race of spirits reputed to feed on a species of canna sees this plant as a sweet potato; so when the Chewong cut down cannas, those spirits see only porcupines rooting up sweet potatoes. Similarly, when a dog eats the excrement that it finds beneath houses, it is convinced it is devouring bananas; elephants, meanwhile, regard one another as human beings. The mode of vision of each species is considered to be a characteristic of its *ruwai* that is unaffected by individual metamorphoses, so that a Chewong who adopts the clothing of a tiger will continue to see the world with the eyes of a human. There is patently a parallel here with the relativism in matters of perception among Amerindians: the identity of beings and the texture of the world are fluid and contingent, resistant to any classification seeking to freeze reality in accordance with the sole evidence of appearances. The Chewong are probably dualists, but in a manner very different from ours: rather than distinguish, deep down, between humans and nonhumans, they draw a line of demarcation between what is near and what is distant, between, on the one hand, communities of persons of heterogeneous aspects who nevertheless share the same mores and habitat and, on the other, the mysterious periphery where other languages and other laws hold sway. Their dualism is of a concentric nature that tones down discontinuities close to home, the better to exclude those beyond the boundary; whereas ours is diametrical and draws absolute distinctions, the better to be inclusive.

The ease with which the Chewong accommodate a world in which nature and society are not separated into different compartments is in no way exceptional in Southeast Asia. In Malaysia itself, ethnographic sources sketch in comparable pictures of other aboriginal peoples, such as the Batek Negritos in the center of the peninsula[32] and the Ma' Betisék in the mangroves of Selangor.[33] Wazir-Jahan Karim tells us that, for the latter, "the exploitation of plants and animals as food resources is fundamentally wrong because it is conceived as the exploitation of humans as food."[34] The same goes for regions farther east, eastern Indonesia, for example, among the Nuaulu on the island of Seram. In his study of the way in which they classify fauna, Roy Ellen concludes that it is impossible to pick out any Nuaulu taxonomy conceived of as a separate domain, that is to say, independent of a more all-encompassing cosmic order, similar to the "chain of being" of the ancient world.[35]

The island of Seram is separated from New Guinea by straits barely two hundred kilometers wide, so it comes as no surprise to find in Melanesia the same absence of a clear-cut boundary between humans and nonhumans. Roy Wagner provides an excellent description of this continuity: "each one of these peoples locates mankind in a world of differentiated, though basically analogous, anthropomorphic entities."[36] This is particularly clear among the societies of the Great Plateau, a highly distinctive biogeographical region well known for its rich and diverse fauna and flora. The cosmology of the Kaluli, for example, is governed by the same kind of perceptive realism as in Amazonia or among the Chewong: multiple worlds coexist within the same environment, inhabited by classes of distinct beings that perceive their fellows as humans but regard the inhabitants of other worlds as animals or spirits. Thus, men hunt wild pigs that embody spirits, while spirits hunt wild pigs that embody doubles of humans.[37] To quote a saying of the Bedamuni people, neighbors of the Kaluli, "when we see animals, we might think that they are just animals, but we know that they are really like human beings."[38] The situation is similar farther to the east, in the Solomon Islands. According to the 'Are'are, their shell currency, cultivated plants, pigs, fish, and men and women are all formed by more or less complete combinations of vectors of identity that, as they circulate among all these entities, link them together in a great cosmic continuum.[39] We are told that, in these same islands, the people of the great Marovo lagoon "hold that the organisms and non-living components of the environment do not constitute a distinct realm of 'nature' or the 'natural environment' separate from 'culture' or 'human society.'"[40]

But it is New Caledonia, farther to the south and a thousand leagues from the regions where we began this inquiry, that provides the most subtle expression of the implications of a world in which humans live enveloped by their environment. We owe this knowledge to a great book, *Do Kamo*, written over sixty years ago by Maurice Leenhardt. In it he draws our attention to a distinctive concept of a person, immersed in the abundance of a world "in which animals, men and plants make exchanges among themselves without boundaries or differentiations."[41] Without differentiations: for the Kanaks postulate an identical structure and substance for the human body and for plants. The tissues, the very processes of growth, and the physiology are in every way analogous, even if the modes of existence are perceived as being different. So this is not a matter of a metaphorical correspondence of a quite classic nature[42] between human development and plant development. Instead, what we find is a material continuity between two orders of life, as is attested by the return of ancestors to inhabit certain trees after their deaths. Leenhardt tells us that this woody body cannot simply be a medium for a particular entity, the kernel of an individual self: embedded as it is in the environment from which it is barely distinguishable, it enables a human to know himself through his experience of the world and "without considering that he might distinguish himself from that world."[43]

The body is animated by *kamo*, a term meaning "life" but implying no clearly defined shape nor any essential nature. An animal or a plant is said to be *kamo* if circumstances suggest that it shares something in common with humans. As in Amazonia, humanity covers far more than the physical representations of human beings. The full scope of humanity, expressed by the terms *do kamo* (true human), is deployed in many kinds of living units distinct from humans as a species. That is why Leenhardt suggests translating *kamo* as "personage," a principle of existence clothed in a variety of appearances, rather than the Western notion of a "person," which presupposes a particularized awareness of the self and of a body clearly circumscribed in space. *Kamo* is defined, not by any closure, but by the relations that constitute it. So when those relations are suppressed (in the case of humans, the network of links of kinship, solidarity, and allegiance), the ego fades away, since it cannot exist in isolation, in the reflexive knowledge of its individuality. The desocialization brought about by the colonial process therefore caused dramatic upheavals, which the education dispensed by missionaries aimed to rectify. That education engendered a consciousness of individuality within an autonomous body. Old Boesoou removed all doubt on the matter in his reply to Leenhardt, who asked him about the effects of schooling: "I risked the following suggestion: 'in short, we introduced the notion of spirit to your way of thinking?' And he objected: 'Spirit? Bah! You didn't bring us the spirit. We already knew the spirit existed. What you've brought us is the body.'"[44]

After the Americas, Asia, and Oceania, let us now turn to consider one more ethnographic continent: Africa, which seems different from the cases examined so far in that there the boundary between nature and society seems more firm, expressed in spatial classifications, cosmologies, and conceptions of what a person is that distinguish quite clearly between humans and non-humans. The clear-cut opposition between the village and the bush thus reappears as a leitmotif in all Africanist monographs: the village is the place of social order, constructed by human labor, maintained by ritual, and guaranteed in perpetuity by a segmentary hierarchy and the presence of ancestors; the bush is a dangerous periphery, inhabited by predatory species and harmful spirits, a disorderly space that is associated with death and is an ambiguous source of masculine powers. Likewise, in Africa, wild animals are seldom endowed with an individual soul, intentionality, or other human characteristics, and when they appear in stories, it is not so much as alter egos of human beings, as in Amerindian myths, but rather as metaphors, archetypes of bad or good moral qualities. They are simply actors in ironic or edifying parables that put one in mind of European fables. Moreover, unlike what happens in other cultural areas, the interactions between humans and other natural species are seldom studied by Africanists (apart from those interested in the Pygmy peoples); and plants and animals figure mainly in analyses of dietary prohibitions, totemism, or sacrifice—that is to say, as icons that express social categories and practices and not as full subjects in the life of this world. And these African specificities were perpetuated in America when African slaves were deported there. This can be clearly seen in the different ways in which the humid forest of the Colombian Chocó is represented by, on the one hand, the Emberá Indians and, on the other, the black populations descended from runaway slaves, who have lived there since the seventeenth century, in constant contact with the Indians. For the Indians, the forest is a familiar extension of a human house, and in it, they engage in ritual exchanges of energy with animals and with the spirits that rule there. Meanwhile, the Africans regard it simply as a wild, dark, dangerous place, to be avoided as far as possible: it is the absolute antithesis of inhabited space.[45]

In Part III of the present work, I shall examine the reasons that might explain this apparent exceptionality of Africa and its puzzling similarity to Europe in the manner in which discontinuities between humans and non-humans are perceived and organized. Actually, this particularism may well, in part, be a product of the intellectual habits that characterize all specialist studies in cultural areas. For these tend to encourage ethnographers to pick out from the society that they are studying those expressions of certain realities that are rendered familiar by the scholarly tradition peculiar to the region under examination, meanwhile neglecting phenomena that do not fit in easily with the interpretive frameworks that this tradition has elaborated. However,

canons of analysis do evolve along with the changes in paradigms that periodically take place in regional studies; and new inquiries in the field may
then throw light upon neglected aspects of cultures that had hitherto been
believed to be well understood. To cite but two brief examples, in Mali and
in Sierra Leone, recent ethnographical works have detected conceptions of
nonhumans that are more similar to what is familiar in America and Oceania
than to the image that has for years been presented by Africanist ethnology.
Thus, the Kuranko of Sierra Leone ascribe to certain individuals the ability to
transform themselves into predatory animals (elephants, leopards, crocodiles,
or snakes), the better to damage their enemies by attacking their livestock or
trampling on their harvests. In the course of his investigations into the ontology underlying such a belief, Michael Jackson has pointed out that it rests
upon a person being conceived as a fluctuating attribute produced by interactions with others rather than as an individualized essence anchored in one's
consciousness of one's self and one's physical unity. The notion of a "person,"
morgoye, thus does not define a singular and stable identity but develops out
of the establishment of more or less successful social relations, at a particular
time, with a whole group of entities, so that the quality of a "person," which depends on position rather than substance, may be ascribed, depending on the
circumstances, to humans, to animals, to bush spirits, to ancestors, to plants,
or even to stones.[46] This blurring of ontological frontiers is just as remarkable
among the Dogon of Tireli, who confer anthropomorphic properties upon
forest plants: healers consult trees in order to acquire their know-how, and
some trees, in particular the kapok, are believed to move around at night in
order to strike up conversations. Stones situated in the vicinity of cemeteries
are also credited with this ability.[47] The opposition between the bush and the
village, which is nevertheless very clear in both these cases, can thus accommodate a multitude of mediations and crossovers, a fact that makes it unlikely
that the respective occupants of the two spaces are distributed according to
categories of essences that are naturally distinct.

Let us now pause in this ethnographic journey that has already borne us
across many seas. Its purpose was to establish that the way of experiencing
the continuity between humans and nonhumans that I had been privileged to
observe in a remote corner of Amazonia was, in reality, widespread; and that
it was unlikely to have emerged from a common ideological source that might
have spread from one place to another and eventually come to permeate a
considerable portion of the planet.
    Some might object that all the peoples that I have mentioned in truth
possess identical structural features that might account for the resemblances

in their respective views of the world. They live, or lived, by hunting and gathering and fishing, and many of them also cultivate tropical root crops that reproduce vegetatively. Dispersed in small communities with a low demographic level, and unable to accumulate substantial surpluses, they depend for their subsistence upon an ongoing, individualized interaction with plants and animals. In most cases the prey presents itself to the hunters in the form of an isolated individual or a small group of animals with which the hunter has to compete in cunning and skill. Meanwhile, the cultivation of cuttings differs from that of cereals in that each plant requires personal attention and is therefore invested with a manifest individuality.[48] It is therefore in no way surprising that anthropomorphic attributes are ascribed to these plants and animals that all become distinctive as they daily receive individual attention.

Furthermore, the societies that we have so far passed in review know nothing of writing, of a central political system, or of urban life. They lack institutions that specialize in the accumulation, objectivization, and transmission of knowledge and so would have been unable to carry out the kind of reflexive and critical program that made it possible for the literate tradition of some peoples to isolate nature and treat it as a field of inquiry from which to draw positive knowledge. In short, and given that it is hard to resist the convenience of evolutionism when challenging explanations based on diffusion, is it not legitimate to assume that the lack of any clear opposition between humans and nonhumans is characteristic of a certain stage in universal history from which the great civilizations have liberated themselves?

A full reply to the above argument would far exceed the scope of the present chapter. So I shall content myself with briefly invoking two examples that cast doubt upon the idea that the naturalization of the world results inevitably from the progress of knowledge made possible by writing and the increasing complexity of means of social integration.

The first example takes us to ancient India, a world steeped in rites that Brahmins are responsible for maintaining by fulfilling their task of organizing sacrifices. Let me borrow the title of a book by Charles Malamoud and say that this task consists in "cooking the world" without let or hindrance, for it is the cooking of sacrificial victims that confirms the gods in their divine status, ensures the regular succession of the seasons, and guarantees the production of foodstuffs appropriate for each different class of beings.[49] However, the sacrificial fires that the Brahmins tend are not designed to change the state of a world that is raw and natural in its original form; they do not stamp the seal of culture upon a formless material mass. All they do is recook a cosmos already transformed by the cooking effected by the sun. It is true that certain spaces seem beyond the reach of the Brahmins' patient labor. The difference between village and forest is very marked in Brahmin India. The "village" (*grāma*) consists first and foremost in the institutions that enable it to exist, in particular sacrifice, and so also in the means of accomplishing that: the domesticated animals, the cultivated fields, and the obligations imposed by the management of farmlands. The "forest" (*araṇya*) is whatever lies outside the village, the gaps between the places that are inhabited, which are characterized not so much by a particular type of vegetation as by the exclusion of sacrifice, which is the symbol par excellence of civilization. But Malamoud shows clearly that this contrast in no way corresponds to an opposition between nature and society:[50] in the first place because sacrifice integrates wild animals, as semivictims, for—unlike domesticated animals—these are not killed but are released. This demonstrates the village's ability to encompass the forest within its ritual space and to bring together things that might have appeared to be separate.

Second, the forest itself, in certain respects, encompasses the village. In Vedic thought, man is characterized and distinguished by the fact that he is both sacrificer and sacrificed, the officiating priest and at the same time the only authentic victim, for whom other animals are just substitutes. From this point of view, man is the chief village animal suitable for sacrifice. But he is also included among the beasts of the forest, and it is because of their resemblance to him that certain species, such as monkeys and elephants, are classified as wild animals. In taxonomies and in practice too, man is of the forest as much as of the village. His double nature finds expression in the doctrine of the stages of life that recommends that once a high-caste man has reached maturity, he should divest himself of his possessions and end his life in the forest, in ascetic solitude, adopting the state of a "renouncer." Some texts indicate that renunciation is not a mortification of the body involving trials sent by an inhospitable nature. On the contrary, it is a way of merging with the environment, nourishing and reviving oneself there, following its rhythm and obeying its principle of existence.[51] Jean-Claude Galey tells us that such teaching still exists in contemporary India: "It is not at all a case of mankind being autonomous but rather of an infinite process of transformations that, without confusing them, envisages all the different categories of living beings within the cosmos as so many links in a continuous and all-including chain."[52] In short, in this refined civilization nature does not appear to have acquired the status of an independent domain any more than it has among the peoples without writing of America and Oceania.

Augustin Berque's fine study on the sense of nature in Japan leads to a similar conclusion.[53] The very term *shizen* by which the concept of nature is translated conveys only one of the meanings of "nature" in the West, the one closest to the original notion of *phusis*, namely the principle according to which a being is what it is in itself: it develops according to its "nature." But *shizen* by no means covers the idea of a sphere of phenomena that are independent of human action, for in Japanese thought, there is no place for a conscious objectivization of nature or for such a withdrawal of humanity from all that surrounds it.[54] As in New Caledonia, the environment is perceived as fundamentally indistinct from the self; it is regarded as an ambience in which a collective identity develops. Berque detects in the syntax of the Japanese language a tendency to block out the individuation of a person, in particular in the relative effacement of a grammatical subject in favor of a context of reference that covers both the verb and individual subjects. Here, the environment should be taken literally: it is what links together and constitutes human beings as multiple expressions of a complex whole that is greater than them.

Such holism helps to clarify the paradox of the Japanese garden. It may seem the height of artificiality, but the aim of this ultimate representation of Japanese culture is not to express an obsessive domestication of nature but to present a purified representation of the cosmos for the pleasure of contemplation.[55] Thanks to it, mountains and water (the sacred dwelling places of spirits and the goals of meditative excursions) are transported in miniature to places fashioned by human beings, but without losing their character or being intrusive. To reduce the landscape to the dimensions of an enclosed space is not to capture an alien nature in order to objectify it by mimetic means. It is to seek, by visiting a familiar space, to recover an intimate connection with a universe that is hard to access. The Japanese aesthetics of landscape does not express a separation between the environment and the individual but shows that the only way for nature to be meaningful is for it to be reproduced by human beings or animated by deities in such a way as to render immediately visible the marks of the conventions that fashion it. Far from being a domain of raw materiality, the garden is the ultimate cultural outcome of a long education of human sensibility.

It is time to bring this lengthy inventory to a close. Its purpose has not been to demonstrate or explain but simply to convey the fact that the modern West's way of representing nature is by no means widely shared. In many regions of the planet, humans and nonhumans are not conceived as developing in incommunicable worlds or according to quite separate principles. The environment is not regarded objectively as an autonomous sphere. Plants and animals, rivers and rocks, meteors and the seasons do not exist all together in an ontological niche defined by the absence of human beings. And this seems to hold true whatever may be the local ecological characteristics, political regimes and economic systems, and the accessible resources and the techniques employed to exploit them.

Over and above their indifference to the distinctions that naturalism fosters, do the cultures that we have surveyed present points in common in their ways of accounting for the relations between humans and their environment? No doubt they do, but not always in the same combinations. The most common procedure is to treat certain elements in the environment as persons endowed with cognitive, moral, and social qualities analogous to those of humans, thereby making it possible for communication and interaction between classes of beings that at first sight seem very different. The practical obstacles created by such a conception are to some extent overcome by drawing a clear distinction between, on the one hand, a principle of individual identity that is stable and able to manifest itself by very different means and in very different forms and, on the other hand, a transitory corporeal envelope, frequently likened to clothing, that can be donned or discarded as circumstances dictate. However, the ability to undergo metamorphosis is circumscribed by certain limits, in particular because the material form in which different kinds of persons are embodied in many cases determines perceptive constraints that cause them to apprehend the world according to criteria peculiar to their own species. Finally, these nested cosmological constructions define particular identities by the relations that institute them rather than by reference to reified substances or essences, thereby increasing the porosity of the frontiers between different classes of beings and also between the interior and the exterior of organisms. Admittedly, all this does not suffice to blur the major differences that exist between the cultures presented here as examples. But it does enable one to put one's finger on an even greater difference, the one that separates the modern West from all those peoples, both past and present, who have not considered it necessary to proceed to a naturalization of the world. The present book will be devoted to examining the implications of this difference, not in order to perpetuate it and enrich it, but rather to try to pass beyond it in full knowledge of the facts.

2

The Wild and the Domesticated

Henri Michaux was not yet thirty when he set off to the Andes to visit an Ecuadorian friend whom he had met in Paris. Fired by the temptation of adventure and despite his fragile health, in 1928 he decided to return to Paris by way of the rivers of Amazonia. This involved one month in a canoe, exposed to the rain and the mosquitoes, all the way along the River Napo as far as the Marañon, followed by three weeks of relative comfort on a small Brazilian steamer, traveling down the Amazon to reach its estuary. It was there, at Belém de Pará that he witnessed the following scene: "A young woman who was on our boat, coming from Manaus, went into town with us this morning. When she came upon the Grand Park (which is undeniably nicely planted) she emitted an easy sigh. 'Ah, at last, nature,' she said, but she was coming from the jungle."[1]

Indeed she was. For this citizen of Amazonia, the forest was no reflection of nature but a disturbing chaos into which she seldom ventured, a place resistant to all attempts to tame it and by no means conducive to aesthetic pleasure. The main park in Belém, with its rows of palm trees and its plots of mown grass planted with a succession of mango trees, gazebos, and stands of bamboo, guaranteed an alternative to the forest: tropical plants, to be sure, but ones tamed by human labor, testifying to culture's triumph over the forest wilderness. This taste for well-groomed landscapes is evident everywhere, as can be seen from the color prints that preside over all the reception rooms, hotels, and restaurants of the little towns of Amazonia. Walls blotched with humidity display nothing but alpine scenes showing flower-decked chalets, cottages snuggling into hedged farmland, or austere rows of yew trees in French-style gardens—all no doubt symbols of exoticism, but necessary contrasts to the excessive proximity of vegetation run riot.

Do we not all, like Michaux's fellow traveler, draw elementary distinctions in our environment according to whether or not it bears the marks of human action? Garden and forest, field and heath, cultivated terraces and shrubland, oasis and desert, village and bush: all are well-attested pairs that correspond to the opposition that geographers draw between ecumene and uninhabited space, that is, between places that humans daily frequent and those into which they more rarely venture.[2] So could it not be said that the absence, in many societies, of any notion similar to the modern idea of nature is simply of a semantic kind since, everywhere and always, people distinguish between what is domesticated and what is wild, between places deeply socialized and others that develop independently of human action? Provided one considers as cultural those portions of the environment that are modified by humans and as natural those that are not, the duality of nature and culture could be saved from the sin of ethnocentrism and even be established upon bases that are all the firmer because they are founded upon an experience of the world that is in principle accessible to all. Doubtless, for many people nature does not exist as an automatic ontological domain, but for them, whatever is wild would take the place of "nature," so they, like us, would be able to see a difference—a topographical one at least, between what stems from human beings and what does not.

Nomadic Spaces

Nothing is more relative than common sense, particularly when it is applied to the perception and use of inhabited spaces. In the first place, it is unlikely that the opposition between wild and domesticated can have been at all meaningful in the period prior to the Neolithic transition—that is to say, during the greater part of human history. And although access to the mindset of our Paleolithic ancestors is difficult, we can at least consider the manner in which hunter-gatherers of our time live within their environment. Subsisting on plants and animals over whose reproduction and numbers they have no control, they tend to move around in accordance with the fluctuations of resources that are sometimes abundant but often distributed in an unequal fashion in different places and in different seasons. Thus, the Netsilik Eskimos, who lead a nomadic life covering several hundreds of kilometers to the northwest of Hudson Bay, divide up their year into at least five or six different stages. In late winter and spring, they hunt the seals in the frozen sea; in summer, they catch fish by building weirs across the rivers of the interior; in early autumn, they hunt caribou in the tundra; and in October, they catch fish through holes cut in the ice covering the recently frozen rivers.[3] Of course, all this involves vast migrations that require the Eskimos, at regular intervals, to familiarize themselves with new spots or else to revert to former habits and places remembered from past visits. At the opposite climatic extreme, the margin of maneuver for the !Kung San of Botswana is more restricted, for in the arid Kalahari environment, they depend on access to water to establish somewhere to live. For them, the collective mobility of the Eskimos is not an option, so each group tends to settle close to a place with permanent access to water. But individuals are constantly on the move, circulating between the various camps, and so spend much of their lives moving to unfamiliar places, of which they have to learn all the nooks and crannies.[4] That is also the case of the BaMbuti Pygmies of the Ituri forest: even though each group successively sets up camp within a particular known territory, the boundaries of which are generally recognized, the composition of their group and their hunting parties constantly changes in the course of a year.[5]

Whether in an equatorial forest or in the Far North, in the deserts of southern Africa or the center of Australia, in all these so-called marginal zones, which for a long time nobody even thought of claiming from their hunting peoples, the same relations between those peoples and the places they frequent always predominate. Their occupation of the space does not spread out from any fixed point. Instead, it comes about through a network of itineraries marked out and punctuated by more or less ad hoc and more or less recurrent stopping places. As Mauss noticed with regard to the Eskimos as early as the beginning of the twentieth century, most hunter-gatherer peoples divide their annual cycle into two phases: a period of dispersion in small teams on the move and a briefer period during which they all gather at a site that affords them the opportunity for a more intense social life and for performing great collective rituals.[6] It would nevertheless be unrealistic to consider this temporary gathering to resemble village life, that is, as a center regularly reactivated in order for them to impose their domination over the surrounding territory. No doubt the surroundings are familiar and are each time rediscovered with pleasure, but their renewed occupation does not turn such areas into domesticated spaces that stand in contrast to the wild disorder of the places that the people visit during the rest of the year.

Because it is constantly revisited and resocialized, the environment of hunter-gatherers at every turn bears the traces of events that have unfolded there and that revivify old continuities right down to the present. In the first place, there are traces of an individual nature that shape a person's existence by enfolding him or her in a multitude of associated memories: the remains, sometimes scarcely visible, of an abandoned camp; a combe, a striking tree, or a bend in the river that calls to mind the site of the pursuit of some animal

or the lying in wait for one; the familiarity of the spot where one was initiated, married, or gave birth; the place where a relative passed away (which, in
many cases, is now to be avoided). But these signs do not stand on their own
as constant witnesses that stamp their mark upon space. At most, they constitute fleeting signatures of biographical trajectories legible only to whoever
left them there and by the circle of those who share his or her intimate memory of the recent past. However, it is true that certain striking features of the
environment are sometimes given an autonomous identity that endows them
with the same significance for everyone. Such is the case in central Australia,
where peoples such as the Warlpiri see in the relief and accidental features of
the terrain—hills, clusters of rocks, salt marshes, or streams—traces left by
the activities and peregrinations of ancestral beings that, through metamorphosis, became components of the landscape.[7] However, these sites are not
petrified temples or centers for civic activities; rather, they are an imprint left
by the passing, in "dream times," of the creators of beings and things. They
only acquire meaning when they are linked together in the itineraries that the
Aboriginals constantly repeat, superimposing the ephemeral marks of their
own passing upon the more tangible ones left by their ancestors. That is likewise the function of the cairns that the Inuit build in the Canadian Arctic.
These heaps of stones indicate a site once inhabited or perhaps a tomb or a
place for hunters to wait for caribou, and they are built in such a way as to
suggest, from a distance, the silhouette of an upright man. Their function is
not to tame the landscape but to call to mind former journeys and to serve as
landmarks for current travelers.

   To claim that hunter-gatherers perceive their environment as a "wilderness"—in contrast to a domesticity that one would be hard put to define—is
to deny that they are aware that, in the course of time, they modify the local
ecology by their techniques of subsistence. Over recent years, for example,
Aboriginals have been protesting to the Australian government against its
use of the term "wilderness" to qualify the territories that they occupy and
by so doing frequently justifying the creation of natural reserves that they do
not want. The notion of a "wilderness," with all its connotations of *terra nul-
lius*, of an original and preserved naturalness, an ecosystem to be protected
against the degradations liable to be introduced by human beings, certainly
runs contrary to the Aboriginals' own concept of the environment and the
multiple relations that they have established with it, and above all it ignores
the subtle transformations that they have produced in it. As a leader of the
Jawoyn of the Northern Territory said, when part of their land was converted
into a natural reserve, "Nitmiluk national park is not a wilderness . . . , it is a
human artefact. It is a land constructed by us over tens of thousands of years

through our ceremonies and ties of kinship, through fire and through hunting."[8] Clearly, for the Aboriginals, as for other hunting peoples, the opposition between wild and domesticated is not very meaningful, not only because of their lack of domesticated animals but above all because they inhabit the entire environment as a spacious and familiar dwelling place, rearranged to suit successive generations with such discretion that the touch of its inhabitants becomes almost imperceptible.

Nevertheless, domestication does not necessarily imply a radical change of perspective, provided the society remains a mobile one. At least, that is what is suggested by the way that space is apprehended by itinerant herdsmen, who, in this respect, present more affinities with hunter-gatherers than with many sedentary livestock raisers. Admittedly, real examples of nomadism have become rare over the past couple of centuries, during which sedentary communities have expanded while herding ones have diminished. However, one example is provided by the Peuls Wodaabe, who remain on the move throughout the year, with their herds, in the Nigerian Sahel.[9] The range of their movements certainly varies: more restricted in dry seasons, when they circulate around the wells and markets of the Hausa area, pasturing their herds on the edges of agricultural land; but more extensive in the winter months, when they undertake a great migration to the rich grasslands of the Azawak and the Tadess. They live in no fixed homes but in all seasons are content with an uncovered enclosure within a semicircular thorny hedge, an ephemeral shelter that is hardly distinguishable from the landscape of stunted bushes of the surrounding steppe.[10]

This model of annual transhumance is the norm in many regions of the world. The Basseri tribe of southern Iran moves en masse northward in the spring and erects its tents in the alpine regions of the Kuh-i-bul for the summer. In the autumn, it returns to pass the winter among the bare hills to the south of the town of Lar. The journey away and the journey back each take between two and three months.[11] During the migrations, the campsites change almost every day, but the groups of tents are less mobile in the summer and the winter, and this is the time when family altercations tend to come to the fore and provoke some groups to split away. Close on fifteen thousand people and several hundreds of thousands of animals—mainly sheep and goats—are involved in these migrations within a band of territory five hundred kilometers long and sixty or so kilometers wide. The Basseri consider the transhumance route, known as the *il-rah*, to be their property, recognized by local populations and the authorities alike as a package of rights conceded to the nomads: the right to pass along routes and over uncultivated land, the right to pasture their herds outside cultivated fields, and the right to draw water everywhere except from private wells.

This way of occupying space has been interpreted as an example of the sharing of a territory by two distinct societies, the one nomadic, the other sedentary.[12] But one may also regard the *il-rah* system along the lines of the Australian model, that is to say as an appropriation of certain itineraries within an environment over which the nomads do not seek to exercise any control. The life of the group and the memory of its identity are attached not so much to an expanse conceived as a whole but, rather, to the unique features that, year after year, mark out the group's journeys. Such an attitude is shared by many nomadic herdsmen in Sahelian and Nilotic Africa, the Middle East, and central Asia. It seems to exclude any clear-cut opposition between a human home and an environment that is self-perpetuating and beyond any human intervention. So distinctions in the treatment and classification of animals according to whether or not they are dependent on humans do not necessarily involve a distinction between what is wild and what is domesticated in peoples' perception and use of places.

But it might be objected that such a dichotomy could well be imposed upon nomads from outside. Whether or not they possess and raise animals or subsist mainly as hunters or, more usually, gatherers, plenty of itinerant peoples find themselves faced with the need to come to some agreement with sedentary communities, whose land and villages manifestly differ from their own nomadic mode of occupying the space. Such perennial sites may be stages in the nomads' itinerary that need to be negotiated or, where the herdsmen are concerned, market towns; or they may be peripheral zones in which to engage in barter, as in the case of Pygmies, who exchange their game for the cultivated products of their farming neighbors; or they may become temporary rallying points, as in the case of the early Christian missions among the Yaghan and the Ona of the Tierra del Fuego or the trading posts for the people of the Canadian Arctic and subarctic.[13] However, whether such sites are to be found adjacent to zones where nomadic peoples pass or constitute enclaves within these zones, they never provide models of domesticity for the nomads, for the values and rules observed in those zones are so very different from their own. And if, in such cases, one persisted in preserving the opposition between "the wild" and "the domesticated," it would, absurdly and paradoxically, be necessary to reverse the meanings of those terms: the "wild" spaces such as the forest, the tundra, the steppes—all habitats that are as familiar to them as the intimate nooks and corners of our own birthplaces are to us— would be classed by nomadic peoples on the side of what is domesticated, in contrast to the stable, but hardly friendly places where the nomads are not always well received.

The Garden and the Forest

Let us now cross over into cultivated land, to see whether the opposition between "wild" and "cultivated" makes more sense among people whose agricultural labor forces them to lead a relatively sedentary life.

Such is the case of the Achuar, already mentioned in chapter 1. In contrast to nomadic or transhumant people, these horticulturists of the upper Amazon do remain in the same place for quite long periods (ten to fifteen years, on average). It is not soil exhaustion that forces them to go and settle on a new site but dwindling supplies of game in the vicinity and the need to reconstruct their houses, which have a limited life span. Evidently, the Achuar are very experienced in the cultivation of plants, as can be seen from the diversity of species that prosper in their gardens (as many as a hundred in the best-stocked ones) and the great number of stable varieties within the principal species: twenty or so kinds of sweet potato and as many of manioc and bananas.[14] It is also significant that cultivated plants occupy such an important place in Achuar mythology and ritual; and the subtlety of the agronomic knowledge manifested by the women is remarkable, for it is they who are incontestably in charge in the realm of the garden.

Archaeology confirms the great antiquity of plant cultivation in the region, for it was in a lake in the foothills of the Andes and close to the present habitat of the Achuar that the first traces of maize in the Amazon basin were found; they date from over five thousand years ago.[15] No one knows if this was an independent center of domestication; but several tropical tubers widely used today originated from the lowlands of South America, where the earliest occupants have had several millennia of experience in the raising of cultivated species.[16] All the indications thus suggest that the contemporary Achuar are heirs to a long tradition of experimentation with plants the appearance and genetic characteristics of which have been modified to such a degree that their forest ancestors are no longer identifiable. Furthermore, these expert gardeners organize their living space according to a concentric pattern of division that immediately evokes the familiar opposition between the domesticated and the wild. Given that the Achuar habitat is widely dispersed, each house is set in the middle of a vast cleared area that is cultivated and weeded with meticulous care and is surrounded by a confused mass of forest, which is the domain of hunting and gathering. All the ingredients of the classic dichotomy would seem to be well and truly in place: an orderly center versus its forest periphery, intensive horticulture versus extensive foraging, and a stable and abundant source of supplies within a domesticated environment versus the chancy resources offered by the forest.

However, such an impression certainly turns out to be illusory once one embarks on a detailed examination of the discourse and practices of the Achuar. In their gardens, they cultivate both domesticated species, that is to say those whose reproduction depends on humans, and also wild species transplanted from the forest, for the most part fruit trees and palms. Yet their botanical taxonomy makes no distinction between the two groups in the garden and, apart from the weeds, all the plants present in a cleared plot are classed as *aramu* (that which is placed in the earth). This term qualifies all plants manipulated by humans and applies both to domesticated species and also to those that are simply acclimatized. The latter may also be called *ikiamia* (of the forest), but only when they are found in their original setting. So the epithet *aramu* does not denote "domesticated plants." Rather, it refers to the particular relationship that links humans and plants in the gardens, whatever the origin of those plants. Nor is the adjective *ikiamia* equivalent to "wild," in the first place because, depending on the context in which it is found, a plant may lose that quality but also and above all because, in truth, the plants "of the forest" are likewise cultivated. They are cultivated by a spirit called Shakaim, whom the Achuar represent as the official forest gardener and whose benevolence and advice they seek before clearing a new plot of land. Furthermore, the layered vegetation of a garden that, in an expert disorder, intermingles fruit trees with palms and manioc bushes with ground-covering plants evokes in miniature the trophic structure of the forest.[17] This classic organization of polycultural swiddens in the tropical belt makes it possible, at least for a while, to offset the destructive effects of torrential rains and high temperature on soils of no more than mediocre fertility. No doubt the efficacy of such protection has been overestimated; all the same, each time they create a garden, the Achuar are fully conscious of substituting their own plantations for those of Shakaim.[18] The terminological pair *aramu* and *ikiamia* thus in no way covers an opposition between the domesticated and the wild. Rather, it applies to the contrast between plants that are cultivated by humans and those that are cultivated by spirits.

The Achuar draw a similar distinction within the animal kingdom. Their houses are enlivened by a whole menagerie of tamed animals: birds that were taken out of their nests and the young of hunted animals, which hunters take in when they have killed the little ones' mother. The young are placed in the care of the women, who nourish them by hand or even at the breast while they are still incapable of feeding themselves, and they soon adapt to their new lifestyle. Very few species, even among the felines, are really resistant to cohabiting with humans. These animal companions are seldom restrained and hardly ever maltreated. And, in any event, they are never eaten, not even when they die a natural death. They are said to be *tanku*, an adjective that might be translated "tamed" or "acclimatized to humans." The term can also be used as a noun that corresponds well enough to the English "pet." So one would say of a young peccary foraging close to the house, "That is so-and-so's *tanku*." But although *tanku* may evoke domesticity, that is to say socialization within the house, it does not correspond to our usual idea of domestication, for the Achuar never try to get their pets to reproduce and establish stable lineages. The term designates a transitory situation that cannot be opposed to a possible "wild" state, particularly since animals may also be tamed in their original state, but by spirits. The Achuar say that the beasts of the forest are the *tanku* of the spirits, which watch over their well-being and protect them from excessive hunting. So what differentiates forest animals from the animals that the Indians become attached to, as companions, is not at all an opposition between wildness and domestication but the fact that some animals are raised by spirits while others are temporarily tended by humans.

The idea of distinguishing places according to whether or not they are transformed by human labor is equally ill-founded. To be sure, in the early days of my stay among the Achuar, I was myself struck by the contrast between the welcoming freshness of their houses and the inhospitable luxuriance of the nearby forest, which I hesitated for a long time to enter alone. But it was simply that I brought to the situation a view reflecting my inbuilt city dweller's attitudes. It was not long before my observation of Achuar practices taught me to see things differently. The fact is that the Achuar mark out their space by means of a series of barely perceptible small concentric discontinuities rather than a head-on opposition between, on the one hand, the house and its garden and, on the other, the forest.

The area of beaten earth immediately adjacent to the dwelling is a natural prolongation of the latter and is the scene of many domestic activities. But it already marks a transition to the garden, for it is there that separate bushes of chili peppers, annatto, and genipapo are planted, along with most of the medicinal herbs and poison-bearing plants. The actual garden, which is the unchallenged territory of the women, is itself partly contaminated by forest behavior: it is the favorite hunting ground for Achuar boys, who keep a lookout for birds at which they can shoot using their little blowpipes. The men, too, lay traps here to catch the plump rodents with delicate, juicy flesh—pacas, agoutis, and agouchis—that nightly invade the garden to root up tubers. Within a radius of one or two hours' walk from the edge of the cleared area, the forest is used as a vast orchard, constantly visited by the women and children to gather berries, collect palm-tree grubs, or catch fish by asphyxiating them in the streams and small lakes. It is an intimately known domain where every fruit tree and palm is periodically visited in the appropriate season. Beyond it, the true hunting zone begins, where the women and children venture only when accompanied by their menfolk. However, it would be mistaken to see this outer ring as the equivalent of an external wilderness—for a hunter knows every inch of the territory in which he roams almost daily and to which he is linked by a multitude of memories. The animals that he encounters there are, for him, not wild beasts but beings that are almost human and that he must seduce and cajole in order to draw them out of the grasp of the spirits that protect them. It is in this great garden cultivated by Shakaim that the Achuar set up their hunting lodges, simple shelters sometimes surrounded by a few plantations, which they visit at regular intervals to spend a few days there with their families. I was always struck by the happy, carefree atmosphere in those encampments, which resembled that of a holiday in a rural cottage more than a bivouac in the depths of a hostile forest. Whoever is surprised by that comparison should bear in mind that Indians get bored with their all-too-familiar environment and, deep in the forest, they enjoy a little change of scene, just as we enjoy a break in the countryside. Clearly, the deep forest is hardly less socialized than the Achuar house with its cultivated surroundings. In the eyes of the Achuar, from the point of view of these visits to it and the principles of existence that obtain there, it bears no resemblance to a wilderness.

There is nothing extraordinary about regarding the forest as one does a garden when one reflects that some Amazonian peoples are fully aware that their cultural practices exert a direct influence upon the distribution and reproduction of wild plants. Until quite recently, this phenomenon of an indirect human impact on the forest ecosystem was unrecognized. Now, though, it has been well described in the studies that William Balée has devoted to the historical ecology of the Ka'apor of Brazil.[19] Thanks to his meticulous work of identifying and counting the plants, he has been able to establish that the clearings abandoned forty or more years ago are twice as rich in useful forest species than adjacent portions of the primeval forest that are, at first sight, almost indistinguishable from them. Like the Achuar, the Ka'apor plant in their gardens many nondomesticated plants that then flourish on the fallow land, to the detriment of the cultivated plants, which, when uncared for, soon disappear. The clearings still in use or abandoned only recently also attract predatory animals, which, by defecating there, disseminate the seeds of the forest plants that they have consumed. The Ka'apor claim that agoutis are largely responsible for spreading copal and several kinds of palms, while capuchin monkeys have introduced wild cocoa and various species of *inga*. As generations pass and the cycle of the renewal of the clearings proceeds, a by no means negligible portion of the forest is converted into an orchard, the artificial character of which the Ka'apor recognize, although they have done nothing deliberate to effect this. The Indians are also skilled at calculating the effects of former fallow land upon hunting. The zones with a high concentration of edible forest plants are more frequented by animals, and in the long term this affects the demography and distribution of game. This fashioning of the forest ecosystem, which has been going on over thousands of years in large parts of Amazonia, has no doubt contributed considerably to justifying the idea that the jungle is a space as domesticated as the gardens. It is true that to cultivate the forest, even by accident, is to leave one's mark on the environment, but unlike a humanly organized landscape, it does not rearrange it in such a way that the legacy of humans is immediately detectable. What with periodically shifted habitats, itinerant horticulture, and low population density, in contemporary Amazonia everything combines to prevent the most manifest signs of the occupation of a site from remaining detectable.[20]

A very different situation prevails among certain horticulturist peoples in the highlands of New Guinea. For example, in the Mount Hagen region, the fertility of the soils has allowed intensive exploitation of fallow land and a high density of inhabitation: among the Melpa, density may rise as high as one hundred and twenty inhabitants to every square kilometer whereas, among the Achuar, it is lower than two inhabitants to every ten square kilometers.[21] The valley floors and hillsides are covered by an uninterrupted mosaic of enclosed gardens, arranged like a checkerboard and leaving only the steepest slopes covered by a thin forest. As for the hamlets, each composed of four or five houses, they are almost all within sight of neighboring ones.[22] This is an organized area, appropriated and developed in every nook and cranny, where clan territories with well-defined boundaries fit alongside one another almost in the manner of hedged farmland. All in all, the arrangement presents a tangible contrast to the residual thickets that sprawl across the mountain slopes.

Yet the inhabitants of the Hagen region seem indifferent to this perception of their landscape, as is shown by an article by Marilyn Strathern unequivocally entitled, "No Nature, No Culture."[23] It is true that people in this region use a terminological pair that may be reminiscent of the opposition between the domesticated and the wild. *Mbo* qualifies cultivated plants while *rømi* refers to everything outside the sphere of human intervention, in particular the world of the spirits. But this semantic distinction no more covers a clear-cut dualism than does the difference between *aramu* and *ikiamia* among the Achuar. As in Amazonia, certain *rømi* spirits afford the forest plants and animals care and protection but allow humans to use them, on certain conditions. The "wild" fauna and flora are thus just as domesticated as the pigs, sweet potatoes, and yams upon which the people of Mount Hagen essentially depend for their subsistence. If the term *mbo* refers to the cultivation of plants, that is because it denotes one particular aspect of it, namely the act of planting. It is associated with the concrete image of placing in the ground, rooting, even autochthony, and in no way evokes the transformation or deliberate reproduction of living things controlled by humans. Nor does the contrast between *mbo* and *rømi* have any spatial dimension. Most of the clan territories incorporate portions of the forest that are appropriated socially according to generally recognized rules. It is there, in particular, that domesticated pigs forage in search of food, under the benevolent eye of spirits that watch over their safety. In short, and despite the strong control that the Mount Hagen inhabitants exercise over their environment, they do not see themselves as surrounded by a "natural environment." Their way of envisaging space in no way suggests that their inhabited places have been wrested from the wild domain.[24]

Admittedly, you could say that the intensification of the techniques of subsistence helps to crystallize the sense of a contrast between a durably organized center of activity and a seldom-frequented periphery. But to be conscious of a discontinuity between portions of space used for different social practices in no way implies that some domains are therefore perceived to be "wild." This emerges clearly from Peter Dwyer's comparison between the customs and representations of the environment in three horticulturist tribes of the highlands of New Guinea, chosen for the degree of the human impact on their ecosystem and for the extent to which they use forest resources as food.[25] The Kubo are a truly woodland people, with a density of population lower than one inhabitant per square kilometer, for whom an opposition between the inhabited center and whatever lies beyond is the more meaningless given that people sleep in little shelters in the forest as often as they do within the village. Spirits, in particular the souls of the dead embodied in animals, coexist everywhere with the humans. One hundred or so kilometers away, the Etolo leave a more consequential mark on their environment: their gardens are bigger and they cultivate pandanus orchards and establish permanent traplines. Their demographic density is in some places fifteen times greater than that of the Kubo. Their spiritual geography is also more clearly defined: the souls of the dead reside initially in birds, then in the fish that migrate to the outer edges of their territory. The Siane, finally, have profoundly and durably modified their habitat. They are decidedly sedentary, engage in intensive horticulture and the raising of pigs, and seldom visit the residual forests that cling to the mountains. Their spirits are less immanent and more realistic than those of the Kubo and the Etolo. They adopt their own particular kinds of appearances, are relegated to inaccessible places, and only communicate with humans using messenger-birds or ritual objects as go-betweens.

If we regard these three examples as so many stages in a process of an increasingly intensified use of cultivated resources, there can be little doubt that a growing transformation of the forest environment surrounding their centers of habitation goes hand in hand with the emergence of a peripheral sector that is increasingly alien to ordinary social relations both among humans and between humans and nonhumans. Nevertheless, Dwyer establishes that there is nothing in either the vocabulary or the attitudes of these peoples to warrant any inference that these increasingly marginal spaces are considered to be "wild," even among the Siane, whose demographic density is only half as great as that of the inhabitants of Mount Hagen.[26]

The Field and the Rice Paddy

Readers may consider that the peoples of the highlands of New Guinea do not present the most telling example of a complete domestication of the environment. Even intensive, horticulture in clearings requires more or less lengthy periods of letting the land lie fallow, during which the woodland vegetation colonizes the gardens for a while, creating a periodic intrusion that blurs the frontiers separating the spaces affected by human influence from their forest margins. A vast and dense network of permanent fields where nothing intrudes to call to mind the disorder of uncultivated zones would doubtless render a manifest polarity between the wild and the domesticated more detectable. Such is the case of the alluvial plains and the loess plateaus of eastern Asia and the Indian subcontinent, which, long before the Christian era, were exploited for cereal cultivation. For whole millennia, all the way from the Ganges plain in India to the area bordering the Yellow River, millions of peasants have cleared, irrigated, and drained the land, taming watercourses and enriching the soil and thereby profoundly modifying the aspect of those regions.

In fact, the languages of the great eastern civilizations quite clearly mark the difference between places over which humans exercise control and those that elude their power. Mandarin Chinese distinguishes between yě, the zone extending beyond the cultivated periphery of built-up areas, and jiā tíng, the domesticated space. Through its etymology, the former term evokes the notion of a threshold, a limit, an interface, and denotes the wild nature of not only places but also plants and animals. *Jiā tíng* refers more strictly to the domesticity of a family unit and is not used for domesticated plants and animals.[27] Japanese also establishes an opposition between *sato*, "the inhabited place," and *yama*, "the mountain," which is perceived not so much as a relief elevation that contrasts with the plain but rather as the archetype of an uninhabited space, comparable to the original meaning of the French or English "desert."[28] In Sanskrit, a rural inhabited space also seems clearly separated from a periphery that has not been transformed by humans. The term *jāṅgala* designates uninhabited land and becomes synonymous with the "wild place" of classical Hindi, while *atavī*, "the forest," refers not so much to a formation of plants but rather to places occupied by barbarian tribes—that is, the opposite of "civilization." It stands in opposition to *janapada*, the cultivated countryside, the terrain where *grāmya* beings, those "of the village" are to be found, including domesticated animals.[29] Yet when one considers the ways in which these semantically distinguished spaces are perceived and used, one is bound to see that in China, India, and Japan, it is hard to discover any dichotomy of "wild" and "domesticated" comparable to that which the Western world has forged. It is hardly surprising that in Asia a distinction is drawn between places that are inhabited and those that are not; but whether that distinction covers a hard and fast opposition between two systems of mutually exclusive values seems more doubtful.

The subjective geography of ancient China seems governed by a major contrast between town and mountain. The town, with its checkerboard layout, is symbolically associated with the cardinal points in an image of the cosmos and is at the same time the center that appropriates the agricultural terrain and the seat of political power. On the other hand, the main purpose of the mountain, a place of asceticism and exile, seems to be to provide pictorial representation with its favorite theme.[30] However, that opposition is less clear-cut than it appears. In the Daoist tradition, the mountain is the dwelling place of the Immortals, elusive beings that merge with the slopes and lend a palpable dimension to the sacred domain. Time spent on the mountain, in particular by scholars, is prompted by a quest for immortality, the most prosaic aspect of which is the collection of herbal remedies ensuring longevity. Furthermore, as Augustin Berque has suggested, the aestheticization of the mountain in Chinese landscape painting may be seen as a kind of recognition of spiritual characteristics that run parallel to agriculture's practical use of the plains.[31] Far from constituting a disorganized space devoid of any civilization, the mountain—the domain of deities and an expression of their essence— provides a necessary complement to the city and village world.

Nor is the town dissociated from the hinterland, even in its most distant reaches, for its situation and the arrangement of its houses are dictated in the smallest details by a kind of space-physiology, *fengshui*, imperfectly rendered in English and French by the term "geomancy." Daoism teaches that a cosmic breath, *qi*, irradiates throughout China from the Kunlun mountain chain, circulating along lines of force comparable to the veins that irrigate the human body. Hence, it is crucial to determine, by divination, the most favorable sites for human habitation and the ways to dispose houses so that they fit in with this network of energy that is deployed throughout the Middle Empire. If it is well situated, well built, and well governed, a Chinese town is in harmony with the world, which—to borrow an expression of Marcel Granet's—"is itself in order only when it is enclosed the way that a house is."[32] The wild thus appears to exert little purchase upon this cosmos so densely regulated by social conventions. And if Chinese thought does recognize that obscure forces that offer an enigmatic resistance to civilization exist, it relegates them to its own domain's periphery, where barbarians live.

In Japan likewise, the mountain is par excellence the space that stands in contrast to terrains in the plain. Symmetrical volcanic cones, thickly forested mountains, and rugged crags can everywhere be seen from the valleys and hollows, imposing their background of verticality upon the flat fields and dykes. But the distinction between *yama*, the mountain, and *sato*, the inhabited place, signals not so much a reciprocal exclusion but, rather, a seasonal alternation and a spiritual complementarity.[33] The gods shift regularly from one zone to another. In the spring, they descend from the mountains and become deities of the rice paddies. Then, in the autumn, they make the return journey to their "interior shrine" (*okumiya*), usually some topographical feature, their true home, where they are believed to have originated. A local deity (*kami*) thus proceeds from the mountain and, within the sacred arc, each year undertakes a journey by which it alternates between the sanctuary of the fields and the sanctuary of the mountains, at the center of a kind of itinerant domestic cult that blurs the boundary between what is within the village domain and what lies beyond it. As early as the twelfth century, the sacred dimension of the mountain solitudes had made them the preferred sites for Buddhist monastic communities, to such a degree that the character signifying "mountain" also served to designate monasteries.[34] And although it may be true that in about the same period in the West, the brothers of the order of Saint Benedict had long since fled the world in order to establish themselves in isolated places, it was as much in order to clear the forest and exorcize its wildness by dint of human labor as the better to rise toward God through prayer.[35] This was altogether different from the situation in Japan, where monastic life was lived in the mountains not so as to transform them but, by walking there and contemplating their sites, to experience a fusion with the sensible dimension of the landscape that constituted one of the guarantees of salvation.

A Japanese mountain is neither a space to conquer nor the seat of a disturbing otherness, so it is not really perceived as "wild," although it may, paradoxically, become so when its vegetation is totally domesticated. In many regions of the archipelago the forests growing on primeval slopes were replaced, following World War II, by industrial plantations of native conifers, mainly Japanese cypresses and *sugi* cedars. For the inhabitants of the mountain villages, the old forest with its deciduous or glossy-leaved species had been a place where harmony and beauty were enhanced by the presence of deities (as well as by a store of resources that were of use to the domestic economy). However, the plantations of resinous trees that replaced it evoke nothing but disorder, sadness, and disorganization.[36] Badly cared for, taking over fields and clearings, and having lost much of their economic value, these "black trees" growing in monotonous serried ranks are now beyond the social and technical control of those who planted them. The mountain is *yama*; the forest is *yama*; uninhabited places are *yama*. The same term is used in all three cases. But although it is wholly domesticated, this artificial mountain forest has become a moral and economic desert; in short, it is much more "wild" than the natural forest that it replaced.

In ancient India the status of places is more complex, for terminological reasons that Francis Zimmermann has illuminatingly explained.[37] In Sanskrit texts, *jāngala*, from which the Anglo-Indian "jungle" is derived, has two main meanings. First, it is, as noted above, an uninhabited place long abandoned and fallow. But—and this is the first paradox—*jāngala* also designates dry land—that is to say, the exact opposite of what "jungle" has evoked for us ever since Kipling. So, in its ancient meaning, a jungle was not an exuberant wet forest. Instead, the word designated semiarid thorny steppes, sparsely wooded savannas, or thin woods of deciduous trees. It thus stood in opposition to marshy land, *anūpa*, characterized by water-loving vegetation: rain forests, mangroves, swamps. The contrast between *jāngala* and *anūpa* reflects a strong polarity in cosmology, in medical doctrines, and in plant and animal taxonomy: dry terrains are valued because they are healthy, fertile, and peopled by Aryans, while marshy terrains appear as unhealthy margins where non-Aryan tribes take refuge. Each type of landscape constitutes a separate ecological community defined by emblematic animal and plant species and by a cosmic physiology that is peculiar to it. Hence a second paradox. How can an uninhabited, apparently "wild" zone also be the seat par excellence of virtues associated with agricultural civilization? Quite simply, because the jungle represents not only a geographical unit but also a potentiality. It was dry terrain that, thanks to irrigation, was colonized, and it was *in the heart of* those uncultivated but fertile regions that Aryan peasants organized their terrains, leaving to peripheral tribes the use of marshy land that was both impenetrable and waterlogged. The contrast between *jāngala* and *anūpa* thus takes the form of a dialectic involving three terms, one of which remains implicit. Upon the opposition between marshy land, the domain of barbarians, and dry land, claimed by Aryans, is superimposed an overarching notion that makes the jungle a space that, although unoccupied, is available, a place devoid of human beings but imbued with the values and promise of civilization. This twofold view prevents the *jāngala* from being considered a wild place that is in need of socialization, since it is virtually inhabited anyway and encompasses, as a project or ultimate possibility, cultural energies that will here find conditions favorable to their development. Meanwhile, marshy land is not wild either: it is simply lacking in attraction and fit only to shelter a few peripheral specimens of humanity in its bushy darkness.

Piling up examples has never constituted a proof, but examples do at least make it possible to cast doubt on a number of established certainties. It now seems clear that, in many regions of our planet, contrasting perceptions of beings and places, depending on their greater or lesser proximity to the world of humans, coincides hardly at all with the body of meanings and values that, in the West, have become attached to the two poles represented by "the wild" and "the domesticated." Unlike the many forms of gradual discontinuity or encompassment whose traces are to be found elsewhere in agricultural societies, those two notions are mutually exclusive and acquire their full meaning only when they are related to each other in a complementary opposition.

Ager and *Silva*

Anything "wild" in Romance languages (*sauvage, selvaje, selvaggio,* and so on) comes from the *silva,* the great European forest that Roman colonization was gradually to erode. The *silva* is an uncultivated space to be cleared; a place for the beasts and plants found there and the rough peoples who inhabit it, for individuals seeking refuge from the laws of the city, and, hence, for those possessed of fierce temperaments and who are recalcitrant to the discipline of social life. However, although these various attributes of wildness no doubt derive from the characteristics attributed to a very particular environment, they form a coherent whole only because they are set, term for term, in opposition to the positive qualities affirmed in domesticated life.

These are deployed in the *domus*, not a geographical unit as the *silva* is, but an environment for living, originally involving agricultural exploitation, in which, under the authority of the paternal head of the family and the protection of the household deities, women, children, slaves, animals, and plants all found conditions that favored the realization of their true natures. Laboring in the fields, raising children, training animals, and dividing up tasks and responsibilities all combined to set humans and nonhumans under the same hierarchical regime of subordination, the perfect model of which was provided by relations within an extended family. The Romans bequeathed to us the values associated with this antithetical pair that was to gain increasing acceptability along with the terminology to express it. For the discovery of other forests, in other latitudes, was to enrich the initial dichotomy without altering its range of meaning. The Tupinamba of Brazil and the Indians of New France would take the place of the Germans and the Britons described by Tacitus, while domestication would undergo a change of scale and turn into civilization.[38] It might be said that this slippage of meaning and periods opened up the possibility of the inversion that Montaigne and Rousseau were to exploit: now, what was wild could be good and what was civilized could be bad, with the former embodying the virtues of an ancient simplicity of which the latter had been deprived though the corruption of its mores. But we should remember that that rhetorical ploy was not exactly new (Tacitus himself had resorted to it) and that, besides, it does nothing to undermine the interplay of reciprocal meanings that make the "wild" and the "domesticated" mutually interdependent.

Possibly because they ignore the impossibility of thinking of one of the terms in that opposition without thinking of the other, some authors tend to turn the "wild" into a universal dimension of the psyche, a kind of archetype that humans have progressively suppressed and pushed aside as their mastery over nonhumans increased. That is the case of the scenario proposed by the environmental philosopher Max Oelschlaeger in his voluminous history of the idea of wilderness. According to him, the Paleolithic hunter-gatherers lived in harmony with a wild environment that had many positive qualities but was hypostasized as an autonomous domain and worshiped within the framework of a "totemic" religion. In contrast, the farmers of the Mediterranean Neolithic shattered that fine entente and set out to subdue the wilderness, thereby demoting spaces not dominated by humans to a lower status until such time as they regained their place of honor thanks to American nineteenth-century philosophy and painting.[39] That may be, but it is hard to see how the very notion of "wilderness" could have existed in a preagricul-

tural world in which it was not opposed to anything, and why, if it embodied positive values, anyone should have felt the need to eliminate whatever it
represented.

Ian Hodder avoids that kind of impasse by suggesting that a symbolic construction of "the wild" was already under way in the early Paleolithic, as a
necessary background to the emergence of a cultural order. For this leader of
the new interpretative Anglo-Saxon archaeology, the domestication of the wild
began with the improvement of the stone tools characteristic of the Solutrean
period, testifying to a "desire" for culture that was expressed in the perfecting
of hunting techniques. His suggestion is that more effective protection against
predators and less chancy subsistence techniques made it possible to overcome
the instinctive fear of an inhospitable environment and to turn hunting into the
symbolic means of exerting control over the wild as well as a source of prestige
for those who excelled at it. The origin of agriculture in Europe and the Near
East could thus be explained simply by an extension of that desire to exercise
control over plants and animals, which were gradually withdrawn from their
own environment and integrated into the domesticated sphere.[40] There is no
way of knowing if this really happened or whether Hodder, carried away by his
imagination, perhaps interpreted ancient vestiges in accordance with mental
categories that are attested only very much later. Whatever the case may be, the
question that remains is why such a movement came about in one particular
region of the world and not elsewhere: the psychological dispositions cited by
Hodder as the sources of a propensity to exercise an ever-increasing mastery
over nonhuman beings are so generally present that it is hard to see why this
process should not have occurred everywhere. However, the domestication
of plants and animals was not a historical inevitability that only technical obstacles could delay here or there, for plenty of peoples throughout the world
seem to have barely felt the need for such a revolution. We should be aware
that some sophisticated civilizations—the cultures of the west coast of Canada
and southern Florida, for example—developed by prioritizing the tapping of
wild resources. Moreover, many contemporary hunter-gatherer groups manifest a certain indifference or even an overt repugnance vis-à-vis the agriculture and stock raising that they see practiced on the margins of their domains.
For them, domestication is by no means a compulsion but a choice that they
continue to reject.

In a more subtle manner, Bertrand Hell suggests the hypothesis according
to which a collective imaginary representation of the wild is present everywhere in Eurasia, and traces of it may be found in its beliefs, rites, and legends
concerning hunting and the treatment of large game.[41] One central theme
structures this symbolic configuration, the theme of "black blood," the thick

blood of a rutting stag or a solitary wild boar, which is both dangerous and desirable, full of generative power and also a source of wildness. For this fluid also runs in the veins of hunters when, in the autumn, they burn with *Jagdfieber* (hunting fever). This takes possession of woodsmen, poachers, and marginal figures in flight from village sociability, who are barely distinguishable from enraged beasts or werewolves. Admittedly, in the Germanic zone from which Hell draws most of his examples, the world of the wild seems to have acquired a certain autonomy along with an ambiguous power of fascination, as if it has been left room to subsist in itself as a source of life and virile success rather than as a negative contrast with cultivated terrains.[42] Yet, although it may not be the strict converse of agricultural dominion, the domain of "the wild" is nevertheless highly socialized. It is identified with the great forest, not the unproductive *silva* that impedes colonization but the *foresta*, the gigantic park filled with game that the Carolingian dynasty, as early as the ninth century, took measures to protect by edicts limiting grazing rights and deforestation.[43] This, then, was wildness highly cultivated and linked with extremely ancient endeavors to manage and improve hunting territories, organized by an elite that regarded the ambushing and tracking of big game as a character-forming school for the development of courage. It is precisely because Hell so carefully reconstructs the historical context within which the imaginary representation of the wild developed in the Germanic world that it becomes difficult to follow him when he attempts to find analogous manifestations in other regions of our planet, as if everywhere and for all time men have been conscious that dark and ambivalent forces have to be placated by means of the artifices of civilization.[44]

Herdsmen and Hunters

We must beware of ethnocentrism: the "Neolithic revolution" of the Near East is not a universal scenario the conditions of appearance and the material and ideational effects of which are transposable, just as they are, to the rest of the world. In other cradles of agriculture, the domestication and management of plants seem to have developed in different technical and mental contexts. As we have seen, these hardly favor the emergence of a mutually exclusive distinction between a domain controlled by humans and a residual sector that is of no use to humans or is destined eventually to fall under their domination. It would, of course, be absurd to claim that the difference between the inhabited and the wild was perceived and expressed only in the West. But it does seem probable that the values and meanings attached to the opposition between wild and domesticated belong to one particular historical trajectory and depend, in part, upon a characteristic feature of the process of transition to the Neolithic that began in the Fertile Crescent more than ten thousand years ago. In a region extending from the eastern Mediterranean to Iran, the domestication of plants and animals took place more or less concurrently within less than a millennium.[45] The cultivation of wheat, barley, and rye was accompanied by the raising of goats, oxen, sheep, and pigs. In this way, a complex and interdependent system for the management of nonhumans was set up in an ambience designed to allow their coexistence. But such a system is at variance with what happened in other continents, where large mammals were for the most part domesticated either quite a while after the plants were or, in the case of East Africa, long before—that is, if they were indeed domesticated at all, for in much of the Americas and Oceania the raising of livestock did not occur, or else was adopted only later on, as a result of the arrival of already-domesticated animals from elsewhere.

In the European Neolithic, a major contrast was thus set up, which certainly opposed spaces that were cultivated to those that were not but also and above all opposed domesticated animals to wild ones and the world of cowsheds and pastureland to the realm of the hunter and of game. It may even have been the case that this contrast was desired and actively engineered so as to preserve domains in which it was possible to deploy qualities such as cunning, physical endurance, and pleasure in conquest that, except in warfare, no longer had a role to play in the carefully controlled setting of an agricultural terrain. Indeed, it is not beyond the bounds of possibility that peoples of the European Neolithic deliberately abstained from domesticating certain species, such as deer, in order to preserve them as a preferred source of game. In that case, the domestication of some animals would have gone hand in hand with a kind of "huntingization" of a few others, and the maintenance of the latter in their natural state would have resulted not from technical obstacles but, on the contrary, from a desire to set up a domain reserved for hunting that was separate from the cultivated one.[46]

The evidence from ancient Greece shows very clearly how, in the Mediterranean world, the antinomy between the wild and the domesticated draws on a contrast between hunting and livestock raising. The Greeks ate only meat that was provided by a sacrifice, ideally a domesticated ox or the spoils of a hunting expedition. In the symbolic economy of foodstuffs and statuses, the two activities were at once complementary and opposed. The cuisine of sacrifice brought humans and the gods together, yet opposed them, given that the former received the cooked meat of the animal while the latter had the right only to the bones and the aromas from the cooking fire. Conversely, as Pierre Vidal-Naquet points out, hunting "determines the relationship between man and nature in the wild."[47] Humans behave as predatory animals do but differentiate themselves from those animals through their mastery of the art of hunting, a *technē* linked with the art of warfare and, more generally, that of politics. Humans, beasts, and the gods constitute three opposed elements in a system in which a domesticated animal (*zoon*) is placed very close to humans, being, on account of its aptitude for living communally, barely inferior to slaves and barbarians (we should bear in mind Aristotle's definition of man as a *zoon politikon*). Such a domesticated animal was clearly differentiated from wild animals (*theria*).[48] The sacrificial victim represents a point of intersection between the human and the divine. Moreover, it is imperative to obtain from it a sign of assent before it is put to death, as if the animal consented to the role allotted to it in the civic and liturgical life of the city. Such a precaution was unnecessary in hunting, where victory was won by competing with the game. In hunting, adolescents demonstrated their cunning and agility, while mature men, armed only with a spear, put their strength and skill to the test. It should be added that agriculture, livestock raising, and sacrifice are closely linked in that consumption of the sacrificed victim must be accompanied by cultivated products such as toasted barleycorn and wine.[49] The habitat of wild beasts thus constitutes a belt of noncivilization that is indispensable to the flourishing of civilization itself. It provides a theater in which it is possible to exercise virile dispositions that are poles apart from the virtues of conciliation required for the treatment of domesticated animals and for political life.

The Roman Landscape, the Hercynian Forest, and Romantic Nature

In this respect, the Latin world offers a contrast. Although founded by a pair of twins raised in the wild, Rome gradually withdrew from the model of heroic hunting and came to regard the tracking of game simply as a way of protecting its crops. By the end of the Republic, Varro was stigmatizing the pointlessness of hunting and how unproductive it was in comparison to livestock raising (*Rerum rusticarum*). This was a point of view that Columella endorsed one century later, in his treatise on agriculture (*De re rustica*). The fashion for extensive hunting brought back from Asia Minor by Scipio Aemilianus did not win over an aristocracy that was more preoccupied by the productivity of its domains than by hunting exploits: wild animals were regarded above all as harmful, and it was the duty of stewards and professional trappers to destroy them.[50] The organization of the rural landscape in the plains was now centered on the *villa* (or large farm). A *villa* was a compact building surrounded by a vast quadrangular territory devoted to the cultivation of cereals and vines and olive trees. It favored a clear segregation between the drained, cultivated land (the *ager*) and the peripheral zone devoted to pasturing free-roaming herds (the *saltus*). As for the great forest (the *ingens silva*), it had lost all the attraction it may formerly have held for hunters and now represented nothing more than an obstacle to the extension of agricultural development. The rational management of resources even extended to game, the numbers of which were fixed and controlled (at least in the great rural properties), thanks to fodder depots to which wild deer were guided in the winter months by the tamed members of their species, which had been specially trained for this purpose.[51]

Under the empire, the Romans' point of view with regard to the forest was certainly ambivalent. In the now almost deforested peninsula, it evoked the setting of Rome's foundation myths and memories of the ancient Rhea Silvia, and its nurturing and sacred aspect was perpetuated only as a faint echo in woods consecrated to Artemis and Apollo or in the woodland sanctuary alongside Lake Nemi, the strange rites of which provided Frazer with the inspiration for his *Golden Bough*. But those residual groves in which the trees produced oracles were by now no more than reduced models of the primitive forest, vanquished by the pursuit of agriculture. As Simon Schama stresses in his commentary on Tacitus's *Germania*, the true forest represented what lay beyond Rome, the limit of the state's jurisdiction, a reminder of the impenetrable tangle of vegetation into which the Etruscans had withdrawn to escape the consequences of their defeat, or, in its concrete form, the vast wooded expanse to the east of Latinized Gaul, where the last savages of Europe still held out against the legions.[52] That "shapeless land" was not to the taste of the Romans: it was agreeable neither to the eye nor to live in. What beauty could it possibly present to the eyes of people who appreciated nature only once it had been transformed by civilizing human action and who definitely preferred the bucolic charms of a countryside marked by labor and laws to the bushy, damp disorder of the Hercynian Forest? This Roman landscape, together with all the values associated with it that colonization had introduced around cities as far away as the banks of the Rhine and in Britain, was the landscape that introduced the notion of a polarity between the wild and the domesticated that we still recognize today. This opposition is neither an objective representation of the properties of things nor an expression of a timeless human nature. Rather, it possesses a history of its own, conditioned by a particular system of organizing space and a particular style of alimentary regime that can in no sense be applied generally to other continents.

In truth, even in the West the line separating the wild from the domesticated has not always been as clearly defined as it was in the countryside of Latium. In the course of the very early Middle Ages, the progressive fusion of the Roman and the Germanic civilizations introduced a far more intensive use of woods and heaths and tempered the contrast between cultivated zones and uncultivated ones. In a traditional Germanic landscape, the nonagricultural space is partially annexed by the village. Around small, widely dispersed hamlets surrounded by arable clearings, a vast forest perimeter extends and this is pressed into collective use. It is the scene of hunting and of gathering, where people go to collect firewood and materials for building and toolmaking and where they let their pigs loose to forage for acorns. The transition from household to the deep forest is thus a very gradual one. As Georges Duby comments, "This intermingling of fields with grazing grounds and forests is undoubtedly the feature that most clearly marked out the 'barbarian' agrarian system from the Roman one, where the *ager* was kept separate from the *saltus*."[53] In the seventh and eighth centuries, the Roman organization of space deteriorated, as a result of changing eating habits and growing insecurity in regions of the plain that were impossible to defend. Lard and animal fats took the place of oil, venison replaced other meats even in the richer households, and the products of the *saltus* and the *silva* became more widely used as the situation of the great agricultural domains worsened. The combination of the dualistic Roman system and the concentric Germanic pattern generated the medieval Western landscape in which, despite appearances, the frontier between the inhabited and the deserted zones was no longer as clear-cut as it had been a few centuries earlier.

It was possibly not until the nineteenth century that the frontier was strengthened, as was, at the same time, the aesthetic and moral dimension that even now still characterizes our appreciation of different places. This was the period when Romanticism invented wild nature and propagated a taste for it. It was the time when essayists advocating the philosophy of the "wilderness" such as Ralph Waldo Emerson, Henry David Thoreau, and John Muir urged their compatriots to seek in the mountains and forests of America an existence more free and authentic than the one for which Europe had long provided the model. It was also the time when the first national park was created, at Yellowstone, as a grandiose representation of the work of the deity. From being gentle and beautiful, Nature now became wild and sublime. The genius of creation found expression no longer in landscapes bathed in a Roman light, the tradition of which Corot perpetuated, but in precipices from which torrents crashed down, superhuman heights from which tumbled a chaos of rocks and tall, black stands of trees of the kind painted by Carl Blechen, Caspar David Friedrich, and Carl Gustav Carus in Germany and by Thomas Moran and Albert Bierstadt in the United States.[54] After centuries of indifference or terror, travelers discovered the severe beauty of the Alps, and poets hymned the delicious horror of glaciers and chasms and succumbed to "the alpine exaltation of the mountain authors" that even Chateaubriand was to deem excessive.[55] There is no need to rewrite the history of this new sensibility, which, amid massive industrialization, discovered an antidote to the world's disenchantment in a redeeming but already-threatened wild nature. Such sentiments seemed self-evident and their effects are everywhere around us: in the favor lavished upon the protection of natural sites and the conservation of threatened species, in the fashion for roaming abroad and the taste for exotic landscapes, and in the interest aroused by vast sea voyages and expeditions to Antarctica. But perhaps this apparent self-evidence is preventing us from seeing that the opposition between the wild and the domesticated is not so patent everywhere or at all times and that it owes its present convincing power to ups and downs in the evolution of techniques and attitudes that other peoples have never shared.

Michaux's traveling companion had no doubt never read *La nouvelle Héloise* or admired the tormented landscapes of Turner. The idea of safeguarding the forest whose resources her fellow citizens were pillaging had never crossed her mind. She, poor dear, was pre-Romantic and was horrified by rampant vegetation, disquieting animals, and swarms of insects. Perhaps she was even astonished by the young European poet's perverse taste for this welter of plants from which she sought to distance herself. On the steamer, descending the Amazon, she carried with her a very particular vision of her environment, a whole baggage of prejudices and sentiments that the local Indians would have found extremely enigmatic had she had the ability and desire to confide these to them. For her, the conquest of virgin spaces was a tangible reality and a desirable goal—but at the same time a distant and confused echo of a more fundamental contrast between nature and civilization. As can be imagined, none of this would have made the slightest sense to the Indians, who see the forest as anything but a wild place to be domesticated or a theme for aesthetic delectation. The truth is that, for them, the question of nature has hardly arisen. It is an obsession that is peculiar to ourselves, and a very effective one too, as are all the beliefs that humans embrace in order to act upon the world.

3

The Great Divide

The Autonomy of the Landscape

Arbitrary though it may be, I cannot resist associating the emergence of the modern concept of nature with a little drawing that I noticed a few years ago in the cold light of a gallery in the Louvre. An exhibition had caused it to be disinterred briefly from the storage cabinet of drawings, to which it has since been returned, not without acquiring short-term notoriety, as it also appeared on the cover of the exhibition's catalog.[1] The drawing shows an austere, rocky ravine opening out, in the background, on to a wide valley, where, in between little copses and seemingly well-to-do farms, a river winds its way in wide meanders (fig. 1). A figure, seen from behind, is seated in the lower-left corner, minute among the huge blocks of limestone. Wearing a cape and a feathered hat, he is busy sketching the view before him from life. He is Roelandt Savery, an artist of Flemish origin who, in about 1606, represented himself sketching a landscape in western Bohemia. Officially classed as a "landscape painter" at the Prague court, where he worked first in the service of Emperor Rudolf II and then in that of Rudolf's brother Mathias, Savery was commissioned to roam the Alps and Bohemia and sketch their remarkable sites in their natural state.[2] The appearance of the rock formations, the exactness of the various planes of relief, and the situation of the fields, roads, and houses all suggest that this drawing reproduces a real view, seen in perspective, although possibly a little foreshortened so as to accentuate the vertiginous character of the mountain.

Savery's *Mountainous Landscape with an Artist* was certainly not the first representation of a landscape in the history of Western painting. Art historians trace the origin of the genre to the first half of the fifteenth century with the invention, by northern artists, of the "interior window" that frames a view of the distant landscape.[3] There, the main subject of the painting generally

Roelandt Savery, *Extended valley, view between two high cliffs*. Louvre, Paris, France. Photo by Michèle Bellot.
Courtesy of Réunion des Musées Nationaux/Art Resource, NY.

remains a sacred scene set inside some building, but the window or arcade
in the background isolates a profane landscape, set within the dimensions of
a small picture, and bestows upon it a unity and autonomy that separates it
from the religious theme embodied by the figures in the foreground. Medieval
painters treated elements extracted from the environment as so many icons
scattered within a discontinuous space, subordinating them to the symbolic
and edifying ends of the sacred image. In contrast, an interior *veduta* organizes these elements as a homogeneous whole that acquires a dignity almost
equal to that of the episode from Christian history depicted by the artist. All
that was then needed was to increase the size of the window to the dimensions of an entire canvas so that the picture within a picture became the actual

subject of the representation and, with the religious reference removed, blossomed into a veritable landscape.

Dürer was probably the first fully to develop this process in the watercolors and gouaches of his youth, painted around the 1490s.[4] Unlike his contemporary Patinir, whose famous landscapes still incorporate sacred scenes as a kind of pretext for representing the natural setting of their action with virtuosity, Dürer does paint real environments from which human figures have disappeared. But Dürer's watercolors were private exercises in style. They were unknown to his contemporaries and exerted no immediate influence on the manner of apprehending and representing landscape. Dürer was also the first painter in the Germanic world to master the mathematical bases of linear perspective that Alberti had codified fifty years earlier. The emergence of landscape painting as an autonomous genre stemmed from its being organized in accordance with the new rules of *perspectiva artificialis*. The positioning of objects and the field in which they were deployed were now governed by the gaze of the spectator, which plunged, as if through a transparent pane, into an exterior space at once infinite, continuous, and homogeneous.

Panofsky, in a famous essay, showed how the invention of linear perspective, in the first half of the fifteenth century, introduced a new relationship between the viewer and the world, between the point of view of the spectator and a space now rendered systematic, in which objects and the intervals separating them were simply proportional variations in a seamless continuum.[5] The foreshortening techniques used in antiquity were designed to restore the subjective dimension of the perception of forms by means of a methodical deformation of the objects represented, but the space within which these were placed remained discontinuous and, as it were, residual. In contrast, modern perspective aims to restore the cohesion of a perfectly unified world in a rational space, mathematically constructed so as to elude the psychophysiological constraints of perception. And this new "symbolic form" of one's apprehension of the world presents a paradox that Panofsky skillfully brought to light.[6] The infinite and homogeneous space of linear perspective is, however, constructed on axes that start from an arbitrary point, that of the direction of the gaze of the observer. So a subjective impression serves as the starting point for the rationalization of a world of experience in which the phenomenal space of perception is transposed into a mathematical space. Such an "objectification of the subjective" produces a twofold effect: it creates a distance between man and the world by making the autonomy of things depend upon man; and it systematizes and stabilizes the external universe even as it confers upon the subject absolute mastery over the organization of this newly conquered exteriority.[7] In this way, linear perspective established in the domain of representation the possibility of the kind of confrontation between the individual and nature that was to become characteristic of modern ideology and of which landscape painting would become the artistic expression. It really is a matter of a confrontation, a new position from which to look—for the projective plane distances things but offers no promise of a true unveiling. As Merleau-Ponty remarked, "on the contrary, it refers back to our own point of view; and as for things, they flee away into a distancing where no thought can follow."[8]

Savery was an heir to this revolution, which began several generations before his time; but on two points, his drawing is innovative. Both his theme and his technique reflect the influence of Pieter Bruegel, who was famous as early as the second half of the sixteenth century for his mountainous landscapes. With the exception of Dürer's watercolors, which had no immediate influence, and one or two striking prints by Altdorfer, the alpine views by Bruegel the Elder are among the earliest pictorial representations that erase human beings from the landscape or testify to their presence solely by referring to their works. But whereas many of Bruegel's landscapes were imaginary compositions that freely interpreted sketches made from nature, Savery's drawing seems to be a faithful enough representation of a real scene. And, perhaps more importantly, Savery appears to have pushed the paradox of perspective formulated by Panofsky to its logical conclusion. Where Bruegel, by omitting human beings from a landscape, simply draws attention to the exteriority of the subject who imbues objective nature with meaning and coherence, Savery reintroduces this subject into the pictorial representation, depicting the very action by which he objectifies a space different from the one in which he finds himself, which itself is different from the space offered to the gaze of the spectator. For the perspective view presented to the latter is not the same as the one that the artist, shifted to the left of the drawing but positioned on the very axis of the ravine, is busy drawing on the paper. This landscape thus presents a double objectivization of reality and, as it were, a reflexive representation of the operation through which nature and the world are produced as autonomous objects, thanks to the gaze that a human being turns on them.

Perhaps we should even be speaking, here, of a triple articulation, if we adopt the distinction drawn by Alain Roger between "artialisation" *in situ* and "artialisation" *in visu*. The former defines the rearrangement of a piece of nature for recreative and aesthetic purposes, usually the art of landscape gardening, while the latter characterizes the representation of a landscape in a painting.[9] The countryside that Savery offers to our gaze is certainly no example of English landscaping, and its almost Arcadian elegance no doubt owes as much to the skill of the artist as to the intentions of its inhabitants. It is safe to say, however, that the latter knew very well what they were doing when they positioned a copse of young elms over here, an apple tree in the middle of a field over there, and, in another spot, a tree providing cool shade in the courtyard of a house. So it is quite possible that the emperor's *Landschafts-mahler* (landscape painter) fully intended to combine in the foreground and the background of his perspective view representations both of a rock formation characteristic of the Silurian mountains of Bohemia and also of the organization of the equally typical rural habitat of the region. The marriage of wild nature and tamed countryside effected by the artist's pen creates the genius loci. And even if that was not the case, the composition of the drawing is sufficiently original to satisfy a fantasy of beholding in it a remarkable representation of the beginnings of a modern production of nature.

In a period of about one hundred and fifty years, from the time of Patinir and Dürer to that of Ruysdael and Claude Lorrain, landscape painting attained total mastery over space. The depiction of scenes in which a succession of planes still evoked a theatrical stage set gave way to an impression of homogeneous depth that masked the artifice of a perspective construction, thereby making it seem as though the subject had withdrawn from the natural scene that he was painting. This way of representing the human environment in all its exteriority was of course indissociable from the movement to mathematize space that in this same period was being promoted by geometry, physics, and optics, ranging from Copernicus's decentralizing of the cosmos to Descartes's *res extensa*. As Panofsky pointed out, "the projective geometry of the seventeenth century . . . is . . . a product of the artist's workshop."[10] The invention of new tools for making reality visible—not only linear perspective but also the microscope (1590) and the telescope (1605)—made it possible to establish a new relationship with the world by circumscribing certain of its elements within a strictly defined perceptive framework that conferred upon them a salience and unity thitherto unknown. The privileged status accorded to sight, to the detriment of other sensitive faculties, led to extension gaining an autonomous status that Cartesian physics was to exploit and that was also favored by the expansion of the limits of the known world that resulted from the discovery and mapping of new continents. Nature, now dumb, odor-free, and intangible, had been left devoid of life. Gentle Mother Nature was forgotten, and Nature the cruel stepmother had disappeared; all that remained was a ventriloquist's dummy, of which man could make himself, as it were, the lord and master.*

---

* Translator's note: This is a reference to Descartes's Discourse on Method: "and thereby make ourselves, as it were, the lords and masters of nature."

For the technical dimension of the objectivization of reality was, of course, essential in this mechanistic seventeenth-century revolution that represented the world as a machine the cogs of which scholars could dismantle, rather than as a composite totality of humans and nonhumans endowed with intrinsic meaning by divine creation. Robert Lenoble has assigned a date to this rupture: 1632, which saw the publication of Galileo's *Dialogues on the Two World-Systems*, from which modern physics emerged in a discussion in the Venice Arsenal between engineers trained in the mechanical arts—far removed from any philosophers' *disputatio* concerning the nature of being or the essence of things.[11] Now the construction of Nature had really begun! It was, to be sure, a social and ideological construction, but it was also a practical one thanks to the expertise of clockmakers, glass producers, and lens grinders and of all the craftsmen who made laboratory experimentation possible. For that experimentation led to ongoing efforts to dissociate and reconstruct the phenomena that produced the objects of the new science. This process then acquired autonomy at the cost of forgetting the conditions of the objectivization of the phenomena. Liberated, thanks to reason, from the dark muddle of the experience of others and rendered transcendent by the severance of the links connecting them to the disorders of subjectivity and the illusions of continuity, the "factishes" of modernity (to borrow Bruno Latour's handy neologism, *faitiches*) now made their appearance.[12] The dualism of the individual and the world now became irreversible: this was the keystone in a cosmology that set in opposition, on the one hand, things governed by laws and, on the other, the thought that organized them into meaningful sets: on the one hand, the body—now regarded as a mechanism—and, on the other, the soul that ruled it, as was intended by the deity. Nature, stripped of its marvels, was now offered up to the child-king, who, dismantling its workings, shook off its power over him and enslaved it for his own ends.

This masterstroke by which nascent modernity finally liberated humans from the matrix of objects both animate and inanimate may seem exceptional in the history of human peoples, but in truth this moment was, after all, no more than a phase. The process had got under way many years earlier and did not culminate until a century and a half later, by which time nature and culture, each now solidly established with its own subject matter and methodology, would mark out the space in which modern anthropology could operate. Historians of science and philosophy have devoted enough scholarly works to this particular characteristic of the West for it not to be necessary, at this point, to present any more than a brief picture of this long process of maturation that eventually established, on the one hand, a world of things endowed with an intrinsic factuality and, on the other, a world of human beings governed by arbitrary meanings. If I do nevertheless take on this brief exercise, it is the better to emphasize that, contrary to the impression given by many excellent studies of the history of the idea of nature,[13] nature has not revealed its essence thanks to the combined efforts of a cohort of great minds and ingenious craftsmen. Rather, it has been constructed little by little as an ontological tool of a particular kind, designed to serve as the foundation of the cosmogenesis of modernity. Seen from the point of view of a hypothetical Jivaro or Chinese historian of science, Aristotle, Descartes, and Newton would not appear so much as the revealers of the distinctive objectivity of nonhumans and the laws that govern them; rather, they would seem the architects of a naturalistic cosmology altogether exotic in comparison with the choices made by the rest of humanity in order to classify the entities of this world and establish hierarchies and discontinuities among them.

The Autonomy of *Phusis*

As usual, everything begins in Greece. But initially progress was slow. It is true that the *Odyssey* contains an occurrence of the term that was later used to designate nature: namely *phusis*; but there it is used to refer to the properties of a plant, that is, in the limited sense of whatever produces the development of a plant and characterizes its particular "nature."[14] That is the sense that Aristotle later clarifies in an overview of all living things: every being is defined by its nature, conceived as a principle, as a cause, and also as a substance.[15] But Homer is not concerned with any such principle of individuation peculiar to particular entities in the world. Nor, a fortiori, does it ever occur to him that things with a particular "nature" might form an ontological set: namely Nature itself, independent of the works of humans and likewise of any decrees from Olympus.[16] On this point, Hesiod differs hardly at all from Homer. His poems trace the origins of deities and heroes, their genealogies and the circumstances of their metamorphoses, and if he does ever mention features of the physical world, it is—as in the Amerindian manner—the better to account for the attributes of mythological figures. Admittedly, in his *Works and Days*, Hesiod does briefly mention a difference that sets humans apart from certain animal species taken as a whole. Whereas fish, wild animals, and birds devour one another, humans have received justice from Zeus and never do so. All the same, this still leaves us a long way from any distinction, even of an embryonic nature, between nature and culture, for the animals that he mentions serve mainly as a foil to humans, who are being urged not to behave as predators. It is also a way of recalling the part played by the gods in the genesis of civic morality. The special attribute of humans, *dikē*, is more an effect of divine benevolence than of an original nature entirely distinct from that of other living species.[17]

When the first philosophers ventured to propose naturalistic explanations for lightning, rainbows, and earthquakes, they did so in reaction against the religious interpretations sanctioned by tradition, in particular the tradition of Homer and Hesiod, who regarded most unusual or frightening phenomena as personal interventions on the part of a whimsical or angered deity. The philosophers and the Hippocratic doctors too were committed to suggesting physical causes for atmospheric events, cyclical phenomena, and illnesses, causes appropriate to each kind of phenomenon—in other words, causes that stemmed from their respective "natures," not from some whim of Apollo, Poseidon, or Hephaistos. In this way, they gradually established the idea that the cosmos is explicable and organized in accordance with laws that can be discovered and that arbitrary divine intervention no longer has any place, nor do the superstitions of ancient times. These were, of course, convictions held by an elite, and they were expressed cautiously so as to avoid the grave consequences of an accusation of impiety. All the same, for Hippocrates and his disciples and for some of the Ionian philosophers and the Sophists, the domain of nature began to take shape as a project and a source of hope. This new regime of beings, which covered all physical phenomena and living organisms and was marked with the stamp of what is regular and predictable, distanced itself from the residue of divine intentions, haphazard creations, and human productions, all of which were effects of artifice.

As we know, it fell to Aristotle to systematize this emerging object of inquiry, to establish its limits, define its properties, and set out the principles by which it functioned. His objectivization of nature was inspired by political organization and the laws that governed it, although he formulated this idea in a back-to-front manner: he suggested that the City conformed to the laws of *phusis*, reproducing the natural hierarchy as closely as possible. It is significant that the theater in which this revolution took place was the turbulent and troubled Athens, which, following the brilliance of the age of Pericles, found its power diminished and its role challenged, so that adversity forced it to examine the conditions in which the sovereignty that was eluding it could be exercised. Reflection upon law as an obligation freely accepted and a means of living together, unaffected by the urgency of immediate decisions, made it possible to seize upon the more abstract features that were to provide a prototype for the laws of nature.[18] *Phusis* and *nomos* became indissociable: the entire multiplicity of things operated within a totality subject to identifiable laws, just as the community of citizens was governed by rules of public action unaffected by particular intentions. These constituted two parallel domains of legality, one of which, however, was endowed with a dynamic and finality of its own, for Nature lacked the versatility of men.

To be sure, Aristotle's nature is not as all-encompassing as that of the Moderns. It is restricted to the sublunary world, that of familiar phenomena and beings. Beyond these extend the incorruptible heavens, in which the divine stars move, no doubt likewise in accordance with regular and predictable rules; but the perfection of those heavens is such that they are exempt from natural accidents. In contrast, in the realm here below, the things of nature are now endowed with an undeniable otherness: "Some things exist, or come into existence, by nature; and some otherwise. Animals and their organs, plants and the elementary substances . . . these and their likes we say exist by nature."[19] When he examines the ontological regime peculiar to these entities that exist *by nature*, Aristotle provides a theoretical basis for one of the current meanings of the word "nature." It is the principle that produces the development of a being that contains within itself the source of its movement and its rest. This is the principle that causes it to realize itself in accordance with a particular type. But Aristotle's *Physics* is complemented by a natural system, an inventory of different forms of life and the structural relations that they share within an organized whole. Here, Aristotle is concerned about Nature as the sum total of beings that are ordered by and submitted to laws. This was a new concept that, after him, was to enjoy a lasting influence. His project consists in specifying each class of beings on the basis of the variations in the characteristics that it possesses in common with other classes of beings within the same form of life. Each form of life, in turn, is characterized by the kind of specialized organs that enable it to realize a vital function: locomotion, reproduction, nutrition, respiration. In this way a species can be defined precisely by the degree of development of its essential organs, which are peculiar to the form of life to which it belongs. The wings of birds, the paws of quadrupeds, and the fins of fish are all organs that serve one and the same function in different forms of life. But the size of the beaks, wings, and organs of nutrition and locomotion that characterize birds would, in its turn, provide a criterion for distinguishing species according to their modes of life. This classification of organisms on a basis of collection and division draws upon the particular "nature" of each being, so as to construct a system of Nature in which species are disconnected from their particular habitats and stripped of the symbolic meanings that were attached to them, so that they can exist solely as complexes of organs and functions that are part of a table of coordinates that encompass the entire known world.[20] A decisive step had thus been taken. By decontextualizing the entities of nature and organizing them into an exhaustive taxonomy of a causal type, Aristotle conjured up an original subject matter that was thereafter to account for many of the peculiar features of Western thought.

The Autonomy of Creation

In Greek thought and particularly in Aristotle's, humans remain a part of nature. Their destiny is not dissociated from an eternal cosmos, and it is by virtue of the fact that they are able to accede to knowledge of the laws that govern it that they are able to find their place in it. So, for the nature of the Moderns to come into being, a second operation of purification was necessary: humans had to become external to nature and superior to it. Christianity was responsible for this second upheaval, with its twofold idea of man's transcendence and a universe created from nothingness by God's will. The Creation bears witness to the existence of God and to his goodness and perfection, but his works were not to be confused with him, nor were the beauties of nature to be appreciated for themselves. They proceed from God but God is not present in them. Given that a human being, too, is a creation, his significance stems from that founding event. His place in nature is therefore not that of an element like any other; he is not, by nature, as plants and animals are; he has become transcendent in the physical world; his essence and his coming-to-be are matters of God's grace, which is beyond nature. The source of a human being's right and mission to administer the earth is his supernatural origin, since God formed humans on the last day of Genesis in order for them to exercise their control over Creation, organizing and arranging it to suit their needs. Just as Adam, having received the power to name the animals, was authorized to introduce his order into nature, so too his descendants, as they multiply on the face of the earth, realize God's intention to impose the mastery of Creation everywhere. But nature is only entrusted to humans on a temporary basis. For now the world has not only an origin but also an end—a strange notion that Christianity inherited from the Jewish tradition and that is at odds not only with the ideas of pagan antiquity but also with most of the cosmologies that ethnography and history have recorded. The Creation is a provisional scene in a play that will continue after the stage scenery has disappeared, when nature will exist no more and only the principal protagonists will be left: namely God and human souls, that is to say, human beings in a different form.

Although obsessed by the idea of the Creation and its consequences, the Middle Ages also retained some of the lessons learned from antiquity. This produced a plethora of syntheses on the unity of nature, combining biblical exegesis with elements of Greek physics, especially from the twelfth cen-

tury onward, when Aristotle's works were rediscovered. The exteriority of
the world acquires a manifest character through a metaphor that runs right
through the Middle Ages: nature, in all its diversity and harmony, is like a
book in which one can decipher evidence of the divine creation. The book
of nature is certainly inferior to the Holy Scriptures, since God, a transcendent being, is revealed only imperfectly by his works. The world should thus
be read as an illustration, a commentary to complement God's word. Many
medieval writers nevertheless set great store by this source of edification, for
it was all that was available to those who, lacking education, had no direct access to the holy text: "even the most simple of men may read the world," Saint
Augustine was to declare.[21] It is worth noting that this bucolic optimism is still
favored by certain missionaries who appear to be in no doubt that the tribes
they are trying to convert are capable of recognizing in their environments
the harmonious nature celebrated by Saint Basil and Saint Francis. Perhaps we
should even see in this one of the earliest formulations of the idea, beloved of
the West, that nature is universally self-evident and no people, however savage, can fail to perceive its unity.

The theme of the book of nature sustains developments in a natural theology that is echoed in a particular Christian view of ecological ethics.[22] This
kind of theology, which examines the effects of divine intentions in the Creation, is, to be sure, no more than an auxiliary to revealed theology, but it nevertheless constitutes a precious complement for the interpretation of nature and
knowledge of God, one upon which Saint Thomas Aquinas drew. His natural
theology relies on the authority of Aristotle to show the respective effects
of final causes (the intellect of God) and efficient causes (natural agents) in
the organization of the world. He likewise picks up the Aristotelian idea that
nature does nothing by chance and commits himself without reservations to
its finalism: everything bears witness to the fact that the forms and processes
of natural objects are those best adapted to their functions; everything also
indicates that Adam's descendants are destined to occupy the supreme position here below in the world and to rule over the hierarchy of inferior creatures, for "the subordination of animals to man is natural."[23] No doubt Genesis
does literally justify such dominion, but it also supports the idea of a common measure between God and human beings. Given that God's intelligence
was at the origin of the creation of living beings, it was appropriate that some
of them should be able to participate in this faculty and thereby be able to
apprehend, in the perfection of the universe, the goodness of God's design.
Humans, who are therefore endowed with reason and knowledge, are thus
set apart from the rest of Creation, enjoying a supremacy that stems from the
divine plan and, in consequence, calls for humility and responsibility. In his

Literal Interpretation of Genesis, Saint Augustine had already emphasized that in the Creation only humans constitute a unique *genus* that stands in contrast to all the animal species. With the support of the authority of this exegesis, the theologians of the sixteenth century were to assert that the human race is unique.[24] The Middle Ages had thus not proved themselves unworthy: what with divine transcendence, the uniqueness of humankind, and the exteriority of the world, all the parts of the mechanism were now in place together, making it possible for the classical period of the seventeenth century to invent nature as we know it.

The Autonomy of Nature

The emergence of modern cosmology results from a complex process in which many factors are inextricably intermingled: the evolution of an aesthetic sensibility and pictorial techniques, the expanding limits of the world, the progress of mechanical skills and the greater mastery over certain environments that this made possible, the progression from knowledge based on an interpretation of similarities to a universal science of order and measure—all these are factors that have rendered possible the construction not only of mathematical physics but also of a natural history and a general grammar. Changes in geometry, optics, taxonomy, and semiology have all emerged out of a reorganization of humanity's relationship with the world and the analytical tools that made this possible, rather than from an accumulation of discoveries and a perfecting of skills. In short, to quote Merleau-Ponty, "It is not scientific discoveries that brought about a change in the idea of Nature. Rather, it is the change in the idea of Nature that has made those discoveries possible."[25] The Scientific Revolution of the seventeenth century legitimated the idea of a mechanical nature in which the behavior of every element can be explained by laws, within a totality seen as the sum of its parts and the interactions of those elements. For this to happen, it was not necessary to invalidate rival scientific theories, only to eliminate the finalism of Aristotle and medieval Scholasticism, relegate it to the domain of theology, and lay the emphasis, as Descartes did, on one single efficient cause. Of course, this was still linked with God, but God purely in the sense of a moving force, at once the original source of a movement conceived in geometric terms and also the guarantor of its constant preservation. Divine intervention became more abstract, less dependent on the functioning of the cogs in the world machine, and it was now confined to the mysteries of faith or to an explanation for the principle of inertia. All the same, alongside the likes of Bacon, Descartes, and Spinoza, who rejected the illusion of an intentional nature, a more discreet trend of thought remained attached to finalist convictions and the idea of a nature organized in accordance with an overall plan, understanding of which would make it possible to account better for the action of the elements that composed it. Kepler, Boyle, and Leibniz were by no means negligible advocates of this conception of nature as a balanced totality and unity, and as we know, they were eventually succeeded by Buffon, Alexander von Humboldt, and Darwin. And the legacy of the latter thinkers, in its turn, no doubt contributed powerfully to the teleological orientations of a particular kind of contemporary biology characterized by a quasi-providential vision of the adaptation of organisms and the homeostasis of ecosystems. In the seventeenth century, however, among both the supporters of a mechanistic world and the partisans of an organicist one, a separation between nature and humanity gained acceptance. Spinoza found himself quite alone when he rejected such a separation, urged that human behavior be considered as a phenomenon governed by a universal determinism, and condemned the prejudices of those who imagined the plan of nature on the analogy of self-knowledge. For the latter, who were in the majority, were in no doubt that natural effects served an end determined by some divine intention, that man, "the viceroy of Creation," was totally distinct from the reality that he tried to understand, and that God "had invested man with power, authority, right, dominion, trust and care . . . to preserve the face of the Earth in beauty, usefulness and fruitfulness," as the English jurist Matthew Hale floridly put it.[26] What now came into existence was a notion of Nature as an autonomous ontological domain, a field of inquiry and scientific experimentation, an object to be exploited and improved; and very few thought to question this.

If the idea of nature acquired such importance in the seventeenth century, it was certainly not because the powerful vibration of the life of the world was suddenly perceived by eyes now unsealed that would in future never cease to endeavor to fathom its mysteries and define its limitations. For that notion of nature was indissociable from another, namely that of human nature, which the former had engendered through a kind of fission when, in order to determine a place in which the mechanisms and regularities of nature could be discerned, a tiny portion of being was detached to serve as a fixed point. As Michel Foucault has shown, those two concepts function as a pair to strengthen the reciprocal link between the two dimensions of representations in that period: the first was the imagination, which was seen as the power, attributed to the human mind, to reconstitute order on the basis of subjective impressions; and the second was resemblance, the property that is possessed by things and that presents thought with a whole field of barely sketched in similarities upon which knowledge can superimpose its work of establishing order.[27] Thanks to the wide generality of their meanings, Nature and human nature allow one neatly to synthesize the new possibility of effecting a readjustment between the ceaseless pullulation of the analogical multiplicity of beings and the mechanism of induction, with its whole parade of images and reminiscences. Understanding and controlling nonhumans are assigned to a subject who knows or one who acts, the scientist in his heated room* or the engineer draining marshland, the physicist manipulating his air pump or the steward of Colbert's forests. They were not the responsibility of humanity as an organized whole, let alone of particular collectivities differentiated from one another by their respective customs, languages, and religions. Nature is there, of course, paired with human nature, but as yet there is no sign of society as a concept and a field for analysis.

Since Foucault's *Les mots et les choses* (translated into English as *The Order of Things*), it has become almost a cliché to say that the birth of a concept of "man" and that of the sciences that explore his "positivities" were events that did not occur in European culture until quite late and are unparalleled in the history of humanity; and also to say that these events were instigated, at the very end of the eighteenth century, by a great upset in the Western episteme, which now witnessed the appearance of a space that brought together organized systems that were comparable to one another thanks to their contiguity in a chain of historical successions, replacing a general schema of representation that simultaneously set in order a whole network of identities and differences. Yet another commonly accepted idea is that, in consequence, the human sciences owed nothing to some vacant domain more or less similar to that once occupied by human nature, now left fallow but well marked out, in which all they would have needed to do was sow some seeds of positive knowledge and, using the more effective tools that they now possessed, bring them to fruition. In short, to quote Foucault's emphatic declaration: "No philosophy, no moral or political option, no empirical science of any kind, no observation of the human body, no analysis of sensation, imagination or the passions, had ever encountered, in the seventeenth century, anything like man; for man did not exist."[28] The results of Foucault's archaeological inquiries into the substrata of the human sciences are now so well known that further commentary is unnecessary. However, we should bear in mind one point that is relevant to the present study. If it was not until the nineteenth century that the concept of society began to take shape as an organized totality and if it was

* Translator's note: In his Discourse on Method, Descartes indicates that he is seated by a wood-burning stove, a seventeenth-century method of heating.

therefore only then that such a concept could be set in opposition to nature, then the genesis of, respectively, each of those notions, and their progressive maturation within an operational field where they could be combined, together with the glimpses of reality that their paired discontinuities rendered possible—all that must result from such a long and exceptional process of multiple filterings and ruptures that it is hard to see how it could possibly have been shared by cultures other than our own.

But at this point a brief comment on Rousseau seems necessary. We know that Lévi-Strauss gave him an important role in the anticipation of modern ethnology. He credited the author of the *Discourse on the Origin of Inequality* with having foreshadowed the method of this science that was yet to be born when he recommended observing the differences between humans, the better to discover the properties that they shared in common. Lévi-Strauss also declared that Rousseau had based his program on a concrete examination of the problem of the relations between nature and culture, seeing it not as an irreversible separation but in a nostalgic and often desperate quest for what, in humans, authorizes and encourages them to identify with all forms of life, even the most humble.[29] Despite the criticisms directed at it, the militant Rousseauism of the founder of structural anthropology can therefore not be regarded as an attempt to extract from the thought of the Enlightenment the beginnings of a dualism between nature and society that twentieth-century anthropology then itself took over. After all, in Rousseau's view, the assembly of citizens in no way constitutes a society in the conventional sense of the term in modern sociology, that is, a unit superior and external to individuals, as it were, a moral entity the needs and aims of which differ from those of the members who compose it—in other words, an autonomous whole animated by a specifically social collective interest that amounts to something more and other than the sum of the desires of individuals. Moreover, Durkheim made no mistake about this when he compared his own conception of collective utility, determined by a social being considered in its organic unity, with the common interest as expressed by Rousseau: "the interest of an average individual," which gave body to the general will by adding to it whatever is useful to each member of the community.[30] There is more than a difference of degree and a different emphasis between Durkheim's transcendent society and the aggregation of individuals all mutually bound by a convention whose conditions of legitimation are spelled out by the social contract. The former is an ontological entity of a new kind, and it is illusory to seek in Rousseau for a promise or prefiguration of it, even if his theory of a social link does offer a fertile source of analogies to those who, like Lévi-Strauss, have managed to detect behind the power that Rousseau grants to feeling and his defense of the idea of virtue an original manner of thinking about ways of getting along with others.

The Autonomy of Culture

But our genealogical account of dualism is not completed by the advent of the concept of society; for contemporary ethnology owes its raison d'être to a notion established more recently: namely the notion of culture, by which it defines the proper field of its inquiries and by which it concisely expresses all that which, in humans and their achievements, is distinct from nature and imposes meaning upon it. Perhaps it was also inevitable that terms as vague as "nature" and "culture," so ready to lend themselves to the successive meanings that have been found for them, so well adapted to gathering together in a single expression this or that region of the welter of aspirations, processes, and forces that the variegated spectacle of the world presents—perhaps it was inevitable that these terms should end up finding in their mutual opposition a definition of their positive qualities and at the same time a seemingly self-evident significance that is greatly increased by their conjunction. The idea of culture assuredly took shape later than the idea of nature, but its development was no less contingent, and the movement in the course of which the range of its meanings came to be restricted was just as complex.

All ethnologists are familiar with the famous critical inventory in which Alfred Kroeber and Clyde Kluckhohn noted most of the definitions of culture.[31] Of the 164 accepted meanings that they list, I shall pick out only two, to make my point. The first, which they label "humanist," envisages culture as a distinctive characteristic of the human condition. Its canonic formulation, by Edward B. Tylor in 1871, is traditionally regarded as, so to speak, the birth certificate of the field of modern anthropology: "Culture or Civilization, taken in its wide ethnographic sense, is that complex whole which includes knowledge, belief, art, morals, law, custom, and any other capabilities and habits acquired by man as a member of society."[32] Here, culture is not distinguished from civilization, in the sense of an aptitude for collective creation governed by a progressive quest for perfection. This was the view adopted by the evolutionary anthropologists of the last third of the nineteenth century. It accepts the possibility and necessity of comparison between a range of societies arranged in order of the degree of development of their cultural institutions, which are more or less elaborated expressions of a universal human tendency to overcome natural constraints and instinctive forces. The strictly anthropological concept of culture did not appear until later. It was only at the turn of the twentieth century, in the ethnographic work of Franz Boas, that there emerged the idea that each people constitutes a unique and coherent configuration of material and intellectual features sanctioned by tradition, that tradition being typical of a certain mode of life, rooted in the specific categories of a language and responsible for the specificity of the individual and collective behavior of its members.[33] The Boasian view, reworked and elaborated in a more systematic fashion by his disciples, was to form the matrix of North American anthropology and lastingly define its "culturalist" character. In this second definition, culture takes a plural form, as a multitude of particular realizations; it is no longer singular, signifying the attribute par excellence of humanity. The grading of peoples according to their proximity to the modern West is supplanted by a synchronic table in which all cultures are equally valid. The optimistic universalism of the theorists of evolution gives way to a relativist method centered on an intensive monographic approach and the revelation of the full richness of the peculiar. The teleological emphasis shifts from faith in a continuous progress in manners and customs to the assumption that every culture inclines toward its own conservation and the perpetuation of its own *Volksgeist* (spirit of the people).

Before reaching a more or less specialized status in ethnology, each of these concepts of culture was crystallized in particular national contexts and in accordance with a process of differentiation, the echoes of which are still perceptible in the theoretical tendencies of various scholarly traditions. Culture, in the universal sense, was, as we have seen, not distinguished from civilization. Up until the beginning of the twentieth century, the two terms continued to be used interchangeably in anthropology, even by Boas. The word *civilisation* is itself relatively recent. It appeared for the first time in French in 1757, penned by Victor Riqueti de Mirabeau, and about ten years later in England, used by Adam Ferguson with an equivalent sense.[34] It meant the state of civilized society, which had resulted from constant progress in virtue and civic skills, in contrast to the mere urbanity of manners or civil behavior, superficial and static qualities. However, as Norbert Elias has shown, "civilization" was to take on a completely different meaning in Germany, in fact a meaning closer to what it was originally opposed to, that is, customs ruled by convention that expressed one's social standing, knowing how to present oneself well and speak well, in short the attitudes of a court nobility aping French taste. "Culture" was the opposite of a civilization of appearances conceived in this way.[35] The term "culture" evoked the character peculiar to certain products of human activity that testified to the genius of a people, revealing its own particular value and enabling it to regard this as something of which to be proud. In Germany, the antinomy between culture and civilization initially took on a social dimension. At least, that was the polemical argument used by a bourgeois intelligentsia, distanced from any real economic and political responsibility by a court aristocracy that gloried in its privileges but was reputed to be incapable of any creative initiative. Following the French Revolution, the antagonism between the values that these two notions (civilization and culture) embodied began to take on a national character: the ideals of the cultivated middle class became emblematic of German culture, in contrast to the idea of civilization that an expansionist and confident France was conveying to the four corners of Europe.

What followed is so well known that I need not dwell on it. We know how Germany reacted to the Enlightenment; how Herder, Fichte, and Alexander and Wilhelm von Humboldt turned away from the quest for universal truths and instead emphasized the incommensurability of collective peculiarities, styles of life and forms of thought, and the concrete achievements of this or that community. We know the degree to which a people denied political unity became obsessed by the question of the bases of its own character; and to what extent its desire to classify, delimit, and consolidate the specific characteristics of a nation as yet still nascent contributed to setting up the idea of culture as one of the central values of nineteenth-century Germany. We also know how much Boas, who emigrated to New York at the age of twenty-nine, owed to his years of *Bildung* (upbringing) in the crucible of German university life, as did his principal disciples, the first generation of American anthropology, most of whom had received a Germanic education; Sapir was born in Pomerania, Lowie in Vienna, and Kroeber amid the German American elite of Manhattan.[36] The roots of the American conception of culture thus plunged deep into German historicism, in the *Volksgeist* (spirit of the people) of Herder, the *Nationalcharakter* of Wilhelm von Humboldt, and the *Völkergedanken* (folk ideas) of Bastian.

Although shaken by the failure of evolutionism, the notion of culture, in the singular, nevertheless did not disappear from twentieth-century ethnology. This was the case even in the United States, where Kroeber, distancing himself from Boas, soon set about defining the specific character of culture as a "superorganic" entity of a particular kind, a hypostasis that took shape as it transcended individual existences and defined their orientations.[37] But it was above all in French and British anthropology that culture continued to exist as a distinctive attribute of the whole of humanity. Yet it did so in an almost underground fashion by reason of the predominance of the Durkheimian school and the preeminence that this ascribed to the notion of society for filling the same function. This belief in "culture" was really an unreflective conviction that was at odds with the particularism of Boas's followers: it was thought

that it was both possible and desirable to find regularities and invariants—
not to mention universals—in the human condition that could account for
a unity of culture that underlay the multiplicity of its particular manifestations. Expressions of this aspiration are to be found not only in Malinowski's
somewhat unconvincing "scientific theory of culture," in Radcliffe-Brown's
insistence on defining anthropology as a nomothetic discipline, and also in
Lévi-Strauss's proclaimed project for a science of the "order of orders." In
fact, this last project illustrates to what extent the two notions of culture, as a
reality sui generis distinct from a Nature that was both the originating condition of humanity and also an autonomous ontological domain providing
symbolic thought with an inexhaustible source of analogies, stemmed from
Lévi-Strauss's philosophical training and his attachment to the rationalism
of the Enlightenment. But as a result of his time spent in the United States
and his acquaintance with Boas, he did pay heed to the lessons of relativism:
the idea that nothing justifies setting up a hierarchy of cultures in accordance
with either a moral scale or a diachronic series.

There can be no doubt that the notion of culture (in the singular) derives
much of its fertility from its opposition to nature. Cultures (in the plural), on
the other hand, make sense only in relation to themselves; and even if the environment in which they have developed certainly does constitute an important dimension in the peculiarities ascribed to them, from a culturalist point
of view their manner of adapting to nature is but one means among others
that helps us to understand them, a means no more legitimate or expressive
of a worldview than is language, a system of rituals, technology, or table manners. So, in itself, a holistic idea of culture does not summon up nature as its
automatic counterpart. Yet, as initiated in Germany and developed in North
America, this was the idea that was to solidify contemporary dualism, not by
disseminating its specialized use in anthropology but by reason of the work
of epistemological purification that was necessary for the idea of culture as an
irreducible totality to win autonomy in the face of natural realities.

The genesis of this idea is indissociable from the intense debates that, in
late nineteenth-century Germany, attempted to spell out the respective methods and objects of natural sciences and sciences of the mind. Battling as much
against idealist philosophy as against positivist naturalism, historians, lin-
guists, and philosophers were trying to set on a firm basis the humanities'
claim to become rigorous sciences, worthy of as much respect as that received
by physics, chemistry, and animal physiology. Within barely twenty years, several fundamental texts on this question were published. The first of these was
the *Principien der Sprachgeschichte* (1880; English translation 1890), in which
the historian of languages Hermann Paul drew a distinction between "sciences

that produce laws" and "historical sciences," which attach themselves to the individuality of phenomena as a product of historical contingency. The second text was the famous *Einleitung in die Geisteswissenschaften* (1883; English translation 1989), in which Wilhelm Dilthey set the sciences of nature in opposition to *Geisteswissenschaften*, which proceed according to "understanding," that is, according to the researcher's aptitude at reliving, through empathy, the concrete situation of a historical actor. The third was the article "Geschichte und Naturwissenschaft" (1894; English translation 1980) by Wilhelm Windelband, who, developing a distinction proposed a few years earlier by Otto Liebmann, established a contrast between the nomothetic method of the sciences of nature and the idiographic method of the historical sciences. Perhaps even Boas should be included in this epistemological debate, for in 1887 he wrote a little essay, entitled "The Study of Geography," in which he set up an opposition between the method of, on the one hand, a physicist (his initial training in Heidelberg was in physics) studying phenomena that possess an objective unity and, on the other, a cosmographer (here Alexander von Humboldt was his model) endeavoring to understand phenomena whose connection is established in a subjective manner.[38]

However, it was Heinrich Rickert, particularly in his *Kulturwissenschaft und Naturwissenschaft* (1899; English translation 1962), who produced the most complete classification of the sciences, the one that distinguished between their respective methods and objects with the greatest logical rigor. At any rate, this was the classification that exerted the most telling influence not only on Rickert's contemporaries, first and foremost his friend Max Weber, but also on great figures of twentieth-century German philosophy from Heidegger to Habermas.[39] In the first place, it fell to Rickert to substitute the expression "the sciences of culture" for the one more usual at the time, namely "the sciences of the mind." This was a novelty that was more than simply terminological. The expression "sciences of the mind" could lead to confusion and, as in the case of Dilthey, suggest that the humanities dealt only with mental life or the spiritual dimension of phenomena, as though this was an intrinsic reality that was presented to us independently of the things that were the object of the natural sciences. As a good Kantian, Rickert held that we live and perceive reality as a disparate continuum whose segmentation into different domains comes about only as a result of the mode of knowledge that we apply to it and the characteristics that we select. The world becomes nature when we envisage it in its universal aspect; it becomes history when we examine it in its particular and individual aspect. Rather than draw a distinction between a nomothetic approach and an idiographic one, we should therefore consider all scientific activity as one and the same: activity that focuses on an object that is itself unique but that does so according to two different methods: (1) generalization, which is typical of the natural sciences, and (2) individualization, which is the prerogative of the cultural sciences. This is why psychology, to which historians lay claim, far from constituting a privileged means of access to human behavior, rightfully belongs to the natural sciences in that its objective is to discover the universal laws governing mental functions. So by what criteria should we identify that which, in the undifferentiated teeming profusion of the world, is likely to lead to generalizations and that which, on the contrary, leads to reducing things to their peculiarities? Rickert's answer is that the cultural sciences aim to study whatever takes on meaning for the whole of humanity or at least whatever is meaningful for all the members of a community. In other words, from the point of view of their scientific treatment, it is in their relationship to values that cultural processes are distinguished from natural ones.

By distinguishing between, on the one hand, objects without meaning whose existence is determined by general laws and, on the other, objects that we apprehend in all their individuality by virtue of the contingent value that is attached to them, Rickert dealt a blow to the foundations of ontological dualism. More or less all reality can be apprehended through one or another of its aspects, according to whether it is considered in its brute and stubborn factuality or from the point of view of the desires and uses invested in it by those who have deliberately produced or preserved it. But such a clarification comes at the price of an implacable epistemological separation between two fields of investigation and two modes of understanding that are now perfectly heterogeneous. This separation is no doubt more impermeable than that which involves simply classifying the entities of the world into two independent registers of existence. Between the human and the nonhuman there no longer exists the radical discontinuity of transcendence or the ruptures introduced by the mechanization of the world. It is only in our eyes that they are differentiated, and differentiated according to the manner in which we choose to objectivize them, for "this antithesis between nature and culture, in so far as it refers to a difference between two groups of real *objects*, is the actual basis for the classification and division of the various sciences."[40] In short, the opposition does not lie in things themselves; it is constructed by an arrangement that makes it possible to discriminate between them, a mechanism that will become increasingly effective as the human sciences abandon speculation on origins in favor of empirical inquiries and, as they accumulate positive knowledge, begin to supply proof of their legitimacy. It matters little, here, that Rickert, like many of his contemporaries, was inclined to classify the study of *Naturvölker* (primitive peoples) among the natural sciences, for the general ruling that he established was to carve out the space in which twentieth-century anthropology would be able to operate. It would be a study of cultural realities, as opposed to the study of natural realities.

The Autonomy of Dualism

Anthropology was to reap the fruits of the long period of maturation that we have just presented, and this would place it in a quite embarrassing position. Let us see what it has made of the situation. Ferocious though the controversies that fuel this discipline may seem to those observing it from afar, they nevertheless rest upon a wide consensus as to its mission. Just as any private altercation implies some common ground that defines the nature and forms of expression of the disagreement, so too, anthropological disputes presuppose a background of habits of thought and shared references on the basis of which oppositions can emerge. That common fund of interests originates in the very terms in which anthropology defines its object, namely Culture, or cultures, understood as a system of mediation with Nature that human beings have managed to invent. This constitutes a distinctive attribute of *Homo sapiens* and involves technical skills, language, symbolic activities, and the capacity to organize individuals in communities that are to some extent not constrained by biological continuities. Whatever the theoretical divergences that run through the discipline, there really does exist a consensus on the fact that the field staked out by anthropology is one in which the universal constraints of life and the contingent rules of social organization—the need for humans to exist as organisms in environments that they themselves have only partially fashioned and their capacity to ascribe a myriad of particular meanings to their interactions with other entities in the world—intermingle and mutually affect one another. All the concrete objects of ethnological investigation lie within this zone of overlap between collective institutions and the biological and psychological factors that confer upon social life its substance but not its form. The autonomy that anthropology claims within the scholarly world is thus founded on the belief that all societies constitute compromises between Nature and Culture and that its task is to examine the many singular expressions of this compromise and, if possible, to try to discover the rules of their formation and destruction. In short, the duality of the world has become the original (in both senses) challenge to which this science of anthropology has tried to respond, deploying a rich fund of ingenuity in order to reduce the gap between the two orders of reality that it found waiting for it in its cradle. The implications carried in the initial definition of the object were bound to influence the way in which that object was grasped. If one agrees that human experience is conditioned by the coexistence of two fields of phenomena that are accessible through two distinct modes of understanding, one inevitably approaches their interface from the starting point of one aspect rather than the other. This starting point may be the determinations that result from the use, control, or transformation of nature, which are universal in their effects but differentiated according to different environments, techniques, and social systems, or one may begin from the particularities of symbolic ways of treating a nature that is homogeneous within its own limits and mode of functioning—particularities that are recurrent because of the universality of the mechanisms mobilized and the unity of the object to which they are applied.

That is why naturalist monism and culturalist relativism continue to prosper in mutually legitimating confrontations. They form the two poles of an epistemological continuum along which those trying to make sense of the relations between societies and their environments must position themselves. Because they have hardened in the course of polemics, the extreme positions reveal in a purified form all the contradictions within which anthropology has been trapped because of its adhesion to the postulate that the world can be divided between two types of reality whose interdependence needs to be shown. When apprehended in its most excessive formulations, the choice thus acquires a pedagogic value: either culture is fashioned by nature, whether this is composed of genes, instincts, and neuron networks or by geographical constraints, or else nature only takes on shape and relief as a potential reservoir of signs and symbols on which culture can draw. Formulated crudely, such an opposition may evoke certain features of the old Scholastic distinction between a *natura naturans* and a *natura naturata*, to which Spinoza imparted new life. For Spinoza *natura naturans* is the absolute cause, constituted by an infinite number of infinite attributes, and is identified with God, as the source of all causality. Meanwhile, *natura naturata* covers the whole collection of processes and objects and also the ways of apprehending them that stem from the existence of *natura naturans*.[41] As Spinoza's contemporaries soon spotted, there is nothing Christian about such a God: as an impersonal causal substance, both the definition and the sum total of all possibilities, *natura naturans* is simply the hypostasis of a logically prior Nature expressed in the phrase "God or Nature" (*Deus sive natura*). In this, the materialists of subsequent centuries were to find a convenient substitute for the divine prime mover. On the other hand, it may be objected that Spinoza's *natura naturata* has very little to do with the modern idea of the autonomy of culture as a distinctive shaping, differing according to the languages and usages of peoples, of organisms, and of objects that come into existence only by virtue of the codes by which they are objectivized. Without wishing to push the transposition too far or to slip into anachronism, it is important to point out that, for Spinoza, *natura naturata* is constituted above all by modes—modes of being, of thinking, of acting, and of the relations between things—some of which are certainly universal but which are incommensurable with the cause that brings them about. They can therefore be studied in themselves, leaving aside that which determines them.

In opposition to an analogical use of the *natura naturans* and *natura naturata* pair, it could also be objected that the terms of such a distinction are mutually exclusive and do not allow for any intermediary states. Plenty of authors—anthropologists, sociologists, geographers, and philosophers—have tried to find a middle way between "crass determinism" (*le déterminisme crasse*) and "airy fancifulness" (*imaginarisme aérien*), to borrow Augustin Berque's expressions;[42] a dialectic way out would make it possible to avoid a head-on clash between the two dogmatisms. These authors hope to establish themselves at an equal distance from, on the one hand, militant positivists and, on the other, the advocates of an unyielding hermeneutics; they endeavor to combine the ideal and the material, the concrete and the abstract, physical causes and the production of meaning. But such efforts at mediation are condemned to failure as long as they are based on the premises of a dualist cosmology and assume the existence of a universal nature to which multiple cultures adapt or which they codify. Along an axis leading from totally natural culture to totally cultural nature, it is not possible to find a point of equilibrium. One is reduced to compromises that are closer to either one pole or the other. In any case, the problem is as old as anthropology itself; as Marshall Sahlins graphically puts it, anthropology is, as it were, a prisoner forced for over a century to pace to and fro in its cell, trapped between the walls of mental constraints and practical causes.[43]

I am ready to concede that such a prison does have its advantages. Dualism is not an evil in itself and it is ingenuous to stigmatize it for purely moral reasons in the manner of ecologically friendly philosophies of the environment or to blame it for all the evils of the modern era, ranging from colonial expansion to the destruction of nonrenewable resources and including the reification of sexual identities and class distinctions. We need at least to give dualism credit not only for its wager that nature is subject to laws of its own but also for its formidable stimulation of the development of the natural sciences. We are also indebted to it not only for the belief that humanity becomes gradually civilized by increasing its control over nature and disciplining its instincts more efficiently but also for certain advantages, in particular political ones, engendered by an aspiration toward progress. Anthropology is the daughter of these trends and of scientific thought and a belief in evolution; and we have no reason to feel ashamed of the circumstances of its birth or condemn it to disappear in expiation of its youthful errors. All the same, its role is hampered by this heritage—for that role is to gain an understanding of how peoples who do not share our cosmology came to invent for themselves realities that are distinct from our own, thereby manifesting a creativity that cannot be judged according to the criteria of our own accomplishments. And this is something that anthropology cannot do so long as it takes our reality for granted as a universal fact of experience, along with our ways of identifying discontinuities and discerning constant relationships in the world and our manner of distributing entities and phenomena, processes and modes of action, in categories thought to be predetermined by the texture and structure of things.

To be sure, we do not apprehend other cultures as completely analogous to our own, for this would hardly be likely. But we see them through the prism of no more than a limited part of our own cosmology, as so many singular expressions of Culture, which stands in contrast to a unique and universal Nature. We thus regard them as cultures that are very diverse but that all fit into the canon of what this double abstraction means to us. Because it is deeply rooted in our habits, this ethnocentrism is very difficult to eradicate. As Roy Wagner rightly notes, in the view of most anthropologists cultures on the periphery of the modern West "do not contrast with our culture or offer counterexamples to it, as a total system of conceptualization; but rather, invite comparison as 'other ways' of dealing with *our own reality.*"[44] By turning modern dualism into the standard for all world systems, we are forced into a kind of well-meaning cannibalism, as we repeatedly incorporate nonmoderns' objectivization of themselves into our own objectivization of ourselves. Primitive peoples were long reputed to be radically "other" and consequently were used as foils to civic morality or as models of now-vanished virtues. But now they are regarded as almost transparent neighbors, no longer the "naked philosophers" praised by Montaigne but preliminary sketches of citizens, protonaturalists, quasi historians, and nascent economists: in short, precursors who fumble at a way of apprehending things and human beings that we ourselves are believed to have discovered and codified better than anyone else. Of course, that is one way of expressing respect for them, but amalgamating them into the categories to which we belong is also the surest way of wiping out their distinctive contribution to the intelligibility of the human condition.

Such ethnocentricity does not make it unjustifiable to study kinship or technical systems using our own terms, but it does become a formidable obstacle to an accurate comprehension of ontologies and cosmologies whose premises differ from our own. Given its essential dualism, anthropology was bound to treat this degree of objectivization of the real that nonmoderns seemed not to have managed to achieve as a clumsy prefiguration or a more or less convincing echo of the objectivization that we ourselves have perfected, a motley mixture of baseless inferences, half-baked logic, and expressive projections bearing witness to the childhood of reason and the contemporary sources of superstition—in short, a residue of positive knowledge that, for us, takes on form and meaning only when set alongside the solid mass from which it has become detached. Ever since Frazer, this remnant of knowledge about nature has been the meat and drink of religious anthropology; and nothing is more symptomatic of the consequent status of the phenomena that interest it than the epithet "supernatural," by which they are still qualified. For even if one watches out for it, it is hard to avoid the illusion that, for many peoples, the supernatural is the part of nature that they have been unable to explain, and that an intuition of a supernatural causality anticipates the idea of a natural causality that could correct that intuition. After all, it is a seductive illusion to surmise that when "magical thought" interprets a rainbow, a flood, or an illness as the result of some invisible force endowed with intentionality, it is betting on a universal determinism that it can identify by its effects, but without discerning its true causes. Yet, as Durkheim saw, quite the reverse seems more plausible: "In order to call certain phenomena supernatural, one must already have a sense that there is *a natural order of things*, in other words that the phenomena of the universe are connected to one another according to certain necessary relationships called laws. Once this principle is established, anything that violates these laws necessarily appears to be beyond nature, and so beyond reason."[45] As Durkheim stresses, such clarifications become possible only late in the history of humanity, since they resulted from the development of the positive sciences undertaken by the Moderns. Far from indicating an incomplete determinism, the supernatural is an invention of naturalism, which casts a complacent glance at its mythical genesis, a sort of imaginary receptacle into which one can dump all the excessive significations produced by minds said to be attentive to the regularities of the physical world but, without the help of the exact sciences, not yet capable of forming an accurate idea of them.

The tendency to pass legitimate knowledge and symbolic residues through a naturalist sieve is illustrated by a taxonomic mania for picking out specialized fields of inquiry that are given the name of a recognized science preceded by the prefix "ethno-." The first two of these were ethnobotany and ethnozoology, but they have now been joined by ethnomedicine, ethnopsychiatry, ethnoecology, ethnopharmacology, ethnoastronomy, ethnoentomology, and many others too. This procedure makes it possible to reify certain blocks of native knowledge by dint of rendering them compatible with the modern division of sciences, for the frontiers of each domain are established a priori in accordance with the classes of entities and phenomena that the corresponding disciplines have gradually picked out from the fabric of the world as their own particular objects. Once each of these ethnosciences has won its institutional autonomy, with its own journals, congresses, professorial chairs, and controversies, it becomes increasingly difficult to escape from the illusion that the objectivation of reality is everywhere organized following a similar natural tendency the progress of which is blocked here and there by big blocks of magical thinking, moving testaments to a still imperfect recognition of the regularities of the physical world and an ambition to exercise firmer control over it. At this point, the distribution of anthropological work becomes inevitable. Specialists in the ethnosciences are responsible for revealing "folk" classifications and knowledge that constitute approximate variants of the scholarly disquisitions of which they are the prototypes; meanwhile, the specialists in "culture" appropriate the study of symbolism, beliefs, and rituals, the precious surface froth that bestows upon a people its own inimitable style.

Yet the multiple and tangled links that every individual is constantly weaving with his or her environment hardly sanction such a cut-and-dried distinction between practical knowledge and symbolic representations—at least not if one allows some credit to the meaning that the members of a collectivity attach to their actions. When an Achuar hunter finds himself within striking distance of his intended prey and sings it an *anent*, a plea designed to win the animal over and lull its mistrust by means of misleading promises, is he suddenly switching from rationality into irrationality and from instrumentalized knowledge into a fantasy? Has he moved into a quite different register, following the long period of stalking the animal, in which he has mobilized all his ethological expertise, his deep knowledge of the environment, and all his tracker's skills: all the qualities that have allowed him, almost by instinct, to link together a multitude of clues and create a thread that will lead him to his prey? In short, should the magic song be interpreted as an illusory representation needlessly introduced into a chain of operations molded out of a combination of know-how, effective knowledge, and confirmed automatic reflexes? Not at all. For if I regard an animal as a person endowed with faculties analogous to my own, an intentional being attentive to whatever I may tell it, it is no more abnormal to speak to it with all the appearance of civility than it is to provide myself with the technical means of slaughtering it. The two attitudes are both part of the tissue of relations that I establish with it, and each has a role to play in the configuration of my behavior toward it.

Does this lead one back to an intellectualist idea that might explain hunting magic by a particular belief of those who resort to it, namely a theory of the world in which such actions are invested with an operational efficacy? Not at all. No Achuar would claim that the *anent*, on its own, makes it possible to flush out his prey and be sure of killing it. The *anent* is but one of the elements that establishes the ontological status of a particular animal, in combination with a whole collection of other, equally relevant criteria relating to its customary behavior, its habitat, and whatever one knows about the circumstances that, at one particular moment, have made it possible for this animal to become associated with the hunter's biography and his past encounters with other members of the same species. The magic incantation is not operational because it is performative or because it may bring about the result that it suggests or make this seem possible in the eyes of the singer. It is operational because it helps to characterize and therefore to render effective the relationship that is established at a particular moment between one particular man and one particular animal; it recalls the links between the hunter and other members of the animal's species, it describes those links using the language of kinship, and underlines the ties of solidarity between the two parties that are present; in short, it picks out from the attributes of each party those that will impart to their confrontation a greater existential reality. So a hunting *anent* cannot be isolated as a symbolic dross that accompanies a technical process. To obtain a useful result is not its primary purpose; it is neither an additive nor a palliative; what it does is make it possible to set up a system of relations already virtually existent, in such a way as to give meaning to a chance interaction between the man and the animal by delivering an unambiguous reminder of their respective positions. In Amazonia, as among ourselves, an organism is established as a significant entity in the environment not solely on the strength of the material and cognitive attributes that make it possible to identify it, kill it, and eat it but also by taking into account a whole collection of properties that are attributed to it and that, in return, call for particular types of behavior and mediation that are appropriate to the nature ascribed to it. Are vegetarians really so different from an Achuar hunter when they refuse to eat veal but not spinach, and are international organizations when they forbid the capture of dolphins but not that of herrings? Are not the differing ways in which we treat different species likewise based on the type of relations that we think we have established with this or that segment of the living world? Rather than regard the former as obvious superstitions and the latter as covert ones, linked more or less reasonably to a system of positive knowledge, would it not be preferable to treat the "symbolic" dimension of our actions in the world simply as one means, among others, of distinguishing, out of the whole network of things, certain ways of proceeding that, as we shall later see, are less random than they may appear?

The Autonomy of Worlds

As we near the end of this outline, what more needs to be said? Is it still plausible to classify as a cross-cultural universal an opposition between nature and culture that was introduced scarcely more than a century ago? Should we continue to scour the four corners of the planet in order to discover how the most diverse of peoples may have expressed such an opposition, meanwhile quite forgetting the altogether exceptional circumstances in which we ourselves belatedly forged it? Is it really so shocking to recognize that the Jivaros, the Samoyeds, and the Papuans may not be conscious of the fact that humans are classed as different from nonhumans by the systems of analysis now applied to them, when our own great-grandparents were not conscious of the fact? In short, should we cling to such a historically determined way of dividing up the world in order to account for cosmologies that are clearly still very much alive in plenty of civilizations or that, now relegated to the shelves of our libraries, await only our curiosity in order to come to life once more? As I am sure must be clear by now, I myself do not think so.

One objection that may spring to readers' minds is the following: my critique of dualism may be either naïve or sophistic; it seems to skim the surface of the insubstantial tissue of words and confuse the absence of concepts with the nonexistence of the realities that they designate. Just because the opposition between nature and culture acquired its definitive form and its operational efficacy only at the beginning of the twentieth century, it does not necessarily follow that people earlier and elsewhere were in practice incapable of discriminating between the two orders of reality that we classify using those terms. In short, I have failed to resist an ingenuous variant of the nominalist perversion. However, the ambition of the present book is to show that this is not at all the case and that a rejection of dualism leads neither to absolute relativism nor to a return to modes of thought that today's context has rendered obsolete, and that it is possible to reflect upon the diversity of customs in the world without succumbing either to a fascination with the exceptional or to a refusal of the positive sciences. I will limit myself, for the moment, to a brief declaration of faith.

It is unlikely that anyone can have failed to notice that nonhumans do not, ordinarily, use language, that it is impossible to have productive sexual relations with them, and that many are incapable of moving by themselves or of growing and of reproducing themselves. Perhaps we should even lend credit

to developmental psychologists when they tell us that all children, whatever
the environment in which they are raised, tend very early on to draw distinctions between entities that they perceive to be endowed with intentionality
and others that are not.[46] In short, in all probability an observer ideally removed from any cultural influences could accumulate many signs indicating
that, between himself and what we customarily call natural objects, a whole
range of differences exists—differences in appearance, in behavior, and in
the manner of being present in the world. However, the signs that indicate a
gradual continuity are equally numerous and have not failed to attract the notice of a handful of rebellious spirits who, from Montaigne to Haeckel and including Condillac and La Mettrie, never ceased to oppose the dominant doctrine.[47] Why should the frontier be drawn at language or poiesis rather than
at independence of movement? Or at independence of movement rather than
at life? Or at life rather than at material solidity, spatial proximity, and acous-
tic effects? As Whitehead observes, admittedly in a different context, "nature
as perceived always has a ragged edge."[48] The ethnographical and historical
ground that we have covered so far shows clearly enough that a consciousness
of certain discontinuities between humans and nonhumans is not in itself
enough to create a dualist cosmology. The multiplicity of forms of existence
that we witness all around us may offer a more fertile terrain for ontological discriminations than the tiny quantum by which we distinguish ourselves
from what Merleau-Ponty calls "associated bodies" (*les corps associés*).[49] The
world presents itself to us as a proliferating continuum, and one would have to
adhere to a truly myopic realism of essences to consider it cut up in advance
into discontinuous domains that the brain is designed, always and everywhere,
to identify in the same manner.

Readers might furthermore argue that the great divide is an illusion since
Moderns never have conformed in practice to the radical distinction upon
which their representation of the world is founded. This original hypothesis,
proposed by Latour, goes as follows: ever since the mechanistic revolution of
the seventeenth century, scientific and technical activity has never ceased to
create mixtures of nature and culture in networks of increasingly complex
structure in which objects and humans, and material effects and social conventions, coexist in a situation of mutual "translation"; such a proliferation of
mixed realities was itself rendered possible only through a parallel endeavor
of critical "purification" designed to guarantee the separation of humans and
nonhumans into two hermetically sealed ontological regions.[50] In short, Moderns neither do what they say nor say what they do. The only thing that distinguishes them from premoderns is the presence of a dualist "constitution"
designed to speed up the production of hybrids and render it more effective,

at the same time concealing the conditions in which this is accomplished. As for premoderns, they—it is claimed—concentrated their efforts on the conceptualization of hybrids, thereby preventing the latter from multiplying. All in all, the argument is very convincing. But in no way does it call into question the absolutely exceptional nature of modern cosmology—a point that, it is true, Latour has no hesitation in conceding.[51] The fact that dualism masks a practice that contradicts it does not eliminate its directive role in the organization of the sciences, nor does it efface the fact that ethnology derives constant inspiration from an opposition that most of the peoples it describes and interprets do perfectly well without. What primarily interests me are the deforming effects of this perspective on ethnology, for it is here that its creation of illusions is the most pernicious. A sociologist of the sciences may well incur Latour's criticism if he believes that humans and nonhumans exist in separate domains, but nevertheless he will remain faithful to one dimension of his object. In contrast, an ethnologist who thinks that the Makuna and the Chewong believe in such a dichotomy would be betraying the thought of those he studied.

I know that the idea of the great divide has had a bad press for some time. Ever since ethnology liberated itself from the grand evolutionist schemas of the nineteenth century under the combined influence of British functionalism and North American culturalism, it has persisted in seeing the magic, myths, and rituals of nonmoderns as prefigurations of, or fumblings toward, scientific thought, as attempts—that are both justifiable and plausible, given the circumstances—to explain natural phenomena and ensure control over them and at the same time as expressions, bizarre in form but basically reasonable, of the universality of humanity's physiological and cognitive constraints. Its intentions were honorable: the aim was to dissipate the fog of prejudices surrounding "primitives" by showing that good sense, observational skills, an aptitude for inferring properties, and ingenuity and resourcefulness are all part of an equally shared human heritage. As a result, it is now hard to refer to any difference between Us and Others without finding oneself accused of imperialistic arrogance, incipient racism, or impenitent nostalgia for the past, resurgences of thought both malign and retrograde that should promptly be consigned to the oblivion of history, there to join the ghosts of Gustave Le Bon and Lucien Lévy-Bruhl. I agree that it may have been useful, in a particular period, to declare that peoples long considered "savages" were nevertheless not in thrall to Nature since, just like us, they were capable of conceptualizing its otherness. The argument was effective when used against those who doubted the unity of the human condition and the equal dignity of all its various cultural manifestations. But there is now more to gain from trying to situate our own exoticism as one particular case within a general grammar of cosmologies rather than continuing to attribute to our own vision of the world the value of a standard by which to judge the manner in which thousands of civilizations have managed to acquire some obscure inkling of that vision.

PART TWO

The Structures of Experience

Whoever truly wishes to become a philosopher will, "for once in his life," have to fall back on himself and, within himself, try to overturn all the sciences so far accepted and attempt to reconstruct them.

EDMUND HUSSERL, *Cartesian Meditations*

4

The Schemas of Practice

Even if we recognize the contingency of the dualism of nature and culture and the difficulties that this introduces into any apprehension of nonmodern cosmologies, we should nevertheless not be led to neglect to seek for structural frameworks that can account for the coherence and regularity of the diverse ways in which humans live and perceive their involvement in the world. However useful a physiology of interactions may be, it amounts to nothing without a morphology of practices, a praxeological analysis of forms of experience. To paraphrase a famous saying of Kant's, structures without content are empty and experiences without forms are meaningless.[1] It so happens that, in one of those swings that are customary in anthropology, the study of structural factors has for some time found itself particularly discredited. It is likened to an icy objectivism that irremediably dissolves all that goes to make up the richness and dynamism of social exchanges. Associated with it is the cliché of an interplay of timeless structures, hypostasized as essences that function in the manner of a series of actions executed by automata lacking any initiative or affects. Against this position (that no one ever held), the emphasis is now laid upon the creativity of the agency of social actors, upon the role played by historical contingency and resistance to hegemonies in the invention and cross-fertilization of cultural forms, upon the self-evident power and spontaneity of practice and the innocence now forever lost of all interpretative strategies.

Yet how can we be blind to the fact that practices and behavior observable within a collectivity display a regularity, a permanence, and a degree of automatism that the individuals concerned are usually at pains to attribute to systems of instituted rules? And how can we ignore the fact that, in societies without writing at least, only a few exceptional figures, so rare that all ethnol-

ogists know their names, have been able to propose even partial syntheses of
the bases of their culture? In truth, such syntheses are, anyway, in many cases
produced just to satisfy the expectations of some inquirer, and their generally
esoteric character rules out regarding them as a charter that everybody recognizes. Such lines of conduct, such routine reactions and choices, and such
shared attitudes toward the world and others are distinctive enough to serve
as an intuitive indication for gauging the differences between neighboring
peoples. However, they are so deeply internalized that they seldom surface
in reflexive deliberations. So how could those tacit dispositions become the
object of public debate, be consciously submitted to reforms, and, by dint of
deliberate adjustments, be made to fit in with the prevailing circumstances?
To claim that this is possible, provided one responds to the bewitching spontaneity of praxis finally released from its alienation, is to perpetuate the old
confusion between, on the one hand, the series of norms instilled by education and, on the other, the cognitive and corporeal templates that govern the
expression of an ethos. It is also to amalgamate models of action objectivized in the form of prohibitions or prescriptions that can be revoked at any
moment with practical schemas that, if they are to be effective, must remain
undetectable, shrouded in the obscurity of habits and customs.

Structures and Relations

There is one major finding for which we should be grateful both to anthropological structuralism and to the pioneering work of Gregory Bateson. It is
a finding that is perceptible even to those who pretend to be unaware of its
source: namely the agenda to envisage social life from the point of view of
the relations that hold it together. This is a choice that presupposes ascribing to the links that relationships establish a structural stability and regularity greater than that of the contingent actions of the elements that they link.
Whatever the domain organized by those relations—be it kinship, economic
exchanges, ritual activities, or attempts to understand the ordering of the cosmos—their range is, logically, far more limited than the infinitely diverse elements that they link together; and that limitation opens up the possibility of a
reasoned and systematic analysis of the diversity of relations between existing
things. The aim of this would, in the first instance, be to set up a typology of
possible relationships to the world and others, be they human or nonhuman,
and to examine their compatibilities and incompatibilities.

However, such a study of structural factors runs into a number of difficulties, many of them interdependent. In the first place there is the problem
of scale: either (1) the structures that are identified are so general that they

cannot explain the specificity of particular cultural configurations, or else (2) they are so particularized by their historical contexts that they turn out to be unsuited to any comparative endeavor. The notion of cultural "patterns" suggested by Ruth Benedict is no longer fashionable, but it does provide a good illustration of the former situation (i.e., 1).[2] Those "patterns," detected by an inductive analysis of no more than three societies, can basically be reduced to the classic Nietzschean opposition between Apollonian peoples and Dionysiac ones. These represent two forms of collective experience that in no sense constitute structures—that is to say, combinations of relational features organized into models that can be connected by transformational laws—since they result from heterogeneous value systems, ethical principles, and normalized types of behavior that are, furthermore, hypostasized in autonomous and transcendent cultures to which each individual would react on a smaller, personal scale.

As for the notion of habitus, this encounters the second difficulty (2). Although this notion may make it possible to avoid the usual hazards presented by a structural approach, in particular the reification of structure conceived in the manner of an autonomous subject endowed with social effectiveness, it makes generalization very difficult. A habitus, as defined by Bourdieu, is certainly a structure identified by analysis, but it is a structure of a particular kind: a system of durable arrangements immanent in local practices, which results from people learning to imitate and internalize the behavior and bodily techniques of those who surround them. These structuring structures, which are predisposed to engender and perpetuate structured structures, therefore constitute the distinctive style of actions within a given social environment without, however, being present in the consciousness of the actors in the form of general rules or series of prescriptions. Because a habitus is a system of cognitive and motivational structures so familiar that we feel no need to examine them, it is, moreover, far more stable than the local theories by means of which it is rationalized and converted into norms of individual and collective behavior.[3] A habitus is nevertheless particularized by history, for "habitus, the product of a historical acquisition, is what enables the legacy of history to be appropriated." It is somehow naturalized by the contexts within which it operates, both those peculiar to the field within which it is deployed and also those at the heart of the context into which the analyst studying it is himself inserted.[4] In this sense, then, and contrary to universalizing forms of experience of the "patterns of culture" type, a habitus may be extremely diverse, for each of its expressions reflects one modality of the multitude of cultural skills that humans have to deploy at one point or another in their history in order to exist together in very varied physical and social environments. However reasonable it may be, this particularization of a habitus nevertheless makes it difficult to compare the modalities of its concrete manifestation and also to grasp, as a structured whole, the diverse combinations in which it operates.

It seems to me both possible and necessary to explore farther upstream, around a kernel of elementary schemas of practice whose different configurations might make it possible to take account of the whole gamut of relations to existing beings—a kind of original matrix from which every habitus stems and a perceptible trace of which they all retain in each of their occurrences. In principle, such a hypothesis is not so very distant from the idea that Lévi-Strauss presents when he writes: "Every newborn child comes equipped, in the form of adumbrated mental structures, with all the means ever available to mankind to define its relations to the world in general and its relations to others. But these structures are exclusive. Each of them can integrate only certain elements out of all those that are offered. Consequently, each type of social organization represents a choice, which the group imposes and perpetuates."[5] It is, however, necessary to point out that those "means ever available to mankind" consist not solely of innate mental structures but above all of a limited number of internalized practical schemas that synthesize the objective properties of all the relations that are possible between humans and nonhumans.

This brings us back to the second difficulty that any study of structural factors encounters: how to assign them their ontological status. Are the structural configurations detected by analyzing any social-reality expressions purged of the concrete relations that constitute the web of that reality, or should they, rather, be considered as operational models constructed by an observer relatively independently of the explicit models formulated by those whom he is observing? And if the latter is the case, how should one evaluate the relevance of those structures and also take into account the fact that they may explain the systematic character of the norms, practices, and ways of behaving without, however, being consciously apprehended? The former, so-called 'realist' position was illustrated most clearly by Alfred Radcliffe-Brown: "I use the term 'social structure' to denote this network of actually existing social relations that hold human beings together in a particular natural environment."[6] This is also the model of a social structure that many contemporary ethnographers and sociologists spontaneously adopt when they describe the structural characteristics of the societies or groups that they are studying: they do not present these as underlying properties likely to feature in vaster combinations (e.g., throughout a whole cultural area or as a particular type of phenomenon); rather, they present this model as an inductive formalization of observable relations between individuals (one frequently inspired by the models by means of which the observed community apprehends and translates the regularity of the behavior patterns within it). At the descriptive level at which it is operational, acceptance of the realist postulate is not unjustified, so long as one is aware of the fact that the results to which it leads, namely an ad hoc interpretation of a particular society, should not be employed as raw material in the elaboration of a structural morphology.[7]

It is, of course, to Lévi-Strauss that we owe the alternative definition of the notion of structure. Blinded by his empiricism, Radcliffe-Brown—we are told—confused social relations with social structure. The former present the material for observation that the ethnologist or sociologist uses so as to elaborate abstract models that render the latter (the social structure) manifest. In short, "the term 'a social structure' has nothing to do with empirical reality but with models which are built up after it."[8] For those models to be truly structural, they need, moreover, to satisfy further conditions. They must be systematic, in the sense that any modification of one of their elements will lead to a predictable modification in all the others. At the level of a family of models, they are furthermore organized in accordance with an ordered variation that defines the limits of a transformational group. Such a structural model presents some of the characteristics of the deductive model of causal explanation that Newton used to account for physical reality and from which Kant drew the philosophical consequences in his theory of synthetic causality. Lévi-Strauss himself invited that analogy when he distinguished mechanical models, the preferred instruments of structural analysis, from the statistical models more generally favored by sociologists and historians. A mechanical model characteristically formulates the relations between the essential elements at the same scale as the phenomena in the real system. In statistical models, in contrast, the behavior of individual elements is not predictable from knowledge of their mode of combination. In the social sciences, these two types of models are equivalent to the difference in physics between mechanics and thermodynamics.[9]

Yet the Lévi-Straussian structural models possess one characteristic that definitely distances them from the deductive model of causal explanation: they are unconscious, or at least, the unconscious models are the most rewarding for structural analysis.[10] As such, they exist as structures buried just beneath the surface in the psyche, where they are often undetected by the collective consciousness of social actors, concealed as they are by vernacular models whose normative functions reduce them to an impoverishing simplification. When an observer constructs a structural model corresponding to phenomena whose systematic character has not been perceived by the society that he is studying, he is therefore not content to assume that the morphology of his formal device represents underlying properties of the society that he is trying to understand; for he furthermore suspects that those properties do have an empirical existence, one that is certainly unseen by those who make daily use of them but that a skillful analysis will be able to bring to the surface. But what is the nature of this structural subconscious? Is it present in each mind in the form of cognitive imperatives that remain tacit despite being culturally determined, or is it distributed among the properties of the institutions that reveal it to the observer? How is it internalized by each individual and by what means does it act in such a way that it may determine recurrent behavior patterns that can be translated into vernacular models?

Lévi-Strauss does not provide very precise answers to these questions. The structural unconscious has no content but it does have a directive or "symbolic" function: to impose very general laws upon forms taken by social phenomena and objectivized systems of ideas such as myths or popular classifications. Thus, the three elementary structures of matrimonial exchange — bilateral, matrilateral, and patrilateral — may unconsciously be constantly present in a human mind, so it is possible for thought to actualize one of them only if it sets up a contrastive opposition to the other two.[11] It is therefore a matter of generative synthetic categories that, through a study of social institutions, may be detected far upstream in the functioning of the mind. This would justify considering the sociological analysis to be simply a stage in an investigation of a primarily psychological nature.

Fruitful though it may be, the hypothesis of the existence of unconscious structural invariants founded on contrastive oppositions does not help to elucidate what happens at the intermediary stage. How could very general structures linked to characteristics of the functioning of the mind possibly engender models of conscious norms or, more importantly, provide an organizing framework for practices that, for the most part, do not appear to be governed by any explicit rules? This last point is particularly crucial since Lévi-Strauss himself was mostly concerned to explain highly formalized domains in social life, such as kinship, totemic classifications, and spatial organization. These domains are codified without too much ambiguity by many societies and described in more or less standard terms by ethnographers; and it is not impossible to conjecture that they are governed by a small kernel of principles directly traceable to certain properties of thought. It is quite a different matter when one is faced by peoples little inclined to reflexive thinking, who present no more than very summary models of their social life, or when one tackles the more shapeless field of daily customs and habits, technical activities, and stereotyped patterns of behavior — in short, all the distinctive automatisms peculiar to a cultural environment, for which it is much harder to find underlying mental determinants.

The fact is that Lévi-Strauss took little interest in cognitive and practical mediations that might make it possible to move on from a highly abstract psychic combination of factors to the remarkable diversity of instituted customs, for that was not the level of analysis that he considered the most productive.[12] The point of view that he recommends is that of an astronomer who is forced, by the great distance separating him from the objects that he studies, to identify only their most essential characteristics. This is quite different from the point of view of a physiologist trying to understand the mechanisms by which the structural regularities that he detects take on a concrete form for the individual of this or that society. Yet, far from being contradictory, those two points of view are, in fact, complementary, in that the latter is indispensable for validating the hypotheses of the former and for guaranteeing that the models that result may indeed be found at a tacit level in the way in which people organize their experience. Lévi-Strauss would no doubt not disagree, but in his case the necessity for that second phase is expressed not so much by circumstantial analyses but rather by a very general conviction that there does exist a dimension of human activity in which such an investigation is justifiable. That, at any rate, is what one famous passage in *The Savage Mind* suggests: "Marxism, if not Marx himself, has too commonly reasoned as though practices followed directly from *praxis*. Without questioning the undoubted primacy of infrastructures, I believe that there is always a mediator between *praxis* and practices, namely the conceptual scheme by the operation of which matter and form, neither with any independent existence, are realized as structures, that is as entities which are both empirical and intelligible."[13]

If we set aside an overly substantive distinction between infrastructure and superstructure, what Lévi-Strauss is here suggesting in general terms is an anthropological project that is radically new. However, it is one that he himself never completed, for he was possessed by the urgency of establishing the methodological validity of gaining an understanding of human realities by means of intelligible structures and therefore neglected the pursuit of a better understanding of the conditions of their concrete existence.

This "conceptual scheme" is supposed to be the key to interaction between what is intelligible and what is empirical. But what does it consist of? Lévi-Strauss is here using this notion in a quite loose philosophical sense that is clearly derived from the Kantian theory of a transcendental schematism understood as a method of thinking through the relation between a concept and the concrete object to which it applies. Presumably, by using the expression "conceptual scheme" Lévi-Strauss has in mind the mediatory synthetic and dynamic properties of a transcendental schematism without, however, recognizing the restrictive definition that Kant applies to it. His idea is probably closer to that of Piaget, himself inspired by Kant, for whom a schema constitutes an internal representation of a category of situations that allows an organism to act in a coherent and coordinated fashion every time that it is faced by analogous situations. However, although Lévi-Strauss did examine the supposed institutional translations of some of those structuring schemas, he was never completely explicit about their identity or their way of functioning. He went only so far as to say that they could not coincide with the general system of our ideas, which, he claimed, only a madman could dream of listing in an exhaustive fashion.[14] Such a warning is not to be taken lightly, so my ambition is more measured. The present book is founded upon a hunch that it *is* possible to reveal elementary schemas of practices and to sketch a summary cartography of their distribution and their ways of operating. But such an undertaking is only justifiable provided one specifies the mechanisms by which structures are reputed to organize systems and mores without, however, rejecting the hypothesis that it may be possible to analyze human relations with the world and with others in terms of finite combinations.

Understanding the Familiar

Understanding how models of relations and behavior can influence practices without rising to the level of consciousness has now become a less formidable task, thanks to progress made in understanding the processes of inference and analogical derivation that govern the construction of mental schemas. That progress itself results from a change of perspective in the study of human cognition, which led to interest in the nonlinguistic dimensions of the acquisition, implementation, and transmission of knowledge. Previously, knowledge had, essentially, been treated as a system of explicit propositions organized in accordance with the sequential logic characteristic of natural languages and computer programming. That type of model offered an unsatisfactory representation of the mental process that makes it possible to recognize certain objects and immediately include them in a particular taxonomic class. But then a shift took place in the study of classificatory concepts, which moved toward a position inspired by the Gestalt psychology, according to which such concepts should be apprehended as global configurations of characteristic features rather than as decomposable lists of attributes whose necessary and sufficient definitions would have already been learned. Following the work of Eleanor Rosch, it is now recognized that many classificatory concepts are formed by reference to "prototypes" that condense groups of particular cases that display "a family resemblance" into a network of associated representations.[15] For example, the concept of a house is not constructed on the basis of a list of specific features—roof, walls, doors and windows, and so forth—the presence of which would have to be verified in order for us to be sure that the object in question truly was a house. In such circumstances, we should be hard put to it to identify as a house an edifice lacking walls or a ruin whose roof had disappeared.[16] If we have no hesitation in describing as houses an ice igloo, a troglodyte dwelling, or a yurt, that is because we recognize in a flash that they conform to a vague and unformulated collection of attributes not one of which is essential to a classificatory judgment but all of which are linked in a schematic representation to which a typical house should conform. Far from being decomposable into a series of definitions of the kind provided by a dictionary, classificatory concepts are based on fragments of tacit knowledge relating to the properties that our theoretical and practical knowledge of the world leads us to ascribe to the objects to which those concepts refer. In this we are guided by our experience of certain concrete expressions of those objects, expressions that seem to us best to exemplify the class to which they belong.

The importance of the nonlinguistic aspects of cognition has also been revealed by increasingly numerous studies devoted to learning how to perform practical activities, whether these depend on a specialized know-how or a mechanical completion of daily tasks.[17] Operations as humdrum as driving a car or preparing a meal mobilize not so much explicit knowledge that can be organized into propositions but rather a combination of acquired motor aptitudes and various experiences synthesized into a skill. They depend on "knowing how" rather than on "knowing that."[18] True, learning to drive involves words, and one can learn to cook from recipe books or by following the instructions printed on the packaging of foods. But in these domains, as in others that involve some practical knowledge, it is possible to execute a task quickly and well only when the knowledge transmitted through the medium of language either oral or written has been absorbed as a reflex rather than in a reflective form, as a series of automatic actions rather than as a list of the operations that need to be performed. Whatever the role that linguistic mediation plays in creating it, in order to become effective this kind of competence requires that language now be bypassed. The person who possesses this skill must be able to work rapidly and with confidence in order to complete a task certain aspects of which may differ from those previously encountered in comparable situations. Such flexibility appears to suggest that, in a practical activity, one becomes dexterous not by memorizing particular cases already encountered or lists of instructions that may be relevant but by developing a specialized cognitive schema that can be adapted to a whole family of similar tasks. The unintentional activation of such a schema is derived from a certain type of situation.

Some of these practical schemas take longer to establish than others because of the great quantity of disparate items of knowledge that they have to organize. Hunting provides a good illustration. The Achuar say that one becomes a good hunter only when one reaches maturity—that is to say, in one's midthirties. It is an assertion that is confirmed by systematic statistics: the hunters who bring home the most game are certainly men of forty or more.[19] Nevertheless, every adolescent already possesses a fund of knowledge of the natural environment and a technical dexterity worthy of admiration. For example, he is able to identify by sight several hundred kinds of birds, to imitate their song, and to describe their habits and habitat. He knows how to recognize a trail from the slightest of signs, such as a butterfly hovering at the foot of a tree, attracted by the still fresh urine of a monkey that has recently passed; as I repeatedly saw for myself, he can fire a dart from a blowpipe into a papaya standing one hundred paces away. But it will be another twenty years before he can be sure of bringing home game from every hunt. What exactly does he learn in the course of that interval that makes the difference? He no doubt completes his ethological knowledge and improves his understanding of interdependencies within the ecosystem. But the most essential aptitude that he acquires is probably an increasingly well-controlled ability to interconnect a mass of heterogeneous information structured in such a way as to allow him to respond effectively and immediately to whatever situation he encounters. Such automatic physical reflexes are indispensable for hunting, in which rapid reactions are the key to success. These are also transposable to warfare, which demands from an Achuar warrior the same accuracy in interpreting tracks and trails and the same ability to make swift judgments. Faced with such expertise, only the effects of which are measurable, a nonhunter is reduced to guesswork, for practically none of all this can be expressed adequately by language.

Yet, since the time when Kant wrote of the schematism of understanding, saying that it was "an art hidden in the depths of the human soul whose true operations we can divine from nature and lay unveiled before our eyes only with difficulty,"[20] some progress has been made in understanding the material conditions required for the exercise of nonpropositional cognition. First, the neurosciences told us that the brain does not function in as compartmentalized a fashion as used to be thought according to the old theory of the faculties. They told us that all perceptive and cognitive processes presuppose a parallel activation of neuronal networks distributed throughout the nervous system, networks that become stabilized and differentiated gradually during the first years of a child's development in close correlation to stimuli received from the environment.[21] Furthermore, over the last few years, the connectionist models developed in the field of artificial intelligence have begun to prove their usefulness, particularly when applied experimentally to robotics. In contrast to the classic models that govern the elaboration of standard computer languages, connectionist models do not function on the basis of lists of instructions that allow them, through predictive calculations, to carry out a series of operations specified by initial data stored in the memory bank. Instead, they consist of a collection of electronic networks that interconnect selectively, depending on the nature and intensity of the stimuli received. This means that they can recognize regularities in their environment and accordingly remodel their internal organization, not by creating explicit rules adapted to a recognized regularity, but by modifying the thresholds in the connections of the processors in such a way that the structure of the knowledge mechanism reflects the structure present in the input.[22] For this reason, they (unlike sequential models) are compatible with the prototypical effect at work in the formation of classificatory concepts and even allow for plausible inferences regarding the reconstitution of structures and forms that appear in an incomplete fashion in the input, in the same way as configurations are recognized in Gestalt psychology.[23] Finally, even if the connectionist models come close to the ideal of a tabula rasa—a criticism leveled at them by partisans of modularity, who believe that much knowledge is innate—they do not in principle exclude the possibility that at the start of ontogeny a small core of specialized mechanisms is supplied in the course of phylogenetic evolution.[24] In short, connectionist models mirror the functioning of neuronal networks; they are capable of learning, react rapidly to certain complex situations, seem to obey formal rules without such a stipulation being introduced into the model, and even create the illusion of a minimum degree of intentionality. These are all properties that make them similar to human cognition when it is faced, not with resolving propositional problems, but with the kinds of situations so familiar to ethnologists, in which people appear to regulate their actions as if these were dictated by cultural imperatives that they are nevertheless not able to express.

Schematisms

The heuristic stimulus provided by connectionist models and the increasing number of studies devoted to the formation of classificatory concepts and the acquisition of know-how have led psychologists and anthropologists to take a more systematic interest in the role played by abstract structures that organize understanding and practical action without mobilizing mental images or any knowledge conveyed in declarative statements. Such structures are now regrouped under the generic heading of "schemas."[25] However, this term now covers such a diversity of mechanisms for processing information, for expressing experience, and for representing routine tasks that a few words of clarification are necessary.

The first thing to do is to distinguish cognitive schemas reputed to be universal from those that stem from a particular acquired cultural experience or the vagaries of an individual's history. The existence of the former is still disputed, either because the link that they assume between biological data and their conceptual or symbolical interpretation remains rather speculative or because such schemas have been inferred on the basis of experiments conducted almost exclusively in Western industrialized societies. For example, such is the case with what developmental psychologists have, in an approximate fashion, called "naive theories" but that it might be better to call "attributive schemas." These are cores of assumptions concerning the behavior of objects in the world that are recognized very early on in the process of ontogeny and that guide children in the inferences that they make concerning the properties of those objects. These schemas affect three domains: expectations concerning human action (the imputation of internal states, in particular intentionality and affects), expectations concerning the mode of being of physical objects (the effects of gravity and conservation of forms and the continuity of trajectories), and, at a later age, expectations concerning the intrinsic nature of nonhuman organisms (animation, growth, and the ability to reproduce). Nearly all contemporary psychologists agree that these attributive schemas are universal, but they disagree as to the question of the stages and modalities of their appearance and therefore as to the degree of their innateness.[26] If the existence of these so-called naive theories were to be confirmed, they would constitute knowledge of an intuitive, nonpropositional nature, which would make it possible to interpret the behavior of salient objects so as to act upon and with them in an effective way.

Without underestimating the role played by possible universal schemas in the formation of ontological judgments, it does seem necessary to agree that it is above all acquired schemas that are at the center of attention of those interested in the diversity of customs across the world, since it is partly through the effect of those mechanisms that human ways of behaving differ. They differ from one individual to another as a result of the influence of idiosyncratic schemas, such as those that make it possible to perform an action as a matter of routine (e.g., to follow a regular itinerary) or those that structure the many protocols that each of us devise in the course of time so as to organize our sequences of daily tasks. It is even possible that, doubtless at a deeper level, a Freudian subconscious prompts such a procedure, given that, in a nonintentional fashion, as the product of a particular individual history, it gives rise to, channels, and organizes structures of feelings and relations to others. These, as is well known, can be verbally objectivized only with the utmost difficulty and always in an unsatisfactory manner. All the same, collective schemas are the ones that are of most interest to ethnologists, for they constitute one of the principal means of constructing shared cultural meanings. They may be defined as psychic, sensorimotor and emotional dispositions that are internalized thanks to experience acquired in a given social environment. These make it possible to exercise at least three types of skills: first, to structure the flow of perception in a selective fashion, granting a preeminence in signification to particular traits and processes that can be observed in the environment; second, to organize both practical activity and the expression of thoughts and emotions in accordance with relatively standardized scenarios; and third, to provide a framework for typical interpretations of patterns of behavior and events—interpretations that are acceptable and can be communicated within a community in which the habits of life that they convey are regarded as normal.

These collective schemas may be either nonreflective or explainable; that is to say, they can be formulated in a more or less synthetic fashion as vernacular models by those who put them into practice. A cultural model is not always reducible to strings of simple propositional rules such as "If X belongs to one class of relatives and Y to another, then they may (or may not) marry." Many cultural models are not transmitted as bodies of precepts but are internalized little by little, without any particular teaching, although this does not prevent them from being objectivized quite schematically when circumstances demand it. This is particularly true of the ways of using space, a domain of collective life that every society codifies to a certain extent, without it being the case that this code is apprehended by individuals as a collection of rules to be consciously applied. A good illustration of this kind of nonpropositional schema is provided, in many regions of the world, by the way that a house is organized: its orientation, structure, the stages of its construction, and, above all, the way it is used constitute an established model that one learns to recognize as procedures become progressively familiar rather than as a result of a series of propositions explicitly passed on. All the same, it is always possible for an observer to obtain precise information about the way in which a dwelling is built and inhabited, a fact that shows that his informants are perfectly capable of clearly explaining the broad lines of the schematic model that guides their practical behavior.[27]

In contrast, nonreflective schemas do not rise to the surface of consciousness, and one has to infer their existence and the way that they organize knowledge and experience solely on the basis of their effects. Mauss's famous essay on bodily techniques and the studies on types of habitus undertaken by Bourdieu and his disciples have by now made this kind of schema so familiar that examples are no longer necessary.[28] We should, however, note that nonreflective schemas are more or less resistant to objectivization. Their degree of coherence and their presence at a conscious level depend both on the domains that they structure—in particular the possibility of delegating to objects, places, and sequences of actions some of the automatisms that they set in motion—and also on the motivations, emotional states, and capacities for introspection and analysis of the individuals using them. The distinction between an objectifiable model and a nonreflective schema needs to be qualified, as it depends so much on the situation. Thus, artistic perspective is both a scholarly cultural model and a "symbolic form" that governs our perception. Treatises are written about it, it is taught in schools, and its history is known. Yet we hardly ever mobilize this type of explicit knowledge when we are looking at a painting, for so deeply have we internalized it as a visual schema that representations that do not conform to it seem intuitively to us either bizarre or clumsy or are identified with figurative styles that are ignorant of the rules of perspective or that deliberately flout them. Furthermore, nonreflective schemas manifest themselves at different levels. Some are highly thematic and can be adapted to a wide variety of situations, while others are activated only in very particular circumstances. Let us call the former "integrating schemas" and the latter "specialized schemas."

There is a wide consensus as to the existence of specialized schemas (perspective composition and different kinds of habitus constitute two examples). They form the fabric of our daily life in that they organize most of our actions, ranging from bodily techniques and scenarios for the expression of emotions to the use of cultural stereotypes and the formation of classificatory judgments. Integrating schemas, on the other hand, are more complex mechanisms, but an understanding of them is crucial for anthropology, given that all the indications suggest that it is their mediating function that to a large extent contributes to giving each of us the sense that we share with other individuals the same culture and the same cosmology. They may be defined as cognitive structures that generate inferences that are endowed with a high degree of abstraction, that are distributed in a regular fashion within collectivities of variable dimensions, and that ensure compatibility between different specialized schemas, at the same time making it possible to generate new ones by induction. Such schemas are not internalized by means of a systematic inculcation; nor do they exist in a realm of ideas all ready to be captured by consciousness. They are constructed little by little, all with identical characteristics, given that the individuals of a group all pass through comparable experiences. This is a process facilitated by a common language and the relative uniformity of the ways in which children are socialized within any given group.[29] The attraction that many ethnologists feel to the study of distant and relatively isolated peoples in no way testifies to a nostalgia for authenticity or an obsession with an impossible cultural purity. It stems more simply from the fact that schemas that integrate collective practices or at the very least their surface effects are more easily detectable in cases where, since contacts with the outside world are less intense and members of the community are less numerous, the register of interpretations open to each individual is limited by the homogeneity of their learning experiences and their living conditions.

How, unless through vague intuitions, can one identify these integrating schemas that imprint themselves on the attitudes and practices of a collectivity in such a way that it appears immediately distinctive to an observer? Without overanticipating subsequent chapters, which will be tackling this question in depth, it is possible, even at this point, to suggest an answer: the schemas that should be held to be dominant are those activated in the greatest number of situations in the treatment of both humans and nonhumans and that subordinate other schemas to their own logic by stripping them of much of their original orientation. Perhaps this is the kind of mechanism that André-Georges Haudricourt had in mind when he drew a distinction between the two ways of "treating nature and others," constituted by negative indirect action and positive direct action.[30] Illustrated by the cultivation of yams in Melanesia and by the irrigated cultivation of rice in Asia, negative indirect action aims to favor the conditions of growth of the domesticated item by improving its environment as much as possible, not by establishing any direct control over it: each seedling is individually cared for so that it can develop as well as its own nature allows. Sheep raising in the Mediterranean region, on the contrary, implies positive direct action, for it necessitates permanent contact with the animals, which depend for their food and protection upon the intervention of humans: a shepherd accompanies his flock everywhere, guiding it with his crook and his dogs, choosing where it should pasture and find water; and it is also he who, when necessary, carries the young lambs and defends the sheep against predators. This difference in attitudes is not due solely to the opposition between domesticated plants and domesticated animals, for the treatment of cereals in Europe requires the same type of positive action as sheep raising does. It involves submitting the plants collectively to a series of coercive operations, in contrast to the "respectful friendship" that every yam elicits. In the earliest days of agriculture, at least, scattered seeds were trampled into the ground by the herds, which also served to thresh the grain after it had been roughly harvested by being pulled up or by scything. In contrast, not all forms of stock raising are characterized by positive direct action: in the countryside of Indochina, water buffaloes are in principle guarded by children, who are certainly not capable of protecting them against the attacks of tigers, so the herd of animals surrounds its little "guardian" so as to prevent the tiger from seizing him.

According to Haudricourt, the opposition between negative indirect action and positive direct action is likewise noticeable in behavior toward humans. The Near East and Europe are dominated by an interventionist attitude, well illustrated by a very ancient, unvarying political philosophy that regards the good shepherd as the ideal of a sovereign. In the Bible, as in Aristotle, the leader commands his subjects, who are seen as a collective body. He guides them and intervenes directly in their destiny, as does the unique God of his faithful people. In contrast, in Oceania and the Far East, a noninterventionist attitude prevails in the way that human beings are treated. In the precepts for good government conveyed by the Confucian Chinese Classics (in which plant metaphors are frequently used to represent human beings), this inclination toward conciliation and a search for consensus is very noticeable. It is likewise present in the modus operandi of Melanesian chiefdoms: the chief does not issue orders but strives to make his actions reflect the general will of the community, having discovered what this is by consulting each of its members.

This opposition is no doubt not convincing on every point, in particular where the treatment of humans is concerned, so wide are the spheres that it covers and so numerous the counterexamples that spring to mind, especially for Asia and Oceania. But that is not the problem. Haudricourt's brief, pithy article has aroused so much interest since its appearance because it draws attention to the possibility that identical very general schemas may activate the ways that humans behave in their relations with entities long considered to belong to quite different ontological spheres. If so, it becomes possible to envisage action on organisms that is structured by similar principles within major unified spheres of technical and social practices, without having first to raise the question of whether or not there is any discrimination between organisms that are human and those that are not. Haudricourt is certainly at pains to speak of "correspondences between the treatment of nature and the treatment of others," and this in no way prejudges the source from which these schemas of action spring. So it is neither a matter of projecting relations between humans upon relations to nonhumans nor one of extending to humans the attitude adopted toward nonhumans. Rather, homologous guiding principles apply in relations with two groups of beings that are hard to dissociate from the point of view of the types of behavior that they provoke.

Differentiation, Stabilization, Analogies

However, it is by no means easy to substantiate schemas of practices peculiar to a group of humans. To help us to do so, there are no bodies of evidence of the kind that structural anthropology used in its analyses: nomenclatures of kinship, marriage, and residence rules, myths and totemic classifications formulated in consensual declarations that observers have collected and more or less standardized so as to form a useful yardstick for comparison. The way in which a human group schematizes its experiences does not lend itself to such simple descriptions. It is certainly discernible in ethnological accounts but one has to be able to reveal it on the basis of disparate signs and to identify its operational principles without allowing oneself to be blinded by ostensible codifications. Such schematization is discernible in customs rather than in the precepts that justify them—in attitudes toward relatives, for example, as much as in the rules of kinship, in ritual mechanisms and the types of interactive situations that they establish as much as in the literal language of myths and ritual formulae, in bodily techniques, forms of learning, and the use of space as much as in theories of ontogeny, taboos, and the geography of sacred sites.

Schemas of practices, consolidated over the course of years of formation, make it possible to adapt to novel situations that are perceived as particular cases of situations already encountered. Like all habits acquired early in life, schemas are not so much modified by experience as reinforced by it. Such persistence in individuals could be explained partly by the role played by affects in the process of schematization: the study of neurochemical mechanisms of memory appears to indicate that an intense emotion that an event triggers helps to reinforce the neural connections that its apprehension activates, thereby fixing the associations of concepts and perceptions that it induces.[31] So it is understandable that the integration of experience into durable schemas comes about above all in circumstances that capture the attention because they break with daily routine by leaving their mark not only on feelings but even on bodies. This will come as no surprise to anthropologists, who know how effectively rites, in particular those of initiation, make it possible to transmit and reproduce norms of behavior and models of relationships by playing upon the unexpected, the paradoxical, and the mobilization of passions. Rites thus constitute valuable indications of the way in which a collectivity conceives and organizes its relations to the world and others, not only because they reveal, in a condensed form, schemas of interaction and principles of the structuring of praxis that are more diffuse in ordinary life but also because they provide the beginnings of a guarantee that the analyst's interpretations will match the lived experience of those who find in those rites a framework suitable for the internalization of models of action. Besides, as psychoanalysis and novels have taught us, the part played by affects in the stabilization of schemas is not manifest solely in ritual contexts: any event that is remarkable for the emotions that it arouses contributes powerfully to the process of learning and to the reinforcement of models of relations and interaction.

An important question remains, one that was often raised in connection with structuralism. It is supposed that "positive direct action" and "negative indirect action," like reciprocity, hierarchy, or any other schema, integrate practices. But how can we be sure that these are anything other than categories constructed "ad hoc" by the observer, for the needs of description and analysis? It might well be the case that types of behavior or interaction that bear a family resemblance at the level of an individual or a collectivity are produced by imitating one another, in a chain of analogies, as Gabriel Tarde would have it, rather than stemming from a preexisting schema whose ontological reality remains hard to establish. Although the question may in the end be insoluble, a naive conviction that favors the second alternative is not totally lacking in experimental corroboration. In fact, studies in cognitive psychology devoted to analogical reasoning show that the recognition of similarities between singular objects or events becomes much easier when it proceeds by induction from a schema already present—or else constructed on the spur of the moment by eliminating differences—than when it develops from a series of analytical comparisons made term by term. Schematic induction is rapid and economical, for it functions as a way of assessing particular cases that constitute so many different examples of a prototype, in contrast to a search for analogies listed one by one, which demands more attention and draws more heavily on memory.[32] Between analogical reasoning in an experimental situation and induction from shared schemas there is a wide gap that separates individual cognition from "collective representations." But how could it be denied that the latter cannot come into existence, be transmitted and invested in practice, without emerging and spreading in individual bodies, experiences, and brains? Without seeking to deny that a collectivity is more than the sum of its components, we are bound to recognize that those components, with all their sensitive faculties and mental properties, are the source of the dynamic substance of the collectivity's creativity and permanence.

Besides, much of the work of bringing into existence norms and meanings that are shared by all the members of a collectivity involves procedures of analogical derivation from the particular to the general and from the general to the particular. If one is willing to concede that there is a difference between (1) publicly instituted models of behavior and interaction, (2) implicit schemas orientating the practices that those models codify, and (3) the infinite vagaries of idiosyncrasies and particular events, then the minimum of coherence that each of us perceives in our conduct and that of our acquaintances must result from our ability freely to transpose rules, tendencies, and situations from one of those domains to the other. The transposition may take place in either direction, depending on whether our experience of the world is organized in accordance with existing paradigms or whether those paradigms are affected by unforeseen events that call for their modification.[33] For example, in the first type of induction one can transpose a concrete event into the ideal model that makes its interpretation possible: such is the classic case of a judgment that something conforms to an accepted norm. One may also transpose a schema into an explicit model or make the schema manifest by means of that model, an operation that, par excellence, defines the institutional creativity of humans. This is what anthropologists have traditionally assumed to be their mission to describe and elucidate. Finally, one can transpose a schema directly into an unprecedented situation in order to render it meaningful or tolerable. But that happens less frequently, for the function of assimilating something new generally devolves upon intermediary models: people resort to it in times of great collective upheavals such as the traumas provoked by colonial conquest or emigration to distant places, when the ordinary parameters of reference cannot deal with circumstances or experiences that are too exceptional, and deeper schemas have to be mobilized in order to cope.

The second type of induction, namely the production of a schema designed to accommodate unusual circumstances, is something that directly contributes to an unfolding of history. It takes place either when an established model is elaborated or altered so as to take account of an unprecedented event (commonly best illustrated by the creation of new laws) or when an unusual situation engenders a new schematization by means of which specialized models, that is to say "bits of culture," are integrated or recombined in a new configuration. This makeshift operation is well known to anthropologists as "syncretism" or "acculturation," which prophetic or millenarian movements, for example, tend to exploit. On the other hand, only very rarely are new schemas produced through a direct transposition of exceptional experiences, since these are generally filtered through models that, because they cannot be matched to unusual circumstances, will be restructured in accordance with the procedure outlined above rather than by an immediate subsuming of the event into a schema.

If one accepts the above analysis, the nature of the relation between a vernacular model and a structural one becomes less enigmatic. It seems that what a structural analysis reveals, when well conducted, is a way of assessing an understanding of the schematization of experience carried out by the members of a collectivity and the manner in which this serves as a framework for the explicit codification systems to which its members adhere. What guarantees that the formal mechanism constructed by the analyst does indeed reveal certain underlying characteristics of the social system that he is trying to understand is the fact that those characteristics express not so much universal properties of the human mind—or only do so at a very abstract level—but rather the tacit frameworks and procedures of objectivization by means of which the actors in the system themselves organize their relations to the world and to Others. In between the model, or action, and the structure, the schema constitutes an interface that is both concrete, since it is incorporated in individuals and put to work in their practices, and particularized, since it reflects some objective property of the relations to existing beings. Moreover, this interface possesses a high coefficient of abstraction, since it is detectable solely from its effects—although that does not mean to say that it emanates from mysterious entelechies such as a collective unconscious or some symbolic function.

All the same, the schematization of experience is not abandoned to arbitrary, fortuitous inventions and unpredictable circumstances. Those no doubt play a role in the emergence of specialized schemas of the habitus type, the wide variety of which is attributable to the diversity of the historical contexts in which they operate. But over and above these many particular capabilities that are immanent in practices, human beings also resort to a much more limited number of more general integrating schemas in order to structure their relations with the world. These schemas manifest themselves in what are, after all, a quite limited number of options available for distributing resemblances and differences between existing entities, and for establishing, between the groups defined by that distribution and within them, distinctive relations of a remarkable stability.

The rest of the present book will be devoted to elaborating this idea, which is founded upon the conjecture that all the schemas at the disposition of humanity for specifying its relations within itself and with the outside world in fact exist in the form of predispositions, some of which are innate while others stem from the very properties of communal life—in other words, from the different practical ways of ensuring the integration of both the self and Others in a given environment. But these structures are not all compatible with one another, and every cultural system, every type of social organization, is the product of a selection and a combination that, although contingent, are frequently repeated in history, producing comparable results. Anthropology that seeks to be consequential has no choice but to gain an understanding of the logic of this work of composition, by lending an ear to the themes and harmonies that stand out from the great hum of the world and concentrating on emerging orders whose regularity is detectable behind the proliferation of different customs.

5

Relations with the Self and Relations with Others

Modes of Identification and Modes of Relation

The hypothesis that will serve as a guide through the analyses that follow is that the integrating schemas of practices whose general mechanisms we have studied in chapter 4 may be reduced to two fundamental ways of structuring individual and collective experiences: two modalities that I shall call "identification" and "relations." Identification extends beyond the Freudian sense of an emotional link with some object and beyond a classificatory judgment that makes it possible to recognize the distinctive character of that object. It covers a more general schema by means of which I can establish differences and resemblances between myself and other existing entities by inferring analogies and contrasts between the appearance, behavior, and properties that I ascribe to myself and those that I ascribe to them. Marcel Mauss translated that another way when he wrote that "man identifies himself with things and identifies things with himself, doing so with a sense of both the differences and the resemblances that he establishes."[1] This mechanism of mediation between the self and the nonself seems to me, from a logical point of view, to precede and be external to the existence of an established relationship with something other, that is to say, something the content of which can be specified by its modalities of interaction, given that the "other" in question here is not one term in a pair but an object that exists for me in a general otherness yet to be identified: an *aliud* then, not an *alter*.

That distinction is certainly an analytical, rather than a phenomenal, one, for identification immediately assumes a correlation to the object that is being provided with an identity: once it is classified in some ontological category or other, I shall be able to enter into some relationship with it. It is, however, important to preserve the distinction between identification and relation insofar as each of the ontological, cosmological, and sociological formulae that the identification makes possible can itself underpin several types of relationship, ones that are therefore not automatically derived simply from the position occupied by the object and the properties conferred upon it. For example, considering an animal as a person rather than as a thing in no way justifies prejudging the relationship established with it, one that is as likely to stem from predation as from competition or protection. A relationship thus adds a further dimension to the primary terms set out by identification. For that reason, and in contrast to a structuralist or interactional stance, it seems necessary to envisage separately those two modes of integrating "the other." Besides, these modes cover the original distinction that logic introduces between judgments of inherence and judgments of relations. In truth, the decision to treat on an equal footing, on the one hand, identification, which involves mainly terms, and, on the other, relationships, which involve mainly the links established between those terms, is one way of correcting the excesses of earlier anthropological approaches that, by granting preeminence to one dimension over the other—suggesting either that relations stem from terms or that terms stem from relations—had difficulty in tackling head-on any study of ontological distributions along with a study of social relations.

Relationships are thus here understood not in a logical or mathematical sense (i.e., as intellectual operations that make it possible to establish an internal link between two concepts) but rather as the external links between beings and things that are detectable in typical behavior patterns and may be partially translatable into concrete social norms. There is nothing surprising about the fact that these links of an anthropological nature correspond, in some aspects, to purely formal relations such as coexistence, succession, identity, correspondence, and origination, for the number of relations identified by epistemology since Aristotle is remarkably limited, so, in all probability, the whole collection of established ways of forging links between existing beings may in the last analysis be reduced to a corpus of logical relations. All the same, given that the declared ambition of this book is to gain a better understanding of collective behavior, the relations that concern us are those that can be detected from observable practices, not those that can be deduced from the formal rules governing logical propositions. Emphasizing that the relations in question concern, so to speak, external links between elements furthermore makes it possible to forestall any misunderstanding regarding the respective statuses of identification and relationships. Although identification defines terms and their predicates, it goes without saying that it also involves a relationship since it is based on judgments of inherence and attribution, but it is a relationship that becomes intrinsic to the object identified once one sets aside the process that established it as such. In contrast, the relations that we shall be concerned with are of an extrinsic nature in that they refer to the connections that this object has with something other than itself, connections that are certainly potential in its identity but without it ever being possible to tell which one in particular will in effect be actualized. That is why I decided to ascribe to modes of identification a logical precedence over modes of relationship, since the former, by specifying the ontological properties of terms, partially influences the nature of the relations that may link those terms, yet without determining the type of relationship that will become dominant. First, then, we shall examine the ontological modalities of identification (part III) and their expressions in social life (part IV), before passing on to modes of relations and the links that connect them with modes of identification (part V).

Even at the general level at which I am considering them here, identification and relationship are by no means the only possible forms taken by the structuring of the experience of the world and of what is Other. To be more thorough, it would no doubt be necessary to complement them by at least five other modes that play a role in the schematization of practices. (1) *Temporality*: the objectivization of certain properties of duration according to various computing systems, forms of spatial analogies, cycles, cumulative sequences, and procedures of memorization or deliberate forgetfulness. (2) *Spatialization*: the mechanisms for organizing and dividing up space that are based on its uses, on systems of coordinates and cardinal points, on the importance ascribed to such or such means of marking out places, on ways of passing through or occupying territories and the mental maps that organize these, and on the possibilities that the environment affords for apprehending the landscape through vision and other senses. (3) The various systems of *figuration*, understood as the action by means of which beings and things are represented in two or three dimensions, using a material medium. (4) *Mediation*: the kind of relationship that depends on the interposition of a conventional device that functions as a substitute, a form, a sign, or a symbol, such as sacrifice, money, or writing. (5) *Categorization*: in the sense of the principles that govern explicit classifications of entities and properties of the world in taxonomies of every kind.

In the present work, I shall not be tackling those modes, partly in order to limit its size and partly because the analyses that follow show that the various combined forms of identification and relations suffice to explain the principles underlying most known ontologies and cosmologies. The reader is thus asked to accept the provisional hypothesis—hardly more than a hunch at this stage—that temporality, spatialization, figuration, mediation, and categorization depend for their expression and their occurrence on the various configurations of identification and relationships (each of which are concrete realizations) that these secondary modes may engender. Three examples of this are cyclic temporality, cumulative temporality, and egocentric temporality. Furthermore, those configurations are probably derived from one or other of the structures made possible by the interplay of the two primary modes.

Each of the configurations resulting from the combination of a type of identification and a type of relationship reveals the general structure of a particular schema for the integration of practices, in other words, one of the forms that may be assumed by the mechanism for generating inferences that is described in chapter 4. It is this mechanism that allows the members of a collectivity to make different classes of specialized schemas compatible with one another while at the same time ensuring the possibility of engendering new schemas that bear a family resemblance to the original ones. Identification and relationships may thus be seen as the sources of the instruments for social life that provide the elementary means for human groups of variable dimensions and kinds daily to piece together a schematization of their experience, without, however, being fully conscious of the endeavor in which they are engaged or the type of object that it will produce. There are nevertheless two ways in which these schemas can be partially objectivized: by vernacular models, which are necessarily imperfect since effective social action depends upon the effacement of the cognitive mechanisms that structure it; and by scholarly models, such as those I shall be describing, whose equally patent imperfection stems, rather, from the fact that they are unable to take into account the infinite richness of local variants. But that is the risk run by any attempt to generalize, which has to sacrifice the spicy unpredictability and the inventive proliferations of day-to-day situations in order to reach a higher level of intelligibility regarding the mainsprings of human behavior.

The Other Is an "I"

Identification, which operates well upstream from the categorizations of beings and things that taxonomies reveal, is the ability to apprehend and separate out some of the continuities and discontinuities that we can seize upon in the course of observing and coping practically with our environment. This elementary mechanism of ontological discrimination does not stem from empirical judgments regarding the nature of the objects that constantly present themselves to our perception. Rather, it should be seen as what Husserl called a prepredicative experience, in that it modulates the general awareness that I may have of the existence of the "other." This awareness is formed simply from my own resources—that is to say, my body and my intentionality—when I set aside the world and all that it means for me. So one could say that this is an experience of thought prompted by an abstract subject. I do not need to know if this has ever existed, but it produces definitely concrete effects since it enables me to understand how it is possible to specify indeterminate objects by either ascribing to them or denying them an "interiority" and a "physicality" similar to those that I attribute to myself. As we shall see, this distinction between a level of interiority and one of physicality is not simply an ethnocentric projection of the Western opposition drawn between the mind and the body. Rather, it is a distinction that all the civilizations about which we have learned something from ethnography and history have, in their own fashions, objectivized. At this stage in our inquiry a brief description of the fields of phenomena that those two levels (interiority and physicality) encompass will suffice.

The vague term "interiority" refers to a range of properties recognized by all human beings and partially covers what we generally call the mind, the soul, or consciousness: intentionality, subjectivity, reflexivity, feelings, and the ability to express oneself and to dream. It may also include immaterial principles that are assumed to cause things to be animate, such as breath and vital energy, and, at the same time, notions even more abstract, such as the idea that I share with others the same essence, the same principle of action, or the same origin: all these ideas may be objectivized in a name or an epithet common to us all. In short, interiority consists in the universal belief that a being possesses characteristics that are internal to it or that take it as their source. In normal circumstances, these are detectable only from their effects and are reputed to be responsible for that being's identity, perpetuation, and some of its typical ways of behaving. Physicality, in contrast, concerns external form, substance, the physiological, perceptive and sensorimotor processes, even a being's constitution and way of acting in the world, insofar as these reflect the influence brought to bear on behavior patterns and a habitus by corporeal humors, diets, anatomical characteristics, and particular modes of reproduction. So physicality is not simply the material aspect of organic and abiotic bodies; it is the whole set of visible and tangible expressions of the dispositions peculiar to a particular entity when those dispositions are reputed to result from morphological and physiological characteristics that are intrinsic to it.

To suppose that identification is founded upon the attribution to existing beings of ontological properties conceived by analogy with those that humans recognize in themselves is to imply that such a mechanism can find in each one of us its self-evidence and a guarantee of its continuity. In other words, it presupposes accepting that every human perceives himself or herself as a unit that is a mixture of interiority and physicality, for this is a state that is necessary if one is to recognize in others or deny them distinctive characteristics that are derived from one's own. Now, the idea that individuals everywhere and always consider themselves to be autonomous and unique entities has attracted strong criticism. So too, and even more so, has the idea that the perception of this singularity, which takes the form of a combination of intentionality and physical experience, is universal. It has become commonplace to cast doubt upon the generality of the idea of the self being conceived as a single unit of experience. It is argued that, in numerous cases, peoples do not consider the body to constitute an absolute limit to the person, since the latter is fragmented into many constitutive units, some of which are distributed among or determined by either human or nonhuman elements in its environment.[2] Common though they may be, such notions do not justify dismissing the fundamental distinction that Mauss, years ago, proposed between, on the one hand, a universal sense of self (i.e., a sense possessed by every human being "of one's individuality, both spiritual and corporeal") and, on the other, the very diverse theories (the components and spatial extension of which are extremely variable) of what constitutes a person that have, in some places, been elaborated.[3]

As Mauss had suspected and Émile Benveniste, following Peirce, clearly confirmed, the universality of the perception of the self as a separate and autonomous entity is borne out primarily by linguistic data, namely the presence in all languages of pronominal forms or affixes such as "I" and "you" that can refer only to the person making the statement containing the linguistic form "I" or, symmetrically, to the interlocutor, addressed as "you."[4] But this semiotic "I" in no way implies that the speaker conceives of himself or herself as an individual subject wholly contained within the boundaries of his or her body, in the manner of the traditional image proposed by Western individualism. There is little doubt that in many societies it is believed that the idiosyncrasy, actions, and development of a person depend on elements exterior to one's physical envelope—elements such as the relations of every kind amid which that person lives. That is most famously the case in Melanesia, which is why Marilyn Strathern has suggested that, in this region of the world, we should describe a person not as an individuality but as a "dividuality," that is to say, a being primarily defined by his or her position and relations within some network.[5] However, without denying the existence of a theory of a "dividual" person in Melanesia, we should bear in mind, along with Maurice Leenhardt years ago and Edward LiPuma more recently, that that theory coexists alongside—or is in some situations supplanted by—a more egocentric conception of a subject; and there is no evidence to suggest that this theory is a product solely of European colonization.[6] But whatever the diversity of the solutions adopted in order to ascribe some of the principles that constitute one particular human body as a person, it is safe to accept as a universal fact the form of individuation that an indexical consciousness of the self renders manifest and that is reinforced by the intersubjective differentiation that stems from the use of "you."

The universality of reflective individuation constitutes a necessary but not sufficient condition for one to feel oneself divided between a plane of interiority and one of physicality. For such a distinction would not be recognized by an ordinary consciousness of the self, which inextricably intermingles a sense of, on the one hand, an internal unity that bestows powers of expression and coherence upon mental activities, affects, and perceptions and, on the other, continuous experience of a body that occupies a position in space, is the source of its own sensations, and is both an organ of mediation with the environment and an instrument of knowledge. We all know that we can "think" with the body as well as with the mind, both within the vast register of internalized abilities and also within the more mysterious one of intuitions condensed in a gesture, such as "speaking with one's hands," which physicomathematical diagrams reveal and the nature of which philosophers of science have tried to pinpoint.[7] Descartes himself, despite his tenet of dualism and the priority that he ascribes to the cogito in one's consciousness of the self, is ready to recognize that the sense of one's individuality, the factor that makes one "a real man," depends primarily on the intimate unity of the thinking soul and the feeling body.[8]

So, sensing a disjunction between one's immaterial self and one's physical self is not a common experience, but it does happen in those more rare states of dissociation in which the mind and the body—to use our usual terminology—seem to become independent of each other. It happens fleetingly but daily in moments when one's "internal life" displays its control, in meditation, introspection, daydreaming, mental monologue, or even prayer: all these are occasions that prompt a deliberate or unexpected suspension of corporeal constraints. It also occurs, more detectably, in memories and in dreams. Even if, as often happens, such an experience is triggered involuntarily by some physical sensation, memory enables one to dematerialize, to escape partially from the temporal and spatial constraints of the moment, the better to be transported by one's mind into some past situation in which it becomes impossible for the conscious mind to feel the suffering, pleasure, or even coenesthesia that we nevertheless know to be associated with the remembered moment. As for dreaming, this provides even stronger evidence of a split, for the vividness of the images that assail one seem out of step with the state of corporeal inertia that is the condition on which dreaming depends for the emergence of such images. Less commonplace, finally, are situations of extreme dissociation induced by hallucinations or by temporary loss of one's senses as in ecstasy or catalepsy, or even those experiences of extracorporeal perception associated with drug taking or near-death experiences, when the self appears to detach itself from its envelope of flesh and to look down upon it from a distance. Yet such situations are not that exceptional: in many parts of the world, the ritualistic use of hallucinogenic substances or trances provoked by alcohol, fasting, or music can provide anyone with repeated proofs of a split between interiority and physicality that is all the more striking because it is deliberately provoked for the sake of the sensations that it procures. But the frequency of such phenomena is not important, for I am not seeking to determine an incontestable source for the sense of the duality of the person, as Tylor was when he suggested that dreams were the origin of the notion of a soul and from that notion stemmed a belief in spirits, which was the basis of an animist religion conceived as a projection upon inert objects of a principle of animation endowed with autonomy.[9] My own intention, which is a far cry from assuming such risky causal links, is simply to emphasize that an awareness of a separation between an internal self and a physical self is not unfounded in ordinary life, as seems to be confirmed by recent work in developmental psychology, which detects in this dualist intuition an innate characteristic of human beings.[10]

Another indication of the universality of this separation between the physical and the moral is the fact that linguistic traces of it are to be found in all the cultures so far studied. It would seem that all languages distinguish between a level of interiority and a level of physicality within a certain class of organisms, whatever may be the extension given to such a class and whatever the words used to convey the two: in the language of Western observers, usually "soul" and "body." Of course, the terms used to translate "soul" are frequently numerous within a single language and therefore require copious commentaries, whereas the term that refers to the body is usually unique. But nowhere do we find a concept of an ordinary living person that is founded solely upon interiority—for instance, a soul without a body—or on physicality alone, that is to say, a body without a soul. Not until the materialist theories of consciousness in the last decades of the twentieth century, those of Antonio Damasio and Daniel Dennett, for example, did such a possibility become envisageable; and even then, such theories provoked stiff resistance to what, for many of our contemporaries, seemed to constitute both an offence to common sense and also an attack on the uniqueness of human nature.[11] For, obviously enough, this duality of a person is a matter of common sense, that is to say it is an empirical intuition everywhere detectable in well-established forms of expression; it does not, of course, involve the complex mechanisms of consciousness of the self such as those that neurobiology strives to understand.

In my assumption of the universality of a conventional distinction between interiority and physicality, I am not unaware that interiority is often presented as multiple, nor that it is believed to be connected with physicality through numerous mutual influences. Even in the West, where the most elaborate forms of dualism can be found, a general consensus exists as to the coexistence of at least three principles of interiority—the soul, the mind, and consciousness—and to these, over the past century, have been added the Freudian triad of the ego, the superego, and the id, plus, even more recently, an extravagant outbreak of multiple personalities in North American psychiatry.[12] In this domain there are no limits to the imagination, and some peoples have proliferated the inner elements of a person by ascribing a whole set of them to each part of the body or a different set to each of the sexes, adding to these or subtracting from them in the course of the life cycle and suggesting an infinite number of functions for each of them so as to render them responsible for the entire range of situations in which an individual may find himself or herself. In Mexico, for example, the Tzeltal Indians of Cancuc attribute as many as seventeen distinct "souls" to a single person, while the Dogon are content, more modestly, with eight.[13]

All the same, however numerous the immaterial components of a person, whether innate or acquired, whether transmitted by the father, by the mother, by accident, or by some benevolent or hostile entity, and whether temporary, lasting, or eternal, immutable or subject to change, all these principles that generate life, knowledge, passion, or destiny take an indeterminate form. They are made of some indefinable substance that usually resides in the innermost depths of the body. To be sure, it is often claimed that these "souls" reside in some organ or fluid—the heart, the liver, bone marrow, or blood—or that they are linked with an element that cannot be dissociated from the living body, such as breath, the face, or one's shadow. It is also said that they experience growth and decline and hunger and sexual desire, just as the organism with which they are associated does, and that part of their essence can be transmitted or alienated by the substance that underlies them or moves them around. But however intimately linked they may be with the nonphysical components of a person, the organs and humors in which these components are incorporated are never any more than imperfect objectivations of them. Their materiality cannot represent the totality of the predicates that one attributes to the elements of one's internal identity: the liver does not move spatially outside the body when the soul believed to inhabit it is said to travel during dreams, nor do the heart and lungs of a dead person move when they liberate the part of the individual that is believed to live on after death. We should, rather, consider these corporeal substances said to shelter souls as hypostases, convenient means for giving concrete expression to agents, essences, and causes the existence of which is usually inferred solely from the effects imputed to them.

The duality of interiority and physicality, which is present all over the world in various modalities, is thus not simply an ethnocentric projection of an opposition peculiar to the West between, on the one hand, the body and, on the other, the soul or mind. On the contrary, we should regard this opposition, in the guise in which it is forged in Europe, together with the philosophical and theological theories that it has prompted, as a local variant of a more general system of elementary contrast. In the chapters that follow we shall examine the mechanisms and organization of this contrast. It may well be surprising to find this dualism of the person, which has become somewhat discredited these days, acquiring a universality that I earlier denied to the dualism of nature and culture. Yet, as we have seen, there is no lack of empirical arguments to justify this preference, in particular the fact that consciousness of a distinction between the interiority and the physicality of the self seems to be an innate aptitude that is borne out by all lexicons, whereas terminological equivalents of the pair constituted by nature and culture are hard to find outside European languages and do not appear to have experimentally demonstrable cognitive bases. But what needs above all to be said here is that, contrary to an opinion currently in fashion, binary oppositions are neither a Western invention nor fictions of structural anthropology but are very widely used by all peoples in plenty of circumstances, so it is not so much their form that should be questioned but rather the suggested universality of their content.

The recognized formulae for expressing the combination of interiority and physicality are very limited. Faced with some other entity, human or nonhuman, I can assume either that it possesses elements of physicality and interiority identical to my own, that both its interiority and its physicality are distinct from mine, that we have similar interiorities and different physicalities, or, finally, that our interiorities are different and our physicalities are analogous. I shall call the first combination "totemism," the second "analogism," the third "animism," and the fourth "naturalism" (fig. 1). These principles of identification define four major types of ontology, that is to say systems of the properties of existing beings; and these serve as a point of reference for contrasting forms of cosmologies, models of social links, and theories of identity and alterity.

Before enumerating the properties of these combinations, I should explain the terms that I have used to designate them. Both because of my distaste for

| Similar interiorities Dissimilar physicalities | *Animism* | *Totemism* | Similar interiorities Similar physicalities |
| Dissimilar interiorities Similar physicalities | *Naturalism* | *Analogism* | Dissimilar interiorities Dissimilar physicalities |

FIGURE 1. The four ontologies

neologisms and also in order to conform with a practice as old as anthropology itself, I have chosen to use notions that are already well established but to confer upon them new meanings. However, this use of old terms may lead to misunderstandings, especially as the definitions of "animism" and "totemism" that I am proposing here are appreciably different from those that I have suggested in earlier studies.

We should remember that anthropologists have been accustomed to using the word "totemism" every time that a group of social units—moieties, clans, matrimonial sections, or religious groups—are associated with a series of natural objects, with the names of each of these units frequently being derived from an eponymous animal or plant. In *Totemism* Lévi-Strauss developed the idea that totemism was not so much an institution peculiar to so-called primitive societies but rather the expression of a universal classificatory logic that uses observable differential gaps between animal and plant species in order to conceptualize the discontinuities between social groups. Plants and animals spontaneously exhibit perceptible contrasting qualities— different forms, colors, habitats, and behaviors—and the differences in species that these render manifest are therefore particularly suited to signaling the internal distinctions that are necessary for the perpetuation of segmentary systems. Certain earlier conceptions of totemism emphasized the intimate association of the terms involved—for instance, a mystical link between a particular group of persons and a particular natural species. But Lévi-Strauss, on the contrary, perceives a homology between two series of relations, the one differentiating a collection of species, the other differentiating a collection of social units, with the former presenting an immediately available model for organizing the latter. Nature thus provides a guide and a framework—what Lévi-Strauss calls "a method for thinking"—that helps the members of certain cultures to conceptualize their social structure and to offer a simple iconic representation of it, one similar to that used by European heraldry.[14]

Lévi-Strauss's intention was to dissipate what he called "the totemic illusion," in order to associate totemism with a universal characteristic of the human mind. So, understandably enough, in his analysis he ascribed scant importance to the dyadic relations between a human and a nonhuman that have sometimes been labeled "individual totemism."[15] My own ethnographic experience among the Achuar has made me realize that, like them, many Amazonian societies ascribe to plants and to animals a spiritual principle of their own and consider it possible to maintain personal relations with those entities—relations of friendship, hostility, seduction, matrimonial alliances, or those involving reciprocal services. Such personal relationships differ profoundly from the denotative and abstract relation between totemic groups and the natural entities that serve as their eponyms. In such societies, which are very common in South America but are also found in North America, Siberia, and Southeast Asia, attributes are conferred upon plants and animals— intentionality, subjectivity, affects, even speech in certain circumstances—including specifically social ones, such as a status hierarchy, behavior patterns based on respect for the rules of kinship or ethical codes, ritual activity, and so on. With a mode of identification such as this, natural objects constitute not a system of signs authorizing category-specific transpositions but, instead, a collection of subjects with which humans day after day weave a web of social relations.

Resurrecting a term at the time seldom used, I had earlier proposed calling this form of the objectivation of natural beings "animism"; and I had suggested regarding it as the symmetrical reverse of Lévi-Straussian totemic classifications. I suggested that, in contrast to the latter, animist systems did not use plants and animals to conceptualize the social order but, on the contrary, employed elementary categories of social practice to think through the links of humans with natural beings.[16] This hypothesis emerged from the Achuar ethnographic findings. Among the Achuar, the women treat the plants in their gardens as children, while the men behave toward hunted animals and their spirit masters in accordance with the norms required in relations with relatives by marriage. Affinity and consanguinity, the two categories that govern the social classification of the Achuar and orientate their relations with "the Other," thus play their part in the prescribed attitudes toward nonhumans. This correspondence between the social treatment of humans and that of plants and animals has turned out to be widespread not only in Amazonia but elsewhere too. I have provided a number of examples in chapter 1 of the present work: solidarity, friendship, and respect for elders among the Cree, marriage alliances with hunted animals among Siberian peoples, and commensality among the Chewong. In all these cases, the most common and valued norms of behavior in social life are thus employed to characterize the relations of humans with plants and animals that are regarded as persons.

However, that definition of animism as the symmetrical reverse of totemism suffered from a serious defect, for it led back to what it claimed to be escaping, in that it surreptitiously imported into the characterization of nondualist cosmologies the analytical distinction between nature and society peculiar to the Lévi-Straussian explanation of totemic classifications.[17] Furthermore, one has to recognize that Lévi-Straussian totemism is not commensurable with animism: the latter is certainly a mode of identification that objectivizes a particular relation between humans and the nonhuman elements in their environment; but the former is a mechanism of categorization that sets up purely logical correlations between classes of humans and classes of nonhumans.[18] In short, despite my desire to avoid an overclassificatory interpretation of phenomena that clearly were ill-suited to such a reading, I had fallen into the pitfall of a dichotomy through sticking too closely to Lévi-Strauss's theory of totemism. That is why my first definition of animism and Lévi-Strauss's definition of totemic classifications could not serve as a starting point from which to characterize modes of identification even though, as we shall see, at a later stage those definitions remain valid as principles for justifying the frontiers between groups of humans and of nonhumans.

I had strayed off course primarily by seeking to define modes of identification, in other words ontological matrixes, starting from relational processes that were expressed by institutions. The mistake was excusable if one bears in mind that, ever since Durkheim, that has always been the way of proceeding. A sociological approach was favored, for at the time it was necessary to open up for the human sciences a positive domain of their own. Inevitably, religious beliefs, theories of the person, cosmologies, the symbolism of time and space, and conceptions of the efficacy of magic were all considered to be explainable, in the last resort, by the existence of particular social forms that were projected on to the world and that modeled practices employed to objectivize that world and make it meaningful.[19] By proposing that the social stemmed from the psychic, Lévi-Strauss certainly avoided that tendency. But, given the uncertainty that still surrounds the laws pertaining to the human mind, that derivation was bound to be inductive: except in the case of his analyses of myth, his starting point was a study of institutions, from which he worked back "toward the intellect," rather than the reverse. However, a relational system can never be independent from the terms that it brings together, if by "terms" we mean entities endowed from the start with specific properties that render them either able or unable to forge links between one another, rather than interchangeable individuals or established social units. I have accordingly had to reject the sociocentric assumption and opt for the idea that sociological realities (stabilized relational systems) are analytically subordinate to ontological realities (the systems of properties attributed to existing beings). That is the price that has to be paid if animism and totemism are to be reborn with new meanings. Now each redefined as one of the four combinations allowed by the interplay of resemblances and differences between the self and the Other at the levels of interiority and physicality, animism and totemism, along with naturalism and analogism, become elementary components of a kind of syntax for the composition of the world, from which the various institutional regimes of human existence all stem.

PART THREE

The Dispositions of Being

To exist is to differ.

GABRIEL TARDE, *Monadologie et sociologie*

6

Animism Restored

If one strips the definition of animism of its sociological correlations, there remains one characteristic that everybody can accept and that the etymology of the term indicates, which is why I chose to preserve it despite the dubious uses made of it in the past. That characteristic is the attribution by humans to nonhumans of an interiority identical to their own. This attribution humanizes plants and, above all, animals, since the soul with which it endows them allows them not only to behave in conformity with the social norms and ethical precepts of humans but also to establish communicative relations both with humans and among themselves. This similarity of interiorities justifies extending a state of "culture" to nonhumans, together with all the attributes that this implies, ranging from intersubjectivity to a mastery of techniques and including ritualized conduct and deference to conventions. All the same, this humanization is not complete, since in animist systems these, as it were, humans in disguise (i.e., the plants and animals) are distinct from humans precisely by reason of their outward apparel of feathers, fur, scales, or bark—in other words, their physicality. As Viveiros de Castro notes in connection with Amazonia, it is not through their souls that humans and nonhumans differ but through their bodies.[1] Durkheim had earlier made the same point when he remarked with his usual perspicacity that "two sorts of elements produced the idea of a person. One is essentially impersonal: it is the spiritual principle that serves as the soul of the collectivity. The principle is the very substance of which individual souls are made. . . . From a different point of view, if there are to be separate personalities, some factor must intervene to fragment and differentiate this principle; in other words, a principle of individuation is necessary. The body plays this role."[2] It matters little that, true to his doctrine, Durkheim confined that differentiating role of the body solely to human communities, for by doing so he put his finger on the general principle that the individuation of existing beings—and, I would add, their assignment to collective groups—can only operate through the interplay of the identities and contrasts that affect the respective attributes of the soul and those of the body.

Forms and Behavior Patterns

Animist systems use this difference in physicalities to introduce discontinuity into a universe peopled by persons with such disparate outward appearances yet at the same time so human in their motivations, feelings, and behavior. But what is the nature of this difference? It consists in the *form* and the mode of life that it prompts, far more than in substance. The fact is that the idea of a material continuity linking all organisms together is common to most animist ontologies. As Alexandre Surrallés notes in connection with the concepts of the Candoshi Indians of Peruvian Amazonia, all the entities in the world are made up of "a permanent potential and universal substratum. This implies a substance common to all material things in consequence of which the categorical boundaries between beings are considerably weakened."[3] Marie Mauzé makes a similar observation relating to the Indians of the Northwest coast of Canada: "They consider that animals are composed of an internal substance which, given that this is essentially human, has been transformed into an animal form by means of the skin."[4] Florence Brunois tells us that among the Kasua of the Great Plateau of Papua New Guinea, the bodies of humans, trees, and animals are all filled with the same substances: *bebeta* (blood), *ma* (a vaginal humor), and above all the omnipresent *ibi* (which means "stomach fat" but also "tilth" and "latex"), which is the source of the materiality of all organic and abiotic bodies.[5] It is perhaps in this sense of a substantial continuity between all organisms that we should understand the words of Leenhardt's Kanak informer that I quoted in chapter 1: "You didn't bring us the spirit. . . . What you've brought us is the body." Old Boesoou no doubt had in mind the absolute novelty of a Christian body (Leenhardt was also a missionary), that carnal principle contaminated by the defilement of original sin, the foil to the spirit and its life-giving immortality.[6] But one could also read into this enigmatic remark a recognition of the discovery of a specifically human body, with its own peculiar kind of matter and internal mechanisms. Such a concept was bound to present a contrast to the pre-Christian concept of the human body in New Caledonia, which was founded on an identity of both structure and substance between human bodies and plants, a principle that is revealed not only by anatomical terminology but also by physiological and eschatological theories. But, as Leenhardt stresses, that identity between humans and plants relates only to matter and not to form, for the two types of organism each have "a different mode of existence," so it would not be possible for them to develop, behave, feed, and reproduce in the same fashion.[7]

Ethnography places beyond doubt the fact that form is the crucial criterion of differentiation in animist ontologies. Thus, Anne Christine Taylor, commenting on the diversity of human and nonhuman "person-forms" among the Jivaros, writes: "The appearance of different species, generated in mythical times, implies the emergence of particular physical forms, and humans, like every other species, possess one of their own," for "what distinguishes one species from another is definitely its outward clothing."[8] According to Kaj Århem, among the Makuna of Colombian Amazonia, humans, animals, and plants each possess a "phenomenological form" that distinguishes them from one another and a "spiritual essence" that they all share.[9] In his study of the Arakmbut of Peruvian Amazonia, Andrew Gray writes: "The physical property of the body separates a person from all others." So it is not the soul that constitutes the unique and essential aspect of a person, for "the body gives a distinct form to a person."[10] In his pioneering article on Ojibwa ontology, Irving Hallowell says more or less the same, but puts it the other way round. Pondering on what constitutes the distinctive characteristic of a person among these Indians of Canada, he decides that it is not his or her anthropomorphic aspect, since there also exist persons "of the other-than-human class" who "do not always present a human appearance."[11] So it is certainly the corporeal form that differentiates between humans and nonhumans, for the soul that all of them possess could not perform that function. Writing about the Chewong of Malaysia, Signe Howell observes: "Consciousness in this sense makes one a 'personage' . . . regardless of one's outer shape (or 'cloak,' in Chewong parlance), be it that of gibbon, human, wild pig, frog, ramboutan fruit, bamboo leaf, the thunder-being, a specific boulder or whatever." The Chewong apprehend the world as being composed "by a series of species-grounded conscious and unconscious beings, each with a different shape."[12]

The question of the discontinuity of bodies is the obsessive theme that Amerindian myths convey at every opportunity. These are unusual stories about a time when humans and nonhumans were not differentiated, a time when, in the case of the Jivaro examples, it was perfectly normal for Nightjar to do the cooking, for Cricket to play the fiddle, for Hummingbird to clear the garden, and for Swift to go hunting with a blowpipe. In those days, animals and plants were masters of all the skills of civilization, communicated with one another with no difficulty, and abided by the major principles of social etiquette. As far as one can tell, their appearance was human, and only a few clues, such as their names and their strange behavior, indicated what they were to change into. Each myth tells of the circumstances that led to a change of form and of the actualization, in a nonhuman body, of an animal or a plant that up until then had existed in a state of potentiality. Jivaro mythology explicitly emphasizes this physical transformation, indicating the completion of the metamorphosis by the appearance of some anatomical feature or the emission of some communicative sound characteristic of that particular species. Thus, the Amerindian myths do not evoke an irreversible switch from nature to culture. Rather, they portray the emergence of "natural" discontinuities from an original "cultural" continuum within which humans and nonhumans were not clearly distinguished. However, this great movement of speciation does not result in a natural order identical to the one familiar to us, since, even if plants and animals now possess physicalities different from those of humans—and also, accordingly, mores that correspond to the biological equipment peculiar to each species—most of them have so far preserved the faculties that they enjoyed before they split into different species. These faculties were subjectivity, reflective consciousness, intentionality, the ability to communicate in a universal language, and so on. They are thus persons, clothed in the body of an animal or a plant, which they occasionally set aside in order to live a collective life analogous to that of humans. The Makuna, for example, maintain that tapirs paint themselves with roucou when they dance and that peccaries play horns during their rituals, while the Wari' claim that peccaries make beer from maize and that jaguars take their prey home for their wives to cook.[13]

For many years such claims were regarded as evidence of thinking that was averse to logic and incapable of distinguishing reality from dreams and myths, or simply as figures of speech, metaphors, or wordplay. But the Makuna, the Wari', and many other Amerindian peoples who make such claims are no more short-sighted or credulous than we are. They are well aware that a jaguar devours its prey raw and that a peccary does not cultivate maize plantations but lays them waste. It is the jaguar and the peccary themselves, they say, who see themselves as performing the very same gestures as humans and who, in all good faith, fancy that they share with the latter the same technology, the same social existence, and the same aspirations. In short, in their myths and in their daily lives as well, Amerindians do not regard what we call culture as the prerogative solely of humans, since there are many animals and even plants that are reputed to believe that they possess a culture and live in accordance with its norms. It thus becomes hard to ascribe to these peoples an awareness or presentiment of a distinction between nature and culture similar to that with which we are familiar but their whole way of thinking would appear to deny.

A last example, this time from New Guinea, will make it possible to form a clear idea of the role that the body plays as an ontological differentiator. According to André Iteanu, among the Orokaiva, the myth of the *ganda* pig serves as a didactic account that underlines the difference between wild pigs and humans. It is a classic story about a cross-species marriage, in this case between a girl and a pig that has taken on the appearance of a magnificently appareled man in order to seduce her. When she discovers the true nature of her husband and his cannibalistic intentions, the young wife returns to her native village, where her parents, assuming that her husband will be coming to reclaim her, wait for his arrival with weapons at the ready. The arrival of the pig-man is described as follows:

> Because he came from very far away, he made the journey in the form of a pig, but at the entry to the village he once again turned himself into a man. First he took his skin off, and as he was now a man, he cut it up to form a loincloth of thin bark. Round his neck he hung an oral *ganda* ornament that he fashioned out of pig's teeth. He attached his snout to a handle and turned it into a club; his bristles turned into a feathered headdress, which he tied to his head. He made his shield from his own ribs, still with their leather covering.[14]

In other words, the pig-form is here an envelope (the skin) and a collection of movable attributes (the teeth, the snout, the ribs covered by their leather carapace), all of which, once shed, reveal an anthropomorphic person and furthermore serve to adorn him as befits a man if he is to be, without question, what he appears to be. Among the Orokaiva, as in other regions of New Guinea and in the Americas, a man-form is thus not an apparently human anatomy in all its nakedness but is an adorned body, enriched and superdetermined by ornaments that, though borrowed from the animal and plant world, nevertheless acquire the function of rendering more tangible external discontinuities in cases where internal continuities may lead to dangerous confusions. For the purpose of making such adjustments to the body-form is certainly not to mark out humans from animals by imposing the seal of "culture" upon "nature," especially given that what are used to create the desired effect are precisely parts transplanted from an animal. The wearing of feathers, teeth, skins, and masks with beaks, fangs, and tufts of bristles makes it possible, by using the very attributes that signal the discontinuity between the species, to differentiate, not men from animals, but different kinds of human species that resemble one another too closely in their original physicality. By sporting ornaments characteristic of particular species of animals, the members of neighboring tribes can manifest in their own appearances differences that are analogous to the differences between nonhuman persons.

The fact that differences of form are more common than differences of substance is hardly surprising when one remembers that animist ontologies seem to borrow some aspects of their operational schema from the model provided by the chain of life. In Amazonia, in the Arctic and circumpolar regions, and in the forests of Southeast Asia, time and again one encounters the same idea that vitality, energy, and fecundity all circulate constantly between organisms thanks to the capture, exchange, and consumption of different kinds of flesh. This ceaseless recycling of tissues and fluids, which is analogous to that which characterizes the interdependence of foodstuffs in the synecological process, makes it possible to understand how it is that all these beings that ingest one another can hardly be distinguished from the matter of which they are made. Furthermore, in animist systems, feeding prohibitions and prescriptions are designed not so much to prevent or promote the mixing of substances reputed to be heterogeneous (as in the case of Chinese or Galenic medicine); rather, their purpose is either to prevent or to render possible a transfer from a banned or an approved species: a transfer of particular anatomical features and the behavioral characteristics believed to stem from them. On the other hand, the place that each being occupies in the chain of life is determined very precisely by its organic equipment, for it is this that conditions both the medium of life that is possible for it—terrestrial, aquatic, or aerial—and also the type of resources that will be available to it, thanks to its particular organs for locomotion and for the acquisition of food.

The form taken by bodies covers more than just their physical conformation; it includes the entire package of biological equipment that makes it possible for a species to occupy a particular habitat and there develop the distinctive mode of life by which we immediately identify it. Thus, Tim Ingold, for example, defines human and nonhuman persons in circumpolar societies as follows: "A fundamental division is always recognized into two parts; an interior, vital part that is the source of all awareness, memory, intention and feeling, and an exterior, bodily covering that provides the equipment and confers the powers that are necessary to conduct a particular form of life."[15] That description holds good for all societies in which an animist mode of identification prevails. Against the background of an identical interiority, each class of beings possesses its own physicality, which is both the condition and the result of particular diets and a particular mode of reproduction. This produces an ethogram, that is, a specialized way of behaving, the detailed characteristics of which could not fail to be recognized by the observational faculties of peoples who depend for their subsistence upon an environment little affected by human intervention.

The Makuna have theorized this concept in their own particular way. As we have seen, these Indians of Colombian Amazonia define as *masa* (people) many plants and animals that are endowed with a soul that is identical to their own but that they daily feed upon. Before consuming any vegetables or meats, they therefore mentally chant an incantation the purpose of which is to decontaminate the food, that is, to strip it of all its harmful principles. Those principles, known as "weapons," are regarded as similar to the powers that each species received as its share at the time of its mythical genesis: powers that determine a species' feeding and reproductive habits and its means of protecting itself in its allotted habitat. Every group of "weapons"—itemized as wooden splinters, feathers, poison, saliva, blood, or semen—thus objectivizes a collection of biological properties and ethological dispositions reputed to be intrinsic to the identity of a species.[16] A corporeal form is therefore indissociable from the behavior that it occasions, and in many myths and anecdotes that tell of a human being's stay among a people whose appearance and manners are altogether human, it is always some unexpected detail in the customs of his hosts that suddenly alerts the visitor to the animal nature of those who have welcomed him; a dish of rotting meat politely served reveals vulture-people, an oviparous birth indicates snake-people, and a cannibalistic appetite points to jaguar-people.[17]

The Variations of Metamorphosis

If animals can, if they so wish, shed the corporeal envelope peculiar to their species and reveal the human dimension of their interiority, without losing the attributes of their behavior, it is because forms are fixed for each class of entities but are variable for the entities themselves.[18] A classic feature of many animist ontologies is the ability to undergo metamorphosis that is recognized to belong to beings with an identical interiority. A human can be embodied in an animal or a plant; an animal can adopt the form of another animal; a plant or an animal can shed its outward clothing and reveal its objectivized soul in the body of a human being. Admittedly, in many cases, such transformations are attested only in myths that are well known to constitute quintessential tales of metamorphosis. But in the Americas at least, mythical figures are seldom relegated to the indefinite past in which they are said to have acquired their distinctive properties, for the effects of their well-meaning or hostile actions continue to be felt even today. Among the Jivaros, Nunkui, the creator of cultivated plants, still acts as the guardian of today's gardens, and Jivaro women actively solicit her assistance. Among the Ojibwa, "it is taken for granted that all the *ätíso 'kanak* [mythological beings] can assume a variety of forms"; and these beings like to come to listen to the myths told about them

or, like "thunder birds," to relay messages to humans.[19] The manifestly lasting presence of these entities mistakenly described as "mythical" is nowhere
more striking than in dreams, in which they usually appear in a human form.
Among the Ojibwa, Hallowell reports that one of his informants, when still
an adolescent, dreamed that he encountered the "master" of golden eagles
in human form. Having transformed himself before the lad's very eyes into
a bird of that species, it invited him to follow it. The boy himself then took
on the appearance of a golden eagle and flew off in the wake of his mentor.[20]

Often enough, it is perfectly "ordinary" human or nonhuman persons,
that is, ones with no mythological antecedents, that are credited with this
capacity of metamorphosis, thereby testifying to the normality of the inter-
changeability of forms among all those who possess the same subjectivity.
However, this plasticity is not total, and some modes of embodiment are less
frequent than others. Conversion from animal to human and from human to
animal is a constant feature in animist ontologies: the former process reveals
interiority, while the latter is an attribute of the power with which certain
particular individuals (shamans, sorcerers, specialists in ritual) are credited,
namely the power to transcend at will the discontinuity of forms and adopt as
their vehicle the body of some animal species with which they maintain special relations.[21] The metamorphosis of a human into a plant or of a plant into
a human is not so common and even less common is that of an animal into
another animal species.[22] As for the possibility of the soul of a living human
invading the body of another human, that does not seem to be attested in any
animist ontologies: a fact that confirms the already classic recognition of the
incompatibility, in principle, between possession and what, for convenience's
sake, is known as "shamanism."[23] The conclusion that may be drawn from this
list of possible and impossible metamorphoses is that the common fund of
interiority stems from the set of characteristics observable in human beings,
while the discontinuity of physicalities is modeled on the astonishing diversity of animal bodies: on the world's stage, the former provides the theme,
while the latter testifies to the diversity of instruments with which it can be
interpreted.

What is the function of this multiplicity of corporeal instruments in the
concert of life, apart from the obvious one of demonstrating a number of irreducible differences between humans, animals, and plants? Its function is to
allow analogous interiorities to avoid an excessive continuity by introducing
between terms differences that are indispensable if those terms are to establish a relationship with one another. The discontinuity of forms and of the
modes of life associated with them separates out distinct collectivities, each of
which possesses characteristics that are defined by the anatomical equipment

of its members and their habitat, and the behavior that these make possible. Among the Chewong, for example, "all 'personages' act culturally and socially, and as long as one behaves in conformity with the moral premises of one's own species, one may not be in any sense condemned for one's actions." In Siberia, relations between animal species are regarded as resembling the relations between different tribes. In the circumpolar region, "animals, like humans, are reputed to establish communities of their own and the members of all those communities can visit one another." The Cree of Canada believe that the animals that they hunt live in social groups similar to those of the Indians. The Oglala Sioux "invariably spoke of all animal categories as representing 'peoples as we are.'" Finally, according to the Makuna, "animal communities are organized along the same lines as human societies. . . . Each species or community of animals is said to have its 'culture,' its knowledge, customs and goods, by means of which it sustains itself as a distinct class of beings."[24] So each species has a basic physical body that constitutes at the same time a body politic and a corpus of precepts; and although a change of form is always possible, such an operation does not affect the intrinsic identity of individuals. In short, what Howell says about metamorphosis among the Chewong can probably be generalized to cover all animist societies: "This can only be done for short periods and it is a risky business."[25]

So what is the point of inhabiting another body? Quite apart from the fact that one risks being unable to regain one's original form—a fate sometimes suffered by overbold shamans and by quite a few human mythical figures— this kind of process, taken literally, requires one to suspend many of the criteria of common sense. Yet, however much one insists that metamorphosis is "symbolic" and belongs to the register of metaphor or figurative speech, many people in different parts of the world, still today, claim that it is a fact "of nature" analogous to the growth of plants and the movement of heavenly bodies. The truth is that it offers a convenient solution, indeed the only one, to the problem of interaction on the same level between human and nonhuman persons that start off with completely distinct physicalities. For the Achuar, the Makuna, and the Chewong do not spend their lives changing into anacondas, tapirs, or tigers. Nor do these animals repeatedly reveal their disguised interiority to human beings. Most of the time each of the predators feeds on its prey with the equipment that it possesses; relations between the different classes of beings are determined by the kinds of physicality that they possess—that is to say, in accordance with their respective ethograms. But given that the interiorities of predators and prey are reputed to be identical, there must arise situations in which their shared ontological destinies can find clear expression in some kind of communication between different collectivities that are separated by their bodies. Not that the moments in which a physical relationship predominates can be clearly separated from moments when two souls communicate. The example of an Achuar hunter mentioned earlier shows that such a distinction really makes no sense. The man is not solely engaged in a tracking operation in which he uses all the knowledge that he has embodied. He is at the same time careful to maintain a tenuous connection that links his interiority with that of his prey, and he does this by means of incantations that he addresses to the animal. However, for a metamorphosis in the strict sense to take place and for it successfully to confirm in a truly intersubjective experience the properties that are ascribed to the beings of the world, a further step needs to be taken, one that breaks through the barrier constituted by forms. And this is possible only in two sets of circumstances: either when plants and animals or the spirits that are their hypostases visit humans, taking on the same appearance as the latter (usually in dreams) or else when humans, generally shamans, go to visit those same entities. In both cases, the visitor assumes a position that puts him on the same footing as his hosts, for this is necessary if he is to establish communication, and this he does by adopting the same costume as those he is addressing. Nonhumans reveal their interiority by taking on the form of human physicality; humans abandon their own physicality in order to take on that of a nonhuman or so as to move freely within the world of interior forms. That is how the visitor signals that he is adopting the point of view of those he has come to meet.

Thus, metamorphosis is not an unveiling or a disguise. Rather, it constitutes the ultimate phase in a relationship in which each party, by modifying the viewpoint imposed upon him by his original physicality, endeavors to coincide with the perspective in which he imagines that the other party sees itself. Through this shift in the angle of his approach, in which each party seeks to "enter the skin" of the other, by identifying with his supposed intentionality, the human no longer sees the animal as he usually does but, instead, sees it as that animal sees itself, that is, as a human, while a shaman is perceived, not as he usually sees himself, but as he wishes to be seen, that is, as an animal. What is involved is really not so much a metamorphosis as an anamorphosis.

Animism and Perspectivism

This merry-go-round of points of view is bound to evoke what Viveiros de Castro calls "perspectivism," the concept by which he designates the positional quality of Amerindian cosmologies. He has developed the nature and implications of this with regard to the definition of animism that I had originally suggested.[26] Viveiros de Castro takes as his starting point the perceived fact that, in the eyes of many autochthonous peoples of the Americas, the following is the case: "Typically, humans see humans as humans, animals as animals and spirits (if they see them) as spirits; however, animals (predators) and spirits see humans as animals (as prey) to the same extent that animals (as prey) see humans as spirits or as animals (predators). By the same token, animals and spirits see themselves as humans; they perceive themselves as (or become) anthropomorphic beings when they are in their own houses or villages, and they experience their own habits and characteristics in the form of culture."[27]

Can this thesis of different perspectives illuminate the problem of animism by providing the key to a better understanding of the exact nature of the difference between humans and nonhumans, all of which are endowed with a human essence? In an attempt to answer this question, Viveiros de Castro first considers the Amerindian ethnonyms usually translated as "human beings," "people," or "persons," which are usually interpreted as signs of an ethnocentric propensity to reserve the generic noun "humanity" solely for the tribe that considers that it has a right to it. However, if one envisages these terms from the point of view of pragmatics, not syntactics—that is, as pronouns rather than nouns—"they indicate the position of the subject; they constitute an enunciative marker, not a name."[28] Far from being indicators of ontological exclusion, such ethnonyms simply characterize the point of view of the speaker ("people" would thus here be synonymous with "us"). Thus, when they say that nonhumans are persons endowed with a soul, Amerindians are in reality conferring upon them a position as enunciators that defines them as subjects: "Whatever possesses a soul is a subject, and whatever has a soul is capable of having a point of view."[29] "Perspectivism" thus expresses the idea that any being that occupies a referential point of view, being in the position of subject, sees itself as a member of the human species. The human bodily form and human culture are deictics of the same type as ethnonymic self-designations. But that is not to say that perspectivism is a relativism in which each kind of subject forges for itself a different representation of a material world that nevertheless always remains identical, since the life of nonhumans is governed by the same values as that of humans: just like humans, nonhumans hunt fish and make war. According to Viveiros de Castro, what are different are the actual things that they perceive: if animals see humans as predator-animals and blood as manioc beer, that is because the point of view from where they stand depends on their bodies and their bodies differ from ours in the intrinsic dispositions that they manifest. The emphasis that animist ontologies lay on the discontinuity of forms should therefore be regarded as a sign of the heterogeneity of the habitus that a body incorporates as the seat of a particular perspective: "Whatever is activated or 'agented' by the point of view will be a subject."[30]

At this point it is not possible for me to comment appropriately upon these subtle propositions, to which my summary does scant justice; and besides, they form part of a more general theory of Amerindian cosmologies that represent work still in progress. So I shall simply discuss their implications with regard to the relations between animism and perspectivism. However, I cannot resist the temptation of first noting a little paradox: this interpretation of perspectivism that Viveiros de Castro presents as an alternative to the sociocentric thesis of a "projection" (of social categories on to the natural world) concurs with a penetrating remark made by Durkheim, the most illustrious advocate of the latter thesis. In his study of the role played by the body as a principle of individuation, to which I have already alluded, Durkheim remarks that such a contrastive function devolved upon it since "bodies are distinct from one another, since they occupy different positions in time and space, each is a special *milieu* in which the collective representations are gradually refracted and coloured differently." Like Viveiros de Castro, Durkheim was inspired by Leibniz: "For Leibniz, the content of all the monads is identical. All, in fact, are consciousnesses that express one and the same object: the world. . . . However, each expresses it from its own point of view and in its own manner. We know how this difference of *perspectives* arises from the fact that the monads are differently placed with respect to one another and with respect to the whole system they comprise."[31] This unexpected antecedent certainly in no way diminishes the originality of the solution proposed by Viveiros de Castro, namely that the human form and culture that Amerindians attribute to animals are, as it were, cosmological deictics that are immanent in points of view. But can this argument be generalized to cover the whole group of animist ontologies?

In "standard" animism, humans maintain that nonhumans perceive themselves as humans because, despite their different forms, they all possess similar interiorities (souls, subjectivities, intentionalities, enunciative positions). To this, perspectivism appends an additional clause: humans claim that nonhumans see humans not as humans but as nonhumans (animal predators or spirits). In short, what we have here is a logical possibility in the interplay between the two positions: if humans see themselves with a human form and see nonhumans with nonhuman forms, then nonhumans who see themselves with a human form should see humans with a nonhuman form. But this crossed inversion of the two points of view, which is a defining characteristic of perspectivism, is by no means attested in all animist systems. A number of fine examples are to be found in the Americas, particularly in myths, and also, albeit much less commonly, in Asia.³² Of course, it may be that sources are laconic on this point, but that seems unlikely when one bears in mind that where cases of perspectivism are reported in a society, they are supported, even in an allusive fashion, by almost all the ethnographers who have visited it. That is a sure sign that this feature is sufficiently noticeable for it to be unlikely to escape the attention of observers, particularly in the Americas, where it is nowadays rare for an Amerindian group to have been studied by only one person.

The most common situation, typical of most animist ontologies, is, rather, one in which humans say no more than that nonhumans perceive themselves as humans. But how do nonhumans envisage humans if perspectivism does not come into it, that is, if they do not apprehend them as nonhumans? On this particular point, ethnographic studies have little to say. But that is no doubt because the answer seems so obvious that, unlike in the case of perspectivism, nobody bothers to record it: that answer is that nonhumans can apprehend humans only in their human form.³³ That is hardly surprising when one bears in mind that humans and nonhumans are reputed to engage in one-on-one personal relationships, characterized by precisely defined regimes of sociability and systems of attitudes (such as friendship, seduction, maternity, affinity, and the authority of elders). Unless they consciously resort to deception, the humans who adopt these regimes vis-à-vis nonhumans are bound to expect that they will elicit from the nonhumans a reciprocal pattern of behavior. If I conform to the conventional way of treating brothers-in-law in my behavior toward a monkey that, I believe, perceives itself as a human, I surely must (unless I prefer to deceive myself) expect that monkey to respond to me in the same fashion, that is, consider me according to a "human code," not a "jaguar code" or an "anaconda code." For a human can establish a prescribed social relationship with a nonhuman that regards itself as a human, whereas a nonhuman could not act toward the human in similar fashion if it did not attribute to him the same humanity that it believes itself to possess; and that humanity is best manifested by the human corporeality that the nonhuman perceives the human to possess. To be sure, the nonhuman might apprehend the human in a nonhuman form, yet still assume that the human apprehends himself as a human being, but that would presuppose that, through a reflective conversion, the nonhuman was aware that it was itself not a human, despite the human form that it believed itself to be inhabiting. However, that does not really seem likely, nor, so far as I know, is it confirmed by ethnography.

So a new question now arises. If the most common situation in an animist regime is one in which nonhumans regard humans as humans, how can they distinguish themselves from humans, given that they also see themselves as humans? From the point of view of ethnography, the only plausible answer is that nonhumans distinguish themselves from humans (and from one another) by the behavior patterns that are determined by the biological equipment peculiar to each species, habits that persist in their bodies even when they regard these to be human. As we have seen, the discontinuity between forms is one means of signifying discontinuities in ways of living, not with respect to the general characteristics of social existence, which are common to both humans and nonhumans, but from the point of view of modes of subsistence, types of habitat, and the specific dispositions that their particular physical conformation both prompts and expresses. Now, if the members of each class of beings regard themselves as humans, they nevertheless do not see other classes as possessing a humanity exactly identical to their own, since the customs peculiar to each class clearly differ from one another. In all probability, a tapir reputed to regard itself as a human being does not perceive humans in a form altogether similar to that which the Indians claim it imputes to itself. In a perfect world (for the tapirs, of course, not the Indians), tapirs and Indians would live together in perfect understanding, maybe sharing the same village and exchanging wives and goods. But the Indians have a distressing habit of hunting the tapirs, as the latter, despite their shared humanity, cannot have failed to notice. Furthermore, as the tapirs see it, Indians live in villages that are different from their own, and their chiefs and shamans are different too and so is their food, particularly since they consume tapirs. Here, the perspectivist solution would be to say that tapirs that suffer attacks from the Indians regard the latter as jaguars or cannibalistic spirits, as certain Amerindian societies do indeed claim, and so, being in the position of prey, they are unable to perceive certain human features (their physical appearance, their villages, and their institutions) that render humans identical to the tapirs' image of themselves. In contrast, in an ordinary animist solution, tapirs do see that humans possess certain social and anthropomorphic attributes that, by and large, resemble those that they think they themselves possess, but they also realize that humans are different from themselves according to other criteria, the kind to which an Amerindian would resort in order to identify members of a neighboring and probably enemy tribe, by referring to their different customs and body ornamentation. In other words, even if nonhuman persons apprehend their own bodies in terms of human morphology, they are also aware of the fact that their bodies differ, mainly through their respective dispositions (e.g., dispositions to flee or attack, daytime or nighttime customs, solitariness or gregariousness). They also know that they differ in the manner in which they present themselves to others when in action (through their costumes, ornamentation, gestures, the types of weapons and tools that they use, and the languages that they speak). For physicality—the basis of discontinuity between species—amounts to more than naked anatomy. It distinguishes that discontinuity in many ways of using bodies, of presenting them and extending their functions. These are all elements that add a particular form of activity in the world to the forms given at birth.

As Viveiros de Castro himself says, perspectivism is "an ethno-epistemological corollary of animism."[34] By postulating the reversed symmetry of points of view, perspectivism ingeniously exploits the possibility opened up by the difference in physicalities upon which animism is founded. But that is a graft that many peoples in the animist archipelago have not attempted, not for lack of imagination or of aptitude for reflective conversion, but perhaps because it introduces an extra layer of complexity into a positional ontology in which, in all the situations that daily life throws up, it is already difficult enough to attribute stable identities to the beings that one encounters. We are a long way away from the reassuring world of Being and existing beings, of primary and secondary qualities, of perennial archetypes and of knowledge as revelation. For all those weary of an overuniform world, that realization is surely cause for a measure of rejoicing.

7

Totemism as an Ontology

Defining animism as a combination of resemblance in interiorities and difference in physicalities led me to return once again to the question of totemism—not totemism as a classificatory method such as Lévi-Strauss's *Totemism* suggested, with an explanation at once authoritative and beguiling, but totemism in its specifically ontological aspects, which Lévi-Strauss set aside the better to open up an intellectualist approach to the phenomenon, an approach that would supersede earlier speculations on the indistinctness of humans and nature in the thinking of primitive peoples. Taking as his starting point the principle that totemism is a mystification, Lévi-Strauss maintains that the artificial unity of this notion stems from a confusion between two problems in the minds of anthropologists: "The first problem is that posed by the frequent identification of human beings with plants or animals, and which has to do with very general views of the relations between man and nature, relations which concern art and magic as much as society and religion. The second problem is that of the designation of groups based on kinship, which may be done with the aid of animal or vegetable terms but also in many other ways. The term 'totemism' covers only cases in which there is a coincidence of the two orders."[1]

It is above all the second of those two elements in the definition of totemism that captures the attention of Lévi-Strauss, for this is what leads to the classificatory solution already sensed by Franz Boas forty years earlier: the homology of differential gaps between, on the one hand, a natural series (that of the eponymous species) and, on the other, a cultural series (that of social segments). As for the first element, that is, the identification of humans with nonhumans, in the solution adopted by Lévi-Strauss it remains as a kind of

mechanism of self-persuasion that reinforces the operational efficacy of totemic classifications in societies in which "a general tendency to postulate
intimate relationships between man and natural beings or objects is put to
good use for concretely qualifying classes of relatives or supposed relatives."[2]
Yet, seen for themselves and not simply in their function of assisting the categorization of humans, in certain totemic configurations these "intimate relations" between humans and other natural beings present features that are
altogether unique. In truth, Lévi-Strauss was himself aware of this aspect, for
he devotes long passages in *The Savage Mind* to societies with totemic clans in
which a deep physical and psychic affinity between humans and their totems
is assumed. Citing the case of the island dwellers of the Torres Strait, of the
Menomini of the Great Lakes, and, further to the north, of the Chippewa, he
emphasizes the fact that, in this kind of case, each totemic group will be considered on its own and will "tend to form a system no longer with other social
groups but with particular differentiating properties regarded as hereditary."[3]
This produces among the totemic segments an intrinsic diversity that is truly
ontological and that likens them to castes. In such systems, in contrast to the
interpretation proposed in *Totemism*, the homology no longer refers to the
differential relations between two series of terms (clan 1 differs from clan 2
just as an eagle differs from a bear); rather, it refers to the terms themselves
(clan 1 is *like* the eagle; clan 2 is *like* the bear). "Two images, one social and
the other natural and each articulated separately, will be replaced by a *socio-
natural* image, single but fragmented."[4] In short, if it is true that totemism
belongs on a quite different level from animism when it is considered in its
classificatory version (the homology of relations), its "fusional" dimension
(the homology of terms) can offer an interesting approach that leads to justifying treating it as a mode of identification.[5]

   Australia is the continent that, at the end of the nineteenth century,
prompted the most extravagant conjectures as to the nature of totemism, so it
will come as no surprise to find that it is here that the exceptional properties
that it manifests are expressed most clearly. Thanks to excellent early ethnographic descriptions, Australia came to illustrate par excellence for Durkheim, Frazer, Rivers, and even Freud, a system of social organization and
a mode of relating to nature that, according to early observers, were characterized by the fact that each individual "belongs to a group of persons, each
of whom bears the name of, and is especially associated with, some natural
object."[6] Ever since that period, specialists studying Australia were struck by
the diversity of the forms of totemism present on this continent and, at the
same time, by the impression of unity nevertheless conveyed by the general

principles of social segmentation and affiliation that were peculiar to the Aboriginals and to their conceptions of a person and of the environment. This apparent contradiction was explained by an endogenous evolution over a very long period of time (close on seventy thousand years), in the course of which the earliest occupants of Australia had scattered in various directions into the country's vast territories and, apart from regional neighbors, had little contact with one another. It was supposed that each group consequently developed its own institutions, borrowing from neighboring groups or in contrast to them and producing many variations to the initial model assumed to have been common to them all. It matters little, at this point, whether this diversification of social organization and rites resulted from a combination of diffusion through migrations and local developments or from an ecological and demographic adaptation of social modes of occupying space in very different environments, which was another possibility.[7] Whatever the source of those variations, the common structural characteristics that they all manifest are obvious enough for it to be possible, in the wake of ethnologists specializing in Australia, to treat this cultural region as a whole that is, in some respects, remarkably homogeneous.

Dreaming

The most original feature of Australian totemism is certainly the fact that it is rooted in a remarkable cosmological and etiological system that it has become customary to call "Dreamtime" or "Dreaming" in English.[8] "Dreaming," known as *alchera*, was described for the first time by Baldwin Spencer and Franck Gillen, who were working among the Aranda of the central desert. At a first approximation, it can be said to evoke all that relates to the time when the world took shape, as this is related in the ritual accounts that accompany totemic ceremonies. These tell of primeval beings that long ago emerged from the depths of the earth at precisely identified sites. Some embarked upon peregrinations punctuated by many ups and downs, the routes and stopping places of which are still detectable in the material environment, in the form of rocks, water sources, woods, and seams of ocher. These beings vanished as suddenly as they had appeared, either in the very place where they had emerged or else where their journeys came to an end, each one of them having left behind some of the many existing beings of today: humans, plants, and animals, together with all their respective totemic affiliations and the names that designate them, religious rites and objects, and all the organic and inorganic elements of the landscape. These beings from Dreamtime, which are both the engenderers and the prototypes of social and physical reality, are generally represented as hybrids, part human and part nonhuman, divided into different totemic groups already at the time of their arrival. They are human with respect to their behavior, their mastery of language, the intentionality that they manifest in their actions, and the social codes that they respect and institute, but they have the appearance and bear the names of plants or animals and are the origin of stocks of spirits deposited at the sites where they themselves disappeared. These spirits have since been embodied in individuals of the species or the object that they represent and in humans who have taken that species or object as their totem.

"Dreaming" is not just an Aboriginal way of referring to the mythical times that many peoples trace back to a fabled genesis of beings and things. For at the time of that "World-Dawn," as Radcliffe-Brown put it, a movement of continuous generation took off, the effects of which can still be felt.[9] The potential left by the beings of Dreamtime in various sites and routes is constantly realized by successive embodiments of their spirits in entities of various kinds and thanks to the rites, the naming procedures, and the repeated journeys by means of which the Aboriginals make the hidden presence of these entities tangible and alive. For they are entities that, by modeling beings and things, gave meaning and order to the world. Dreamtime is thus neither a remembered past nor a retroactive present. Rather, it is an expression of the eternity that is confirmed in space, an invisible framework for the cosmos that guarantees the permanence of its ontological subdivisions. As for the beings of Dreamtime, they cannot be likened to classic mythical heroes, since their organizing impetus, partly given solid material form by various features in the landscape, has continued without interruption even since they abandoned the earth's surface. Nor are they ancestors, in the strict sense, since every existing being, whether human or nonhuman, is linked to the entity that determines it in a direct relationship of duplication, actualization, or formation rather than through an affiliation that unfolds from one generation to the next. Thus, in Australia, totemic organization, that is to say, this association between nonhuman entities and phenomena and groups of human persons, stems from a process that both is originating and also continues ceaselessly to stabilize essences and forms of life that are already differentiated into classes and types, within which social and physical components are inextricably intermingled. As Spencer and Gillen write in their study of the Aranda, "the identity of the human individual is often sunk in that of the animal or plant from which he is supposed to have originated."[10] But that mixed identity itself combines behavioral features, ritual instruments and objects, taxonomies at once sociological and biological, names and stories, and sites and journeys. All are elements that it would be hard to distribute to one side or the other of an imaginary line drawn between nature and culture.

An Australian Inventory

The cosmological framework of Dreaming is, by and large, valid for the whole of Aboriginal Australia, allowing for a few variations concerning greater or lesser latitude in the elaboration of a totemic interpretation of dreams that prompt ritual innovations, the degree of the personalization of the Dream-beings, and the extension in space of their itineraries. On the other hand, the relations between individuals and their totems vary widely, as do modes of totemic affiliation and the part that these play in social organization, the definition of statuses, and the interplay of matrimonial alliances. In the 1930s, Adolphus P. Elkin produced the first reasoned inventory of the diverse variants of Australian totemism, an undertaking conducted in the spirit of the functionalism of the period, that is, essentially based on the manner in which totemic divisions play an integrating role in the various social systems recorded throughout the continent.[11] But before tackling Elkin's typology, a brief ethnographic reminder of the nature of these systems and their distribution is necessary.

In a few regions along the north coast and in the southeastern quarter, there were tribes organized in local exogamous groups that recognized no internal divisions. However, the great majority of Australian societies were characterized by a more or less complex segmentation into classes. The simplest forms were represented by societies with exogamous moieties in which every individual belonged to one or other of the two named classes and had to find a spouse in the opposite class. Such forms were to be found in a number of different regions that varied according to whether the moieties were of patrilinear or matrilinear affiliation. The societies with patrilinear moieties were mostly located in the northern part of the continent, between Dampier Land and the Cape York peninsula, while the societies with matrilinear moieties mostly occupied the southern zone. As well as these societies with exogamous moieties, there were also groups with endogamous and generational moieties. Nowadays these are represented by the Aluridja tribes of the south, where a man or a woman can marry only within his or her own moiety, not into the moiety that encompasses older generations (his or her father and mother) and younger ones (his or her children). Societies that have a "four-section system" may be considered logical extensions of the system of exogamous moieties on to which a criterion of residence is grafted: for example, two matrilinear moieties (the most common case) called A and B whose members are distributed into two local groups known as 1 and 2, with the wives and children living with their husband/father, since in Australia residence is always patrilocal. In such a case, a man from moiety A of local group 1 (A_1) is obliged to marry a woman from moiety B of local group 2 (B_2), and their children are affiliated to B_1 since they belong to the moiety of their mother (B) and the local group of their father (1); the B_1 children will themselves have to marry into the opposite moiety and into a local group distinct from theirs (A_2). These four-section systems, often labeled Kariera, after a western coastal tribe, were mainly present in the desert regions of the northwest, the northeast, and in much of the southeast. Systems with eight subsections follow the same principle, but with four local groups instead of two. In a society with matri-moieties, such as the Aranda, a man from moiety A and local group 1 marrying a woman from moiety B and local group 3 will have children classed as B_1; an A_2 man marrying a B_4 woman will engender B_2 children; an A_3 man marrying a B_2 woman will engender B_3 children; and an A_4 man marrying a B_1 woman will engender B_4 children. Similarly, switching moieties, a B_1 man marrying an A_4 woman will have A_1 children; a B_2 man marrying an A_3 woman will engender A_2 children; a B_4 man marrying an A_2 woman will engender A_4 children; and a B_3 man marrying an A_1 woman will engender A_3 children. These systems with eight subsections are common among tribes in central Australia and can be found in the north as far away as Arnhem Land and the Cape York peninsula. Finally, we should note that although the names designating sections or subsections may differ from one language or dialect to another, the general classification system remains similar, and this makes it possible to integrate individuals born in other tribes into the class that corresponds to them.

Falling with a greedy curiosity upon the Australian facts, nascent anthropology had assumed that there was a direct link between these class systems and the institution of totemism as an operator of exogamy, with the obligation to marry outside one's totem constituting a convenient imperative the better to integrate atomized local groups through marriage. But Elkin's inventory split Australian totemism into a multitude of apparently heterogeneous types and unambiguously showed that some of those types played no role at all in the functioning of matrimonial alliances. Elkin thus apparently ruined any hope of demonstrating a systematic link between totemic classifications and forms of social organization throughout the continent. Lévi-Strauss's criticisms of him on this score were all the more vehement because that was precisely the objective that he himself had in mind.[12] My own ambition is quite different, so it is not this consequence of Elkin's typology that arrests my interest but rather certain characteristics that it reveals relating to the specific ontological characteristics of Australian totemism.

The first form of totemism that Elkin considers is the so-called individual totemism. Among the tribes of the southeast, he describes a particular relationship between a sorcerer and an animal species, generally of reptiles. Members of this species act as the sorcerer's assistants, carrying disease or a cure to distant places and acting as his spies. Among the Kurnai, it is said that the sorcerer carries within him the spirit of the species that assists him and that this can also be externalized and materialize in a tamed animal. Among the Yualayi, a sorcerer can entrust an animal of his particular totemic species (what Elkin calls his alter ego) to a sick person in order for its power to cure him or her. The Yualayi also claim that a wound inflicted upon a totemic animal causes suffering to the sorcerer associated with that species. A whole series of differences are immediately detectable when one compares this individual totemism of the Australian southeast with the particular links forged between humans and certain animals in animist systems. The relations between an Amazonian or Siberian shaman and the spirits of his animal assistants, or between an ordinary man and his animal guardian or companion in North America, always involve individual creatures, not whole species, even if the animal may sometimes serve as an intermediary among its fellow creatures. In contrast, in Australia a relationship is established with a species considered as an indissociable whole, and the tamed animal that the sorcerer parades is no more than an individual expression of the characteristics that are peculiar to the species in general. Furthermore, in animist systems, human and animal persons are clearly distinguished, and it is precisely this that makes it possible to construct a wide range of dyadic relations between the two kinds of individuals. In contrast, an Australian sorcerer's person seems completely fused with the animal species that he has adopted as his totem. The essence of that species has become his own essence, and he himself physically feels everything that affects any member of the animal group whose destiny he has now espoused. So here, it is not a matter of an alliance or a contract of assistance between the sorcerer and his totemic species. Instead, a hybridization is both sought and assumed, the end purpose of which is certainly social (i.e., either the treatment or the dissemination of misfortune among humans). But to produce a concrete realization of this, it is necessary to acquire properties that are shared with an animal species.

"Sexual" totemism is likewise common among the tribes of the southeast. This involves dividing the sexes into two mutually exclusive totemic classes, each symbolized by some species, usually an animal one: the bat for men, the owl for women, for the Kamilaroi and the Wotjobaluk; the bat and the woodpecker, for the Worimi; and so on. The exact nature of the relationship between the sexual group and the eponymous species is not clear from the data. The Wotjobaluk say that "a bat's life is a man's life," thereby implying an affinity between their forms of existence, while the Kurnai instead emphasize a shared affiliation: "Every descendant of Yeerung [emu-wren] is a brother, every descendant of Djeetgun [superb warbler] is a sister."[13] So here one certainly detects the general idea that humans and nonhumans share certain common properties that are stable enough to be passed down from one generation to another. However, the idea is expressed much more vaguely than it is in the case of individual totemism.

Although Elkin brackets alongside sexual totemism the "conceptional" totemism of the Aranda and the Aluridja, the principle seems quite different from that of sexual totemism. The totem of each child is not determined by sex or filiation but by the place where the child's mother became aware of her pregnancy, either by actually being there or by visiting it in a dream. The place in question is, of course, a totemic site, that is, a place where a Being from Dreamtime has deposited the child-souls of its totemic species, one of which is said to penetrate the womb of the mother and there to form the newborn child. An Aranda child will thus not necessarily have the same totem as its father, its mother, or its brothers and sisters, since here the subsections that function as matrimonial classes bear no relation at all to totemic affiliations. We shall be returning in more detail to Aranda conceptional totemism, but we can already learn something from it. Sexual totemism allows for collective categorizations on the basis of a homology of differences (men are to women what wrens are to warblers). But conceptional and individual totemisms clearly stem from a different model: both are primarily determined by the ontological definition of a human person conceived as sharing certain intrinsic characteristics with a particular totemic species.

Do the other collective totemisms that Elkin studies really operate differently? At first sight and as in sexual totemism, the function of the totems of moieties, sections, and subsections seems to be to use distinctive emblems to overdetermine classes of individuals that appear to be organized by and for marriage. However, the justifications put forward in each case for the totemic affiliation allow us to glimpse other principles at work. Let us start with the totemism of moieties. In its matrilinear variant it symbolizes sharing a common life founded on an inheritance of the same flesh and blood passed down by mothers. This is an identifying substance the origin of which, as we shall later see, can be traced back to the moieties' eponymous animals, which are generally two species of birds. Meanwhile, the totemism of patri-moieties instead refers to two species of kangaroos and is combined with local totemic cults the responsibility for which is usually passed down a paternal line. The exogamy of moieties is not as strict or as automatic as its dualist organization might suggest, for, according to Elkin, here totemism is first and foremost a means of distributing all existing beings within two major classes, the members of which—humans, animals, plants, objects, and totems—present affinities with the two species that serve as the principal totems.

From this point of view, the totemism of sections presents the same characteristics as the totemism of moieties: it operates according to a fourfold partition of the entities of the cosmos "on the basis of the kinship which is held to exist between the human beings and the natural species."[14] The same principle applies for the totemism of groups with eight subsections, but with two variants and one exception: either the totems of the subsections are directly associated with sites of totemic child-souls and thus find themselves invested with a generative function that reinforces the common attributes shared by the human members of the subsection and their localized totems; or else they are more specifically categorial and may exist alongside a totemism of child-soul sites and a religious totemism, which are totally distinct from it. The third possibility, as among the Aranda, is that totemic affiliations have no link at all with subsections nor, therefore, with marriage. As can be seen, the characters of the kinds of totemism present in the various class systems are extremely diverse: most clearly have a classificatory dimension of a cosmological or ontological type rather than a strictly sociological one, the general idea being that there exist shared properties, even if they are only vaguely defined, between humans, nonhumans, and the totems that encompass them. But the totems may or may not be associated with matrimonial classes, transmitted through filiation or linked to ceremonial sites and local deposits of child-souls left by the Dream-beings.

Such diversity is even more noticeable in the last major type of totemism envisaged by Elkin, namely "clan" totemism. Australian clans may be either patrilinear or matrilinear, but some are also "native" in the sense that they incorporate all individuals conceived or born at the same totemic site. Matrilinear clan totemism is based on the principle that all persons linked in an ascendant matrilinear line share the same corporeal substance (flesh and blood) derived ultimately from the totemic entity from which the clan emerged. This shared physicality leads to strict exogamy and a prohibition against the consumption of the totemic species, since no individual should ingest the same substance as itself. In the tribes to the northwest of Victoria, this material indissociability of certain humans and certain nonhumans is confirmed by the belief that to kill a member of a person's totemic species causes that person to suffer a real wound, as was also the case in individual totemism. Here, the totem "is more than a name or emblem; something of the life of man is in the life of the totemic species, and *vice-versa*."[15] Finally, as in the case of moieties, the principal totem and the species that embodies it constitute the apex of a hierarchy of secondary totems and species, so that the combination, within a single society, of all the totems, subtotems, and affiliated species takes on the aspect of an exhaustive system for categorizing the cosmos.

In contrast to matrilinear clan totemism, patrilinear clan totemism allows for a perfect coincidence between a clan and a local exogamous group whose link with the totem is materialized by and in the territory that the two inhabit together: the spirits or essences of each of the members of the local group are reputed to proceed, generation after generation, from the sites of which they are the guardians and which were the scenes of the exploits of Dream-beings belonging to the same totem as themselves. In the case of a matrilinear clan, the relation between the clan members and their totem is of a substantial nature. But in a patrilinear clan it stems from an intimate solidarity between the humans and the totemic beings, a solidarity that is nourished and strengthened by an identical spiritual genesis and an identical sacred geography—in short, by the same identificatory rooting in what may, justifiably, be called the genius of the place. Finally, native clan totemism is simply a way of associating in one sui generis group individuals who share the same totemic class of child-souls because the latter were incorporated into their mothers at their conception (among the Aranda) or at their birth (in southwestern Australia), on the very same totemic sites formed by the Dream-beings. This kind of totemic clan has nothing to do with marriage (it is not exogamous) and should instead be regarded as a religious collective, the depository of etiological stories, secret knowledge, and rites concerning the Dream-being from which its members are descended. The latter are in duty bound to use their esoteric knowledge and prerogatives in ceremonies designed to celebrate their totem and ensure the well-being and fecundity of the totemic species produced from the same site as themselves, whose essence and destiny they share. Just as in patrilinear classic totemism, religious totemism (and "dream totemism," which is one of its individual variants) is thus based on the spiritual identification of humans, totems, and the species affiliated to them: each of these is present in the world as a particularized expression of one and the same immaterial prototype with a physical embodiment.

By cutting up Australian totemism into a dozen distinctive forms, Elkin rendered null and void the idea that it might constitute a single regulating mechanism that applied throughout the continent and was associated with a certain type of institution or marriage rule. In many tribes, several forms of totemism coexist, fulfilling different functions. Thus, in the northwest of southern Australia, an individual may be linked in diverse ways to as many as five heterogeneous classes of totems: he possesses or is possessed by one or several moiety totems but also by sexual totems and the totems of a matrilinear clan, of a religious site inherited from his father, and, secondarily, of another religious site inherited through the matrilineal line of his mother's brother, although this is one that he cannot transmit to his children. All the same, is it legitimate to infer from this painstaking deconstruction that Australian totemism does not exist, at least not in the form of a systematic whole, but simply amounts to an anthropological fiction that mixes together, in a great dogmatic potpourri, social and natural taxonomies, concepts of a person, and rites, myths, and beliefs between which no logical link exists? That would be to leap too hastily to a conclusion and to ascribe more importance to ostensible differences than to certain resemblances that Elkin's inventory reveals.

Admittedly, Elkin himself, although convinced of the underlying religious unity of Australian totemism, provides scant help for elucidating its principles. His clearest contribution consists in noting that all the forms that he has identified are based on a belief in the "oneness of life, which is shared by man and natural species," adding that laying claim to a totemic name is not prompted solely by the need for a group to have a distinctive emblem, "for the name stands for a community of nature between the group and its totem."[16] Apart from his tirelessly repeated assertion that humans share the same "form of life" as their totemic species, Elkin has little to say when it comes to defining exactly wherein lies this common nature. At the very most, his inventory indicates the prevalence of two major varieties of hybridization between humans and nonhumans, totems included. One type refers to the sharing of one and the same substance (flesh, blood, skin) and concerns above all matrilinear totems, those of moieties and clans, and also the totemism of subsections when this is linked to localized religious sites. The other is based on an identical essence or principle of individuation that is engendered by the regular incorporation of the child-souls of a totemic site into both humans and nonhumans. This is most clearly manifest in conceptional totemism, religious totemism, and patrilinear clan totemism. Only the individual totemism peculiar to sorcerers seems indubitably to combine both modes of hybridization. This constitutes a somewhat meager conclusion, but it is enough to warrant an inquiry into the possible ontological unity of Australian totemism. For in his day, Elkin was one of the most remarkable connoisseurs of aboriginal Australia, and we cannot discount his opinion when he writes—probably in opposition to Durkheim—that the divisions and subdivisions of totems are not only a method of classifying nature "but an expression of the idea that man and nature form one corporate whole—a whole which is living and social." It was an assertion that this minister of the Anglican Church no doubt did not make lightly.[17]

The Semantics of Taxonomies

To gain a better understanding of these presumed totemic hybridizations, we must now consider what the Aboriginals themselves have to say about them and therefore in the first instance explore what the semantic indications suggest. This is what the linguist Carl Georg von Brandenstein set out to do in a book devoted to a comparative study and interpretation of the names of totems and totemic divisions throughout Australia.[18] His first task was to examine the meaning of the various terms by which the Aboriginals designate the concept that we call a "totem"; and we should bear in mind that the word was borrowed from the language of the Ojibwa of the Great Lakes of North America before becoming generalized in the anthropological terminology of the second half of the nineteenth century. Brandenstein shows unambiguously that the great majority of these generic terms refer to elements of a human or animal body or to physiological substances, some of which are explicitly regarded by the Aboriginals as vectors of a shared identity. The most current of these terms belong to an anatomical vocabulary and may be translated as "flesh" (or "meat"), "skin," "head," "forehead" (or "face"), "eyes," "side," "liver" (or "temper"), or "color" (in particular that of the skin). Next come polysemic terms that designate both corporeal humors or dispositions and also the qualities associated with them, such as *ngurlu*, the word for matrilinear totems among nine tribes of central northern Australia, which means "interior" or "temperament," and its probable cognate *ngarlgi*. The latter term is used by the Yanyula of the Carpentaria Gulf to designate totems and to qualify "that which comes from somewhere," such as armpit sweat, behavior, color, exudate, odor, perfume, skin, taste, tune, voice, and an identifying essence.[19] On the other hand, terms that denote a relationship or sharing are much less common; they include "moiety," "section," "friend," and "same name." In short, with very few exceptions, in which the idea of segmentation or kinship predominates, what we call a totem, that is to say both the entity itself and the class that it symbolizes, is designated in Aboriginal languages by terms that refer to very concrete physical predicates that are frequently hypostasized into moral qualities.

The reason for those semantic choices appears more clearly in the light of the analysis that Brandenstein then produces—an analysis not of generic terms denoting the concept of a totem but of particular terms used to designate this or that totem, essentially those associated with different class systems. Contrary to authors such as Peter Worsley, who maintains that the assignment of a totem (and a natural species) to a social group is totally arbitrary,[20] Brandenstein argues that the whole Australian totemic system is governed by a single immanent logic whose most complete expression, in societies with subsections, is based on eight combinations of three pairs of primary properties. Each combination characterizes the totem or totems of each subsection, along with the humans and nonhumans affiliated with it. He adopts a progressive method, starting with a study of moiety societies in the Kimberley and southwestern region, where totemic species are usually a pair of birds or snakes. Among the Wunambal and the Ngarrinjin of Kimberley, for example, the dualist classificatory schema is governed by two opposed principles, one of which is embodied by the *kuranguli*, the *Grus rubicunda* crane, the other by the *banar*, the *Eupodotis australis* bustard. Each of those two totems subsumes a collection of twenty or so moral, physical, and behavioral attributes that oppose term for term and that qualify all the human and nonhuman entities grouped into the two moieties. Those attributes are explicitly recognized by the members of these tribes, and Brandenstein sums them up by setting in opposition the two principal qualities "quick" and "slow," which themselves refer to a series of pairs exemplified by "smart" and "fool," "active" and "passive," "slender" and "plump."

The next stage involves examining the names and characteristics conferred upon the totems of societies with four sections. The system is quite simply doubled: the "quick"/"slow" contrast between moieties is now accompanied by a new contrast that Brandenstein describes as an opposition between "hot-blooded" and "cold-blooded." Thus, among the Kariera, the "quick" moiety was subdivided into two sections. The first was called *karimarra*, which may be translated "which acts vigorously," with, for its totem, a species of kangaroo and the attribute "hot-blooded." The second was known as *pannaga*, meaning "supine," with, for its totem, a species of goanna (a reptile) and the attribute "cold-blooded." The "slow" moiety, for its part, was also composed of two sections: the first called *pal-tjarri*, meaning "supple" or "malleable," with, for its totem, a different species of kangaroo and the attribute "hot-blooded"; the second called *purungu*, meaning "massive," with, for its totem, a different species of goanna and the attribute "cold-blooded." Those "who act vigorously," namely the quick and warm-blooded *karimarra* kangaroos, thus married the "supple ones," namely the slow, warm-blooded *pal-tjarri* kangaroos, while the "stretched ones," namely the quick, cold-blooded *pannaga*, married the "massy ones," namely the slow, cold-blooded *purungu*. The qualities of "warm-blooded" and "cold-blooded" synthesize a collection of physical attributes intrinsic to the members of the sections and their respective totems: for instance, a more or a less dark-colored blood but also the antithetical dispositions that those attributes were believed to encourage, such as vigor or languor, aggressiveness or passiveness, determination or nonchalance. These contrasts were fully recognized by the Aboriginals, as is attested by the manner in which the Kabi of Queensland describe the rules for marriage between different sections: "The lighter class of the light-blood phratry married the lighter class of the dark-blood phratry, and the darker class of the light-blood phratry married the darker class of the dark-blood phratry."[21]

From his study of the totemic names of thirty or so groups with subsections and of the qualities attributed to the members of each of them, Brandenstein finally draws the conclusion that these eight-class systems introduce yet another pair of attributes, which he subsumes under the contrast between "round" and "flat." As with the preceding ones, this pair of attributes refers to both physical and moral characteristics: "tall" and "short," "in front" and "to the side," "principal" and "secondary," "wavy-haired" and "straight-haired," "broad-faced" and "narrow-faced," of a "choleric" disposition and of a "phlegmatic" one, and so on. The totems and members of each subsection are thus identified by a specific combination of three properties that define a type of behavior (quick or slow), a type of humor (hot-blooded or cold-blooded), and a dimension or volume (round or flat). So a "round–quick–warm-blooded" man should marry a "round–slow–warm-blooded" woman, a "round–quick–cold-blooded man" should marry a "round–slow–cold-blooded woman," while a "flat–quick–warm-blooded" man should marry a "flat–slow–warm-blooded" woman, and a "flat–quick–cold-blooded man" should marry a "flat–slow–cold-blooded" woman. Such a system seems at first sight very constricting since a man from a subsection whose members are reputed to be plump, squat, with wavy hair, a broad face, and of small stature should take a wife from the subsection prescribed by the rules of marriage whose members, for their part, are reputed to be slim, with smooth hair, narrow-faced, and tall. Their children are expected to inherit some attributes from their father and others from their mother, the combination of which is different from that of each of their parents and will be supposed to correspond to the attributes of the members of the subsection in which they themselves will be classed. In fact though, Aboriginals are not particularly bothered when the physical characteristics of an individual do not correspond to his or her subsection's norm. All the same, among the Murinbata of Arnhem Land, for example, it does sometimes happen that children are classed in the subsection that best corresponds to their physical qualities in cases where these are too different from the norm recognized in what is officially their allotted subsection.[22]

The human members of a totemic class thus share a collection of substantial and immaterial properties that are peculiar to them all. How is this
common patrimony connected with the natural species that serves as their
principal totem? Particularly in the cases of animals (since these constitute
almost three-quarters of the recorded names of totems), but also in those of
plants, the totem is said to embody, in exemplary fashion, the particular attributes of the behavior, humors, and appearance recognized as characteristic of
the humans whom they represent. But there is more to it: according to Brandenstein, in many cases "the animal is named after the quality which is its
main characteristic, never the quality after the animal."[23] So the section name
padtjarri, which is common in a number of variants in western Australia and
means "malleable" and "gentle," also serves as the name for the hill-kangaroo
that is generally the totem for this section. Similarly, among the Nungar of
the southwest, the moieties were called *maarnetj*, which may be translated as
"the getter," and *waardar*, meaning "the watcher," two terms that also served
to designate their respective totems, the white cockatoo (*Cacatua tenuirostris*)
and the crow (*Corvus coronoides*). In other words, the names of the totemic
classes are terms denoting properties that designate the eponymous animal
also, rather than the reverse, that is, names of zoological taxons from which
the typical attributes of classes would be inferred. It therefore becomes difficult to maintain the interpretation of totemic classifications for Australia proposed in *Totemism*, that is to say, the idea that totems are borrowed from the
natural kingdom because the ostensible differences between species where
appearance and behavior are concerned provide a suggestive model for conceptualizing the segmentation of human groups. The fact is that the primary
difference here is between aggregates of attributes common to both humans
and nonhumans within classes designated by abstract terms, not between animal and plant species that are able, through their ostensible differences, to be
the natural source of an analogical model that would serve to organize social
discontinuities.

It is doubtful whether this "Aboriginal World Order," as Brandenstein calls
his general model of Australian totemic properties, is as perfectly systematic
and coherent at the scale of an entire continent. Nevertheless, in the form in
which he presents it, he provides us with valuable insights into the nature of
totemism in Australia. By means of subtle semantic corroborations, he explains the modus operandi of this totemic hybridization to which Elkin drew
our attention: in class systems, the identity of the totemic group is founded
upon a specific collection of physical and moral attributes shared by all its
members, whether human or nonhuman. This constitutes a kind of ontological prototype of which the totemic species constitutes the emblematic expres-

sion, not the concrete archetype, from which those qualities are derived. This makes it possible, where Australia is concerned, to remove two difficulties raised by the Lévi-Straussian classificatory theory.

The first difficulty stems from the fact that some names of totems designate not plants or animals but human elements (boy, breast, clitoris, corpse, cough, foreskin) or artifacts (anchor, boomerang, rhombus, canoe) or meteors or other natural phenomena (cloud, hailstone, lightning, river, tide). These are certainly few in number: they represent no more than 15 percent of the names in the list of 524 totems collected by Brandenstein. But although they constitute a minority, they should nevertheless be taken into account in any general interpretation of totemism. Yet that is ruled out by the hypothesis of a homological transposition of natural discontinuities into social discontinuities since, unlike the differences between animal or plant species, the referents of these totems are not experienced by the senses in the way that spontaneous systems of discontinuities are. But if we accept that these "nonspecies" totem names are nothing but more or less iconic labels denoting a class of properties with which they have only a metonymic relationship, then the difficulty disappears. As for the predominance of animals among totems, no doubt this may, as Lévi-Strauss supposed, be explained simply by reasons of cognitive economy, albeit not those that he suggested: the contrasts in behavior and appearance presented by animals are more striking and noticeable, so it was logical, although not indispensable, to prefer them to other entities as more likely embodiments of the groups of attributes for which they are not the referential source.

The intellectualist interpretation of totemism is also hard put to account for the hierarchized stacks of totems and secondary species that are subsumed by the principal totems. This is particularly evident in moiety systems. To return to the example of the white cockatoo and the black crow that head the Nungar moieties, it is—at a pinch—possible, provided one ignores the significance of their names, to accept that these birds might, by reason of their respective ethologies and morphologies, present a major contrast that native thought seized upon in order to symbolize the dualist division of society.[24] But was it really necessary to turn to the animal species to find an elementary dualist schema that any number of other oppositions—such as those between the day and the night, the sky and the earth, or the sunrise and the sunset— could equally well have motivated? Above all, why should it be necessary to reinforce that contrast, as the Nungar did, by a series of minor oppositions between the eagle and the crow, the white cockatoo and the black one, the pelican and the pair comprising the heron and the sea eagle, the tiger snake and the brown snake, the mosquito and the fly, the whale and the seal, the male and the female kangaroo, and the male and the female dingo? From a strictly taxonomic point of view, all this involves a pointless redundancy that simply blurs the initial contrast between the white cockatoo and the crow and undermines the relevance of its primary function as a dichotomic matrix. It seems more likely that each of those secondary species (or each of the sexes, where members of the same species are concerned) provides a less forceful expression of certain attributes of the moiety that the principal totem illustrates far better. For in the case of the human members of the two moieties concerned, those attributes are clearly defined by the Nungar. The people in the "Getter" moiety have pale chocolate-colored skin, some are tall and well-built while others are small and frail, but they all have rounded faces and limbs and wavy hair and are endowed with an impulsive and passionate temperament, at the same time maintaining an open and agreeable demeanor. Meanwhile, the people of the "Watcher" moiety have a darker and duskier skin color, are very hirsute, thickset, and squat, with small hands and feet, and are reputed to be surly, vindictive, and secretive. These qualities are not suggested by observation of the white cockatoo and the crow. Within the order of physical and moral characteristics ascribed to humans, they express series of antithetical properties that are of a more abstract nature but that those two emblematic species are said to share and embody far better than the secondary species that their respective classes include. To employ, or rather adapt, the language of contemporary studies on ethnobiological classifications, one could say that our two birds are prototypes, that is, the "best examples" of their respective classes, but for reasons that are not exclusively morphological (as Brent Berlin, for example, claims), for they also have to do with inferred properties suggested by their customs, their habitats, and their diets.

The types of hybridization that Brandenstein's analysis illuminates thus confirm Elkin's intuitions and do seem to bear out the existence, in Australia, of a mode of identification founded on an interspecies continuity of both physicalities and interiorities. The identity of numerous components of physicality is patently clear when humans and nonhumans of various kinds are said to all share collections of properties both material and behavioral and to be moved to act as they do by identical humors. For, as we should remember, it is correct to say that temperament and character stem from physicality, as I have defined it, if they are considered to testify to an influence exerted upon behavior patterns by particular corporeal substances and anatomical dispositions. It is, in fact, that very corpus of common attributes that primarily defines a totemic collective, a corpus that is synthesized in a name denoting a quality that identifies both the class and the emblematic (rather than eponymous) species that expresses its organic unity.

As for the continuity of interiorities, there can be no doubt about it where classes are associated with Dreaming sites, where the child-souls that are to be incorporated into both the human and the nonhuman members of the totemic group are stored. Such is the case of the totemism of patrilinear moieties (in central Australia, in northern Kimberley, and in the eastern part of Arnhem Land) and also of the totemism of subsections that are attached to "religious sites" (in eastern Kimberley and among the Mangarrayi and Yangman tribes). Here, a soul should be understood as a principle that produces the identity and individuation that stems from the stock of totemic essences, conferring upon each of those in which it lodges a kind of guarantee of conformity to the eternal ontological paradigm that a Dream-being instituted in the distant past. However, this idea that members of a totemic group conform to an ideal type is also subliminally present elsewhere, even where there are no explicit connections between class totems and child-soul sites. It finds expression particularly in metaphors of kinship, of particular affinity, and of shared filiation rooted in an identical origin, and it takes on a public character in the custom of subsuming all the members of a totemic group, both the humans and the nonhumans, under a generic name. The fact is that it is the class itself, with all its physical and moral attributes, that here constitutes the vector and symptom of a shared interiority. Each and every member of a totemic group, humans and nonhumans alike, possesses the same intrinsic characteristics that define the group's identity as a species. The essence that defines them all stems partly from the substances that they share in common, as the vocabulary used sometimes clearly reveals: we should remember that the term *ngarlgi*, by which the Yanyula designate totems, connotes not only characteristics of both a material and a moral nature but also an "identifying essence."[25]

The above considerations suggest that we should treat with circumspection the sometimes-suggested hypothesis of a clear-cut opposition between, on the one hand, a patrilinear totemism founded solely on a shared spiritual identity proceeding from totemic sites located in the paternal territory and, on the other, a matrilinear totemism founded solely on a shared identity of substance that is inherited from the mother. Quite apart from the fact that, as we have seen, certain class totemisms combine transmission from both types of attributes, totemic hybridization seems everywhere to occur simultaneously at the levels of both interiority and physicality, albeit according to variable modalities. It is not possible to demonstrate this generally for all Aboriginal societies, since, at the time of the European conquest, there were, after all, close to five hundred different languages among them. So I shall limit myself to a brief illustration featuring two contrasting ethnographic cases of subsection systems, the one characterized by a semimoiety patrilinear totemism, the other by totemism of the conceptional type.

Varieties of Hybrids

The totemism of the Mangarrayi and the Yangman living to the south of Arnhem Land, studied by Francésca Merlan, is characterized by being associated not with the eight subsections that govern matrimonial alliances but with four semimoieties each of which is composed of a pair of subsections designated by a term that combines the names of both the subsections concerned.[26] So these semimoieties have nothing to do with marriage but constitute a form of totemic segmentation that divides up larger groups that encompass the members of two generations who are linked by patrilinear filiation. Known by the generic name *marragwa*, the numerous totems peculiar to each semimoiety include plants, animals, natural phenomena, mythical figures, and abstract entities. And even though informers who are asked to name their totems always first cite a small number of plants and animals, there is no formally hierarchized system in which major totems head the list of subtotems, as happens in societies divided into moieties. A quadripartite grid of totems may be seen as an inclusive classification of all elements in the cosmos, although it is not organized as a taxonomic tree: for example, all the catfish species may well be affiliated to the same semimoiety but that is not the case of other equally typical forms of life such as snakes, fish, or lizards, different species of which are distributed among all the semimoieties. In short, the Lévi-Straussian principle of the conceptualization of social discontinuities by means of natural discontinuities does not work here. We must therefore turn to mythical ontogenesis to understand the reasons for the totemic groupings.

Among the Mangarrayi and the Yangman, Dream-beings are hybrids, part human, part animal, that are known by the generic name *warrwiyan* and are distributed among the semimoieties. Each of them brought to its site beings from its semimoiety that now stay there in the form of trees, rocks, or other features of the landscape. These are also called *warrwiyan* but are furthermore given particular names that constitute the inherited stock of names of the human members of that semimoiety. Although their feats are recounted in myths, *warrwiyan* have not confined their generative activities to a distant past. One of Merlan's female informants told her that her child-soul was taken from one place to another by *wirrilmayin*, a type of goanna, and one of the *warrwiyan* of her semimoiety. What relations do *warrwiyan* Dream-beings maintain with the totems of *marragwa* semimoieties? Dream-beings may be considered particular realizations of an ever-vibrant creative potential, whereas totems express the direct and continuous link between humans and the entities of the cosmos that were instituted by the Dream-beings. As Merlan tells us, because humans, totems, and all other existing entities "were placed in the social-and-natural order by *warrwiyan*, there is an unchanging relationship of *common origin and substance* between them, regulated by a system of categorization (the semi-moieties) that pre-existed, and in terms of which the *warrwiyan* were already differentiated among themselves."[27] Thus, mythical accounts relate not to an initial undifferentiated state but to a world already divided into substantive essences that were actualized as classes of particular entities thanks to the intervention of the Dream-beings.

The contrast with animist mythologies, those of Amazonia, for example, is striking. In both cases, the beings whose adventures are recounted are certainly a mixture of humans and nonhumans living within a regime that is already both cultural and social through and through. But there is a difference. Amerindian myths tell of separate events that occasioned the introduction of discontinuities between the species that had all been part of an original continuum (plants and animals dissociating themselves from humans through their forms and behavior, yet retaining an interiority that is shared by all). But Australian mythology evokes a process of parthenogenesis unfolding actually within the classes of hybrids already constituted. When this process was complete, each of those classes of existing beings contained a vaster number of species, including varieties of humans who nevertheless remained in conformity with the essential and material particularities of the ontological type peculiar to the subdivision in which they had come to be.

Now let us return to the Aranda tribes of the central desert. As we have seen, their totemic groups are constituted by all the individuals linked with the site of the Dream-being under whose sign they were conceived. This makes the totemism of the Aranda even more independent of matrimonial classes than it is among the Mangarrayi and the Yangman, since members of a subsection can claim several distinct totemic affiliations. These depend on the peregrinations that their mothers have happened to engage in and their visits to this or that reservoir of souls presided over by some Dream-being, for one of those souls enters the woman and becomes the existential and categorial principle of her as-yet-unborn child. It is true that, with residence being quite stable, people from the same locality generally frequent the same totemic site, where ceremonies periodically take place, so the chances are that, given that the mothers have regularly visited this site, the children of a particular subsection will all have the same totem. However, there is nothing systematic about this, in particular on account of the long journeys that entail visits to different totemic sites. As a result, a group of coresidents may well be composed of individuals who identify with quite distinct totems.

How is this identification conceived? Spencer and Gillen insist on the fact that what they call the "reincarnation" of a Dream-being in a human leads to that human being identified completely with the totemic species of the site. "The totem of any man is regarded . . . as the same thing as himself."[28] At first sight, then, this is identification with at once a generating principle, a class of totemic entities, and the animal or plant that symbolizes this class. This is illustrated by an anecdote concerning a man of the Kangaroo totem who said "'That one,' pointing to his photograph which we had taken, 'is just the same as me; so is a kangaroo.'"[29] All the same this perfect identity posed a problem for Spencer and Gillen, given that they subscribed to a Frazerian concept of totemism, which was understood above all as a special relationship of protection and mutual respect between humans and the totemic species from which they are believed to be descended. However, among the Aranda there is no sign of either mutual respect or protection, since it is not forbidden to kill one's own totem, although one is advised to eat of it no more than sparingly. Moreover, mythical accounts and fables suggest that long ago it was customary to feed above all upon one's totem. The totemic animals and plants were therefore not treated as relatives that it would be wrong to harm. Furthermore, the ceremonial prerogatives of totemic groups include the performance of rites known as *intichiuma*, in the course of which they increase the number of individuals of their totemic species so that other totemic groups can also draw upon these as food. How can one both set up a relationship of profound identification between a human and a nonhuman and at the same time accept that the former brings about or is complicit in the destruction of the latter?

The answer to that question is no more than hinted at in the studies that Spencer and Gillen devoted to the Aranda. The first thing to note is that the child-souls that the Dream-beings deposited in sites are, in principle, differentiated: some come to be actualized in humans, others in animal or plant species that the Dream-being has at some moment adopted as its form. Dream-beings are thus not plants or animals that undergo metamorphosis and change into humans, nor are they humans that change into plants or animals. Rather, they are original and originating hybrids, concrete hypostases of physical and moral properties that can thus transmit those attributes to entities all with their own individual forms but each of which is regarded as a legitimate representative of the prototype from which it came. Any example of my totemic species is, for me, not an individuality with which I can maintain a personal relationship (as would be the case in an animist ontology). Instead, it constitutes a living and contingent expression of certain material and essential qualities that I share with it, qualities that will not be affected if I kill it so as to feed on it, since they stem from an immutable matrix from which both of us have emanated. Far from mutually apprehending each other as subjects engaged in a social relationship, humans and nonhumans are merely particularized materializations of classes of properties that transcend their own existences.

In her synthetic study of the Aranda materials, Marika Moisseeff confirms this. Stressing the "constitutional hybridization" of Dream-beings, she reminds us that this is in fact intrinsic to all existing entities—at least it is if one is to believe the myths of ontogenesis.[30] Myths of origin that are quite distinct from the accounts of the peregrinations of Dream-beings evoke an earlier period in which the earth carried no life apart from semiembryonic masses produced by the incomplete transformation into human beings of various plants and animals, all amalgamated together in their hundreds. These conglomerates, known as *inapatua* (incomplete beings), could neither move nor see nor breathe. There then arose other beings called Numbakulla (issued from nothing), quite distinct from the Dream-beings, and these brought into being the celestial vault, the sun, the stars, and the watercourses. Two of them also set about segmenting the *inapatua* with stone knives and extracting the rough shapes of human forms and modeling these. As Moisseeff explains, "it was only once it was individualized out of the common mass of matter that each human being became associated with the nonhuman element, either an animal or a plant, from which it had at first been separated. This element . . . was to become its totem."[31] Because humans were hewn out of a composite material, their morphological singularity was accompanied by an inevitable substantial hybridization that remained a reminder of their totemic association with the plant or animal from which they had been separated. This is how it is that their identification with specific nonhumans can be manifested at two levels: that of the common matter from which they emerged and that of the essence of Dream-beings, themselves hybrids, that was incorporated in them.

A Return to Algonquin Totems

The ontological formula of totemism as illustrated above assumes an exemplary character in Australia, even if it is not everywhere presented equally clearly. Nowhere else do we find such a vast gathering of peoples that has so systematically, explicitly, and uniformly developed the idea that there exists a moral and physical continuity between groups of humans and groups of nonhumans. However, on other continents—even, in an attenuated form, in Europe—one does come across institutions that may also be described as totemic, in the traditional sense of the term, to the extent that the names of natural species and phenomena are used to designate clearly delimited social segments. In most of these cases, the Lévi-Straussian interpretation based on the homology of differential gaps can legitimately be applied without the necessity of introducing a substantive distinction between nature and culture: the discontinuities between species constitute an easily observable phenomenon and hence an ever-available source of labels that make it possible to designate distinctive groups. In contrast to Australia, this classificatory tool generally possesses a purely denotative aspect and in no sense implies any recognition of material or spiritual continuities between the humans and their eponymous species. My use of the term "totemism" to characterize the particular ontology for which Australia provides the model may therefore lead to some confusion since it adds a new sense to the meaning that has been generally accepted ever since Lévi-Strauss's analyses in *Totemism*. To get around this difficulty and the better to emphasize the specific features of Australian totemism, specialists of that continent have lately tended to substitute the word "Dream" for the word "totem." The inevitable consequence is that they thereby reduce the scope of the concept, which is now confined to one particular—albeit vast—ethnographic region.

I am not in favor of such semantic cosmetics for, although the Australian formula of totemism is certainly remarkable for its coherence and its degree of elaboration, it is not at all unique. Rather, we should regard it as the expression, in a particularly purified form, of a more general ontological schema of which sporadic or residual examples are to be found elsewhere. Such is the case in the southeastern United States in certain societies with totemic clans that Lévi-Strauss considered to be hybrids, a mixture of totemic systems and caste systems, since their internal subdivisions were so very accentuated by a differential repertory of physical, moral, and functional features believed to be derived from those eponymous species.[32] For instance, the Chickasaw attributed to each eponymous clan, or even each hamlet, definite particularities of behavior, diet, costume, temperament, means of subsistence, and physical aptitudes. It was said of Puma people that they had an aversion to water, lived in the mountains, and fed mainly on game; Wild-Cat people slept in the daytime and, thanks to their keen sight, hunted at night; Red-Fox people lived by plundering, deep in the forest, and prized their independence; Raccoon people fed on fish and wild fruits, and so on.[33] Of course, here, unlike in Australia, it was not a matter of identifying all the human and nonhuman members of a particular totemic class by the properties of an ideal prototype whose eponymous species was simply a materialization more striking than others. In a more classic fashion, here animals and their mores constituted concrete paradigms for the humans, who were said to be descended from the species from which they derived their clan name. Nevertheless, the general inspiration for the totemic mode of identification is preserved, since each group of humans claims to share with a group of nonhumans a collection of physical and psychic dispositions that distinguishes them, as an ontological class, from others.

We should furthermore remember that modes of identification are ways of schematizing experiences that prevailed in certain historical situations and are not empirical syntheses of institutions and beliefs. Each of these generative matrices that structure practice and peoples' perception of the world certainly predominates at particular times and in particular places, but is not exclusive: animism, totemism, analogism, and naturalism can each tolerate a discreet presence of other emerging modes, for each of them is a possible realization of a combination of elements that are universally present. Each one may thus introduce nuances and modifications into the expression of the locally dominant schema, thereby engendering many of the idiosyncratic variations that are customarily called cultural differences.

This is certainly what happens in totemism as I have described it on the basis of the Australian data. I will provide only one illustration, which will return us to the country where the term "totemism" originated, namely the northern region of North America. The terms *totam* and *totamism* appear for the first time in the memoirs of John Long, a fur trader operating at the end of the eighteenth century among the Ojibwa Indians north of the Great Lakes.[34] As many authors have pointed out, the birth of these terms seems from the start to have been dogged by confusion, for Long mentions the term *totam* in the context of an anecdote in which one of his Ojibwa companions uses the word to refer to a bear that is apparently his own personal guardian spirit, not the eponymous animal of his clan. It is important to note at this point that the Ojibwa people, like most of the northern Algonquins, customarily established an individual personal relationship with benevolent and protective entities that Hallowell calls *pawagának*. These would manifest themselves above all in dreams, although even in a waking state one could sometimes encounter them in an animal form.[35] Furthermore, unlike other tribes that speak an Algonquian language and live farther north, the Ojibwa of the Great Lakes were organized into patrilinear clans named after animals (bear, crane, loon, moose, and so on), membership of these social subdivisions being indicated by possessive constructions based on the root *-dodem*, which expresses a relationship of kinship or coresidence: for example, *ododeman*, "my cousin" (of either sex), or *makwa nindodem*, "the bear is my clan." It was thus concluded that Long had made a mistake when he applied the word *totam* (a term reserved for collective social affiliations) to what was actually an individual animal spirit of the *pawagának* type. To avoid this confusion, anthropologists then, in the second half of the nineteenth century, took to drawing a distinction between totemism in the proper sense, namely various types of association between social groups and their eponymous species, and "individual" totemism, a relationship between a person and an entity in the form of an animal or a plant. In some cases, as indeed among the Ojibwa, the two forms of totemism coexisted.

That was how the matter rested until Raymond Fogelson and Robert Brightman cast some doubt on the reality of the confusion imputed to Long.[36] We should note that Long knew the Ojibwa well, had spent several winter seasons with bands of them, and was fluent in a simplified form of the Ojibwa language that was used for fur trading. Moreover, Long was well aware of the existence of collective totemism. For example, at the beginning of his book, he records the fact that each of the five "nations" in the Iroquois League was divided into three tribes or families known respectively by the names Tortoise, Bear, and Wolf. So it seems unlikely that he would not have realized that the Ojibwa people also had clans named after animals.[37] Finally, Long was not alone in making this purported mistake. Half a century later, Father De Smet, a Jesuit missionary famous for his ethnographic descriptions, mentioned an identical use of the word "totem" (which he spelled "dodeme") among the Potawatomi, an Algonquin-speaking tribe neighboring the Ojibwa to the south. The term was used of an animal that appeared to a young man in a dream and became his guardian spirit in an association that was clearly of an intimate nature, since it implied the adoption of the animal's name as a personal name and permanently sporting some distinctive emblem (a paw, feather, or tail) that evoked the animal metonymically.[38]

These two independent occurrences of the word "totem," in situations said to be different from those in which it is ordinarily used and reported by observers whose word we have no good reason to doubt, encourage one to examine in greater detail the semantics of the term in Algonquian languages. In Proto-Algonquian, /*o.te./ is a verbal root that may be translated as "to live together as a collective" and from which may stem nouns, generally employed in a possessive form, such as /*oto.t.e.ma/, "someone's coresident." Considering thirty or so uses of this root in North Algonquian languages and the various Ojibwa dialects, Fogelson and Brightman conclude that the terms and expressions in which it figures always refer to a social link, usually of a localized nature and in many cases characterized by some kind of connection. In the Ojibwa language, for example, /-do.de.m/ designates both a patrilinear clan and also its eponymous animal, and /odo.de.man/ expresses the kinship between an individual and his cousin of either sex, for its use may cover all the Ego's relatives. Among the Woods Cree, /nito.ti.m/ means "my relative" or "my friend." Among the Penobscot, /-tottem/ may be translated as "friend," as may /-tuttem/ in the Micmac language. Among the Fox, finally, William Jones ascribes to /oto.te.ma/ the meanings "his (elder) brother," "his eponymous clan-animal," and "his provider of supernatural power."[39] As can be seen in this last case, the term may be used indifferently so as to denote either kinship or a totemic association or a link with an individual animal spirit. This is not at all surprising, given that all the variants considered in other Algonquian languages denote some personal relationship, whether it be kinship, coresidence, or friendship.

Now let us return to Long. The word *totam*, which he explains in a long commentary, stems from an account confided to Long by one of his Amerindian companions and related totally in the Ojibwa language. The man tells him that his guardian spirit, a bear that he calls *nin, O totam*, is furious with him because he has killed a fellow bear. In consequence, Long's confidant fears that he will no longer be capable of hunting. The expression *nin, O totam* is probably an approximate transcription of /nindo.de.m/, meaning "my relative" or "my friend" and here used in the generic sense of a relationship of familiarity and intimacy between persons living in the same place, which corresponds well enough to the tonality of the links that exist between a man and his individual guardian animal. In other words, although Long is at fault in that he has decontextualized the term *totam* by turning it into a noun, he is nevertheless not mistaken when he reports the use of this polysemic term in an apparently unusual context. On the contrary, it seems fair enough to assume that the Ojibwa, or the Potawatomi described by Father De Smet, were not as strict as anthropologists later were when it came to distinguishing between what the anthropologists called "social totemism" and "individual totemism." As the example of the Fox shows, depending on the pragmatic situation of enunciation, it is not at all incongruous to use one and the same word to refer sometimes to a clan relative, at other times to one's clan's eponymous animal, and at yet other times to one's individual animal spirit.

Should such semantic polyvalence be considered to indicate that the totemic complex and the complex of guardian spirits were not as dissociated as had at first been claimed? At first sight, the two registers of a relationship with an animal do seem to be clearly differentiated. As I have already several times had occasion to point out, the Ojibwa, and the northern Algonquins more generally, undoubtedly can be connected to an animist mode of identification, given that they attribute an interiority of the same nature as their own to nonhumans that are seen as persons. As for the totemic groups among them, these are not characterized by the kind of continuity both physical and spiritual between humans and eponymous species that prevails in Australia and in certain tribes of the southeastern United States. Rather, they seem to be governed by the mechanism, detected by Lévi-Strauss, of a relationship that is metaphorical, not inwardly motivated, between two series of discontinuities. But in any case this kind of segmentation is far from general: the most northern Ojibwa groups have no totemic clans at all.

Nevertheless, even if the two systems are governed by different logics (the one truly ontological, the other classificatory), they are not on that account heterogeneous. For even if the guardian spirit takes on the appearance of one particular animal, it is also an emissary of the species and, as it were, its representative to the man whom it assists, in particular by facilitating his hunting of its fellow animals. So the typically animist relationship that links a human person and an animal person is compounded by a special relationship between that human person and the whole animal species. This clearly suggests a totemic aspect, especially when the latter relationship is prefigured by the fact that at birth the human has been given the name of an animal species whose "onomastic twin" (*nijotokanuk*) he then becomes, as is the case among the Ojibwa of Big Trout Lake, who, however, have no totemic clans.[40] Similarly, the purely denotative totemic association between a class and an animal species may shift toward an animist relationship where a man acquires as his individual guardian spirit an animal belonging to the eponymous species of his clan. For him, this species now becomes something more and other than merely the referent of a collective name: it makes it possible for the human to identify immediately with a class of nonhumans that are now personalized. That being said, it is true that the phenomenon of identifying with the animal species remains on the individual level and does not take the classic Australian form of sharing material and spiritual attributes that belong to groups of both humans and nonhumans.

Yet a rough version of a truly collective continuity between humans and animals does exist among the northern Algonquins, but in a society without descent groups. The Penobscot of Maine did in fact possess what Frank Speck called "game totems." Of the twenty-two local groups of which they were composed at the end of the nineteenth century, thirteen were named after an animal species reputed to be particularly abundant in the winter hunting grounds of the band that had adopted its name: lobster, crab, eel, beaver, sturgeon, raccoon, wolf, squirrel, wolverine, otter, wildcat, hare, yellow perch.[41] The identification between the local group and its eponymous species rested upon the fact that the members of this band hunted or fished mainly for the animal whose name it bore, either for food or for trade, and they therefore depended acutely on it for their subsistence or, sometimes, for their very survival.

Such collective specialization may not have resulted solely from the technical constraints of adapting to the differential distribution of species to habitats, which was always an essentially relative matter. Speck establishes a parallel between the Penobscot and the Mistassini Cree regarding their relationships to the game that they hunted, noting that the "totems" of the band in the former case and the guardian spirits in the latter were always the animals that they hunted for preference. Now, the Cree considered the animal species to be the legitimate proprietors of the hunting territories that they allowed humans to use, and the same may well have been true of the Penobscot; in which case, the eponymous species would have lent the band of hunters not only its name but also the use of its territory, that is to say the possibility, day after day, to take from it whatever was needed for the humans' survival. Here, the totemic names were not based on some arbitrary correspondence between natural and social discontinuities but on an accepted material relationship of dependence reached between the human groups and the nonhuman groups that had imprinted the mark of their identity on to the territory. Such a situation puts one in mind of certain aspects of Australian totemism and shows clearly enough that totemism, as I have defined it, may be present, in a minor mode or potentially, in animist ontologies even where, in the absence of any groups segmented by descent, there are no truly totemic institutions.

8

The Certainties of Naturalism

If one accepts that identification is a fundamental modality for the schematization of experience, one must also assume that the forms it takes are organized in accordance with systematic relationships that make it possible to throw light on not only the properties of its constituent parts but also those of the totality that results from their combination. Insofar as animism and totemism differ from each other without being opposed term for term, the two other ontological formulae that complete the schema of identification must possess structural characteristics that render them compatible with the first two, so that the coherence of the whole is assured by some simple rules of transformation. Seen from this point of view, the counterpart of animism is not totemism, as I had earlier supposed, but naturalism. For the naturalist schema reverses the formula of animism: on the one hand, articulating a discontinuity of interiorities and a continuity of physicalities and, on the other hand, reversing their hierarchical order, with the universal laws of matter and life providing naturalism with a paradigm for conceptualizing the place and role of the diversity of the cultural expressions of humanity.

When, in earlier works, I characterized naturalism as a straightforward belief in the self-evidence of nature, I was simply following a positive definition that goes back to the Greeks. According to this, certain things owe their existence and development to a principle that has nothing to do either with chance or with the will of humans: a principle that our philosophical tradition has successively qualified by the terms *phusis* and *natura* and subsequently by the various terms derived from these in European languages.[1] This reductionist definition remained imprisoned within a conceptual genealogy internal to Western cosmology. It thereby forfeited the advantage of the use of contrastive features that were less welded to a historical situation that a systematic comparison with animism could have provided. So when Viveiros de Castro commented upon my incomplete distinction between naturalism and animism, he was quite right to emphasize that the fundamental opposition between those two modes of identification was essentially based on a symmetrical inversion. According to him, animism is "multinaturalist," since it is founded upon the corporeal heterogeneity of classes of existing beings that, however, are endowed with identical souls and cultures. Meanwhile, naturalism is "multiculturalist" in that it uses the postulate of the oneness of nature to support recognition of the diversity of both individual and collective manifestations of subjectivity.[2] One might question the use of the term "multinaturalism" in such a context, since the multiple natures of animism do not possess the same attributes as the one and only nature of naturalism: the former more or less evoke the ancient Aristotelian sense of a principle for the individuation of beings, including humans, whereas the latter, with its one and only nature, refers directly to the mute and impersonal ontological domain, the contours of which were definitively drawn by the mechanistic revolution. However, even if it might be preferable to formulate that opposition in more neutral terms, it still certainly remains relevant.

The notion that modern ontology is naturalist and that naturalism can be defined by the continuity of the physicality of the entities of the world and the discontinuity of their respective interiorities truly seems so well established by the histories of science and philosophy that it may seem hardly necessary to produce any circumstantial justification for it. That is all the more true as the origin of this great divide has already been by and large described in chapter 3. But let me briefly summarize the argument. For us, what differentiates humans from nonhumans is a reflective consciousness, subjectivity, an ability to signify, and mastery over symbols and the language by means of which we express those faculties, and furthermore the fact that human groups are reputed to distinguish themselves from one another by the particular manner in which they make use of those aptitudes by virtue of a kind of internal disposition that used to be called "the spirit of a people" but that we now prefer to call "culture." For one does not need to profess an intransigent relativism in order to agree with the general opinion that when it comes to customs and mores, behavior varies according to the arbitrary conventions and signifying regimes by means of which humans like to particularize themselves collectively, despite belonging to the same species. However, since Descartes and above all Darwin, we have no hesitation in recognizing that the physical component of our humanity places us in a material continuum within which we do not appear to be unique creatures any more significant than any other organized being. To be sure, we no longer share with the animals a structure of springs and pneumatic devices in the manner of Vaucanson's automata, for we are aware now that it is the molecular structure and metabolism inherited from our phylogeny that indubitably link us to the humblest of organisms, just as the laws of thermodynamics and chemistry link us to nonliving objects. As Bouvard and Pécuchet discover with a slight sense of humiliation, we must get used to the idea that our bodies "contain phosphorus as do matches, albumin as do egg whites, and hydrogen gas just as do streetlamps." As for "consciousness," a term whose use in the French language was popularized by Descartes, it continues to prosper as an emblematic sign of humanity, even if philosophy nowadays prefers the concept of a "theory of mind."

Unlike the other modes of identification, so familiar are the ontological distinctions drawn by naturalism, even if they are not always apprehended reflectively, that it will not be necessary to examine them in detail for the benefit of readers of the kind that I imagine will be interested in a book such as this. Where the general principles of our shared cosmology are concerned, what I need to do is not so much supplement insufficient information, as I have tried to do in the cases of animism and totemism, but rather sift through the superabundant supply of knowledge in order to pick out the main guidelines. For naturalism has emerged from a climate of critical discussions and empirical investigations that has bestowed upon it the unique characteristic of constantly giving rise to heterodox points of view that call into question the distinctions that it draws between the singularity of human interiority and the universality of the material features ascribed to all existing beings. While the doctrinal corpus of our ontology does not require the in-depth examination that more exotic modes of identification do (at least within the framework of the objectives of this book), it is nevertheless indispensable that we evaluate its claims to hegemony in the face of alternative formulations produced from the same historical crucible—claims that appear to strip it of its robust simplicity and to challenge the system of oppositions upon which it is based.

An Irreducible Humanity?

First we need to recognize that, in the course of the last few centuries, plenty of critical minds have objected to the ontological privilege granted to humanity, calling into question primarily the ever unstable boundary by means of which we try to distinguish ourselves from animals. Among those who have criticized the attribution of an absolute singularity to humans thanks to their inner faculties, Montaigne is without doubt the most famous and the most eloquent in his indictment of our presumption toward other creatures. As Bayle observed, "An Apology for Raymond Sebond" is partly an "apology" for animals because, in it, Montaigne challenges the idea that the use of reason is humanity's prerogative. He argues on the basis of his own observations and the testimony of the Ancients that animals differ from ourselves in neither their behavior, their technical abilities, their aptitude for learning, nor even their "discourse," understood here as the faculty of reason. Just as we are, they are able to free themselves from the rule of instincts, for "there is, I say, no rational likelihood that beasts are forced to do by natural inclination the selfsame things which we do by choice and ingenuity. From similar effects we should conclude that there are similar faculties. Consequently, we should admit that animals employ the same method and the same reasoning as ourselves when we do anything."[3] Philosophers such as Descartes, Locke, and Leibniz, after Montaigne and often in opposition to him, maintained that the phrases pronounced by talking birds are certainly no indication of their humanity since those animals cannot adapt the impressions they receive from external objects to the signs that they imitate. Contrary to them, the author of the *Essays* is convinced that the facility with which blackbirds, crows, and parrots reproduce the human language shows that they have "an inward power of reasoning which makes them teachable—and willing to learn."[4] Like contemporary ethologists, he is struck by the ability to solve problems that animals manifest in their technical operations: "Why does the spider make her web denser in one place and slacker in another, using this knot here and that knot there, if she cannot reflect, think or reach conclusions?"[5] So it is ridiculous to perpetuate any idea that humans possess an intellectual and moral supremacy over animals, given that both humans and animals are subject to the same natural constraints, and animals cope with them rather better in that they organize their little world in a more sensible and unprejudiced manner. In short, wisdom dictates that "we are neither above them nor below them. . . . Some difference there is: there are orders and degrees: but always beneath the countenance of Nature who is one and the same."[6]

It has to be said, however, that Montaigne was an exceptional case on more than this particular count and that his judgments on animals, even before Descartes refuted them, were hardly shared by common opinion in his own day. In the very decade in which Montaigne's *Essays* appeared, an author now long forgotten published a "defence and illustration" of the anthropology of the Bible, which was reprinted many times during the author's lifetime, a fact that suggests that its influence was considerable. In his *Suite de l'Académie française en laquelle il est traité de l'homme . . .* (an address to the French Academy on the subject of man), Pierre de la Primaudaye opposes Montaigne's arguments by reasserting that in the Creation man's place is defined by the opposition between matter and soul.[7] Actually, the adversary of this

former adviser to Henri III was not so much Montaigne as the atheist wits of
the court who claimed to follow Epicurus and trampled the mysteries of faith
underfoot, brandishing the hammer of reason. Although La Primaudaye's argument in support of the preeminence of man is essentially based on biblical
exegesis, it constitutes a good synthesis of the orthodox view on this subject
at the dawn of the classical period. The justification in Genesis could hardly
have been more widely accepted: if man, and only he, is capable of intelligence
and reason, that is because God created him last of all and in his own image,
unlike anything created before him, in order that his faculties should enable
him to know and glorify his creator. The exceptional status that this conferred
upon man constituted "the true difference between him and the other animals, which are nothing but brute beasts."[8]

However, La Primaudaye adds to the authority of the scriptures an outline
of an ontology whose details are, in the present context, more interesting. In
it, he first separates spiritual creatures such as angels from corporeal creatures, taking care to specify that all the latter, humans included, are linked by
a physical continuity, for "the composition of man's body consists of the four
elements and all their qualities, just as do all the bodies of all other creatures
under the sun."[9] The true difference within physical beings lies in whether or
not they possess life and above all the nature of their respective souls. Among
living creatures, four types of soul should be distinguished, corresponding to
different regimes of existence that are characterized by increasing degrees of
complexity: the "vegetative" souls of plants; the "perceptive" souls of lower animals such as sponges and oysters; the "cognitive" souls that confer upon those
that possess them "a certain virtue and vigor such as thought and knowledge
and memory, so that they know how to preserve their lives and how to behave
and control themselves as is natural to them. This is the type of soul possessed by brute beasts." Finally, a "rational" soul is peculiar to humans alone;
"it has all the faculties of the earlier species but also something that is more
excellent, for it participates in reason and intelligence."[10] Aristotle's influence
is patent, even though the dialectical subtlety of the *De anima* is lost in this
summary typology from which all that emerges is an assertion that the material continuum between humans and other existing beings is accompanied by
a discontinuity of internal faculties. All the same, one can see that Descartes,
despite his rejection of Scholasticism, was not building on nothing when, a
few decades later, he proclaimed an absolute separation between matter and
spirit, between extension and intellect, and between everything mechanical
and all that stems from understanding turned inward upon itself.

There can be no doubt that after Montaigne there was a scattered minority who may be described as "gradualists" and who persisted in challenging

the concept adopted by the Moderns, namely that man had an exceptional place in Nature thanks to his internal dispositions. But we should exaggerate neither the volume of those dissident voices nor the scope of their opposition to the dominant naturalist ontology. Condillac is a case in point, despite the fact that he was repeatedly accused of having abolished the separation between animal sensation and human understanding by suggesting that the difference between the two was one of degree, not of nature. The *Traité des animaux* (Treatise on animals; 1755) does indeed seize upon the pretext of a refutation of Buffon's mechanistic approach in order to develop a sensualist theory of animals' thought that is inspired by Locke (Condillac was one of his most zealous disciples in France). Condillac declares that, to the extent that "beasts compare, judge, and have ideas and memory," it is not possible to assimilate them to automata.[11] So, given that animals and humans have the same needs, the same habits, and the same elementary knowledge and that both groups learn solely from experience, where does the difference between them lie? The break between them occurs with language, which enables humans to rise to the level of reflective thought, whereas animals are incapable of abstraction and unable to wonder about themselves. Man, in contrast, can compare himself to all that surrounds him: "he turns inward, into himself, then comes out again." Thanks to language, he has access to introspection, inferences, and generalizations; his knowledge grows and, surpassing animals in the use and development of the capacities that they nevertheless share, he ends up by distancing himself from them.[12]

Although he is indubitably a gradualist and despite anticipating evolutionist theories of cognition in some respects, Condillac's psychology does recognize the existence of an irreversible threshold in the development of internal faculties, a threshold that only humans have crossed. Besides, even if humans and animals do possess comparable faculties of feeling and thinking, the souls from which those faculties stem are not comparable: a human's soul is immortal; an animal's is mortal. This amounts to more than a passing tribute paid to theology by Abbé Condillac. It should be seen as a deep conviction that the origin of the unequal development of aptitudes must lie in a more fundamental ontological difference: "The faculties that we have been allotted . . . show that if we could penetrate the nature of those two substances [the souls of humans and those of animals], we should see that they are infinitely different. So our human soul is not of the same nature as that of an animal."[13] Clearly, it is not easy, even for an original mind, to shake off the influence exerted by the schemas of perception and thought peculiar to a dominant mode of identification.

Condillac's ambivalence is symptomatic of an essential paradox of modern naturalism, which persists in regarding an animal either as the lowest common denominator of a universal image of humanity or else as the perfect counterexample that makes it possible to define the specific nature of that humanity. Faced with the combined evidence of, on the one hand, physical similarities and, on the other hand, differences in their respective dispositions and aptitudes, the opportunities that a naturalist ontology offers for comparative speculation are strictly limited. One can either underline the connection between humans and animals mediated by their biological attributes (if necessary, adding a more or less large dose of common internal faculties to make the transition more gradual), or else one can relegate that physical continuity to the background and lay the emphasis primarily on the exceptional nature of the internal attributes by which humans are distinguishable from other existing beings. In the West, it is the second of those two attitudes that has for a long time prevailed and that is still largely dominant when it comes to defining the essence of humanity. As Ingold rightly points out,[14] philosophers have seldom asked, "What makes humans animals of a particular kind?," the typical preferred question about naturalism being "What makes humans different in kind from animals?" In the first of those questions, humanity is a particular form of animality defined by membership in the *Homo sapiens* species; in the second it is an exclusive state, a self-referential principle, a moral condition. Even the greatest naturalists have not avoided such prejudices. In his *Systema naturae* (1735), Linnaeus positions the *Homo* genus within a general taxonomic filiation based on contrasting anatomical features, but he nevertheless separates humans from all other species with the injunction "*Nosce te ipsum*": it is through reflective thought and by knowing the resources of one's soul that one will seize upon the distinctive essence of one's humanity.[15]

Hence the problem posed by an exact understanding of that old Western oxymoron: "human nature." If beings are reputed to be split into two, with their bodies and appetites on the animal side and their moral condition on the side of divinity or transcendent principles, how can they have a nature of their own? Should we, like Condillac and contemporary ethologists, regard that nature as the culmination of a series of faculties and behavior patterns that is also present, and easier to observe, in nonhuman animals—that is, as truly the nature of our species, which guarantees the singularity of our genome? Or should we, like anthropologists, consider it to be a predisposition to pass beyond our animality thanks, not so much to our possession of a soul or mind, but rather to our ability to produce cultural variations unaffected by genetic factors? By underlining interspecific continuities in physicality, the first approach makes it hard to account for intraspecific discontinuities in public expressions of interiority (i.e., in cultures). Meanwhile, by seeing *an-*

thropos above all as something that animals do not appear to be, namely an inventor of differences, the second approach forgets that he is also *Homo*, a unique biological organism. So it is not hard to imagine the astonishment of a Jivaro, a Cree, or a Chewong when faced with this strange, shifting human figure. They might well say, "How can you not see that our bodies and behavior patterns are very different from those of other organisms, even if they are made up of identical substances? And how can you be sure that animals do not possess an interiority identical to our own, even if we never catch them talking? Why should reflective consciousness, intentionality, and a moral and civil sense be limited to the human species, when so many indications show us that that is not the case?" An Australian Aboriginal might be just as puzzled, albeit for other reasons. "Why attach such importance to the literality of things?" he might say. "Why concentrate on the superficial differences of forms and capacities between existing beings when it is far simpler to think, rather in the manner of that Greek philosopher whom you rate so highly, that the world has always been divided into a whole collection of physical prototypes and spiritual generators of specific qualities, all of them fertile sources that bring forth those great aggregates of humans and nonhumans that you call hybrids simply because your ontological classifications differ from ours?"

Animal Cultures and Languages?

It is also true that the naturalist ontology has evolved along with the progress made by the sciences and that, contrary to common opinion and certain ill-informed essayists, scholars are now less quick to affirm an obvious discontinuity in the interiorities of humans and nonhumans. That is particularly the case of ethologists such as Donald Griffin, who has no hesitation in attributing conscious and subjective thought to animals on the strength of his observation of their behavior, which seems to testify to action prompted by real planning. This is now reputed to be possible by virtue of the animals' internal representation of their desired goals.[16] Griffin also points out that, despite its incomparable adaptability, human language does not really differ from the communication systems used by the great apes and certain birds and that it is perfectly legitimate to call these means of exchanging messages "language." Griffin is thus close to Condillac when, on the apparently more solid bases that evolutionary biology and cognitive ethology provide, he argues that there is a continuity of mental faculties between humans and animals, rejecting as an anthropocentric prejudice alien to scientific thought the idea that the two groups differ in their natures.[17] However, such views are by no means universally accepted among the community of ethologists:

a matter about which I shall have more to say later. For the moment, let me simply note that those views do at least have the merit of drawing attention to conflicts over the interpretation of modern ontology when this is confronted by possible empirical counterevidence and, in particular, to the foremost of those conflicts: the one in which naturalist monism clashes with cultural-ist dualism. For when contemporary continuists postulate mere differences of degree between the cognitive faculties of animals and those of humans, they always take as their comparative term for the process of evolution the figure representing humanity best known to psychologists, that is to say, a Western adult. And even if no scientist would these days dare to claim that peoples once called "primitive" represent an intermediary stage in between the great apes and ourselves, one cannot but be disturbed by the interest that evolutionary psychologists take—from afar, admittedly—in the present-day mental functions of hunter-gatherers, whom they implicitly assimilate to our Pleistocene ancestors and who, we are led to believe, must therefore be closer to nonhuman primates than any Stanford professor.[18]

When seen in the extremely long-term view of evolution, the cognitive differences between humans and animals are indeed only a matter of degree. And that is a legitimate view to support, provided one does not succumb to the pernicious form of ethnocentrism that involves extending the scale of gradations within *Homo sapiens sapiens* and scouring the Kalahari, the Canadian forests, or Amazonia for ethnographic examples that would illustrate a biobehavioral stage in cognitive adaptation, one as yet not too contaminated by "culture." In short and to be frank, the suggestion would be that where ideas are simple and limited in number and where the norms are rudimentary, it should be easier to understand how behavior and choices are dictated by natural selection. The point is that, even while rightly denouncing such prejudices and reminding us that present-day hunter-gatherers have undergone several tens of millennia of historical transformations and, in consequence, cannot be treated as fossilized evidence of the earliest stages of hominization, ethnologists cannot help falling for the other dogma of naturalism, which is essential to their own disciplinary field: that of the absolute uniqueness of humanity, the only species capable of internally differentiating itself by means of culture. In other words, while the anthropocentrism of ethnologists leads them to neglect the continuity of physicalities between humans and all other organisms, the acknowledgment of this continuity by modern gradualists renders them incapable of apprehending the discontinuity of interiorities other than as a variable external factor labeled "culture," the effects of which on cognitive aptitudes should be easier to evaluate among the least modern of human beings.

You may well say that this kind of dispute is by now on the way out, for it persists only at the level of spats between the rear guards of naturalist monism and culturalist dualism. And there is, indeed, no denying that the naturalist consensus amid which such altercations used to thrive nowadays seems somewhat undermined by a number of developments in the sciences, ethics, and law. Initially, it was probably under the influence of ethology, in particular that of the great apes, that modern ontology began to waver once one of its most generally recognized principles was called into question: namely the absolute uniqueness of humans as a species capable of producing cultural differences. Ethnologists do not, as yet, seem to have taken full measure of this revolution, despite the fact that it was to them that, in 1978, William Mc-Grew and Caroline Tutin addressed an iconoclastic article that was published in the prestigious British periodical of social anthropology *Man*. In it, they defined chimpanzees as cultural animals and called for a comparative ethnographical study of them. They argued that these animals that are so close to us genetically also satisfy most of the criteria by means of which we define culture: observation shows that new individual patterns of behavior appear in populations living in the wild, that they spread within the group and become durably implanted, and that they differ from other patterns of behavior present in other, quite distinct groups.[19]

This behavioral variability relates essentially to the techniques that Mc-Grew, a few years later, listed in a meticulous inventory in his classic work, *Chimpanzee Material Culture*. In this, he studies almost twenty instances of the use of tools. These range from fashioning probes for catching ants to cracking nuts with a hammerstone and anvil and also include the use of clubs and projectiles.[20] But it was in 1999 that a decisive stage was reached in bringing matters up to date, when eight famous ethologists, including McGrew, published in *Nature* a synthesis devoted to chimpanzee cultures.[21] This was a decisive step since being published in *Nature* amounts to the seal of orthodoxy where scientific results are concerned. And those results were by no means slender. On the basis of numerous independent observations carried out over an extended period of time and on groups of chimpanzees living far away from one another, the authors unambiguously show that different groups elaborate and transmit very different sets of techniques. Since these kinds of variations could apparently not be explained by the evolution of behavior adapting to ecological constraints, the authors were led to attribute distinctive cultures to the chimpanzees; in other words, they concluded that the latter were free to invent responses of their own to the needs of subsistence and a communal life.

This eruption of an animal species into the domain of culture, shattering though it was, was not unprecedented. Other examples of technical innova-

tions and of a diffusion of new behavior patterns among animals have long
been on record. Some even made it beyond the pages of scholarly publications and passed into folklore. One case in point is that of British tits, which,
in some localities, took to opening the milk bottles left by milkmen on their
customers' doorsteps; another is that of the macaques of the little island of
Koshima, in Japan, which wash their sweet potatoes before eating them, copy-
ing the example set by one particularly imaginative female. This phenomenon
was soon classified by Japanese primatologists in the categories of "proto-
culture," "preculture," or "infrahuman culture."[22] But the *Nature* article goes
further, recording a far wider range of distinctive behavioral traits and establishing beyond doubt the variability of the techniques that different groups of
chimpanzees employ in order to accomplish the same task.

But does this mean that one of the defensive locks of naturalism has been
blown now that it is recognized that humans are no longer the only animal
species capable of inventing and transmitting practices that are unaffected by
instinctive or environmental causes? That is by no means certain, for, according to naturalist ontology, the distinctiveness of humans rests primarily on
their recognized ability to produce cultural peculiarities by using the internal
faculties that characterize them. To cut naturalism down to size, it would be
necessary to show that the chimpanzees draw upon psychic resources identical to our own when they engage in cultural activities. But on this point
chimpanzee specialists have little to say. Behavioral ethology reveals observed
variations in the technical systems of wild animals and provides detailed descriptions of the procedures by means of which they are passed from one
individual to another. But it remains vague when it comes to the mental and
neurophysiological conditions necessary for doing this, except for referring to
a general aptitude for imitation, which, in the case of the great apes, may stem
from an ability to manipulate the attention of other individuals.[23] Meanwhile
though, experimental psychologists engaged in comparing social learning
among human children and captive chimpanzees challenge the very idea that
the animals may be capable of imitation. They stress that children learning
to use a tool make a representation of the aim of their instructor, whereas the
chimpanzees are content to regulate their behavior by watching one another
and then making successive readjustments in the course of repeated occurrences that prompt emulation.[24]

An intense debate is therefore ongoing between ethologists working in
the field, who are inclined to ascribe to the animals they are observing mental
properties that may account for their actions, and laboratory-bound ethologists, who claim that they find no trace of those hypothetical properties in the
animals that they study. Perhaps the question is, after all, irresolvable, for the

animals are not the same in the two cases, even if they do belong to the same species. To show that the behavior of wild chimpanzees is affected by cultural variations because their cognitive faculties are identical to our own, it would be necessary to have them perform, in a laboratory, various tasks that would make it possible to compare them systematically to humans. But behavioral ethologists point out, precisely, that a laboratory context is so particular, by reason of the interaction of the captive animals with the experimenters, that any results obtained in this way could hardly be generalized to cover chimpanzees in the wild. In short, recognition of the existence of "cultural" traditions among the chimpanzees is, in the short term, unlikely to threaten the central belief of naturalist ontology according to which humans are the only species that possesses the psychic equipment capable of engendering cultural differences.

However, that is not the end of the matter, for other branches of ethology also note disturbing similarities between the faculties of humans and those of animals and find them in a domain that closely concerns the dogma of discrimination on the grounds of interiority, since it involves the system for communicating internal states, which is what we call language, the conventional, intentional, and referential properties of which were for a long time considered by naturalist ontology to be the best distinctive sign of humanity. The fact is that many works on the semantics of animal communication seem to lead to the conclusion that humans should be denied exclusive possession of this precious attribute. The literature on this subject is both vast and riddled with controversy, so I shall limit myself to considering the data that is more or less generally accepted and shall exclude research into nonsonorous signals, such as the famous "bee-dance" and the tracking systems that animals leave for the guidance of their fellows.[25] Ever since Peter Marler's pioneering studies on the dialects of finches, it has been established beyond doubt that, first, the songs of certain birds are not stereotyped for the entire species but, on the contrary, manifest great individual and regional variations. The same point has been made for the sound signals of several species of terrestrial and marine mammals. In the case of birds and certain primates, we also know that their ability to conform to a repertory of vocalization that is specific to one particular dialect is something that is learned; in the case of singing birds, it is learned from an adult, usually the father. Furthermore, it now seems established that the sound signaling of certain birds adapts to circumstances (such as the presence or absence of a listener of the same species) and differs according to the messages to be transmitted: for instance, cries of alarm differ according to the type of predator located. This referential dimension has also been noted in the case of the cries emitted by vervet monkeys in Kenya.[26] It is therefore possible that intentionality may be behind the sound signals emitted by certain species with regard to an external referent (such as the detection of either food or a predator) since such signals vary in the frequency of their production depending on whether a conspecific animal is likely or not likely to hear them. This would appear to be confirmed by cases of manifest deception in the cries signaling supplies of food among domesticated chickens and among rhesus macaque monkeys. In such cases the cheater is punished if its trick is discovered.[27]

Even if the sound signals of animals do not attain the semantic and syntactic complexity and richness of human language, it is thus hard to continue to claim that they are no more than simple instinctive expressions. Arbitrary variations and innovations within a species, learning by imitating, a stable correspondence between a vocal signal and what is signified, and the possible intentionality of a message combined with anticipation of the effects of its reception: all these are features that suggest that we should accord to the communication systems of certain animal species the status of at least very elementary language.

What interior resources are animals believed to call upon when they activate this ability to produce a limited symbolic system? Are they endowed with a mind that renders them capable of controlling their behavior and making interventions in their environment by means of representations that they can transmit to their fellows? Are we ready to accept that some of them may have an interiority comparable to our own, which would open up a considerable breach in the citadel of naturalism? The fact is that, unlike Griffin, most cognitive ethologists jib at attributing true conscious thought to animals, preferring to regard animal language as the product of a genetic predisposition encoded in the brain, which Marler calls learning instinct, the characteristics of which vary according to the species' genome. He suggests that among songbirds, where these phenomena have been most fully studied, the capacity to recognize the sound signals of fellow conspecifics and the ability to learn a song are both innate and vary greatly from one species to another, while the phonological and syntactical characteristics that a subject selects in order to form its vocal repertory remain homogeneous within a single species.[28] Animal language would thus proceed from a neurophysiological cause, gradually rendered specific through experience, so there is no need to explain it by introducing the mediation of complex representations, that is to say, propositional attitudes thanks to which the animal would objectivize its own internal state (its emotions, beliefs, and aims) and would interpret those of other organisms present in its environment. In short, recognition that animal species do possess the ability to produce individual and collective variations by means of a conventional and referential system for exchanging sound signals in no way results from the attribution to nonhumans of an interiority identical to that of humans. On the contrary, it is based on reducing their linguistic faculty to a fundamental physicality—that of the genome, which epigenesis would then modulate within strict limits. Naturalism is thus safe and sound: to concede to birds and monkeys the privilege of being distinctive thanks to language is in reality to revert to the idea of the universality of nature.

Mindless Humans?

Let us now return to humans and the distinctive interiority with which they are traditionally credited in the ontology of the Moderns. Do we still adhere to such a principle other than as a popular belief? Do humans still live, as in Descartes's day, under the regime of a separation between a more or less immaterial mind and an objective physical and corporeal world—that is, a world whose properties are specified even before any knowledge of it is acquired? The overall answer is "yes," even among scholars. All the same, there are exceptions that we need to examine so as to evaluate how they might contribute to a rejection of the naturalist mode of identification. One current of cognitive science strongly opposed to dualism rejects the idea that we could be acting in the world and ascribing many meanings to it simply because each one of us is granted at birth the privilege of occupying some kind of command center to control behavior patterns and the handling of perceptive information, in the same way as Turing's computer did. One of the most novel attempts to bypass this standoff between a computational interior and an already-structured exterior is the theory of cognition as embodied action, which has been developed by Francisco Varela, Eleanor Rosch, and Evan Thompson.[29] On the basis of the philosophical intuitions of Merleau-Ponty, these authors defend the thesis that cognition stems from the experience of a subject endowed with a body that must guide its actions in situations that are constantly changing because they are modified by its activities. The subject's point of reference is no longer an autonomous mechanism dealing with information forthcoming from a world independent of perceptions. Instead, it is a whole combination of the subject's sensorimotor mechanisms that are constantly modulated by the events that occur in an environment from which the subject is not separate and which provides it with the opportunity to interact in various ways. With the support of experimental illustrations, these authors declare that, far from being reducible to a representational interiority that gives form to passively received stimuli, "cognitive structures emerge from the kinds of recurrent sensorimotor patterns that enable action to be perceptually guided."[30] The mind, if it can still be called a mind in such circumstances, becomes a system of emergent properties that result from continuous retroaction between an organism and its environment. So it has lost any intrinsic interiority and become no more than an attribute or epiphenomenon of physicality.

The ecological theory of vision proposed by the neurophysiologist James Gibson is even more radical, since it leads to the total elimination of the mind as a supposed seat of the higher mental functions.[31] In its classic form, the principle of "affordance" developed by Gibson has become familiar: the environment of animals, humans included, possesses properties that are irreducible to the physical world or to phenomenological experience since they stem from possibilities, or "affordances," that an observer perceives there for engaging in action in accordance with his or her sensorimotor capacities. For a human or a sheep, for example, the edge of a cliff presents, on the one hand, the possibility of a walk along it and, on the other hand, a fall into the void, whereas for a vulture this spot might invite it to take off in flight. The fact that it is possible to engage in a variety of actions in this place is not an intrinsic property of cliffs themselves that might be studied by a geomorphologist. The particular attributes of these features of the landscape only become what they are for organisms that are able to make use of them. Gibson furthermore maintains that there exist enough invariances in the topology of the ambient light to make it possible to specify the properties of the environment (and these include "affordances") without the mediation of any internal representations. Perception is thus immediate and consists in detecting those optical invariances and also the affordances that they reveal; and this happens independently of any action on the part of the animal, since affordances are always there, ready to be perceived. Such a redefinition of perception in its turn implies a redefinition of the operations of the mind, to the extent that the extraction and abstraction of optical invariances by any organism stem from both perception and from knowledge, the latter being simply an extension of the former. It is thus no longer necessary to invoke an intellect in order to account for processes such as memory, thought, inference, judgment, and anticipation. As Gibson remarks, "I am convinced that none of them can ever be understood as an operation of the mind."[32] So it's goodbye to that mysterious interiority! Away with those strict distinctions between human animals and nonhuman ones! Gone is the structural coupling of a sensorimotor mechanism and the environment! All that remain are optical regularities awaiting actualization by a suitable receptor.

With this ecological theory of perception of his, Gibson offers a powerful and coherent alternative to the form of cognitive realism that has for several centuries constituted the virtually unchallenged epistemological regime of modern naturalism. He does not set up an autonomous subject endowed with a mind capable of processing sensorial information extracted from an objective world by means of representations that are a combination of innate dispositions and culturally acquired abilities. Instead, he invites us to regard knowledge as a schooling of attention undertaken by an organism engaged in the daily realization of tasks whose successful accomplishment requires only a continually enriched ability to detect the most striking aspects of its environment and to adjust to them increasingly well. It is not hard to understand the fascination that this program has exerted on authors such as Ingold and Berque, confronted as they are, in the societies that they study, by modes of relating to the environment whose local formulations hardly fit in with the classic dualism of the world and the mind, subjects and objects, intellectual activity and sensation.[33] Although Gibson himself has remained evasive with regard to the social and cultural implications of his ecological theory of perception, this theory does make it possible to envisage a very different way of apprehending human sociability. It can be seen no longer as a structuring of experience made possible by a filtering of sensible data by means of a system of collective representations, but as a state that existed prior to any cultural objectivization and that is based on the practical engagement of bodies which can detect the same affordances and which, on that account, can react in similar fashion in any given environment.

Theories of knowledge that postulate bodies plugged directly into the environment thus seem to topple the entire edifice of naturalism. A mind is no longer a requisite for human action and thought; cultures are no longer seen as substantive and well-differentiated blocks of normative representations and patterns of behavior waiting to be inculcated into individuals; and animals can be raised to the dignity of subjects since they, like us, are organisms whose sensorimotor faculties offer them the possibility of understanding the world. In short, that distinctive interiority completely disappears, giving way to a harmonious continuity of physicalities. However, this effacement of ontological discrimination that is based on the criterion of the mind leads to a new exclusion, for it concerns only one category of existing beings, those lucky enough to have at their disposition a body capable of perception and movement. Inanimate nonhumans remain pure objects even if, like computers, they can execute mental operations similar to ours. By making thought the product of an interaction between perception and action that is gradually laid down in a body involved in a specific *Umwelt*, anti-mentalists deny computers any ontological affinity with humans (or animals): not because they lack intentionality or consciousness of the self, which is the classic argument developed by the philosophy of mind, but because they are, as it were, purely minds, and it is the body, not some neuronal or electronic processor, that is home to the kind of memory of the experience of self that constitutes subjectivity. Even robots capable of modulating their actions following an autonomous learning period find no favor in their eyes, for their mechanism is inspired by connectionist models of the mind. And, as Ingold writes, connectionism "is still grounded in the Cartesian ontology that is basic to the entire project of cognitive science—an ontology that divorces the activity of the mind from that of the body in this world."[34] Having been eliminated as a factor of ontological exclusion at the heart of complex organisms, interiority thus resurfaces as a default attribute of a class of existing beings. The "mock-mind" that computers possess will never make them comparable to humans, precisely because humans do not have minds, at least not in the form of a computing mechanism that is independent from a body. It is thus the sham interiority that is ascribed to certain nonhumans that tips them into radical otherness, and it is in the name of that interiority, which can no longer separate us from animals since neither they nor we possess it, that new ontological distinctions are invented.

Beneath its iconoclastic appearance, the new phenomenology of perception thus renders visible, as in a negative image, traits characteristic of the naturalist ontology that it claims to undermine. Behind an apparent continuity of physicalities (between humans and animals) that is no longer broken by any discrimination on the grounds of a mind that is now abolished lurks a new and contradictory discontinuity of interiorities between, on the one hand, machines that possess interiorities because human artifice so designed them and, on the other, human and nonhuman animals, which, given their intrinsic vitality, can dispense with interiorities altogether. A comparison with the animist mode of identification is most instructive at this point. When an Achuar or a Cree says that an artifact or an inorganic element in the environment has a "soul," what he means by this is that those entities possess an intentionality of their own that is of the same nature as that of humans and so does not stem from the type of molecular substratum in which it is lodged nor from the type of process through which it eventually comes into existence. Differences of form and behavior are recognized, but they do not constitute sufficient criteria for excluding a blowpipe or a mountain from the advantage of a shared interiority. In contrast, when one says that an animal resembles us because it thinks with its body but that a computer, even if it speaks and plays chess, does not resemble us because its parody of interiority is not lubricated by vitality, what returns to the forefront of the argument is a distinction between an objectivized physicality (a machine) and a subjectivizing physicality (a body). In other words, whatever the anti-cognitivists may claim, what we have here is the barely readjusted topography of the extremely dualist distribution of existing beings between subjects and objects.

At the opposite extreme from theories of embodied or ecological cognition, a tendency fueled by recent developments in the neurosciences has likewise challenged the naturalist schema of an autonomous human interiority. It does so by dissolving that interiority into the internal properties of physicality. However, the material substrata in the two cases differ, for now thought is no longer the result of a link between a sensorimotor apparatus and an environment but is the product of the activity of the brain, an organ long associated with the higher mental functions. Ever since the earliest hesitant pronouncements of phrenology, there has certainly been nothing new about the idea that mental states may be reducible to the mechanisms of cerebral activity or, more generally, of the central nervous system. But the progress made by neurobiology and the attention that psychologists and philosophers pay to it have, over recent years, made it possible to envisage this hypothesis with greater lucidity and wariness than in the days of Gall and Broca. Most biologists do express doubt regarding the possibility of an absolute reductionism that would make it possible to fuse into a universal theory any explanation of the behavior of all physical entities, humans included. Those adopting an intermediate position, traditionally known as "physicalist," are content to postulate that all elements of reality, including mental states, stem from material processes or states that it is possible to study experimentally. Thus, to cite Jean-Pierre Changeux, "To consider mental processes as physical events is not to take an ideological stand but simply to adopt the most reasonable and, what is more important, the most generative working hypothesis."[35] It is true that if one accepts the proposition that there can be no causal efficacy between events of any kind without there being some physical relation between them, then the mental event that consists in the formation of a representation could not come about without the help of a suitable material instrument, in this case the brain. The idea of a separation between mental activity and neuronal activity becomes obsolete: if mental phenomena intervene causally in the behavior of an individual in whom they are lodged, which is hard to deny, those mental phenomena must possess a physical dimension that can be described in molecular and physicochemical terms. Clearly, despite the abyss that seems to separate them from Gibson, the physicalists believe no more than he does in the existence of an immaterial interiority that produces mental representations. To quote Changeux again: "What is the point of speaking of 'mind' or 'spirit'?"[36]

All the same, even when they subscribe to conflicting theories, philosophers, even Monist ones, are more prudent on this point than neurophysiolo-

gists. Donald Davidson, whose analyses have been so influential among supporters of a materialistic theory of mind, thus maintains that physical reality
and mental reality possess heterogeneous properties: physical reality can be
objectivized by a causally self-contained theory, whereas mental reality cannot, in that an explanation of the formation of mental states depends upon
imputing to the observed subject preexisting characteristics, such as the fact
that he holds as true the propositions that he produces and that they are indeed true. Davidson calls this methodological necessity "the principle of charity." Because the contents of the thoughts of others are always interpreted on
the basis of their principle of rationality and coherence, no data independent
of those interpretative norms can provide the theory with a fixed point, since
those norms come to constitute the data to be interpreted. That is why Davidson supports a thesis of occasional physicalism according to which a mental
event is indeed identical to a physical event, just as Changeux maintains, but
only in isolated instances, without it ever being possible to be sure that that
coincidence is reproduced in a series of repeated occurrences, which would
justify the formulation of a law. So it is claimed that a mental event "supervenes" upon a cerebral one to the extent that the former is determined by the
latter, even though its properties remain irreducible to those of the physical
event upon which it supervenes.[37]

Although this notion of "supervenience" is borrowed from Aristotle, it
seems too contradictory to serve as the basis of a satisfactory philosophical
interpretation of a thought being determined by the brain. As Vincent
Descombes has pointed out, the supervening element is added to something
that it cannot complete, so it oscillates between two statuses, "that of something additional and that of something superfluous."[38] At the very most, one
may interpret this as Quine does, in a minimal fashion, as a supervenience
of mental differences upon physical differences, which is a complicated way
of translating the idea that every mental difference corresponds to a physical
difference. But whereas a physical difference may be measured, it is not always
possible to measure a mental difference, for mental states are of a different
nature from physical ones, given that they do not succeed one another in the
same fashion. To be sure, cerebral imaging makes it possible to correlate the
production of certain statements and the resolution of certain problems with
the activation of certain parts of the brain, but this is not possible in the case
of many ordinary mental states that cannot be divided into separate temporal
units and that philosophers of mind call *qualia*. I feel happy this morning because the weather is fine and I have received some good news (at least, this is
how I interpret my state). But when did this state start and when does it end?

Is it continuous or discontinuous? At what point is it present in my consciousness, and at what point is it no longer present? This is a mental event that one
hopes will be frequent and that may influence my behavior in a causal fashion, yet it would be very difficult to make it correspond to a neuronal event,
even occasionally and in accordance with the principle of supervenience. In
short, even if we grant physicalist explanations the benefit of the doubt, there
seems to be still a long way to go before those explanations will be capable
of equating all the properties of human interiority with neural mechanisms.

However, that is not the point here. In no way is my purpose to pass judgment on contemporary theories of cognition at an empirical, philosophical,
or epistemological level. Rather, it is to examine to what extent those theories
could undermine the foundations of modern naturalist ontology. And, as we
have seen, physicalism still falls short of achieving such an objective. In the
strategy that it adopts in order to do away with the distinctive interiority of
humans (and solely of humans, for most materialist philosophers of mind
are, like Davidson, not prepared to concede thought to animals),[39] physicalism nevertheless manifests a trait that is characteristic of the naturalist ontology. The latter takes as its starting point the principle that the specificity of
humans stems from the fact that they can differentiate themselves from one
another, both as individuals and as groups, thanks to an immaterial faculty
that is internal to each subject although partly modulated by the values and
representations peculiar to each culture. The only way to challenge the individual and collective existence of this interiority, which has so long eluded direct observation, is therefore to de-singularize the mind by reducing it to the
universal material properties of the brain, in other words to dissolve interiority in a complementary thesis of naturalism according to which differences
in physicality are differences of degree, not of nature. Hence, the role played
in this task, both in psychology and in the neurosciences, by techniques of
functional cerebral imaging that make it possible to map the brain's activities becomes increasingly important. If it is reducible to cerebral operations,
human interiority sheds much of its mystery and density since it is now possible, by at last making it partly visible, to strip it of the major attribute that
justified its hypothetical existence. Nevertheless, positron emission tomog-
raphy and functional magnetic resonance imaging are still not able to allow
us to see in vivo such obstinate remains of interiority as consciousness of the
self, the individuation of meanings, and how a cultural representation affects
a propositional judgment. So it seems that the mind can still look forward to
a number of days of serenity before it unveils its physical nature completely to
the inquisitorial gaze of ideography.

The Rights of Nature?

It is in quite different domains that naturalist ontology may run the most serious risks of being whittled away, namely the domains of moral philosophy
and law. The discontinuity between humans and other existing beings is occasioned in modern ideology by the concept of a doubly subjective interiority:
consciousness of the self produces subjectivity, then subjectivity makes moral
autonomy possible, and moral autonomy is the foundation for responsibility
and freedom, which are the attributes of a subject in the sense of an individual with rights and duties to the community of his or her peers. Plants
and animals, which are traditionally defined as lacking those properties, are
therefore excluded from civic life. Because they lack the status of a subject it
is not possible to enter into political or economic relations with them.[40] But
this subordination of nonhumans to the decrees of an imperialistic humanity
is increasingly being challenged by moral and legal theorists working toward
an environmental ethic liberated from the prejudices of Kantian humanism.

It is mainly in the United States, Australia, Germany, and the Scandinavian
countries that, since the 1970s, a new strand of moral thought on the relations
between humans and their natural environment has emerged. France and
the Latin nations have essentially distanced themselves from this movement,
which they treat with a mixture of irony and suspicion, regarding it, at best, as
an insult to reason and technological progress and, at worst, as a reactionary
attempt to undermine the universality of the ideals of the Enlightenment and
the inalienable rights attached to the person of a human.[41] I will not attempt,
here, to disentangle the complex reasons that in certain countries have favored
the emergence of a truly moral approach to the duties of humans toward the
whole collectivity of living entities and the rights that this collectivity might
intrinsically possess. Protestantism, with its combined values of individual responsibility and community ethics, has no doubt played a role here, as has the
very particular function played in the formation of national consciousness
in the United States and Germany by a variety of identifications with nature
in the wild, which may strengthen an inclination to regard the simple life, in
contact with an environment that is innocent of affectation, as the best antidote to the artifices of a society that is forgetful of the virtues of *Gemeinschaft*.
At this point, let us be content simply to recognize that environmental ethics
prosper above all in countries where Anglo-Saxon Puritanism has prevailed
and in the northern regions of Europe, which, in the nineteenth century, saw
the emergence of diverse variants of the *Naturphilosophie* to which the land of
Descartes and Comte has remained obdurately impermeable.

But in truth environmental philosophies derive their inspiration from a variety of very different sources. It has become customary to distinguish within them between, on the one hand, extensionist ethics that propose to extend to a greater or lesser range of nonhumans the benefit of moral consideration that used to be attached solely to humans and, on the other, holistic ethics in which the emphasis is placed on the responsibilities of humans in the preservation of a balance between ecosystemic communities, which is seen as an imperative in itself—that is to say, quite apart from the status and future of the entities that compose those communities.[42]

Extensionist ethics are somewhat anthropocentric, although not all to the same degree. Thus, Peter Singer includes in the domain of the application of practical morality a large number of nonhumans on the grounds that they, like humans, are capable of feeling pleasure and pain and so have interests of their own that should be taken into account.[43] The rights that stem from this situation should be comparable to some of those that protect humans— notably respect for life and the proscription of cruelty—even if the origin of those rights does not stem from a specifically human attribute that could be extended to animals. Singer's ethics is based on the utilitarian doctrine of Bentham: if one accepts that it is in the interest of all sensitive beings to protect themselves from suffering and perpetuate themselves in life, then to recognize that interest only in the case of humans constitutes "speciesism," an attitude analogous to racism in that it establishes unfounded discriminations between classes of existing beings that all have the same properties. However, in the course of time Singer has moved toward a position that is definitely more anthropocentric and eventually asserts that the life of certain sensitive beings is intrinsically more valuable on account of the fact that they are en- dowed with faculties that are clearly derived from those that naturalism im- putes to humans, such as consciousness of self, a capacity to think and project oneself into the future, and the ability to communicate complex information. This affects only a very small number of animals, chimpanzees among them, which thus become invested with the status of persons by reason of their proximity to humans with regard to their interiority. The logical and strongly contested corollary to this position is that humans who lose such faculties as a result of serious cerebral lesions or malformations may not fully rate as persons and therefore have no automatic right to life.[44]

Although Singer's ethics is presented as a radical criticism of the anthro- pocentric thesis that reserves the juridical rights of the status of a person solely for the human species, it cannot be denied that it does not fundamentally call into question the basic principles of the naturalist ontology. In fact, it exploits all its possibilities, since the "patho-centric" argument for extending the right to life to sensitive beings rests upon stressing a similarity in the physical di-

mension of existing beings at least in the case of organisms endowed with
a central nervous system, while the extension of the status of a person only
to certain animals is based on the fact that these share with "normal" humans an interiority of the same nature. The ontological boundaries have certainly slipped a bit, giving rise to crucial and passionate debates over what it
is that justifies the right to existence for humans and nonhumans. However,
this movement has developed in predictable directions that are set out by
the guidelines of naturalism: a physical continuity, on the one hand, and a
discontinuity in the mental faculties, on the other. So the animals excluded
from the restricted circle of persons remain confined to an inferior position,
given that they are not recognized to possess the quality of autonomous subjects. They may be objects of moral concern on the part of humans, but they
do not possess rights that they could defend. As for plants and abiotic elements in the environment, since they lack sensibility they remain condemned
to the mechanical and impersonal fate that naturalism used to reserve for all
nonhumans.

The ethics of the animal condition developed by Tom Regan is definitely
more inspired by anthropocentricity than that of Singer. It nevertheless distances itself more vigorously from the ontological conventions of naturalism.
Regan sets out from an overtly individualist position: the sources of morality
and rights are to be found only in individuals—that is, in beings that possess
an inherent value in that they are true "subjects-of-a-life" and not simply the
objects of the moral consideration of humans, which is always tainted by a
condescending commiseration. To be recognized as a moral agent, it is necessary to possess, if not the reason required to understand the law and the
freedom to regulate one's behavior with reference to it (as modern theories of
law insist), at least a set of abilities that testify to an autonomy of action and
a form of intentionality: consciousness of the self, an ability to act in accordance with the aims that one sets oneself, and the possibility of forming representations.[45] Regan, who is more generous than most ethologists, imputes
such attributes to a small number of mammals, in particular primates, which
thus become fully juridical subjects, not simply beneficiaries of the protective
rights conceded to them by sympathetic humans.

To be sure, just as for Singer, it is by virtue of the internal properties that
they are believed to possess in common with humans that these animals can
switch categories in this way. But the new status that they acquire by virtue
of their own merits opens a more serious breach in the naturalistic mode of
identification since they are finally recognized to possess the quality of a subject, just like humans, and this is an intrinsic distinctive characteristic. That
being said, this reordering of ontological boundaries is far from rendering

this extended variant of naturalism proposed by Regan comparable in every way to the distribution of properties produced by animism. That is because, in the first place, an interiority similar to that of humans is imputed to a few animals only, by reason of indications that suggest convincingly that they do indeed possess one, rather than, as in the case of animism, on account of a principle according to which, given that subjectivity is not always discernible from its empirical effects, there is no valid reason to deny it to plants and artifacts. Second, it is because the interiority that Regan attributes to great apes does not make them into collective subjects since, for him, only individuals can give rise to rights, unlike animism's tendency to regard all kinds of classes of existing beings as communities sui generis, organized according to principles analogous to those that govern humans. And, finally, it is also because here physicality does not play a disjunctive role; only interiority does so, in contrast to the distinctions that animism establishes between collectives of subjects by reason of their anatomical equipment and the behavior patterns that this induces. Even Regan's extensionism would probably seem absurd in the eyes of a Makuna or a Montagnais. Regan insists that certain animals should be protected for what they are, namely subjects, but at the same time accepts that, to claim their rights, they need representation. The Montagnais or the Makuna have long accepted that most animals are subjects, but it is by very reason of this essential autonomy that it becomes absurd to infringe upon it by involving oneself at all costs in their defense. Clearly, the misunderstandings between, on the one hand, associations bent on protecting wild fauna and, on the other, the autochthonous hunters of Amazonia and the subarctic are not about to be dissipated.

In contrast, holistic ethical systems seem closer to animism, for they lay the emphasis not on individuals or species endowed with particular properties but on the need to preserve the common good and not inconsiderately upset the relations of interdependence that unite all the organic and abiotic components of an environment. All that matters is the connection of all the parts to the whole, for the only value and significance of each element in that whole lie in the position that it occupies in the economy of vital exchanges. However, on account of their greater disruptive capacity, humans are invested with a decisive moral responsibility in the maintenance of ecological balances. It is a role that they can fulfill only if they understand their position in the chain of life. And such understanding of those interactions can be attained only by humbly observing nature and endeavoring to identify with the obscure teleonomy that animates each of the actors in the great terrestrial community.

This is an endeavor exemplified by Aldo Leopold, the great inspirational figure behind holistic environmental philosophy, as expressed in his rightly

famous *Sand County Almanach*, published posthumously in 1947.[46] Leopold
was a forestry engineer trained at Yale and an ecologist well versed in the
management of natural resources. Furthermore, ever since adolescence he
had also been a hunter and had never suffered from any guilty conscience on
that account. It was as an experienced hunter, rather than as a philosopher
or a moralist, that he apprehended the complexities of the environment and
tried to shape his own concept of it. It finds expression in an allusive, even
allegorical style, in the course of reminiscences evoking forty years of his intimate and diverse experiences of nature in America. One fundamental guiding
theme runs through these reminiscences: knowing how to hunt is knowing
how to find one's game, and knowing how to find it is knowing how to adopt
the point of view of the animal that one is seeking, perceiving things as that
animal does and putting oneself in its place. In short, it involves abandoning
a superior vantage point in order to seize, from within, upon this tangled
web of destinies and desires that weaves together the world in motion. Such
an attitude is reminiscent of the manner in which Amerindian hunting communities envisage the metamorphoses that mark relations between humans
and nonhumans, such as exchanges of viewpoints in the course of which each
party, modifying the observational position imposed by its body, endeavors
to slip into the skin of the other in order to see things from its point of view.

All the same, we should not push this analogy too far, for the technical
and cognitive needs peculiar to solitary hunting support it only partially. The
fact is that Leopold's "land ethic" in no sense calls into question the ontological distributions of naturalism, which it, on the contrary, accepts without a
qualm. To be sure, in order for humans to form a fitting idea of their place
and responsibility in synecological interactions, it may be useful for them un-
pretentiously to imagine the aims and lifestyle of the other components in this
superorganism that they help to animate. Hence, there is an educational need
to—as Leopold puts it—"think like a mountain," the better to evaluate the
balance between wolves, deer, and vegetation to be respected on its slopes; or
to imagine the odyssey of an atom carried through the cycle of its successive
incorporations by a kind of inchoate intentionality.[47] But all this is a matter of
experiencing salutary thoughts of a kind to give substance and a live urgency
to abstract ecological learning; in no sense does it constitute a profession of
animist faith. Even if the poetic license taken by his formulations may sometimes prompt interpretations that are ambiguous, Leopold never does impute
to nonhumans an interiority analogous to that of humans, for the awareness
of a future with which he sometimes credits them is nothing but a metaphor
for the general teleonomy of nature, which, he believes, reverberates within
each one of them. Above all, he never ascribes to animals or to plants any

ability to lead the existence of a species characterized by cultural conventions, since, for him, the latter are strictly the prerogative of humans. Leopold in effect adheres without argument to the usual version of the naturalist schema, together with its essential dualism: "Wilderness is the raw material out of which man has hammered the artefact called civilization. . . . [The wilderness] was very diverse and the resulting artifacts are very diverse. . . . The rich diversity of the world's cultures reflects a corresponding diversity in the wilds that gave them birth."[48] Nothing much new there, clearly.

No doubt we should not expect a forestry engineer of the early twentieth century, however perceptive and original in his thinking, to detach himself totally from the mental frameworks within which he was trained. It is true that Leopold's followers have managed to disengage themselves from the misleading symmetries of dualism and of partitioned finalisms to which their mentor sometimes succumbed. But they then reverted to the more robust certainties of the natural sciences and derived a model for moral action from the laws of ecological interdependence. The most interesting of them, John Baird Callicott, defends a vision of ecosystemic solidarity that Durkheim would not have disowned.[49] Although he rejects the idea that the biotic community may be regarded as a society, the properties that he imputes to it put one very much in mind of the conditions for the exercise of organic solidarity, in particular the fact that the unity of the whole exists independently from the individuals who compose it and whose belonging to that whole implies contractual obligations vis-à-vis its members, on account of the system of functions that they fulfill. The ecosystem comes to transcend its elements and these, both human and nonhuman (and herein lies the great difference from Durkheim), are stripped of any ontological substance and so become mere cogs in a network of relations in a constant state of reorganization. Nature and culture lose their raison d'être in such a cosmology, which is no longer biocentric or anthropocentric. Instead, it is ecocentric, that is, subject to the regulatory mechanisms of energy in the environment. That being said, some process of evaluation must take place in order for the totality to behave in a moral fashion and preserve its systemic integrity, or at least the ability to regenerate itself, to the possible detriment of one or other of its components. What are needed are thus skilled agents capable of conferring a value upon that which intrinsically has none. And it comes as no surprise to find that these are recruited solely from among humans, preferably those who are well versed in the natural sciences. Inevitably, one gets a sense of déjà vu: human subjects who possess a rational interiority and a moral conscience and who recognize the essential principle of physical continuity and the material interdependence of all entities in the world assume the mission of preserving that continuity and that interdependence, often in the face of opposition from their fellows; and they do all this in the superior interest of all, which they alone are capable of discerning and representing. That could be an excellent definition of naturalist ontology seen from the point of view of all its positive practical consequences.

The point of my critical analysis should not be misunderstood. Some people, myself among them, may see in an ecocentric ethics such as that favored by Callicott a philosophical foundation solid enough for humans to engage in a less conflictual coexistence with nonhumans and to endeavor in this way to erase the devastating effects of our lack of concern and our voracity for the global environment, for which we are mainly responsible, given that our means of acting upon it bear no comparison to those of other actors in the terrestrial community. However, that is not the concern of the present book. My ambition in examining the ontological consequences of a variety of environmental ethics was simply to measure the possible differences between them in relation to the habitual norms of naturalism in order to assess how likely they are to subvert those norms. However, there is no avoiding the fact that, no more than the categorial shifts effected by ethology and the cognitive sciences, have those introduced by environmental philosophies really endangered the typical organization of naturalism. At least, the variations that I have noted are not of a kind to suggest the emergence of an utterly new mode of identification or even of one comparable to those already encountered.

All the same, the very existence of such variations and their increasing numbers over the past decades in themselves suggest that the naturalist schema can no longer be taken for granted (which is why a book such as this one has now become possible) and that a phase of ontological recomposition may be beginning, the results of which are as yet unpredictable. It is suggested that proof of this is provided by recent evolutions in the law, a domain that no doubt does testify more faithfully than any philosophical or ethical treatises to a mutation in the principles that govern our statuses, our practices, and our relations with the world. A thousand leagues away from the arguments between the partisans of animal liberation and the defenders of Kantian anthropocentrism, the jurist Jean-Pierre Marguénaud has recently shown that, in French law at least, domestic animals, tamed ones, and those kept in captivity already possess intrinsic rights just as moral persons do, given that the law recognizes interests of their own, that is, interests distinct from those of whoever is their master, and it also provides them with the technical possibility of a voice to represent their cause.[50] Alongside crimes and offenses against persons, against property, and against the state, the new penal code has created a new category of infractions, those against domesticated animals, thereby showing that, although not yet defined fully as persons, these are already no longer considered as goods, that is, as things. This intermediate status is probably destined to evolve in penal law into a more clearly defined personification, for there is nothing to prevent non–wild animals from being invested with a juridical personality in the same way as any moral persons or corporate bodies recognized to have interests of their own and the means to defend them. As for organs that might legally represent the distinct interests of what Marguénaud calls an "animal person," even if they run contrary to those of their master, many such organs have already sprung up in the shape of animal-protection associations. Without the nonspecialist public realizing it and in anticipation of the establishment of the necessary jurisprudence, dogs, cats, cows (whether mad or not), budgerigars, and the chimpanzees in our zoos would now appear, like us, to be able to assert their rights to life and well-being; and this is no longer by virtue of the humanitarian reasons used to justify the former Grammont law of 1850, namely, the public scandal that could be caused by their mistreatment. Rather, it is because they have become, if not quite legal subjects, at least quasi persons whose prerogatives are clearly derived from those that we ourselves are recognized to possess. The concession of a legal personality to animals that are dependents of humans certainly does not call naturalist ontology into question, since the discontinuity of moral faculties remains unchallenged. Nevertheless, the extension of the status of a subject to a few nonhumans at least shows that there was nothing "natural" about the discrimination of which they used to be the objects.

Naturalism's supreme cunning ploy and the purpose of the term that I use for it are to make it seem to be "natural": partly because the divisions that it authorizes between the world's various entities are presented as spontaneous self-evidence in the eyes of those who use them as the principle for their schematization of experience (as is also the case with other modes of identification), but above all because the undeniable character of those self-evidences stems from the fact that they are said to be founded upon nature. This is an irrefutable argument when it comes to disqualifying rival ontologies. That is how it is that the naturalist formula turns out to be a total inversion of the animist formula: in animism, the universality of the condition of a moral subject and the relations between humans and nonhumans that this authorizes override the physical heterogeneity of the various classes of existing beings; in contrast, in naturalism, human society and its cultural contingencies are subordinated to the universality of the laws of nature. Darwin proposed the canonical version of this incorporation of culture in nature in *The Descent of Man* when he sought to extend to human societies the theory of descent modified by natural selection by suggesting that the latter had affected not only organic variations but also social instincts, in particular the obligation to be of assistance, otherwise known as altruism.[51] A number of divergent interpretations of this inclusion of the cultural properties of humanity in the history of nature have certainly been proposed. In the cases of sociobiology and social Darwinism in the mode of Spencer, this exegesis has been restrictive and reductionist, but under the pen of Patrick Tort, it takes on a more liberal and subtle character, for in Darwin he detects "a reversive effect of evolution," that is to say, a specific effect of natural selection when it is applied to humans: here, it favors a form of social life "whose progressive advance to what we call 'civilization' tends increasingly, through the interplay of morality and institutions, to exclude eliminatory types of behavior."[52] But never mind those variations, since the general idea that culture can only be understood in reference to nature has spread far beyond its Darwinian formulation and has been converted into a basic principle of naturalist ontology. (The anthropological effects of this have been briefly examined in chapter 3.) And if the opposite idea of a "cultural construction of nature" is currently enjoying a degree of favor, it is at the price of an offhand ignorance of the regressive paradox that such a notion implies: to construct nature within culture, there has to be a precultural nature that can be adapted to such a construction; there has to be a brute fact that is imaginable without the meanings and laws that convert it into a social reality; there has to be a precondition fated stubbornly to reemerge every time that it is believed that, by reversing the values of the dualist schema, it is possible to reduce it to a conventional representation.[53] For if nature became completely cultural, there would be no reason for it to exist, nor for the culture by means of which this process is supposed to be accomplished, for the disappearance of the object to be mediated presupposes the pointlessness of any mediating agent. Whether nature is *natura naturans* or *natura naturata*, it thus reaffirms *a contrario* its dominance and culture's subordination.

9

The Dizzying Prospects of Analogy

Naturalism and animism are all-inclusive hierarchical schemas that are the polar opposites of each other. In the one, the universality of physicality extends its system to cover the contingencies of interiority; in the other, the generalization of interiority becomes a means of attenuating the effect of differences of physicality. Totemism, in contrast, appears as a symmetrical schema characterized by a double continuity of both interiorities and physicalities, the logical complement to which can only be another symmetrical schema, but one in which a double series of differences are regarded as equivalent. I have called this "analogism." By this I mean a mode of identification that divides up the whole collection of existing beings into a multiplicity of essences, forms, and substances separated by small distinctions and sometimes arranged on a graduated scale so that it becomes possible to recompose the system of initial contrasts into a dense network of analogies that link together the intrinsic properties of the entities that are distinguished in it. This way of distributing the differences and correspondences detectable on the world's surface is very common. For example, it finds expression in the correlations between microcosms and macrocosms that are established by Chinese geomancy and divination, in the idea, common in Africa, that social disorders are capable of provoking climatic catastrophes, and also in the medical theory of signatures that bases the etiology and therapy of illnesses upon the apparent resemblances between, on the one hand, substances or natural objects and, on the other, symptoms and parts of the human body. What is immediately striking in such systems is the inventiveness deployed in order to track, for practical purposes, all the similarities and resonances that observation offers for inference: the quest for well-being or for the causes of misfortune is based on the hypothesis that the qualities, movements, and structural modifications of certain existing beings exert an influence on the destiny of humans or are themselves influenced by the behavior of those humans. This obsession with analogy becomes a dominant characteristic that is affirmed with a vigor that becomes increasingly manic the more its effects in daily life are reputed to be crucial. That is why the label "analogical" seemed to me the best suited to designate this schema.

However, analogy here is no more than a result or a consequence. It becomes possible and thinkable only if the terms that it compares are initially distinct and if the ability to detect similarities between things and thereby partially to remove their isolation is applied to single items. By bringing together through an operation of thought that which was previously separate, any resemblance certainly suspends the difference for a moment, but only to create a new one, this time in the relation of objects to themselves, for they become alien to their earlier identity as soon as they intermingle in the mirror of correspondence and imitation. In short, analogy is a hermeneutic dream of plenitude that arises out of a sense of dissatisfaction. Noting that the general segmentation of the world's components is based on a scale of small differences, it nurtures the hope of weaving these slightly heterogeneous elements into a web of meaningful affinities and attractions that gives the appearance of constituting a continuity. All the same, the ordinary state of the world is one of differences infinitely multiplied, while resemblance is the hoped-for means of making that world intelligible and bearable.

The Chain of Being

An early sketch of what might constitute an analogical ontology is provided by the concept of a world plan and structure that was close to hegemonic in Europe throughout the Middle Ages and the Renaissance. It is generally known as "the great chain of being." Working back to trace the genesis of this remarkable configuration, Arthur Lovejoy detects its origin in Plato, in what he calls "the principle of plenitude." He suggests that this results from a tension between, on the one hand, the infinite multiplicity of eternal Ideas that form immutable archetypes of which every material and immaterial entity is simply a lesser copy and, on the other, the synoptic unity conferred upon one of those Ideas in particular, that of the Good, upon which the existence of the world is founded and which showers its perfection upon all the entities that the world contains.[1] Thanks to this dynamic essence, no potentiality of being, however insignificant, can fail to be realized. The cosmos is thus better—that is to say, closer to the ideal of the Beautiful, the Good, and the True—the greater the quantity and diversity of the distinct things that it contains. To this cosmos saturated a priori with all conceivable beings, Aristotle adds the rigorous hierarchies of his natural history: the genera are fixed, the species are indivisible, and living creatures are arranged in accordance with the degree of their perfection, each in its place in a *scala naturae* that also takes account of the differences in the functions of the types of souls with which each organism is endowed. Plotinus and the Neo-Platonic philosophers then produced the full formulation of this ontological and cosmological schema of the chain of being that was to govern the *Weltanschauung* of the West right down to the early seventeenth century. It was composed "of an infinite number of links ranging in hierarchical order from the meagerest kind of existence, which barely escaped non-existence, through 'every possible' grade up to the *ens perfectissimum* . . . every one of them differing from that immediately above and that immediately below it by the 'least possible' degree of difference."[2]

The theory of the chain of being presents a particular intellectual problem that is probably typical of analogism: namely, how do the continuous and the discontinuous fit together? When seen in the full scope of its development, the hierarchy of world entities seems continuous, for each element finds its place in the series because it possesses a degree of perfection that is scarcely greater than that of the element that it succeeds and is likewise scarcely less great than that of the element that it precedes. Through this contiguity that tolerates no gap or break, a general solidarity is established throughout the chain, from top to bottom and from bottom to top. However, the difference between each ontological link, which is certainly infinitesimal in relation to its immediate neighbors, turns out to be ever greater when one compares a link to others more distant from it. It thus introduces between them an essential inequality that unquestionably implies discontinuity. As time passed and depending on personal inclinations or the pressure that orthodox doctrines exerted, emphasis was laid either on the difference in nature that confers upon each thing its unique identity or on the connection that links all things so intimately that it becomes impossible precisely to determine the borders that separate them.

In Neo-Platonic philosophy and medieval theology it is the theme of multiplicity that appears to dominate. In Plotinus, for example, the generative world soul that, through its emanations, creates the chain of being has one essential property, that of creating otherness; for if the universe is at peace with itself, even if its parts are often in conflict, it is because this conforms with reason, and the unity of reason stems from the contraries that it encompasses. Reason makes things different from one another, in fact as different as possible: "So by making one thing different from another in the highest degree, it will necessarily make the opposites and will be complete if it makes itself not only into different things but into opposite things."[3] While rejecting Plotinus's theory of an immanence of the prime mover in the order that it creates—which is hardly compatible with the attributes of the Christian God—Saint Augustine nevertheless does pick up on the thesis of the diversity of ordered things. All things would not exist if they were all equal (*non essent omnia, si essent aequalia*), and from the point of view of the divine plan, the whole that they form is the only perfect one.[4] This insistence on the differences between the entities of the world is crucial for medieval theology, for it makes it possible to explain the existence of bad things. If everything proceeds from a perfect creative intention that is benevolent and that transcends God's works absolutely, how can we explain the imperfection, evil, and suffering of which our world provides so many examples? Did God really will the existence of the lion that devours the lamb? Yes, says Saint Thomas, for in its infinite wisdom, divine rationality willed that each species should act in accordance with its nature and that relations between them all should balance out so that not one of them becomes predominant: "The diversity and inequality of created things are not the result of chance but of the intention of God Himself, who wills to give the creature such perfection as it is possible for it to have."[5] It takes all kinds to make a world; so it is necessary that there should be differences between existing beings, so that they are able to deploy themselves within the ordered plenitude of all possible diversities.

In later conceptions of the chain of being, those of the seventeenth and eighteenth centuries, it was, on the contrary, the idea of continuity that seems to have predominated, above all in Leibniz but also in Spinoza. To be sure, the God of Leibniz, even more than that of the medieval philosophers, fills the world with as many things as possible: "Among the infinite combinations of possible series, that one actually exists by which the most of essence and of possibility is brought into existence."[6] However, the multiple monads are interconnected far more intimately than in the gradations of a linear chain. They are organized in the manner of a trellis in which every node, "a perpetual living mirror of the universe," expresses and synthesizes as one whole all the relations existing between every point in that whole. In this cosmology, in which every position is a point where a multitude of influences meet, the force of the principle of continuity is so strong that all the kinds of natural beings "are so closely linked one to another that it is impossible for the senses or the imagination to determine precisely the point at which one ends and the next begins."[7] Albeit expressed with less vigor and less visionary originality, this preponderance of an emphasis on harmonious unity is also present in Locke, Bolingbroke, Buffon, and Kant. This testifies to a robust optimism with regard to the general quality of the world plan and also indicates a new ontology in which the recently introduced clash between human nature and nature alien to man was mitigated by the recognition of a material continuity between existing beings. In fact, from the early seventeenth century onward, the scale of beings gradually lost its analogical dimension and soon was employed only as a familiar metaphor in the service of naturalist ontology. It was a handy formulation of the principle of the continuity of physicalities that the knowing subject probably needed in order to affirm the uniqueness of his mind without doubt or remorse.

The Renaissance was probably the period in which analogism shone the most brightly in Europe, before fading into an underground existence from which it surfaces from time to time as a reducer of uncertainties. It is to the great surprise of positivists that it does this in the ancient guises of astrology, numerology, alternative medicines, and all the techniques for decoding and making use of similarities that remind naturalism how fragile it is and how lacking in ancient roots. As Foucault writes, "Up to the end of the sixteenth century, resemblance played a constructive role in the knowledge of western culture."[8] His pages devoted to modes of deciphering the "prose of the world" in The Order of Things are so well known that we need not now dwell upon the forms taken by that resemblance. Let us simply note some of their characteristics that seem likely also to be at work in any analogical system, even if only as tentative tendencies.

In the elusive world of analogism, resemblance becomes the only means of introducing order, for this is a priori a chaotic and inflated world, since it contains an infinite number of different things, each in a particular place and each at the heart of an idiosyncratic network. In order to reduce this dizzying atomist perspective, the links of similarity that justify repeatedly moving along certain meaningful paths need to be identified. Such links may be metaphorical if they present a similarity between terms, or metonymic if they concern a similarity in relations. Among the former group of links are those that establish a connection in space, by means of which things that are placed in a relationship of proximity, of "convenientia," are united by their immediate closeness; in this group, imitation likewise plays a part, for it likens dispersed things because they appear to be mirror images of one another, albeit usually on different scales. Metonymic links include, in the first place, analogy in the strict sense, which applies to similarities among, not things themselves, but the relations that they maintain. Analogy is a flexible and polyvalent means of producing resemblances that is likely to make use not only of symmetry but of various forms of inversion, encompassment, and division. To this may be added links of attraction or sympathy, that is, action at a distance, which is also metonymic at least in the sense that it brings together in a sui generis relationship the previously separate relations that each thing had with its neighboring things. Furthermore, this network of resemblances should be discernible from tangible signs, so that the theory of signatures, far from being confined to the prehistory of Western medicine, is bound to manifest its pleasing imaginativeness everywhere in an analogical mode of identification. It does so in particular thanks to lists that indicate marks that are visible on the surface of things and that thus make it possible to reduce the multiplicity of appearances to occult properties, many of which can be organized into polar opposites of sameness and difference. Finally, the same applies to the exceptional emphasis placed on relations between the macrocosm and the microcosm, which was certainly particularly noticeable during the Renaissance, in its Neo-Platonic form, but the purpose of which may be presumed to be identical in all analogical systems, and for the same reasons as those identified by Foucault in connection with the *epistemē* of the sixteenth century. The obsession with correspondences between humans and the cosmos made it possible to establish one privileged creature as the seat of a denser focus of such correspondences, which checked both the proliferations of signs at that level and also their limitless reverberation within a closed world. This seemed to guarantee that an ordered system of knowledge and a restorative practice were possible, that in the unremitting flood of similarities, a guiding map was available.

Marcel Granet explains that, in ancient China, "society, man, and the world formed the object of an all-encompassing knowledge constituted solely by the use of analogy."[9] And it is indeed hard not to regard the way that this civilization accounted for its experience of things as a fine illustration of the analogical mode of identification, carried to a very high level of subtlety and refinement by several millennia of learned speculation. We shall nevertheless not linger over this exemplary case, for to do justice to its complexity and to the unity of the whole system that emerges from it would require following up too many lines of thought to cope with here. Let us simply note that Chinese philosophy most fully reveals what appears to be a central feature of any analogical ontology, namely the difficulty of distinguishing in practice among the components of existing beings, between that which stems from interiority and that which stems from physicality. This is expressed by the aphorism found in a treatise more or less contemporary with Aristotle, the *Xi ci*: "The *wu* (beings) are made up of *jing* and *qi*."[10] By *wu*, we should understand each of the types of things both animate and inanimate, collectively known as the "Ten Thousand Things" (*wan wu*), the exact number of which, however, calculated on the basis of the sixty-four hexagrams used in divination, would actually be 11,520, and these would correspond to the same number of particular situations, states, and emblems. Each *wu* is constituted by emanations from Heaven, which is ruled by Breath (*qi*), and from Earth, which produces nurturing essences (*jing*), so that every "nature" (*xing*) results from a more or less harmonious and balanced combination and dosage of heterogeneous elements that proceed from Water, Fire, Wood, Metal, and Earth. In short, the manner of being, personality, temperament, idiosyncrasy—in other words, the *xing* of an existing being—are not produced by a dynamic opposition between mind and matter but express the distinctions that are established between the states of elements and the proportions of their respective mixtures. This immeasurable multiplication of the elementary parts that make up the world is reflected within each one of those parts (including human beings, who are each fragmented into numerous components that are themselves repeated in successive interlocking situations). This seems to be a distinctive property of an analogical ontology and the surest means of identifying it. Intentionality and corporeality seldom surface as autonomous entities, for they are distributed in chains of pairings that bring the material and the immaterial together at every level in the respective scales of the microcosm and the macrocosm. So my earlier definition of analogism as a combination of the differences of interiorities and the differences of physicalities should not be taken altogether literally, so indefinite do the contours of those two groups seem to be. Rather, we should regard it as an approximate way of describing this teeming host of more or less harmonious singularities, which fragments the self-evidence of the physical and the moral, the better to ensure their union.

A Mexican Ontology

Sidestepping China and the formidable erudition required to study it, our inquiry into analogism now takes us to the central plateau of Mexico. My choice is no doubt justified by my firmer ethnographic acquaintance with this region of the Americas but is also prompted by less contingent reasons. To select the Han civilization as the principal illustration of an analogical ontology, or indeed India, which, I suspect, would exhibit similar properties, would be to risk reducing this mode of identification to an "oriental" paradigm coextensive with a vast and hypothetical domain of Asiatic "high cultures." This would be a lazy way of suggesting a kind of unity (even if a reminder of our own ancient "chain of being" should suffice to dispel the idea of any such geographic exclusiveness). We have delved into the lowlands of South America and the northern zone of North America to find numerous examples of animism. Now let us turn to Mesoamerica (though Andean America would have served equally well). This will, by contrast, present an opportunity to make the point that ontological schemas are distributed all over the world in accordance with peoples' preferences for this or that way of organizing their behavior in the world and vis-à-vis others, not because these schemas are the emanations of great cultural clusters or are products of rashly reconstructed diffusions of ideas. Certain ideological themes certainly are present in much of Native America, but they are tacked on as nuances or enrichments of more elementary modes of identification whose contrasting structures are for the most part unconnected with any common substratum. The Mexico of the Conquest furthermore presents a rare case of an analogical system of knowledge that has been transmitted to us mostly by observers who were themselves already immersed in an analogical way of thinking, that of sixteenth-century Europe, to which, whatever one might say, the Aztecs must have seemed less mysterious than they do to modern researchers. The analogical ontology is, moreover, so common in every latitude of the world that it seems preferable to investigate the details of one of its actualizations in order to pick out unvarying relations that are useful for comparison rather than to construct an abstract type on the basis of disparate facts.

Although they were distributed among a multitude of city-states, chiefdoms, and principalities all more or less politically dependent on the huge town of Mexico-Tenochtitlan, the Nahua peoples who occupied the central plateau of Mexico at the time of the Conquest presented a remarkable homogeneity in their conceptions of a universe in which the macrocosm and the microcosm were closely integrated. Of these two domains of existence, one remained relatively unknown for a long time, for although the Aztec cosmology has been the subject of many publications, only more recently have the Nahua theories of the body and the person received the systematic attention that they deserve, thanks to the study devoted to them by Alfredo López Austin.[11] López Austin's work is based on philological analyses of sources written in the Nahuatl language, on a critical use of sixteenth-century Spanish ethnography, in particular the admirable *General History of the Things of New Spain* by the Franciscan brother Bernardino de Sahagún, and on the ethnology of the modern Nahuas. It constitutes an unprecedented summation of the ontology of the ancient Mexicans, and I shall be drawing heavily upon it in the present work.

The Nahuas recognized the existence of four principal components in a human person (*tonacayo*, *tonalli*, *teyolia*, and *ihiyotl*), which we shall need to examine closely for, apart from the first of them, it is hard to find simple translations for these terms. *Tonacayo*, "all our flesh," was a term commonly used to designate the body as a substantial reality that formed a totality on its own. It was used to refer not only to humans but also to plants, maize in particular. López Austin defines the three other components as "animist centers," that is, the centers of an organism that govern life, movement, individuation, and psychic functions, both in humans and in nonhumans.

The most individualized element of an existing being appears to be its *tonalli*. In humans this is situated in the head and it spreads its influence throughout the body (by means of the blood, according to present-day Nahuas). *Tonalli* is an impalpable emanation that sometimes materializes in breath, and when it happens to absent itself from the body, it adopts an invisible shape identical to that of the body in which it lodges. But it cannot remain for long without a protective envelope, and so, if it is a human *tonalli*, it takes refuge in an animal or a plant. *Tonalli* may be translated as "irradiation," but depending on the context, it may also mean "the destiny of a person according to the day of its birth" or "something that is a property peculiar to one person in particular."[12] This is a force or essence made manifest in the world in the form of heat or light, but it is unique for each person, depending on the sign that corresponds to the day of his or her birth and the name, which is kept secret, that he or she will in consequence be given. *Tonalli* is not present at birth but has to be incorporated in a ceremony featuring a ritual bath, which completes the person of the newborn child and defines the framework for his or her future achievements.

This identity marker, which has every appearance of a simple astrological predestination, nevertheless also functions as a principle of animation and a mental faculty. It provides vigor, determination, and the capacity to grow; it regulates the body temperature and makes consciousness of the self possible. *Tonalli* may temporarily leave the body (at times of drunkenness, sickness, dreaming, or sexual intercourse) or abandon it forever, which is a symptom of imminent death, for life without *tonalli* is possible for only a short space of time. Nahua sources mention *tonalli* above all in reference to humans, but it is certainly not a human prerogative: gods, plants, animals, and even inanimate objects also possess it. Modern equivalents to *tonalli* among Mexico's non-Nahua indigenous groups possess analogous characteristics. The *šūti* (soul) of the Otomi of the Sierra Madre and the *sombra* (shadow) of numerous Mesoamerican communities are likewise liable to detach themselves from the body, creating a perilous situation since they thereby expose themselves to the risk of being captured by a sorcerer.[13] For the Tzotzil, who speak a Mayan language, each and every thing possesses a *ch'ulel*, which is "the intangible replica of its material form and qualities": among humans, this principle of individuation absents itself during sexual intercourse, dreaming, and drunkenness and can then enter into communication with the *ch'ulel* of other existing beings. Above all, and to the extent that *ch'ulel*, like *tonalli*, is diffused throughout the entire organism, elements of the body that become separate from it (such as nail parings and hair) continue to maintain an intrinsic link with it, while at the same time being infused with a *ch'ulul* of their own.[14] Finally, we should note that every individual has a specific *tonalli*. It sometimes happens that two persons receive similar *tonalli*s and destinies if they are born on the same day and under the influence of the same planet. Such an accidental link might lead to an amicable and ritualized affinity. On the other hand, identical *tonalli*s were incompatible in marriage (for they devoured each other), so it was important to consult specialists before any matrimonial union in order to ascertain that the respective *tonalli*s of the future spouses were definitely not the same.

Teyolia is situated in the heart but should not be confused with it. As one of the Nahua informers of Brother Alfonso de Molina told him: "When one is dying, something resembling a person . . . issues from the mouth and goes there [with the supreme gods]. . . . The heart which leaves is what makes one alive and once gone, the dead body remains. The heart does not go away, only that which keeps one alive here."[15] *Teyolia*, which can be broken down into /yolia/ (that which animates) and /te/ (a possessive suffix), is in effect the part of the person that goes off into the world of the dead; and this concept was very soon assimilated to *anima*, the Christian soul, both by the Spaniards and by the Hispanicized Nahuas. Unlike *tonalli*, *teyolia* never leaves the body during life. It is apparently lodged in the embryo by the protective deities of the *calpulli*, the localized descent group to which the newborn child will be attached. This is the component of the human person that, through its permanence and properties, seems to correspond most closely to an idea of interiority: it is the source of sensibility, memory, "states of soul," and the formation of ideas ("to think" was "to make something inside alive").[16] But *teyolia* also controls feelings in that these reflect a lasting temperament, which is expressed in a specific kind of behavior that is identified with the type of "heart" received at birth. Depending on the type of *teyolia* with which an individual is endowed, he or she is said to have a heart that is "white," "hard," "sweet," "bitter," "sad," "raw," or "cold." For example, a "bitter" heart predisposes one to effort, sadness, and regret, and it immunizes one against attacks from sorcery. As with *tonalli*, every human is endowed with a *teyolia* that is very individualized, for there are a great number of varieties of this component. But that being said, possession of a *teyolia* is no more the privilege of humans than is possession of a *tonalli*: animals, plants, and even mountains, towns, and lakes were all provided with one. Nowadays the Mayas of the highlands and the Totonacs even attribute one to crosses and to houses. This confirms that a human heart is only a hypostasis, or even a metaphor, for a *teyolia*. It is not the substantial incarnation of a faculty.

In a human body, the *ihiyotl* is linked with the liver and the bile, but here again the organ is simply the means of localizing a function, since inorganic entities also have *ihiyotls*. *Ihiyotl* can have the meaning of "breath" and was commonly used to designate the face. It is described as an extremely dense luminous gas that emanates from a human, an animal, or an object and acts as an attractive force and seat of influence over all that surrounds it. *Ihiyotl*, which is present as early as the embryonic stage of life and survives after death in the form of a dangerous exhalation, engenders and channels the feelings that are directed toward any object (desire, anger, appetite, a desire to harm), and it must be constantly revitalized by the air that one breathes and the food that one ingests. The *ihiyotl* of humans combines the register of emotions that prompt action and that of the civic virtues associated with such actions; as a "face," it is peculiar to each individual, for the Nahuas maintain that a physiognomy reflects the idiosyncratic qualities that are recognized by the collectivity and are emblematic of the various statuses that are reflected in the social hierarchy: fame, a good reputation, humility, splendor, experience, dignity.

If one wished at all costs to distribute the Nahua components of existing beings between the categories of interiority and physicality, the solution most respectful of the facts would probably be to place *tonalli* and *teyolia* under the heading of immateriality, while the *tonacayo* body, the *ihiyotl*, and the assignation of these to one particular place would define the material aspect of an individual. Although they refer to organs in living beings, *tonalli* and *teyolia* are insubstantial. The former is an irradiation that cannot survive for long without a protective envelope; the latter is a principle of animation that may call to mind the Christian soul. Both express or render possible functions peculiar to interiority: consciousness of the self, sensitivity, thought, an individual essence, and vital energy. Meanwhile, *tonacayo* is totally substantial since its very name derives from "flesh" (*nacatl*), here understood as matter that constitutes certain organisms by which humans are nourished. *Ihiyotl* is harder to classify. In its ordinary form it is certainly not material as a part of the anatomy is, but it is much more concrete than *tonalli* and *teyolia*. It is a vaporous exhalation similar to an aura and recognizable from the disagreeable odor that it emits after birth and death. The Chortis of Guatemala, a group belonging to the Maya linguistic family, confirm the rank stench of *hijillo* (the Hispanicized version of *ihiyotl*) and claim that it is so dense that one can sometimes make out its outline.[17] *Ihiyotl* moreover helps to model the physicality of individuals in a characteristic fashion, revealing the temperament's dominant traits in a person's physiognomy and bearing. As for the topographical aspect, considered as an ontological attribute, this follows from the fact that every existing being must occupy a place appropriate to its identity, in both physical space and social space. This is well illustrated by the meaning of the term "misfortune" (*aompayotl*); literally, it is "the condition of something outside of its place."[18] It is worth noting that the physical determination of the entities of the world by the position that is assigned to them also appears in ancient China, where space was considered, not simply as an extension resulting from the juxtaposition of homogeneous parts, but as a collection of concrete sites that served to classify beings and things from the point of view of action.[19] In fact, this way of using position in space as an additional means of particularizing each existing thing seems to be a common feature of most analogical systems.

All the same, the distribution of the components of a person in accordance with whether they are mainly material or mainly immaterial is not what is important here. The dominant feature of Nahua ontology, as of any analogical system, is the grouping within every existing entity of a plurality of aspects the right coordination of which is believed to be necessary for the stabilization of that entity's individual identity, for the exercise of its faculties and dispositions, and for the development of a mode of being in conformity with its "nature." The great diversity of types of *tonacayo*, *tonalli*, *teyolia*, and *ihiyotl* and the virtually infinite variants rendered possible by combinations of these types thus make each entity in the world, whether human or nonhuman, quasi-unique. Among the ancient Nahuas, this obsessive differentiation found expression in the constant attention paid to the disparities between humans according to their age, their sex, the color of their skin, their odor, their degrees of vigor and heat, their conformity to the canons of physical normality, and their vulnerability to danger and the attacks of sorcerers or malevolent deities: all of these constituted characteristic signs peculiar to the constituents of each entity and the way in which they were assembled. The scale of differences was just as marked in other existing beings, as was manifested by their gradational distribution along a continuum that stretched from hot to cold, in which there was a specified place for—in addition to humans—plants, animals, minerals, heavenly bodies, foodstuffs, illnesses, deities, and many other things besides. This, in short, was a system of universal classification that is still strong in Mesoamerica and to which we shall return.

At first sight, Nahua analogism seems close to animism. Animals, plants, stones, and mountains are all endowed with "animist centers" analogous to those of human beings. There are existing beings of every kind whose interiorities communicate with one another in dreams: for example, trees from which one begs forgiveness before felling them and which are honored once felled.[20] Is such a world, humming with conscious life and saturated with objects credited with intentionality, really distinct from the world of the Indians of Amazonia and Canada? The first point to note is that the ancient Nahuas and likewise the present-day Tzotzil attribute interiorities more liberally than the Jivaros or the Cree do. For the former pair, all visible and invisible entities in the environment possess at least one of the components that assure humans of subjectivity, memory, vital force, and volition. Furthermore, every existing being is different from every other on account of the plurality of its components and the diverse modes of their combination. This is at odds with the unity of the internal faculties that animist ontologies ascribe to humans and to certain nonhumans. In an analogical regime, humans and animals do not share the same culture, the same ethics, and the same institutions. By taking multiple precautions, humans manage to cohabit with plants, deities, houses, grottoes, lakes, and a whole mass of multifaceted neighbors within a closed universe in which each entity, anchored at a particular spot, pursues the ends that destiny has fixed for it in accordance with the dispositions that it has been allotted. Each entity is, willy-nilly, connected to every other entity by a tangle of correspondences over which it has no control. In contrast to the freedom of action that animism allows to existing beings endowed with similar interiorities, analogical worlds are burdened by the weight of destiny. Given that every entity is made up of a multiplicity of components in an unstable equilibrium, their tendencies to roam are thereby facilitated. So the transmigration of souls, reincarnation, metempsychosis, and, above all, possession all constitute unequivocal signs of analogical ontologies. Indeed, the invasion of an alien interiority into an existing being and the former's temporary or definitive domination over the autochthonous interiority—the minimal definition of possession—appear to be unknown in animist systems. True, it is sometimes said that certain Amerindian or Siberian shamans are invaded by their "auxiliary spirits," but this is a way of conveying the shaman's deliberate communication with alter egos that are invited to help him and whose actions he controls. It does not involve the total alienation of an individual by a power that changes his or her identity.

The Nahuas provide many examples of this effacement of personality that is characteristic of possession. Its effects often proved disastrous: certain bouts of madness, for instance, were imputed to an invasion of the demented person by the minor deities of rain. In such a case, the victim was said to be *aacqui*, "one who has suffered an intrusion." Meanwhile, the *teyolia* of *cihualpipiltin*, women who had died in childbirth, which accompanied the sun in its cycle, "became manifest" in its victims by provoking paralyses.[21] However, possession might also be sought for its beneficial consequences. When someone drank *pulque*, the alcohol made from the agave, one of the four hundred rabbit deities (*centzontotochtin*) that resided in the beverage invaded the body of the drinker. If he had reached the required age for partaking of *pulque* (fifty-two years) and if he used it in moderation and for valid ritual reasons, then the deity would bestow strength and beauty upon him. Otherwise, the deity would take offense and propel the contravener into a demeaning pattern of behavior. Such possession was extremely individualized, for the same rabbit deity would always seize upon the same drinker and transmit into his drunkenness the characteristics of its own personality: gay, melancholic, or aggressive.[22] Exactly the same thing would happen if one ingested psychotropic substances such as *peyotl* or hallucinogenic mushrooms, all of which were inhabited by deities, which by this means took possession of the bodies of humans, there to reside for a short period. This is strikingly different from analogous practices in animist Amazonia. Here, the ingestion of hallucinatory substances such as *ayahuasca* (*Banisteriopsis* sp.) is in no sense supposed to introduce an alien interiority that would then establish a hold over the one already present. On the contrary, it serves to free the interiority from its physical receptacle by increasing its acuity and clairvoyance and eventually making it possible for it to be free of the body and so be able to interact with its fellows without constraint.

The wandering among other bodies that is undertaken by the components of a person is well documented by the early Nahuas and offers us the opportunity to reflect a little on the typically Mesoamerican phenomenon known as "Nagualism." So many different factors have been intermingled in the use of this term and over such a long period (all the founding fathers of anthropology make abundant use of it) that a preliminary clarification seems called for. The word *nagual* (or *nahual*) designates all or some of the following things: (1) an animal double whose life cycle runs parallel to that of a human, since it is born and dies at the same time as that human and everything that affects the integrity of one of them also affects the other; (2) the zodiacal sign under which a child is born (and the day of its birth), which determines the child's particular character and attributes; (3) sorcerers reputed to be able to change themselves into an animal or a ball of fire, usually with the intention of doing harm; (4) the animal into which a sorcerer is incorporated; and, finally, (5) a component of a human person. Upon reexamining the "Nagualism" file, George Foster has established that the ability to be embodied in an animal, which was ascribed to the Nagual sorcerers of Mexico and Guatemala, was totally independent of any belief in an exclusive link established at birth between a human and an animal—a belief that the Nahuas of the central plateau do indeed not appear to have held.[23] It thus seems preferable to reserve the word *nagual* (and "Nagualism") for a sorcerer able to turn himself into an animal and to apply the term *tona* to a human's animal alter ego, for the latter is a term that is in current use in many regions of Mesoamerica.

What exactly are the mechanisms mobilized in these processes of onto-logical embodiment and pairing that appear to efface the boundaries between humans and animals? A *tona* (or *wayjel* among the Tzotzil) is a wild animal that is born on the same day and under the same sign as a human and with which that human shares temperamental characteristics: among the Tzotzil, if the animal is a jaguar the person will be stubborn, willful, violent, and can-tankerous; if the animal is a hummingbird, the person will instead be pa-tient, gentle, and understanding.[24] Such a connection with a plant is more rare and ambiguous: among the Teenek of Huasteca, for example, young trees are chosen by healers to serve as godfathers to children, their mission being in general to protect them without their realizing it, although in this instance there is no coincidence between the dates of birth nor any correspondence between the character imputed to the tree and those imputed to the child.[25] Although their destinies run parallel, no explicit relation exists between a human and his *tona*, so in most cases the identity of the *tona* is not known and there is always the risk that the human may harm it and thereby do him-self damage. As Jacques Galinier writes on the subject of the Otomi, "everyone knows that he can accidentally kill his [animal] companion when hunting in the bush, and thus bring about his own death."[26] All the same, a *tona* is not really an anonymous double in the sense of a moral and biographical coun-terpart that capricious deities or ancestors choose for a human in order to make his existence more unpredictable. For the common destiny that unites them regardless of their own respective wills rests upon the fact that as soon as he is born, a fraction of the human—part of his *tonalli* according to López Austin—installs itself in his animal alter ego, where it remains until death.[27] Neither projection of a personality on to "virgin wax" nor materialization of twinned attributes, the *tona* is at once different from and similar to its human twin, since it provides a receptacle for a fragment of delocalized interiority that eludes any conscious control (for this is purely a matter of destiny) even as it continues to influence the individual from which it proceeds.

As for the term *nagual*, it goes beyond the figure of a sorcerer with the ability to change into an animal, although that is the illustration most fre-quently offered. Among the early Nahuas, as in much of present-day Meso-america, deities, the dead, and animals are likewise able to adopt an animal form (in the last case that of an animal of a different species), not by changing their own appearances but simply by infiltrating the body of another entity. No metamorphosis is involved. Rather, according to López Austin, we should

consider nagualism "a kind of possession that men, gods, the dead and animals effect by sending one of their animistic entities, *ihiyotl* or *nahualli* to
take cover in various beings, animals predominantly, or by placing themselves
directly inside their victims' bodies."[28] This being so, a *nagual* (or *nahualli*)
is at once a being that can separate itself from its *ihiyotl* and provide it with
another being to serve as its envelope, the *ihiyotl* itself, and also the being that
takes in the *ihiyotl* of another.

This helps to explain why "tonalism" and "Nagualism" have so often been
confused, even in indigenous formulations. Both cases involve the exporta-
tion of one component of an existing being into another existing being and
their fates becoming so closely linked that anything that concerns the one will
produce consequences for the other. But there are also differences between
the two. In the one case the element exported is *tonalli*, and in the other it is
ihiyotl; as for the link that is established, in the one case it is involuntary and
permanent, and in the other transitory and intentional; the receiver is in the
one case a particular animal, and in the other a random entity. The qualities required for shifting a part of oneself are also different, since all humans
unknowingly externalize part of their *tonalli* into an animal, whereas only
experts can consciously transport their *ihiyotl* into another being. However,
these differences between the two modes of exteriorization count for very
little in comparison to the major contrast that they both present with regard
to the metamorphosis that is at work in animist ontologies. If Nagualism involves the introduction of a foreign element of a generally physical nature
(*ihiyotl*) into an independent entity while tonalism involves the introduction
of an element of interiority (*tonalli*), then there is certainly either a lasting or a
transitory coexistence of ontological principles of different origins within one
and the same existing entity. This amplifies the effect of multiplicity already
engendered in normal circumstances by the huge number of combinations
between the many different kinds of components that make up individuals.
In metamorphosis, in contrast, the interiorities of both humans and nonhumans, identical in their dispositions, remain constant, unitary, and autonomous; only their corporeal envelopes change, in accordance with the point
of view from which they are apprehended. To lodge a part of oneself in an
animal that one thereby takes over, as a Mexican *nagual* does, is not the same
as assuming an animal appearance or one perceived as such, as an Amazonian
shaman does. The Mexican *nagual* decomposes and disperses the elements
of his person as he wills; an Amazonian shaman retains the stable identity of
his interiority.

A world of singularities patched together from disparate materials in permanent circulation, constantly threatened with collapse on account of the be-

wildering plurality of its inhabitants, requires powerful mechanisms for pairing off, structuring, and classifying for it to become representable or, indeed, simply livable for those who inhabit it. And it is here that analogy serves as a compensatory procedure of integration, making it possible to create chains of solidarity and links of continuity leading in every direction. All the levels of the cosmos, the visible and invisible parts and ingredients of humans, plants, and animals and the relations between family members, social strata, occupations, specializations, atmospheric phenomena, foodstuffs, medicaments, deities, celestial bodies, illnesses, temporal divisions, sites, and cardinal points: for the early Nahuas, all these elements were interconnected by a thick web of correspondences and mutual influences, as they still are for many of the peoples of Mesoamerica. No doubt the full extent and structure of this knowledge, about which Mexicanists have written many volumes, were accessible only to a small group of specialists who were extremely knowledgeable about divination, astrology, and medicine, but even ordinary people, the *macehualtin*, must have possessed scraps of knowledge that were useful for carrying out the rituals of daily life and sufficient for them to sense the density of the relations between the constituents of the universe. That is certainly what is suggested by the ethnography of present-day Indian communities, which confirms that ordinary folk possess knowledge in this domain that is quite solid, even if not always as precise as that of the recognized experts: healers, visionaries, *hechiceros* (bewitchers), and midwives.

Whether found in Renaissance Europe, in China, or among the Nahuas of the period of the Conquest, this web of intercommunicating signs is often reduced by analysts to the classic formula of a correspondence between the macrocosm and the microcosm. But this conceptual device is not an easy one to handle. This is because it is universal if taken at its highest degree of generality: everywhere analogies are drawn (and are well attested in vocabulary) between parts of the human body, parts of plants and animals, and elements of the inorganic environment; everywhere houses are apprehended as a microcosm intermediate between the human body, of which it forms an extension, and the world, which it reproduces in miniature; everywhere links are found, sometimes of a very allusive nature, between, on the one hand, functions, dysfunctions, and biological substances and, on the other, climatic or seasonal events and cycles. In short, our body offers such a rich and immediately available reservoir of anatomical and physiological particularities that it would have been surprising if people all over the world had not made the most of it to construct networks of analogies and metaphors that in some cases reach right up to the sky. However, only analogical ontologies have managed to systematize these straggling chains of meaning into ordered and interdependent sets that for the most part are designed to be effective practically: ways to cope with misfortune, the orientation of buildings, calendars, predestination, eschatology, divinatory systems, the compatibility of marriage partners, good government—everything is interconnected in a web so dense and so charged with consequence that it becomes impossible to tell whether it is man who reflects the universe or the universe that takes man as its model. Chains of transitive causality so long and so luxuriant are seldom to be found in animist or totemic ontologies, and in present-day naturalism they appear only as incomplete fragments, nostalgic survivals from an enchanted epoch on which horoscope watchers, adepts of alternative medicines, and the followers of New Age sects all tend to draw.

So it cannot be said that analogism has established man at the intersection of all the lines of meaning that connect things. As Foucault says when speaking of the Renaissance, the macrocosm-microcosm correspondence is really a superficial effect. But the privileged position that analogism grants to the human being, as a hermeneutic standard, makes it possible to reduce the proliferation of resemblances by means of an interpretative guide that can be mastered since it is founded on the properties imputed to a human person. It should be added that the ecology of an organism constituted by many wandering elements that cohabit in a more or less harmonious fashion must surely evoke the image of a world in miniature—better, at least, than the simpler combinations used by other ontologies. There is nevertheless nothing anthropomorphic about analogical systems: despite the preponderant epistemic position filled by humans, the diversity of the parts that compose the systems is so great and their structure so complex that one single creature could not possibly constitute an overall model.

Another way of imparting order and meaning to a world full of singularities is to distribute these into great inclusive structures that stretch between two poles. In this way, the teeming mass of attributes can be contained by an operation of classification into a simplified nomenclature of perceptible qualities. Two such nomenclatures are very common: that which opposes the hot and the cold and, sometimes combined with this, that which opposes the dry and the wet. In fact, these perhaps constitute the most obvious indications of an analogical ontology. The early Nahuas made use only of the former, but they employed it regularly and exhaustively in order to divide all existing things into two classes. On the side of the hot they placed the celestial world, light, the masculine, what is above, strength, fire, the eagle, the day, the number 13, life, and so on. On the side of the cold they lined up the chthonic world, darkness, the feminine, what is below, weakness, water, the ocelot, night, the number 9, death, and so on. This duality is still very much present in Mesoamerica, where it continues to order the whole mass of visible and invisible entities: plants, animals, minerals, celestial bodies, days of the week, months, spirits, foodstuffs, physiological states; everything can be reduced to the polarity of the hot and the cold.

As can be seen from the nature of the elements classified, assignation to the one or the other class depends not on its actual temperature but on the properties attributed to it and the associations that its situation and function suggest. The hot and the cold, subjective and contrastive qualities par excellence, here serve as abstract and conventional rubrics under which to classify, not empirical indicators of a material state, but pairs of contraries. According to the Mayan people of Yucatan, for example, the heat of an oven transmits a "cold" quality to food because of the analogies with the underworld that it suggests, whereas foodstuffs cooked on a *comal*, an earthenware plate placed directly on a fire, acquire a "hot" quality in keeping with that of the sky.[29] Although it is a dichotomy, the polarity between the hot and the cold also allows for gradations, in particular in the domain of medicine, where it is a matter of restoring the equilibrium of organisms either by heating or by cooling them by suitable means, usually treatments based on plants. Most plants are said to be either hot or cold, but some plants can change between hot and cold depending on the use to which they are put. A case in point is found among the Tzotzil, who sometimes classify a small number of plants both as *sik* (cold) and as *k'ixim* (hot).[30] Finally, there are also certain entities that intrinsically combine the two qualities. For the Totonacs of the Sierra de Puebla, one such is maize.[31] The degrees of heat or cold imputed to things and states thus function as highly polyvalent parameters that make it possible both to structure the world in a taxonomy of the same and the different and also to define relative positions that suit the circumstances, so as to indicate what kind of action should be taken.

The authentically Mesoamerican character of the polarity of the hot and the cold is not universally recognized, and an important polemic has developed around this subject, about which a few words should be said. The perplexing coincidence between this pair of concepts and its homologue in the ancient European theory of the humors, in which it likewise plays a preponderant part, led Foster to maintain, in a well-known article, that the dichotomous classification based on the hot and the cold was a legacy from Hippocratic medicine, which was transmitted to the New World by the Spaniards.[32] This thesis was soon adopted by a number of Mexicanists and helped decisively to stimulate a whole flood of studies on the part played by Iberian grafts in the formation of the great cultural and social melting pot of New Spain. This is an area of study that had certainly long been neglected, but the present vogue for it sometimes causes one to forget that the Indians of Mesoamerica have kept plenty of features of their pre-Columbian past very much alive. There can be no doubt that several centuries of colonial domination brought about notable changes in indigenous systems of thought, some of which made an impact even as early as the first decades of contact, in particular among the Mexican elite, who constituted the principal source of information for Sahagún and his associates. That being said, however, the arguments that support the idea of a pre-Hispanic origin for the hot/cold opposition seem more convincing than those suggesting that it is an imported belief. Without going into the details of this polemic, we may follow López Austin, an outspoken partisan of the autochthony of this polarity, in particular when he points out that it is curious that one part only of the theory of the humors crossed the Atlantic Ocean, for the complementary opposition between the dry and the wet, which is central to the European doctrine of the four elements, has made very little impact in Mesoamerica. It is also reasonable to follow him when he notes that the earliest sources written in Nahuatl mention classifications according to the hot and the cold that are not directly related to questions of health, and this was at a time when Spanish medicine had not yet established its influence. And we should also follow him when he emphasizes that the field structured by this pair of concepts extended much further than that of medicine at the time of the Conquest, as it still does today,[33] for more or less everything can be included in it. Furthermore, we should note that the crucial importance ascribed to the hot/cold polarity in other regions of the world where the Hippocratic influence is either out of the question (China, the Ayurvedic system in India) or is possible but unlikely (West Africa) tends likewise to favor an independent origin in the case of Mesoamerica.[34]

If we accept that the great inclusive classifications based on pairs of perceptible qualities are one of the most typical features of analogical ontologies, then the controversy over the origin of the hot/cold polarity will seem quite beside the point. In truth, what we have here is no more than a partial coincidence (given that the dry/wet dichotomy never became established in native Mesoamerica) between two modes of classification that are similar, since they both developed in comparable analogical contexts, but are geographically separate. The structural convergence of the autochthonous nomenclature and part of the European nomenclature thus does not pose a major problem.[35] We know that the Europeans were scandalized by some aspects of early Mexican civilization that went too far against the teaching of the Gospels. However, they manifested no surprise when faced with Mexican divinatory and medical techniques but rather stressed the resemblances to their own practice. As one commentator on the Codex Borgia forthrightly wrote: "Everything was well organized and in agreement and they used the same methods as astrologers and doctors employ among ourselves."[36] And if the conquerors did sometimes dismiss certain aspects of indigenous medicine, that was certainly and with good reason not because of its use of the hot/cold opposition as an etiological and pathological indicator but because some of the therapeutic applications that resulted were contrary to Hippocratic orthodoxy.[37] So these were no more than squabbles between experts who shared the same principles of qualitative physiology and who, as in the medical treatises of the Renaissance, voiced their disagreements chiefly on the subject of the clinical consequences to be drawn from this or that case.

Just as one everywhere comes across rough versions of correspondences between the macrocosm and the microcosm, there is probably nowhere in the world where human beings have not from time to time been tempted to classify things according to whether they are said to be hot or cold, or dry or wet. However, inserted into circumstantial statements and nomenclatures, as they are, those oppositions do not turn into vast all-inclusive and explanatory systems of the kind to which analogical ontologies have recourse for ordering the multiplicity of entities with which they people the world. It is remarkable that there is no trace of a general hot/cold polarity in totemic Australia, nor in Siberia, subarctic America, or indigenous Amazonia, which are the animist regions par excellence.[38] Naturalism still retains a few traces of it in popular taxonomies that are a tenacious legacy from the ancient theory of the humors, which sometimes even infiltrates scholarly thought. According to Bachelard, it is to just such a survival that we owe the word "calories," which translates the nutritive value of foodstuffs.[39] Rather than regard the hot/cold or dry/wet opposition as a universal invariant, we would do better to regard it as a handy mechanism for the reduction of singularities. It is, to be sure, based on universally recognized salient qualities, but it takes the form of an all-encompassing classificatory system only when the level of ontological diversification is such that specialized nomenclatures are no longer able to set reality in order for the benefit of both thought and action and when a more general principle becomes necessary to ensure the integration of a whole range of classificatory mechanisms.

Echoes of Africa

Perhaps we need to complement this example of Mexican analogism coinciding with that of sixteenth-century Europe with a brief counterpoint from another part of the world. This provides an opportunity to turn to Africa, a continent so far barely mentioned in the present work. A memory evoked by the Malian anthropologist Amadou Hampaté Ba will explain the reasons for this choice: "Every time my own mother wished to talk to me, she would first summon my wife or my sister and tell her, 'I wish to talk to my son Amadou but I would like, first, to know which of the Amadous that inhabit him is there at the moment.'"[40]

The part of West Africa that corresponds roughly to the Mandé-Voltaic region (Mali, Burkina Faso, the eastern fringes of Senegal, and the northern part of the Ivory Coast) is dominated by a concept of a human person that is remarkably close to that of the Indians of Mexico: each individual is made up of a multiplicity of mobile components whose combinations, all different, produce particular identities. The example of the Bambara, studied by Hampaté Ba, could not be clearer. There are two terms for a person: *maa*, the person itself, and *maaya*, "the person's persons," that is to say, the various aspects of *maa* present within the person. Hence, the Bambara have a traditional saying "The persons of a person are many within the person."[41] This state of affairs had its origin when the demiurge Maa-nala, having created beings none of which could communicate with him, took a tiny portion from every existing being and mixed all those fragments together to create a hybrid being, a human that contained a scrap of each and every entity in the universe. The psychic and moral attributes of each of the persons cohabiting in an individual are reflected in his or her face, the signs being distributed among the forehead, the eyebrows, the eyes, the ears, the mouth, the nose, and the chin.[42]

Among the Samo of Burkina, Françoise Héritier found a similar multiplicity of components within a person. According to her, every human contains the following components: a body, *mɛ*, the flesh of which is bestowed by the mother; blood, *miya*, received from the father; breath, *sisi*, carried around by the "blood of the heart"; vital energy, *nyìni*, diffused by the "blood of the body," of which every living being contains its own portion and which is made manifest by heat and sweat (*tàtáre*); a psychic personality, *yí:ri* (understanding, consciousness of the self, memory, imagination), which is totally idiosyncratic but may in some cases be a reincarnation of some ancestor; a "double," *mɛrɛ*, an immortal essence that is absolutely specific to each individual and is partially recognizable from the characteristics of the individual's shadow (*nysile*) and with which plants, animals, and certain inorganic elements such as clay and iron are also endowed; an "individual destiny," *lɛpɛrɛ*, which is partly conditioned by that of the mother and which determines length of life; also, finally, other unique attributes such as a name or even a "surreal homonym," *tōma*, that is derived from a bush genie's approval and that is identified by a diviner at the child's birth.[43] Every existing being thus appears as a particular combination of very diverse material and immaterial elements that confer upon it an identity of its own. Humans are the product of a more complex combination than those of other entities in the world, which leads Héritier to define a Samo individual as a "layering" of elemental components.[44]

However, in this region of Africa, it is the Dogon who have carried the diversification of a being's components the furthest. Germaine Dieterlen tells us that, for them, every human is made up of a body, *gódu*; eight "souls," *kikinu* (a contraction of *kindu kindu*); eight "clavicle seeds"; a great number of parcels of "vital force," *ɲàma;* as well as an animal double.[45] The eight *kikinu* souls are divided into four "body souls," which are themselves divided into two pairs of twinned souls, one of each sex (the *kikinu sáy*, or "intelligent souls," associated with mental faculties, which are spread throughout the body and are capable of detaching themselves from it; and the *kikinu búmonɛ*, or "crawling souls," which are reflections of the former that manifest themselves in the individual's shadow and seldom leave the body); and four "sex souls," which are, as it were, doubles of the "body souls" and which serve procreative functions and are themselves also divided into two pairs of twinned souls of opposite sexes. The eight *kikinu* souls of each human being are altogether peculiar to him or her and are not transmitted to his or her descendants. A child receives a specific group of these at the very beginning of its life in the womb and retains them to the day of its death. They are conferred by Nommo, the master of water and the genitor of humanity, and are the product of stocks of *kikinu* located in the water, in particular in sacred "family" ponds that are allocated to every extended lineage. As for the two clavicles, these contain symbols of the eight primordial seeds, four to each clavicle, that were engendered by the Creator right at the start of the genesis (small millet, white millet, shadow millet, female millet, the bean, sorrel, rice, and the *Digitaria*), the whole collection being likened to a miniature barn that makes it possible for an individual to profit from the energy, *ɲàma*, of the cultivated plants that he consumes. The contents of the clavicles and the way that they are organized vary for each person in accordance with his or her sex, tribe, caste, function, and so on. Furthermore, the position of the seeds within the bone changes each time the carrier changes status in consequence of the numerous rites of passage to which he submits and also every time that he takes part in a collective ceremony. Finally, the vital force, *ɲàma*, is placed under the direct control of the *kikinu* souls. According to Marcel Griaule, it may be defined as "an energy that is present, impersonal, unconscious, distributed among all animals, vegetables, supernatural beings, and natural things and that tends to preserve the vehicle to which it is assigned temporarily (in the case of mortal beings) or eternally (in immortal beings)."[46] However, the *ɲàma* of a human is not an undifferentiated fluid. It is formed from a combination of eighty particles from a variety of provenances. That combination is specific to each individual and links him or her to ancestors, both direct and indirect. Under the aegis of the male *kikinu* of the "body," forty *ɲàma* are grouped. These are headed by that of the father, and under the aegis of the female *kikinu* of the "body," forty others are headed by that of the mother. These two groups are established in the clavicles, and each day a new pair of *ɲàma* particles stemming from the two sets come to watch over the person, totally occupying his or her body in a cycle that alternates every forty days. On top of all this, every human acquires supplementary portions of *ɲàma* that are provided by the powers which that individual worships. These are portions that do not mix in with the initial stock. An individual is thus the depository of a multitude of *ɲàma* of diverse origins that maintain his relations with a whole crowd of beings that have transmitted portions of vital force to him, "each one of them helping to ensure his spiritual integrity and thus maintain the balance of his physical strength."[47] In short, not only does each Dogon form a composite and absolutely unique alloy of a prodigious quantity of both material and immaterial components, a veritable world in miniature, with its own ecology and laws of compatibility and incompatibility; but, moreover, the constant mobility of his constitutive parts turns him every day into a being different from the one of the day before.

In the African examples considered, qualities similar to those of humans are certainly attributed more parsimoniously to nonhumans than in the case of Mesoamerica, where almost all existing beings are credited with components that are similar to those of humans, albeit organized differently in each case. All the same, we are still a long way from the ontological partitioning of naturalism, with its strict segregations between humans credited with an interiority and the generic mass of natural beings without consciousness or free will. We should remember that, among the Dogon of Tireli, certain trees like to move around at night in order to hold discussions, as do stones situated near cemeteries.[48] Furthermore, as we have seen, *ɲàma*, the general principle of animation and identity, is distributed liberally among both humans and most nonhumans. The Bolo of Mali and Burkina entertain a similar notion, that of *nyama*. It is recognized by all the peoples of the Mandé region and takes the form of a life-force that bathes the whole universe and is condensed in all kinds of entities, humans, animals, and also spirits.[49] Among the Samo, *mɛrɛ* is a stable and eternal essence that carries the identity of a human or a nonhuman and that survives as a principle of individuation even after the physical disappearance of the entity that it individuated. Thus, the death of a human causes all his constitutive elements to disappear, with the exception of the *mɛrɛ*, which goes off to begin a new life in the village of the dead and, to this end, re-creates an entirely new person with new components. When this existence in the world of the dead comes to an end, the process is repeated in a second "life of the dead," after which the *mɛrɛ* of the deceased passes into a big tree that itself possesses a *mɛrɛ.*

As among the Mexicans, the constitutive elements of beings are extremely mobile, constantly recomposing and partly located outside their physical envelope. That is the case of the Samo *mɛrɛ*, which wanders about from one physicality to another, where it sometimes coexists with the *mɛrɛ* of other organisms. Among the Dogon, this is even more striking. One of the "body souls," the female "intelligent" soul (*kikinu sáy*) of a man, will sometimes take up its abode in the water of the family pond, as will the male *kikinu sáy* of a woman; one of the "crawling souls" (*kikinu búmonɛ*) of a man may inhabit the sanctuary of his ancestral cult, while the other one will settle in the clan's prohibited animal. Every rite of passage (name giving, male circumcision, female circumcision, marriage, or funeral) will provoke a displacement of one or several of the individual's components, as will participation in some collective ceremony. Furthermore, every human possesses an animal double born at the same time and of the species associated with his family. According to Ogotemmêli, Griaule's famous informant, when the eight human ancestors of the Dogon were created, eight animals were born in the sky at the same moment and each human-animal pair shared a common soul. In the same way as with Mexican *tona*, "the animal is like the human's twin . . . ; it is certainly distinct from him, born somewhere else and apparently with a heterogeneous form, but it is of the same essence."[50] Every animal twin itself has a twin of another species, as does the latter, and so on, with the series extending gradually all the way to plants, so that every human being who is a member of one of the primordial ancestors' eight lineages finds himself linked in a chain with nonhuman individuals, a chain whose appearance was triggered by his own birth and that encompasses one-eighth of all the living beings in the world.

As in Mesoamerica, vast networks thus connect every human to a multiplicity of existing beings, through the intermediary of a limited number of common elements, forming veritable chains of beings that incorporate every singularity in an interlacing of mirrored causes and attributes controlled by the ancestors. The Dogon have no doubt carried this obsession with correspondences between macrocosm and microcosm to extremes and with a coherence so meticulous (and so meticulously reported by Griaule and his collaborators) that it may well seem doubtful whether any of them, Ogotemmêli included, were able to form an overall view of this world, bogged down as it is in countless filaments of analogies and meaningful echoes, and whether it is possible for anyone to make all his actions conform with the precepts that govern the good functioning of this overpopulated cosmology. But what the Dogon have carried to extremes is also present in the rest of the Mandé-Voltaic region. Among the Bambara, for example, a body is regarded as "a sanctuary in which all beings are to be found in interrelation"; and among the Samo, an individual is a "contingent concretization at a crossroads, at the intersection of lines both surreal and real, which themselves straddle two worlds, that of the Universe and that of Humanity."[51] It is not hard to see how very incongruous it would be to say such a thing of the Jivaros, the Naskapi, or the Chewong, whose ontological organization conforms to a reassuring duality and who connect with nonhumans simply through daily intercourse with the interiorities present in social life, not through multiple interconnecting branches of the various strata that constitute their person, which link them with this or that sector of the cosmos. On the other hand, one may speak in almost the same terms of the ontology of the Mexicans or the Chinese, and for the very same reasons. This region of Africa is part of the great analogical archipelago that is scattered across the surface of the earth in a multitude of islands and islets. No diffusionary network could possibly account for the uniformity of such a structure.

Pairings, Hierarchy, and Sacrifice

Let me rapidly summarize the properties of the mode of identification that confers their distinctive character upon the inhabitants of this archipelago. Interiority and physicality are here fragmented, in every being, into multiple components that are mobile and partly extracorporeal, the unstable and haphazard grouping of which produces a permanent flux of singularities. At the heart of this gigantic collection of unique existing beings, humans constitute a privileged cohort, for their persons offer a reduced and therefore manageable model of the relations and processes that govern the mechanics of the world. Hence, there is a constant concern to preserve an ever precarious balance between the constitutive parts of individuals, a concern that finds expression especially in systematic recourse to theories relating to the dosage and compatibility of humors and physiological substances, and also in an ever-present fear of being invaded by an intrusive and alienating identity or of seeing an essential element in one's own identity disappear. Hence, there is also a need to keep workable and efficient channels of communication open between all the parts of all beings and to maintain the many circumstances and influences that ensure their stability and proper functioning. The weight of these dependencies makes it essential to pay obsessive attention to a whole sheaf of prohibitions and prescriptions. So constraining are these that aid is usually required from specialists who are well versed both in the interpretation of signs and the correct execution of rituals and also in developing particular techniques for reading the future, such as astrology and divination. To find one's way through the forest of singularities, one needs a whole battery of symbols and emblems to make it possible to code all this diversity in a hermeneutic grid. To this end, semiautomatic systems for computing and combining, along with certain artifacts, many of which may be found in our ethnographic museums, are pressed into service. They are used to clarify an overcomplex cosmos by plotting all its points of connection and major lines of force in manageable configurations.

Analogism thus uses analogy to cement together a world rendered fragile by the multiplicity of its parts; and it does so in an admirably systematic fashion. The interplay of connectivity among places and contiguity among times makes it possible to arrange things in classes based on their position in a particular site and in a particular series. This provokes an unparalleled proliferation of spatial coordinates and divisions of time: cardinal points, quarters, strict topographic segregations, calendars, and—above all—long cycles of genealogy. It is especially by means of these long-drawn-out lines of filiation that the great skein of intergenerational solidarities can be woven. It is a convenient way of justifying the permanence of groups of attributes and prerogatives that continue to be transmitted even with the passing of time; and it accounts both for the preponderant place that ancestors frequently occupy in this mode of identification and also for the fearful reverence that surrounds them. All this stands in total contrast to animism and totemism, from which these cumbersome ancestral figures are absent. As we have seen, great dual classifications (or quadripartite ones produced by doubling the duality) are in general use because these offer the most economical solution for the arrangement of existing beings in accordance with the qualities ascribed to them, and for adding on all the hidden similarities that they conceal behind their phenomenal diversity. Analogism is also very different from the totemic dualisms that are common in Australia. The latter set up primitive classes of intangible properties to which are attached a variable number of entities that express them, whereas binary classifications of the hot/cold type are simply a way of organizing elements according to the predicates one attributes to them. In the former case, the class comes first and specifies the ontological characteristics of what it should contain; in the latter case, the class is no more than a powerful taxonomic tool used to subsume qualities recognized to be possessed by entities whose ontological composition remains independent of the indicators used to list them under one or another rubric.

Another expedient way of managing such a flux of singularities is to set them in a hierarchical order. The model of the chain of being is thus by and

large transposable to all analogical ontologies, although the criteria for the hierarchical levels may vary considerably. The difference where animism and totemism are concerned is a matter of scale, for in these the distinctions between
collections of structurally equivalent entities are set out solely on a horizontal
plane and not in these superpositions of castes, classes, and functions, these
accumulations of powers and divinities, with which analogical civilizations,
with their sprouting polytheisms, have made us so familiar. The trouble is that
overlong hierarchies become hard to handle: so there is a call for mechanisms
by which to structure their linear gradations and for ways to diminish the
range of the discontinuities that are involved. We may place in this category
the organizational schemas brought to our attention by Louis Dumont in his
analyses of the hierarchy of castes and varnas in India: for example, within
each subdivision of the hierarchy, the principles that govern its general structure are repeated. In such a hierarchy, at the level of the units that compose
it, each caste reproduces the global model of distribution of which it is itself a
result.[52] Dumont calls this holism, by which he means a system of values that
subordinates the place of each existing being in the hierarchy, and the cohesion of that hierarchy itself, to a totality that transcends its parts. But holism
is not so much a characteristic by which nonmodern societies as a whole
are differentiated from modern individualism; rather, it is a means employed
solely by analogical ontologies to make it possible to manage such a mass of
singularities. The same applies to the reversals of dominance that, in China,
accompany changes in levels: the left, rather than the right, is preeminent in
the upper part of the body and of the cosmos, while the right is preeminent
over the left in the lower part.[53] Thanks to the interplay of rules founded upon
analogy, reversion, and pairing, a universe that is fractured by multiple discontinuities becomes intelligible in all its connections, and provided total deference is observed toward ritual obligations and the prescriptions of etiquette,
this universe becomes habitable for one and all, with no confusions of place
or status.

One last pairing mechanism needs to be mentioned, if only as a hypothesis,
for which I beg the reader's indulgence. It is impossible not to notice that sacrifice is present in regions dominated by analogical ontologies (in particular
Brahmanic India, West Africa, ancient China, where it was above all associated with political functions, the Andean zone, and pre-Columbian Mexico),
whereas it is virtually unknown in totemic Australia and the regions that are,
par excellence, animist, namely Amazonia and subarctic America. Of course,
one could point out that, with the exception of dogs in North America, stock
raising is absent or has been introduced only recently in those regions. Without domesticated animals to immolate, sacrifice becomes impossible.[54] How-

ever, to invoke such a practical reason would merely be to shift the question, for it would then be necessary to explain why there should be an incompatibility between animal domestication and animist and totemic ontologies. (This is a problem that will be addressed in part V of this book.) Besides, in such cases it would theoretically be possible to sacrifice humans; for it is probably fair to generalize the precept of Vedic India according to which the only genuine victim is the person offering the sacrifice, for it is he who initiates the rite and expects to be affected by it. The animals are merely substitutes for him, ones that can be replaced by other things for this function.

Nor, in the absence of domesticated animals, would there be anything to prevent the ritual slaughter of wild animals captured for this purpose and then partially socialized within the village sphere. Such a period of familiarization would render them altogether suitable to represent the humans who have fed and taken care of them just as they do with domesticated animals raised as livestock. Indeed, such cases are not unknown in the animist world. The Cashibo of Peruvian Amazonia regularly organize a great ceremony in the course of which they slaughter a tamed tapir, the flesh of which is then consumed in a feast that brings several local groups together. The family that raised the tapir sings its praises and laments it disappearance, adopting all the signs of mourning usually reserved for a deceased human relative. The "Bear festival" held by the Ghiliak (or Nivkx) of the Amur River valley and Sakhalin Island was based on an analogous principle: a bear captured when young and carefully tended for several years was ritually slaughtered and then eaten in a collective banquet in which, as a sign of respect and affection, a portion of its own flesh was offered to its remains.[55] But in neither of these two typically animist societies was the killing of the animal anything like a sacrifice: the bear or tapir was not a victim consecrated to some deity that needed to be conciliated; the ceremony was not expected to produce any benefit, certainly no change of status for those who had raised or slaughtered the animal. Moreover, finally, that animal could not be replaced in the festival by a substitute, not even by one of the same species.

The characteristic feature of a sacrifice is precisely the fact that it establishes a link between two terms initially unconnected, the purpose of the operation being, to cite Lévi-Strauss's definition, "to establish a relation, not of resemblance but of contiguity, by means of a series of successive identifications. These can be made in either direction, depending on whether the sacrifice is expiatory or represents a rite of communion: thus, either of the persons offering the sacrifice [the sacrificant], or of the sacrificer with the victim, or of the sacralized victim with the deity; or in the reverse order."[56] Such a chain of mediations would be as pointless and incongruous in the case of the tapir or the bear, both of which were reputed to possess an interiority resembling that of humans and so would be treated as persons, killed with consideration, and not considered replaceable by another entity. They had no role that linked them to any (in this case nonexistent) transcendent power. On the other hand, making use of sacrifice to forge such a relationship of contiguity between initially separate entities may well seem necessary in an analogical ontology, in which all existing beings are singularities between which links need to be established. Just as one cannot leave out any links in the chain of being without compromising its structural integrity, so too the link between two distant and heterogeneous entities such as a sacrificer and a deity can only be constructed by a mechanism of gradual and transitive identifications between the intermediate elements.

But in this case why put the sacrificial victim to death, for this would seem, in spectacular fashion, to break the connection that one was seeking to establish by means of these cascading identifications? Here too, Lévi-Strauss comes up with an ingenious answer: once the relation between the sacrificant and the deity is assured by the consecration of the victim, that victim's destruction at the hands of humans interrupts the continuity previously established, filling whoever the sacrifice is destined for with a desire to renew contact by dispensing the hoped-for favor. The abolition of the term connecting the "human reservoir" and the "divine reservoir" thus creates a brutal gap in contiguity, and this void prompts an appeal that is believed to initiate some compensatory reestablishment of contiguity.[57] This is a beguiling interpretation. But it is perhaps excessive to speak here of "reservoirs," as if it were a matter of two perfectly autonomous domains that need to be linked by some conduit. On the contrary, the effectiveness imputed to the practice of sacrifice stems from the fact that the victim is presented as a composite package of diverse properties some of which are identical to those of the sacrificant (e.g., it is endowed with life and has been socialized within a human community). Other properties are identical to those of the deity (e.g., it can take on the aspect of its body, be descended from it, contribute to its subsistence). And yet others are identical to those of substitutes that may replace it (e.g., it is looked after by humans and may be eaten). And it is precisely this decomposition of the victim's attributes, against the background of a general splitting of existing beings into a mass of components, that allows it to serve as a link thanks to each actor in the rite identifying with at least one of its properties. Moreover, there are many cases of sacrifice, in Africa in particular, where the beneficiary of the rite is not a person but a concrete or abstract entity with only incidental links with the sacrificant, whether the latter be an individual or a group. In some cases, indeed, it is not a matter of bringing about or consolidating some kind of status or of procuring some advantage but rather that of dissolving an earlier relationship, as in the sacrifice that the Nuer offer up in cases of incest: whether the sacrificial victim is a cucumber, a goat, or an ox, it is always cut in two lengthwise. This operation is called *bakene rual*, "the separation of incest into two," the purpose of which is to dissociate two groups of relatives that an undesirable, potentially lethal relationship had brought together.[58] Sacrifice could thus be interpreted as a means of action developed within the context of analogical ontologies in order to set up an operational continuity between intrinsically different singularities. It is a means of action that, to this end, makes use of a serial mechanism of connections and disconnections that functions either as an attractor (to establish a connection with something else) or as a separator (to break a connection that already exists at a different level and that one seeks to destroy).

10

Terms, Relations, Categories

Now that we have completed this tour of ontologies, both exotic and familiar, we can define and enrich the table of modes of identification with more precision. Depending on what characteristics humans discern in existing beings, judging on the basis of their idea of the physical and spiritual properties of their own persons, continuities and discontinuities of varying proportions are established between the entities of the world, classifications based on identity and similarity come to seem self-evident, and frontiers emerge, consigning different categories of beings to separate regimes of existence. The distribution of the four combinations of resemblances and differences is organized on the basis of two vertical axes. One is characterized by wide dichotomous separations, by the preeminence of continuity over discontinuity and by the inversion of the poles of hierarchical inclusion. In animism, the continuity of interiorities between humans and nonhumans that share the same "culture" takes on a universal value (in contrast to the particular and the relative introduced by differences in forms and biological equipment). Meanwhile, in naturalism it is the continuity of physicalities within the unified field of nature that plays this role (in contrast to the particular and the relative introduced by cultural differences). The other axis favors chromatic continuities and, in a paired symmetry, juxtaposes a system of resemblances tending toward identity (totemism) and a system of gradual differences tending toward continuity (analogism) (fig. 2).

It might reasonably be objected that the world and its ways are far too complex to be reduced to this kind of combination of elements. But we should remember that modes of identification are not cultural models or locally dominant forms of habitus. Rather, they are schemas for integrating experience,

Wide gaps (encompassment)				Small gaps (symmetry)
• **Similar interiorities** (continuity of souls) • **Dissimilar physicalities** (discontinuity of forms, which may lead to heterogeneous points of view)	*Animism*	*Totemism* Australian model		• **Similar interiorities** (soul essences are identical and all members of a class conform to one type) • **Similar physicalities** (substance and behavior are identical)
• **Dissimilar interiorities** (discontinuity of minds) • **Similar physicalities** (continuity of matter)	*Naturalism*	*Analogism*		• **Dissimilar interiorities** (gradual discontinuity of the components of existing beings) • **Dissimilar physicalities** (gradual discontinuity of the components of existing beings)

FIGURE 2.   The distribution of existing beings according to interiority and physicality

which make it possible to structure, in a selective fashion, the flux of perceptions and relations. They do this by noting resemblances and differences between things on the basis of the same resources that every human carries within himself or herself: namely a body and intentionality. Given that the principles that govern such schemas are *ex hypothesi* universal, they cannot be exclusive, and we may suppose that they coexist potentially in all human beings. One or another of the modes of identification certainly becomes dominant in this or that historical situation and is consequently preferred and mobilized both in practical activities and in classificatory judgments, although this does not prevent the three other modes from sometimes infiltrating the formation of a representation, the organization of a course of action, or even the definition of a field of customs. Thus, most Europeans—and I am no exception—are spontaneously naturalists by virtue of their education, both formal and informal. But that does not prevent some of them, in certain circumstances, from treating their cat as though it has a soul, from believing that the orbit of Jupiter will affect what they do the next day, or even from identifying with one particular place and its human and nonhuman inhabitants so closely that the rest of the world seems to them to be of an entirely different nature from that of the community to which they are attached. This does not mean to say that they have become animist, analogical, or totemic, for the institutions that provide the framework for their existence and the automatic behavior patterns acquired over the passing of time are sufficiently inhibiting to prevent such episodic slippages into other schemas from eventually endowing them with an ontological grid that is completely distinct from that which dominates their own environment.

It might also be objected that those two major axes of identification are not of the same nature. The first one combines resemblances and differences by reversing the fields in which they are manifest, whereas the second juxtaposes a pairing of resemblances and a pairing of differences: in totemism all discontinuity seems to disappear; in analogism all continuity does. However, that is just an effect of a skewing of the perspective adopted for defining the modes of identification on the basis of some abstract individual that objectivizes regularities in the world thanks to the attributes that one detects in oneself. Seen from this point of view, the original identification framework of an Australian Aboriginal is certainly his totemic class, characterized by an internal continuity of physical and moral properties that is shared by a group composed of both humans and nonhumans, all derived from one and the same prototype. This framework is not viable on its own, however. For a social life to flourish, what are needed are other totemic groups that are similar but each of which is founded on collections of different properties. These units become complementary at the level of the combination that they form within a tribe or even a wider community. An aspiration toward a homogeneous togetherness, peopled by hybrids unconcerned about some of their apparent dissimilarities, can only become plausible and functional if each of those members of the collective assumes a position in contrast to the rest in such a way that a flux of signs, persons, and values can circulate among them in accordance with a code to which they all adhere. It is at this point that discontinuity recovers its rights, as a condition for totemic segments to become integrated and to form a system by playing on their intrinsic differences (fig. 3).

The same applies to analogism, but in reverse. Its initial state is certainly

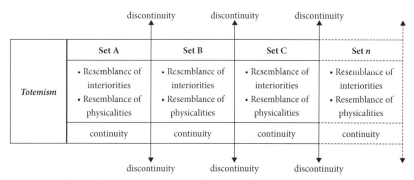

FIGURE 3. The relation between continuity and discontinuity in totemism

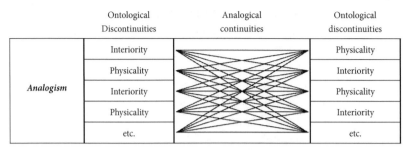

		Ontological Discontinuities	Analogical continuities	Ontological discontinuities
Analogism		Interiority		Physicality
		Physicality		Interiority
		Interiority		Physicality
		Physicality		Interiority
		etc.		etc.

FIGURE 4. The relation between continuity and discontinuity in analogism

a general fragmentation of existing beings and their components. But that accumulation of discontinuities may be seen as a preliminary state of affairs that is logically necessary for the vast movement of recomposition destined to reverse the disjunctive effects of the initial atomism. A world saturated with singularities is almost inconceivable and is in any case extremely inhospitable; so among its premises analogism must include the possibility of modifying that infinitely teeming mass of ontological differences by means of a reassuring continuity that is ceaselessly woven together by correspondences and analogies between its disparate elements (fig. 4).

Encompassments and Symmetries

So far, we have been envisaging the classes of entities carved out by modes of identification solely from the point of view of their intrinsic characteristics. However, from their properties and the contrastive positions that they occupy it is also possible to infer some of the relationships that they may establish between one another. In the animist schema, for example, the physical differences between the various categories of existing entities in no way prevent their respective members from establishing intersubjective relations with one another. The fact is that the ostensible heterogeneity of humans and nonhumans that is defined by their specific forms and patterns of behavior comes to be largely wiped out by the symmetrical links that those entities are able to establish by calling upon the resources of their interiorities. When a man treats an animal as an affine or a ceremonial friend, he expects his attitude to be appreciated by the nonhuman person at whom it is directed and that this person will respond in accordance with the same conventions. As a result of the imputation of human behavior to nonhumans, which is made possible by the resemblance of their interiorities, a large part of what we call "nature" is annexed into the sphere of social life. This constitutes a movement of hierarchical encompassment in which the fact of sharing a mutual relationship counts for more than the physical difference between the terms thus brought together. It is true that the monkey and the bear are different from me by reason of their physical equipment, but that does not stop us from maintaining a personal relationship at another level. This accounts for the fine unanimity with which ethnographers of Amerindian, Asiatic, or Melanesian animist societies all emphasize the relational character of the cosmologies that they describe, and also the fact that individual identities consider themselves defined above all by their contrastive positions. In this mode of identification, relations count for more than terms.

In naturalism, quite the reverse attitude prevails. From the point of view of their physicality, all existing beings depend on the same physicochemical elemental mechanisms, and furthermore, many of them can be fitted into a long evolutionary series of phylogenetic continuities. The universality of nature encompasses them all in a network of common causalities in which they vary from one another only in the degree of complexity of their molecular and systemic organization. All the entities in the world resemble one another in that, whatever their differences of form, behavior, and internal organization, none elude the jurisdiction of the laws of matter. Such entities may be found in the collections of specimens displayed in museums of natural history. They constitute huge ontological inventories arranged according to the rules of systematic classification, which form a cosmos in miniature in which each kingdom, every side branch, each order, each family, each genus can lie at rest there, all together, in their drawers, glass cases, and bottles, protected from the hazards that synecological interactions introduce into the real world. Within those repertories of decontextualized beings, no relations take place, apart from one of general inclusion in the classificatory system. However, in most of those museums there are also a few rooms set aside for ethnography: humans and their artifacts (both classified as primitive) have a niche of their own, flouting the initial unifying ambition that aimed to assemble all existing beings within one and the same taxonomic regime. For great confusion reigns in these ambiguous places where classifications of all kinds—racial, linguistic, cultural, technological, geographical, and stylistic—overlap and intertwine and where culture and its products indicate their resistance to being set into an order dictated by the natural sciences. It is here that dissimilarities start to proliferate—first, between nonhumans and humans, the latter being particularized by their minds, with their ability to create a limitless flux of objects, relations, and signs and, second, between humans themselves, with their kaleidoscope of institutions, symbols, and techniques. Humans constitute a strange species whose members are hardly distinguishable physically and are without question included in nature's great register, yet turn out to be differentiated in so many ways once one examines how they make use of the world and give it meaning. This singularity of theirs means that no relations are transferable; none provides a model that can be generalized to include both humans and nonhumans, for none does any more than cover a circumscribed field of interactions within a circumscribed segment of existing beings. Gift giving, links in the food chain, justice, parasitism, servitude, symbiosis, hierarchy: everything is diversified, nothing is common to all humans. So in this mode of identification, in contrast to animism, what takes precedence, given the heterogeneity of relations, is the material continuity of its terms.

Unlike the hierarchical encompassing tendencies peculiar to both animism and naturalism, the totemic schema is perfectly symmetrical. All the human and nonhuman entities included within the same class of existing beings share a collection of identical attributes that stem from both their interiorities and their physicalities. Morphological differences are not considered a sufficient criterion for making ontological discriminations within any particular class. The human and the nonhuman members of each totemic group also share a relationship in common—a relationship of origin, of kinship, of similarity, or simply of inherence—and all the groups are situated together in a relationship of equivalence since they constitute homologous elements in the more widely encompassing collective constituted by their juxtaposition at the level of a tribe. Here there is no trace of that incipient ontological duality that animism introduced with its distinction between different physicalities and that naturalism turns into a dogma with its distinction between different interiorities. Nature and culture are completely beside the point, as can be seen from the periphrases that ethnographers of Aboriginal Australia must resort to when it comes to describing an order that is at once "social and natural" (Merlan), the "identity" of humans and other natural species (Elkin), or Dreaming as "a culture but also as nature" (Glowczewski). Those expressions all indicate the semantic difficulty of situating totemism within the old dualist polarity. Lévi-Strauss made his own contribution to that collection of circumlocutions when he described certain totemic organizations as presenting "a socio-natural image that is unique but fragmented."[1] Seen solely from the point of view of each class and not from that of the general system that they all form together, Australian totemism is thus a balanced structure characterized by a double identity, that of both its terms and its relationships—a structure that echoes the double ontological identity of interiorities and physicalities. Whereas animism ensures the preeminence of relations over terms, and naturalism that of terms over relations, Australian totemism places interdependent relations and terms on an equal footing. This is a source of perplexity to anthropologists and probably accounts for their oscillation between two antithetical explanations for the phenomenon: one favors the identity of terms (the "participatory" interpretation), and the other emphasizes the homology of relationships (this is the Boasian or Lévi-Straussian classificatory explanation).

Analogism too plays on symmetry, but a symmetry of differences, not resemblances. Existing beings are all particularized and are formed from dissimilar components that both muddle and extend the subjective duality of the body and intentionality: for interiority is often partially externalized, while physicality is invested with spiritual properties. All the same, no more than weak ontological differences separate these countless singularities, while multiple pairing devices are designed to link them in a web of correspondences that plays on certain qualities that they appear to manifest: they are adjacent in space, one seems an imitation of another, or they are mutually attractive. They are certainly all intrinsically different, but it is possible, indeed necessary, to detect points that they share in common. This is where the paradox of analogism lies: it postulates a difference of principle between different terms that in other ways resemble each other. However, the paths that analogy may follow are numerous, so numerous that it is always possible to find several possible avenues or chains of correspondences that link two entities. Relations, like the things that they bring together, are thus extremely varied although several may be applied to the very same existing beings. The combination of these two systems of differences between terms that resemble each other and between relations that bear on the same terms is what confers upon the analogical mode of identification its strange and beguiling ambivalence: the cosmologies that it renders possible are so perfectly integrated and coherent that they border upon a totalitarian order while allowing each of their inhabitants a large measure of hermeneutic liberty. Here too, as in totemism, terms and relations are interdependent, but on the vaster scale of a whole iridescent world, all of whose reflections are relentlessly noted in the vain and magnificent hope of rendering it perfectly meaningful.

The four modes of identification thus imply different connections between terms and relations that one is likely to see resurfacing in the concrete cosmological and sociological objectivations for which each of these modes provides a schematic principle. To describe these arrangements in a synthetic fashion, we may resort to the handy distinction between metaphor and metonymy that Roman Jakobson proposes: metaphor is a connection of internal similarity between terms (which appeals to one's ability to select and substitute words in the organization of a meaning); metonymy is a connection of external similarity between relations (which brings into play one's ability

Wide gaps			Small gaps
• **Difference between terms** (by reason of the differences of physicality and despite the resemblance of interiorities) • **Resemblance between relations** (a way to efface the differences of physicality) *Relations are more important than terms*	*Animism*	*Totemism*	• **Terms are identical** (by reason of their common origin and despite differences in form) • **Relations are identical** (by reason of the discontinuities between classes: correspondence of differential gaps) *Terms and relations are interdependent within each class*
• **Resemblance between terms** (by reason of the resemblance of physicalities and despite the difference of interiorities) • **Difference between relations** (correlating with the differences of interiorities) *Terms are more important than relations*	*Naturalism*	*Analogism*	• **Difference between terms that resemble one another** (by reason of analogies between properties and despite differences of interiority and physicality) • **Difference between relations that affect the same terms** (several types of analogy possible between the same terms) *Terms and relations are interdependent at the level of the general system*

FIGURE 5. The distribution of existing beings according to terms and relations

to combine linguistic units in a referential relationship).[2] In animism, the absence of metaphorical resemblances between existing beings (by reason of their differences of physicality) is compensated for by metonymy (by reason of the relations that they establish). In naturalism, however, it is the absence of metonymic resemblances (the heterogeneity of relations) that is compensated for by a metaphorical link (by reason of the material continuity). However, in both totemism and analogism, metaphor and metonymy are mutually supportive, although in different ways. The similarity between the components of a totemic class provides the basis for the relationship that characterizes these classes as a whole (with the same series of differential gaps). Metaphor at the level of the classes is thus the condition for metonymy at the level of the system. As for analogism, it endeavors to find relations between terms considered to be dissimilar and multiplies dissimilar relations in order to discover a similarity between terms. An absence of metaphor leads to metonymy and an absence of metonymy leads to metaphor (fig. 5).

Differences, Resemblances, Classifications

The modes of identification also differ from one another from the point of view of the classificatory mechanisms that they mobilize. In the field of ethnosciences, it has become customary to oppose categorization according to attributes to categorization by prototypes, as if the use of the one were incompatible with the use of the other. The former method was in vogue around the mid-twentieth century, with its "componential analysis" that consisted in breaking down the terms of a nomenclature into matrices of contrasting features that were assumed to be used in assessing attributions. The latter became the dominant hypothesis with Eleanor Rosch's work on the categorization of colors and that of Brent Berlin on ethnobiological taxonomies, two domains in which it is conjectured that classifications are constructed around typical representatives, or "natural prototypes," which provide the basis for a class because they are the most salient at the perceptive level.[3] But, rather than regard those two cognitive mechanisms as mutually exclusive, it is more reasonable to suppose that we use them alternately, depending on the objects to be classified and along with other classificatory schemas such as spatial contiguity, origins, and spheres of activity. Thus, in folk taxonomies of plants, inclusion within a class always seems to be based on a prototypical classification: in French, the common oak, *Quercus pedunculata*, is the prototype for the taxon *chêne* (oak), for it is perceived as a better example of this class than the English oak (*Q. robur*), the holm oak, the dwarf oak, and the cork oak, all of which are subsumed into it with a descriptive adjective, the better to distinguish one from another. But in certain contexts plants are grouped together according to habitat (reeds accompany willows, osiers, and alders and all the other plants of wet zones) or according to provenance (the olive, the vine, the fig, the cypress, and the umbrella pine, all of which are features of the Mediterranean landscape) or according to use (vegetables, fruits, medicinal herbs, decorative plants, etc.); some are objectivizable by a lexeme of their own, but for the most part these groupings are not marked at a linguistic level.

Furthermore, different criteria may overlap, provided they are not too numerous, and this produces a classification according to attributes. Such is the case with, for example, the French taxon *agrume* (citrus fruit), despite the fact that it is hard to see to which prototype it might correspond: there is no reason why the orange or the lemon should be said to constitute better examples of this class than the grapefruit, the mandarin, or the citron. Nevertheless, *agrume* may be defined in a contrastive fashion within the semantic field of fruit by a taste—acidity (which contributes to the etymology of the French term but does not exhaust its meanings), by a provenance (the Mediterranean region), by a habitat (an orchard), by a temporality (winter ripening), or even by a dominant hue (yellow/orange). Many of those criteria are necessary in order to specify the taxon, possibly even when they are not automatically present in one's mind as one decides on where to classify the object. It is true that the result is not altogether identical to the contrastive matrices of componential analyses since, unlike components, contrasts remain implicit: it is fair to assume that acid is here opposed to sweet, Mediterranean to northern, the orchard to a field, winter to summer. All the same, in the wider sense, this is classification by attributes; and it is very common.

The animist schema seems to rely chiefly on prototypical generalization. Unlike the way that ethnobiological classifications work, here the prototype is characterized not by a form or appearance but by a condition or state. It is humanity, a composite package of affects, intentionality, reflective consciousness, linguistic and technical aptitudes, and the ability to invent arbitrary norms, that provides the ontological model by means of which to evaluate and classify existing beings: and it is a human with his overwhelming interiority, not a human as a biological species, that constitutes the best example of the class of persons into which nonhumans are incorporated by virtue of their assumed identity. Of course, at the level of perception, such a prototype is counterintuitive, a fact that seems to undermine the very definition of such an object: after all, on the face of it, what do I have in common with a bear, a toucan, or a manioc plant, apart from that somewhat vague predicate, life? But this is because we customarily ascribe an exaggerated importance to the perceptive dimension of a prototype and tend to overlook other less ostensible dimensions. To credit a monkey or a sweet potato with an interiority identical to my own, all that is required is for me to replace a salient perceptive feature by a salient psychological trait that is glimpsed sporadically: the kind that one senses in dreams or when we succumb to the urge to impute intentionality to nonhumans, as we all sometimes do. Such a substitution is, in any case, neither complete nor definitive but is simply a matter of context. Just as we all do, the Achuar, the Makuna, and the Naskapi make use of inclusive taxonomies of plants and animals that are based on a prototypical generalization of some salient perceptible feature; but that certainly does not prevent them, in certain situations, from apprehending plants or animals on the basis of the model of interiority of which they are themselves the prototype.

The totemic mode of identification also appears to be governed by generalization from a prototype. The repeated use of the very term "prototype" by ethnologists of Australia in itself indicates its relevance to an understanding of the way in which a totemic group is structured. No doubt it will be agreed that in this case the prototype is even more abstract than that used by animism, for it does not exist as a phenomenal object. In totemism, the prototype under which a class of humans and nonhumans is subsumed is not, strictly speaking, the Dream-being that has engendered the model of this class, nor is it the principal totem from which the class takes its specific name. Rather, it is the core of physical and moral properties that identify each of its members, one of which—usually the one after which the class and the totem are named—synthesizes the characteristics of all the rest. To borrow Brandenstein's terminology once again, all the human and nonhuman members of a totemic class can be "round," that is to say, "large," "choleric," "primary," "broad-faced," and so on or, alternatively, "flat," that is to say, "small," "phlegmatic," "secondary," "narrow-faced," and so on. It might be objected that this constitutes a list of qualities and so seems more like a classification by attributes. But what we need to remember is that, in a classification by attributes, those attributes are contrastive. And indeed they are so at the level of the complete totemic system, but not at the level of the class itself, which for us is the starting point for the process of identification, since each attribute expresses a complementary characteristic derived from the initial prototype that confers coherence upon this class. And, above all, we need to remember that attributes are decomposable, just as an inventory is. The point is that totemic identification does not proceed first by listing common properties, even though those may be stated when the circumstances demand it. Instead, totemic identification presupposes massive and unthinking adhesion to the fact that this or that existing being is identical to me because we both come from the same ontological mold, in other words because we are materializations of the same generative model. It is only on that condition that it is possible to say, as Spencer and Gillen's informant did, that a kangaroo is "just the same" as himself. Here again, the prototype is counterintuitive because it pays no attention to differences in form; nevertheless, it is prodigiously normative given that its very abstraction makes it impossible for experience to invalidate it. From this point of view, it is similar to certain ideal notions that are in common use, such as "all God's creatures" or "the humanist culture."

As for the analogical mode of identification, this mode does classify according to attributes and, indeed, excels at doing so. Every existing being is decomposable into a multitude of elements and characteristics that may be paired with others opposed to them, so that a table of correspondences is always at the same time a table of contrasts. Consider, for example, the correspondences established by the *Hong fan*, probably the most ancient Chinese treatise, between the elements, the human faculties, and the celestial signs: the five phases (Water, Fire, Wood, Metal, and Earth) certainly constitute a field of contrasts, but each is connected with one of the human activities (gesture, speech, sight, hearing, and will) and with one of the celestial signs (the rain, the *yang*, the hot, the cold, and the wind), and these constitute two other semantic fields that are correlated contrastively.[4] Furthermore, this is a rudimentary nomenclature, so Chinese ritualists and philosophers had no compunction in extending it by adding other series of elements. The fact is that the repertory of analogies and contrasts is in principle limitless for anyone seeking to make the most of all the correlations in the world. It seems reasonable to suppose that such a type of knowledge, if it truly strives for exhaustiveness, will not for long be able to do without the help of writing or at least of some graphic means in order to increase the columns in the tables of attributes without unduly taxing the memory.

The naturalist mode of identification also operates according to a classification by attributes, one that, in truth, is extremely elementary: humans are what they are because they have a physicality *plus* an interiority; and nonhumans are what they are because they have a physicality *minus* an interiority. Many refinements may of course be added to this contrastive opposition whose persuasive force stems from its very simplicity; but most of them relate to physicality. Once man was separated from the rest of the world by his moral faculties, he had to be reinserted into the general economy of nature by means of the elements shared in common with other existing beings, that is, his anatomy, his physiology, and his functions. So it is that the place that he occupies in the huge, branching taxonomies of a Buffon or a Linnaeus is determined, as for all organisms, by successive dichotomies of contrastive features that specify his physical attributes in relation to those of his closest nonhuman neighbors. Actually, even within the human species, distinctions were conceived above all in terms of physical variations in the eighteenth century, a period when it was deemed that nothing should elude the taxonomic efficacy of classification according to differences. Blumenbach, for instance, classified humans into five races that differed from one another in their skin color, the nature of their hair, and the shape of their faces. This is an example of a system of classification by attributes that posterity has not seen fit to abandon: in the United States, some of its categories are still accorded an official status (the famous "Caucasian," "African," and "American Indian" types). Of course, there had long existed tables of national characteristics—a Spaniard was proud, an Italian was disposed to love, and so on—but without any scientific pretensions, even if Buffon probably was influenced by them when he mentioned "what is natural" (*le naturel*) among his criteria for the differences between races. It was only with the first babblings of anthropology that people also became intent on methodically classifying human institutions into contrastive typologies that embraced the world's entire surface. At this point, opposed pairs that were less superficial and were hierarchized in terms of evolution came to the fore: oppositions between classificatory kinship and descriptive kinship, between consanguineous families and *gens*, or between gentilitial organizations and state societies. It is as if naturalism, established by a break between humans and nonhumans on the basis solely of a difference of interiority, then endeavored to wipe out all memory of its crude ontological origins by producing a multiplicity of classifications according to more diversified criteria that made it possible to restore humans to the sphere of natural history and to distinguish between humans by varying degrees of interiority. Naturalistic thinking harbors a predilection for classifications expressed in tables of attributes, as can be seen from the classifications of the sciences that take the form of those great charts of retroactive authentication produced, for example, by Comte and Ampère; and as can also be seen from the present book, as its readers will no doubt already have noticed.

PART FOUR

The Ways of the World

'Tis said that the views of nature held by any people determine all their institutions.

RALPH WALDO EMERSON, *English Traits*

11

The Institution of Collectives

Modes of identification are polyvalent, for the assumption is that they relate to universal dispositions. They come to have a public existence in the form of ontologies that favor one or another of them as the principle according to which the regime of existing beings is organized. Each of those ontologies, in its turn, prefigures the kind of collective that is particularly suited to assembling within a common destiny the various types of beings that it distinguishes and also to expressing their properties in practical life. Understood in this way, a collective corresponds in part, but only in part, to what we call a social system.[1] If we pay serious attention to the very diverse ideas that peoples, in the course of history, have forged concerning their institutions, we are bound to notice that they seldom result in isolating the social domain as a separate regime of existence, with precepts that govern solely the sphere of human activities. In fact, not until naturalism reached maturity did a body of specialized disciplines take as their object the social domain and in consequence undertake to detect and objectivize that domain of practice in every part of the world and with scant regard for local concepts, just as if its frontiers and content were everywhere identical to those that we Westerners fixed for it. And even when local "sociological theories" were taken into consideration, they were in many cases so truncated that all that remained was whatever concerned the government of human beings. Concepts of kinship, of power, of the division of labor, of status hierarchies: all these were seen against the background of the political philosophy and sociology of the Moderns; and, set against that standard, they immediately became incongruous. So anthropology set out to justify them with copious explanations that it felt obliged to provide in order to explain the unity of social dispositions that was masked by the apparent differences in the ways that they were institutionally expressed. However, far from being the presupposed basis from which every-thing else stems, sociality on the contrary results from the ontological work of assembling together and distributing subjects and objects to which every mode of identification leads. So sociality is not an explanation but, rather, what needs to be explained. If this is accepted and if it is recognized that, until recently, most of humanity did not make hard and fast distinctions between the natural and the social and did not think that the treatment of humans and that of nonhumans stemmed from entirely separate mechanisms, then we should regard the different modes of social *and* cosmic organization as a mat-ter of distributing existing entities into different collectives: what or who gets to be ranked alongside what or who, and in what way, and for what purpose?

A Collective for Every Species

The animist mode of identification distributes humans and nonhumans into as many "social" species as there are different forms and behavior patterns, so that the species endowed with an interiority analogous to that of humans are reputed to live within collectives whose structures and properties are iden-tical to those of human collectives. They are fully complete societies with chiefs, shamans, rituals, houses, techniques, and artifacts, societies that come together, coalesce, quarrel, provide for their own subsistence, marry in accor-dance with the rules, and lead a communal life that, as described by humans, would appear to be covered by all the habitual rubrics of an ethnological monograph. Here, the term "species" does not extend solely to humans, ani-mals, and plants, for practically all existing beings have a social life. As Walde-mar Bogoras notes in his study of the Chukchees of eastern Siberia: "Even the shadows on the wall constitute definite tribes and have their own country, where they live in huts and subsist by hunting."[2] Throughout the territories where animism prevails, the members of each tribe/species thus share the same appearance, the same habitat, and the same feeding and sexual behavior and are, in principle, endogamous. Admittedly, unions between different spe-cies are not unknown, above all in myths, but they require, precisely, that one of the sexual partners should shed the attributes of his or her species so as to be regarded as just the same as his or her partner.

It may also happen that a member of a tribe/species enjoys a kind of ex-tra affiliation to another tribe/species. This is so in particular in the case of shamans, who, par excellence, are able to pass between human collectives and animal collectives. Thus, among the Wari' of Brazil, a man becomes a shaman when an animal spirit (*jami karawa*) implants in him elements of

its own food that it carries distributed throughout its own body; these generally consist of roucou pods, seeds, or fruits. By means of this action, which
comes down to establishing a relationship of commensality, the animal spirit
forms a strong link with the human, one that makes it possible for the latter
to mobilize the assistance of the corresponding species. These *jami karawa*
look like ordinary animals but are invisible to ordinary people. Their bodies
are inhabited by a spirit in human form that a shaman, for his part, is able to
recognize, beneath the features of some Wari', at least in the case of the representative of the species that has chosen him. Following that transplantation of
nourishment, the *jami karawa* becomes the shaman's friend and his potential
father-in-law, since the man, after his death, will turn into an animal of the
same species as his companion and will marry one of his daughters. The link
thus created forbids the shaman to kill and eat any animals of the species that
has chosen him and that, in return, makes it possible for him to intercede
with them when an illness that they have sent strikes down a human in his
own community.[3] Among the Huaorani of Ecuadorian Amazonia, it is, on the
contrary, the animals that ask to be integrated into a human collective, not
the humans who are invited to become affiliated with an animal collective:
shamans (*meñera*, literally "parents of jaguars") are chosen to be adoptive
fathers by a jaguar spirit that manifests its intention in the course of dreams
and thereafter regularly visits its new family at night, expressing itself through
the mouth of the shaman.[4] In both cases, the fact of being incorporated in
another tribe/species as a kind of honorary citizen in no way suspends the
man's membership in his original tribe/species, nor does it at all imply that
he loses the attributes of form and behavior that go with it.

Animist "nature" and "supernature" are thus peopled with social collectives with which humans establish relations that conform with the norms supposed to be shared by all, for when this happens, humans and nonhumans
are not content simply to exchange perspectives. They also, and above all,
exchange signs, which sometimes leads to an exchange of bodies or, at the
very least, indications that, in their interactions, they understand each other.
Those signs cannot be interpreted by either side unless they are underwrit-
ten by institutions that legitimate them and make them meaningful, thereby
ensuring that misunderstandings in the communications between the two
species are kept to a minimum. It is specifically as a son that the Huaorani
jaguar asks to be adopted, not as a son-in-law; it is as a father-in-law that a
Wari' jaguar chooses a shaman, not as a father; and it is as a brother-in-law,
not a brother, that a woolly monkey presents itself to an Achuar hunter. Each
of these registers is expressed in statements reputed to be intelligible to both

interlocutors, not only because they are formulated in a common language but also because both conform to a system of attitudes and obligations that is shared by the members of both the related collectives.

What is the model according to which these isomorphic social collectives are conceived? Clearly, the model is that of a human society, or at least that of the particular society that ascribes its own internal organization, system of values, and mode of life to the collectives of the nonhuman persons with which it interacts. However, that is not the obvious answer to everyone, certainly not to authors who criticize its implicit sociocentrism. Ingold, in particular, has reacted strongly against the idea that hunter-gatherers may rely on their experience of relations between humans when they seek a conceptual model for their relations with nonhumans. He claims that "actions that in the sphere of human relations would be regarded as instances of practical *involvement* with the world come to be seen in the sphere of relations with the nonhuman environment, as instances of its metaphorical *construction*."[5] Ingold formulates this remark in a critical review of an article by Nurit Bird-David in which the latter develops the hypothesis that hunter-gatherers conceive their environment not as a neutral place that provides means of subsistence but as an entity that, like a parent, is careful to feed its children, with no thought of any reciprocation. Bird-David suggests that this perception of the environment may thus be governed by an unconscious metaphor, "forest is as parent," which, as it happens, is something that the Nayaka of Tamil Nadu and the BaMbuti Pygmies of the Congo do indeed say explicitly.[6] Ingold, however, objects that in such a case one cannot speak of a metaphor: for the hunter-gatherers, there is not one world of society and another of nature, with the former projected on to the latter as an organizing principle. Rather, there is a single world within which humans are seen as "person-organisms" that maintain relations with all other existing beings indiscriminately. No absolute demarcation lines can be drawn between these implied different spheres. At the very most, one may isolate contextually delimited segments within a single field of relations. So the relations that govern interactions with plants and animals cannot be apprehended as metaphors of those that structure interactions between humans.

Ingold's criticism is certainly relevant and also applies to some interpretations of the societies that I call "animist." So I should at this point make it clear that the use that these societies make of categories borrowed from the field of relations between humans in order to qualify relations with nonhumans (or between nonhumans) does not in any sense stem from any metaphorical projection. As Ingold notes, such an interpretation would only lead back to a distinction between nature and society that is alien to local practices. In animist collectives, social categories serve simply as handy labels that make it possible to characterize a relationship, regardless of the ontological status of the terms that it links together. Within the limited number of relationships that it is possible to enter into with existing beings, each human group selects ones to which it ascribes a regulating function in its interactions with the world. Now, the ethnography of animist societies shows clearly that these polyvalent relations are systematically formulated in the language of the relations instituted between humans, not in that of relations between nonhumans. In Amazonia, in subarctic America, and in northern Siberia, the links that bind animals or spirits together and those that bind them to humans are always qualified by a vocabulary drawn from the register of sociability between humans: friendship, marriage alliances, the authority of elders over the young, adoption, rivalry between tribes, and deference shown to the elderly. With regard to the metaphorical interpretation, Ingold points out that one might just as well say that "a parent is as the forest" as say that "the forest is as a parent." And that is quite true, except that that is not what is usually said (except, precisely, in metaphorical speech) any more than one says that humans are to the forest as plant parasites are to their hosts or as plants are to the earth that makes them grow.[7]

While it is fair enough to criticize the sociocentrism of anthropologists, it is absurd to blame the populations that they study for it. The fact is, though, that in animist societies there are no examples in which the relations between human beings are specified by expressions that denote relations between nonhumans, except in rare cases in which the two types of relations coincide perfectly because of the similarity of the actions that they involve. For instance, the vocabulary of warfare sometimes calls upon a terminology that evokes the behavior of predatory animals. Nor, as a general rule, does one find in these societies specific terms that designate ecological relationships between nonhuman organisms such as parasitism or symbiosis, despite these being easily observable. The absence of such terms is noticeable even where, in practice, such relationships are certainly known and are frequently exploited in myths for their contrastive properties and their analogical benefits. But in such myths they will not be specifically named, for the mere mention of the plants or animals that they concern suffices to evoke them by metonymy.[8] In short, in the animist world, relations between nonhumans or between humans and nonhumans are characterized as relations between humans, rather than the reverse.

It is true that to define affinity, friendship, and respect as typical human behavior could be seen as anthropocentric prejudice that might cause one to apprehend common terms and expressions that designate codified attitudes as if, originally, they had applied solely to the domain of human realities. But could one not assume that their semantic configuration right from the start included relations with nonhumans so that its use in their domain should not be seen as an extension of its original field of application? In truth, that seems doubtful, since the altogether concrete relations between humans by means of which interactions between humans and nonhumans are described appear to be used as such (i.e., with their fully human implications) neither in the relations that humans maintain with plants nor in the relations that nonhumans establish between one another.

Let us see how all this works out among the Achuar. They distinguish between three major types of relations between humans and nonhumans. The first is the maternal relationship between women and the plants (mainly manioc) that they cultivate; the second is the relationship of affinity established between men and the animals that they hunt; and the third is the relationship between humans and tamed animals living in the home—animals saved at an early age when their parents were hunted and killed or young birds that were removed from their nests. As regards the first of those relationships, it is true that maternal behavior is also detectable among nonhumans. All the same, the maternal link that Achuar women establish with their manioc and that they maintain with a ceaseless flow of incantations addressed to the souls of their leafy children is quite different from the kind of bond that they establish with their human children or that they can observe elsewhere in their environment: they do not give birth to the seedlings, even if they behave as though they do when they propagate them by means of cuttings; nor do they breast-feed them, but on the contrary they protect themselves from the plants' vampire-like inclinations, for it is said that the manioc sucks the blood of those who touch its leaves; nor do they eat their human offspring, whereas they do consume their plant-children, in fact they even use the latter to feed to the former. So the two relationships are not literally equivalent. The one, a woman's relationship with her human children, sets the general atmosphere that justifies describing the other as a maternal attitude, that is to say, a compound of solicitude and firmness, in equal measure. As for the relationship of affinity, typically that which links brothers-in-law, this is nowhere to be found among nonhumans: a hunter has no sexual relations with the females of the species of which he is a generic brother-in-law; nor is he feudally subservient to the spirit masters of his prey in the way that he is beholden to his own father-in-law. Furthermore, however attentively he observes the woolly monkeys and toucans that he hunts, he will never discover grounds for inferring that they practice an exchange of sisters (as it is said that they do), which the Achuar recommend for themselves. Here again, it is the atmosphere of affinity between men, which is a compound of rivalry, bargaining, and real or potential hostility, that sets the tone for a hunter's relations with his prey.

The taming of animals is a special case. This very common relationship that is established when an animal is turned into a family member does not solely involve wild animals that have been acclimatized to living in a human home. It is also characteristic of the links established between shamans and their animal or spirit auxiliaries, which, as Carlos Fausto has pointed out, is a practice that is widespread throughout Amazonia.[9] Furthermore, this relationship, which involves both a relative dependence and a relative control that humans manage to impose on nonhumans of various kinds, is also used in certain contexts to designate a particular relationship between humans: namely the process that involves the tender and progressive habituation that brings a husband and a wife together in the course of their married life. The use of such a description underlines the human dimension of a taming relationship, for it is always initiated by the Indians themselves. Sometimes this relationship involves animals that the humans wish to include within their domestic community—in which the animals in question are treated with the rather brusque affection usually reserved for orphans. But it sometimes involves a shaman's assistants, its purpose being to get these to agree to place their nonhuman faculties at his disposal. It should be added that the adoption of the young of one species by another species is a very rare phenomenon among animals and so would be unlikely to provide an analogical model for the taming process that is undertaken by humans. The Achuar certainly declare that the spirit masters of the game animals that they protect consider the latter as their pets, but no Achuar has ever told me that he has seen a spirit (who would be invisible anyway) taming a herd of peccaries. In the case of the Achuar, as in all animist societies, we are therefore bound to conclude that general schemas of relations that involve both humans and nonhumans become representable and describable only by reference to the usual forms that such relations take when they are established between humans. They do not draw upon the register of phytosociology or the behavior patterns of animals.

There are perfectly good reasons why animist peoples favor a "sociocentric" formulation for relations between nonhuman persons. In the first place, relations between humans unfold immediately before the eyes of all and sundry, in daily life, and linguistic terms always exist to describe them, even if only in the vocabulary of kinship, whereas relations between nonhumans are either formally similar to those between humans and so can be expressed using the same terms (e.g., maternity, conjugality, rivalry, predation) or else they are more difficult to describe with any precision. We should remember that (1) it was not until the twentieth century that phenomena such as parasitism, commensality, biotic succession, the food chain, and the overlapping of niches were defined and named by scientific ecology; (2) relations between humans seem to be more formalized, their content specified by explicit rules of conduct and their normality shored up by the predictable repetition of the prescribed attitudes; and (3) those relations authorize wider variations than the observable interactions between nonhumans do, in that they can be modified by practice and their conformity to a rule can be subject to public evaluation. Moreover, differences in established expressions for them become more manifest when they are compared, with a critical eye, to the forms that they take in neighboring societies. That is an exercise in which all peoples like to engage. Relations between humans thus appear as abstract and reflective schemas that are easier to handle, to memorize, and to mobilize for wide use than the relations that are detectable in the nonhuman environment. For all these reasons, human relations are predisposed to function in animist ontologies as flexible and effective cognitive models that make it possible to conceptualize human-type relations for all entities possessed of an interiority analogous to that of humans.[10]

An animist collective thus appears as a species whose relations are qualified by means of those that humans set up between one another, but it is a species of a very particular genus and corresponds hardly at all to the definition that a naturalist would provide. Of course, in both cases the species is a collection of individuals who conform to a particular type. However, the natural sciences rule out introducing the point of view of the members of the species when it comes to characterizing its attributes and taxonomic boundaries, except perhaps with regard to that minimal mutual form of identification that a community of reproduction implies. With the sole exception of the human species—which can objectivize itself as such, thanks to the reflective privilege conferred upon it by its interiority—the members of all species are thus reputed not to know that they belong to an abstract set that the external gaze of some systematizer has picked out from the web of living creatures in accordance with classificatory criteria of his own choosing. In contrast, the members of an animist species are said to know that they form a particular collective with distinctive formal and behavioral properties; and this self-awareness of each of them as an element in a wider whole furthermore stems from a recognition that the members of other species apprehend them from a point of view different from their own, a point of view that they need to appropriate in order to feel fully themselves. In the naturalist classification, species A is distinguished from species B because species C decrees this on the strength of the singular faculties of rational discernment that its humanity confers upon it. In an animist classification, however, I am aware that I am a member of species A not just because I differ from members of species B, as our respective attributes show, but also because the fact of the very existence of B enables me to know that I am different, since he does not see me from the same point of view as I do. In short, the perspective of the presumed classifier must in this case be absorbed by the classified in order for the latter to perceive himself truly as different from the former.

This mechanism of constitutive otherness is not at all the same as simply representing oneself through the mirror provided by another, which is a universal way of seizing upon one's own individual and collective identity since, in certain conditions, it results in a complete identification with the point of view of that other person. In Amazonia, this mechanism takes an exemplary form that Viveiros de Castro, writing about Tupi groups, has felicitously called the "cannibal cogito"; the ritual anthropophagy of the Tupi-Guarani is not a narcissistic absorption of qualities and attributes, nor is it a contrastive operation of differentiation (I am not the one that I am eating); it is, on the contrary, an attempt to "become other" by incorporating the enemy's position vis-à-vis me, for this will open up a possibility for me to get out of myself so as to see myself from the outside, as a singularity (the one whom I am eating defines who I am).[11] Exo-cannibalism, head-hunting, the appropriation of various parts of the enemy's body, taking captives from neighboring tribes—all these phenomena that are indissolubly linked with warfare in the lowlands of South America are responses to one single need: the only way to construct a self is by concretely assimilating alien persons and bodies, not as life-giving substances, trophies that bestow prestige, or captives who provide labor, but as indicators of that external gaze that they bring to bear on me, by reason of their own provenance.

Warfare is not the only way to achieve this result. Still, in Amazonia, the various tribes that make up the Pano linguistic group use the word *nawa* both as a generic term indicating strangers in a slighting way and also as an affix for the construction of autonyms: it designates both that to which one is opposed and that with which one identifies. Numerous elements in the social life of Pano groups confirm this paradoxical situation, leading Philippe Erikson to write as follows: "One can even go so far . . . as to say that a stranger not only is seen as a kind of reservoir of brute force that needs to be socialized . . . but is also more precisely defined as a model, or even as a guarantee, of the essential virtues of society."[12] It is here that the theme of perspectivism developed by Viveiros de Castro acquires its full meaning. For even in animist collectives in which it is not claimed literally that animals that regard themselves as humans apprehend humans as nonhumans, many indications suggest that

identity is primarily defined through the point of view from which members
of other collectives see oneself, for these are placed in the position of external
observers; such is particularly the case with the dead, whites, game animals,
spirits, or even an ethnologist (who may well occupy several of these positions at once). So one does not have to be bellicose and have enemies in order
to see oneself through the eyes of another tribe/species: the extremely pacific
Chewong of Malaysia do so when they impute to animals or to spirits a point
of view on the world and therefore on themselves that is quite different from
their own. In the eyes of a Chewong, the tiger and the elephant are perhaps
mistaken when they take him to be what he is not, but that mistake, for the
very reason that it testifies to an ability to have a point of view that is different
from his own, is indispensable for him to situate himself in his own collective.
In short, the assumed misunderstanding plays an essential part in the characterization of an animist species as a collective, in contrast to the definition
of a naturalist species, which, on the contrary, seeks at all cost to singularize a
particular class unambiguously.

Asocial Nature and Exclusive Societies

Naturalism's sociological formula is the simplest of all to define and the most
intuitive, for it corresponds to the sense of self-evidence that modern *doxa* has
instilled in us. It is the formula that we learn at school, that the various media
transmit, and that learned thought elaborates and comments upon: humans
are distributed among collectives that are distinguished from one another by
their respective languages and customs, in other words, their cultures, and that
exclude anything that exists independently of them—that is, nature. There is
no need to dwell on examples of this foundational and seldom-questioned
dogma that is shared by philosophy, the sciences, and common sense, particularly as part I of the present work has already traced its historical genesis
and underlined its characteristic features. So let me just recall a scattering of
facts that testify to its ongoing vigor at the dawn of the twenty-first century.

   As we have seen, plenty of ethologists are prepared to recognize that groups
of chimpanzees may be distinguished from one another by their technological
"cultures," while the older notion of "animal societies" continues to provoke
doubts and controversy. "Social" species certainly do exist in the sense that
their members, with few exceptions, can live and survive only in collectivities.
However, as is frequently repeated, even if those collectivities are highly integrated and possess considerable solidarity, they are not equivalent to human
society, for they lack not only a consciousness of forming a unit as a result of
a reflective choice to live together but also the faculty to devise new rules by

exercising free will. Ethologists studying the higher primates are haunted by the risk of veering into anthropomorphism by interpreting the behavior of the great apes using exaggerated analogies with human behavior. Hence, there is an abundance of ad hoc notions designed to keep animal ethology clearly separate from the sociology of human beings: dominance is not domination, cooperation is not reciprocity, and altruism, despite its ambiguity, is not quite the same as heroic self-sacrifice for the good of the community. In contrast, ordinary thinking about race has desisted from referring to the natural differences between humans that racist theories used to emphasize (an inhibition that is perhaps prompted by the public condemnation of their horrible consequences). Now they justify their aversion to otherness only by referring to the danger of mixing up incompatible cultures: to each his own world and customs, clearly, provided that those are firmly fixed in distinct territories. The ethologists most inclined to concede a culture to the great apes thus support the principle that human collectives have no parallel in nature, while even the xenophobic Westerners who are least open to differences between humans nevertheless do recognize as a fact both the heterogeneity of cultures and the biological unity of the human race.

It goes without saying that, for naturalism, the paradigm of collectives is human society—preferably that which has been developing in Europe and the United States ever since the late eighteenth century—which stands *in contrast* to a lawless nature. Humans come together freely, make rules for themselves, and create conventions that they may choose to flout; they transform their environment, they share out tasks necessary to provide for their subsistence, they create signs and values that they disseminate, they consent to some form of authority, and they assemble to deliberate upon public affairs. In short, they do all the things that animals do not do. And it is against the background of this fundamental difference that the unity of the distinctive properties ascribed to human collectives stands out. As Hobbes remarks, with his robust concision, "To make Covenants with bruit Beasts is impossible."[13] To be sure, social evolutionism has introduced gradations in that original break with the world of nonhumans, and they persist as prejudices: some cultures are said to be closer to nature (nowadays this has become a positive feature) because they do little to modify their environment and do not display the heavy apparatus of states, with all their social divisions and instruments of coercion. But nobody, even among the most diehard of racists, would go so far as to claim that those cultures have borrowed their institutions from animals.

Even if animism and naturalism both set up human society as the general model for collectives, they do so in very different ways. Animism displays a limitless liberalism in its attribution of sociability, while naturalism, more parsimonious, reserves the whole apparatus of sociability for all that is not natural. Conventional anthropology would formulate this by saying that, in the case of animism, "nature" is thought of by analogy with "culture," while in the case of naturalism "culture" is thought of as what is different from "nature." It has also become customary to label those two attitudes ("projective" openness and dualist closure, respectively) as variants of anthropocentrism. But in truth only naturalism is anthropocentric, in that it defines nonhumans tautologically by their lack of humanity and claims that humanity and its attributes represent the paragon of moral dignity that other existing beings lack. Nothing of the kind is to be found in animism, since here nonhumans share the same condition as humans, and the only privilege that the latter claim for themselves is that they can engage with nonhumans in relations founded upon common norms of conduct. Animism is thus anthropogenic rather than anthropocentric in that it derives from humans all that is necessary to make it possible for nonhumans to be treated as humans.[14]

Hybrid Collectives That Are Both Different and Complementary

For over a century, totemism has been regarded as a form of social organization in which humans divide into interdependent groups whose distinctive characteristics are borrowed from the realm of natural species either in that the humans imagine that they have inherited certain of the attributes of those species, or in that they derive inspiration for their own internal differentiations from the contrastive distinctiveness that those eponymous species exhibit. However, this sociocentric view unfortunately introduces an analytical dichotomy between the social system and the natural system, a dichotomy that appears to be absent from the ontological concepts of the "totemists" par excellence, namely the Australian Aboriginals. It is therefore preferable to describe totemism as a system in which humans and nonhumans are *jointly* distributed between isomorphic and complementary collectives (totemic groups), in contrast to animism, where humans and nonhumans are distributed *separately* between collectives that are likewise isomorphic, but autonomous. In the Cockatoo moiety of the Nungar of southwest Australia, we certainly find, as well as cockatoos, not only the human moiety of the tribe but also, for example, eagles, pelicans, snakes, mosquitoes, whales—in short, a whole aggregate of disparate species that could never be found together in groupings detectable in the environment. In contrast, in an Achuar tribe there are only Achuar persons; in a peccary tribe there are only peccary persons; in a toucan tribe there are only toucan persons. While the structure and properties of animist collectives stem from those attributed to human collectives, the structure of totemic collectives is defined by the differential distinctiveness between packets of attributes that nonhumans denote in an iconic fashion, while the properties attributed to their members do not proceed directly either from humans or from nonhumans, but from a prototypical class of predicates that preexist them.

Although animist collectives are distinct from one another by reason of the monospecific composition of their populations, they are homogeneous from the point of view of the principles that dictate their organizations: for the Makuna, the tapir tribe has the same type of chief, shaman, and ritual system as the peccary tribe or the howler monkey tribe and, of course, the Makuna tribe. In the case of totemic collectives, that is not so, for, although likewise different, they are homogeneous at the level of the system that encompasses them, since they are hybrid by virtue of their content and, above all, heterogeneous in the principles that dictate their composition. For, in Australia at least, there are many types of totemic collectives. Under the aegis of one or several totems, humans can be grouped in communities by sex, by generation, by cult, by a shared place of conception or birth, by clan affiliation, or by matrimonial classes; and it is common to belong to several of these collectives at once. Some of these totemic units (matrimonial classes, single-sex moieties, clans) are exogamous either in principle or in fact; others (ceremonial groups and those groups, in many cases identical to the former, whose members received their child-soul at the same site) are not; yet others (e.g., generational moieties) are explicitly endogamous. This confirms that a natural species—or the natural differences between species—do not constitute an analogical model that makes it possible for the totemic group to see itself as a totality sui generis, since, unlike plants and animals that are endogamous within the species, the human components of a totemic collective usually have to find a spouse in a collective other than their own. In fact, it is even because humans and nonhumans together form interspecific collectives that have nothing in common with the collections of individuals that species represent that unions become possible between groups of humans despite their being intimately associated with distinct species of plants and animals that cannot be paired off together.

In this respect too, the contrast to animist collectives is considerable, for the latter are, on the contrary, founded upon the corporeality of a species, since affiliation with each "society" depends upon sharing the same physical appearance, the same habitat, the same feeding habits, the same type of reproduction, and, ipso facto, being apprehended from the same point of view by other tribes/species. It is definitely in animism, not in totemism, that the biological species serves as a concrete analogical model for the composition of collectives; and this is possible because, in just the same way as species, these collectives are never integrated into a functional totality at a higher level: above an Achuar tribe/species, a toucan tribe/species, or a peccary tribe/species there is no common link other than the abstract predicate that anthropologists who study them call "culture." Totemism is altogether different, for, as Lévi-Strauss perceived, the encompassing collection formed by the different totemic groups cannot be represented on the basis of the groupings offered by the natural world: the only available model would be a species, since a genus is a taxonomic fiction; but a species, precisely, cannot be broken down into contrastive segments analogous to totemic collectives.

However, at this point a distinction should be drawn between, on the one hand, the principle of ontological recruitment into totemic collectives, which does not discriminate between humans and nonhumans, and, on the other, the different functions fulfilled by the various kinds of collectives. In Australia, those functions can be listed right through a continuum that passes from an instrumentalization of nonhumans by humans to instrumentalization of humans by nonhumans, passing through an intermediate situation in which humans intervene as the agents of both a human and a nonhuman purpose in that they act as the ritual mediators and the beneficiaries of cosmic fertility. The matrimonial classes provide the example par excellence of totemic groups of the first type: the totemic entities arranged in moieties, sections, and subsections alongside humans, together with the plants and animals that are affiliated with them, have nothing to gain from the taxonomic divisions or the exchanges of marriage partners that these exogamous units serve to bring about at the initiative and to the exclusive profit of the humans. It makes no difference to the kangaroos, bandicoots, and goannas if a kangaroo-woman marries a bandicoot-man and brings into the world a goanna offspring. The plants, animals, totems, and Dream-beings all remain outside this interplay of alliances and affiliations by means of which the human elements in the collectives reproduce themselves by combining the resources of the various totemic groups. Indeed, that is all the more true since, in contrast, the animals and the plants reproduce themselves within their own species, that is to say, actually within the totemic collective. And because they perpetuate themselves without the complex mechanism of exogamous exchanges that govern the human marriage classes, in these they play only a subordinate role as convenient indicators that synthesize the contrastive attributes activated in the matrimonial alliances of the humans (in the case of the totems) or as illustrations of the exhaustive and coherent nature of the general classification of the cosmos that the classes provide (in the case of the species attached to them).

For the various forms of conceptional totemism, the situation is different.

In this kind of totemic group, the human members of the collective are expected to perform periodic rites designed to ensure the fertility of the species associated with their totem. They do this at the very site where a Dream-being once appeared and from whom their totemic identity stems, since each one is a product of the actualization of an identical child-soul that proceeds from the stock deposited in that locality by a Dream-being at the same time as the child-souls of the species in question. These "multiplication" rites, which are very common throughout the continent, have been well described by Spencer and Gillen in the case of the Aranda, among whom they are known as *intichiuma*. Two examples will suffice to explain their purpose. In the multiplication rite of the Emu totem of the Strangeways site, the initiates attached to the totemic center pour some of their blood on to a small area of earth previously brushed smooth, and on the red surface obtained in this way they paint the inner parts of an emu—its fat, intestines, and heart—and also the creature's eggs at various stages in their development. The purpose of this operation and the songs that accompany it is, in mimetic fashion, to retrace the process of an emu's gestation and thereby encourage the species' fertility. In the rite of the Witchetty-Grub totem at the Alice Springs site, the initiates visit and honor each of the rocks that represent the concrete presence and corporeal manifestation of the Dream-being from which this species is derived. The rocks, which are of various shapes, represent the insect's eggs, its chrysalis, the adult creature, and also the body parts of the Dream-being. A hut is then constructed, representing a chrysalis, inside which the initiates sing the praises of the insect at each stage of its development.[15] These rites are performed just before either the emergence or the coupling of the species concerned and they are designed to favor its development and increase by means of this condensation of the stages of its biological reproduction.

The human members of a conceptional totemic group are thus responsible for watching over the propagation of an animal or plant component of their collective. The task devolves upon them by virtue of the fact that they share with it the same ontological origin and participate in the same prototypical class of attributes. It would be going too far to say that, in this partially delegated reproduction process, the nonhumans make use of the humans in order to achieve their own ends, for the multiplication rites of plants and animals are also to the advantage of the human members of other totemic groups that feed on them, and furthermore, this kind of collective also provides the framework for rituals exclusively designed for the individualization of humans. Nevertheless, here humans and nonhumans are, at the very least, bound in solidarity in an ambition to perpetuate life in each of its embodied classes.

Multiplication rites may also take place in the context of clan totemism, as is the case among the Warlpiri, where this is combined with conceptional totemism. All the components, both human and nonhuman, of a patri-clan share the same "Dream-fathers" and are therefore of the same stock. For example, the humans of the Opossum/Black Plum clan call those marsupials and those fruits "fathers" and "brothers" and are invested with the mission of ensuring their ritual reproduction in the sites where their common "Dream-father" deposited their respective stocks of child-souls. This also benefits other clans, which reciprocate by watching over the species in their own care. The multiplication mechanism differs from that used by the Aranda. Here, the human and nonhuman members of the clan are inhabited by their own kind of imagistic and dynamic totemic essences, known as *kuruwarri*, which can only be activated when they are summoned to appear in a ritual. The rite prompts the *kuruwarri* of the plants and animals to function, and in this way their propagation is ensured.[16]

Collectives based on the sharing of a common totemic filiation or of a conception site serve not simply to propagate their nonhuman components but are also the means by which, through appropriating the reproductive process of humans, these totemic entities choose to perpetuate themselves. Throughout the continent, representations of conception are all in agreement on one point, which Ashley Montagu already emphasized many years ago: "Neither male nor female parent contributes anything whatever of a physical or spiritual nature of the being of a child."[17] As Merlan shows clearly in her comparative study of Aboriginal theories of human reproduction, children are always the product of a mother's incorporation of a child-soul deposited in a totemic site by a Dream-being. Before taking the form of a fetus, a child-soul leads an autonomous life, often in the shape of an animal or plant that its mother may then ingest, for she is seen as a mere receptacle, a kind of incubator that allows the child-soul to develop until its birth. These seeds, which are said to be of a playful nature, wait for a human body that they then endow with the totemic attributes peculiar to the Dream-being from which they proceed. Essentially, they "look for mothers from whom to be reborn."[18] Ethnologists' descriptions are in no doubt at all that the humans are seen as no more than vectors of an actualization sought by a totemic entity. On the subject of *maroi*, the child-souls of the totemic sites of the Belyuen community of the Cox peninsula, Elizabeth Povinelli tells us that "they preconceive an image of the child before making it." The intentionality ascribed to child-souls is central to this reproductive mechanism, in contrast to the relatively passive role played by the humans: "*maroi* intentionally hide in foods and create children. Men and women unintentionally capture and ingest them."[19] Furthermore, this autonomy of the *maroi* persists after birth, for it is claimed that they exert an irresistible influence on their hosts, determining the choice of the game that they hunt, the foodstuffs that they consume, and the sites that they frequent. A similar situation obtains among, for example, the Aranda. For them, "the incarnation of a child-soul, a *kuruna*, comes about, in the first instance, from its desire to be embodied."[20] The parents are therefore no more than an adoptive father and a bearer-mother, the consenting instruments for perpetuating one of the dimensions of a totem that objectivizes itself in a human being who thereby herself becomes a component forever already present in the intrinsically hybrid collective established long ago by a Dream-being.

The same process is at work in totemisms transmitted through clan filiation. The impregnation of the woman usually takes place on the site that harbors the child-souls of the clan, and the newborn child quite naturally becomes a part of the collective whose continuity was ensured by his maternal and paternal ancestors, who shared the desire of the totemic entity to perpetuate itself. Thus, in the Belyuen community, the filiation totems known as *durlg* "preconceive the descent of themselves in the form of humans before they are actually born into a new generation."[21] It thus seems legitimate to wonder if, in such circumstances, one should even speak of human ancestors, since the whole of human life seems to be nothing but a vehicle of which the filiation totems take possession in order to become manifest in each successive generation. Like all patrilinear filiation totems, the *durlg* are anchored in sites scattered across the clan's territory, and it is traditionally claimed that they legitimate their members' rights to use the resources of the place (in particular when conflicts over land use arise with non-Aboriginals). The exercise and transmission of such rights are incontestably crucially important for ensuring the subsistence of the Aboriginal humans and for their identification with a space still animated by the properties with which a Dream-being infused it. But we should also note that the clan members are not merely guardians with rights of usufruct over the sites that are home to their totem and over the territory that it long ago fashioned in its peregrinations; they, along with the landscape, are also embodied emanations of it and the channel through which its creative action remains vibrant in a particular place. As Povinelli writes, "rather than humans passing down sites from generation to generation, the interior mythic power of sites passes itself down through the human body."[22] There could be no clearer way of saying that here humans are the zealous auxiliaries of an immanent and unique finality that both encompasses them and is beyond them.

The multiplicity of the types of totemic collectives in Australia and of the functions that they fulfill, along with the multiple affiliations authorized by this diversity, are all no doubt necessary if each of the human and nonhuman members that compose them is to be given its due. The humans need to identify with a place and a prototypical class of attributes; the nonhumans need assurance that they can continue to reproduce themselves thanks to the deliberate or involuntary mediation of humans. Each element in these hybrid units depends on the rest of them in a great exchange of services in which their respective contributions end up becoming confused, so powerful is the cement that federates them all within an ontological totality rooted in a common space. From this point of view, the totemism of matrimonial sections should probably be relegated to the rank of a subordinate—and probably late—phenomenon, despite the importance that anthropological literature has granted to these institutions. Understandably fascinated by the elegant formal complexity of the eight-section marriage systems, kinship specialists have failed to take sufficiently into account the fact that, for the Aboriginals, these models were probably prompted more by an exercise of intellectual virtuosity than by a procedure for organizing the daily existence of collectives and their reproduction. For even if matrimonial classes certainly are, like other totemic units, specific syntheses of physical and moral attributes shared with nonhumans, they have nothing to do with one fundamental dimension of Australian collectives, namely the relationship to a particular place, the space that produces an identity. They are nominal categories, as it were, anthropometric filing systems that prescribe the criteria for the general classification of humans—and therefore also for the pairings that are permitted or proscribed for them. But they are not principles for association that make it possible to develop a social life and that attach one to a territory and all its resources. In contrast, conceptional totemism and clan totemism do constitute the true bases of concrete collectives, for they bring about the aggregation of humans into separate groups, invested with responsibilities and rights with respect to the places from which they draw their subsistence and that are perpetuated through their bodies and thanks to the rituals that they perform there.

It is also reasonable to ponder upon, not so much the functions assigned to different kinds of totemic collectives, but the very purpose of such segmented organization. For at first sight this seems quite strange and counterintuitive, since it intermingles humans and nonhumans with the same interests within specific totalities that might have remained autonomous while at the same time forcing these apparently self-sufficient units to exist within the vaster collectives that are formed by their combination. One of the primary functions of this form of the distribution and association of existing beings is no doubt of a practical nature, although that is not to say that this suffices to explain it. As Lévi-Strauss rightly noted, the functional specialization characteristic of totemic order is analogous to that of a caste system in that it makes it

possible to optimize the management of the means necessary for life. It introduces a strict distribution of ontological work among complementary groups
that are all qualified in the production and reproduction of the localized resources with which these groups identify, even without, themselves, consuming them.[23] The paradox of this generalized foraging economy that is applied
throughout the whole gigantic continent is that it seems to involve a constant
endeavor to fabricate and maintain what would appear to be given naturally:
both the products indispensable for subsistence (by means of rites for the
multiplication of species) and also the humans indispensable for their production (since each totemic group places "incubator women" engendered within
it at the disposition of other groups). In other words, Aboriginal totemic collectives are highly specialized mechanisms for the creation and maintenance
of certain types of resources, either for the benefit of other collectives ("bel-
lies" to carry their child-souls, and plants and animals to feed them) or, within
the collective itself, for the mutual benefit of its human and nonhuman components. They ensure the reproduction of totemic species, for which humans
are responsible, the perpetuation of totems by means of women's bodies, and
access to hunting and gathering territories through totemic affiliation. Without going so far as to imply that all this is a matter of a necessary functional
adaptation, one cannot help thinking that, given the strategic character of the
management of unpredictable resources in a hunter-gatherer economy, it is
indeed a good policy to entrust to specialized organs the job of watching over
each of those resources by identifying with its fate.

When seen in its collective dimension, the totemic ontology thus acquires
an extra specification that is both peculiar to the particular morphology of
this kind of organization and also indispensable if it is to become truly functional. As a mode of identification, totemism recognizes only one basic unit,
the totemic class, which constitutes an integral and self-sufficient totality since
it provides the framework for the identification of its human components. As
an emu-man, I ascribe to myself physical and moral attributes derived from
the Emu Dream-being, attributes that are also present in emus and in other
existing beings with which I share a common origin and the tangible source
of which lies in particular sites and features of the landscape. That is all I
need in order to know who I am, whence I come, and with what elements of
the world I belong. But although my totemic class is certainly what fundamentally provides me with a prototypical identity, it is not, on that account, a
sufficient condition for me to act effectively in the world. In order to do so, I
need to establish relations with other existing beings, and that is possible only
if the terms in these relationships are clearly distinct from myself, that is, if
they are external to the ontological community that I form together with all

the human and nonhuman members of my class. The essential unit constituted by a totemic class is thus not enough in itself if it wishes to escape from
solipsism and extend its action beyond the frontiers that its form assigns to
it. It needs other segments of the same nature but of different compositions,
for these are indispensable if productive interactions are to occur and a sociocosmic dynamism is to be created, recalling the multiple relationships that
the Dream-beings engaged in with one another long ago, so as to animate the
world and diversify it.

However, simply juxtaposing totemic collectives does not ipso facto lead
to a higher-level totality that can be clearly represented as a unique entity.
In Australia at least, the combination of depopulation and the migrations
provoked by the European conquest has brought about a wide movement of
ethnic recomposition that in many cases rules out classifying as a separate
totality of the "tribal" type an association formed locally between heterogeneous clans with different languages and territorial origins. Furthermore, the
itineraries of the Dream-beings and the totemic affiliations that stem from
these form networks that cover extensive areas, so that totemic classes that
are identical since they emerged from distinct portions of the same original
itinerary end up in different "tribes" that are not necessarily adjacent to one
another. Faced with the ambiguity of the criteria that might make it possible
unequivocally to define the principles of recruitment and the contours of a
tribal "macrocollective" that integrates these totemic classes, each segment is
thus obliged to seek from other segments the resources necessary in order to
achieve complementarity with them in a wider combination.

But totemism does offer a means of ensuring the functional integration
of segments without their being subsumed into some preexisting composite whole, for the identity, not of the individuals within the collective, but
of the collective itself as a pluralized individual, necessarily depends on an
awareness of what it is different from, that is, other collectives. This involves
a contrastive specification that does not need to be made at the level of each
of its individual elements, for these derive from their prototypical class all the
intrinsic characteristics necessary to define their own being. The individuation of segments is thus conditional upon recognition of an otherness against
which background the differential specificity of the segment stands out clearly
and so, in consequence, does that of each of its members vis-à-vis members
of other segments. As Stéphane Breton notes in a critique of the classificatory interpretation of totemism, totemism is operational as a social system
only because the members of a totemic group that is, by definition, closed are
able to apprehend themselves through outside eyes by identifying with an-

other segment whose function is to reflect their own image to them as a third party.[24] This alter ego collective and the segment that it has made it possible to particularize then come together to form a functional whole at a higher level than that of totemic units, and this constitutes the principle underlying the mechanism that justifies both their difference and their equivalence on a vaster scale. By having recourse to the *clinamen** of contrastive identity, totemism overcomes the initial obstacle introduced by the autonomy of self-referential classes and thus accedes to a veritable sociological existence based on the interdependence of collectives of the same type within an encompassing whole. This would have been inconceivable within the terms solely of the ontological premises initially posited.

Unlike animism and naturalism, which set up human society as the paradigm of collectives, totemism operates an altogether new fusion by intermingling within hybrid sui generis wholes both humans and nonhumans that make use of one another in order to produce social links, generic identities, attachments to particular places, material resources, and generational continuity. But it does so by fragmenting the constitutive units in such a way that the properties of each of them are complementary and their association is dependent upon the differential distinctions that they present. To describe such a system, traditional anthropology has oscillated between a definition that emphasized the continuity between nature and culture (a "participative" logic) and one that contented itself with a cognitive interpretation of the phenomenon (a classificatory logic). The problem here is that although totemic collectives are certainly the basic units in the system that organizes the universe, for the Aboriginals at least they stem neither from an extension of the social categories that govern the life of humans (the sociocentrism of Durkheim) nor from the model offered by the discontinuities between natural species (the intellectualism of Lévi-Strauss). If we strive to be faithful to what the Aboriginals say about the principles that structure the existence that they lead in common with a many-faceted crowd of nonhumans, it would be better to say that their totemism is "cosmogenic." Just as animism is anthropogenic in that it borrows from humans the minimum indispensable for nonhumans to be treated as humans, totemism is cosmogenic in that it derives from cosmic groups of attributes that precede both nature and culture all that is necessary for it to be impossible ever to separate the respective parts of those two hypostases in the life of collectives.

---

* Translator's note: in the doctrine of Epicurus the unpredictable swerve of atoms that provides the impetus for natural phenomena to occur.

A Mixed Collective That Is Both Inclusive and Hierarchical

The analogical mode of identification does not find expression in forms of
collectives that are as specific to it as those of animism and totemism. In an
analogical ontology, the totality of existing beings is fragmented into so many
examples and causes that the associations between all those singular units may
follow many kinds of paths. However diverse the morphology of the groups of
humans and nonhumans recognized by analogism, those groups are nevertheless always presented as being constitutive units in a collective that is vaster by
far, given that it is coextensive with the whole world. Here, the cosmos and society are equivalents, almost to the point of being indiscernible, whatever the
various types of internal segmentation that such an extensive whole requires
in order to remain operational. For a relevant example that will be more help-
ful than a whole clutch of illustrations, let me take you to the southern Andes,
to the Chipayas of Bolivia, to whom Nathan Wachtel has devoted a remarkable
monograph.[25]

Lost on a high semidesert plateau in the province of Carangas, at an alti-
tude of close to four thousand meters, despised by their Aymara neighbors,
who dismiss them as "rejects," and by now reduced to barely one thousand
individuals, the inhabitants of the village of Chipaya dilute their poverty and
abandonment in a microcosm of prodigious richness in which, on a reduced
scale, it is possible to make out all the structural features of more grandiose
and populous analogical collectives. The Chipaya, who speak a Puquina language, are the last Urus to survive as an autonomous unit in Bolivia. At the
time of the Conquest, they made up one-third of the country's autochthonous
peoples. Their territory is shaped like a rectangle. It spans roughly thirty kilometers from east to west and is twenty or so kilometers wide, bordered on
the south by Lake Coipasa. It is divided along a north–south axis into two
sectors of more or less equal size. These are known as Tuanta (east) and Tajata
(west), as are the two moieties who live there, each of which corresponds
to what, in the Andes, is called an *ayllu*, that is, a group of bilateral descent
(figs. 2 and 3). Situated approximately at the center of the territory lies the village of Chipaya, which is also divided into two moieties along a north–south
axis; and each moiety is furthermore divided into two quarters along a west–
east axis. The four quarters, Ushata, Waruta, Tuanchajta, and Tajachajta, are
grouped around four chapels and each is occupied by several lineages that all
recognize a common ancestor. The quadripartite organization is repeated at
the scale of the territory, except that the moieties' internal subdivisions do not
follow the orthogonal pattern of the village but are given geographical limits
in the form of riverbeds. In the Tajata moiety, the Tajachajta and Tuanchajta

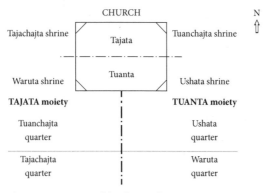

FIGURE 6. The quadripartite organization of the Chipaya village

sectors are thus separated by a north–south axis, while in the Tuanta moiety, the Ushata and Waruta sectors are marked off by an axis running from north-west to southeast. The lineages of each quarter of the village possess, in their particular sector of the territory, hamlets consisting of a few huts that they occupy for part of the year. Here they benefit from the use of the pastureland that surrounds them, which is allotted to them by the *ayllu* of the moiety to which they belong. Finally, just as the territory can be seen as a projection of the organization of the village, the church presents a reduced model of that organization. The church, which is dedicated to Santa Ana, the patroness of Chipaya, is used by both moieties and stands, to the north of the village, in the space that separates them. It is a simple adobe construction, rectangular in shape, with a door opening to the east. The members of Tuanta always position themselves in the moiety on the right in relation to the east, while the members of Tajata position themselves on the left, the men being on the right-hand side within each moiety, the women on the left. The church is surrounded by a walled patio flanked by a tower and extended by a longer patio. At each of the four corners of these patios and on the four walls of the tower are placed sacrificial altars, which are reserved for each of the quarters. Their positioning in space (i.e., in relation to the east) respects the general quadripartite schema of the village and the territory (fig. 6).

The interactions between the various levels of these interlocking units follow the classic logic of segmentary affiliations: the members of one lineage stand together against those of another lineage, as do the lineages of one quarter against those of another quarter and the quarters of one moiety against the other moiety; and all the Chipayas stand in solidarity against the Aymaras. This repetition of a contrastive structure at the various levels of social and spatial affiliation seems central in the organization of the Chipaya collective.

As Wachtel notes, "it constitutes the principle of a veritable mental schema in which a number of categories that organize the world interact."[26] However, the units are not all equivalent. True, there is no political superiority of one moiety over another, for the exercise of authority regularly alternates, in accordance with the traditional principle that is recognized in the Andes; and as for disparities of wealth, which in any case are minimal, they are unaffected by the quadripartite structure. However, the dualist organization does imply a classificatory order for the moieties and quarters, which is structured around a series of pairs, the first term of which symbolically predominates over the other one: east over west, right over left, masculine over feminine, upper over lower. The Tuanta moiety (to the east and on the right) is thus superior to the Tajata moiety (to the west and on the left); and the Ushata quarter (to the east of the east) is superior to the Waruta quarter (to the west of the east), just as the Tuanchajta quarter (to the east of the west) ranks above the Tajachajta quarter (to the west of the west).

Nonhumans are also subject to this segmented division. In the first place, every year each *ayllu* delimits, rearranges, and redistributes its fields of quinoa and its pig pastures by means of collective labor involving ditch-digging, irrigation, and drainage in its own portion of the territory, without ever soliciting the collaboration of its opposite moiety. But it is above all the various kinds of deities that are equitably distributed among the subsections of Chipaya, in particular the deities that reside in the *silos* and the *mallku*. The *silos* (from the Spanish *cielo*) are small chapels consecrated to saints, aligned at regular intervals along four straight lines that are oriented on the cardinal points and mark out an immense cross stretching right across the territory, with the village positioned at the intersection (fig. 7). Each line of *silos* corresponds to one of the quarters, the last *silo* (the one farthest from the village) being the most important in the series because it is consecrated to the patron saint of the quarter. Although these chapels appear to refer to Christian values, that attribution is weakened if one accepts, as Wachtel does, that the alignments of *silos* follow the same principle as the *ceques* system at Cuzco in the Inca period and that, like the latter, they are linked with the cult of the sun.[27] The *ceques* formed a set of forty-one imaginary lines radiating out from the Temple of the Sun along which 328 sacred sites, or *huacas*, were positioned. Each of the forty *ceques* (but not the forty-first, which was associated with the family of the Inca) was linked with a group of honorary Incas (non-Inca autochthonous individuals allied with the sovereign by virtue of matrimonial alliances) and was oriented toward the place where the group lived. The Cuzco *ceques* imposed order upon the geographical, social, and ritual space of the capital of an empire conceived by its rulers as a cosmological system, and they

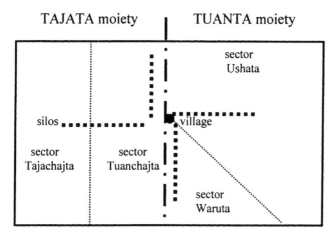

FIGURE 7. The quadripartite organization of Chipaya territory

also served to divide up time. The whole installation constituted a veritable calendar laid out on the ground, which was also linked with an irrigation system. The same can be said, on a more modest scale, of the *silo* alignments. The saints are honored in a regular succession in each quarter in turn, in accordance with a rotation that covers the entire year, moving clockwise, with the summer (the rainy season) being associated with Tuanta and the winter (a dry and very cold season) with Tajata.

The cult of the *silos* represents the celestial part of the relations that the Chipayas maintain with their deities. The other part, which is typically Andean, brings together elements linked with the earth and is organized around the cult of the *mallku*, male and individualized chthonic deities that dwell, together with their spouses, in small conic adobe monuments known as *pokara*. Each moiety celebrates its own *mallku*, of which there are four, and the *pokara* that correspond to them respectively are distributed in the space between the quarters. In each of the moieties, there are also other *pokara* that are the seats of two *mallku* that are common to all the Chipayas—Marka Qollu, a female deity assimilated to Pachamama or Mother Earth, and Lauka Mallku, the male deity of terrestrial water. Finally, the most important of all is Torre Mallku, which is shared by the two moieties. This is, in fact, nothing but the church tower, on the summit of which, at carnival time, sacrifices are made and offerings are placed, requiring, just for once, collaboration between the two moieties. Torre Mallku is the father of the other *mallku*, so these are all brothers, although they are split into pairs, one element of which is assigned to one of the moieties, and the other to the second moiety. As for Marka Qollu and Lauka Mallku, which are unique, although each is assigned to two *pokara*, their incarnation in each of the moieties is regarded as the twin of the other. The *mallku* are analogous to the mountain deities of the Aymaras, which, in similar fashion are likewise endowed with an active interiority, and it is because the desolate plateau to which the Chipayas were in the past relegated is totally flat that they have had to erect miniature substitutes for hills, namely their *pokara*.

It is not possible, here, to go into the details of the complex and minute rituals that are performed in each of the sites mentioned above. Suffice it to say that their primary function is to put the multitude of Chipaya deities in contact with one another and "get them 'to talk' to each other, so that the universe can be in harmony with itself."[28] The assignment of deities to social units, subdivisions, and spatial regions, periods of the year, and technical specializations divides up a liturgical economy. The effect of this is, at a suitable moment, to get a subgroup of humans, which is a different one each time, to organize the mobilization of the cohort of nonhumans involved in the dominant activity of the moment. Each kind of deity is responsible for mediating with this or that portion of the population of the cosmos whose assistance is required in one or other of the four great domains of human intervention, all of which are very localized: namely agriculture, the exploitation of the resources of lakes, livestock raising, and hunting. Some deities are concerned with celestial water, others with underground water; some control the winds; and others protect the domesticated animals or rule the aquatic birds that the Chipayas capture in their nets. And given that "the world is an immense field of forces and flux, in which everything echoes everything else,"[29] it is essential that humans, through their offerings and supplications, be able to win organized cooperation from the deities, which are basically heterogeneous and distributed, as the humans themselves are, in their clearly separated segments of the great collective that they form all together. It is only on that condition that the beneficial complementarity and cooperation of the nonhumans will amplify the efforts that the Chipayas themselves make in the hope of fulfilling themselves, despite their differences, in the plenitude of a shared destiny.

In its most general principles, the organization of the Chipaya world differs hardly at all from that of the Aymara and the Quichua communities of Bolivia, Ecuador, and Peru or even, on a quite different scale, from that of the Tawantinsuyu (Inca Empire). In fact, its merit is that it reveals the structural characteristics of any analogical collective with exceptional clarity. In the eyes of those who compose it, this kind of collective conforms to the dimensions of the entire cosmos but is divided into interdependent constitutive units structured by a system of interlocking segments. Lineages, moieties, castes, and descent groups of various kinds extend the connections between humans and other existing beings, stretching from the underworld to the empyrean, but at the same time maintain a separation, in many cases an antagonistic one, between the various channels through which these connections are established. Although not totally ignored, whatever is beyond the collective becomes an "out-world," prey to disorder, at times disdained, at times feared, at times destined eventually to become a part of the central apparatus, as a new segment whose potential place already awaits it. This latter status was that accorded, for example, to the barbarian tribes that imperial China annexed to one of its regions, and likewise to the "savages" who lived alongside the Tawantinsuyu on its Amazonian flank and who, although they had never been conquered, in principle belonged to the Anti section of the Inca quadripartite system. In similar fashion, the Moogo kingdoms of the White Volta valley considered those in their peripheries to be subhuman but would nevertheless periodically raid there to acquire captives to attach to the exclusive service of their royal lineages.[30] The segments that strengthen and stabilize the architecture of the universe do not intermingle but may always integrate peoples along their margins.

Analogical collectives are not necessarily empires or statelike formations. In fact, some, as the case of the Chipayas testifies, involve quite modest numbers of human beings who know nothing of stratifications of power or disparities of wealth. Nevertheless, what they all share in common is the fact that their constituent parts are arranged in hierarchical order, even if only at a symbolic level with no direct political consequences. The hierarchical distribution is in many cases repeated within each segment, thereby marking out subgroups that find themselves in unequal relationships similar to those that obtain between units at a higher level. The classic illustration of such a situation is provided by the caste system in India, in which the general schema of subordination is repeated in a whole succession of interlocking groups at lower levels. (This happens in the subcastes that compose the castes, in the clans that compose the subcastes, and in the lineages that compose the clans.) A similar process operates in the organization into endogamous "sections," or *kalpul*, of the Tzotzil and the Tzeltal of Chiapa. These are units that do not really qualify as moieties since some communities include three or five of them, yet they do have all the same attributes. As at Chipaya, these are social and cosmic segments in which humans and nonhumans are intermingled with moral persons who control landholdings and individuals within their respective jurisdictions. When only two sections are involved, as is usually the case, they are divided by a line running through their sloping common territory at the level of the village, so that the moiety that is preeminent at the ritual, symbolic, and demographic levels is situated in a higher position that is associated with mountains and the autochthonous deities that live in them. The patron saint of that moiety is also that of the entire community. Meanwhile, the subordinate moiety is associated with the lowlands, agricultural abundance, and the world of demons and non-Indians. The numerical and ceremonial superiority of the upper moiety simply expresses the more general schema of the segmentation of the universe into complementary pairs of elements, one of which is said to be the "elder" or "major" one, the other the "younger" or "minor" one. Every "major" mountain is paired with a "minor" one, every "elder" cave with a "younger" one, and the same goes for many other elements that are positioned within the *kalpul*. They range from fountains to statues of saints in the churches and include political and religious posts at every level of the community hierarchy.[31] Although less formalized, the positioning of lineages in certain West African societies abides by the same principles. In some cases, the lineages are organized into a hierarchy in accordance with the order of successive segmentations spreading out from the original root lineage. In others, there are, as it were, lineage castes that distinguish between the descendants of chiefs, masters of land, blacksmiths, and captives, with the distinction between "elders" and "youngers" operating contrastively at every level. Finally, even where the "standard" hierarchy is expressed in terms of political domination or economic supremacy, in many cases it may be reversible at another level. The exercise of authority may be accompanied by religious subordination; a unit associated with what is spatially a preeminent region may find itself in a subordinate position in ritual circumstances; and in commemorative foundation rites, conquering segments may become the dependents of autochthonous segments.

Some of the collectives that I call analogical are sometimes said to be "totalitarian," as in the cases of the Inca Empire and some lineage-based societies in West Africa.[32] That is one way of expressing the extraordinary interlocking of elements in societies that are holistic yet very compartmentalized, in which the freedom of individual maneuver seems reduced and, in our eyes at least, the control over conformity exercised by the totality over its parts seems almost insupportable. It is also a way of saying that nothing is left to chance in the distribution of existing beings between the various strata and sections of the world, and that each one finds itself fixed in a place that suits, if not all its own expectations, at least what is expected of it. That is why nonhumans also find themselves enrolled in the segments that make up the collective and are expected, in the place assigned to them, to serve the segment's interests. Llamas, millet, and rain certainly exist as generic entities whose properties are known to all, but it is through their relation to the segment upon which they are dependent that they acquire an authentic meaning and a practical identity, as the herd of llamas of such or such a lineage, the millet fields of such or such a group of descendants, the rain that such or such a mediator is responsible for causing to fall at the opportune moment. This fundamental singularization becomes even more clear-cut with one particular kind of nonhuman entity: deities. In contrast to Australian totems and to the "spirits" that inhabit animist universes, an analogical deity is the object of a real cult that takes place in one precise spot: there it receives offerings; sacrifices and prayers are addressed to it at the allotted times; and, in return, it is expected to grant the wishes of its faithful worshipers in the particular domain of expertise that it is recognized to control. The immanence of these deities is thus partially counterbalanced by their material presence at a particular site or in a particular object, by their affiliation to a segment of the collective that may produce liturgical specialists responsible for glorifying them, and by the specialized field of intervention that is generally assigned to them. The miracle of monotheism is to have fused all these particularities into one polyvalent God, unattached to any particular place or any segmentary membership: an operation so extraordinary that it did not take Catholicism, with its cult of the saints, long to restore the functional distribution peculiar to analogism.

Analogical collectives are thus alone in having veritable pantheons, not because they are polytheist (a more or less meaningless term), but because, as has often been pointed out, the organization of their little world of deities extends that of the world of humans with no break in continuity. It is, indeed, the same world, with an identical social division of labor and an identical compartmentalization of the sectors of activity, rivalries, and antagonisms among its segments. So it is understandable that, just as in the case of the Chipayas, the various units of a collective strive, by setting up cults, to get their own particular deities to accomplish whatever they are destined to do and endeavor to mobilize their obstinately separate characters for the benefit of all in certain undertakings in which their cooperation is indispensable. It is equally understandable that analogical pantheons should be so flexible: it certainly makes sense for an empire to welcome the deities of the peoples that it absorbs, for their cooperation is necessary the better to integrate within a cosmic totality all the disparate elements of which it is composed. But conversely, it is also perfectly normal that analogical collectives subjected to Christianization should enthusiastically recruit the Catholic saints, along with the powers that each of them is recognized to possess, into the regiments of nonhumans that already exist in each segment. Indeed, it was perhaps partly because they had no gods of this kind nor any segments in which to lodge them that, despite all attempts to conquer them, the Indians of the Amazonian foothills remained resistant to their annexation by the great Inca analogical machine, just as the Germans for so long remained impossible to assimilate into the Roman Empire.

There is one more characteristic that the Chipayas illuminate: the general use, in every dimension of existence, of spatial and temporal symmetries and endless repetitive structures. Quarters, cardinal points, and levels all reflect one another; the cosmos periodically turns back on its axis and the past is repeated in the future. The relics of deified ancestors are put on show and icons are set up in order to keep alive the link that connects them to the present. Everything possible is done to ensure that no singular unit remains outside the great network of analogical connections. In this kind of collective there are no solitary beings. Or if there are, it is by dint of extracting themselves utterly from those shared kinds of servitude and those endless hierarchies, as the "renouncers" in India do and the one God did in his cradle of the Near East. Apart from them, none can make the most of their multiple differences unless these are rewoven into the interlocking meshes and isomorphisms maintained by the net of coordinates in which every entity, whether human or nonhuman, is caught. This feat is achieved thanks to the combination of multilevel segmentation and the analogical obsession with correspondences. What was dissimilar at one level appears similar at another in relation to a new stream of differences, although intrinsic particularities are never effaced, since everything is a matter of perspective. Thus, it often happens that, at the summit of the hierarchy, where all points of view meet and toward which all divisions converge, one unique being is enthroned, so that all those successive integrating layers finally become totalizable: the Inca, the pharaoh, some creative deity, or, more sensibly perhaps, the tower of the Chipaya church, silhouetted against the lunar immensity of the Altiplano.

The configurations of existing beings that analogism renders possible may not be as specific as the animist and totemic collectives, nor as purified as the naturalist ones, but they nevertheless present a number of remarkable features (fig. 8). In contrast to the multiple collectives of humans and nonhumans in which all are of equal status and the composition of which is homogeneous (the tribes/species of animism) or heterogeneous (the totemic classes), all of which are designed to enter into relation with one another, the analogical collective is unique, divided into a hierarchy of segments, and relates exclusively to itself. It is thus self-sufficient, for it contains within it all the relations and determining factors necessary for its existence and functioning, unlike a totemic group, which is certainly autonomous at the level of its ontological identity but requires other collectives of the same type as itself in order to function. In an analogical collective, the hierarchy of the units that constitute it is contrastive, that is to say, definable solely by the reciprocal positions held

	Animism	Totemism	
• Humans and nonhumans are distributed separately in different collectives with the same structures and properties (isomorphic "social" collectives). ↳The structure and properties of the nonhuman homogeneous collectives are indexed to those of humans. • Modernist translation: "nature" derives its specifications from "culture" ("projection"). • Anthropological label: **ANTHROPOGENISM**			• Humans and nonhumans are distributed jointly in isomorphic collectives (complementary segments of "social" collectives). ↳The structure of hybrid collectives is indexed to the differences of hypostasized attributes in nonhumans, while their properties are indexed to the identity of the attributes of humans and those of nonhumans. • Modernist translation: "nature" and "culture" are continuous ("participation") but internally segmented by the properties that nonhumans embody (correspondence between differential gaps). • Anthropological label: **COSMOGENISM**
	Naturalism	Analogism	
• Humans are distributed in different collectives (cultures) that exclude nonhumans (nature). ↳The structure and properties of collectives of humans are indexed to the difference between humans and nonhumans ("dualism"). • Modernist translation: "culture" derives its specifications from its differences from "nature." • Anthropological label: **ANTHROPOCENTRISM**			• Humans and nonhumans are distributed within a single collective (the world), organized in mixed segments arranged in hierarchical order. ↳The structure and properties of the collective are indexed to the ontological differences between existing beings grouped into complementary units on the basis of analogy. • Modernist translation: "nature" and "culture" are continuous within a cosmos organized as a society (a sociocosmic order). • Anthropological label: **COSMOCENTRISM**

FIGURE 8. The consequences of ontological distribution for the structures and properties of collectives

within it, which is why its segments do not form independent collectives of the same nature as totemic classes, which derive from within themselves and from the sites and prototypical precursors peculiar to them, the physical and moral bases of their distinctive character. The moiety of the East only exists in that it complements a moiety of the West, whereas the totemic Kangaroo group, even if it may need the totemic Emu group on many occasions, nevertheless derives the legitimation of its absolute singularity solely from the circumstances of its own origin.

The segments of an analogical collective are thus fundamentally heteronomic in that they only acquire meaning and a function in relation to the whole that they form conjointly, a whole that, for its part, is perfectly autonomous. It is true that, as we have seen, animist collectives also allow for a measure of heteronomy; but it is of quite a different kind since the external specification in this case is mediated by a series of identifications with individual and intersubjective otherness from various provenances. It is not produced by a superdetermination of the elements by the structure that organizes them. The enemy whose otherness—that is to say, the gaze with which that enemy sees them—a Jivaro or a Wari' absorbs by capturing his head or eating his body, or an animal-person whose perspective both the Jivaro and the Wari' sometimes try to adopt, certainly all come from collectives that are different from that Jivaro's or Wari''s own. However, characteristics intrinsic to those collectives are not what gives that enemy or that animal-person the ability to singularize an individual. What is important is simply their external position in relation to that individual. Accordingly, the members of tribe/species A are differentiated from the members of tribes/species B, C, and D because they perceive themselves as distinctive entities through the gaze that those other tribes/species direct at them when certain codified interactions occur. That is why, in the case of animism, nothing predetermines which kind of collective is likely to fulfill this function of specification from outside. Depending on the context, it may be one or several tribes/species of animals, one or several tribes/species of spirits, one or several tribes/species of humans, or a combination of all those.

As for a purely physical incorporation of an external point of view, that becomes a fortuitous luxury reserved for only a few animist collectives, as does the cannibalism that constitutes the most usual means of doing so. In an analogical collective, in contrast, the members of segment A are, as a whole, differentiated from the members of segment B, insofar as A and B are elements in the hierarchical structure that encompasses them all. In philosophical language, one could say that their positions and relations are the effect of an expressive causality. The dependence of analogical segments upon the collective that defines them is thus essential to their mode of being. They need to be able to create exteriority (from themselves) out of elements that are interior (to the collective).

The relations between analogical collectives and naturalist ones are more complex and ambiguous by reason of the historical contiguity that connects the emergence of the latter with the dissolution of the former. With the emer-

gence of the modern world, to which the best minds of the last two centuries
have devoted their analyses, the hierarchical segments of collectives based on
levels of status have crumbled, giving way to an immense mass of human individuals who are legally equal but who continue to be separated by concrete
disparities both within the particular communities in which they are distributed and also within the formal aggregate that they all constitute together in
the "concert of nations." The mixed worlds that each collective had tailored
to suit it have become diluted in an infinite universe that is recognized by all
those who, regardless of their position on earth, recognize the universality
of the nonhuman laws that govern it. Above all, the City of God has fragmented into a multitude of "societies" from which nonhumans have been
banished—in law, at least, if not in fact. This has given rise to collectives of
the same nature that are, therefore, comparable even though for a long time
they were judged not to be equal according to evolutionary criteria, principally owing to the fact that some of them appeared to be incapable of expel-
ling from the heart of their social life plants, animals, mountains and lakes,
and ghosts and gods.

The features peculiar to analogism may well have facilitated this new distribution. In effect the nonhumans that analogical collectives mobilize in their
segments preserve their particularities, unlike in totemism, in which they are
fused with the humans, and—of course—in animism, in which their physical
and behavioral differences are very clearly evident, given that they are distributed among monospecific "societies." Analogical segments are thus not
hybrid but mixed. The entities that they encompass retain their intrinsic ontological differences—as the nature of this mode of identification dictates—
but those differences are attenuated by the multiple relations of correspondence and cooperation that their sharing in the common ends of the segment
weaves between them. The deified ancestor of a lineage is no longer altogether
human, even if he is represented by a mummy or an anthropomorphic sculp-
ture; a mountain is not really human, even if the group of humans that worship it expects it to heed its prayers and contribute to its well-being. When
the sections that compose an analogical collective split asunder, the human
and nonhuman members of each of them ostensibly seem to recover their
ontological singularities, which the united actions in which they engaged had
partially erased. They thus became available for the radical differentiations
and massive regroupings that naturalism is forced to introduce in order to
organize this chaos of singularities without resorting to a segmentary system.
The old cosmocentric order disappears, given the absence of intermediary
bodies able to embody its hierarchical series of levels, and it can now be supplanted by an anthropocentric order in which the world and its constituent

units find themselves divided up according to whether humanity is directly present, present through delegation, or not present at all. Then, like so many solemn tutelary powers, societies with all their conventions, religion with its gods, artifice, and the objects that this creates, Nature and all that it determines—in short, all those familiar things whose reassuring ordinariness we have learned to appreciate—at last emerge into the light of reason.

12

Metaphysics of Morals

When Marx said that "mankind always takes up only such problems as it can solve,"[1] he was right, provided that it is clear that particular problems and fitting solutions arise not only from the historical developments of material life with all its contradictions but also from the fact that, faced with analogous situations, not every fragment of humanity asks the same questions or they at least formulate them in such different ways that other fragments may have some difficulty in recognizing in them the very questions that they themselves have set out to elucidate. Now, most of those questions may be grouped as problems whose expression will take altogether different forms depending on the ontological, cosmological, and sociological contexts in which they arise. If we accept that the distribution of the properties of existing beings varies according to the modes of identification that we have been examining, then we must also accept that, likewise, the cognitive regimes, the epistemological positions that make those modes of identification possible, and the resulting ways of tackling a problem will all vary to the same degree. Lévi-Strauss provides an example when he compares the methods of investigation adopted by the Spanish and the Amerindians when faced with the question of their respective humanity. While the churchmen wondered whether the savages of America possessed souls, the Indians of Puerto Rico immersed the whites that they captured in water for weeks on end to see whether they would rot. The former posed the problem of the nature of man in terms of moral attributes; the latter did so in terms of physical ones.[2]

Logically enough, given its reformative ambitions, what modern epistemology presupposes as the starting point for its researches is an abstract, cognizant, but individualized subject, endowed with faculties of perception, intellect, and reason that, on the basis of the knowledge and technology of the period, make it possible for that subject to produce verifiable hypotheses about the state and structure of the world. However, the present work will adopt a different way of proceeding. Rather than assume the existence of a universal subject, it will be necessary to determine what kind of a subject is produced by each mode of identification—in other words, to clarify the nature of the entity that occupies a position from which legitimate statements can be made about the state of affairs and that constitutes the seat from which action in the world can proceed. Each of these protean subjects, the product of a particular ontology and acting within a specific collective, will necessarily be confronted by distinct epistemological and metaphysical problems that he will endeavor to resolve in his own way and with the means that are at his disposal, thereby establishing zones of objectivity, of nonsubject, for which he will have to elaborate a suitable kind of treatment. Many of the misunderstandings that are described as "cultural," some of them comical, others tragic, result from the fact that the various collectives that populate the world do not really understand the fundamental questions that engage other collectives. Or, believing mistakenly that they can detect the shape of a problem that they themselves confront, they have no hesitation in applying to it the solution that they have devised for themselves. Some of those solutions no doubt do have a universal application—human rights and scientific procedures, for instance—but it is illusory to think that that they can definitely resolve questions that are formulated in other places and in other contexts and that concern mysteries not even suspected. Dissolving such questions in the acid bath of reason will not remove their relevance for those who are preoccupied by them, at least not until such time as the latter themselves disappear from the human scene along with the problems that worried them.

An Invasive Self

Animist subjects are everywhere, in a bird that is disturbed and that, protesting, takes to flight, in the north wind and rumbling thunder, in a hunted caribou that suddenly turns to look at the hunter, in the silk-cotton tree swaying in a light breeze, and in a clumsy ghost that reveals its presence by stumbling over a dead branch. Existing beings endowed with an interiority analogous to that of humans are all subjects that are animated by a will of their own and, depending on their position in the economy of exchanges of energy and on the physical abilities that they possess, hold a point of view on the world that determines how much they can accomplish, know, and anticipate. The jaguar that, the Wari' insist, thinks in all good faith that he is taking his prey home for his wife to cook, the elephants that, the Chewong claim, visit one another and live in their own country just as humans do in theirs, the sea lions that, according to the Tsimshian, go to consult a shaman when they have been wounded by an arrow, and the Ke'let spirits that, the Chukchees say, live in villages, practice divination, and move around on sledges: all these beings may consider themselves humans and practice human skills, but that does not mean that they live in a land of mirages or willful illusions. To say that they are persons in effect comes down to recognizing that they possess autonomy, intentionality, and a point of view of the same nature as those of humans, but they are situated within spheres of practices and meanings that are peculiar to each of them, since each shares only with its conspecifics what von Uexküll calls an *Umwelt*, a lived and "acted" world, characterized by whatever the animal in question is capable of doing in it with the physical advantages at its disposal. It is this ability to perceive, in a subjective fashion, a world that extends their own organs and needs that converts animist entities into subjects, and it is because they are recognized to be subjects that they are said to have souls.

The fact that this interiority is described as similar to that of humans is not at all surprising, nor is the fact that it enables nonhumans to live a "cultural" life in social collectives. For it is humans and their institutions that provide the most accessible model for specifying what a subject is: namely a singularity occupying a position from which autonomous actions, perceptions, and statements are all possible. A soul is thus the concrete and quasi-universal hypostasis of subjectivities that, however, are definitely singular since they proceed from forms and behavior patterns that determine the situation and mode of being in the world that are peculiar solely to the members of the species collective that has been endowed with those particular attributes. This interiority is shared by almost all beings, but the mode of its subjectivization depends on the organic envelopes of the beings that possess it. That this is a strange paradox is shown by Viveiros de Castro when he writes of Amazonia as follows: "Animals see in the *same* manner as we do *different* things from those that we see, because their bodies are different from ours."[3] The tranquil certainty that things are indeed as we perceive them to be does not, here, stem from the apodictic power of a well-constructed demonstration, nor even from the persuasive effect of a rhetorical argument that one may come round to believing oneself. Rather, it stems from the conviction, anchored in a definite perceptive apparatus, ethos, and situation, that the world conforms with the way that we use it: it is a perceptible extension of the body, not a representation.

The animist theory of knowledge involving a generalized subjectivity that is particularized by bodies is clearly poles apart from the cognitive realism to which most of us adhere spontaneously even if we are not always able to explain it theoretically. The philosophies of the self, which, in the West, accom-

panied the rise of the positive sciences, postulated a radical break between
words and things, between the abstract ideas used in understanding and the
reality that they apprehend, between mental representations and their objects. But animism, unlike them, does not consider the work of knowledge
to be a formalization of a world of preexisting substances. Perhaps one could
generalize what I once wrote about the Achuar: "They are probably closer
to the immaterialism of a thinker such as Berkeley in this respect, for they
appear to found the existence of cognizant entities and the elements of their
environment more or less entirely upon the act of perception. To paraphrase
the famous formula of that Irish bishop, it is the perceptive qualities that,
in a single movement, constitute at once things themselves and the subject
who perceives them." I then went on to say that the entire Achuar cosmology stems from this relational concept of belief: "The hierarchy of animate
and inanimate beings is founded, not upon the degree of perfection of Being
or upon a gradual accumulation of intrinsic properties, but upon the various modes of communication that are made possible by the apprehension
of perceptive qualities that are unequally distributed."[4] In short, among the
Achuar, the act of knowing, and the specification of subjects and objects that
it renders possible, do not proceed from one fixed point in a view that sets in
order the diversity of a neutral reality. On the contrary, they result from the
pragmatics of communication between entities distinguished by their respective positions and by the type of perception that they can mobilize as they
apprehend one another. What I said then of the Achuar (and here comes my
excuse for citing it at such length) later found confirmation for Amazonia in
general, for Viveiros de Castro has, for example, made the following observation: "Amerindian souls, be they human or animal, are thus indexical categories, cosmological deictics whose analysis calls for . . . a theory of the sign
or a perspectival pragmatics."[5]

Let us generalize a little further. As a first approximation, animism seems
to lead to a relativist approach to knowledge, not so much with regard to the
source of the point of view expressed about it—for it is always the human
point of view that prevails, since it is humans that speak for nonhumans—
but rather with regard to the conditions that render it possible. Each type of
physicality corresponds to a type of perception and action, and so to a type of
Umwelt, that is to say a relation to things that are definable not by their absolute properties but by perceptions and uses that vary according to the kinds of
subjects dealing with them and the possibilities for their objectivization that
they offer those subjects. But animism also manifests a decided universalism
in that it refuses to confine subjectification to humans alone: every entity in
possession of a soul accedes to the dignity of a subject and can lead a social

life as rich in meaning as that ascribed to *Homo sapiens*. Here we are faced by interiorities that are generalized and physicalities that are particularized. It is a combination that is decidedly enigmatic, for it reverses our own *doxa*, term for term: if we stuck to the time-honored phraseology, we should have to speak here of a natural relativism and a cultural universalism—an insurmountable contradiction for any well-formed modernist epistemology.

From the point of view of its very singular premises, animism is constantly confronted by a problem both doctrinal and ethical that we have already several times glimpsed beneath the surface: how can one be sure that humanized nonhumans are not indeed humans? Of course, their bodies are manifestly different, as are the behavior and mores that are determined by their biological apparatus. And it is primarily that difference of physical envelopes that makes it possible for humans to feed daily upon animal and vegetable persons without sinking into routine anthropophagy. But the resemblance between interiorities is so powerful, affirmed so vividly in all the circumstances in which humans are involved with nonhumans, that it becomes really difficult to ignore it completely when it comes to cooking and eating. A niggling doubt always lingers: beneath the body of the animal or plant that I am eating, what remains of its human subjectivity? What guarantee is there that I am not munching (or worse) on a subject just like me? That is precisely the point made by the Inuit shaman Ivaluardjuk, to which I have already referred: "The greatest peril of life lies in the fact that human food consists entirely of souls." It is indeed a serious peril if one goes so far as to admit that eating a person, even one covered by fur, feathers, or foliage, cannot quite be dismissed as a symbolical sleight of hand.

Humans endeavor to face up to this problem by resorting to various methods, often combining them. First, one can do one's best to de-subjectivize this food, to make it just "a thing," by eliminating everything that recalls the being that provides it, all the shreds of interiority that still adhere to the tissues because they synthesize the dispositions peculiar to the species. As we have seen, that is what the Makuna are doing when they decontaminate their foodstuffs by dint of incantations designed to send the "weapons" of each species back to the site of their origin. Another ploy, favored by the Piaroa and the Barasana, is to treat the game as though it were a plant: a somewhat hypocritical way of demoting dangerous foodstuffs by several notches in the hierarchy of entities that display affinities with humans.[6] However, the more usual ploy is to accept the calculated risk of eating nonhuman persons but to take the precaution of compensating for this neo-cannibalism by, in exchange, making offerings to the animals or to their masters. In some cases the exchange is perfectly symmetrical, as among the Desana, where the shaman returns the souls of dead humans to the animals' master so that he can convert them into game. An edible soul that will be clothed in flesh is traded in exchange for a soul consumed along with the flesh that has clothed it.[7] Conversely, one may take the line that subjectivity is unaffected by the eating, so the integrity of the animal person survives for as long as its interiority does. That is the solution adopted by the hunters of the Siberian North, who ceremoniously thank the souls of the slaughtered game and return to the animals only that which they claimed to have taken, namely flesh, with which they punctiliously feed the various types of *ongon*. The Ma' Betisék of Malaysia likewise offer food to the animal and plant species that they feed on, "because they are perceived as humans who have been wronged,"[8] although this does not prevent the victims whose indulgence they have tried to buy from avenging the wrong done them anyway, by causing the humans to suffer from wounds and sickness. The fact is that no measures of compensation, however well intentioned, can ever totally dissipate the brutality of the following recognized fact: the maintenance of human life involves the consumption of nonhuman persons. It is therefore quite common in the animist world for the nonhumans upon which humans feed to be blamed for sickness, misfortune, or death, usually through the mediation of the spirits that govern the destiny of the hunted animals. Some of these, in Siberia and Amazonia, make it their specialty to hunt human souls and feed upon them. Fair enough, perhaps: if to eat a person (not just an animal) is *also* to eat its soul, the reprisals seem perfectly equitable.

Putting quasi-similar beings to death and eating them is far more disturbing metaphysically than the passing prick of conscience that certain Westerners may feel when they eat meat.[9] It is not so much a sense of culpability that grips the Amazonian or Siberian hunter when he takes an animal's life, but rather a muffled anxiety when faced yet again with the manifest porosity of ontological frontiers. Which will win out, the difference in bodies or the similarity of souls? Against this background of angst peculiar to animism, metamorphosis takes on its full meaning. As we have seen, here it is more a matter of anamorphosis, the *experimentum crucis* of the relationship between a human and a nonhuman: by changing one's corporeal envelope, one can slip into the skin of another in order to fuse with the subjectivity anchored in its body. If that is so, metamorphosis allows interiorities trapped within heterogeneous physicalities and points of view to find grounds for an accord, in which social interactions can unfold without altogether flouting the constraints of verisimilitude. It is, in the end, metamorphosis that testifies to the humanity of animal-persons and plant-persons, and so it is metamorphosis that principally fuels the animist dilemma concerning the true nature of what is eaten. But even as it instills doubt, metamorphosis helps to dissipate it, since in this way it makes supremely manifest the separability of interiority and physicality. If humans can take on the outward appearance of animals and animals can cast off their costume and reveal their subjectivity within a human appearance, then the flesh of a hunted animal and the substance of plants become more clearly dissociated both from the souls that they shelter and from the behavior patterns for which they provide the material. Furthermore, the phenomenon is repeatable, transitive, and reversible—at least, it is when outside the temporal regime of myths—unlike other types of metamorphosis, such as the transformation of the Australian Dream-beings into elements of the landscape or into totemic entities, or indeed the changes of form, from human to animal, that the jealous gods of antiquity sometimes delighted in imposing upon mortals.[10] Animist metamorphosis is a contingent meeting of two points of view at the level of perceptible experience. In this way, through its periodical sidelong shift, it helps to objectivize the duality of interiority and physicality by distinguishing the domains of autonomy open to each.

But the autonomy of souls is relative, since they are all alike. So it is, rather, in bodies, with all their variations of forms, functions, and potential uses, that animism finds signs of otherness and, against the background of a moral condition common to most existing beings, endeavors to distinguish self from nonself. The body, an objective seat of difference that constitutes both the source and the matter of knowledge, becomes par excellence the object of speculation, the one that is the most rewarding for thinking about the diversity of the world and organizing it. It comes as no surprise to find that animals rank highest in the cohort of others (*alter*) whose limits need to be determined. Their physiology, their habits, and the intentionality that they seem to display in their actions all easily indicate them to be subjects of the same nature as humans, even though they stand out as being different by virtue of a mass of anatomical and behavioral details that prevent them from being regarded as altogether identical. As Brightman notes when writing about the Cree, animals are "social others." In the Canadian Far North, as in all animist territories, they are the emblematic incarnation of social otherness.[11] In particular, they present a vast range of feeding regimes, that is, of bodies feeding on other bodies, and still according to the model of the food chain, this makes it possible to specify ontological taxonomies by means of the multiple interactions and hierarchies of the eaters and the eaten. Here, it is not really a matter of the universal phenomenon of marking out a collective identity by the ostensible difference in feeding habits; nor even of the equally common idea that it is commensality or the repeated sharing of the same foodstuffs that makes the eaters identical. Rather, the point here is the postulate that every existing being is defined primarily by its position within a network of relations in which it is predator to some and prey to others.

Humans are not spared this destiny, as we have seen, since they must ceaselessly "pay in person" in exchange for the nonhumans that they devour. It is those humans' living flesh that the animal masters consume by disease; their blood that cultivated plants daily suck (e.g., among the Achuar); their dead flesh that the beasts of the Inuit and the Siberian North devour and that the *ongon* take back to the Spirit of the forest for it to gorge upon. And it is their souls that will provide the starting point for new animal flesh from which the bodies of their descendants may benefit. It is hardly surprising, then, that it is often by means of cannibalism or its diverse more or less metaphorical variants that humans subjected to this regime strive to carve out between them zones of identity and otherness. The souls of the members of neighboring tribes make them subjects, just like me, but their bodies objectivize them as different from me. They are decorated, painted, and tattooed differently; the weapons, tools, and utensils that are extensions of their bodies differ from mine (as do the forms of the jaws, beaks, and claws or talons of animals); the houses that shelter those bodies are not the same as the one in which I live; and the language by means of which they act upon the world is not the one that I speak (any more, indeed, than is the language of the peccary or that of the bear, or at least the one attached to their specific forms). Here, the social body is not an abstraction; it is an organic community of subjects with similar bodies, subjects who, to borrow a formula that Terry Turner applies to the Kayapó of Brazil, "apprehend their subjectivity as immanent to their concrete physical activities."[12] This is probably a characteristic of animist collectives in general. Each variety of humans perceives itself with a bodily form of its own and thus constitutes a kind of independent species, so that eating an enemy is not, strictly speaking, anthropophagy (or allelophagy) since, just as with an animal person that one hunts and eats as game, the victim comes from a neighboring tribe that is distinguishable by its physical attributes. It is not the case that the enemy is reduced to the rank of a nonhuman—for the whole world bears traces of humanity—but he is a human of a particular type and differs from his predator in the same way as a tapir-person differs in its body, not its "culture," from the hunter tracking it.

In an animist regime, objectivizing a human who is different consists first and foremost in noting the singular properties of the physical envelope in which he appears. This is very clearly the case in the lowlands of South America, where one does not usually seek to act upon an "other" by changing the nature of its soul (that is an old missionary obsession), but instead tries to do this by appropriating features of his body: occasionally, quite literally, eating him, but more often by taking from him elements that generate his identity (head, penis, scalp) or even, more generally, by capturing fertilizable wombs and their products (captive women and children, who are integrated following treatment that alters their original appearance and habitus in a kind of one-way metamorphosis). The goal of all these practices is not to capture substances and fluids from which to derive power and energy. Rather, what flesh, bones, and hair provide in a metonymic fashion for those who appropriate them are dispositions peculiar to a particular situation and physical form: the mode of being peculiar to a particular species.[13] The otherness that one absorbs along with bodies is thus neither a vital force whose distant provenance renders it desirable nor a second-order identity to be annihilated so as to mark one's own triumph. On the contrary, it is something that is indispensable if one is to perceive oneself as distinctive. Eternally in quest of an elusive completeness and surrounded by misleading forms and concealed souls, an animist subject can be sure of only one thing: he eats and will be eaten.

The Thinking Reed*

What can be said of the epistemology of naturalism that has not already been repeated a thousand times? At the risk of advancing shocking simplifications, let us therefore content ourselves with a very brief synthesis. A subject both cognizant and political (for the two are for once united) takes the form of an abstract human capable of reasoning and exercising free will. That excludes nonhumans from superior forms of knowledge and action (those belonging to the nonperceptible realm). Within that domain, though, not all humans appear to be equally competent. One has but to remember anthropology's ceaseless attempts to impose the idea that "savage thought" too was in some respects rational and that "a science of the concrete" constituted a worthy *bricolage*! Whereas animism extends to a general multitude of existing beings the position of a moral and epistemic subject, naturalism confines this to one species and surreptitiously introduces a hierarchy within that species. Furthermore, with the exception of scholars and philosophers, who, it is said, know how to rise above this condition, the general mass of more or less rational subjects remains, for most of the time, trapped in the prison of habits and prejudices. Groups of these subjects thus differ from one another with regard to their customs, languages, and conventions and also individually, within each culture, by reason of their education, their native environment, and their talents. Not only is intersubjectivity impossible between humans

---

* Translator's note: a reference to Pascal's famous definition of man.

and nonhumans, but it also turns out not to work very well between humans themselves, so varied are their beliefs, values, and institutions, as are the sign systems by which they try to translate those fleeting constructions in communications that are always threatened by misunderstandings. Happily, a grand and beautiful certainty unites the wisest of the inhabitants of this tower of Babel. Behind the welter of particularities that man ceaselessly engenders, there exists a field of realities with reassuring regularities, knowable by tried and trusted methods, and reducible to immanent laws whose veracity cannot be impaired, whatever the processes by which they are discovered. In short, cultural relativism is only tolerable or even interesting to study when set against the massive background of natural universalism to which minds in quest of the truth can turn for help and consolation.

All the same, not everything is resolved, for the persistence of cultural arbitrariness introduces a source of persistent anxiety as to science's claim to account for everything that exists and to do so better and more completely than religion used to. Why does culture remain intractable to the models of explanation and the causal links that chemistry, physics, and biology employ with such success? Can one be satisfied with this state of affairs or should one place one's confidence in the human and social sciences in the hope that they will put a stop to this scandal? As can be seen, the epistemological problems faced by naturalism are the exact opposite of those facing animism. Whereas the latter wonders about the place of the "natural" (physical differences) in a world that is almost wholly "cultural," the former is not too sure where to place Culture (moral differences) within the universality of Nature. The solutions found are scarcely more than half measures, just as metamorphosis was for animism. They consist in obstinately oscillating between two ways of eliminating the question: the first is naturalist monism, with its ambition to reduce the autonomy of culture—which has become a system of adaptation determined by genetic and environmental constraints; the second is radical relativism, with its ambition to reduce the autonomy of nature—which has become purely a system of signs with no objective referent. I have already spent too long on that dialogue of the deaf to return to it here. Let us just remember that it is totally vain to hope to discover a third way, at least it is so long as one identifies with a naturalist epistemology whose explicit foundations rest upon an irreconcilable duality between two fields of incompatible phenomena. But just as the problem of the humanity of nonhumans provides animism with an inexhaustible and fascinating object for speculation, the problem of the status of moral phenomena in material determinisms offers naturalism an endless opportunity for philosophical controversy. Those who fancy reflective subtleties and well-turned arguments will not be complaining.

While animism sees signs of otherness in the discontinuity of bodies, naturalism finds them in the discontinuity of minds. I am different from someone who, speaking another language, believing in other values, thinking according to other categories, and seeing things according to another "worldview," is no longer just like me because the "collective representations" to which he adheres and that condition his actions are so very different from mine. A bizarre custom or an enigmatic or repugnant practice can thus be explained by the fact that those who adopt them cannot do otherwise than believe (think, represent to themselves, imagine, judge, suppose . . .) that this is the way to proceed if one wishes to achieve such or such an end. It is all a matter of "mentalities"—a fertile domain for history—and if these are reputed to be understandable up to a certain point from the traces that they leave in public expressions of them, it is nevertheless not possible to penetrate their ultimate sources, for I cannot quite slip into the mind of someone else, even someone very close. For naturalist subjects, there is unfortunately no mental equivalent to metamorphosis; all we have at our disposal are the unsuccessful attempts made by poetry, psychoanalysis, or mysticism. In these circumstances, it is understandable that radical otherness seems to lie on the side of those either devoid of minds or who do not know how to use them: savages (in the past), the mentally ill (today), and, above all, the immense multitude of nonhumans, animals, objects, plants, stones, clouds, all this material chaos that exists in a mechanical fashion and with laws of composition and functioning that humans, in their wisdom, work busily to discover.

Representing a Collective

For an ethnologist used to Amazonia, one of the most disconcerting features of Australian totemism is that the organic elements of the environment are not treated as persons, despite the crucial place that the fauna and flora occupy in the ontology and economy of the Aboriginals. There are no rituals designed to obtain the indulgence of some vindictive hunted animal, no shamans managing the relations between human societies and animal societies, no dialogues between the soul of a hunter and that of his prey, and no indication that kangaroos, emus, and wild yams might possess an interiority that needs to be taken into account.[14] It is not that these kinds of entities leave the Aboriginals indifferent. On the contrary, in a mode of subsistence based on hunting, fishing, and gathering, plants and animals are, understandably enough, the subject of very elaborate knowledge and also of the constant attention of those who live among them and depend upon them for their existence. It is important to know about them, for some are good to eat; moreover, they are all "good to think with," to judge by their eminent position in totemic classifications. But they are not "good to socialize with," at least not in the form of autonomous alter ego communities with institutions analogous to those of humans. It is true that animal and plant species are included in totemic collectives because this or that one shares in common with this or that class of humans an origin and certain prototypical attributes. Nevertheless, their members are not invited to participate in social activities except as subordinate witnesses, that is, as essential parts of the décor set in place long ago by the Dream-beings, as edible provisions to be renewed (through rites of multiplication), and as impersonal signs and vectors of the presence and intentions of the original Demiurges. They represent various objectivizations of those Demiurges, just as humans do. In short, in Australia as in the modern West, animals and plants are not granted the dignity of subjects.

Does this mean that such a privilege is reserved for humans, who alone hold a point of view on the world and an ability to transform it? That seems extremely doubtful, given the extremely slender margin of independence that Aboriginals enjoy vis-à-vis the totemic entities of various kinds that borrow human bodies in order to perpetuate themselves. We should remember that totems of filiation, conceptional totems, child-souls, and even totemic sites all treat humans as instruments by making use of their dynamism and vitality in order, generation after generation, to reproduce the great segmented order of which those ceaselessly active forces are the creators, guarantors, and concrete expressions. However, this does not turn humans into puppets manipulated by ventriloquist totems, even though their subjectivity appears to stem largely from the properties incorporated in the myriad real and potential objects that were placed in the world by the Dream-beings when they bestowed form and meaning upon it. Nancy Munn has helpfully illuminated all this in her study of the mythical thought of the tribes of the central desert.[15]

According to the Warlpiri and the Pitjantjatjara, the whole of their present environment constitutes a kind of register that records the countless traces left by the Dream-beings. Each singularity that it contains can be traced to a metamorphosed part of their infinitely productive bodies, to the vestige of an action in which they engaged, or to the automatic realization of a plan that they decided to imagine. Every existing being is thus linked to one or another of those prototypical figures in a relationship that is both essential and consubstantial. Speaking of a small stretch of water, an Aboriginal may say that "it *is* the body" of such or such a Dream-being, and the same could be said of the offspring that the latter has left in a site, in the form of child-souls, and ritual objects that embody that Dream-being's presence.[16] Thus, the emergence of the landscape, of the so-called natural species and of humans, does not, strictly speaking, result from a process of creation—which would pre-suppose autonomy for the things produced in relation to the instrument of their coming-to-be. Rather, it is the effect of a movement of objectivization in the course of which those original subjects engendered classes of things out of themselves—by partial metamorphosis, separation, or imprint—in such a way that those things to this day bear signs of the active subjectivity of which they are the concrete consequence. The real subjects of this totemic activity and the ever-vibrant order that it instituted are certainly the Dream-beings, that is, the initially mobile agents that long ago actualized out of themselves parcels of beings and collections of objects in hybrid groups that, as a result of the circumstances in which they appeared, all share properties in com-mon. All the same, despite the realistic tone of the stories that retrace their adventures, the Dream-beings elude any faithful description of their original hybrid character. Moreover, they have infused themselves into entities that are morphologically so diverse that it is hard to imagine them as singulari-ties with appearances of their own. As a hypostasis of a process of segmented engendering, the active subject here is thus really an abstraction, a concept objectivized in a multiplicity of things: it is a prototypical class of human and nonhuman elements, all with the same origin and represented by a named collective.

With this perspective, it is not possible to claim that humans are subjects except by derivation or procuration, for their physical and moral identity de-pends on the identity of the primordial entities from which they proceed. That is made quite clear by, for example, the fact that a Pitjantjatjara iden-tifies with the Dream-being of his birthplace when he says "I" in order to refer to that Dream-being. Similarly, it is said of beauty spots, moles, and birthmarks (*djuguridja*, "that which belongs to the ancestors") on the bodies of humans that these constitute reminders of the distinctive markings borne by the Dream-being from which they stem. Those markings are still detect-able in the particular features of the form into which the Dream-being has transformed itself.[17] The subjectivity of any human individual thus operates essentially by means of objects with which he maintains a relation of intrin-sic solidarity (elements in the landscape, child-souls, and sacred objects), for those manifest and render operational the still-quivering subjectivity of the Dream-beings and so also of his own subjectivity inasmuch as it is sustained by that of the Dream-being. The identity of an Aboriginal is thus "alienated" in the full sense of the term, in that it resides in the traces left in things by the entities that have produced the class of which he is a member, a class that in itself is an entity whose presence he himself helps to actualize by performing rituals. As Munn observes, "For human subjects, objects which come to embody 'intimations of themselves' already contain 'intimations of others'—who are superordinate to them and precede them in time."[18] In this dialectic that may be either materialist or idealist (it is hard to determine which), those original subjects, thanks to their subjectivity, founded the state and dynamics of everything, by objectivizing the world. Meanwhile, humans find themselves objectivized as subjects through the intermediary of the objects that the Dream-beings have subjectivized.

So, given that humans themselves are hardly more than personifications of a reality that determines them both physically and morally, it is not surprising that animals and plants are not persons. Everything in the world is linked to those primordial Dream figures that were responsible for the distribution of beings and things into different classes. Everything forever depends on those agents that imposed order, whose essence and material properties find expression in the most insignificant of objects. So there is no reason why plants and animals should not be both condensations of attributes stemming from totemic essences and also generic substances with no real interiority, easily converted into nourishment since destroying and consuming them will in no way affect the enduring source from which springs a constant stream of ontological irrigation. An Opossum-man who eats an opossum does no harm to the "Opossum quality" by which both are defined since each, in its own way, is no more than a provisional embodiment of it. However, the irremediable destruction of the Opossum site from which both proceed (possibly as a result of being buried beneath a golf course or a supermarket) not only causes the annihilation of their generic identity but also, and above all, makes it impossible for them to perpetuate their respective descents, since they now lack the totemic seeds that prospered in that place. Amid all these separate ontological streams, it would be hard to distinguish a purely objective materiality that could be separated from a structuring intentionality and from a creative project immanent in everything and to which everything testifies. As for subjects, they are at once everywhere and nowhere: everywhere since everywhere there are tangible signs of that active subjectivity attributed to the Dream-beings, yet nowhere because, being incorporated in the landscape and having detached existing things from their own bodies, those original subjects have desisted from making themselves visible as representable individualities. So there is nothing universal about the properties of matter and nothing homogeneous about this mass of subjects submerged in things. If one wished at all costs to place this curious metaphysics in the Procrustean bed of our epistemology, one would probably have to describe it as a double relativism, at once natural and cultural, but somewhat tempered by an obsession with classification unequaled elsewhere.

In view of the depersonalizing effect on the consciousness of individuals produced by what we may rightly call "collective representations," it is not hard to discern the problem that totemism faces: how, without ambiguity, to pick out human from nonhuman individuals, given that they are all fused within a collective; how to separate out existing beings that are amalgamated into a hybrid class as a result of a mode of identification that minimizes discontinuities? If the totemic group attached to a particular site does indeed constitute the preeminent form of a subject as a moral person assimilated to a Dream-being, then the elements gathered together in such a group become particularly difficult to distinguish since they all stem from the same prototypical matrix, and over and above differences of form, each one of them is simply a fleeting actualization of the attributes associated with that matrix. But within the collective there is a need for at least a minimum threshold of differentiation that renders possible interactions between terms that would otherwise be too similar.

In the case of fauna and flora, the solution lies in dissociating the attributes of an individual, seen as a singular member of a biological species, from the attributes of the species, seen as a component of a totemic collective. An example of my totemic species is not, for me, a subject with which I establish a personal relationship; rather, it is a living expression of certain material and essential qualities that I share with it. That is how Spencer and Gillen's informant, whom I have cited above, could say of a kangaroo that "it is just the same as me."[19] However, that is not an absolute identity, or at least it is only as regards certain predicates reputed to be relevant when it comes to assessing an attribute that affects an ontological membership. In such a case, what will be concerned are the same origin, the same essence, and certain common substances, certain shared physical and behavioral traits, and the same taxonomic name, which, as we have seen, is usually derived from an abstract property rather than from the species' name. In other respects, the morphology is different, as are feeding habits, forms of communication, and many other features too. Such differences are originally occasioned by the fact that the stocks of child-souls of a single totemic class are clearly dissociated: some embody themselves in humans, others in plants or in animals. It is these divergent attributes, which are obliterated in the context of ontological identification, that attract attention in practical experience, thereby introducing singularities within a totemic collective. When circumstances demand it, they make it possible for humans and nonhumans, even if fused within a single group, to be treated as distinct entities.

Such an operation is much harder to carry out when it is a matter of individualizing humans within a totemic collective, since each one, produced from the same reservoir of child-souls, conforms in the same way to the properties of the prototypical class that he or she objectivizes in his or her person. The solution here is, rather, to overdetermine the attributes of the individual in relation to those of his or her class by particularizing the basis of his or her identity, that is to say, the characteristics of his or her child-soul. This is one of the purposes of the initiation ceremonies and of the ritual objects used in them, as the function of the *churinga* among the Aranda illustrates well.[20]

The term *churinga* (or *tjurunga*) designates, among other things, religious objects of various kinds, kept at a totemic site and serving to support the identity of the Dream-being that originally established that site. Among these objects, it is important to distinguish between, on the one hand, the collective *churinga* (known as *knanja*), which are stationary stones and rocks that incorporate the child-souls of totemic species that are nonhuman and that are used essentially in rites of "multiplication," and, on the other, the individual *churinga* (known as *indulla-irrakura*), which are all different from one another and each of which objectivizes a human child-soul. These consist of planks of wood and oval or rectangular flakes of schist engraved or painted with abstract motifs and normally tucked away in a hollow tree or a rock crevice on the totemic site. The motif that adorns each individual *churinga* is entirely original and represents the singularity of, not so much the individual with whom it is associated, but rather the child-soul that animates his or her existence as a particular member of the totemic collective. But how is such singularity possible, one wonders, given that the child-souls of all humans at one totemic site proceed from one and the same Dream-being and so are ontologically identical? The answer is, quite simply, because every *churinga* and therefore every human child-soul can be seen as a kind of fractal expression of the general structure of the properties of its totemic class, in that it illustrates a different stage in the conditions of its objectivization. This "representation of the unrepresentable," to borrow Moisseeff's formula, can be achieved by remarkably limited means. The motifs of circles, semicircles, spirals, and continuous or discontinuous lines that are painted on to the surfaces of the *churinga* each represent one portion of the journey of a Dream-being, along with the traces left by it in this or that place and following this or that event. So each individual, that is, each incarnation of a child-soul, becomes an actualization of one of the successive stages through which passed the genesis of the collective identity peculiar to the group to which he or she belongs. Against the background of a common ontological specificity, individuals are differentiated from one another thanks to the distribution, to each of the human members of the totemic class, of different segments of the initial history that has brought them together as a homogeneous class. Each of those segments takes the form of a miniature landscape animated by that founding event.

What form can otherness take in such a regime, with subjects that are everywhere present in the objectivized effects of their instituting action yet impossible to apprehend in the phenomenal guise of their original singularity? The first point to note is that totemism is, in itself, a useful mechanism for defining the thresholds of discontinuity between oneself and others, since its primary purpose is to distribute parcels of contrasting properties among the various classes of existing beings. Thus, anyone who, because he or she belongs to a different totemic collective, possesses physical and moral attributes different from my own can be defined as different from myself. Nevertheless, at least in the case of humans, the ontological gap is not so great that it prevents common life within a vaster composite unit, let alone exogamous unions between the members of different totemic groups. Far from being incompatible, differences in both materiality and interiority between totemic segments on the contrary complement one another in a harmonious fashion. In fact, coexistence between heterogeneous collectives is even a condition of survival that is necessary for all those involved, since the human members of each totemic group work hard to ensure the subsistence of the rest by multiplying, for their benefit, the plants and animals for which they are responsible and also by allowing them to make use of the resources to be found on the territories associated with the sites of their own emergence. Nor is there any incompatibility between parents who belong to different totemic species, since the physical and moral characteristics of their children depend not on themselves but on the totemic entities under whose aegis they are born or conceived. In fact this constitutes a remarkable case of rational cohabitation between "ontological races" that, despite considering themselves as utterly different with regard to their essence, substance, and the places to which they are attached, nevertheless adhere to values and norms that render them complementary. Indeed, they make use of the grid of otherness on which they find themselves placed in relation to others in order to produce an organic solidarity out of taxonomic heterogeneity.

This is not the case where plants and animals are concerned. Like the humans, they are primarily distinguished from one another by their totemic affiliations, but in their case it is not possible to transcend that original division and intermingle freely since, unlike the humans, they cannot pair off together if they come from different totemic segments, nor can they do so even within the same totemic collective if they belong to different species. Despite the totemic links that bind it to other categories of existing beings, each biological species of nonhumans is thus confined to a confrontation with itself. Furthermore, although humans gladly recognize that they share with their totemic species a profound identity of both essence and substance, they nevertheless consider the individuals that make up those species as objects lacking the type of creative interiority that permits themselves, as humans, to declare themselves the principal emissaries of the Dream-beings. In the eyes of the humans, these plants and animals that are "exactly like themselves" are no more than accidental vectors of qualities that characterize all of them: they are not subjects to be mobilized in any project of communal life. The totemic category of otherness thus plays upon a subtle dialectic interaction between the level of an individual and that of a species. It includes indiscriminately humans, when one chooses to apprehend them as a species (according to their totemic affiliation) and not as individuals (social partners), and the myriad collection of nonhumans that are treated either as individuals considered as things despite their species membership (within the totemic group) or both as foreign species and as individuals with no identity of their own (outside that totemic group).

The Signature of Things

Animist cosmologies teem with persons that are clearly individualized and easily identifiable from the diversity of their outward apparel: such or such an animal scrutinized me, such or such a great tree came and spoke to me in a dream, such or such a distant human has come to visit me. Analogical subjectivities also proliferate everywhere, but in a far more diffuse and ambivalent manner, refracted as they are in unexpected receptacles from which they must be picked out by means of tiny indications and signs that are hard to decipher. In a world saturated with a prodigious quantity of singular existing beings, themselves composed of a plurality of unstable mobile components, it becomes hard to attribute a continuous identity to any object: nothing is ever really what it seems, so exceptional ingenuity and great attention to the context are demanded in order to manage, even in a provisional way, to make out a definite individuality behind the equivocal fog of appearances and misleading indications. No doubt humans lay claim to a less indecisive singularity, given that they assume the privilege of interpretation by taking themselves as models in their task of imposing order and bringing meaning into the world. Even then, though, when dealing with one of them one needs to be sure of his or her true nature. As the mother of Amadou Hampaté Ba so aptly put it, "I should like to know which of the Amadous who inhabit him is there at this moment." Indeed, who, really, is Amadou? Which of his many personalities is in charge at the moment that one speaks to him? And what can be said of the old Nahua man possessed by his little deity of drunkenness, of the initiate to the *candomblé* ridden by his *orisha*, or of the witch inhabited by her demon? Are they still autonomous subjects, even if they are versatile and composite, or has the entity that has alienated them become so intrusive that they will always carry within them traces of its subjectivity? And what can be said of the *tona* of the Mexicans, an animal double that is host to a fragment of a human's interiority? Is it a double subject, the Siamese twin of the person whose destiny it shares? Or is it an independent being that coexists with another, partially delocalized subjectivity? In short, analogical subjects seem to be back-to-front versions of Pascal's God: their circumference is everywhere, their center nowhere. They exist only by virtue of their surface effects, deploying themselves in concentric waves of variable amplitude and in constant interaction with one another. But it would certainly be hard to determine a focus for them, even an infinitely multiple one. Far from being "one everywhere and wholly present in every place," they are fragmented into multiple parts that never form a stable whole.

While the parts of beings vary constantly in their dosages and combinations, the materials that constitute them seem, for their part, to be reassuringly stable. The diversity of forms and the singularity of their compositions matter little here, provided that a limited range of substances and material states guarantees both a kind of elementary physical continuity between existing beings and also the possibility of pairing or opposing them in accordance with the affinities and incompatibilities of the substances of which they are composed. Analogical physics is simple, at least insofar as an inventory of its materials is concerned. Whether it is a matter of the ancient doctrine of four elements, the Chinese or Ayurvedic theory of five elements (which are not quite the same), or the interplay of opposites between masculine and feminine humors or between the flesh of plants and that of animals, it is always the same fundamental substances and the same principles of attraction or repulsion that form the basis for the litany of sympathies and discordances endlessly produced by medical wisdom, dietary prescriptions, and ritual requirements. Perhaps that simplicity as regards components is indispensable if analogical worlds are to remain intelligible and manipulable. When each and every thing is seen as a virtually unique specimen, it has to be possible to reduce its singularity by decomposing it into a small number of elements that can define its nature and explain its behavior vis-à-vis other things. Supported by therapeutic practice and the understanding of materials acquired through metallurgy, pottery, and the chemistry of pigments, this qualitative physics is not without an empirical plausibility. Above all, and to transpose a hypothesis produced by Lévi-Strauss concerning magic thought in general, could one not consider the rigor and precision evident in these presumed associations and causalities between a few elementary substances "as an expression of the unconscious apprehension of the *truth of determinism*, the mode in which scientific phenomena exist? In this view, the operations of determinism are *divined* and *made use* of in an all-embracing fashion before being *known* and *properly applied*."[21]

This would make the transition between analogism and naturalism a little less mysterious. Despite all the "changes of paradigms" and the "epistemological ruptures" between the Renaissance and the classical period, one conviction remains unchanged: that the elementary materials of the world have the same knowable properties everywhere and that the different combinations that they allow are everywhere valid. All the same, that is where the resemblance stops. For what analogism deploys against the background of this universalism that one hardly dares to describe as "natural" is not a teeming mass of singular societies. Rather, it is a universalism of a different order, that of myriads of diffused subjectivities that animate all things with a will yet to be discovered, a meaning yet to be interpreted, a connection yet to be revealed. This, then, is a "spiritual" universalism, if not a strictly "cultural" one. And that is probably one reason for the persistent success of "Eastern wisdoms" in the disenchanted West. In one swoop, sweeping aside the irritating question of cultural relativism, Zen, Buddhism, and Daoism offer a universalist alternative that is more complete than the truncated universalism of the Moderns. Human nature is not shredded into bits as a result of the force of customs and the weight of habits, since every human being, thanks to meditation, is reputed to be able to draw from within himself or herself the capacity to experience the plenitude of the world without preestablished foundations—that is to say, liberated from the particular foundations that a local tradition might assign to it. Understandably enough, biologists and physicists with monist aspirations may have been won over by this aspect of analogism that was provided by Asiatic philosophies in a reflective form already highly elaborated but easier for scientists to accept than the analogical doctrines of the Renaissance, against which their own scholarly disciplines were built in reaction.[22]

If one accepts that analogism functions by taking the line that "everything is in everything and vice versa," then the epistemological problem that it faces is exactly the reverse of that of totemism, for it is a matter not of singularizing amalgamated entities but of amalgamating singularized ones. And it has to be recognized that this is a by no means minor problem. How can one aggregate existing beings in a mode of identification that places the emphasis on their discontinuities? How can one justify an assembling point of view in a cosmos of particularized immanences? How can one account for a division into parts within a totality that is its own justification? There are certainly ways of classifying, segmenting, and ordering that organize this medley of heteroclite beings, for, as we have seen, that is precisely the function of various types of analogy, of great classificatory structures with two qualitative poles or hierarchical divisions. However, these mechanisms of internal organization are not self-sufficient. To become effective and tolerable, they need to be legitimized and motivated by something that is bigger than they are, something whose position and status transcend the dispersion of particular subjectivities. Who or what is responsible for the division of the Chipaya world into two moieties and the complementary relations between their inhabitants, both human and nonhuman? What brings about the pairing of an Otomi Indian and his animal *tona*? What is the basis for the hierarchical levels of Indian castes and their inegalitarian characteristics? Who guarantees the permanence of the chain of being and the stability of its divisions? As soon as one asks these questions, one can see that there is no single answer. Just as analogism finds expression in a wide variety of collectives, it allows for a wide range of justificatory perspectives.

It is, however, possible to discern one regular feature in the institution of the totalizing structure that makes the analogical hierarchy meaningful and ensures that it functions satisfactorily. Whatever its configuration, it always results from a process that hypostasizes the world collective, the stability of which must be ensured and the segmentation of which must be perpetuated. The most common hypostasis takes a metonymic form: one exceptional singularity comes to embody not so much the whole collection of other singularities but, rather, the permanence of the ordered totality that structures it. It may be the Inca, the divine being, the vital center of the cosmos and the original model of all things; or it may be Pharaoh, the son of the Sun and the mediator between gods and humans, the guarantor of justice, prosperity, and victory; or it may be God, the architect of the chain of being and the preserver of its integrity. A similar metonymic movement may result in one segment of a collective becoming responsible for representing the bases of the sociocosmic order and maintaining the conditions in which it operates. The role played by the ancestors in West Africa or in Japan, those dead who are still active in the existence of the living, comes to mind. They are the guarantors and painstaking guardians of norms and values, eminent members of the various segments of the collective whose continuity they sanction and from whom proceed the rights and privileges of their descendants. Or it may be that one particular class of humans is invested with the mission of maintaining the world through their liturgical activities: for example, the Brahmins in India.

Far more rare, finally, are attempts to hypostasize the cosmic order itself by condensing it into a principle, or even in a word, which it then becomes difficult to define other than by illustrations, allegories, and precepts. This was the course adopted, for example, by the Chinese, with their *dao*, although that did not stop them from also having recourse to the ancestors—for in most cases, faced with the scope of the task, one tends to take the wise precaution of combining several different totalizing principles.

However, given the need, day in and day out, to ensure that singularities are all collected into an effective hierarchy, most mechanisms of aggregation and subordination remain very abstract. This is why the political function becomes decisive in analogical collectives, particularly when very numerous items are involved. It is through the political function and the coercion that it exerts that every individual, every segment, and every aspect of the world is kept in the place fixed for it. Here, the example of India is the most instructive. We know that the Brahmin class was superior to the class of the *kshatriya*, the warrior princes from whom monarchs proceeded, and that their dominant position was justified by the crucial role that sacrificial activities played in the preservation of the sociocosmic order. Yet, despite this official ideology that placed a Brahmin above a sovereign, the Brahminic orthodoxy itself promoted an even more fundamental division, that between the "eaters," namely the princes who held the power, and the "eaten," their subjects, whose allotted role was to be obedient and productive. Charles Malamoud provides a good account of this in his commentary on a passage of the *Çatapatha-Brâhmana* concerning the reasons for using two kinds of bricks in the construction of a fire altar.[23] Some bricks are individualized and represent the class of warrior princes, while others are not differentiated and represent the masses of the "eaten." But even though each of the princely bricks is singular, they are unified because, as each is laid, the same formula is pronounced. This is a way of indicating what these particularized beings all have in common. Even if each of the kings and princes enjoys power, they all resemble one another and display solidarity in their use of force. In contrast, each plebeian brick is treated to a formula of its own, to show that they are all different. More precisely, "the masses are made up of elements that are not individuals nor are parts sufficiently similar to constitute a whole unless, to hold them together, there are 'hole-fillers' constituted by the princely bricks that 'fill in the gaps.'"[24] There could be no better way of indicating that, behind the empowering function ostensibly conceded to the Brahmins, the real work of totalizing and adjusting singularities here falls to those who hold coercive power.

It is probably safe to generalize and include analogical world collectives in Granet's remark, cited in chapter 2, about the Chinese cosmos, which "is itself in order only when it is enclosed the way that a house is." The boundary between what is the same and what is other is, in this case, brilliantly simple: beyond the limits of the home, which are usually marked out in a quite literal fashion, there lies an "out-world" populated by outsiders, the indistinct mass of barbarians, savages, and marginal peoples, which is a constant source of threats and a potential breeding ground for co-citizens who can be domesticated. All those peoples behind the mountains, on the borders of the deserts, beyond this or that river, and in the depths of impenetrable forests obstinately refuse to share the totalizing point of view that an analogical collective has chosen and the wise laws that it has introduced; and they do so because they do not recognize the authority of the sacred king, they know nothing of the benevolent presence of the ancestors, or they reject the aid proffered by divine enlightenment. Unlike what happens with other modes of identification, here otherness is external in a purely spatial sense, for even in the most extremely subdivided hierarchical systems, such as that of the Indian castes, the inequalities between segments are not so decisive that they cannot be compensated for by functional complementarities and the integrating effects of the schema of distribution by which they are organized. Each caste is certainly different from all the rest by reason of its specialization, its way of life, its prerogatives, and its reproductive endogamy, but together they form an integrated totality, given that they produce goods and services for one another and, in solidarity, depend on the great sociocosmic model of which each expresses a particular facet. In contrast, animism, naturalism, and totemism have all installed otherness at the very heart of their collectives: animism does so by highlighting discontinuities of bodies, naturalism by attributing it to the discontinuity of minds, and totemism by playing on the difference between the levels that separate individuals and species (fig. 9).

Readers have a right to raise one more question: what starting point do you need to adopt in order to feel justified in classifying the points of view of others in combinations that only you elude? From what do you derive and how can you justify this bird's-eye point of view from which you organize the different kinds of problems that human beings tackle, meanwhile avoiding those that your own approach raises? In the first place, it goes without saying that my own starting point is without doubt rooted in the familiar soil of naturalism. It is no easy matter to escape from one's origins and from the schemas of apprehending reality that have been mastered through education and strengthened by being accepted as common practice. Although we may from time to time indulge in the type of ontological judgments that other modes of identification suggest, it is out of the question for any modern subject fully

	Animism	Totemism	
• Generalizes the position of a social subject and relativizes objective materiality (each subject sees the world from its own position). ↳Natural relativism ≠ cultural universalism. • **The problem** for animism: how to account for the nonhuman form of humanized nonhumans (what is the place of "nature")? ↳Solution: metamorphosis. • Definition of the "other" (the *alter*): those (humans and nonhumans) whose physicality is different.	*Animism*	*Totemism*	• Relativizes the position of the subject, which is embodied by the creators of the totemic groups, and relativizes the forms of materiality (nonhumans are at once bodies without interiorities and totemic essences). ↳Cultural relativism + natural relativism. • **The problem** for totemism: how to singularize individuals (humans and nonhumans) within a hybrid collective? ↳Solution: distinguish between the attributes of the individual and those of the species. • Definition of the "other" (the *alter*): nonhumans as individuals but not as a species, humans as a species but not as individuals.
• Relativizes the position of a subject (reserved for humans, variable depending on cultures) and universalizes objective materiality. ↳Cultural relativism ≠ natural universalism. • **The problem** for naturalism: what place to assign to culture within the universality of nature? ↳Solution: oscillations between naturalist monism (denial of culture) and absolute relativism (denial of nature). • Definition of the "other" (the *alter*): those whose interiority is different and/or those that have no interiority ("natural" objects).	*Naturalism*	*Analogism*	• Generalizes the position both of subject and of objective materiality: everything is in everything and vice versa. ↳Natural universalism + cultural universalism. • **The problem** for analogism: how to authenticate a point of view that includes everything in a world of singular immanences? ↳Solution: hypostasize the world, a singularity, or a segment of the collective. • Definition of the "other" (the *alter*): those who do not share the same all-inclusive point of view.

FIGURE 9. How ontological distribution affects the definition and properties of a subject

to become animist or totemist (as ethnographic experience attests) or even to return consistently to the ancient attractions of analogism. It is not possible to adhere to philosophies of knowledge that tend to oppose the relativity of bodies to the universality of mind or to combine objective materiality and moral subjectivity as two relativisms or two universalisms. In these circumstances, how can one extract oneself from the dilemma of naturalism and its all-too-predictable oscillation between the monist hope of natural universalism and the pluralist temptation of cultural relativism? Above all, how does one turn one's back on the consoling idea that our culture is the one that has carved out for itself access to a real understanding of nature, while other cultures have nothing to go on except representations that are approximate but worthy of interest in the opinion of charitable minds, false and pernicious in the view of positivists who fear their power of contagion? This epistemological regime, which Latour calls "particular universalism,"[25] is the foundation of the whole development of anthropology and legitimates its successes, so it is hard to imagine rejecting its hospitable welcome without incurring ostracism and risking sterile, if fascinating, wanderings among the mirages of singularities.

However, there is one way that would make it possible to reconcile the demands of scientific inquiry and a respect for the diversity of states of the world, a way not yet properly opened up but whose twists and turns the present book would like to indicate. I am content to call it *relative universalism*, not to be provocative or out of a taste for apparent contradictions, but giving the epithet "relative" the sense that it carries in the expression "a relative pronoun"—in other words, where it describes a relationship. Relative universalism takes as its starting point not nature and cultures, substances and minds, nor discriminations between primary qualities and secondary ones, but, instead, the relations of continuity and discontinuity, identity and difference, resemblance and dissimilarity that humans everywhere establish between existing beings, using the tools that they have inherited from their particular phylogenesis: a body, an intentionality, an aptitude for discerning differential gaps, an ability to weave with any human or nonhuman relations of attachment or antagonism, domination or dependence, exchange or appropriation, subjectivization or objectivization. Relative universalism does not demand that an equal materiality should at the outset be ascribed to all beings, along with the possibility of giving to them contingent meanings. It is content simply to detect salient discontinuities both in things and in the mechanisms of their apprehension and to accept, at least as a hypothesis, that the options for making use of that recognition are limited, either when one ratifies a phenomenal discontinuity or when one invalidates it by a continuity.

It is not hard to detect in this project the legacy of structural analysis according to which an element in the world acquires meaning only by contrast to other elements. However, the project that I have in mind is innocent of any methodological clause that insists that these elements and their relations be divided between the black boxes of culture and nature. Relative universalism has no need of any transcendental subject or any disembodied and immanent mind that acts as a catalyst of meanings. All that this program requires is a subject with no preconceptions as to the lived consciousness of others that would be based on his own experience of consciousness, but who nevertheless recognizes that the world offers to all and sundry the same kinds of ways of coming to grips with it, whatever cognitive and practical uses these lend themselves to: what is needed is a subject more attentive to the reality instituted by the intentional activity of the very diverse subjectivities whose products he studies than to the misleading self-evident assumptions of his own fundamental intentionality. For the latter constitutes no more than an imperfect filter, invariably contaminated by the historical causes that no *epochē** can reduce. To be sure, that filter is indispensable but only because it is the only one available, and the subject in question needs to manage to objectivize it from outside, simply as one variation that is provisionally invested with the function of totalizing understanding by reason of the circumstances that surround him.

---

* Translator's note: a suspension of judgment, in philosophical language.

PART FIVE

An Ecology of Relations

We need one, we need two, we need . . . Nobody is ubiquitous enough to be his own contemporary sovereign.

(Il en faut un, il en faut deux, il en faut . . . Nul ne possède assez d'ubiquité pour être son contemporain souverain).

RENÉ CHAR, *Faire du chemin avec . . .*

13

Forms of Attachment

Modes of identification broadly schematize our experience of things, distinguishing between parcels of ontological properties distributed in accordance with the arrangements of existing beings, arrangements whose structural characteristics we have examined above, each in turn. It is a distribution of beings according to their attributes, the principles according to which sociocosmological collectives are organized, the dominant regimes of knowledge and action, and the boundaries of identity and otherness. Each of these forms of identification defines a specific style of relations with the world. Long-established expressions of these relations are to be found in geographical regions, many of which are immense, and over very long periods. Yet we cannot use those styles as criteria for distinguishing between singular collectives with contours limited both in time and in space—the kind that historians, ethnologists, and sociologists usually choose to investigate. Rather, we should regard those stylizations of experience as what are usually called "worldviews," "cosmologies," or "symbolic forms," all of these being terms of vague epistemological status yet that constitute a handy intuitive way of synthesizing under a simple label (such as "the modern West" or "shamanistic societies") "families" of practices and mind-sets that seem to display affinities despite the diversity of their concrete manifestations. However, within those great archipelagoes marked out by a shared mode of identification one comes across numerous kinds of collectives that consider themselves to be very different from one another (and that are, indeed, perceived as different by those who study them). This is not only on account of their different languages, institutions, and, more often than not, the discontinuity of their territories but also because the interactions within them present remarkable contrasts. For even when the ontological distribution of existing beings and the ways that they come together are based on identical principles, the links that they weave between one another, the ways that they affect one another, and the manner in which they treat one another can all vary through and through. It is thus primarily the general form of the local *relations* that structure the connections between entities that are all distinguished by the same process of identification, which makes it possible for collectives to differentiate themselves from one another and for each to display the singularity of their own particular ethos, of which any observer soon becomes aware.

Like modes of identification, relational modes are integrating schemas; that is to say, they stem from the kind of cognitive, emotional, and sensorimotor structures that channel the production of automatic inferences, orientate practical action, and organize the expression of thoughts and feelings according to relatively stereotyped patterns. A relational schema becomes dominant in a collective when activated in a whole range of very different circumstances in relations with humans or nonhumans. The effect of this is to subject all relations to its particular logic, either by limiting their field of application or by subordinating this to the achievement of the ends that the dominant schema embodies. But unlike modes of identification, dominant relational modes are also identifiable thanks to the fact that in many cases they express the greatest possible difference from those in action in the immediate neighborhood. It is as if each collective concentrates its greatest efforts on whatever it judges to be capable of distinguishing it most effectively from the collectives surrounding it and with which it coexists: namely the styles of interaction and behavior that its human members are led to adopt in the course of daily life. However, the nature and the limits of a collective of this kind are never fixed a priori since it is, on the contrary, the area covered by the dominant relational schema that establishes them in the first place. A collective defined in this way does not necessarily coincide with a "society," a "tribe," or a "class," all of which are misleading terms to use because of the substantive closure that they imply. Rather, it is characterized primarily by the discontinuity that is introduced all around it on account of the ostensible close presence of other principles for the schematization of relations between existing beings. Its existence is thus positional, not intrinsic, and is revealed through comparisons.

When seen as dispositions that bestow form and content upon the practical links between myself and a human or nonhuman *alter*, relational schemas can be classified according to whether or not that *alter* is or is not equivalent to me on an ontological level and whether the connections that I establish with it are or are not mutual. So numerous are the kinds of relations that can be established between the entities that fill the world that it is clearly not possible to summarize them all. So let us concentrate here upon no more than one group of six types of relationships that appear to play a preponderant role in the connections that humans establish between one another and also with nonhuman elements in their environment. Whether they are identified by the words that I use or are given other names, these relations have for many years attracted the attention of the social sciences, some of them even to the point of becoming key concepts. The relations in question are those of *exchange, predation, gift, production, protection,* and *transmission.* These relational modes that come to modulate all modes of identification may be divided into two groups. The first is characterized by potentially reversible relations between terms that are similar. The second is characterized by univocal relations that are founded upon connections between nonequivalent terms. The first group covers exchange, predation, and gift; the second covers production, protection, and transmission.

Giving, Taking, Exchanging

The relations at work in the first group correspond to three formulae that ensure the movement of something valuable between two terms of the same ontological status, terms that may themselves actually contain that value and therefore circulate in such a way that one may be led to disappear physically as a result of being absorbed by the other. The first relationship, that of "exchange," appears as a symmetrical one in which any agreed transfer from one entity to the other requires something in return. The other two are asymmetrical. In the one, entity A takes something of value from entity B (perhaps its life, its body, or its interiority) without offering anything in exchange: "predation" is what I call this negative asymmetry. In the other, entity B offers something of value to entity A (maybe even itself) without expecting any compensation: I call this positive asymmetry "gift." At least two of the terms that I use to qualify these relations have a long anthropological history, so I need to specify their meaning in relation to previous definitions.

As is well known, Lévi-Strauss ascribes a crucial role to exchange in the developing and functioning of social life. The prohibition of incest is a rule of reciprocity in that it instructs a man to renounce a woman for the benefit of another man who, in turn, rules out his use of another woman who thus becomes available for the first man. The prohibition of incest and the exogamy that is the positive side to it would therefore simply be a means of instituting and guaranteeing reciprocal exchange, which is the basis of culture and a sign of the emergence of a new order in which the relations between groups are governed by freely accepted conventions. But culture does not play a totally innovating role here. According to Lévi-Strauss all it does is codify universal mental schemas that preexist the norms that bring them into play. Among these categorical imperatives that are written into the architecture of the mind before the emergence of the symbolism that makes it possible to express them, one finds "the notion of reciprocity regarded as the most immediate form of integrating the opposition between the self and others; and the synthetic nature of the gift, i.e. that the agreed transfer of a valuable from one individual to another makes these individuals into partners and adds a new quality to the valuable transferred."[1] The preeminence of reciprocity and gift thus results from the fact that those two means of founding and maintaining the social link are a legacy of human phylogenesis, a reminder of the function of natural predispositions in the structuring of the "being together" that is organized by culture.

It is no doubt not necessary to go as far as Lévi-Strauss and postulate an innate neural basis for reciprocity and gift in order to agree with him that those two relational schemas do indeed orientate many forms of human behavior. Besides, there is nothing new about the idea. The suggestion that reciprocal exchange and gift constitute the true cement of all social life seems to be a leitmotif in Western political philosophy, in which it is hard to sort out how much of the idea stems from empirical observation and how much from a moral ideal regarding the most desirable way of ensuring that a collective of equals sticks together. Although he does not explicitly acknowledge it, Lévi-Strauss is thus positioned along the main line of development from a tradition recorded as early as antiquity. Aristotle, for instance, declares that reciprocity in relations of exchange "is the bond that maintains the association"; and Seneca declares that gift "constitutes the chief bond of human society."[2] However, this venerable precedent should not deter us from asking two questions. Is it legitimate to associate reciprocity and gift within the same set of phenomena? And is it certain that every collective considers those two values as the basis of its social life?

In answer to the first question, we must briefly look back to Marcel Mauss's famous "Essay on the Gift" and consider this text's influence on Lévi-Strauss.[3] Although critical with regard to certain aspects of this essay, Lévi-Strauss does confirm the conception of the gift that Mauss presents there, namely "a system of total prestation" characterized by the three obligations of giving, receiving, and giving back. Lévi-Strauss does not challenge that definition, but he does criticize the way in which, he claims, Mauss explained the reciprocity involved in the exchange of gifts and countergifts, namely by resorting mainly to a local theory centered on the Polynesian notion of *hau*, a mysterious force that resides in the given gift, which forces the gift receiver to reciprocate. Lévi-Strauss claims that Mauss allowed himself to be mystified by a deliberate interpretation put forward by a group of native specialists instead of endeavoring to discover the underlying realities of exchange where they could be found, that is, "in the unconscious mental structures that may be reached through institutions."[4] If exchange plays a founding role in social life, according to Lévi-Strauss that is because it constitutes an absolutely primitive phenomenon, "a synthesis immediately given to, and by, symbolic thought."[5] What is paradoxical about this famous critique is that Lévi-Strauss seems not to have realized that Mauss's characterization of the gift, with which he himself does not disagree, was in truth derived from another theory, every bit as native as that of the *hau* but also truly Western. For Mauss implicitly echoes his own cultural tradition when he interprets the gift as resting upon the obligations of giving, receiving, and giving back. As Denis Vidal has shown, this is a common interpretation that goes back to the well-known ancient image of the Three Graces. These constitute a most precise allegory of the three obligations that surround gifts, as Seneca makes perfectly clear: "some would have it appear that there is one for bestowing a benefit, another for receiving it, and a third for returning it."[6] Despite his extensive knowledge of classical culture, Mauss never mentions this line of thought on the theme of gifts, which commentaries on the Three Graces have highlighted from Chrysippus right down to Pico della Mirandola. But it seems unlikely that that unacknowledged source did not affect his conception of the nature of gifts (the three obligations). It may also have affected his desire to see restored the values associated with it, namely generous behavior, in particular the euergetism of prominent figures, that testifies to a reputedly more authentic sociability as illustrated by archaic societies.[7]

In view of its antecedents, it thus seems reasonable to question whether this concept of the gift bequeathed by the ancients, which anthropology then took to its heart in the wake of Mauss, really does match the practice that it claims to characterize. Unlike exchange, the gift is above all a one-way gesture that consists in abandoning something to someone without expecting any compensation other than that, possibly, of gratitude on the part of the receiver of the gift. If the notion is given its literal meaning, reciprocal benefaction is never guaranteed where a gift is concerned. To be sure, reciprocation is a possibility that one may well hope for, either as a tacit wish or as an out-and-out calculation, but the realization of such a wish remains independent of the actual act of giving, which would, ipso facto, lose its meaning if it was conditioned by an imperative to obtain something in compensation. Alain Testart is thus quite right to draw a clear distinction between exchange and gifts: the former consists in handing something over in return for something else; the latter, in doing so with no expectation of reciprocity.[8] Thus, the presents that

I receive from those close to me on the occasion of my birthday cannot in any way be regarded as a deferred return in exchange for the presents that I gave them on their birthdays, for there is no obligation inherent to the custom according to which these gracious transfers take place that would make the present given to me conditional upon the gifts that I offered. It is true that one may say that one is "much obliged" by the gift that one receives. But, contrary to what Mauss claims, the fact that one is "obliged" in no way makes a countergift obligatory, at least not in the sense in which an initial favor might be accompanied by a compelling clause such as those that stem from a contract or responsibility and that, ignored, might well lead to sanctions. In the case of a present, the obligation to repay one's benefactor in some way is purely moral. If one evades it, one may eventually be despised, lose face, or be labeled stingy by the gift giver, although for the latter there can be no recourse to any means of obtaining reciprocity for something freely given and that he would never even think of demanding. If the gift gives rise to any obligation, it is, strictly speaking, neither obligatory nor obliging.[9]

In this respect, a gift is profoundly different from an exchange. Every gift constitutes an independent transfer by reason of the fact that nothing can be claimed in return. There are, of course, societies where it is customary to respond to a gift with another gift, as in the potlatch of the Indians of the Northwest Coast of America, which is very much to the fore in "Essay on the Gift": the riches offered during a ceremony provided the opportunity of presenting some appropriate countergift in the course of some later ceremony. Yet no one was, strictly speaking, obliged to honor a gift with a countergift. In societies that placed generosity at the pinnacle of their values, not to do so certainly meant that one's honor was seriously sullied, and one's access to the highest spheres of political prestige was compromised wherever that political prestige was founded above all on one's reputation for liberality. But even if, as in many other societies too, the fear of being discredited no doubt constituted a powerful motive to respond with a countergift, that was not the same as the obligation to repay that would have been implied in a contractual and quasi-legal way by the fact of accepting the original gift.

Exchange, in contrast, requires as a necessary condition that something be obtained in return. Regardless of whether or not it is equal in value to the thing received, it is this return that represents both the purpose and the means of the exchange, whether this be immediate or deferred and whether or not it be a commercial deal. For even when its nature is not explicitly stipulated or when the time allowed for repayment is not specified, some kind of reciprocation can always be demanded: each party gives away the goods that he has only in exchange for other goods. In this sense, as Testart also notes, the essence of exchange lies in two transfers in opposite directions, transfers that are intrinsically linked, since each of them results from an obligation the raison d'être of which lies in the other. The whole operation is thus a closed system, which may, of course, be inserted into a whole series of similar transactions, but each of which is formed by an independent combination of two elementary mirrored operations.[10] Unlike a gift, which is a single transfer that may eventually prompt a countertransfer, but for motives other than the principle of liberality that made it possible in the first place, each of the two transfers that an exchange involves is both the cause and the effect of the other. A reciprocal relationship is inherent to this kind of deal and is peculiar to it: I give to you so that you give to me, and vice versa.

This is why the all-too-vague notion of reciprocity should be set aside when analyzing transfer relations. Literally, reciprocity designates only what happens between term A and term B and subsequently between term B and term A. There is no overt indication of the nature of the obligations that link the two terms. Thus, a gift may be reciprocal when it is followed up by a countergift, although reciprocity, even so, does not constitute an intrinsic characteristic of this type of transaction, given that a gift in return is not obligatory or binding as it is in an exchange. On the other hand, exchange does necessarily imply reciprocity, since it is precisely the obligation to respond with a counterpart that defines it. I shall therefore use the word "exchange" to refer to what Lévi-Strauss sometimes means by "reciprocity," namely a transfer that requires something in return, and contrary to the use established by Mauss, I shall use the term "gift" to refer to an accepted transfer with no obligation to provide a countertransfer. It is difficult to avoid altogether the cinematic illusion that leads to characterizing transfers of things or persons by the directions in which they move (and I am aware that I myself did that in my initial definition of exchange, predation, and gifts). But if one takes into account the form of the transfers according to the obligations that they impose, it becomes possible largely to correct that distortion of perspective. In any case, it encourages one to distinguish between phenomena arbitrarily grouped under the same rubric simply because they involve the circulation of things between particular terms. It then becomes impossible to continue to set on the same level the exchange of goods in all its different forms, the exchange of signs in language, the exchange of women in marriage alliances, the exchange of deaths in a vendetta, or the sequence of gifts and countergifts.

Whether understood in the general sense that Lévi-Strauss lends it or in the more specific sense that I give it, exchange is certainly present in all societies and takes such diverse forms that it is not hard to understand the point of view of those who have wished to see it as the principal "bond that maintains association." Gifts are also common in every latitude. From the Stoics down to Mauss, many authors have hinted at their nostalgia for a hypothetical golden age in which this disinterested practice was more widespread and have expressed their desire to see a generalization of benevolent practices that would give some idea of the consideration that people have for one another. All the same, no moralist has ever seriously thought that gifts could become the key regulatory institution in any real society. So what grounds do I have for saying that gifts might constitute the integrating relational schema in certain collectives? How can one even think of undermining the preeminence of exchange by suggesting that patterns of behavior founded on the principle of agreed gracious transfers may have been adopted as an ideal norm by certain human communities? These rhetorical questions prompt a reminder: a mode of relations does not become dominant because it has successfully supplanted schemas of interactions that do not accept its logic. It does so because it provides the most effective cognitive model for a simple and easily remembered synthesis not only of many patterns of behavior but also, and above all, of those recognized to be the most distinctive of the collective not only by its members but also by outside observers. Just as with modes of identification, no relational schema is hegemonic. The most that can be said is that one or other of them acquires a structuring function in certain places, even if it is not always possible to put a name to it, when, in an immediately recognizable manner, it orientates many attitudes vis-à-vis both humans and nonhumans. It is not the case that exchange disappears when the ethos of gifts dominates, for in truth it is simply encompassed by the latter.

If one accepts this, one has to agree that there are plenty of collectives that do seem to place the logic of the gift at the heart of their practices. Without anticipating the ethnographic case studies that will be discussed in the next chapter, I would like to draw attention to the importance granted to the action of "sharing" in recent studies devoted to hunter-gatherer societies, in order to characterize both their internal relations and those that they maintain with plants and animals. Bird-David has played a decisive role in this domain, at least at the terminological level, by forging the expression "a giving environment" to synthesize the conception that the Nayaka of Tamil Nadu have of their forests. Just as humans share everything between them with no thought of obtaining anything in return, similarly the environment unstintingly hands out its liberalities to the Nayaka, so that the human and the nonhuman components of the collective find themselves integrated into one and the same "cosmic sharing economy."[11] The idea and practice of the gift constitute among the Nayaka a habitus so deeply rooted that it is inconceivable not immediately to give someone whatever he asks for. When, very exceptionally, the Nayaka do not want to part with something, "rather than disrupt the ongoing sense of sharing—the rhythm of everyday social life—they hid it away or avoided people."[12] For Bird-David, the values of sharing and the gift are typical of hunter-gatherer societies in general, a point of view that Ingold takes up and elaborates. His view is that what characterizes the so-called sharing relations of this kind of society (both with other humans and with nonhumans) is simply "trust," that is, a particular combination of autonomy and dependence. According to him, to place my trust in a person is to act vis-à-vis him or her in the expectation that he or she will behave toward me in the same favorable spirit as I am manifesting and will continue to do so for as long as I do nothing to limit his or her autonomy, that is, his or her option of acting differently. This is thus a situation of dependence that is freely entered into and that places a high value on my partner's choice to adopt toward me the same attitude that I adopt toward him. In short, "any attempt to *impose* a response, to lay down conditions and obligations that the other is bound to follow, would represent a betrayal of trust and a negation of the relationship."[13] The difference between, on the one hand, giving or sharing and, on the other, exchanging could not be expressed more clearly. The former is unconditional: even to suggest that it is not condemns it immediately to vanish and give way to the latter. Disinterested trust is then replaced by a tacit or contractual obligation.

Hunter-gatherers—to use the current term—do not constitute the only kind of collectives that are characterized by the high value that they set upon sharing. Those are also the terms that Joanna Overing and some of her disciples use to analyze indigenous sociability in Amazonia, when this is apprehended at the level that seems to them the most significant, namely within the framework of a local group with consanguineous kinship relations. It appears that this domestic and village sphere is marked above all by relations of mutual trust that are confirmed by productive cooperation, daily and festive commensality, an affectionate solicitude for others, and a constant flow of gifts and countergifts. This is a kind of moral economy based on intimacy, free of calculation and ambiguities, the effect of which is to render those within it so consubstantial that they consider themselves to be of the same species. Within this "aesthetic of conviviality," sharing plays a central role in that it testifies to a disposition to open oneself up to others with generosity and compassion and thus, through concrete acts, expresses the ethical insistence on unreservedly helping one another that informs the whole of social life.[14] Further examples are really not necessary, for our account need not ratify all the ethnographical interpretations that we have mentioned. At this stage in our inquiry all we need do is recognize that there are at least some very diverse societies that, as anthropologists confirm, are animated by an ideology of sharing, here

understood as the preeminence of the role played by reciprocal gifts in interpersonal relations.

The opposite of a gift is seizing something, making no offer of anything in
return. It is an action that creates no more obligations for its perpetrator than
the gift does for the gift's recipients. If one wishes to underline the illicit and
generally condemned aspect of the operation, it may be called theft, seizure,
or wrongful appropriation. However, the term "predation" seems preferable
here, in that it conveys the idea that an appropriation of this kind may not result from a desire to harm or some fleeting need. Instead, it may be prompted
by the fundamental constraint to which the lives of animals are subjected.
Every animal needs to replenish its sources of energy at regular intervals by
consuming some prey, a body originally distinct from itself but that the animal in question ends up assimilating in such a way that it becomes a part of its
own organism. Humans are not excepted from that imperative, for they have
obeyed it for tens of millennia, even if, thanks to the development of livestock
raising and the deferred consumption of products already transformed by
agriculture and herding, the evolution of techniques of subsistence has by
now succeeded in partly blurring the memory of the intrinsic link between
the capture and the ingestion of prey. Nevertheless, predation remains a central mechanism in the preservation of living creatures, an elementary way in
which animals are related to their environment, so much so that René Thom
has constructed a mathematical model of the "predation loop" that seems
applicable to many biological processes.[15] Predation is thus a phenomenon of
productive destruction that is indispensable for the perpetuation of individuals: far from being an expression of gratuitous cruelty or a perverse desire
to annihilate others, it on the contrary transforms the prey into an object of
the greatest importance for whatever creature ingests it. Indeed, it is the very
condition of that creature's survival.

But is it legitimate to transpose a biological phenomenon to the social
sphere and claim that collectives have simply converted predatory patterns of
behavior into a dominant relational schema? First, we should bear in mind
(indeed, how could we forget?) that the primacy of exchange and sharing is
not accepted by all those who have reflected upon the foundations of political
existence. Hobbes was by no means alone in emphasizing, following Plau-
tus, that man's original condition is to be a wolf to his fellows, for his egois-
tic awareness of his own interests constantly leads him to try to dispossess
others. And although Hobbes's pessimism has, not without reason, above all
been interpreted as an unconscious naturalization of competitive interpersonal relations within a nascent market economy, it cannot be reduced solely

to that. For there is no denying that violent appropriation and the destruction of others are not the doubtful privileges of individuals fashioned by a bourgeois society. Traces of both are to be found in every period, in every latitude, and it would be as ridiculous to deny this predatory propensity as to claim it to have been the dominant characteristic of human nature up until such time as the latter was pacified by institutions introduced by the social contract. Predation is a disposition that, among others, is a legacy of our phylogenesis, and if certain collectives have adopted it as their own particular ethos, this means, not that they are more savage and primitive than others, but simply that they have found it a paradoxical means of incorporating the deepest kind of otherness while remaining faithful to themselves.

My ethnographic experiences among the Achuar led me, some years ago, to come to that conviction and to apply to the Achuar the notion of "predation" in order to explain a style of relating to both humans and nonhumans that is based on capturing principles of identity and vital substances reputed to be necessary for the perpetuation of the self. This predatory attitude was evident not only in warfare and its rituals but also in many aspects of daily life; and it was not peculiar to the Jivaro groups. I noticed very soon that signs of it were detectable here and there among other indigenous Amazonian societies, in total contrast to the philosophy of equal exchange by which the Amazonian form of social life had long been exclusively defined. However, it was not at all my intention to substitute one hegemonic relationship for another, for it was also perfectly clear that some of the peoples in this vast cultural region did, for their part, adhere fully to the obligations that exchange imposed.[16] At about the same time and in parallel fashion, Viveiros de Castro was developing his own thoughts about the ontological foundations of cannibalism and warfare in the Tupi world, and this led to a model of "the symbolic economy of predation" on the basis of which he set out to elucidate the sociological peculiarities of Dravidian kinship in Amazonia. Far from being symmetrical, as in other Dravidian systems, here the opposition between affinity and consanguinity seems to be characterized by a hierarchical reversal that is dynamically inspired by a diametric structure. Although masked at the level of a particular local group by the behavior patterns and values associated with consanguinity, in relations with other local groups affinity seemed to predominate and was itself subordinated to a more totalizing relationship for which it provided a specific code: namely cannibalistic predation on enemies.[17]

With the passing of time, and despite a few minor divergent interpretations, the idea that, for many Amazonian societies, predation constituted the cardinal schema for relations with "others" has become widely accepted.[18] But it has also encountered resistance and given rise to many misunderstandings.

Without going into the ethnographic details, which we shall examine in the next chapter, I should make it clear that predation is above all a disposition for incorporating otherness, both human and nonhuman, because this is reputed to be indispensable for a definition of the self: in order truly to be myself, I must take possession of another being and assimilate it. This can be done by means of warfare, hunting, real or metaphorical cannibalism, the seizure of women and children, or ritual methods of constructing the person and mediating with ideal affines, in which violence is confined to the symbolic level. Predation is not an unbridled manifestation of ferocity or a deadly impulse set up as a collective virtue. Even less is it an attempt to reject as inhuman some anonymous "other." It constitutes recognition that without the body of this other being, without its identity, without its perspective on me, I should remain incomplete. This is a metaphysical attitude that is peculiar to certain collectives, not a troubled exaltation of violence that some ethnologists might be guilty of, as they project their own fantasies upon the Amerindians.

The trilogy of the gift, exchange, and predation seems to present affinities with the distinction that Marshall Sahlins draws between the three forms taken by reciprocity in tribal societies: "generalized" reciprocity qualifies altruistic transfers within the local group and requires no automatic reciprocation; "balanced" reciprocity corresponds to a direct exchange of equivalent values within the tribal group; "negative" reciprocity consists in trying to obtain something for nothing, sometimes in a dishonest or violent fashion, and is a feature of intertribal relations.[19] But the resemblance is no more than superficial, in the first place because neither the gift nor predation involves reciprocity. In both cases what is involved is a unilateral operation: the gift comes unaccompanied by any binding obligation to return the favor; and a predatory act is unlikely to imply that the perpetrator ardently hopes for a reciprocal response. Such a response is always possible and in fact often takes the form of reprisals, but it is certainly not constitutive of the intention that prompted the action. Besides, the three kinds of reciprocity affect the direction of movements and the balance sheet (positive, negative, or equal) of the passage of objects, not the causes and obligations inherent to each of those kinds of transfers; and it is precisely those causes and obligations that make it possible to distinguish exchange, predation, and gift as classes of heterogeneous phenomena. Finally, the typology of reciprocity describes modes of circulating goods that are to be seen everywhere in operation and that, when combined within a single society, are differentiated from one another above all by their position along a continuum defined by the greater or lesser spatial and kinship distance between the agents in those transfers. In contrast, in the sense in which

I understand them here, exchange, predation, and gift are general relational schemas that concern far more than the circulation of goods, since one or other of them may come to structure the ethos of a collective in a distinctive fashion.

Producing, Protecting, Transmitting

The relations in the first group allow for reversibility of movement between the terms: this is indispensable for an exchange to take place, and it remains possible, though not always desired, in predation and gift. In contrast, the relations in the second group are always univocal and operate between terms set in a hierarchy. This is particularly clear in the case of production. The genetic antecedence of a producer over his product does not allow the latter, in return, to produce its producer (even if it may help to support him), and this places the product in a situation of dependence vis-à-vis the entity to which it owes its existence, at least initially. Marx dispels any doubt about the matter. Production is both a relationship that humans weave among themselves according to well-defined forms in order to procure jointly their means of existence (the relations of production); and it is also a specific relationship to an object that one creates for a particular purpose. In the famous pages of his "General Introduction" to *A Contribution to a Critique of Political Economy*, Marx stresses that "the act of production is, therefore, in all its aspects an act of consumption as well."[20] This is because, in the first place, the individual who develops his faculties by producing something expends energy in this operation and consumes raw materials, which are the means of production; this is "productive consumption." But consumption is also, in an immediate fashion, a production, in the sense that all consumption, whether of food or other things, contributes toward creating the body and the conditions of subsistence of the subject who produces it; this is "production geared to consumption." "In the first [productive consumption], the producer transforms himself into things; in the second [consumptive production], things are transformed into human beings."[21] Although an identity is established between production and consumption, this is only possible thanks to a mediating movement between the two terms: "Production furthers consumption by creating material for the latter, which otherwise would lack its object. But consumption, in its turn, furthers production, by providing for the products the individual for whom they are the products."[22] However, this extremely original dialectical parity between objectivizing production and subjectivizing consumption fades away a few lines further on, when Marx forthrightly reaffirms the primacy of production over consumption. In effect, consumption is simply a particular moment in production since, once the individual who has produced an object returns it to himself by consuming it, he is acting as a productive individual who is thereby reproducing himself; in consequence, "production forms the actual starting point and is, therefore, the predominating factor."[23]

Marx's position is indicative of the more general tendency of modern thought to regard production as the element that determines the material conditions of social life and as the principal way for humans to transform nature and, by doing so, transform themselves. Whether or not one is a Marxist, it is now commonly thought that the history of humanity is primarily founded on the dynamism introduced by a succession of ways of producing use value and exchange value of the materials that the environment provides. But it is fair to question whether this preeminence ascribed to the process of productive objectivization applies generally to all societies.[24] To be sure, humans have always and everywhere been productive; everywhere they have modified or fashioned substances intentionally in order to procure themselves the means of existence, thereby exercising their capacity to behave as agents who impose specific forms and purposes upon matter that is independent of themselves. But does this mean that this kind of action is everywhere apprehended in accordance with the model of a relation to the world known as "production," a model so paradigmatic and familiar to us that we have become accustomed to use it to describe extremely heterogeneous operations carried out in very diverse contexts?

It seems hardly necessary to recall first that the idea of production by no means suffices to define the general manner in which many hunter-gatherers conceive of their subsistence techniques. That is why some specialists of those societies now prefer to use the term "procurement" rather than "production," the better to underline that what we call hunting and gathering are primarily specialized forms of interaction that develop in an environment peopled with intentional entities that are comparable to humans.[25] But the inadequacy of the notion of production is also obvious when it comes to accounting for the way in which great non-Western civilizations conceptualize the process by which things are engendered. François Jullien shows this clearly, in the case of China, in his commentary on the oeuvre of Wang Fuzhi.[26] For this seventeenth-century neo-Confucian scholar, who systematizes a fundamental intuition of Chinese thought, the whole of reality can be conceived as a continuous process resulting from the interaction of two principles, neither of which is more fundamental or more original than the other: for example, *yin* and *yang*, or Heaven and Earth. From this stems a logic of a mutual relationship with no beginning and no end that excludes any external founding agent, any need for a creator-agent as an initial cause or prime mover and any reference to some transcendent "otherness." The process of rest alternating with movement that is given dynamism by the primacy of movement acts in a totally impersonal and unintentional manner. "So order cannot be imposed from outside by a deliberate act of some subject or other implementing a certain plan . . . ; it is inherent in the nature of things and stems totally from their continuous development."[27] In short, the world is not produced by the intervention of an actor with a plan and a will. It results solely from its own internal propensities (*lishi*), which manifest themselves spontaneously in a permanent flux of transformations.

This self-regulated process is a far cry indeed from the heroic model of creation as developed in the West and proclaimed as an unquestioned fact on the twofold authority of the biblical tradition and Greek thought. The idea of production as the imposition of form upon inert matter is simply an attenuated expression of the schema of action that rests upon two interdependent premises: the preponderance of an individualized intentional agent as the cause of the coming-to-be of beings and things, and the radical difference between the ontological status of the creator and that of whatever he produces. According to the paradigm of creation-production, the subject is autonomous and his intervention in the world reflects his personal characteristics: whether he is a god, a demiurge, or a simple mortal, he produces his oeuvre according to a preestablished plan and with a definite purpose—hence the abundance of craftsmanship metaphors that are used to express the origin of this type of relationship. In the Psalms, the Creator is compared to a well-sinker, a gardener, a potter, and an architect. In the *Timaeus*, the demiurge creates the world, fashioning it as a potter would. He carefully composes the mixture that he is about to work on; he turns it on his wheel to form a sphere, then he rounds it off and polishes the surface.[28] Here, the image of fabrication, poiesis, is central; and so it remains in the modern conception of the relationship of a producer and that which he produces. What also remains is the idea of the absolute heterogeneity between them: the creator, craftsman, or producer possesses his own plan of the thing that he will bring into existence and gives himself the technical means to realize his intended purpose by projecting his will upon the matter that he manipulates. In the same way, just as the Creator and his creation are incommensurable in Christian dogma, in the Western tradition there is no ontological equivalence between the producer and whatever he brings into being.

Nothing could be more alien to the manner in which the Indians of Amazonia construe their relations with the entities upon which they feed. For the Achuar, for example, it would be meaningless to speak of "agricultural production" or "hunting production," as though the aim of those activities were to bring into being a consumable product that would be ontologically dissociated from the material from which it came—even if such operations may come to be quantified and assessed vis-à-vis the potential productivity of resources, as by myself in the past.[29] Achuar women do not "produce" the plants that they cultivate: they have a personal relationship with them, speaking to each one so as to touch its soul and thereby to win it over, and they nurture its growth and help it to survive the perils of life, just as a mother helps her children. Achuar men do not "produce" the animals that they hunt. They negotiate with them personally, in a circumspect relationship made up, in equal parts, of cunning and seduction, trying to beguile them with misleading words and false promises. In other words, here it is the relations between subjects (humans and nonhumans) that condition the "production" of the means of existence, not the production of objects that conditions (human) relationships.

In Amazonia, even the production of artifacts seems not to fit into the classic model of the demiurge-craftsman. This is what is suggested by Lúcia van Velthem's studies of the wickerwork of the Wayana of the northern Pará, who, like some of their Carib and Arawak neighbors, are noted for the diversity and refinement, both technical and aesthetic, of the objects that they plait.[30] Wickerwork is a masculine activity that is both valued and prestigious, complete mastery of which is acquired only quite late in life, at least in the creation of the most difficult pieces such as the great *katari anon*, the carrying basket that is entirely decorated by plaited motifs that differ on each of the external and internal sides. However, the Wayana regard the fabrication of baskets, not as a virtuoso fashioning of a raw material, but rather as an incomplete actualization, in slightly different forms, of the bodies of animal spirits that they reconstitute using plant fibers that are assimilated to human skin. Their baskets, receptacles, trays, mats, and plaited containers in which they press manioc are thus, as van Velthem puts it, "transformed bodies."[31] Each has an anatomy—a head, limbs, breasts, a trunk, ribs, buttocks, and genitals—and the motifs that adorn them are stylized representations of the being of which they constitute a transmutation. The designs on the inner sides of baskets even represent that being's internal organs: the point is to evoke in this way the predatory capacity of assimilation of an animal's spirit, which, however, is rendered inoffensive in the artifact by virtue of its incompleteness. Since the fiber body differs from the threatening body of the prototype of which it is an actualization, given that it is not recomposed altogether identically, it lacks the intentionality of the original. However, that is only so in the case of domestic basketry, the daily use of which makes it necessary somehow to "devitalize" it. Objects woven for ceremonial use are said, on the contrary, to be complete materializations of the bodies of animal spirits. The most expert of the basket makers are even credited with the ability to recompose in their handiwork the non-visual characteristics of the prototype, such as its movements, sounds, and smells. This ontological mimetism allows these objects to function, in their turn, as agents of transformation. They are used extensively in healing rites, since they possess properties identical to those of the entities of which they are reincarnations. Far from being apprehended as the production-creation, out of inanimate material, of a new thing informed by the art and purpose of an autonomous agent, the work of a Wayana basket weaver is regarded as something that can make a veritable metamorphosis possible; that is to say, it can produce a change in the state of an entity that already exists as a subject and that preserves all or part of its attributes throughout this operation.

As a way of conceiving action on the world and a specific relationship in which a subject generates an object, production thus does not have a universal applicability. It presupposes the existence of a clearly individualized agent who projects his interiority on to indeterminate matter in order to give form to it and thus bring into existence an entity for which he alone is responsible and that he can then appropriate for his own use or exchange for other realities of the same type. Now, to return to our two examples: the production model does not correspond either to the concept of a continuous autopoietic process as expressed in Chinese thought or to the priority that, in Amazonia, is granted to reciprocal transformation over fabrication ex nihilo. For this reason, anthropologists are perhaps unwise when they succumb to the convenient temptation to use the familiar language of production to interpret the very diverse phenomena by means of which a reality, whether or not of a material nature, comes to be instituted. To speak of the "production" of a person, of social links, of a subject, or of the difference between the sexes outside the Western context, in which, for several millennia, this notion has encompassed an altogether singular relationship, is at best, in most cases, an abuse of language that leads to false parallels.

Protection, too, implies the nonreversible domination of the protector over the one who benefits from that protection. But although it is never reciprocal, the relationship may certainly be reversed in the course of time. The care that parents devote to their children right up to the dawning of adulthood will perhaps be repaid by their children when the parents grow old. It also sometimes happens that a protector is himself protected by someone more powerful, in particular in relations of patronage that sometimes take the form of a hierarchical chain of dyadic links of clientship. And, finally, frequently protection is mutually profitable in that it guarantees the protector not only the gratification brought by receiving the real or supposed gratitude of the person protected but also the possibility of enjoying help from the latter and also whatever advantages stem from the situation in which the latter is placed. But even where there is a reciprocal interest, the relationship remains inegalitarian, for it is always founded on the fact that the offer of assistance and security by which it is manifested stems from the initiative of the party who is in a position to make that offer. A child who is a minor is no more able to refuse the protection of its parents than a citizen is able to refuse that of the state or than pandas are in a position to refuse the protection offered by their ecologist defenders.

In relations with nonhumans, protection becomes a dominant schema when a group of plants and animals is perceived both as dependent on the humans for its reproduction, nurturing, and survival and also as being so closely linked to them that it becomes an accepted and authentic component of the collective. The most complete model of this is probably the extensive kind of herding that pastoral societies practice in Eurasia and Africa. Of course, some of the herded animals are consumed by the humans, either directly or indirectly, but it is seldom this utilitarian function that is foremost in the herdsmen's idea of their relations with the animals that they tend on a daily basis. They commit themselves above all to take charge of the animals, to help them and watch over them, and to offer them care in every domain of life, since the control that wild animals possess over their destiny is here passed over to humans. The latter must therefore see that the animals are fed, if only by choosing the best pastures and waterholes for them. They also have to ensure that the animals reproduce, providing a collective of descendants in the most favorable conditions; and they do this by selecting the reproducers, organizing fertilization, and aiding the newborn. Furthermore, they must defend the herd against predators and care for any diseased animals. Although the term "production" is sometimes used to designate this way of making it possible for the animals to live, it hardly seems suitable, since the direct action exerted upon the animals is of an entirely different order from the work of a craftsman or worker fashioning an artifact out of inorganic material. Whatever the degree of standardization achieved by selection, each animal remains different, with a character of its own and its own whims and preferences. So the idea of protection is the one better able to suggest the mixture of constant attention, individualized control, and well-meaning forms of constraint that define the relationship between the herdsman and his animals. In fact, in some cases, such as Nilotic societies, those duties take on the appearance of a total subjugation of humans to the mission of satisfying their animal partners. As Evans-Pritchard wrote, "The cow is a parasite on the Nuer, whose lives are spent ensuring its welfare."[32]

East Africa is also where the famous "cattle complex" of nomadic herds-men has been best described. What this expression implies is a supervaluation of the herd, the effect of which is to make all utilitarian aims seem to disap-pear, producing a situation in which this sole source of wealth comes to play a mediating role in social relations generally: humans are named after the beasts that they control; the possession of those beasts provides both the means of exchange and the principles upon which social aggregation and transmission are based. As Evans-Pritchard, again, observes in connection with the Nuer, "They tend to define all social processes and relationships in terms of cattle."[33] Godfrey Lienhardt asserts the same of the Dinka, adding that these neigh-bors of the Nuer "conceive their own lives and the lives of cattle on the same model."[34] Such interdependence between the domesticated animals and the human society cannot be reduced to the classic interpretation of fetishism, which regards relations with nonhumans as the basis of interhuman relations. Here, the interdependence indicates that the animals are indeed full members of the collective, and so are not just a socialized segment of nature serving as a metaphor or idiom for relations between humans that are external to it. Lienhardt furthermore emphasizes that the Dinka do not anthropomorphize their animals but, on the contrary, seek at every level to imitate the character-istics and behavior of their cattle, which is why these constitute the best pos-sible substitutes for humans. In other words, the relational schema here seems to be twofold: the humans' protective attitude toward the livestock is com-bined with relations of a different nature between the humans themselves; and these, paradoxically, are copied from those that structure the world of the cattle. The organization of the herd, the competition between bulls, and the relations between the male and female animals serve as models for thinking about political and spatial organization, about the bellicose nature of men, and about the relations between the sexes. This is why, despite the exorbitant role played by cattle raising among the herders of East Africa, protection does not play the role of a general principle of action that structures all the interac-tions between humans and nonhumans, however fully the latter are integrated within the collective.

To find clearer illustrations of what Haudricourt calls "the pastoral treat-ment" of humans, we need to turn to the ancient Mediterranean civilizations: the Roman world, for example, where under the imperious but protective "crook" of the paterfamilias, a little cohort of dependent beings would de-velop. Within the order and relative safety of the living conditions guaranteed by their master's authority, women, children, slaves, and flocks all found the means to contribute to the common prosperity by fulfilling their respective roles. Virgil, better than anyone, sketched in the ideal picture of this agricultural Arcadia, in which a diligent laborer, through wise management of his dependents, "provides sustenance for his country and his little grandson and . . . for his herds of kine and faithful bullocks."[35] Two of the four books that make up the *Georgics* are devoted to care for the animals, the measures to take to protect them against danger, the services that they render, and the benefits that they provide. Thanks to their virtues and their sense of duty, the fat oxen, the powerful bulls, the mettlesome chargers, and the industrious bees all behave like responsible citizens under the enlightened supervision of their owner, just as he himself flourishes on his land in Campania under the aegis of Augustus, the defender of the power and prosperity of the state. Under Virgil's pen, submission is sweet, and even slavery is almost tolerable, given that all that is required is a little obedience and a lot of hard work in return for the security that one's master offers!

The mutual benefits that protection is believed to procure are often part of a long chain of dependence that links several ontological levels by a series of duplications of asymmetrical relations. Just as humans take care of the animals and plants from which they derive their subsistence, they may themselves be protected by another group of nonhumans: the deities, who derive from their patronage the most substantial of advantages, namely their own raison d'être. These deities, who are in some cases hypostases of a plant or an animal particularly important to the local economy, are thus seen as founding ancestors and guarantors of the humans' well-being. At the same time, they are regarded as the condition (or even the direct creators) of the effective domination over the nonhumans that the humans use and protect. This is clearly illustrated by the example of the Exirit-Bulagat, a group of Buryat herders in Cisbaikalia.[36] For these people, herding, although adopted only relatively recently, has become their dominant activity and the motor of their social and ceremonial life; so much so, indeed, that they claim to have been engendered by a heavenly bovine, Buxa Nojon, "Lord Bull," the tribe's principal deity, upon which minor ancestral figures depend. Several times each year, mares are sacrificed to the Lord Bull and to the ancestors to ensure good luck and wealth and to persuade them to protect the herds and ensure their growth. The victims are sacrificed to the deity in order that it will then fill their meat with grace and so too the humans when they consume it. Furthermore, every herdsman has in his herd a "consecrated" bull that must never be maltreated or mounted or sold or castrated. This is the embodied emissary of the Lord Bull and of his inexhaustible virility, and it guarantees and promotes the fecundity of the domesticated animals. The care that the humans lavish upon this bull represents, as it were, a service that they render to their bull-ancestor to thank it for its fertilizing power, while the souls of the sacrificed mares that are offered up

to this deity, as a substitute for human souls, constitute a propitiatory gift motivated by the hope that the deity will concede its benefits to the humans and
its protection to their herds. By distinguishing between these oblations—on
the one hand, a restitution of life through care for the sacred animal and, on
the other, a restitution of souls through the death of the mares—the humans
avoid having to repay the bull the debt that they have incurred toward its
hypostasis. In this way, protection can become the all-encompassing value
of a system of interactions that combines two asymmetrical relationships: a
relation of predation in which one takes the lives of nonhuman dependents
without allowing them any direct recompense, and a gift-giving relation in
which one offers protected nonhumans to nonhuman protectors so as to encourage the latter to perpetuate the domination that they allow the humans
to exercise over the former.[37]

As I understand it, transmission is above all what allows the dead, through
filiation, to gain a hold over the living. We may owe many things to those
who have preceded us: material goods and land received as bequests, prerogatives that are inherited (responsibilities, hereditary statuses and functions,
and symbolic attributes such as a name or the possession of certain kinds
of knowledge), and also physical, mental, or behavioral characteristics reputed to be inherited. The extent of this material and immaterial patrimony
through which we are indebted to previous generations varies enormously
from one civilization and social situation to another, but it largely depends
not only on the quantity of transmitted items but also and above all on the
importance ascribed to the very phenomenon of transmission, understood
as an accepted dependence upon more or less distant ancestors. In every collective, things pass down from one generation to another in accordance with
precise and recognized norms. However, it is only in certain circumstances
that this ceding process acquires the form of a veritable debt owed by the
living to the dead, the former considering themselves to be debtors of the
latter with regard to more or less everything that conditions their existence.
This includes the order and values according to which they live, the means of
subsistence placed at their disposition, the differential advantages that they
may enjoy, and even their very persons, inasmuch as a person is formed by
principles, substances, and in some cases a destiny that stems from one's direct parents and those who, in the past, engendered them. To transmit such
things, real and fictitious genealogies are certainly needed, genealogies that
go back quite a long way and explicit indications stipulating what each individual has the right to receive by way of the identity, privileges, and obligations that are transmitted through these channels stretching down from

the past. It seems reasonable to assume, however, that initial conditions are less important than the institutional consequences that the preponderance of some specific schema of relations with others may gradually have acquired. The depth of genealogies, the rules unequivocally confirming a maternal or paternal filiation, the segmentation into different descent groups that act in the manner of moral persons, and the legitimation of rights stemming from particular ancestral groups: all these are mechanisms that for a long time anthropologists failed to recognize were by no means universal. Now, however, it seems that they should be regarded as the means that certain collectives employ in order dogmatically to perpetuate the sovereignty that the dead exercise over the living through relations of transmission.

The clearest expression of this relationship can be found where the dead are converted into ancestors to whom a cult is devoted. These are close ancestors, not the distant and more or less mythical figures also conventionally called "ancestors" who are sometimes placed at the origin of clans or tribes but are nevertheless not accorded any direct influence over the destiny of those they have created. Immediate ancestors are individualized, named, and often given material form on domestic or lineage altars, and nothing that concerns the living eludes their meddlesome jurisdiction. West Africa is one of the places that such ancestors favor most, as can be seen from the example of the Tallensi of Ghana.

The patrilineages of the Tallensi, which are localized, set in segmented hierarchies, and enjoy a relative political independence, trace their identity and solidarity back to the cult that each devotes to a group of agnatic masculine ancestors, which goes back twelve generations at the most. In his *Oedipus and Job in West African Religion*, Meyer Fortes describes the despotic domination that the ancestors exert over the living, a domination that is analogous in its content to the absolute authority of a father over his sons. Just as a man has no economic rights, legal status, or ritual autonomy as long as his father is living, similarly the members of a lineage depend upon the ancestors for access to land, the exercise of political responsibilities, and the well-being of each one of them.[38] A son does not, in any case, succeed his father in his rights and privileges until such time as he has executed the funerary rites that turn his father into an ancestor, thereby transforming his own subordination to a living individual into an authority delegated to him by earlier generations. The power of the ancestors manifests itself at two levels. Collectively they require that the living should conform to the moral precepts and respect the values upon which their sociopolitical organization is founded. Every death is thus interpreted as a sanction organized by the ancestors on account of a misdeed that an individual or even his father or an agnatic relative may have committed, in many cases inadvertently. But every human being is also flanked by a specific ancestor deemed to watch over him or her provided he or she submits to its will, as this is revealed by a diviner—hence the importance of the ancestor cults, which take the form of sacrifices, prayers, and libations. As Fortes explains, "their solicitude is gained not by demonstrations of love, but by proofs of loyalty."[39] The prerogatives that may be enjoyed within the framework of a lineage, the possessions at one's disposal, and the quota of happiness or misfortune allocated to each individual are all fixed by the ancestors, who extend over the living a cloak of justice as impossible to question and as terrible and inaccessible to human understanding as that which the suffering Job eventually credited to his god.

Among the Tallensi, as in other West African civilizations, the cult addressed to the ancestors is thus not so much a way of honoring them and thanking them for all that they transmit; rather, it is an attempt to conciliate them and dispel their anger, an attempt that one can never be sure will be crowned with success. The movement between the generations is strictly one way, for what one's forebears have given can never be returned to them, starting, for all of us, with the lives we have received from our parents. Nor, in the present case, is it a matter of the ancestors acting with liberality, since they have no choice but to transmit, in their turn, whatever they themselves received, and by doing so they commit their descendants to a spiral of dependence from which they can never free themselves. The debt that the living inherit is thus passed on inexorably from one generation to the next, as the indebted members of the collective join the mass of the dead and so become creditors; they can now make their descendants pay, just as they had to, for the right to existence and all that makes this possible, in return for unswerving obedience to the power that they hold. For the ancestors, this constitutes a precious guarantee of survival of a sort. Like Aeneas, fleeing from Troy, every man carries his father on his back, but also his father's father perched on his father's back and so on, in a by no means metaphorical pyramid, the weight of which crushes the freedom of movement of the living. In these collectives, the burden both vital and deadly of the ancestors is perpetuated by a filiation that cannot be rejected, and it is fair to apply to them what Pierre Legendre says of the subject of transmission in general: "The genealogical institution functions against the background of the subject's distress."[40] However, in Africa, that distress does not encompass a tragic dimension such as that which pervades the particular destiny of an individual faced by capricious gods or the hermetic purposes of the Christian god, since all concerned, including the ancestors, share the fate of dependency upon earlier generations, for better or for worse. So, despite the reference to Oedipus in the title of Fortes's book, it is unlikely that a Tallensi would lament using the words that Sophocles puts into the mouths of the chorus surrounding Laius's son: "Not to be born comes first by every reckoning."[41]

Transmission is not only a relationship within the segments of a collective that links in a chain of dependency, on the one hand, living people, who are destined to become ancestors, and, on the other, the dead, who live on and whose power and will are felt in all circumstances. It is also what distinguishes one collective, with all its elements, from another, for some collectives claim as the principal source of their contrastive identity the fact that they have their own particular groups of ancestors from whom stem both their legitimacy as an autonomous social body and also all the attributes attached to it. The latter range from the right to live in a particular space and exploit its resources—echoes of which are to be found in the notion of a fatherland—to a consciousness of sharing certain hereditary physical and moral properties. This use of transmission in the definition of collectives and their properties is altogether specific to certain regions of the world and should not be confused with the universal phenomenon of ceding certain material and immaterial assets from one generation to the next. In Indian Amazonia, for example, nowhere does one find the kind of hold exerted by the ancestors that exists in Africa and in China. In Amazonia, the very idea of an ancestor seems incongruous. The recently dead are supposed to disappear as soon as possible from the memory of the living, and if anything of them does remain for a while, it is in the form of more or less malicious spirits whose company is to be shunned. Moreover, genealogies seldom go back further than the grandparents' generation, and descent groups, in the rare cases where these exist, control neither access to the means of subsistence nor the devolutions of the latter; and they may anyway concern only a fraction of the population, as is the case of the Sanumá of Brazil. No cult is addressed to the dead, and if there is anything to be inherited from them, it will be, not so much a meager physical patrimony (their objects are usually destroyed) but, rather, symbolic attributes: names, songs, myths, the right to make certain garments or to wear certain ornaments.[42] In short, the dead are excluded from human collectives and have no power over them.

This is probably a feature of the animist regime in general. So when Ingold criticizes the use of the model of a genealogical tree and the primacy of ancestral principle as a means of explaining the relations of indigenous peoples to one another and to the space that they occupy, he finds most of his examples in the kind of collectives that I call animist: the Chewong of Malaysia, the Nayaka of Tamil Nadu, the Ojibwa, the Cree, and the Yup'ik of North America, and so on. According to Ingold, the image of a rhizome, which he borrows from Gilles Deleuze and Félix Guattari, is far more appropriate for characterizing the reticular relations that these people, who are indifferent to unilinear filiation, maintain with the various components of their environment.[43] Ingold's point is fair enough provided one does not go to the other extreme and declare that all reference to transmission and the ancestral principle should be banned if the aim is accurately to restore the idea that "indigenous peoples" have of themselves.[44] For there is no reason to exclude the Tallensi or the Malgaches from the benefit of autochthony and a distinctive identity or to believe that they have succumbed to the Western perversity of the genealogical principle and a cult of *lares*. By choosing to ascribe considerable importance to their dead and all that these transmit and control, some collectives have made the matrix relationship to the ancestors the main linchpin of the precepts and values that organize their common lives. Others have preferred to ignore that dimension of human life and instead to base their individual and collective identity on a dense and shifting network of multipolar relations with a mass of entities both contemporary and of the same status as themselves. Just because anthropology has for a long time tended, when interpreting the practices of animist collectives, to adopt as a standard the institutions of the ancestor worshipers, there is no reason why the contribution made by the latter type of collective to the diversity of world states should be considered suspect or allowed to fall into oblivion.

The relational modes that we have just considered fall into two groups: the first covers potentially reversible relations between substitutable terms, since the latter are situated at the same ontological level (exchange, predation, and gift); the second covers one-way and irreversible relations between nonsubstitutable terms, since these are intrinsically hierarchical (production, protection, and transmission). The former are characteristic of the symmetrical or asymmetrical movement of something of value between subjects of equal status whose identity or essence is not transformed by the actualization of the relationship that links them. Meanwhile, the latter imply a connection of a genetic, spatial, or temporal order between the agents and the objects of an action by means of which the disparity of their respective positions is either created or maintained (fig. 10).

A place in this inventory could no doubt be found for many other relational modes. Most, though, can be included as the complement either to one of the relationships that we have considered here or at least to one of its dimensions. There is no protection without dependence, no liberality without gratitude, no exchange without obligation. As for domination and exploitation, the absence of which might well be criticized in view of the role that

Relations of similarity between equivalent terms		Relations of connection between nonequivalent terms	
Symmetry	*EXCHANGE*	*PRODUCTION*	Genetic connection
Negative asymmetry	*PREDATION*	*PROTECTION*	Spatial connection
Positive asymmetry	*GIFT*	*TRANSMISSION*	Temporal connection

FIGURE 10. The distribution of relationships according to the type of relations that exist between the terms involved

they have played in history, those can be fitted into other relationships, as one of their components: domination is inherent in protection and transmission, and exploitation manifests itself in the relations of force that are established at the time of dictating the conditions of production or exchange. Moreover, unlike the relations that I have picked out, only rarely are exploitation and domination seen as what they are by those whom they concern. More often, they affect the appearance of a relationship involving an exchange of services that to some extent masks their fundamental inequality: payment in exchange for work, protection against forced labor, prosperity in return for subservience. But that is really beside the point—for, I repeat, my intention is not to examine all the relations that occur between existing beings and that are given an institutional form. Rather, it is simply to mark out a few major schemas of action that structure the lives of collectives in order to examine how compatible or incompatible they may be with the modes of identification picked out earlier. So this typology makes no claim other than to group together a few of the elementary structures that make up the great variability of ways of intervening in the world; and that variability is so rich that it would not be possible to propose any more than a rough syntactical sketch of them.

Although relational schemas are based on specific cognitive mechanisms, such as schematic induction, analogical transposition from one domain to another, or the influence of affects upon memorization, they are not categorical imperatives written into the architecture of the human mind. Rather, they should be considered as objectivized properties of all collective life. They are properties that are embodied in mental, affective, and sensorimotor dispositions by means of which behavior patterns stabilize in distinctive forms of interaction. Giving something or oneself to another, taking from another, receiving from another, exchanging with another, but also appropriating another, protecting him, producing him, or placing oneself in his dependence are all actions inherent in the phylogenetic evolution of social primates. They are actions that all humans perform both within the family unit and also in wider contexts. They provide a register of combinations upon which all collectives draw, selecting (we do not really know why) one field of relations rather than another, in order to orientate their public behavior. But none of these practical schemas, on its own, dictates the ethos of a collective. Rather, each schema constitutes an indeterminate ethical landscape, a style of mores that one learns to cherish and by which one differentiates oneself from one's neighbors: a style of mores that colors one's daily attachments to beings and things, with underlying nuances. However, this does not rule out other types of relations to others, ones that individual idiosyncrasy, the unpredictability of feelings, and the arbitrariness of conventions all make it possible to express more discreetly in less stereotyped situations.

14

The Traffic of Souls

Between identification, a means of specifying the properties of existing beings, and relations, a means of specifying the general form of the links between those beings, two kinds of connection are possible. Either the plasticity of a relational schema makes it possible for it to structure interactions in a variety of ontologies, which will then present a family likeness despite the heterogeneity of their essential principles; or, alternatively, one of the modes of identification is able to accommodate several distinct relational schemas and this introduces into an ontological configuration widely distributed in space (a cultural region, for example) the kind of concrete diversity of customs and norms from which ethnologists and historians love to draw their material. The second case is what we shall now consider. However, the combinations made possible by the conjunction of a mode of identification and a relational mode are too numerous for us to consider them all in a systematic and detailed fashion, especially since some of them turn out not to be possible for reasons of logical incompatibility, as we shall soon see. So let us limit ourselves to considering the variations of ethos that various relational schemas imprint upon one particular mode of identification: this will be animism. The demonstration will certainly not be complete, but it will at least provide the beginnings of a proof that anthropology can always hope to find when it enters into some detail in a comparative study of a number of cases. As Mauss, mobilizing John Stuart Mill in his support, declared, "a well-made experiment is enough to demonstrate a law."[1]

If I have chosen animism for this experiment, that is because, in one of its geographical variants, it raises an exemplary problem in the interpretation of the question before us. Whatever theoretical line they take, all the specialists on the Indians of Amazonia sketch in an ethnographic picture of the societies that they study in which the features of the animist ontology are easily recognizable. However, that is no longer the case when it comes to describing a specific style of social philosophy that is valid for the whole of Amazonia. Here, total disagreement reigns, with each anthropologist tending to project on to other peoples of the region the values and practices that he or she has observed in one particular ethnographic context. Ever since Lévi-Strauss, in one of his earliest articles, drew a parallel between intertribal trading and warfare in the lowlands of South America, it has become common to say that the paradigmatic relationship in this region is one of exchange: men exchange marriageable women (the model being a swap of sisters), goods (often identical ones), and the dead (in vendettas and warfare); women exchange among themselves plant cuttings, foodstuffs, and tamed animals; chieftains exchange the right to polygamy in return for a duty to be generous; hunters exchange offerings to the animals that they hunt in exchange for their meat. In short, everything seems to circulate in an unending round of reciprocity.[2] More recently, as we have seen, some anthropologists have laid the emphasis on an altruistic variant of exchange, defining Amazonian sociability as a mutual production of persons amid generous conviviality, while others have, on the contrary, insisted on the cannibalistic dimension of the incorporation of others as a typical mode of interaction. Should we accept, along with Viveiros de Castro, that "generalized predation" is "the prototypical modality of Relationship in Amerindian cosmologies,"[3] or should we believe Overing and her disciples, who regard an intimacy based on sharing as the dominant feature of the Amazonian *socius*? Is the ethical horizon of these populations a fair exchange between partners of equal status, an ideal "togetherness" lubricated by mutual help and gifts? Or is it a bellicose seizure of others? The self-evident answer is that all these relational modes are certainly present, but distributed in different collectives.[4]

Predators and Prey

I shall seek an illustration of what predation may amount to once it becomes a dominant relational schema by turning to a people who have gradually become familiar to my readers. Until they were "pacified" by missionaries between 1950 and 1970, the various Jivaro tribes were reputed to be of a bellicose disposition and seemingly anarchic in their collective life. Their ceaseless wars were a source of perplexity to observers and a motive for anathema. Yet they did not indicate any disintegration of the social fabric or an irrepressible propensity for violence. On the contrary, they constituted the principal mechanism for structuring individual destinies and links of solidarity and also the

most visible expression of one key value: namely the obligation to acquire
from others the individuals, substances, and principles of identity that were
reputed to be necessary for the perpetuation of the self. Head-hunting among
the Jivaro tribes—the Shuar, the Achuar, the Huambisa, and the Aguaruna—
and likewise the unending vendettas between members of the same tribe
were, in effect, expressions of one and the same need to compensate for every
death within a kindred group by capturing real or virtual persons from close
or more distant neighbors. Shrinking the heads of enemies made it possible,
by means of a long and complex ritual, to strip the dead person of his original
identity in order to transfer that identity to the murderer's local group, where
it would become the principle for the production of a child yet to be born.
By dint of shrinking the head, which preserved the dead man's physiognomy
and, along with it, his individuality, the victorious warrior captured a virgin
identity that would allow his kin to multiply without incurring the obligations inherent in a marriage alliance. Consequently, the enemies who were
beheaded had to be neither too close nor too distant if they were to provide an
identity that was culturally usable yet at the same time perceived as different:
they were invariably Jivaros but were selected from a neighboring tribe that
spoke a different dialect and with which no relationship of kinship had been
established in the recent past.

Vendetta warfare did not involve capturing heads, but the principle that
governed it was nevertheless identical. Whatever the vengeful motives that
sparked an armed confrontation between two kindred groups, the assassina-
tion of an enemy belonging to the same tribe in effect often led to the seizure
of his wives and young children. The wives took their place alongside the
victor's earlier wives, while the young children were adopted and treated by
him as his own offspring. Thus, even if the capture of the women and children
of neighboring local groups was never an explicit and sufficient reason for
undertaking a vendetta, it was in many cases an expected or even hoped-for
outcome. For the victorious warrior, the advantages gained were twofold: the
death of his enemy was regarded as payment for a real or imagined slight,
and at the same time, he enlarged his domestic group without incurring the
obligations of reciprocity upon which marriage alliances were founded. To
be sure, both head-hunting and vendettas were likely to lead to reprisals, but
these were obviously not sought for as such, and efforts would be made to
avoid them. The violent and reciprocal appropriation of others within the
Jivaro group was thus the product of a rejection of pacific exchange, not a
deliberately engineered result of an exchange of human lives in the course of
a bellicose interaction.[5]

Furthermore, both vendettas and head-hunting were carried out against persons that the Jivaros classified as affines even if, in actual fact, the enemies killed in the fighting might be consanguineous or, on the contrary, have no genealogical link with the murderer. A few words about social organization will help to explain this identification of enemies with relatives by marriage. The traditional Jivaro habitat is widely dispersed, with each house belonging to a single, very often polygamous family and constituting an autonomous, political, and economic unit separated from neighbors by distances that it takes between a few hours and one or two days to cover, either on foot or by canoe. Here and there, though, one comes across larger local groups comprising ten to fifteen houses strung out along a river, the members of which are more closely linked by consanguineous kinship and marriage alliances. The latter follow the rule of union between bilateral cross-cousins. Now, like other Amazonian societies of the same type, these small endogamous networks tend to regard themselves as ideal consanguineous communities, for the links of affinity within them are in practice obliterated as a result of manipulations of the kinship terminology. These tend to divide affinity and consanguinity between the sexes in such a way that an exclusively masculine affinity is matched by a marriage alliance based on paradoxically consanguineous unions.[6] By dissociating affinity from actual marriage, the Jivaros give themselves the means to convert it into a logical operator for thinking through relations with the outside world, as can be seen, for example, in the practice of transforming into affines consanguineous relatives if these reside outside the endogamous network. The local group's utopian closure on itself in effect presupposes a symmetrical opposite: namely an affinity that is clearly objectivized, given that it is free from any consanguineous contamination. Although relations outside the endogamous network are usually hostile, they are graduated according to the scale of social distance or relative otherness. This finds expression in the form of a schematization that is increasingly marked by the affinity relationship the further one moves away from the focal point where it effectively orientates the marriage alliances.

Internal wars usually break out following conflicts between local neighboring groups over some real or supposed infringement of the rules of marriage alliance. When a quarrel breaks out within the endogamous network over matters linked with rights over women, payment of compensation and the mediation of a great warrior generally suffice to prevent the outbreak of a vendetta between close kin. If an amicable arrangement proves impossible, it is usually because the guilty party or the victim of the infraction comes from another endogamous network—for endogamous closure is an ideal. In fact, though, thanks to a strict application of the principle of uxorilocality, a variable percentage of exogamous unions always make it possible to introduce into a local group men who are natives of a neighboring network. These foreign sons-in-law find themselves in a difficult situation to the extent that affinity instituted by alliance with distant kin is far looser than the more fundamental affinity instituted by a prescriptive exchange. So when a serious incident occurs, the transplanted in-law naturally enough tends to flee and seek help and protection among his direct consanguines. Through marriage alliances, each local group thus maintains a tenuous network of links of affinity with adjacent groups that may serve as the basis of a temporary coalition or, on the contrary, provide the pretext for a factional confrontation. In short, in these conflicts between neighbors, the enemies are unequivocally identified as real affines, who are sometimes described collectively as "givers of women."

In contrast to a vendetta, intertribal warfare has as its sole objective the capture of heads from neighboring Jivaro tribes in order to celebrate the *tsantsa* ritual. The difference between "ordinary" Amazonian trophy heads and the shrunken Jivaro heads is that the former rapidly lose any traces of a specific physiognomy, whereas the latter—for a while, at least—perpetuate the unique representation of a face. That is the sole objective of extracting the skull, desiccating the tissues, and modeling the features so as to obtain a resemblance of the victim. When the *tsantsa* is produced, its role is that of an easily transportable condensed identity. However, the *tsantsa* is not a miniature effigy of a particular person but a formal expression of a purely existential individuality indicated by any distinctive facial trait, provided the head is that of a nonrelated Jivaro. For the Jivaros, an individual identity is contained not so much by the physical features of the head but by certain social attributes of the persona: a name, speech, the memory of shared experiences, and face-paintings. To be used in the ritual, the *tsantsa* must therefore be relieved of any referential residues that might remain to prevent it from embodying a generic Jivaro identity: it is never called by the patronymic, if indeed that is even known, of the one whose head has been taken; its face is carefully blackened to obliterate the memory of the patterns painted on it; and finally all its orifices are sewn up, thereby consigning the sense organs to an eternal phenomenal amnesia.

The depersonalization of the *tsantsa* renders it suitable for a rite whose discontinuous phases extend over rather more than a year. In the rite, the *tsantsa* functions as a logical operator—both as a term and as a relationship— in a series of permutations between terms and relations that are themselves affected by variable values. First called "profile," then "soft thing," the head either simultaneously or consecutively occupies different positions, from the point of view of gender and kinship, in a series of univocal or reciprocal relationships, which may be either antagonistic or complementary, with the killer, his kin and affines of both sexes, and a number of other ceremonial groups. By the time this topological ballet is completed, the *tsantsa* has played every role in a symbolic procreation: nonparent, giver of women, taker of women, wife, and finally embryo. The very real fruit of this simulated alliance—a child to be born within the murderer's kindred group—is thus perfectly consanguineous without being incestuous. As a virtual existence obtained from strangers, the child owes his procreation to the staging of an ideal affinity, the only kind truly satisfactory for the Jivaros because free of any obligation of reciprocity: this is, in short, an affinity without affines. Seen from this point of view, this intertribal war is really indistinguishable from the intratribal warfare of which it constitutes a logical, or even historical, extension. For repeated confrontations between coalitions of different blocks of local networks can only consolidate antagonistic regional identities, thereby contributing to the continuous process of tribal differentiation that is necessary for the perpetuation of head-hunting. Between stealing women and children from potential affines who have been excluded from the kinship community and stealing identities that will produce children from non-kin with whom one simulates an ideal affinity, the difference is one of degree, not of nature.

Whether waged against close enemies or distant ones, Jivaro warfare is the motor for the fabrication of collective identities. In a society without chiefs, without villages, and without lineages, it renders possible a temporary coagulation of factions, a renewal of solidarities that have slackened as the result of such a dispersed habitat, and a stimulation of the social link brought about by the federating sensation of sharing a common enemy. It is through that warfare that groups of relatives acquire their substance and the principles for their renewal, by means of poaching persons and identities, all of them rare and precious, from affines either real or symbolic, who are treated as prey. To be sure, armed clashes are not permanent, but in everyone's mind warfare is always present. At any moment a smoldering conflict is ready to burst into flame, providing the main topic of conversation and orienting the political dynamic of alliances and the interplay between factions. In a society in which the word for "peace" is unknown and the only collective rituals are those that announce or conclude the exercise of collective violence, warfare is by no means an unfortunate accident: it is the very stuff of social life.

Likewise, it is through warfare that individual masculine identities are forged. As soon as boys reach adolescence, they are pressed to enter into contact with an *arutam* spirit, in the course of a visionary trance induced by severe fasting and continuous absorption of green tobacco juice and other hallucinogenic liquids. This terrifying experience enables the adolescent to establish a personal and secret relationship with the ghost of a deceased Jivaro warrior who will pass on to him his strength and protection. *Arutam* first appears in a frightening guise—a glowing head jerking from side to side, a couple of intertwined giant anacondas, or a gigantic harpy eagle—which noisily disintegrates as soon as it is touched, then returns in human form to deliver a message of assistance. The young man will from then on identify with his *arutam*, in particular by painting his face with red dye in a design that recalls the monstrous figure in which the spirit first revealed itself to him. The immediate effect of this identification is an irrepressible desire to manifest the bravery unleashed upon him by his encounter with his protector spirit—by plunging wildly into warfare. However, the quest for *arutam* needs to be regularly renewed, for the power that a man obtains from it disappears every time he takes part in a victorious expedition or kills an enemy. It then leaves him defenseless. Since the physical survival of a warrior is subjectively dependent on his ability to restore his skill at killing, the mechanism of the acquisition and subsequent loss of *arutam* thus contributes to a kind of uncontrollable increase in his individual propensity to accomplish his destiny in the exercise of violence.

The predatory attitude that the Jivaros manifest in their relations with others, the need that they feel constantly to incorporate the bodies and identities of their neighbors in order to persist in being themselves, even while being partly determined by that which they capture and assimilate, and their stubborn rejection of any freely accepted reciprocity: all these are traits that reappear in their relations with nonhumans. In this domain, the Jivaros set a higher value on their violent appropriation of substances and fluids than on the free play of their circulation. Yet, as we saw at the beginning of this book, many plants and animals are regarded as persons who share some of the ontological attributes of the humans with whom they are linked by relations of consanguinity and alliance. However, nonhumans are not integrated into a network of exchange with humans, and they are allowed nothing in exchange when their lives are taken. To be sure, the Jivaro hunters do address *anent* incantations to the game that they hunt, to the spirit masters of the animals, and to the prototypes of each species, so as to establish with them a relationship of connivance: hunting is regarded as an expression of the complicity between relatives through marriage alliances, in which the ultimate end, the killing, is masked by ludic formulae. Hunting *anent* are absolutely explicit in this respect: the animals are always described as brother-in-laws, with whom one communicates in the slightly jokey tone of forced affability that is usual in such a relationship; and sometimes the sisters of the hunted animal are even referred to as potential wives for the hunter. But treating one's prey as an affine is really nothing but a deceit designed to disguise the basically inegalitarian nature of the relationship between the men and their animal victims. The point is to allay the mistrust of the animals so that they will not elude the hunter's darts or make him pay for his cannibalistic intentions. As in many societies in which hunting plays a predominant role, it is not unknown for excesses to be punished. If one kills more game than is needed, one risks a snakebite or a fatal accident in the forest. But in such a case, this is purely revenge on the part of the animals—or rather their spirit master and protector—and is designed to punish a hunter's hubris; there is no question of it being a process of voluntary exchange founded on parity between the two parties.

Even relations with plants are not free from this predatory ideology, so one should not see it as a simple rationalization of the productive destruction that characterizes any form of hunting. Manioc, the main foodstuff for the Jivaros and the most common plant in their immediate environment, is reputed to suck in through its leaves the blood of those who brush by them, but it mainly attacks the women who cultivate it and also their young children. It is a threat that is not taken lightly, and the death of a baby is often attributed to anemia provoked by manioc vampirism. Consequently, the women have to sing special *anent* incantations to this plant, in an attempt to switch its thirst for blood toward other, undesirable visitors to the garden. The women treat the manioc as a child, but one who will eventually be eaten by those who have raised it. Meanwhile, the manioc is itself a child that seeks to bring about the death of human children, whose sole nourishment for several years is, precisely, constituted by a kind of manioc porridge. Beneath its benign appearance, gardening in truth implies a mortal competition between the human and the nonhuman young. For the women, it is a matter of reproducing and raising young plants, whose flesh the humans will consume, meanwhile taking care to prevent the manioc plant from retaliating by consuming the blood of the human young who come into contact with it.

The capture of real or virtual persons from close or distant enemies, the furtive seizure of game, and the cunning warfare against the cannibalistic manioc thus all, in different domains, express an identical rejection of exchange in relations with others. This predatory tension is what structures the relations that the Jivaros maintain with a whole mass of subjects of many different kinds, in that it integrates their experience of the world in many domains ordinarily distinguished by the misleading analyses of dualism, and it is applied, without distinction, to both humans and nonhumans, to both kinship relationships and techniques of subsistence, and to both territorial organization and ritual. One property of relational schemas is to embrace vast areas of practice without discriminating between terms according to their ontological status or the situations in which they relate to one another. These schemas are thus at the source of the stylistic effect perceived by an observer of a "culture" that is different from his own. It is an ineffable and perhaps illusory feeling, but it can be traced back to the thematic patterns of behavior that feed the stereotypes that every group of humans adopts toward its neighbors.

This example presents an opportunity to return to considering how an ethos comes to be incorporated as a way of acting according to behavioral principles that are, however, never made explicit. For example, the schema of predation upon affines is not regarded by the Jivaros as an explicitly transmitted norm. Given that the concepts of predation and affines are not expressed by any words in their language, their tendency to behave toward others in this way is something very internalized that has become implanted, as time has passed, ever since their earliest days and has been constructed not so much through the assimilation of a system of "collective representations" as by successive inductions based on constant observation of the conduct of adults. There are plenty of opportunities for children to be alerted to the behavior patterns that they sense: the differences in the way that various persons are treated, the interminable discussions about the ongoing vendettas in which the shifting cartography of intimacies and alliances can be sensed, the commentaries that punctuate hunting stories or that accompany the butchering of the game, participation in ceremonies that are still mysterious but in which contrastive blocks of oppositions emerge, some heavy-handed joke or even an anodyne remark that remains imprinted on the mind: all these play their part in supplying reference points, prompting automatic responses, infiltrating attitudes, in short, instilling the confidence necessary to enter as an actor into the world into which one has been born.

Among the Jivaros, as elsewhere, this process is fueled by affective responses, through apprenticeship and the reinforcement of models of interrelations and interaction that occur in the first instance on the occasion of events that are remarkable because of the emotions that they arouse. This applies to warfare, of course, with all its attendant mourning and victories. It also applies to the relations of lethal complicity with hunted animals that are forged by the handling of corpses that are still warm and the excitement of the first experiences of tracking and killing one's prey. And for people who know nothing of "natural deaths," it applies to the obsession with shamanistic aggression to which, from time to time, physical accidents or misfortunes testify. Here, predation upon others is not just a synthetic norm of behavior or some anthropological idea: at an early age, Jivaro children are bound to come into contact with it both physically and mentally. By experiencing the pain of a loss and a desire for revenge, the excitement of triumph and the pleasures

of resentment, every Jivaro learns to cultivate all these identifications and antagonisms that an ethnographer then dutifully logs.

There are now so many rich and detailed ethnographical works that interpret the logic behind the actions of this or that ethnic group in the lowlands
of South America according to the schema of generalized predation that the
case of the Jivaros no longer seems exceptional. Among the most striking examples are the Juruna and the Araweté of the Xingu Valley, the Parakanã of
the Tocantins Valley, the Mundurucú of the Tapajós Valley, the Pirahã of the
Madeira Valley, the Wari' of Rondônia, the Yanomami of Brazil and Venezuela, and, farther south, the Nivacle of the Gran Chaco.[7] All these peoples
confer the position of an intentional subject upon a large number of members
of the cosmos. These thus find themselves in a situation of formal equality at
the ontological level while the relations between them are, on the contrary,
defined in effect by a circumstantial asymmetry, with each of these humans
and nonhuman subjects striving to incorporate the substance and identity
of others, in permanent denial of any reciprocity. A similar situation is not
unknown in North America, as is testified by, among others, the Sioux of the
Great Plains and the Chippewa of the southwestern edge of the Great Lakes.[8]
Other cases are also to be found, for instance, among the Kasua of the Mount
Bosavi region of New Guinea and the Iban of Sarawak.[9] However, these seem
more rare, although it is hard to say whether the apparently greater concentration of predatory animism in the Americas results from particular features of the continent's development in isolation from the rest of the world or
simply from the greater attention that ethnographers studying autochthonous
peoples there pay to certain details of their relations with plants and animals.

The Symmetry of Obligations

We need not look far afield to find a perfect counterexample to the Jivaros.
Whereas the latter do all that they can to escape the obligations of exchange,
the Tukanos of Colombian Amazonia, on the contrary, strive to respect such
obligations meticulously in all their interactions with other inhabitants of the
cosmos.[10] Yet these two ethnic groups, each of which is composed of several
tribes, do share many characteristics in common. In the first place, they are
relatively close spatially, separated by no more than five hundred kilometers,
which, given the scale of Amazonia, is a mere nothing. The environments in
which they live are also similar: they are dominated by the equatorial rain forest. There are, to be sure, certain local differences in the availability of certain
resources, but this imposes the same kinds of ecological constraints upon
both groups. The Tukanos and the Jivaros have responded in similar fashion

to these constraints. In both cases, they are dispersed in residential units of relatively small numbers of people; their itinerant slash-and-burn horticulture consists mainly of manioc (sweet in the one case, bitter in the other); they acquire their protein by means of a combination of hunting and fishing, hunting being more important for the Jivaros, fishing for the Tukanos. And, finally, the way they see their environment is altogether similar: both categorize humans, plants, and animals as "people" (*masa*, in the Tukano languages) or as "persons" (*aents* in the Jivaro languages), all of whom possess an analogous interiority. This makes it possible for most of the species to lead the same kind of social and ceremonial life despite the differences in their physicalities. It is on this basis that humans can maintain with plants, animals, and the spirits that protect them individual relations governed by a code of behavior similar to that which prevails among the Indians themselves.

Both the Jivaros and the Tukanos unquestionably belong to the ontological regime of animism. But the principles and values that guide their relations with others could not be more different. The Desana, one of the sixteen tribes that make up the Tukano group, offer a good starting point for an examination of those differences, for an ethnographic study of them has provided Reichel-Dolmatoff with the material for the "thermodynamic" model of the cosmos mentioned in chapter 1, with which many societies in the Amazonian northwest are now credited.[11] According to this model, the universe was created by Father Sun, an omnipotent and infinitely distant being for whom the actual daily sun is, as it were, a delegate to this world. The fertilizing energy that emanates from Father Sun animates the entire cosmos and, through this cycle of fertilization, gestation, and growth, of humans, animals, and plants, ensures their vital continuity. It is likewise the source of other cyclical phenomena such as the revolutions of the heavenly bodies, the alternating seasons, the variations in nutritional resources, and periodical recurrences in human physiology. However, the quantity of energy produced by Sun is finite and is deployed in an immense closed circuit that encompasses the entire biosphere. To avoid entropic losses, exchanges of energy between the various occupants and regions of the world therefore have to be organized in such a way that the quantities of energy that humans extract can subsequently be reinjected into the circuit. For example, when a Desana hunts and kills an animal, a portion of the potential of the local fauna is cut off and is transferred into the human domain when that game becomes food. It is therefore necessary to ensure that the needs for human subsistence do not endanger the good circulation of the flows of energy between the different sectors of the world. And it is the responsibility of the Desana to keep a watch on the situation and compensate for the losses that are caused by what they take from nonhumans.

The most common means to achieve this result is sexual abstinence. By checking his carnal desires, a hunter effects a retention and accumulation of sexual energy that can then rejoin the general stock of fertilizing power that is in circulation in the universe and thereby benefit the reproduction of hunted animals. This balance can also take more direct forms. For the Desana, the relation between the hunter and his prey is above all of an erotic nature: in the Desana language, "to hunt" is rendered as "to make love to the animals."[12] So men try to win the favors of their prey by means of love philters, aphrodisiac perfumes, and seductive invocations. Charmed by these ploys, the animals fearlessly allow themselves to be approached and even visit men in their dreams or daydreams in order to copulate with them; and this reproductive operation helps to multiply the members of the species to which the animals belong. Although the Jivaros and the Tukanos conceive of their relations with animals as being governed by relations of affinity, the content that they ascribe to those relations could not be more different. Whereas the Jivaro hunter treats his prey as a brother-in-law who is potentially hostile and to whom nothing is owed, the Desana hunter treats it as a spouse whose line of descent he is fertilizing.

Even more direct is the principal process of energy feedback. Human souls are traded against animals that can be hunted. After his death a Desana generally enters the "Milk House," a region of the cosmos conceived as a kind of uterine paradise. In contrast, the souls of those who have not respected the exogamous prescriptions go off to great underground or underwater houses where the Vaí-mahsë live. These are the spirits that govern the destinies of hunted animals and fish. There the human souls become animals, as a kind of enforced compensation from those who have not respected the rules of exchange between humans. But this is not the most common mechanism for the renewal of the fauna. The most common operation is the responsibility of shamans. These periodically pay visits to the Vaí-mahsë during trances brought on by narcotic drugs, in order to negotiate a provision of forest animals for the members of their communities to hunt. Every animal thus made available for hunting must be compensated for by the soul of a dead human that will change into an animal of the same species, destined to be included in the stock of animals amassed by the animals' master. The humans destined to become animals after their deaths usually come from neighboring groups but are selected by a consensus. It is said that shamans from the various Tukano tribes meet in the house of the Vaí-mahsë to decide together who, among the members of their respective collectivities, will have to die to ensure that hunting continues to be good. Negotiations for a future exchange of souls in return for game, arranged in an amicable fashion by the shamans of several tribes, thus precede the exchange of souls that each shaman negotiates with the animals' spirit master.

The negotiation that the shaman conducts with the Vaí-mahsë aims to bring about a scrupulous equivalence between the objects involved in the transaction. Once the two parties have reached agreement, the shaman enters the house where the animals are kept, suspended from the rafters like quarters of meat in cold storage. He then shakes one of the posts to dislodge the hunk of game that he fancies for his group. But if he shakes the beams too roughly and detaches more animals than the agreed quantity, a new bout of bargaining is required in order to achieve parity. In this way, humans and animals enjoy an equal status in the living community's access to energy; both groups help to maintain a balanced flow of it, and their functions are reversible in this quest for a perfect balance, based on strictly equal transfers. The freely accepted obligation of mutual dependence is equally central to the nonhuman communities. So the spirit master of the terrestrial animals and that of the fish regularly visit each other for festivals and dances accompanied by all their families. These are opportunities to exchange women and to render one another's respective communities fecund. As can be seen, egalitarian exchange is at the heart of the relations that the Desana weave with nonhumans; its demands color all their actions affecting the environment.

It is true that certain aspects of Reichel-Dolmatoff's proposed model of the Tukano cosmology have prompted disagreement, in particular the correctness of translating the Desana notion of *bogá* (current) by the thermodynamic concept of a closed circuit of a finite quantity of energy. Another Tukano specialist has recently proposed an alternative model, based on his study of the Makuna, in which recyclable energy is replaced by an open-ended flow of "spiritual" forces, which sometimes increase and sometimes decrease.[13] According to Luis Cayón, every tribal territory of the Tukano group is animated by a particular essence regarded as one of the manifestations of the mythical hero Yurupari, whom all of them recognize. This essence resides concretely in the musical instruments that are used in the periodic Yurupari rite but that are ordinarily deposited in some stream or river. The essence thus travels through the rivers of all the territories and thereby, through the interconnections of the hydrographic network, mingles with the essences from other tribal groups. On the occasion of the Yurupari ceremony, which all the tribes celebrate at the same time, the forces of fertility circulating in the rivers reach a high level of concentration and bring fecundity to the forest, to the rivers and streams, and to the nonhuman inhabitants of the cosmos. So, for the Makuna, vital power comes not from Father Sun but from the submerged instruments of Yurupari: since the quantity of energy carried in the rivers fluctuates depending on the

rainfall, it falls to humans to divide it up in a balanced fashion, thereby allowing nonhumans to benefit from it. In this undertaking, a crucial role is played
by the ritual specialists, for it is they who are responsible for fertilizing the
nonhuman occupants of the territory in the course of a ceremony known as
"the healing of the world" (*ümüâri wânôre*). It is also up to them to go and
negotiate with the master of the animals for the more than usual quantity of
game required for organizing a great collective festival. This they obtain in exchange for offerings of coca and tobacco that the master immediately converts
into fertile power for the animals.

Ordinary men, too, take an active part in encouraging animal life. As may
be remembered, it is a Makuna hunter's duty to send the spirit of a slaughtered animal back to the house of its species so that it can be reborn there.
They manage this by dint of an incantation that they chant silently before
eating any game. In this incantation they retrace the mythical origin of the
particular species that they are about to eat. It is a symbolical way of recon-
stituting its collective genesis in such a way as, practically, to reconstitute the
essence of an individual that has temporarily been taken away from its fellows.[14] It is even said that, thanks to this process, two new subjects of an animal species are born for each animal killed, an increment for which Reichel-
Dolmatoff's homeostatic model makes no allowance. The exchange made with
nonhumans thus takes the form of an obligation on the part of the Makuna
to regenerate those that they destroy. It is a way for the animals to perpetuate themselves and for the humans to continue to feed on them. In short,
even though Cayón and Reichel-Dolmatoff diverge as to ethnographic details,
they are certainly in agreement on the fact that parity in the exchanges made
between the Tukanos and their nonhuman neighbors is indispensable for the
survival of the world. As Cayón remarks, "the fact that reciprocity is the axis
of the system is beyond question."[15]

The social organization of the eastern Tukanos is governed by the same
principle of reciprocal dependence as that which rules their relations with
animals. The traditional form taken by the habitat is that of a large house for
several families that make up an agnatic descent group, known as a *maloca* in
the Spanish of this region. The physical and symbolic reproduction of the local communities results from matrimonial exchanges and the distribution of
ritual functions within a group composed of at least sixteen exogamous units,
which I have been calling "tribes," for the sake of convenience.[16] But that term
is not really appropriate. It is true that each of those exogamous units is characterized by a distinct language and a specific name (Desana, Makuna, Tatuyo,
Barasana, and so on); each claims descent from its own founding hero; and
each holds the privilege of making and using certain types of ritual objects.

However, each unit also observes a strict rule of exogamy that stipulates that it should obtain its wives from groups that speak a different Tukano language or even from groups that speak Arawak or Carib. Furthermore, at present, none of these "tribes" occupy a continuous territory. A *maloca* is composed of men who communicate together in the language of their own linguistic group, and of women who come from several adjacent linguistic groups and who continue to speak their own languages, for multilingualism is general throughout this region.

Clearly, each of the exogamous linguistic groups does not form matrimonial alliances with all the other sixteen, in the first place because there are certain pairs of linguistic groups between which unions are prohibited (phratries); and second because marriages are usually arranged with neighboring groups: the Desana with the Pira-Tapuya, the Bara, and the Tuyuka, for example, and the Barasana with the Tatuyo and the Tuyuka. Matrimonial exchange thus makes it possible to structure the whole intertribal system, since the women identify both with their husbands' groups and with the group in which they themselves were born. In this way, they serve as intermediaries between clearly differentiated local units, ensuring that they all become integrated. This close complementarity of different linguistic groups is reinforced by the idea that each possesses its own economic specialization (hunting, fishing, or horticulture), which complements those of the others, even if all of them are polyvalent in the techniques of subsistence. Thus, the Desana regard themselves as "hunters," and for preference, they marry women from the Pira-Tapuya unit, which is classified as a tribe of fishermen. Furthermore, each of the units engaged in such exchanges is associated with one sex in particular, depending on the nature of its specialization. Thus, the Desana "hunters" consider the Pira-Tapuya "fishermen" as a whole as a feminine element, while regarding themselves, collectively, as a masculine unit.[17]

As well as linguistic exogamy, there are other factors that combine to create solidarity between the peoples of northwest Amazonia, welding them into an inclusive regional organization. One factor is mythology, which unites all these linguistic groups in a common origin and assigns to each of them a territory and a place set in a hierarchical order according to the site and order of their appearance in the cosmogony. This is related in stories that all have a common structure. Each narrative describes a series of episodes in a mythical journey to the sources of the rivers made by a group of primordial anacondas that halted at various sites characterized by a chaos of rocks and rapids. In each of these sites, one of the anacondas emerged from the waters and a portion of its body was transformed into a group of human ancestors, each of whom then gave birth to one of the numerous patrilineages that compose each linguistic group. This process of progressive and itinerant segmentation is often represented as a canoe journey that produced all the successive ancestors of the descent groups of the various Tukano "tribes." The most prestigious in the symbolic hierarchy are those who were the first to land in the lower reaches of the hydrographic network.

Moreover, all the Tukano linguistic groups (and a few non-Tukano ones too) celebrate the cult of Yurupari in the course of a series of ceremonies during which masculine initiations take place; but the principal objective of these is to renew contact with the founding heroes and the ideal norms of existence that they established long ago.[18] Every time a *maloca* organizes one of these ceremonies, members of the various neighboring "tribes" are invited, along with their musical instruments that contain the Yurupari essence of their own particular descent groups. This complementarity of linguistic groups in a rite commemorating the etiology of the totality that encompasses them all reaffirms the vigor of the intrinsic links that unite them. The regional division of crafts likewise confers upon each "tribe" a reputation of excellence and hence exclusivity thanks to their production of a kind of object necessary in the daily lives of all of them. Canoes come from the Bara, cassava presses from the Tuyuka, basketry sieves from the Desana, drug pipettes from the Tatuyo, stools from the Tukanos, and so on. This specialization engenders a system of artificial rarity that is very common in Amazonia and that encourages a generalized circulation of artifacts that accentuates the sense of a voluntary mutual dependency. Finally, these links of mutual dependency are strengthened by the systematic practice of paying long visits to one another, visits that sometimes last for several weeks, and by regular drinking festivals during which the invited affines offer their hosts vast quantities of smoked meat and fish, just as the latter will to the former on a subsequent similar occasion. These systematic exchanges of food and hospitality between residential units that are totally autonomous where their subsistence is concerned help to strengthen sociability and a sense of belonging to a single group. Despite the diversity of their languages, each *maloca*, each descent group, and each Tukano linguistic group thus feels it is an element within a metasystem and that it owes its material and symbolic survival to regular exchanges with the others who are part of the whole system. As in their relations with animals, it is the logic of parity in compensation that governs relations between humans here.

No doubt the eastern Tukanos and their neighbors in northwest Amazonia have carried to a degree seldom attained elsewhere their obsession with maintaining a close network of relations of equitable exchanges with the many kinds of persons that compose their world. Although it may elsewhere assume a slightly less systematic form, the constant attention paid to maintaining a balanced reciprocity of transfers as a cardinal schema of action is by no means rare in the animism archipelago. Good examples of similar behavior are found in the Guianas, in particular among the Wayãpi and the Akuriyó, and, on a wider scale, by the kind of confederation that is formed by the indigenous peoples of the upper Xingu River, which is similar in many respects to the regional system of northwest Amazonia.[19] The hunting peoples of the Siberian forest provide another illustration. As Hamayon observes, here "the very act of hunting, of killing game . . . is governed by a logic of marriage alliances . . . modeled on behavior toward a human partner." In fact, the two relationships are two of a kind, to the extent that "the hunting system [is] analogous to the matrimonial system."[20] The same principles of equivalence seem to be at work among the Moï peoples of the high forests of central Vietnam: here, the Reungao establish extremely formal alliances with the spirits of animals, plants, and meteorological phenomena, some of which are characterized by obligations analogous to those that stem from kinship links and association pacts between humans.[21] In all these cases human and nonhuman "others" are treated as alter egos with whom it is possible to live amicably only if an agreement of egalitarian exchange is scrupulously observed.

The Togetherness of Sharing

Our second counterexample is likewise situated no more than a few hundred kilometers away from the Jivaros, but this time to the south: the Campas form a pluri-ethnic community in which generosity, solidarity, and the predominance of common welfare over the interests of individual parties have been elevated to the rank of a supreme canon of behavior that is far more comprehensive than the rules of equal and complementary exchange that the Tukanos like to respect. "Campa" is the generic name given to a cluster of tribes that speak Arawak languages in the upper central Amazonia of Peru—the Ashaninka, the Matsiguenga, and the Nomatsiguenga—who, together with the Piro and the Amuesha (or Yanesha) make up the sub-Andean Arawak group. All of them live in a foothill equatorial forest similar to that of the Jivaros, in the valleys of the Urubamba and the Perené Rivers. Moreover, they are all diversified producers living in dispersed, small, autonomous local communities that combine swidden horticulture with fishing, hunting, and gathering. Finally, the Campas all agree on the fact that animals, plants, and the spirits that protect or embody them are social beings, endowed with an interiority and faculties of understanding similar to those of humans. All these persons with different appearances are primarily distinguished by their detachable bodies, which are assimilated to *cushma*, the long cotton tunics traditionally worn by the Indians of this region. But despite all these resemblances, a greater distance than that which separates the Campa ethos from the Jivaro ethos could not be imagined.

The cosmologies of the Campa tribes are all organized according to the same dualist principle that divides human societies, animals, and spirits into two distinct and mutually antagonistic ontological domains.[22] One domain possesses a positive value and includes all the entities that share a common essence: namely the Campa tribes and some of the forest tribes that surround them (in particular the Cashibo and the Shipibo-Conibo, who speak Panoan languages), the deities of the heavens (Sun and his father, Moon), the spirit masters of hunted animals, and the animals themselves. The other domain is totally negative and is defined by its radical difference from the first one. It encompasses all humans who come from the Andes, whether Indians or whites, sorcerer-animals and their masters, who are bad spirits. Most of the hunted species and their masters stem from a race of good spirits whom the Campas call "our people" or "our fellows" (*ashaninka*) and who are reputed to be well disposed toward the Indians. These live on the periphery of the known world, immediately above or below the terrestrial strata, along the margins of the territory, and on the mountain peaks. They have a human appearance that is invisible to the Campas and so, when visiting, they adopt the form of lightning, thunder, or various animal species. Some of them control important resources. Otters, gray herons, and egrets are the masters of fish and ensure that these swim back up the rivers every year in the spawning season so that the Campas can fish for them in the shallow waters of the dry season. The swallow-tailed kite is the father of edible insects: the shaman pays regular visits to its wife to ask her to allow her children—who are regarded as the shaman's brothers—to accompany him so that humans can feed on them. Most of the birds that the Campas hunt are themselves embodiments of good spirits. Their slaughter is only an illusion; after the hunter has asked the bird for its clothing, out of compassion for him it deliberately presents its carnal envelope to his arrows, at the same time preserving its immaterial interiority, which is immediately reincarnated in an identical body or else resumes its invisible human appearance. The bird thus suffers no damage and its act of benevolence requires no reciprocation except, perhaps, a feeling of gratitude. Certain very common species of game birds, in particular toucans, penelopes, and hoccos, are not reincarnations of spirits but instead are protected by them. And those good spirits offer them freely to the humans, for them to hunt. The reason for this generosity is the fact that the good spirits, their animal transformations, and the species that they control are all identical to humans at the ontological level. The Campas regard them as close kin, and the gift of their bodies is seen simply as evidence of the dutiful generosity that people of the same kin owe one another. The solidarity that such a link presupposes is expressed in exemplary fashion when the good spirits associated with hunting descend, in their invisible form, among the humans in order to dance and sing with them. In so doing, they are not seeking compensation for any services rendered but simply wish to show their affectionate closeness and their desire to share in a conviviality that is free from any obligations.

The status of the mistress of peccaries makes it possible to contrast this dutiful generosity with the imperative of exchange that characterizes hunting in the Tukano groups; among the Campas, this is a feminine entity, described as a generic sister, who keeps the peccaries in an enclosure at the top of a mountain.[23] From time to time a shaman comes to intercede with her, asking her to part with one member of her herd. She then tugs out a tuft of bristles from the back of one of the animals and blows it away so that it will eventually produce many more peccaries, which she will then send down to the humans for them to hunt. This is an action of pure benevolence. It certainly creates certain moral obligations for the hunters. In particular, they must make sure that they kill the peccaries with a single arrow shot, so as not to cause them to suffer. However, unlike among the Tukanos, no compensation is demanded. The same goes for fishing: the fish, filled with pity, allow themselves to be caught on the fisherman's hook and line, after he has repeatedly and sadly mumbled, "My bag is empty, my bag is empty."[24]

The good spirits have no sexual activity. This is a feature that sets them firmly apart from the usual figures of the masters of game in Amazonia and the animist world in general. Among the Tukanos, the spirit masters of animals are characterized by their superabundance of sexual energy, and as we have seen, they send their protégés to copulate, in dreams, with the hunters, a ploy that is perfectly understandable, given that the spirits are responsible for the reproduction of the animal species. To that end, they need assistance from the reproductive powers of humans, who, for their part, are happy to oblige in exchange for the vital force that they absorb when they consume the animals. The good animal spirits of the Campas are quite different. Although they exist as two sexes, they reproduce without coitus. In their human reincarnation they are said to possess atrophied genital organs, and their women give birth by parthenogenesis, simply by shaking out their tunics. Furthermore, also in contrast to Tukano hunters, who seek to win the favors of the animals by making themselves attractive to them by using charms and perfumes to enhance their erotic appeal, Campa men endeavor to purify themselves as completely as possible before setting out on a hunting expedition. They expunge all residual signs of their sexual relations with women, in particular any defilement left by contact, even of an indirect nature, with menstrual blood. The horror that the good spirits feel for anything that draws attention to the physiology of reproduction and its cycles and their disgust at the uncontrollable desires and the flow of substances necessary for existence indicate clearly that the relations between humans and these entities that supply them with game have nothing to do with the exchange and recycling of fertilizing energy and principles of individuation that characterize such relations in northwest Amazonia. The bodies that the good Campa spirits deliver up to the hunters are nothing but carnal envelopes stripped of any subjectivity or principles of animation, and this manifestation of generosity in no way affects the perennial integrity of these beings that are forever unaffected by the contingences of organic life.

Nevertheless, this Campa world is not without negative aspects. It teems with evil spirits that live in close proximity to the humans and are a constant danger to them. These are known as *kamari* and they assume as many different forms as the good spirits do. Most of them have monstrously large sexual attributes. Some have a gigantic penis that causes the deaths of the women and men whom they violate, while others take the forms of attractive incubi and succubi that beat their partners to death after coitus. Moreover, many evil spirits adopt animal forms that may be permanent, as in the cases of insects, bats, or felines, which the Campas are careful not to approach or kill. Others, though, are transient: these are species that are normally edible— toucans, monkeys, birds—but whose outward appearances the *kamari* adopt and then, if the humans laugh at them, transform themselves into incubi or succubi. Evil spirits of the class known as *peári* sometimes even take on the disguise of some ordinary hunted animal, which, if it is killed and eaten, causes those who consume it to die. In all such cases, the human victim then becomes an evil spirit of the same kind as the one that attacked him or, worse still, changes into a white. Finally, *kamari* may be masters of sorcery, which they use to harm the Indians. Shamans then do their best to cure the latter with potions and by rubbing them with medicinal herbs.

The Campas' relations with nonhumans are not confined to accepting the benefits of food that the spirit masters of animals lavish upon them, for at the same time a cohort of evil spirits preys upon the Campas and may slip into the skins of even the animals with the most inoffensive appearances. On the one hand, hunters receive the gift of meat that they ask for, without offering anything in exchange; on the other, they themselves are hunted, powerless to avert their own fate as game. However, it would be mistaken to interpret this reversal as a sign that predation or exchange might be recovering their rights. For that to be the case, either the Campas would have to be the active instigators of this violent alienation, which they are not (for they are its victims and try by every means to protect themselves from it), or else the persecutions that they suffer would have to be regarded as a compensation to which they consent in exchange for the game that they are given (which is clearly not the case). The good spirits and the evil spirits, the Campas and the people of the Andes, and the generous provisions of meat and the animals that have become sorcerers are all divided into two hermetically sealed ontological domains that are in perpetual conflict. One domain is ruled by the constantly reaffirmed values of sharing and solidarity; the other, which is the agent for the evil that every lucid mind can detect in the world, embodies a cruel and senseless otherness that nothing can moderate.

No system of relations between humans can be ruled exclusively by a logic of gift; and the Campas are no exception to that rule. The altruism and prodigality that the good animal spirits manifest when they offer their bodily remains are less apparent in the rules that govern symmetrical exchange in the system of Dravidian kinship or intertribal bartering than they are in the ethos that is characteristic of daily life and in which trust, generosity, and a horror of constraints predominate. The Campas have carried to extreme lengths their desire to eliminate dissent and otherness in their community by reducing to a minimum the differences between individuals that are indispensable if a relationship, be it reciprocal or predatory, is to be established. This point has been emphasized in particular by ethnographers of the Matsiguenga. Writing about them, France-Marie Renard-Casevitz notes that they manifest "a constant concern to reduce oppositions between the self and others that might affect the entire social field." Meanwhile, Dan Rosengren observes that, among them, "sharing is highly valued . . . and almost imperative" and that "emphasis is put upon harmony and social balance, as positive values to strive for."[25]

The Campas are famous for their heavy reproof of internal violence, for it is a source of lasting animosities and a factor that undermines social cohesion. This is illustrated by the oral jousts between Matsiguenga men forced apart by some disagreement, in which verbal provocations and offers of peace alternate. Such a joust ends when one of the protagonists, deciding to turn his aggression upon himself, starts to beat himself repeatedly and is immediately imitated by his opponent. Violent or mean individuals and those who indulge in scandalous behavior become the subjects of public disapproval. This is first expressed by a woman, who mentions the facts but without naming the culprit; then, if the reprehensible behavior continues, other women gradually join in the denunciation. If the situation drags on, a quarantine is imposed, and the individual who has deliberately cut himself off from the network of solidarities is ignored, as if he were invisible, by the entire community. If all these measures fail, the woman who initiated the complaint has no option but to commit suicide so that her death will wipe out the separation and the disorder that her accusations have created.[26] The principle of generosity reputed to govern the behavior of game animals is expressed, as it were, in reverse, in that all positive attempts that are not followed by the desired results are interpreted as an indication of a personal failure caused by an untimely initiative that has placed someone else in a situation in which he is forced to stand apart from me in response to my intention.

The Amuesha have given a particularly clear form to this philosophy of sharing and harmonious conviviality, for they, like Aristotle, consider that love is the source and principle of the existence of all things. They distinguish between two forms of love: *muereñets* means the giving of oneself in the creation of life and is characteristic of the attitude of the deities and religious leaders in an asymmetrical relationship; meanwhile, *morrenteñets* denotes the mutual love that is indispensable for all sociability and is expressed by a constant, uncalculating generosity that is exempt from any expectation of reciprocation.[27] This is a far cry from a constructed and negotiated distinction that makes it possible to regard "others" as a term in a reciprocal relationship, as the Tukanos do, or as prey that is necessary for one's own reproduction, as the Jivaros do. The model of the behavior most favored by the Amuesha and likewise the Campas seems, rather, to be the relationship between parents and their children, in which you unstintingly give affection, care, and protection to those who depend upon you.

Obviously, it is within local communities, in kindred groups welded together by mutual aid and daily interactions, that the schema of generosity and sharing is most clearly manifest, both in the precepts taught to children and also in the customary practice of one and all. However, a disturbing parallel is detectable within the vaster group of sub-Andean Arawak tribes. These maintain two different kinds of relationships with two kinds of nonhuman groups: on the one hand, the gift-giving animals that donate food to humans and, on the other, the evil spirits that practice predation. In parallel, their relationships with two antagonistic networks of humans also stand in marked contrast to each other. The fact is that these people of the foothills have never ceased to engage in warfare along their Andean frontier, even as they reject it within their own midst, where they favor a system of regional interactions and alliances, mostly founded upon the trading that takes place between linguistically linked ethnic communities that share the same concept of civic virtues and social concord. The interethnic complementarity of the products exchanged is reminiscent of the craft specializations of the Amazonian northwest: the Shipibo are renowned for their painted fabrics, the Matsiguenga for their bows and arrows, the Piro for their canoes, the Nomatsiguenga for their fine cottons, while the Amuesha and the Ashaninka produce not only much-sought-after ornaments but also salt. The links developed through the circulation of material goods cement this mosaic and reinforce the sense of belonging to a community federated by common values. Nothing could provide a better illustration of this than what the explorer Olivier Ordinaire has called "the moral decalogue," a ritual litany that was recited whenever two members of different Campa tribes met and that enumerated the reciprocal duties that they owed each other on account of their belonging to the same community.[28]

Fernando Santos suggests that condemnation of endo-warfare is characteristic of a pan-Arawak ethos, and that may be so.[29] But in the case of the Arawak of Peru, internal peace was matched by a remarkable ability to resist external enemies by mobilizing the Campa tribes in large military coalitions along with some of their Pano allies. This exo-warfare was purely defensive, its purpose being to defend their territorial integrity against the attempts to annex land on the part of all kinds of invaders from the Andes. These range from the Inca armies of the early sixteenth century to the columns of Maoist guerrillas of the present day and include the forces that the viceroy of Peru and subsequently the young Peruvian Republic dispatched, without success, into the foothill forests to subdue these intractable Indians and subject them to the sovereignty of the central authorities. So it is hardly surprising that the *puna runa*, the "highland peoples," just like the evil spirits and their animal incarnations, should have been seen as perfect embodiments of an otherness that was as radical as it was harmful, for ontologically they were all identical since they all proceeded from the same mythological origin. Incas, Spaniards, and hostile animals all had to be opposed and confined to the margins of the Campa territory: their negativity had to be expelled from a Campa land of homogeneous togetherness. Here, the perpetuation of an ideal of closeness without indebtedness or calculated expectations comes at a price: namely respect for rules of exchange and complementarity between honorable neighbors whose help may be needed to prevent the Campas from being wiped out by other neighbors who treat them as prey.

The Campas are by no means the only representatives of the archipelago of animism to have sought to put this ideal into practice, and some have done so more successfully than they have. Thousands of kilometers away from the Peruvian rain forest, the northern Algonquins present an example of a people who engage in similar relations with both humans and nonhumans but do so free from the threat of predation and likewise of the constraints of exchange that make it possible to face up to such predation.[30] In the early pages of this book, we saw that the Cree and the Ojibwa groups regard the subarctic region, despite the seemingly strict limitations that it imposes on human life, as a benevolent environment that is inhabited by entities that are attentive to the needs of humans. It is always out of a feeling of generosity that a hunted animal delivers itself up to the hunter. Moved by compassion for humans in the grip of hunger, it presents him with its carnal envelope, as a gift, without expecting any compensation. That manifestation of generosity is of no consequence since, as among the Campas, the animal's soul is soon reincorporated in an individual of the same species, always providing that its corpse receives the appropriate ritual treatment. Relations between humans obey an identical schema. Warfare was banned between the bands of Montagnais, Naskapi, Cree, and Ojibwa, and the sharing of all possessions and resources was an absolutely imperative rule, especially among the coresidents of small winter hunting camps.[31] As Emmanuel Désveaux writes in his study of the Ojibwa of northern Ontario, "the sociological horizon of the Indians knows nothing of otherness."[32] A similar attitude prevails farther north, among the Inuit, as it also does far away, among the Chewong of Malaysia and the Buid of the Philippines.[33] As for the disinterested trust, the spirit of liberality, and the commitment to sharing that Bird-David attributes to the Nayaka and the Pygmies and that she considers to be typical features of the relationship that hunter-gatherers weave between themselves and their environment, both human and nonhuman, we should recognize that these amount to far more than a possible correlation with a particular mode of subsistence. For they denote a general schema for the treatment of others to which animist ontologies offer a special point of anchorage, whatever other techniques they employ to make the most of their environment.

The Ethos of Collectives

The prevalence of a relational schema in a collective leads its members to adopt typical behavior patterns, the repetition and frequency of which are such that ethnographers who observe and interpret them feel justified in describing them overall as normative "values" that orientate social life. The need for sharing among the Matsiguenga and the Ojibwa, the bellicose spirit of the Jivaros, and the obligation of exchange among the Tukanos all provide examples. But no relationship is absolutely predominant because, all together, they constitute the panoply of methods at the disposal of humans for organizing their interactions with other occupants of the world.

To return to the example of the Jivaros, it would be absurd to claim that everything in their daily existence stems from violent incorporation. The schema of predatory assimilation constitutes, rather, a moral horizon that orientates many fields of practice, each of which reflects it in its own way. It tolerates and encompasses other relational schemas that are elsewhere preponderant but here are relegated to particular niches that, however, are always under threat from insidious contamination by the dominant schema and the influence that this exerts. Thus, the Jivaro kinship system, which is of the Dravidian type, is founded on the ideal model of an exchange of sisters between cross-cousins. This form of union, which is, in practice, very common, establishes and perpetuates within localized kindred groups an island of reciprocity and solidarity between real affines; and this is probably indispensable for the development of a predatory attitude toward more distant affines, whether these be real, potential, or ideal. It indeed seems likely that the generalized hostility toward all that lies more than one day's march away necessarily engenders, in reaction, a central kernel in which symmetrical exchange makes it possible to count on a relative security. However, the fall-out rate from the system is considerable: brothers may become deadly enemies if they become rivals for the same potential spouses or if they feel slighted when, in accordance with the levirate rule, the widows of one of them are distributed among the deceased's brothers. Similarly, a son-in-law may attack his father-in-law if the latter refuses to let him marry the sister of his first wife. In such cases, murders and seizures of women are not uncommon. Despite all the measures taken to minimize the fracturing effect of affinity at the heart of a local network, the possibility of this is always present, as a fermenting agent of dissension capable of blowing sky-high the fragile balance of reciprocity between the closest members of a kindred group. Fair exchange is thus formally present in the logic of the Jivaro alliance system, but it remains peripheral to the Jivaro ethos.

Conversely, predation is not absent from the Tukano groups, even if warfare between them has long since disappeared, possibly as the result of a deliberate choice to favor pacific exchanges instead. We know, at any rate, that the Tukanos used to draw a clear distinction between, on the one hand, raids to procure wives from linguistic groups with which wives were not normally exchanged and, on the other, murderous, more long-distance expeditions. The first type of raid seems to have been quite common. Generally, no bloodshed occurred, and the raid was assimilated to a hunting expedition and considered as a possible alternative to ordinary exogamous exchanges. In most cases these abductions were subsequently regularized through negotiation between the two parties, and this could then lead to the establishment of a cycle of matrimonial alliances of the classic type. Exchange would thus recover its primacy following an occasional act of predation.[34] Although very rare, the murder of a man in a distant Tukano tribe constituted a far more drastic form of violence in that it affected the procreative power of another group and thus caused a loss harmful to the whole system. However, unlike in Jivaro head-hunting, this gratuitous destruction cannot be assimilated to an act of predation since it implied no gain of energy or genetic power for the murderer's group. For this reason, a warrior who was "a killer of a man" (*masa sīari masa*) was regarded as the most negative figure in any possible interaction between Tukanos.[35]

As can be imagined, the Tukanos' relations to nonhumans are likewise not exempt from a predatory dimension. Emphasizing this aspect, Århem even chose to describe what he called the ecocosmology of the Makuna as a world envisaged from the point of view of a hunter, that is to say, as a network of eaters and eaten.[36] He defines the limits of the system by two poles: at one extreme, the supreme predators (jaguars, anacondas, certain other rapacious species, and Yurupari spirits), which feed on all living beings and are not prey for any of them; and, at the other extreme, edible plants, the very lowest level in the food chain. Between these two poles lie most of the organisms whose fate is to be at once predators and prey. That is, in particular, the case of humans, whose souls, when they die, are captured (literally "consumed") by the spirit founders of their clan, so that they can be reborn in another form. Such formulations are hardly unexpected, since all animist cosmologies seem to derive their functional principles from the model of the food chain, regardless of the nature of their most favored relational schema. Even Århem admits that these relations between the eaters and the eaten are regarded by the Makuna as exchanges, not as acts of predation: "In this cosmic society, where all mortal beings are ontological 'equals,' humans and animals are bound by a pact of reciprocity. . . . The relationship between the human hunter and his prey is thus construed as an exchange, modelled on the relationship among affines."[37] The subordination of predation to exchange could find no better expression. Finally, regarding the Campas, one just needs to recall that the gift schema occupies a dominant position at the heart of human and nonhuman kindred groups only because it is set against a background of predation from which they can protect themselves only by maintaining a system of exchanges with neighbors identical to themselves.

The three cases studied in this chapter prompt a more general interpretation of the nature of what I have called a "collective." Even if such an entity acquires part of its apparent homogeneity from the mode of ontological identification that characterizes it, that is not enough to differentiate it from other entities that are similar to it in this respect. So the limits of a collective are above all defined by the prevalence within it of a specific relational schema. But the resulting unit does not necessarily tally with the customary divisions into ethnic groups, tribes, linguistic groups, and so on.

The example of the Jivaros will serve to illustrate this point. The way in which I have been describing them up till now might suggest that, despite internal dialectical and cultural differences, they constitute an altogether separate group. However, some of their southern neighbors, such as the Shapra and the Candoshi, share with them not only the schema of predatory appropriation but also the institutions associated with it, and do so despite differences in language and in many features of their social organization and their material culture.[38] On their eastern frontiers, in contrast, the Jivaros maintain enduring relations of commercial exchange and sometimes intermarriage with communities speaking the Quichua language, the *sacha runa*, even though the Quichuas do not share the Jivaro predatory ethos.[39] At first sight, the scale of contrasts between the forest Quichuas and the Jivaros seems neither greater nor less great than that which differentiates between the Jivaros and the Candoshi or the Shapra. Nevertheless, it is reasonable to treat the latter two peoples as if they were part of a "Jivaroid" continuum, whereas the Quichuas, despite many resemblances, have attained a higher level of differentiation. This is borne out by the customary behavior of the interested parties. Although the Jivaros may "Quichuarize" themselves in a peaceful fashion through marriage, and vice versa, such an incorporation is always prompted by an individual initiative. In contrast, the Candoshi and the Shapra maintain with the Jivaros a collective relationship of essential otherness that is sufficiently close for them to be included in the code of head-hunting and abduction of women, whether as victims or as aggressors. The Shapra and the Candoshi are thus essential players in the constitution of the Jivaro "self," whereas the Quichuas, for their part, offer the alternative of "becoming different" to all those tempted by a change of identity.

The unification of a mosaic of peoples through the sharing of a dominant relational schema is even clearer in the interethnic cluster of the Amazonian northwest. We should bear in mind that the flows of reciprocity peculiar to this region include not only the eastern Tukanos but also Arawak groups (Baniwa, Wakuénai, Tariana, Baré, Kabiyerí, and Yukuna), a Carib group (the Carijona), and the Maku, hunter-gatherers speaking an independent language who trade game in exchange for the products cultivated by the riverside communities of sedentary horticulturists. It is true that linguistic exogamy is limited to the Tukano tribes, with the exception of the Cubeo, who dispense with it. But all the components of the metasystem subscribe to the same conviction: that the harmony of the cosmos can be maintained only by dint of a constant and balanced exchange of goods, principles of individuation, and reproductive elements between the various communities of humans and nonhumans that inhabit it. As for the various Arawak peoples of the Peruvian foothills, I hardly need to repeat that they know they belong to the same network of solidarities, structured by their shared values of generosity, egalitarianism, and openness toward others—values that are all the more cherished and respected because, in every way, they stand in opposition to the negative attributes ascribed to the Andean invaders.

In short, it is not so much linguistic limits, the perimeter of a commercial network, or even the homogeneity of modes of life that mark out the contours of a collective. Rather, it is a way of schematizing the experience shared by a more or less vast collection of individuals, a group that may well present internal variations—of languages, institutions, and practices—that are sufficiently marked for one to consider it, on a different scale, as a transformational group composed of separate units. Even if it cannot be a complete substitute for the habitual categories—culture, civilization, ethnic or linguistic group, social milieu, and so on—which may well remain useful in other analytical contexts, such a definition at least makes it possible to avoid the snags of essentialism and to sidestep the almost automatic tendency to apprehend the particularities of human groups on the basis of the characteristics to which they themselves draw attention in order to distinguish themselves from their close neighbors. This way of proceeding is the reverse of that which Benedict adopts in order to reveal her "patterns" of culture; instead of casting one's eye over a group with preassigned limits, to which one ascribes an abstract and transcendent unity that is a mysterious source of regularity in behavior patterns and representations, it is better to seek out a field covered by certain schemas that bring together the practices of collectives of very variable sizes and natures, the frontiers between which are not fixed by custom or by law but simply reflect the breaks that separate them from other ways of being present in the world.

Stripped of any functional or purposive dimension (such as a desire for togetherness), that notion of a collective is also somewhat different from Latour's definition of one: namely a specific association of humans and nonhumans as put together, or "collected," within a network at a particular given moment and in a particular given place. Likewise, for me, a collective is a group combining entities of many kinds. But it is not, strictly speaking, one organized as a network whose frontiers—inexistent in effect if one decides to include all their ramifications—can only be drawn by the analyst's arbitrary decision to limit his field of study to data that he is in a position to take into account. If, instead, one recognizes that the limits of any collective are coextensive with the area of influence of this or that schema of practices, then its definition will depend above all on the manner in which the humans in it organize their experience, in particular in their relations with nonhumans.[40] The task traditionally assigned to anthropology, namely to set in order and compare the discouraging multiplicity of circumstances in this world, will in this way perhaps be rendered less difficult, providing grounds for hope for those who persist in believing in the worth of such a mission and a sign of encouragement for those who wish to devote themselves to the task.

15

Histories of Structures

The many kinds of collectives that we have studied so far have been composed of entities with stable attributes and unchallenged positions. They are rendered homogeneous by great relational schemas that unify their practices, and they have confronted particular problems that they have gradually solved in their own original ways. They seem, however unlikely it may be, to have defied the test of time. My choice of method is largely responsible for this impression. Extracted from their context at an arbitrary point in their historical trajectory, the examples chosen appear as ideal types rather than as the products of contingent events that have made them be as we know them at the moment at which observers describe them. But it is also true that cultures and civilizations do display a remarkable permanence when envisaged from the perspective of the "worldviews," styles of behavior, and institutional logics that indicate their respective distinctive characters. In this respect, it is easier to spot the contrastive oppositions that differentiate them from one another in the synchronic space of an analysis than it is to pick out the structural breaks that each one, taken in isolation, may have undergone between two successive stages in its development. Yet those breaks do exist, as historians of the long-term view of history are careful to point out. One particular distribution of existing beings and their attributes gives way to another; a mode of treating "others" is superseded and another, previously marginal, acquires a dominant position; what has been considered normal now seems impossible and what has seemed unimaginable eventually becomes common sense. Such mutations usually remain unnoticed by those who live through them, for they may be drawn out over a long period of time, spanning many generations. The effect of a threshold that helps one to see that there has been a shift into a new system is perceptible only to a historian bold enough to divide agelong eras into a series of different periods or, by dint of other methods, to an anthropologist who decides to envisage a spatial continuum of comparable societies as if they were transformations of one another—without, however, suggesting that some of them must constitute simpler forms from which the rest must have evolved. Leaving aside questions of genesis and antecedent causality, and instead adopting a resolutely synchronic approach, it is possible to illuminate the structural properties of the combinations that I have put forth and also the positive or negative conditions of their transformations.

One of those conditions seems to be the replacement of one dominant relational schema by another. Even if, as we have seen in the last chapter, a single mode of identification may be modeled by entirely different relational configurations, there are limits to how far this can be taken. Certain ways of treating "others" that are present in a minor form in one mode of identification sometimes come to play a more predominant role that soon renders them incompatible with the ontological regime in which they have developed; and this makes it necessary to alter that ontological regime or transfer to another mode of identification that is better suited to a different way of treating others. Such transformations frequently accompany striking mutations in technological systems, but that does not necessarily mean to say that the latter were the cause of the former. In plenty of cases it would, on the contrary, seem that the generalization of a previously secondary way of relating, by reorienting the interactions between the components of the world, opens up the way for technical innovations, which, in their turn, strengthen the hold that the new dominant relationships wield over practices and the ways in which these are regarded. Let us consider just one example, that of the way in which variations may affect a protective relationship as a result of changes in the relations with the animal in question.

From Caribou-Man to Lord Bull

Herds of caribou numbering as many as several hundred animals are prime game for the native peoples of subarctic America. Caribou are migrant animals, equally well adapted to a forest environment as to the more northern regions of tundra, and their passage through a locality is of crucial importance to the hunters there, who keep an eager watch for their arrival and the promise of abundant supplies of meat that it offers. So it is not really surprising that the apparently erratic migrations of these animals are reputed to be controlled by some master, a spirit that behaves as their herdsman. It is a way of attributing a particular intentionality to a plurality of behavior patterns all of which tend toward the same collective aim. The Montagnais Indians call this spirit the Caribou-Man. He has a human appearance, white and bearded, and he lives in a cave deep within a hill to which access is gained by a narrow passage. In this cavern, he—like Polyphemus—keeps his immense herd. And it is from here that he sends out his beasts on their annual migrations, having previously decided which animals and how many of them may be killed and by which particular hunters. The souls of the slaughtered caribou return to the cave, where they are reincorporated into new animals that will be sent out to the hunters on another occasion. Although the hunters never approach the cave or the zone surrounding it, a ritual specialist may sometimes intercede with the Caribou-Man, begging him to spare some of his beasts to the humans when the latter are passing through particularly lean times.[1]

This, then, is a typical case of "gift-giving" animism: the world is inhabited by intentional entities with a benevolent attitude toward humans. The Caribou-Man and all the spirits that govern the destinies of other species of game offer up their animals out of the goodness of their hearts, expecting no compensation, provided the ethics of hunting remain respected. As for the caribou themselves—whose master is a kind of hypostasis that the Rock Cree describe as a gigantic male—they deliver themselves up to the hunters with all the abandon of a woman in love. The Mistassini Cree say that a caribou is of a feminine nature and can seduce the hunters, taking on the form of a beautiful girl who sometimes visits them in their dreams; and the killing is assimilated to the sexual act.[2] This erotic symbolism of hunting recurs in many regions of the world, but here it is particularly relevant, for it is by a caribou being killed by a man that a new animal can be engendered. However, although gift giving dominates as the general form of relationship between the world's various entities, in the relationship between the Caribou-Man and the animals in his charge, that gift giving gives way to a very different kind of behavior. The Caribou-Man is the absolute master of the animals' fates; he looks after them day in, day out, is attentive to their well-being, controls their reproduction, and is the sole judge of the moment when they must die. In short, like a livestock raiser, he extends over them a cloak of protection that authorizes him to dispose as he will of the animals that he controls.

On the other side of the Bering Strait, in northeastern Siberia, the Chukchees also hunt caribou. When these are found in Eurasia, they are usually known as "reindeer," but the species is the same: *Rangifer tarandus.* Wild reindeer are the game par excellence of the Siberian taiga. From the Ob River across to the Pacific and from the edges of the Mongolian plateau across to the shores of the Arctic Ocean, reindeer have been ubiquitously present, everywhere regarded as difficult prey and everywhere enthusiastically hunted. As in North America, the destiny of the reindeer is ruled by spirits. Among the

Chukchees, the master of wild reindeer is called Pičvu'čin: he is described as a tiny man, with a sledge made of grass stalks, who sees the mice that pull it as reindeer. Just like humans, he devotes much of his time to hunting and his favorite game is the lemming, which for him takes on the appearance of a bear, for both species possess the ability to stand upright on their hind legs (a fine case of "perspectivist" animism, as is worth pointing out in passing). Pičvu'čin lives with his reindeer in an underground den that can be reached by a deep ravine, and it is from there that he sends his herds out to the humans for them to hunt, except when they fail to show him respect and treat his charges with cruelty. But Pičvu'čin is also a livestock raiser, and he uses the wild reindeer that he sends to the Chukchees in the same way as they use their own domesticated reindeer, as draft animals that they also ride.[3]

Unlike in North America, where the autochthonous peoples have never domesticated the caribou, all the Siberian peoples have more or less domesticated the reindeer. It seems that this domestication was undertaken both by means of hunting and for the purpose of hunting. Animals were captured alive as lures for their fellows, and they were also used to carry the belongings of the small, extremely mobile human groups who roamed in search of wild herds.[4] The reindeer in Siberia are saddled and ridden or harnessed to light sledges and also provide meat and milk. Admittedly, it is frequently just a matter of semidomestication in which actions affecting the animals are minimal. In the tundra zones, the Nenec, Iakoutes, Dolganes, and Tunkusi possess large herds and follow their migrations. But in the taiga regions, the beasts number no more than a few dozen animals, which are left to their own devices for part of the year. To the west, among the Xant and the Selkup, they are left at liberty during the summer and are rounded up at the first snowfall, for the hunting season. To the east, the Evenks milk the females and so keep the herd close to their camps during the summer. In the winter, they let them loose in the forest. Then, when the snows begin to melt, they recapture them, as though they were wild. All the same, even if domination over the animals remains weak and sporadic, a decisive step has been taken: whereas in subarctic America, protection remains an ideal relationship, confined to the links that the spirits in control of the game maintain with their animals, the peoples of Siberia have not been content to leave the animals' protection to the reindeers' spirit masters but have themselves taken a hand in it.

The Chukchee master of the reindeer belongs to a class of spirits known generically as ke'let. These spirits all possess herds of domesticated reindeer, which they use to pull their sledges. In accordance with good perspectivist logic, some of them use mammoths to draw their sledges when they descend to the depths of the chthonic world. So domestication does not solely con-

cern the wild reindeer, which, throughout Siberia, are believed to be raised
by herding spirits. For the Evenks, for example, all wild species of animals
and fish upon which humans feed live in herds controlled by their masters.[5]
Meanwhile, the Yukaghir regard the masters of game as jolly fellows who pass
their time drinking and playing cards, using the animal species in their care as
stakes. A species may thus change hands depending on the luck of the game,
a factor that explains sudden migrations.[6]

Although, like the humans, the masters of the animals subsist mainly by
hunting, the relations that the former establish with the latter take the form of
relations of exchange between livestock raisers. By way of compensation for
the wild reindeer that Pičvu'čin sends them, the Chukchees give him tobacco,
sugar, flour, and trinkets obtained from the Russians. No doubt these goods
are not strictly equivalent in value to the animals obtained; but in contrast to
the unqualified generosity of the Caribou-Man toward the Montagnais, here
there is a clear idea that the master of the reindeer must, even if only in a symbolic fashion, be compensated for the losses that his herds incur as a result of
human hunting. Furthermore, the wild reindeer of Pičvu'čin are greatly appreciated in the rutting season, when, attracted by the females in the humans'
herds, they venture into range of the Chukchees' encampments. It is then easy
to shoot them down, first making sure to incite them, by means of invocations, to mate with the tamed females, for the offspring from such couplings
are reputed to be particularly robust. When the males are eventually killed,
they are thanked with offerings of food, and their heads are taken into the
tents, where they are entertained with music.[7] As in northern America, in Siberia likewise the hunting of big game is assimilated to sexual coupling: wild
reindeer appear to men in dreams, in the guise of beautiful young women,
the daughters of the master of the deer tribe, and the men make love with
them. The wild male animals thus render to the herds of the Chukchees the
same sexual services as the Chukchees render to the daughters of the master
of reindeer. The result on both sides is pregnancies that help to increase the
livestock.[8] The theme of matrimonial exchange, so widespread in Siberia in
relations with nonhumans, here acquires the perfection of a balanced symmetry: the humans provide the wild males with domesticated spouses from
their herds, for those males to impregnate, in exchange for the wild spouses
that they impregnate themselves in their dreams for the benefit of the master
of the reindeer. Where the Montagnais hunter is content to accept the sexual
gift sent to him by the Caribou-Man, the Chukchee hunter offers his own
female animals in return, in a not entirely disinterested gesture of reciprocity.

Like the wild reindeer, the domesticated reindeer of the Chukchees depend on a nonhuman protector, the Reindeer-Being, an entity with some-

what vague attributes whose mission is to watch over the well-being of the herds. The Reindeer-Being is totally distinct from Pičvu'čin, the master of wild reindeer, and belongs to a class of benevolent powers, the *va'IrgIt*, that are hypostases or individual expressions of a general principle of existence that animates the whole world, humans included. The *va'IrgIt* entities are associated with cardinal points and may be named after them, and it is to these, in particular Zenith and Dawn, that slaughtered domesticated reindeer are consecrated. The Chukchees, like the Greeks, slaughter and consume animals that they have raised only within the framework of a sacrifice. But this is nothing like an offering made to a deity. The various kinds of harmful or beneficent spirits (*ke'let*) (e.g., the master of wild reindeer) act like persons and are sometimes organized into tribes, and humans maintain with them relations of hostility or exchange. In contrast, the *va'IrgIt* are impersonal and localized manifestations of cosmic vitality with which no kind of interaction is possible. The sacrifices of domesticated reindeer to the *va'IrgIt* are therefore not transfers from one group of individuals to another, which call for reciprocation—as in the case of the food given to the master of wild reindeer. Rather, they are a way for humans to contribute to the general circulation of the flow of life that is carried by the blood of the sacrificial victims. The ones to whom this flow is directed—that is, the *va'IrgIt*—regenerate it and return it to humans in the form of good health, abundance, and prosperity for the livestock.[9]

Each herd is also placed under the protection of a little fire-board, strictly for family use, which is carved into a vaguely anthropomorphic form. Over and above its basic purpose, the Chukchees regard it as a particularized expression of the Reindeer-Being: the holes bored by means of the friction of a bow drill are considered to be its eyes, while the grinding noise made by the drilling is the sound of its voice. When sacrifices are made, the members of each domestic unit daub their fire-board with the animal's blood, which they also use to paint their faces in their own particular patterns. They say that in this way they resemble the Reindeer-Being that protects their herd.[10] The Chukchees' relationship to the guardian power that watches over their domesticated reindeer thus contrasts with the one that they maintain with the figure that raises wild reindeer. They endeavor by every means to identify with the Reindeer-Being, joining their efforts to his, the better to ensure protection for their herds, in the expectation that he will bring to bear on them part of the beneficent power of which he is a reflection and which they themselves help to activate by means of their sacrifices. In contrast, in the case of Pičvu'čin, who is a clearly individualized spirit, endowed with an altogether human disposition, it is more a matter of maintaining balanced relations based on an exchange of services and reciprocal transactions.

In effect, as regards all that concerns dealings with existing beings that elude the jurisdiction of humans, in particular the deer species and those who control them, the Chukchee world differs little from that of the hunters of northern America. In both cases we find animist cosmologies peopled by intentional entities organized into collectives. The only difference between them is the dominant relational schema, which is based on gift giving to the east of the Bering Strait but on exchanging to the west. In the Chukchee region, however, the link with certain classes of nonhumans is subtly modified according to the hold, slight though this is, that the humans have established over them. Their field of protection has been extended beyond the masters of game to include human reindeer raisers and the entity that supports them. That expansion is possibly facilitated by the fact that most visible things, ranging from rainbows right down to the bundles of pelts prepared for trading, are reputed to depend on a nonhuman master.[11] Furthermore, a few features characteristic of an analogical identification are now becoming perceptible in a rough form: the components of the world begin to multiply and above all to vary in nature. Some, namely the *va'IrgIt*, no longer belong to a particular species and have even lost their form and are no longer confined to the framework of autonomous collectives within which other categories of existent beings go about their activities. They have become active, fluid, and mobile principles whose impersonal permanence must be fixed in objects and cardinal points. The task of getting them to communicate harmoniously falls to humans, who must act as mediators by means of their sacrifices.

The ontological diversification of the entities in the world is still embryonic among the Chukchees, but it becomes increasingly manifest as one moves farther south. This phenomenon has been noted by specialists on Siberia. It takes the form of a series of contrasts in social organization and religious beliefs between the people of the northern zone and those of the southern zone. The remarks that follow are based on the oppositions established by Morten Pedersen, whose typology presents the advantage of referring to analytical categories that I had myself suggested.[12] According to this author, the northern fringe is dominantly animist. This covers the regions of tundra and taiga of northeastern Siberia and the extreme east of Russia. It is inhabited by ethnic groups of the Paleo-Asiatic phylum (Chukchees, Koriak, Yukaghir, etc.) and Turkish families (Iakoutes) and Altaic ones (the Tunkusi group and its Evenk and Even offshoots). The southern zone, that is, the steppes of the Mongolian plateau and its forested fringes, is inhabited chiefly by peoples from the Ural-Altaic family (Buryats, Halx, Darxad, etc.). Here, the egalitarian relations between collectives of human and nonhuman persons with identical attributes, as found in the north, have disappeared. They have been supplanted by vertical relations of differentiation that Pedersen calls "totemic," although he recognizes that there are no true cases of totemism in Siberia: even if clans and moieties do often receive animal names, there is no trace of any identification between their members and the eponymous species. In fact, upon closer examination, the "totemic" characteristics that he attributes to southern Siberia turn out to be much closer to what I call the analogist system.

On the basis of his ethnography on the Darxad and Caroline Humphrey's study on the Daur, two Mongolian ethnic groups, Pedersen emphasizes the movement of ontological differentiation and pluralization that is peculiar to southern Siberia: certain nonhumans—mountains, animals, and trees—are still regarded and treated as persons, but to most existing beings are attributed very heterogeneous and idiosyncratic properties that, however, can be linked together by segments of analogist chains that are revealed in ritual specializations. Thus, among the Daur, mature men are made responsible for harmonizing the elements, for they are on the side of the sky and hence of meteorological phenomena; women have to deal above all with social mobility, for they are associated with rivers, which are expressions of flux; the elderly, who are linked with fire, the sign of light, manage hierarchies; the shaman, who is capable of metamorphosis, is close to wild animals and their whole range of specific aptitudes; midwives, whose field of competence is fertility, are linked with the womb and caves, symbols of maturation.[13] No totalizing principle is introduced to unify this conglomeration of autonomous domains and independent spheres of intervention that are linked only by discontinuous parcels of short associative series in which the lineages of ancestors stand out as fixed points. Animist features are still present, one being shamans, who, alone, are able to cross frontiers in this hierarchical set of separate areas and to transcend the ontological fragmentation. But the shamans mobilize above all the spirits of the dead, not the animal auxiliaries of their fellow shamans in the north. In short, differences are beginning to multiply, and with them, relations of a different nature are established between existing beings.

The example of the Exirit-Bulagat, already briefly evoked to illustrate the general protection schema, will help to explain this.[14] We should remember that these Buryat herders of Cisbaikalia, who are organized into exogamous clans, adopted extensive horse and cattle raising only in the seventeenth century, although that did not stop them hunting wild reindeer, elk, and roe deer. As with the domestication of reindeer farther north, the borrowing of horses from the Mongols of the steppes was motivated by their effectiveness in hunting, which is here practiced by large groups of mounted beaters. The Exirit-Bulagat treat their herds of horses in the manner of reindeer raisers; that is to say, they turn them loose for part of the year. Like the hunters of subarctic America and northern Siberia, they assign the control of wild deer to a spirit that we have already come across, known as "Rich-Forest" (Bagan Xangaj). This spirit is described as a very large reindeer or elk and is seen as a kind of generic father-in-law who gives game to his human sons-in-law when they copulate in their dreams with his daughters. So far, this is all very classic: in their relations with wild animals, structured by a logic of alliance with intentional entities, the Exirit-Bulagat differ little from the Siberian peoples. But this pocket of animism has become residual, as has the hunting that used to provide it with a framework of practical experience. For the progressive predominance of livestock raising goes hand in hand with the establishment of a vertical relationship of protective domination—of humans over domesticated animals, human ancestors over their descendants, and a mythical begetter of the tribe over both its members and its herds. This presents a strong contrast to the egalitarian relations between humans and nonhuman persons that are characteristic of northern Siberia.

The founder of the tribe is reputed to be Buxa Nojon, "Lord Bull," a celestial animal that came down to earth, where he impregnated a girl and then took in and raised the child that he had fathered. The lines of ancestors descended from this union each live on a precise site of the mountain at the foot of which their descendants are established. Horses are sacrificed to them to persuade them to grant their protection to the herds and make them prosper. The meat from the victims consecrated to them is impregnated with "grace," *xešeg*, which the ancestors place there so that it will be incorporated by the humans who consume it. In the course of a long ceremony held in July, mares and geldings are sacrificed to Lord Bull in equal numbers and for identical reasons. The souls of the horses, substitutes for those of humans, are regarded as a propitiatory gift offered to the deity in the hope of obtaining in return happiness and wealth, which are the concrete expressions of the grace dispensed to them. However, unlike the balanced exchange involved in the relations with Rich-Forest, this sacrificial oblation to Lord Bull does not always prove effective. The humans beg for his grace, backing up their pleas with offerings and flattering words, but can never be sure that they will receive the hoped-for protection, because, on the part of the deity, that protection is simply an expression of the power that it holds as a result of its position.[15] Far from constituting anticipated compensation offered in exchange for future benefits, the animals sacrificed to the ancestors and the celestial bull represent tokens of devotion addressed to figures whose designs remain impenetrable, figures that may choose not to concede the good fortune that they can dispense as and when they wish to. Just as the lives of the animals dependent upon the humans are at the mercy of those who supervise their well-being, so too the fate of the humans dependent upon ancestors and deities is governed by the goodwill of the latter. At any moment, protection may be withdrawn, in the case of the beasts when they are slaughtered and of the humans when the entities to which they sacrifice remain deaf to their pleas.

The preponderance of this relation of protective dominance is accompanied by a cascade of particularized hierarchies in which many features of an analogical collective are discernible. Despite a seminomadic life, the links with localized ancestral lineages, which are maintained by various forms of a cult of the dead, constitute the source of segmentary identities. The ancestors that each constitutive unit in the tribe claim as the source of their distinctive autonomies are the masters of the places that their descendants occupy in the summer period, and those masters control the destinies of both the latter and their herds. As guarantors of the integrity of the lineages, the dead thus continue to animate with their presence the places that their members frequent for part of the year. It is moreover said that they lead an existence similar to that of the living, contracting intermarriages and giving birth to children. The lineages, which are spread out along a scale of gradations of prestige based on the antiquity of their founders, are like moral persons in a permanent situation of rivalry who, however, on occasion know how to unite to make a common stand against the external world. The Exirit-Bulagat thus certainly constitute a collective divided into separate hierarchical and complementary units, each of which is attached to particular sites and composed of a mixture of entities of various kinds. The collective is structured by a logic of segmentary interlocking which favors the expression of differences yet at the same time limits its dissolvent effects. Despite the superficial resemblances, this is no longer the world of the Chukchees, with its multiplicity of egalitarian and monospecific collectives of humans, spirits, and animals, in which there is as yet scarcely any sign of impersonal entities that stand apart and are no longer included in the solidarities and allegiances of the group.

In contrast to that world, the Exirit-Bulagat collective extends to the very limits of the cosmos and integrates within it a diversified multitude of nonhumans, each with its own domains but linked to the rest of the existing beings, including humans, by a network of correspondences and influences. As Hamayon writes, "Representations of supernatural beings start to proliferate."[16] As well as the lineage territories controlled by ordinary ancestors, many localities are placed under the jurisdiction of the spirits of dead individuals, either because they were born there or because they encountered a premature death there: for example, a hunter who died of exhaustion in a far corner of the forest is thereafter in control of access to the game there and must be begged to supply it. As well as controlling particular sites, these dead also become the masters of particular diseases, activities, properties, and modes of existence that oppress human beings, who either long to be free of them or to gain control of them, if only the dead will agree to this. Another form of dependence is that linking all humans to "destiny spirits" (*zajaan*), which are produced by the dead of shamanistic lineages. These are said to be extremely active and excessively imaginative, and they allocate to each human a destiny that becomes intrinsic to him or her, to the point of being regarded as a component of his or her personality. These spirits may be either masculine or feminine; each is attached to a particular site and specializes in particular types of destinies. They are sufficiently numerous to provide all the biographical trajectories that are necessary for the normal diversity of existing beings. This predestination is accompanied by another factor of particularization, namely the "essences" (*udxa*). These are aptitudes inherited from ancestors, which predispose individuals to exercise particular functions, such as those of a shaman, a blacksmith, a saddler, or a fletcher. Each essence is a potential quality that is transmitted and is necessary for the practice of some special activity. However, it may possibly not be actualized by whoever possesses it. Even so, in order to avoid the wrath of the ancestors, it is imperative not to let it go to waste, that is, to remain unrepresented in the world of the living. Over and above individual destinies, this innate quality thus introduces into the collective differences that are, strictly speaking, "essential," albeit complementary, between different categories of humans. Finally, far more distant from humans but organized according to the same segmentary logic, at the summit of the hierarchy there is a quarrelsome community of "Heavens" (*tengeri*). They are divided into two rival groups, the elder faction of fifty-five white Heavens of the east and the younger faction of forty-four black Heavens of the west. These are individualized entities associated with atmospheric states and are the creators of particularities, insofar as everything that they do has a predetermined function. Each Heaven is thus the depository of one specific attribute, which it helps to maintain and diffuse: a spirit of initiative, jealousy, cunning, or malevolence, each of which is characterized by a color and a particular cardinal point.

Among the Exirit-Bulagat, pockets of animist identification certainly do remain, particularly in the domain of the treatment of wild animals and of Rich-Forest, the master of the deer species, and even in certain properties attributed to domesticated animals, such as the souls of the horses sent to the spirits to which sacrifices are dedicated. But, in contrast to the ontological regime of animism, in which the persons, both human and nonhuman, distributed among differentiated collectives all nevertheless share certain similar attributes, all the elements in the collective to which the Exirit-Bulagat belong seem to be particularized: places, beings, social segments, the dead and the living, the sectors of the cosmos, the deities, the fields of activity, the spheres of skills, predispositions, destinies, qualities—all are dissociated, and everything stems from an obsessive particularism that analogism strives to recompose in an always incomplete network of partial similarities. Even the nature of shamanism has changed and begins to move in the direction of the forms of possession by spirits that are so common in analogical ontologies: whereas a shaman in northern Siberia maintains with his animal auxiliaries a collaborative relationship, the Buryat shaman in a trance physically incorporates the spirits of the ancestors and Lord Bull. Perhaps, in this case, it is not strictly speaking a matter of possession, since it seems that the intrusive powers do not replace the intentionality of their host to the point of alienating him completely; but it comes close to possession especially when, having incorporated the spirit of Lord Bull, the shaman begins to low and drops to all fours as if he had himself become a celestial bull.[17] In short, despite the geographical continuity and superficial resemblances, this world fragmented by vertical relations, teeming with autonomous entities and qualities in quest of hosts, hierarchized by ancestors, and differentiated by essences and destinies is utterly different from that of northern Siberia. Here, right on the edge of the analogical archipelago, in order to become an integral part of it, all that is required is to expel the memory of Rich-Forest and, along with him, the little troop of animals, trees, and mountains that remain aquiver with an interiority similar to that of humans.

Moving from northern America to the fringes of the Mongolian plateau, we have passed in a series of minimal transformations from a system dominated by gift-giving animism to a different system in which protective analogism is beginning to take hold (fig. 11). For this to happen, it was enough that the protective relationship spread beyond the restrictive framework of the raising of wild animals by spirits that watch over them, in order to infiltrate the embryonic domestication of those same animals that is undertaken by humans. That was but a small step to take and one seemingly without grave consequences so long as relations, now of symmetrical exchange, persisted between humans and the collectives of nonhuman persons. But those relations eventually become residual when, spilling over from the practices of occasional livestock raisers, the need for protection contaminates even those dispensing it. At this point, the hierarchies of dependencies, which are felt to provide the necessary conditions for security, have to be extended upward and humans have to enter a cycle of voluntary servitude vis-à-vis their ancestors, their elders, their deities. Now they have to fill the world with beings and principles that are made responsible for the unexpected twists and turns of

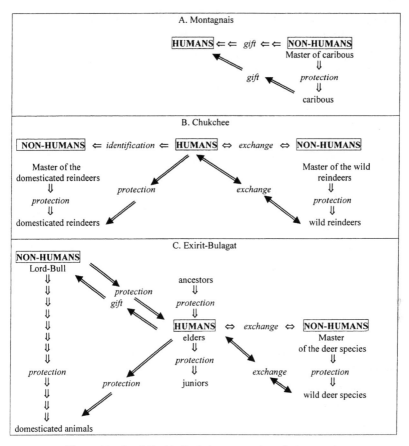

FIGURE 11. The transition from "gift-giving" animism to protective analogism

destinies. They have to implore the benevolence of masters whose silence is feared, and they have to flatter them with sacrificial offerings; they are obliged ceaselessly to interpret signs that bestow meaning upon a compartmentalized and heterogeneous cosmos in which even the assurance that each thing is in its place cannot quite dissipate anxiety regarding the unpredictable consequences of the intervention of certain of those things into human daily life.

Hunting, Taming, Domesticating

The domestication of animals no doubt did play a role in the "Siberian transition," but it does not suffice to explain it. For the availability of a domesticatable animal does not necessarily lead to its domestication, since every technical innovation stems from a choice, that is to say, an opportunity to retain or exclude certain options, depending on whether or not they seem compatible with the other elements of the system within which the technique must be integrated. This is borne out by the fact that the peoples of subarctic America abstained from taking the same path as their Siberian neighbors, who did domesticate their reindeer. Moreover, they abstained from doing so even though the protective relations implied by livestock raising were potentially present in the figure of the master of the caribous and concretely present in their own extremely longstanding domestication of dogs.

Besides, even the example of the practical advantages of livestock raising does not guarantee that it will be lastingly implanted, as is shown by an experiment carried out in Alaska at the end of the nineteenth century.[18] Faced with the decline of the caribou herds in the Seward Peninsula, the representatives of the federal administration had the idea of importing from northeastern Siberia domesticated reindeer along with their Chukchee minders, in order to teach the Yup'ik Eskimos the techniques of livestock raising and thereby procure for them a source of meat that did not depend on the hazards of hunting. The autochthonous Eskimos used sledges drawn by dogs, but the Chukchees also introduced their own sledges harnessed to reindeer as a means of getting around. This was greeted with enthusiasm by the authorities, who then proceeded to promote their diffusion by appealing to Sami, large numbers of whom were brought from Finland and Norway with their own more docile reindeer and better-adapted sledges. With a view to keeping pace with the development of colonization at the time of the gold rush, the governmental program for the raising of reindeer ended up by being almost exclusively directed toward providing transport for prospectors, for trading posts, and for the postal service, leaving to the missionaries the task of trying to convince the native peoples of the advantages of livestock raising. The results of the campaign failed both to meet initial hopes and to repay the efforts expended. The Yup'ik continued to prefer hunting caribou to raising them and were happier moving around on their sledges drawn by dogs than with harnessed reindeer. Only a handful of them, under pressure from the missionaries, agreed to remain far from their villages for most of the winter in order to supervise herds of reindeer. It is hard to say with certainty whether this failure resulted from the inadequacy of the techniques employed to meet the conditions of local life (the dog-drawn sledge was better adapted for the Yup'ik; they found itinerant livestock raising too restricting; the zones for pasturing the reindeer were too widely scattered; etc.) or whether the failure was attributable to reasons of a more moral nature, such as the autochthonous Yup'iks' distaste at the idea of raising an animal that they usually hunted and consuming the meat that they had "produced" rather than obtained within the framework of a person-to-person trade-off with the entities that controlled the hunted animals. As in many similar cases, those two types of causes were no doubt both in play. At any rate, the fact remains that, unlike in northern Siberia, where the environment and modes of existence were not very different, to the east of the Bering Strait no one spontaneously switched to the domestication of the caribou.

We now need to digress at length in order to gain a better understanding of this phenomenon. It will take us among other peoples who have likewise abstained from domesticating the local fauna, even though they possess great practical experience of animals raised in semicaptivity. Throughout Amazonia, Amerindians cohabit in their homes in perfect harmony with many species of animals.[19] These animals are the young of game killed by hunting or baby birds that have been taken from their nests. They are either fed by hand (in the case of birds) or breast-fed and thus receive what ethologists call a substitute "imprint" that leads them to attach themselves to their masters to the point of following them wherever they go. The Amerindians know all about this mechanism, which is indispensable for the taming process, and they are skilled at evaluating the period, which is quite short but differs for each species, during which the imprinting phenomenon is likely to take place. Among the species usually tamed, the ones most suitable for domestication are no doubt the larger rodents (the paca, the agouti, the acouchi, and the capybara), the two species of peccary, the tapir, and certain birds, principally terrestrial ones, which already live a farmyard-type existence around the houses of the Amerindians: the *Cracidae*, the *Tinamidae*, and the trumpet-birds, the latter widely used throughout the region as sentinels. Provided they have been familiarized with humans at a relatively early age, all these animals are fairly docile and adapt well to captivity. So it is quite common to find a peccary the size of a wild boar peacefully snoozing by the fire or a tapir weighing five hundred kilograms gamboling in the river with its master or swimming in his wake when he travels by canoe. Now, although they represent a potential source of meat, none of these household animals are ever killed to be eaten, except in a few altogether exceptional cases such as the ritual slaughtering of a tapir among the Pano, to which I have already referred.[20]

Nor have the Amerindians attempted to breed, in captivity, the animals that they have tamed nor, a fortiori, to select the best of their offspring. Beyond the Andes, where members of the camel family and guinea pigs were domesticated at least six thousand years ago, the only autochthonous domesticated animal of tropical South America is the Barbary duck, which was probably domesticated at the beginning of the Christian era along the northern coast of the continent. However, the raising of this creature has spread extremely slowly to other regions in the lowlands, where it is still relatively rare even today. Despite the very ancient tradition of domesticating the principal plants cultivated in non-Andean South America, there has been no equivalent movement toward the domestication of animals, here understood in the traditional sense defined by Isidore Geoffroy Saint-Hilaire: as the reduction to a state of domesticity of "a succession of individual animals produced one from another, under human control."[21]

The first possible explanation for this state of affairs obviously relates to techniques of rearing animals: even though many species of South American fauna allow themselves to be tamed without difficulty, none would appear to be suitable for true domestication. But plenty of indications suggest that this is not the case. Thus, a study of the livestock-raising potentialities for a variety of wild species, expressed in terms of meat productivity and ethograms, has picked out, for South America, in particular the capybaras, the peccaries, and the agoutis.[22] Intensive raising of these three species on modern farms has become quite common in South America, with the capybaras even serving as ordinary butcher's meat in certain regions of Venezuela. It is also known that a tapir will allow itself to be trained if it is captured at a very early age and that it has occasionally been used as a draft animal by the Caboclos of the interior of Brazil.[23] As for the paca, the agouti, and the acouchi, at a zoological and ethological level, these are very close to the guinea pig, long a principal source of meat for Andean peasants. Finally, it should be noted that, with the exception of the tapir, all these species of mammals are light in weight (less than forty kilograms) and have a medium rate of reproduction, which models of evolutionary ecology consider to be the most favorable conditions when it comes to deciding to switch from hunting to domestication.[24]

However, of all the mammals of the tropical fauna of South America, it is the collared peccary (*Tayassu tajacu*) that presents the most characteristic ethogram of a species suitable for domestication: it is gregarious and sexually promiscuous within a framework of relatively large groups that are both diversified and arranged into hierarchies; it can maintain a high speed only over short distances and adapts well to environmental changes; furthermore, its feeding habits are not very specialized.[25] The experience of zoos moreover shows that the reproduction of this peccary in captivity raises no particular problems.[26] In view of all this, the fact that they have not been domesticated by the Amerindians has caught the attention of a number of authors.[27] Although it is true that male peccaries sometimes become uncontrollable when they reach adulthood, in South America it would have been perfectly possible to adopt the technique of pig-raising practiced in New Guinea, where the sows are left to roam freely in the bush surrounding the villages, where they copulate with stud boars that have remained wild. In Amazonia, tamed peccaries and tapirs are very seldom confined to an enclosure but are left to roam as they please around the inhabited areas, returning to be fed only when their masters call them. Feeding a whole herd would not demand any great intensification of horticultural resources, because at present these are under-exploited and also because the sweet potato, one of the first plant species to have been domesticated in America, is already widely used in Amazonia for feeding another domesticated animal, namely the dog. Its introduction into New Guinea contributed, precisely, to the raising of pigs, in the famous "Ipomean revolution."

It is true that in Papua, gardens are often protected from the incursions of pigs by solid barriers the construction of which is quite hard work, an investment of energy that the Amerindians, whose gardens are not enclosed, might be unwilling to accept. Nevertheless, it would be perfectly possible to keep the peccaries themselves in enclosures, given that such a procedure was probably employed in Brazil in the past, as a hunting technique, by the Mundurucú: herds of peccaries were driven into a corral where they were kept and fed before being slaughtered when the need for food arose (not that this stocking of food on the hoof ever led to any attempt at their controlled reproduction).[28] This example in fact underlines the difference in the Amerindians' attitudes to, on the one hand, animals captured for food but kept collectively outside the village and, on the other, individuals of the same species that are never eaten since they have been mothered and socialized in inhabited places. Furthermore, the raising of European pigs in enclosures is not unknown in Amazonia. Certain societies in upper Amazonia that are in regular contact with the Andes have apparently practiced this for a long time, feeling no particular scruples about eating pork. So it would seem, here, not to be so much a distaste for domesticated animals in general but rather a repugnance felt for the domestication of animals that are usually hunted as game.[29]

The explanation for such a repugnance might, of course, be the simple fact that it is more economical to procure meat by hunting relatively abundant animals than by going to the trouble of raising them. It is now known that contemporary Amazonia is not the "proteinless desert" formerly imagined by some advocates of cultural ecology and that the Amerindians are by no means lacking in game, even if ecological circumstances did introduce notable disparities in its accessibility. Many studies establish definitively that Amerindian hunting is highly productive, and one has even used a mathematical model to compare, among the Piro, the actual yield of meat from hunting collared peccaries with hypothetical yields were they to be raised in captivity. This study demonstrates that it is more profitable for this population to continue to be hunters.[30] No doubt the Amerindians had no need to know how to calculate the allometric relations between density, biomass, and levels of reproduction in order to come to an identical conclusion in many regions of Amazonia with ecological and demographic conditions similar to those of the Piro. It also seems likely that certain animal species were domesticated in the first place, not in order to be eaten (since they could perfectly well be hunted), but rather in order to obtain access to secondary products (milk, leather, wool, transport, etc.).[31] From this point of view, with the exception of the trumpet-bird (which acts as a sentinel) and parrots and macaws (whose feathers are prized as ornaments), the Amazonian fauna has little to offer. That being said, in most major centers of animal domestication, in particular in the Near East, domestication was fully developed only once sedentary living and demographic growth in circumscribed territories had increased to such a degree that dependence for food on the products of livestock raising became irreversible, relegating hunting to a supplementary activity. However, the low population densities that nowadays make it possible, in the interfluvial regions of Amazonia, to acquire adequate supplies of animal protein by hunting have not always been the norm. Sedentary and extremely dense societies, which were destroyed at a very early stage in the European colonial expansion, had developed in the course of almost two millennia on the rich alluvial terraces of the great rivers and in the foothills of the Andes; but even those societies never judged it necessary to resort to the domestication of the peccary, the agouti, or the capybara in order to compensate for whatever hunting could no longer deliver. Instead, they preferred to exploit alternative sources of protein, in particular the intensive cultivation of maize and, to a lesser degree, aquatic fauna. Keeping live tortoises inside enclosed pens was in any case common along the Amazon, although this conservation technique cannot be assimilated to livestock raising since no direct human action was exercised on the animals. It would thus appear that, between the taming of game animals and their domestication, there is a boundary that the Amerindians of the tropical regions have always refused to cross.[32]

This is all the more remarkable given that, in Amazonia just as much as in North America and Siberia, hunted animals are believed to live under the control of spirits that behave toward them as breeders. Even if the term generally used to designated this relationship denotes "taming," this really is a matter of livestock raising for, unlike the Amerindians themselves, who neither eat their pet animals nor try to get them to reproduce, the spirit masters of hunted animals often do feed off their herds or at any rate zealously promote their propagation. Not only are relations of protection for animals concretely present everywhere in Amazonia, taking the form of taming, but they also obtain potentially in all the decisions relating to livestock raising that are taken in the management of wild animals by nonhuman herders. And it is perhaps this duality in the treatment of protected animals that explains why the Indians of Amazonia have not domesticated the peccary, the capybara, or the agouti. For household animals have a status of their own; they socialize in the house in which they live at liberty, are fed and mothered by the women, are playmates for the young boys and girls, and are assimilated to preadolescent children, a fact that is sometimes invoked to explain why they do not reproduce themselves. In contrast, in Amazonia, hunted animals and their masters are usually regarded as affines—sexual partners or brothers-in-law in the case of the animals, parents-in-law in the case of the spirit masters. This is a feature that, as we have seen, is characteristic of many animist systems both in this part of the world and elsewhere. By regarding the young of hunted animals as adoptive children, the Amerindians distance them from the relations of alliance that they maintain with the spirits that protect the fauna, and they themselves fill the place of those spirits when they assume the function of a livestock raiser feeding his animals. But that substitution is both partial and temporary, for the humans are careful neither to encourage the protected animals to reproduce nor ever to kill them in order to eat them. In short, they "play" at being livestock raisers, possessing all the required zoological and ecological skills but without pushing such behavior to its logical conclusion.

In the lowlands of South America, taming animals is thus in no sense an incomplete attempt at "protodomestication."[33] The reason it has not led to veritable livestock raising lies in the manner in which relationships with animals are apprehended in this region. Game is either an alter ego, in a position of absolute exteriority when it is hunted, or else, when it is tamed, it is so close to humans that it cannot be eaten. In an animist regime, it is not surprising that animal-persons that live in their own independent collectives should be perceived as exterior. And as for the excessive proximity of household animals, it is occasioned by the fact that these orphans, separated from their own collectives and integrated into those of humans, have, despite their persistent differences of form, lost most of the attributes typical of their tribal-species origins. Being, in most cases, the only one of their kind in the house that takes them in, they interact no longer with their fellows but with humans or with animals of other species placed in the same situation. They no longer find their food in the habitual manner but eat whatever is prepared for them. They no longer occupy their own habitat but live in an environment created by others. Since they no longer reproduce in the mode that is characteristic of their species, they remain without sexual partners in the state of sexual immaturity of eternal children; even their bodies change, for they are sometimes massaged and shaped as if to make them more like humans, as may happen with the malleable bodies of infants, so that they acquire the perfection desired by their parents.[34] In short, in adopting some of the habits of those who have tamed them, the animals have lost their initial distinctive properties and have come to resemble the humans. That is why they do not end up in the cooking pot. Just as one does not eat the children who are captured from enemies and then integrated into the family of the murderer of their parents, where they are treated as distant blood relatives, likewise one does not eat the young animals whose parents have been killed, for they have now acquired the habits and customs of the collective into which they have been welcomed.

Yet this naturalization through adoption does not totally abolish the tamed animals' dependence on the masters of game, who continue from afar to ensure their protection. Under pain of arousing the anger of the spirits that watch over these temporary guests, there can be no more question of mistreating them than of inflicting pointless suffering on the animals that one hunts or of failing to respect them. The fact is that, in the social imaginary, most animals are already domesticated by their spirit masters and far more completely so than as a result of their adoption by humans; and, in a way, this rules out the humans themselves attempting to domesticate them. That would in effect imply, not so much a practical process prefigured by the taming of the animals, but rather a total transfer of subjection to which the masters of game would have to consent. Totally abolishing the exteriority of animal-persons and integrating them into human collectives would result in a situation that would upset the ontological frontiers of Amerindian cosmologies and also the principles by means of which relations between humans and nonhumans are put into practice. In contrast to pigs in New Guinea or cattle in Africa, which are the objects of a metonymic transfer that enables them to express the qualities and aspirations of whoever owns them, and consequently to serve as substitutes for humans in certain exchanges, an animal in tropical South America can only be seen as the subject, both individually and as a member of a group, of an egalitarian relationship between two persons. Here, the rejection of the technique of domestication is thus not so much the product of a conscious choice independently made by thousands of different peoples; rather, it is an effect of the impossibility, for them, of transforming their schema for relations with animals by generalizing vis-à-vis certain species a protective attitude that is the prerogative of nonhumans and that restricts the human taming of animals to no more than a few individual creatures. Of course, this blockage was necessarily a matter of accident, but it has been maintained ever since the pre-Columbian period right down to the present day. This is borne out *a contrario* by the failure of attempts made by developmental bodies in Amazonian societies to implant model farms in which to raise agoutis or peccaries as alternative sources of meat in regions where the environment has been degraded to the point of reducing the yield from hunting to almost nothing.

Provided certain conditions are met, it is far easier to adopt a new technical object than to invent a new technical relationship. The Indians of Amazonia immediately understood the advantage of metal tools, firearms, and, more recently, outboard motors and power saws, which, far more effectively than their old wooden and stone tools, perform exactly the same functions: cutting, dispatching projectiles, propelling canoes, and so on. Nor, in some cases, did they hesitate to learn from the whites elementary techniques of smelting and fashioning metals so as to make or repair the weapons that they needed in order to rid themselves of the presence of the very people who, with great naivety, had instructed them in this art.[35] The introduction of domesticated European animals among the Amerindians, foremost among them dogs, also took place without major difficulties, since the technical and ideological modalities of the treatment of animals were mostly transmitted along with the animals themselves, and all that was required were a few adjustments in taxonomies.[36] But it was an altogether different story when it came to the domestication of autochthonous animals, despite the fact that the principle was already present by analogy with the supposed behavior of the animals' spirit masters (and also, in some regions, by almost five centuries of familiarity with European domesticated animals). The trouble was that the adoption of such domestication would have necessitated a serious reorientation in the modes of relating to nonhumans and would have entailed modification to their ontological status.

It would, of course, have been possible to separate animals of the same species into two more or less sealed-off domains according to whether they were raised or hunted, as the Chukchees do with reindeer and certain Papuans do with pigs. In both these cases, minimal protection for the semidomesticated animal coexists without problems alongside predation upon their wild fellows, with the consent of the spirits that raise these.[37] The Indians of Amazonia did not follow this course with their peccaries, nor did those of subarctic America with their caribou, for reasons upon which it would be hazardous to speculate. Let us simply note that this kind of rectification of ontological frontiers comes about very gradually over a very long period of time. The reindeer that originated in America began to be domesticated in northern Eurasia almost five thousand years ago, probably by populations that had arrived from the south with longstanding skills as horse breeders. But their domestication took several millennia to become diffused in Siberia, where in certain regions it now dates from no more than a few centuries ago, and it remains embryonic wherever wild reindeers are abundant.[38] As for the domestication of the pig, it is still at no more than a midway stage of taming in some regions of New Guinea, where the inhabitants are content simply to capture wild piglets, which they then raise.

The Genesis of Change

It is not technical progress in itself that transforms the relations that humans maintain between themselves and the world but rather the sometimes tiny modifications made to those relations. It is these that render possible types of action previously considered unrealizable with respect to some particular category of existing beings, for every technique is primarily a mediated or immediate relation between an intentional agent and inorganic or living material, which may include the agent himself. For a new technique to appear or to be adopted with some chance of success, it must certainly be seen to possess a real or imaginary use and also to be compatible with the other characteristics of the system in which it finds a place. Above all, the original relationship that it implies must be possible to objectify—that is, it must correspond to a preexisting schema of interactions that, however, has so far been confined to a subordinate or specialized position because it affects only one particular well-defined class of objects. In this sense, a technical choice presupposes both a reconfiguration of elements already present and also the application of a specific type of relation to entities that were not previously concerned with it. This is what happens in animal domestication, with an expansion of the protective relation beyond its original niche, in which it affected above all the nurturing behavior of parents toward their children and the control that they consequently exerted over the conditions of the latter's existence. That control might even extend as far as the right (which many societies recognize) for parents to dispose of their children's lives, if only through a lack of care, abandonment, or exposure to the elements.

Understood in this way, a technical relation is remarkably stable over a long period of time, in contrast to the instrumental means that it employs and the organization of the operational chains in which it finds expression, for these may undergo setbacks within quite brief periods of time. The range of possible relations with oneself or some other living or inert being is far more limited than the whole collection of objects that those relations may engender and than the gamut of usable methods to achieve one's aim. Technical evolution could therefore be envisaged, not as a gradual complexifying of tools and processes of transformation, but rather as a limited and more or less cumulative series of objectivizations of new relations. The transition from cart to automobile or from the belted loom to the Jacquard loom was in no way inevitable or predictable, but at least it seems compatible with the features of such operations and the nature of the results inherent to those categories of artifacts. However, that is by no means the case with the objectivization of a new technical relationship, such as the domestication of plants or animals (the two do not necessarily go together), which constitute unprecedented revolutions in the apprehension and treatment of the frontiers between oneself and others. Instrumentalization is another of those major revolutions, probably the first one, since the idea of transferring an organism's physical function to an object that will facilitate it germinated in other species before flourishing so spectacularly as human beings evolved. Among such new relations with things, we should include the storage of foodstuffs, that is, the accumulation of energy for the reproduction of life, a phenomenon that is quite independent from domestication (for some agriculturalists do not practice it while some hunter-gatherers do) and is the probable source of the first economic inequalities.[39] Making no claims to be exhaustive, we might add to this short list the invention of cognitive artifacts (from the Inca quipus to writing and passing by way of the abacus and pictograms) and also the separation of skills in the organization of tasks, this time involving relations between humans, which came about when the multiple abilities of each individual, previously employed in collective operations with no explicit coordination, were redirected by an overseer in order to facilitate the accomplishment of the various specific tasks that were assigned to every individual: the nature of the skills mobilized did not change, but modifying the relations of different parties to the whole made specialization possible and, with it, introduced a social division of work. In all these cases, objectivization takes the form either of an externalization of human properties and physical and mental functions or of an artificialization of some nonhumans, both processes rendered possible by transposing previously developed skills or relations to meet new ends.

With the exception of the stocking of goods, none of these breaks in relations to matter presupposes or even results in a radical modification of social and economic conditions, for the actualization of the productive potentialities contained in the new technical relations is by no means automatic. Perhaps the best illustration is provided by the domestication of plants, an extraordinary mutation in the treatment of nonhumans but one that cannot be considered the deus ex machina of political stratification, demographic growth, or the exploitation of others: we should remember that plenty of hunters–cum–swidden horticulturalists are barely distinguishable from hunter-gatherers from the point of view of their sociopolitical systems, the organization of subsistence, and their strategies for occupying and managing a certain space. In contrast, societies founded exclusively on the tapping of natural resources (the Indians of the northwest coast of North America and those of southern Florida) have presented inegalitarian features—disparities in wealth, the use of servile labor, hierarchical political structures—that are nowhere to be found among most cultivators of tropical tubers.

In the domain of technical innovations as in historical evolution in general, it is not so much movement that needs explaining as stability. Every day brings its quota of tiny discoveries; curious minds everywhere speculate about the world and its mysteries; at any moment strong personalities may embark on enterprises with unpredictable consequences; so conditions are always suitable for things not to remain as they are but, instead, through an accumulation of minuscule mutations, to transform themselves at a pace said to vary depending on the standard adopted for measuring change. If we try to avoid the shortsightedness of the present moment that causes us to assess a general movement according to the way in which we ourselves sense it in the course of the ups and downs of our own existence, we cannot fail to recognize that the major frameworks for the schematization of human experience change very little, in particular ontological regimes and the dominant relational modes that structure praxis; and this does not apply solely to the societies that Lévi-Strauss called "cold" because they seek to neutralize the effects of historical contingency. Stability, then, is due, not to an unlikely absence of movement, but to a suppression of movement or, more precisely, to the obstacles placed in the way of its normal course by mechanisms that inhibit its immediate consequences. One of those obstacles, possibly the most common of them, lies in the difficulty of extending the field of certain relations to include new objects, thereby encouraging them to change in status in order to conform to the expected characteristics of the class of existing beings to which those relations originally applied. The nature of the terms involved constrains the nature of the relations that can be established between them, which is why, in my view, ontological identification must logically precede relationships. For this reason, terms cannot easily be transferred from one relationship to another, and this ontological resistance constitutes the most decisive obstacle to the movement of transposition that characterizes an objectivization of the original technical relationship.

This is what happens in tropical South America with the coexistence of different modalities of relations to two distinct classes of animals: namely, on the one hand, the treatment of animals habitually hunted and, on the other, the raising of domesticated European animals, the most common of these being dogs and chickens. While the protection of certain individuals from the former group remains provisional and conditional upon their being tamed, for the second group, which is totally subordinated to the humans, it becomes absolute; and this tendency explains why it was more or less inconceivable that animals hunted as game could be slipped into a domesticating relationship. Where a transfer from one relationship to another has occurred, it happened because nonindigenous terms came to be included in the original relationship, not the other way around. For instance, in savanna regions several cases are known in which feral cattle that have reverted to a wild state have been turned into game animals by Amerindians, but there is no record of any game animals being turned into domesticated ones.

Such persistent resistance to change is nevertheless rare. More usually, a class of existing beings that is preeminent on account of the role that it plays in some sector of the existence of a collective finds itself gradually subsumed into a relational schema that was previously marginal and that now comes to acquire a preponderant position. The way is then clear for the relationship that initially characterized the treatment of those objects to lose its importance. Thus, although it took a very long time in Siberia, the strengthening of a protective attitude toward certain animals was bound to cause a decline in the person-to-person relationship that previously prevailed with them and, little by little, to lead either to the disappearance of the patterns of behavior previously followed toward nonhumans that were believed to possess attributes identical to those of humans or else, possibly, the consignment of those original relationships to the vault of folkloric survivals. All the same, such a mutation can only come about if the mechanisms that inhibit change have themselves been inhibited by the consequences of events sufficiently exceptional for creative imagination and a sense of innovation to come into their own, upsetting habits transmitted from one generation to the next. Generally, this happens when the terms likely to be objectivized by extending the field of a previously secondary relationship are either totally new or else already deeply modified by the progressive weakening of the relationship that previously objectivized them. Although the first case may be typical of phenomena involving borrowing and diffusion, experience also shows that the arrival of a new entity—a new domesticated animal, for example—does not necessarily imply that it will be adopted if the relationship that objectivizes it (i.e., a certain type of relation to the animal) remains too alien to the locally dominant schemas of interaction and systems of skills. And even if its use is eventually accepted, it will tend to remain confined to a niche that will impede its transposition to other objects. So the second condition, namely the disintegration of a previously preponderant relationship, is fundamental to the process of change. It usually comes about when circumstances generated by the vagaries of history, climate change, or the unintentional effects of human action on the environment force peoples to adapt to different milieux or to ones in which the usual characteristics have changed for the worse. Long-distance migrations under pressure from invaders or bellicose neighbors, expansion as the result of conquest, containment within a territory subjected to more intensive exploitation, the human degradation of an ecosystem or its progressive transformation in the wake of climatic accidents: all these things oblige humans to modify their strategies for subsistence and, above all, upset the relations that unify them with others and with the world, thereby making them more receptive to drastic measures that they would otherwise regard with suspicion.

It is not that innovation is inevitably born of necessity. Rather, a lasting transformation in the relations with real or imaginary entities whose destiny we share can only get under way in the tumultuous and sometimes very lengthy periods in which humans open up to new experiences because the links that they had woven between one another in the ordinary course of things give way before the onslaught of contingency and begin to reshape in a different form. But this reorganization does not follow an altogether random course. Even though, in the evolution of organisms, as in that of the collectives in which they cohabit, chance and arbitrariness are indispensable in the gestation of a new order or equilibrium, that new order, without being altogether predictable, does come about following certain organizing rules and principles of compatibility that are less fortuitous than the events that prompted its development. Destruction can be wreaked in a thousand different ways, but reconstruction can be achieved only with whatever materials are available and by following a limited number of plans that respect the architectonic constraints peculiar to any edifice. All the rest, all that catches the eye in the first instance and provides the pleasures of diversity, is no more than ornamentation.

Epilogue
The Spectrum of Possibilities

Despite the alternatives offered, one after another, by a variety of different structural approaches, ever since its inception anthropology has been more or less overtly fascinated by the robust simplicity of etiological explanations. There are many ways of accounting in this way for a particular institution: by means of appealing, in the manner of nineteenth-century evolutionism, to its supposed genesis or to earlier circumstances or external influences, as do contemporary anthropologists discovering the somewhat outworn virtues of a purely descriptive history. Alternatively, one can try to discover the adaptive function that that institution would fulfill in a given environment or to regard it as an expression of archaic influences or presumed archetypes. All such approaches are no doubt reassuring for minds in quest of certainties, but they do not really make it possible to answer the only question that matters: namely why is a particular social fact, belief, or custom present in one place but not in another? A multitude of reasons have been suggested to explain sacrifice, cannibalism, and ancestor worship, including some provided by those who practice such things, but we are no closer to a better understanding of the motives that led some to adopt them but others not to, let alone how it is that in one place cannibalism cohabits with sacrifice or ancestor worship but in another place it excludes them. Why is there no totemic royalty? Why are nonhumans not represented in parliaments on the grounds of their particular qualities? Why does an Inca or a Pharaoh not eat his enemies? Why do Amerindian shamans not make sacrifices? Those are pointless questions, you may say, and do not deserve serious attention. Yet they are the questions that matter when one tries to account for differences in the ways of inhabiting the world and giving it meaning. We should not be striving to reduce the diversity of established practices by assigning to them unverifiable origins, functions of a general nature that is not very illuminating, or hypothetical biological or subconscious bases. Rather, we should ask ourselves what it is that renders these practices compatible or not compatible with one another, for that is the first stage for an inquiry into the rules that govern the syntax of these practices and their organization into systems. The structural typologies sketched in earlier in this book were prompted by precisely that ambition. For one cannot hope to reveal the principles according to which certain elements are combined unless one has first defined the elements that they affect and has defined them sufficiently precisely for the table of those elements to remain accessible to further additions. If anthropology were ever to discover a source of inspiration in a better-established science, it should turn to chemistry rather than to physics or biology, although the latter are often invoked as models for the anthropological discipline even if the relationship to them is never developed beyond a metaphorical level. It is true that humans are capable of producing new combinations and of thereby modifying the properties of whatever is combined, but whatever the apostles of creative action may claim, except in myth or fiction it is not possible for them to create functional hybrids out of components that possess irreconcilable properties.

That may be something that one is beginning to sense at the end of this long journey through the labyrinth of ways in which things are used. In a schematization of the different aspects of experiencing the world and others, identification and relationships can be divided into a whole range of modalities the intrinsic characteristics of which differ, either permitting or ruling out their coexistence in any particular collective or, in the case of relations, their interaction between a dominant form and one or two minor forms. I have chosen to examine four modes of identification and six relational modes, so, for the picture to be complete, it would be necessary to review the twenty-four configurations that the combinations of those modes produce. But that would be to carry the analogy with chemistry and a spirit of systematization to unreasonable lengths. Besides, some of those combinations are fanciful and only exist in the domains of Utopia or the pages of science fiction, where their contradictory fusions are most successful at momentarily lightening the burden of an all-too-predictable reality. So at this point I will limit myself to evoking a few types of compatibility and incompatibility, leaving readers better versed in comparativism to decide whether some of the impossible collectives I left separated really are so in fact.

Animism and naturalism may be seen as antithetical ways of discerning the properties of things. Animism lays the emphasis on the physical differences between existing beings (they have dissimilar bodies) while recognizing that they maintain similar interrelations (given that they share an analogous interiority). Naturalism, on the contrary, lays the emphasis on the physical continuity between the world's elements (all are subjected to the laws of nature), the better to note the heterogeneity of the relations that may bring them together (these are said to depend on their capacity or incapacity to manifest interiorities of various kinds). So it seems reasonable to examine these two schemas of identification together, seen from the point of view of the relational modes that they are able to sustain.

Despite the patent discontinuities in the biological equipment and the ethograms that animist subjects display, they maintain between one another a permanent dialogue of souls, and this intersubjective communication is the basis for the principle of an unrestricted sociability that encompasses both humans and nonhumans in its universal network. The differences in physical dispositions do not constitute an obstacle to communication and are partly wiped out by the interpersonal relations that are established between terms that can be substituted for one another since they are positioned at the same level of the ontological scale. In animist cosmologies, in which entities of equal status are defined by the positions that they occupy vis-à-vis one another, the only structuring relations possible are those that operate with potentially reversible links between subjects, whether human or nonhuman, whose identities are not affected by the realization of the relations that bring them together: that is to say, the relations of predation, exchange, or gift giving. Conversely, intransitive relations of the production, transmission, or protection type are bound to remain marginal given that they presuppose a hierarchy between terms whose ontological disparity is rendered effective by the very action that one exerts upon another within the relationship. With gift giving, exchange, and predation one subject ratifies the other; with production, protection, and transmission, the subject establishes a dependent subject or a subordinate object.

In that an Achuar hunter regards the animal that he pursues as an alter ego, he actualizes in a particular context the general relationship of predatory affinity that exists between the hunters and the hunted; possibly he reinforces it, but through this interaction he modifies neither the ontological properties of his interlocutor nor the nature of the relations that he establishes with it. The same can be said of the exchange relations that the Tukanos weave between themselves and their environment, and of the gift schema that ideally directs the actions of the Campas and some of the nonhumans with which they cohabit. But in relations of production as these are traditionally conceived by Moderns, the situation is altogether different (even if that conception proves contrary to what practical experience shows). We know that matter resists and imposes its own constraints upon whoever works upon it; yet it is that producing agent who comes to the fore when he is declared to impose a specific form and function upon matter lacking any autonomy, in order to produce a new entity for which he alone is responsible even when he does not, in effect, own it. The object that results from his actions exists with its own particular attributes only insofar as a genetic relationship has brought it into being, as a repeated example of other, similar actions prompted by the same project. As is suggested by the example of the Wayana basket makers, this is why it is mistaken to speak of "craft production" in the case of animism: the artifacts here are not realizations ex nihilo that reinforce the position of subject held by those who fashion them; instead, they are transformed subjects that preserve some of their original ontological attributes.

Protection implies control over the biological functions such as reproduction and feeding, by means of which existing beings can be distinguished from one another. Similarly then, protection cannot constitute a general relational schema suited to animism. Stripped of its freedom to behave in every way in accordance with the physical habits of its species-tribe, the protected subject loses its independence and eventually even its quality as a subject. So protection is truly acceptable only in particular niches of animism and always in a minor mode—such as the prerogative held by the spirit masters of animals that is sometimes extended to humans engaged in semidomestication, although it may happen that its attractions (security for some, domination for others) eventually prove so powerful that a new ontology is required to accommodate it fully.

As for transmission, a way of guaranteeing and reproducing the physical and moral dependence of the living on the dead, it instantly eliminates the possibility of treating animals and plants as subjects, since all its efficacy rests upon a relationship of hierarchical subordination between one generation and others: the central articulation of collectives is formed of human lines of descent that are differentiated one from another and maintain relations solely through reference to groups of ancestors from which they have inherited riches, rights, and all the components of personalities and destinies. It is hard to imagine any way in which such an arrangement could be adapted to the animist abundance of species-tribes of human and nonhuman subjects, which, for their part, distinguish themselves from one another by their dispositions for action, which are determined by the physical form that remains identical for every generation, thereby perpetuating their various modes of life. The cumulative and anthropocentric transmission of substances, patrimonies, and predestinations would thus run counter to the need for every subject, whatever its physical envelope, to re-create at every moment the conditions for a sui generis existence founded on interaction with others. That is why it is necessary to wipe the dead from memory and to destroy their meager possessions and why any tradition that they may transmit must be disassociated from their person.

By rejecting or marginalizing certain relations, animism provides a negative template of all that it rejects. Throughout its territory, there will be no sign of any exclusive livestock raisers, no castes of specialized craftsmen, no ancestor cults, no lineages that function as moral persons, no creative demiurges, no taste for material patrimonies, no obsession with heredity, no arrow of time, no excessively wide-ranging filiation, and no deliberative assemblies. Some perspicacious observers who have noticed those absences have interpreted them as lacks. But they are, of course, nothing of the kind. The price to be paid for populating the world with subjects—each day re-creating the experience of indecisive identities—appears too high only to those who, enclosed within a reassuring block of institutions, are content to measure the promises of the present by the yardstick of whatever the past has bequeathed.

The same remark could well be applied to naturalism, so hypnotized are Moderns by the attenuated variant of transmission constituted by historical consciousness. It is a variant that is certainly attenuated, for even if the dead and their legacy of objects and ideas do combine to define our individual and collective identities, and even if their achievements have circumscribed the field of what we ourselves can accomplish, nevertheless our liberty as human subjects is also reputed to stem from our ability to transform the achievements of the present with a view to improving what happens in the future. This is why, despite our pronounced taste for commemorations and despite the ceaseless celebration of heroes of the past, and the devotion with which it is considered seemly to surround the dead, there will be no trace among Moderns of that subjugation to the ancestors that is a sign of the purest forms of transmission. For us, the dead are not still-active despots who regulate our daily lives. They are just benign puppets to which we turn when involved in affairs that no longer concern them. Far from characterizing transmission, it is in naturalism that this blandness seems to be the rule—naturalism, within which a variety of relations can coexist, many of them in a derivative or incomplete form. This is because of the very properties of the naturalist ontology. For even if the continuity between existing beings links them all together in a network of shared determinations in which they are differentiated only by degrees of complexity, the singularity that is ascribed to humans on account of their distinctive interiority has the effect of preventing any relational mode from occupying a hegemonic position: some relations are deemed suitable for connections between humans, others for connections with nonhumans, but none has the power to schematize the principal interactions between all the world's elements.

Exchange (of a mercantile type) and protection (of citizens by the state) are thus central values for modern democracies; but their advantages do not extend to nonhumans: these are pushed to the peripheries of collectives on account of their lack of any reflective consciousness and moral sense. One does not enter into a contract with plants, animals, machines, or genes, all of which are objects, not subjects, of transactions. The protection afforded to them stems from the interest that humans derive from controlling them and preserving them, not from any rightful inclusion of them in the sphere of social interactions, as would be the case in the forests of Amazonia or the savannas of Nilotic Africa. It is true that, in its capitalist variant, naturalism has been able to disguise this subordination by emphasizing the production of nonhumans as a condition for exchanging them. Where commodity fetishism prevails, labor relations between persons tend to be seen as connections in which things become linked, unlike in animism, for example, in which, to use the language of Marx, it is more a matter of things linking together, on the assumption that they are establishing a connection between persons. But that charade is never perfect since, in order to conceal the sources of capitalist alienation beneath an impenetrable veil, it would be necessary to grant to things an autonomy greater than that of persons, by recognizing them to possess, not only free will, but also the ability to dispose, without hindrance, of those who produce them and exchange them. However, that is far from being the case, even if the trend for treating production and mercantile exchange as natural phenomena that exist in themselves is continually increasing in the assertions of latter-day capitalism. Abstract generalities, such as "the economic environment," "growth," or "profit margin" may, it is true, have acquired the status of independent intentional entities; but all the same, it is hard for those who undergo their effects to believe fully and constantly that it is these things that, in themselves, govern the destiny of billions of humans, not the individuals who act as their by-no-means-disinterested oracles. Thus, even though in naturalist collectives production has little by little become the central schema of relations with nonhumans—a fact that the proliferation of genetically modified organisms has made patently obvious to all of us—the use of production has not yet succeeded in becoming general in relations between humans, even if the fantasies prompted by reproductive cloning show how greatly some people wish to see it extend its influence.

As a consequence of the dissociation that it introduces between human subjects and nonhuman objects, naturalist ontology furthermore condemns itself to perpetual compromises, even as it clings to the utopian hope eventually to see the establishment of a dominant relationship capable of eliminating the segregation upon which it is founded. Unfortunately, in such a clearly apartheid regime, it is impossible to set up between all existing beings a schema of interaction with the synthesizing power and simplicity of expression of the relations that structure nonmodern collectives. That is a painfully self-evident fact that feeds the widespread nostalgia for a world untouched by disenchantment. Despite superficial analogies, transmission, as we have seen, remains imperfect: a veneration for history is not the same as veneration for ancestors, sites of memory are no substitute for lineage altars, nor do laws of inheritance fully replace the rules of descent. Marginalized by mercantile exchange, gift giving fares even worse, despite pious attempts to resuscitate its social virtues; it survives only in rites of intimacy and humanitarian charity, and possibly also in a providential notion of the generosity of good Mother Nature, which, however, would appear not to be very convincing given the outrages that we heap upon her. Nor, despite appearances, does predation lie at the heart of naturalism, at least not if predation is regarded as an incorporation of "others" that is indispensable for the definition of the self. The thoughtless ransacking of the planet's resources and the destruction of its biotic diversity may well contribute to increasing the wealth of the very rich, but they result from our forgetting the belief that prevailed in the first ages of modernity, namely that the splendid otherness of nature is necessary for the manifestation of the specific qualities of humanity. As for the annihilation of strangers who speak a different language, display a different skin color, practice another religion or other customs, which is the hackneyed chauvinist expedient for consolidating a contrastive identity, what this rejects in others are precisely the qualities required to fulfill the role expected of them. Such destruction is a negation of what a human embodies and not, as in animism, a recognition of the position of exteriority that must be assimilated if one is to be fully oneself. Naturalism is thus destructive rather than predatory in its behavior toward certain categories of both humans and nonhumans—not that it is any more constant in this relationship than it is in others, as is shown by the versatility that the colonial powers have demonstrated over the past two centuries. The records of ordered production and mercantile exchange that predominated in the metropolitan capital were effaced overseas by the plundering of natural riches and of workforces—plundering that was, furthermore, frequently presented as a protective mission. Was this cunning? Cynicism? A sarcastic negation? No doubt a bit of all those, but it also demonstrated that naturalism does not possess the means to develop within a single relational mode.

The inability of Moderns to schematize their relations with a whole diverse range of existing beings by means of an all-encompassing relation takes on an almost pathetic aspect when they are faced with the temptation to establish a genuine reciprocity with nonhumans. To effect a deal with nature, or at least with certain of its representatives, is one of the most ancient and elusive dreams of those who are disappointed by naturalism. The strange varieties of *Naturphilosophie* that flourished in the nineteenth century, the aesthetics of the Romantics, the current success of neo-shamanistic movements and New Age esotericism, and television's and cinema's taste for cyborgs and desiring machines—all these reactions to the moral consequences of dualism, and many others too, testify to the desire lurking within each of us, with various degrees of anxiety, to recover the lost innocence of a world in which plants, animals, and objects were fellow citizens. However, the Moderns' nature can emerge from its silence only by means of all-too-human intermediaries, so that no exchange, no negotiation, no contract with the host of inanimate beings is now conceivable. This assessment should not be seen as an attack on technological society. On the contrary: the contradictions of naturalism, in particular its inability to subsume different regimes of behavior into one dominant relationship, are what give it its fascinating plurality. This entails the more or less pacific coexistence of would-be collectives, all of which try with considerable ingenuity to explore paths leading to an exclusive style of behavior to which, however, they will never be able to conform by reason of the ontological constraints with which they start out. This is what bestows upon postindustrial societies their hybrid iridescence and meanwhile provides sociologists with an inexhaustible terrain to explore.

In contrast, totemic and analogical collectives present greater internal uniformity because, even if they contain a constitutive hybrid element, this is tucked away in the composite nature of the existing beings that they gather together and not, as in the case of naturalism, in mixtures of genera into which the relations that structure them are forced. We should remember that the humans and nonhumans included within a totemic group, despite their different forms and modes of life, all share the same collection of physical and moral attributes. This ensures their identity—in both senses of that word: that is to say, a distinctive character and also an equivalence as members of the prototypical class whose properties they embody. As they see it, they thus all stem individually from the same mold while, to an outsider's eye, they seem collectively heterogeneous. This identity of composition is rendered possible and also reinforced by the identity of the relations that determine them. In the exemplary case of Australia, they share the same origin (a Dream-being), inherence (in the class that that Dream-being instituted), and parity (in the attributes that they received from it). In this sense, no veritable relations can exist between the members of a totemic group—at least none of the kind that stamp their vigorous mark on practices and inject the dynamism necessary for each collective to act in an autonomous way in the world. That is not to say, of course, that there are no interactions between the elements that make up a totemic group, for this does include men and women, parents and children, plants and animals, material entities and immaterial ones, all squeezed together in a complex and contradictory tissue of affects, interests, and obligations. But the excessive proximity of these terms in permanent quest of individuation forces them to look outside the group that they form, to other totemic classes, for partners sufficiently different from themselves for a relationship of complementary opposition to become possible. This is the only way for them to escape from the ontological enclosure by which their distinctive existence is determined. Therein lies the principal paradox of totemism, which is what makes its nature so hard to determine: within the framework of a collective, it produces a perfect synthesis between a multitude of existing beings that, at first sight, seem heterogeneous, but it does so at the cost of a paralyzing immobility that prevents this collective from being self-sufficient and obliges it to establish with others the relations that it is incapable of setting up within itself.

Although differentiated by their respective properties, the totemic groups that are forced to enter into contact are all positioned at the same ontological level: they all derive their singular identities from the same type of genesis, the same type of reference to a prototype, and the same type of attachment to particular places. So it is hardly surprising that exchange should be the dominant schema into which their links are subsumed, since this, more than other schemas, makes it possible to establish connections between whole groups (meanwhile also permitting individual associations) and above all is particularly suited to terms with status parity but which have to maintain between each other a situation of mutual dependence (the permanence of the relationship being guaranteed by the cycle of obligations that go with it). Exchanges of women, exchanges of services, exchanges of foodstuffs, and exchanges of resources: the round of transactions is incessant and it is easy to see how it was that Aboriginal Australia provided Lévi-Strauss with not only the most complete model of generalized exchange in matrimonial alliances but also with striking confirmation of his no doubt more ancient conviction that exchange in all its forms constitutes the indestructible basis of social life.

On the other hand, no univocal relations involving nonequivalent terms can be established externally between totemic collectives, nor, a fortiori, internally, within them. Thus, despite a superficial resemblance that in the past was the source of much confusion, the perpetuation of the physical and moral properties that each totemic class embodies, generation after generation, can in no way be assimilated to the transmission of a patrimony. The Dream-beings are not distant ancestors in whose debt the living must always remain but are prototypes endowed with a still vibrant creative potential. Far from transmitting the attributes of which they are the guardians, they instead transmit themselves in the form of attributes into the bodies of the humans and the nonhumans that they choose to actualize by their presence. As for production, in the exemplary sense in which naturalism employs it in the fabrication of objects, that too is a relational mode that has no place in totemism, even in the form of the rites designed to multiply animal and plant species. Ceremonies of the *intichiuma* type are the means whereby the human members of a totemic group encourage the propagation of a class of nonhumans that is likewise affiliated to their collective, for the benefit of other totemic groups that feed on them. This they do by stimulating fertility and favoring the incorporation of its essences by means of actions that, in mimetic fashion, retrace the various stages of pregnancy. So the humans here play the role of midwives assisting the birth of quasi fellow beings, not that of autonomous creators of objects; they facilitate a process of engendering that they do not control, rather in the way that, in certain animist collectives, a hunter must be sure to collect the bones of the animal that has allowed itself to be killed by him and whose flesh he has consumed, so that the animal's interiority, which is unscathed, can, thanks to these material traces of its singularity, be reborn as a new individual.

While totemic collectives have to project themselves outward in order to introduce a relational movement into their all-too-inert togetherness, analogical collectives can, on the contrary, establish links only within themselves. Since each is coextensive with the world and is able to receive within it all that the world contains, outside it no partner worthy of an authentic relationship can exist—only, at the very most, muddled collections of unfamiliar existing beings whose sporadic growth has to be contained and whose chaotic nature must be reduced by absorbing them into the sociocosmic order in which a place has already been prepared for them. The proliferation of particularized entities with dissimilar components that analogism sets in order, and the multiplicity of graduated differences that result from this, are tempered by an obsession to detect common features, signs of correspondence and themes of agreement, for these are the bases of the general system of a segmented hierarchy from which no singularity can be left out. The paradox of totemism is that in principle it posits an identity between terms that are thus forced to seek outside their mixed intimacy for the means to produce something different that will generate relationships. Meanwhile, the paradox of analogism is that it posits in principle differences between terms that in some respects resemble one another but do so in ways so diverse that the relations that may be used to organize them into a common project depend less on ontological properties than on an imperative need to integrate them all into a single functional whole.

So here the relations that predominate are those best suited to cope with differences and to discipline heterogeneity. One such relationship is that of transmission, which is by nature hierarchical and dispenses order. Its temporal continuities encompass long parallel lines of humans both dead and alive, which are distinguished one from another by the contents of whatever they pass down from one generation to the next. Transmission is an ingenious way of cementing their solidarity by distributing among them complementary prerogatives and functions. Another is the relationship involving protection, often combined with the segmentary logic of ancestrality, whose field of activity it helps to expand by extending a cascade of dependencies reaching all the way from plants and animals up to the summit of the pantheons. Each unit owes its security, its well-being, and even its existence to another—even the tutelary deities, who owe all this to the beliefs of the humans who instituted them. In many cases, these hierarchical relations take the form of a division of tasks through the medium of exchange: exchanges of goods and specialized services between the Indian castes, the exchange of an assurance of stability in the cosmos guaranteed by a pharaoh or an Inca in return for forced labor and tribute, and the circulation of work, products, and women between autonomous descent groups. But here the exchange is not so much a cardinal value that schematizes relationships; rather, it is a way of moderating the original disparity between the terms that it brings together through an illusion of equivalence in the obligations that fall to them when they engage in exchange. In these circumstances it matters little if the exchange is unequal or maintains subordination since it does manage to link elements that are sometimes very distant on the scale of statutory positions, and through this interdependence, it helps to ensure their coherence in an all-inclusive system. The only thing that really counts in an analogical collective, whatever the relational arrangements employed to achieve it, is to integrate within an apparently homogeneous whole a host of singularities that are inclined to fragment spontaneously.

This is why the ideology of a collective of this type is bound to be functionalism—that is, the idea that each of its constitutive elements contributes, in its well-defined place, to the perpetuation of a stable totality. In all probability, the sway that was exercised in the United Kingdom by the "functionalist" anthropological doctrine resulted partly from the circumstantial fact that British anthropologists tended to study the social organization of the peoples in the African and Eastern possessions of their vast colonial empire; and most of those stemmed from analogical collectives. These peoples represented themselves as functional groups, and their members had no qualms about explaining their integrating mechanisms in detail to those observing them. The same can certainly not be said of animist collectives, above all those in the Americas, which were tacitly neglected by the functionalist school because of their ostensible lack of institutional cohesion. It was not until the developments of structural anthropology that the singular manner in which these collectives introduced discontinuity within themselves by means of their relational system began to be better understood. If confirmation is needed, this vindicates the effort of abstraction and decentering that must be made if objectivizing reflection upon collective experience is to manage, at least to some degree, to move aside from the collective schemas that subjectivize experience.

Now that the time has come for me to bring this book to an end and I cast a retrospective and almost detached eye over the propositions that it contains, I cannot help feeling a stab of apprehension regarding the misunderstandings that they may occasion. Even though, for some essayists, their no more than superficial understanding of the themes that they tackle has seldom acted as a brake, one might well raise the question of competence: by what right does an ethnologist whose scholarship was for many years confined to one particular region in South America pass judgment on all these civilizations about which he possesses only a limited knowledge? How can one presume to say anything about the Australian Aboriginals if one has read no more than a fraction of the ocean of monographs and articles that have been devoted to them? Is it possible to comment seriously on the concepts of a person among the ancient Mexicans if one has not acquired a command of Nahuatl philology? Above all, how can one treat in such a cavalier fashion the history of the West, the philosophy and epistemology of the Moderns, and the sociology of industrialized societies, to which so many distinguished scholars have devoted so many sleepless nights and even then only manage to explore certain fragments in an incidental fashion? Those are classic questions that a specialist may well address to those who dare to compare and that may be deflected only by an avowal of humility such as that made by Max Weber in the introduction to his *The Protestant Ethic and the Spirit of Capitalism*. I should like to echo his words, so faithfully do they reflect my own state of mind: "It is quite evident that anyone who is forced to rely on translations, and furthermore on the use and evaluation of monumental, documentary, or literary sources, has to rely himself on a specialist literature which is often highly controversial, and the merits of which he is unable to judge accurately. Such a writer must make modest claims for the value of his work."[1]

However, such an act of contrition would hardly seem sincere were it not accompanied by some justification of the scope of the undertaking that motivated it. No doubt some of my analyses will be regarded as simplifications of phenomena that are very much more complex, or as flawed by an excessive fidelity to exegeses that are not accepted by all experts. It is even possible that, as a result of the kind of blindness that conviction engenders, I have failed to discern the true implications of factors that might run counter to my own interpretations. Those are criticisms that I would accept with equanimity provided it is recognized that the hypotheses set out in this work are above all of a heuristic nature and that the sole aim of the ethnographic and historical examples by which I support them is to sketch in what might be a different way of treating social facts: what I mean is, not by seeing them from the start as characteristics that confer dignity upon our species, but by trying to gain a better understanding of the principles according to which humans schematize their experience of things in such very different ways, welcoming nonhumans into their collectives with varying degrees of liberality and either actualizing the relations that they discern between existing beings in concrete systems of interactions or not doing so. Now, however varied the expressions that they take may be, those forms of relating to the world seem to me neither limitless nor incommensurable. Their motley effects are disconcerting only if, fascinated by the multiplicity and richness of motifs and convinced that one can do no more than comment upon them and propose stylistic ways of reordering them, one ends up rejecting the idea that common structures may govern their organization. In the present book, I back the converse assumption, in the wake of many others who have likewise sought to find in fundamental constants (ranging from laws governing the mind to the constraints of material life) the sources of regularity in human patterns of behavior and their collective frameworks. For these may to some extent dissipate the chaotic appearance that they present to our eyes. In the present context, those constants are reduced to the minimum, and no doubt a philosopher would find them somewhat unsophisticated. I have postulated that identification and relations constitute the warp and weft of customs in the world and that the ways in which they intertwine mark out some of the major configurations in which those customs have become established in the course of history. However, I have absolutely no desire to add a small contribution of my own to some hypothetical theory of human nature. I wish only to propose a more effective and less ethnocentric way of accounting for what is usually called cultural diversity. So it matters little to me if the conjectures from which I start out are criticized, provided that, as I trust, the combinations that they allow for make it possible to create a more economical way of accommodat-

ing a greater quantity of material and ideal entities than the classic opposition
between the universality of nature and the contingency of human societies
does; and also provided that, as I am convinced, those premises prove less
easily assignable to a particular cosmology, however respectable the tradition
from which it emerged may be.

Much remains to be done before an enterprise of this kind becomes acceptable and before, having possibly caught the interest of those who may
find in it suggestions leading to a better understanding of the matters that
preoccupy them, it can, with their help, begin to bear fruit. Before expecting
more abundant harvests, it may be necessary to prune away certain branches
that seemed solid to me, to graft on to the trunk new varieties that I did not
know existed, and to train back certain wayward limbs. To take but one domain in which anthropology has for many years excelled, it is clear that the
way in which I have described types of collectives is still much too summary
for it to take into account all the delicate variations in the social structure and
organization of networks of kinship that a host of observers and analysts have
for many years, and with great success, been describing and systematizing. I
also appreciate that numerous facets of human experience have been ignored
in this book and that it is by no means certain that they can easily be fitted
in with the models whose features I have described. So even though I have
found certain empirical foundations for advancing the hypothesis that identification and relationships are what in part define other schemas of practice—
configurations, temporality, and categorization, for example—that intuition
has yet to be justified by well-sustained arguments and rigorous investigations. Finally, and although this is something that I have mentioned before, it
may be useful to remind readers that the precedence ascribed to the discovery of structural configurations over research into the causes of their genesis
is no more than a methodological priority and that, however imperfect our
understanding of structural configurations may still be, this should not be
considered a reason to defer a study of the causes of their genesis. The same
applies to the elucidation of the mechanisms of change and what it is that
so often inhibits it. Understanding how one mode of identification changes
into another or how, on the contrary, its principles are perpetuated and how
it is that a particular relationship loses or preserves its prevalence are clearly
tasks of urgent importance, which have been no more than outlined in the
preceding pages. These remarks will no doubt have made it clear that, unlike
the harmonious and polished constructions that the dualism of nature and
society has accustomed us to erect, the present endeavor remains a work in
progress, a building project whose site manager has decided to hand it over
prematurely solely in the hope that those interested in it will, in the fullness

of time, bestow upon it not only an aspect and potential that may be very
different from what was anticipated but also the look of an edifice that can
truly be hospitable to all.

Might such an edifice provide a home for occupants other than engineers
of social mechanisms, technicians of networks of solidarity, and experts in
cultural distribution? Might humans of every kind, all with their own ideas
about the collectives to which they belong, animals and machines, plants and
deities, genes and conventions, in fact the whole immense multitude of actual
and potential existing things, find a more welcoming refuge in a new kind of
regime of cohabitation that would once again reject discrimination between
humans and nonhumans, yet without resorting to the formulae tried out in
the past? Maybe, but that is not what I have in mind. For although one may
hope for a cosmology, a social system, or an ideology that could offer such
hospitality, that is not a role that befits an anthropological theory such as the
one that I have roughly sketched in. Its aim is limited to establishing the bases
for a way of conceiving the diversity of the principles of a schematization of
experience that is free of the preconceptions that modernity has led us to
maintain regarding the state of the world. Its purpose is not to propose models of communal life, of new forms of attachment to beings and things, or a reform of practices, mores, and institutions. That such a reform is indispensable
is clearly indicated by everything around us, ranging from the revolting disparity between the conditions of existence in the countries of the South and
the countries of the North across the board to the alarming degradation, as
a result of human action, of the major bases of equilibrium in the biosphere.
However, it would be mistaken to think that the Indians of Amazonia, the
Australian Aboriginals, or the monks of Tibet can bring us a deeper wisdom
for the present time than the shaky naturalism of late modernity. Every type
of presence in the world, every way of connecting with it and making use of it,
constitutes a particular compromise between, on the one hand, the factors of
sensible experience that are accessible to us all, albeit interpreted differently,
and, on the other, a mode of aggregating existing beings that is adapted to historical circumstances. The fact is that none of those compromises, however
worthy of admiration some may be, can provide a source of instruction valid
for all situations. Neither nostalgia for forms of living together, the muted
echoes of which are conveyed to us by ethnographers and historians, nor the
prophetic wishful thinking that animates certain quarters of the scholarly
community offers an immediate answer to the challenge of recomposing into
viable and unified groups an ever-increasing number of existing beings need-
ing to be represented and treated equitably. It is up to each one of us, wherever we may be, to invent and encourage modes of conciliation and types of

pressure capable of leading to a new universality that is both open to all the world's components and also respectful of certain of their idiosyncrasies. We might then hope to avert a distant point of no return when, with the extinction of the human race, the price of passivity would have to be paid in another fashion: namely by abandoning to the cosmos a nature bereft of its recorders simply because they failed to provide it with genuine modes of expression.

Notes

Preface

1. In a splendidly bold political essay, Bruno Latour has sketched what such a refoundation might constitute (Latour 2004).

2. Marx 2010, 300. It is above all in this part of the *Grundrisse*, entitled "Forms Which Precede Capitalist Production," that Marx engaged in his project of regressive history; see the luminous commentary provided by Maurice Godelier in his preface to *Sur les sociétés précapitalistes: Textes choisis de Marx, Engels, Lénine* (1970, 46–51).

3. Marc Bloch 1978, xxvi–xxx.

1. Configurations of Continuity

1. For more details, see Descola 1994a.

2. At any rate, the Achuar constitute an example considered sufficiently typical to have already served as an ethnographic illustration for authors who challenge the universality of the opposition between nature and society (Berque 1995, 1990; Latour 1993).

3. Århem 1996, 1990.

4. M. Brown 1986; J.-P. Chaumeil 1983; Grenand 1980; Jara 1991; Reichel-Dolmatoff 1976, 1996a, 1996b; Renard-Casevitz 1991; Van der Hammen 1992; Viveiros de Castro 1992; Weiss 1975. For similar ideas among the Amerindians of the Pacific coast of Colombia, see Isacsson 1993.

5. Van Der Hammen 1992, 334.

6. Belaunde 1994.

7. B. Chaumeil and J.-P. Chaumeil 1992.

8. B. Berlin 1977.

9. Rivière 1994, for other similar examples.

10. Lima 1996; Viveiros de Castro 1996.

11. Recent works in historical ecology have established that swidden horticulture and the cultivation of trees, practiced for over several thousand years by the native peoples of Amazonia, have produced deep transformations in the composition of forest flora. In particular, they contributed to encouraging the concentration of certain nondomesticated species along with domesticated ones that then reverted to a wild state. The most common are various species of palm trees (*Orbignya phalerata, Bactris gasipaes, Mauritia flexuosa, Maximiliana* sp., *Astrocaryum* sp.)

and trees bearing edible fruit (*Bertholettia excelsa, Platonia insignis, Theobroma* sp., and *Inga* spp.). It also seems that many stands of bamboo (of the *Guadua* genus) and "liana forests" are often the result of human activity. See Balée 1989, 1993.

12. Lévi-Strauss 1966, 214.

13. Reichel-Dolmatoff 1976.

14. Ibid., 316.

15. Ethnographic information relating to the conceptualization and treatment of nonhumans, mainly animals, is particularly rich for groups speaking Algonquian languages—the Cree of Labrador and the southwestern area of Hudson Bay and the northern Ojibwa; but essentially these concepts and practices tally with the more heterogeneous data that is available on the tribes of the Athapaskan group, who inhabit the territory stretching from the northwestern area of Hudson Bay right across to the Pacific side of the Rockies and Alaska. On the Algonquins, see Brightman 1993; Désveaux 1988; Feit 1973; Leacock 1954; Lips 1947; Speck 1935; Tanner 1979. On the Athapaskans, see Nelson 1983; Osgood 1936.

16. The "shaking lodge" ritual is common to the entire subarctic Algonquin area. A man of some experience, in many cases a shaman, withdraws at nightfall into a small hut or tent, where he sings invocations to animal spirits. When these approach, they cause the fragile structure to shake. Throughout the ceremony, the spirits converse among themselves, with the officiant, and with the public seated all around the tent, either in a known language or in an incomprehensible gobbledygook, which the medium interprets (see Désveaux 1995; Brightman 1993, 170–76).

17. See Scott 1989; Tanner 1979, 130, 136; Speck 1935, 72; Brightman 1993, 3.

18. Personal communication from Daniel Clément.

19. Désveaux 1995, 438.

20. Ingold 1996, 131.

21. Blaisel 1993; Fienup-Riordan 1990; Saladin d'Anglure 1990, 1988.

22. Rasmussen 1929, 56.

23. Lévi-Strauss 1970, 8.

24. On Siberia, I have mainly consulted the remarkable synthesis produced by Hamayon, (1990); see also Lot-Falck 1953; Paulson, Hultkrantz, and Jettmar 1965; Zelenin 1952.

25. For the subarctic area, see Brightman 1993, 91. For Amazonia, see Descola 1994a, 260–61.

26. Leroi-Gourhan 1946.

27. Perrin 1995, 9–12.

28. Ibid., 5–9.

29. Hamayon 1982.

30. Eliade 1964, 333–36. Alfred Métraux (1967, 234–35) suggests an identical explanation to account for certain features of the shamanism of the Araucans, who live in the extreme south of South America.

31. Howell 1996, 1989.

32. Endicott 1979.

33. Karim 1981a, 1981b.

34. Karim 1981b, 1; and again, "the Ma' Betisék do not have a general term to describe nature. Animate objects which are non-human (plants and animals) and inanimate objects which are part of the physical environment (wind, sky, thunder, rain, water, etc.) are not collectively categorized as objects of nature" (ibid., 7).

35. Ellen 1993, 94–95.

36. Wagner 1977, 404.

37. Schieffelin 1987.

38. A. Van Beek 1987, 174.

39. Coppet 1995.

40. Hviding 1996, 170.

41. Leenhardt 1979, 172.

42. See Maurice Bloch's analysis (1992) in the context of a Madagascar society.

43. Leenhardt 1979, 20.

44. Ibid., 164.

45. Losonczy 1997.

46. M. Jackson 1990.

47. W. Van Beek and Banga 1992.

48. As André-Georges Haudricourt pointed out in an article (1962) in which he drew a contrast between, on the one hand, "the positive direct action" exercised upon living things by a cultivator of cereals or a shepherd of southern Europe and, on the other, "the negative indirect action" of tuber cultivators, who lavish personal care upon every young plant. For a commentary on this opposition, see chapter 4.

49. Malamoud 1996.

50. Ibid., chap. 4.

51. Ibid., 91.

52. Galey 1993, 49.

53. Berque 1986.

54. Ibid., 176.

55. Berque 1995.

2. The Wild and the Domesticated

1. Michaux 1970, 118.

2. Part of this chapter reproduces my article "Le sauvage et le domestique" (2004). For a distinction between "the ecumene" and the "uninhabited space," see Berque 1986, 66-67.

3. Balikci 1968.

4. Lee 1979, 51-67, 354-59.

5. Turnbull 1965.

6. Mauss 1904-5. We now know that this alternation is fairly generalized among hunter-gatherer people, whatever their latitude (Lee and De Vore 1968).

7. Glowczewski 1991. For similar ideas among the Pintupi, see Myers 1986.

8. Cited by Marcia Langton (1998, 34).

9. Dupire 1962.

10. Ibid., 63n1.

11. Barth 1961.

12. Godelier 1996, 92-95.

13. See Bridges 1988 on Tierra del Fuego, and Leacock 1954 on Canada.

14. Descola 1994a, 160-74. The Aguarana, who are neighbors of the Achuar to the south and who share their material culture, do even better, with approximately two hundred varieties of manioc; see Boster 1980.

15. Piperno 1990.

16. It is thought that the sweet potato, manioc, and the American yam were domesticated about five thousand years ago and *Xanthosoma* taro probably much earlier (Roosevelt 1991, 113).

17. Clifford Geertz was probably one of the first to emphasize this analogy when, on the subject of swidden gardens in the Indonesian archipelago, he described them as "a tropical forest in miniature" (Geertz 1963, 24).

18. For a critical appreciation of the ecological and agricultural efficacy of swidden horticulture, see the special issue of *Human Ecology* (11, no. 1 [1983]) devoted to this subject.

19. Ballée 1989, 1994 (esp. chap. 6 of the latter work).

20. It must be said that this was not always or everywhere the case in the lowlands of South America. In the savannas of the Llanos de Mojos in Bolivia, in the forests of the Ecuadorian upper Amazon, and on the island of Marajó at the mouth of the Amazon, many vestiges of roads, sunken paths, raised fields, residential mounds, and canals testify to the fact that populations of horticulturalists effected modifications to the landscape that no longer have any equivalent among present-day Amerindians. See Denevan 1966; Roosevelt 1991; Rostain 1997; Salazar 1997.

21. A. Strathern 1971, 231.

22. Ibid., 8–9.

23. M. Strathern 1980.

24. Ibid., 193.

25. Dwyer 1996.

26. Ibid., 177–78.

27. I am grateful to Anne Henry for this information.

28. Berque 1986, 69–70.

29. Zimmermann 1987, 10–55.

30. In the Chinese pictorial and literary tradition, "landscape" is expressed by the word *shanshui*, a combination of mountain (*shan*) and waters (*shui*); see Berque 1995, 82. For this passage on China I have relied heavily on this work and also on Granet's two classics (1998, 1968).

31. Berque 1995, 84.

32. Granet 1968, 285.

33. Berque 1986, 73–74.

34. Ibid., 89.

35. As Jacques Le Goff (1990, 131) remarks: "A religion born in the east under the shelter of palms made a way for itself in the west at the cost of trees, for these were a refuge of pagan spirits, and were pitilessly attacked by monks, saints and missionaries."

36. Knight 1996.

37. Zimmermann 1987, chap. 1. For a different interpretation, see Dove 1992.

38. This later antonym for "wild" has been adopted in English (the opposition between "wild" and "civilized") and also in Spanish (*salvaje* and *civilizado*).

39. Oelschlaeger 1991.

40. See, e.g., Hodder 1990

41. Hell 1994.

42. In German, unlike in other European languages, the word "wild," *sauvage* in French, has no automatic antonym. Depending on the context, it may be opposed to a whole collection of terms: *zahm*, "tamed," or, in the case of children or animals, "docile"; *gebildet* or *gesittet*, "cultivated," or, in the case of adult humans, "civilized"; not to mention the many terms derived from *Kultur*, in both their literal sense—*Kulturboden*, "cultivated space or terrain"—and also their figurative sense, *Kultiviert*, "civilized," and *Kulturvolk*, "civilized people," etc.

43. Hell 1994.

44. Ibid., 349–53.

45. On the domestication of animals, see Digard 1990, 105–25. On the transition to the Neolithic in the Near East, see Cauvin 2000, 55–86.

46. This is the hypothesis suggested by Vigne (1993).

47. Vidal-Naquet 1988, 144.

48. Vidal-Naquet 1975.

49. Vidal-Naquet 1988, 144.

50. Hell 1994, 22.

51. According to Columella, cited in Bodson 1995, 124.

52. Schama 1995, 81–87.

53. Duby 1974, 24.

54. In the United States, the transition to a new sensitivity to landscape took longer to develop than in Germany. In 1832, Washington Irving was still describing the landscapes of the Far West by evoking Salvator Rosa and Claude Lorrain (in *A Tour on the Prairies*, cited in Roger 1997, 43n2).

55. On the occasion of his expedition to the Saint-Gothard Pass: "It is vain for me to exert myself to attain the alpine exaltation of the mountain authors: I waste my pains" (Chateaubriand 1902, 286).

3. The Great Divide

1. Legrand, Méjanès, and Starcky 1990.

2. Ibid., 60, 93–94.

3. Gombrich 1966, 107–21. Alain Roger (1997, 73–76) notes that one of the first examples of the use of the device of a "Flemish window" was probably *The Madonna with a Wicker Screen* by Roger Campin, known as "the Master of Flémalle," circa 1420–25 (National Gallery, London).

4. Roger 1997, 76–79.

5. Panofsky 1991.

6. Ibid., 67–72.

7. Ibid., 66.

8. Merleau-Ponty 1964, 50.

9. Roger 1997, 16–20.

10. Panofsky 1991, 58.

11. Lenoble 1969, 312.

12. Latour 1996.

13. This applies to three remarkable studies, with respect both to their erudition and to the subtlety of their judgments: see the above-cited book by Father Lenoble, Moscovici 1977, and Glacken 1967. Although they forthrightly affirm the historicity of the idea of nature, these works do not avoid the preconception that consists in regarding nature as being gradually objectivized on the basis of a universal "given," the externality of which is said to be patently clear to all humans. For a similar view, see Collingwood 1945.

14. This is what Odysseus says: "The Argeiphontes gave me the herb, drawing it from the ground and showed me its nature (*phusis*). . . . Moly the gods call it" (*Odyssey* 10.302; Homer 1919, 381). This was the plant that allowed Odysseus to elude the spells of Circe.

15. Aristotle, *Physics* 2.192b (1929, 109).

16. As is noted by Geoffrey Lloyd (2000, 22): "There is in Homer no over-arching concept or category that picks out the *domain* of nature *as such*—as opposed either to 'culture' or to 'the supernatural'" (italics in original).

17. Hesiod 2006, 275. Marcel Detienne (1979, 57) interprets this passage as a sign of the radical opposition, in Greek thought, between humans and animals, the latter, in contrast to humans, being condemned to devour one another. However, not all animals eat other animals. Hesiod mentions only fish, wild beasts, and birds. Besides, the devouring of one another seems to be an internal feature of each of those categories rather than a general feature of the entire animal kingdom. So it is hard to follow Detienne on this point and to regard allelophagy as a global distinction that the Greeks drew between humans and animals as a whole. I should like to thank Eduardo Viveiros de Castro for drawing my attention to this passage in Hesiod and to Detienne's commentary on it.

18. See the interesting parallel drawn by Lenoble (1969, 60) between the increasing number of statutory guarantees granted to Athenian metics, fixing their different status within a particular legal framework, and the new perception of the externality of a physical world subject to certain laws.

19. Aristotle, *Physics* 2.192b (1929, 107).

20. On the principles of the Aristotelian system, see Atran 1985.

21. Augustine 1956, 45, sec. 7.

22. Arnould 1997.

23. Thomas Aquinas, *Summa theologiae*, pt. 1, question 96, art. 1 (1989, 146).

24. See Duvernay-Bolens 1995, 98.

25. Merleau-Ponty 1994, 25.

26. Spinoza, *Ethics*, pt. 1, appendix to proposition 36 (1910, 30–36); Sir Matthew Hale, *The Primitive Origination of Mankind* (London, 1677), 370, cited in Glacken 1967, 481.

27. Foucault 1970, 71.

28. Ibid., 344.

29. Claude Lévi-Strauss, "Jean-Jacques Rousseau, fondateur des sciences de l'homme," republished in Lévi-Strauss 1978, chap. 11.

30. Émile Durkheim, "Le 'Contrat social' de Rousseau," *Revue de métaphysique et de morale*, March–April 1918, 138–39, cited in Derathé 1974, 239.

31. Kroeber and Kluckhohn 1952.

32. Tylor 1871, 1:1.

33. Stocking 1968, 195–233. While recognizing the role played by Boas in the emergence of the concept of culture in North American anthropology, Adam Kuper (1999, 47–72) considers that the stabilization of that concept in contemporary usage and the elaboration of a veritable culturalist research program came about only much later, thanks to the work of Talcott Parsons and his influence on Clifford Geertz and David Schneider. Although it is true that Boas himself remained unforthcoming on the theoretical implications of the notion of culture that he had introduced in the United States, the importance of his contribution in this domain seems to me to have been underestimated by Kuper.

34. Benveniste 1971, 289–96.

35. Elias 1994, 1:3–41.

36. On the influence of the German tradition on Boas and his disciples, see Stocking 1998.

37. Alfred Kroeber, "The Superorganic" (1917), republished in Kroeber 1952.

38. Boas 1887.

39. Rickert 1962.

40. Ibid., 22.

41. Spinoza, *Ethics*, 1.29, scholium (1910, 24).

42. Berque 1986, 135, 141.

43. Sahlins 1976, 55.

44. Wagner 1981, 142 (italics in original).

45. Durkheim 1995, 24. See also the chapter that Clément Rosset devotes to the relations between nature and religion in philosophy (Rosset 1973).

46. Keil 1989.

47. For fuller details, see chapter 11.

48. Whitehead 1955, 50.

49. Merleau-Ponty 1964, 13.

50. Latour 1993.

51. Ibid., 12.

4. The Schemas of Practice

1. "Thoughts without content are empty, intuitions without concepts are blind" (Kant, "Transcendental Theory of Elements, Introduction to Part II," in Kant 1997, 193–94).

2. Benedict 1934.

3. This is a point that some anthropologists seem to forget when, in the name of the primacy of praxis, they ascribe to the schemas that generate it a flexibility and contingency that more likely characterize the ad hoc elaborations that their informers produce of those schemas.

4. Bourdieu 2000, 151.

5. Lévi-Strauss 1969a, 93.

6. Radcliffe-Brown 1956, 190.

7. On this subject, see Dan Sperber's (1985, chap. 1) excellent analysis of the distinction between interpretative knowledge and theoretical knowledge in anthropology.

8. Lévi-Strauss 1972, 279.

9. Ibid., 284.

10. Ibid., 281–83.

11. Lévi-Strauss 1969a, 443.

12. This point of view is made clear in his polemic with David Maybury-Lewis over dualist systems. The latter complained that Lévi-Strauss had proposed for the spatial and social structure of the Bororo and the Winnebago diagrammatic models that were altogether different from the way in which the peoples themselves codified the dualist organization of their habitat and their internal divisions. To this Lévi-Strauss replied that the purpose of structural analysis was not to apprehend social relations as they manifested themselves empirically but to understand them by constructing ad hoc models that, when manipulated, would reveal properties that could not be observed directly in those relations (Lévi-Strauss 1978, 71–81).

13. Lévi-Strauss 1966, 130.

14. Ibid.

15. Rosch 1973, 1978.

16. An example borrowed from Maurice Bloch (1998, 5).

17. See, e.g., K. Gibson and Ingold 1993; Lave and Wenger 1991.

18. Varela, Rosch, and Thompson 1991, 208.

19. Descola 1994a, 244-51.

20. Kant 1997, 273.

21. On the role of epigenesis in the stabilization of neural networks, see Changeux 1985; for an evolutionary theory of phylogenetic stabilization, see Edelman 1987.

22. For good syntheses of connectionist models, see Bechtel and Abrahamsen 1991; Quinlan 1991.

23. Bechtel and Abrahamsen 1991, 54-55.

24. Strauss and Quinn 1997, 79-82.

25. On psychology, see Mandler 1984; Schank and Abelson 1977; on anthropology, see Strauss and Quinn 1997; D'Andrade 1995; Shore 1996. Roy D'Andrade (1995, 142) gives a good general definition of "schema": "To say that something is a 'schema' is a shorthand way of saying that a distinct and strongly interconnected pattern of interpretative elements can be activated by minimal inputs. A schema is an interpretation which is frequent, well organized, memorable, which can be made from minimal cues, contains one or more prototypic instantiations, is resistant to change, etc. While it would be more accurate to speak always of *interpretations with such and such a degree of schematicity*, the convention of calling highly schematic interpretations 'schemas' remains in effect in the cognitive literature" (italics in original).

26. Thus, Susan Carey (Carey 1985; Carey and Spelke 1994) adopts a neo-epigenetic position when she postulates that the properties implicitly attributed to nonhuman organisms are constructed little by little by differentiating them from the properties ascribed to persons, while Frank Keil (1994, 1989) thinks that "modes of construal" of the environment—whether mechanical, intentional, teleological, functional, etc.—which are at the origin of the formation of "naive theories," are "givens" right from the start. We should note that, even if their universality were confirmed, the possible existence of ontological categories such as "person," "artifact," and "natural object," whether innate or acquired in the first years of development, does not necessarily imply the universality of an ontological distinction between culture and nature or between humans and nonhumans. The properties that these categories schematize are activated in particular situations, frequently ones of an experimental type, and coexist perfectly well alongside counterintuitive beliefs concerning the behavior ascribed to certain members of those categories. Thus, the possible universality of an attributive schema making it possible to distinguish intuitively between humans and animals in no way prevents the Dorzé of Ethiopia (to borrow an example from Dan Sperber) from asserting in good faith that a leopard literally respects the fasting periods prescribed by the Coptic calendar or that humans can turn into were-hyenas at night (Sperber 1975, 129-30).

27. See Bourdieu's famous analysis of the Kabyle house (1979) or, in an altogether different cultural context, my own analysis of the Achuar house (Descola 1994a, chap. 4).

28. Bourdieu 1984; Mauss 1935.

29. In their essential properties, what I call integrating schemas in many ways resemble what Bradd Shore calls "foundational schemas" (1996, 53-54). But they differ on two points, which I mention briefly here but will explain more fully later on. In the first place, "foundational schemas" are characteristic above all of modes of organizing space or of arranging things in space, at least that is what they do to judge by the examples that Shore provides of the modular distribution of North American institutions, the contrast between the center and the periphery in Samoa, and the "Dream-times" itineraries of the Australian Aboriginals. In contrast, integrating schemas are more likely to structure relationship systems. Furthermore, Shore

seems to assume that every culture is defined by its specific foundational schemas, whereas integrating schemas seemingly stem from a general repertory within which only their combinations vary.

30. Haudricourt 1962, 41-43.

31. See, e.g., Squire 1987, 39-55.

32. Gick and Holyoak 1983. For a discussion of this work and the contributions that cognitive psychology has made to the theory of schematism, see Shore 1996, 353-56.

33. As B. Shore perceives when he borrows concepts from Piaget to designate these two phases: "assimilation" is the organization of novel experiences in relation to preexisting schemas, whereas "accommodation" is where the schemas themselves are transformed (or even created) by their encounter with novel experiences (1996, 367-68).

5. Relations with the Self and Relations with Others

1. Mauss 1974, 130. See also Durkheim (1995, 240): "If primitives confuse things between which we distinguish, conversely, they distinguish between things that we associate."

2. See, for example, the studies collected in Lambek and Strathern 1998 and Godelier and Panoff 1998. We should note that the editors of the latter work forthrightly recognize in their introduction that "the question to resolve is why humanity . . . seems to have been led to represent a human being as being composed of two parts, one perishable and one that continues to exist and act long after death" (xiv).

3. Mauss 1950, 355.

4. Benveniste 1971, chaps. 20-21.

5. M. Strathern 1988, 268-70.

6. Leenhardt 1979; LiPuma 1998.

7. In particular, the late Gilles Châtelet (2000).

8. "It is not sufficient that it [the soul] be lodged in the human body exactly like a pilot in a ship, unless perhaps to move its members, but that it is necessary for it to be joined and united more closely to the body, in order to have sensations and appetites similar to ours, and thus constitute a real man" (Descartes 1912, 46).

9. Tylor 1871, chaps. 11-18.

10. Bloom 2004.

11. Damasio 1999; Dennett 1991.

12. On the latter theme, see Hacking 1995.

13. Pitarch 1996; Dieterlen 1973.

14. Lévi-Strauss 1969b.

15. For Lévi-Strauss, this kind of relationship has nothing to do with totemism, even if it is sometimes found to be combined with it, as in the case of the Ojibwa, where the "*Manido* system" (individual animal spirits) and the "totem system" (eponymous animals) are juxtaposed (ibid., 86-92).

16. Descola 1992, 1996a.

17. That is the perfectly relevant objection that Eduardo Viveiros de Castro made to my initial theory of animism, although he was charitable enough to address it to an author who had taken over the theory in an overhasty formulation (1996, 120-23; 1998, 472-73).

18. Viveiros de Castro 1996, 121; 1998, 473.

19. Gabriel Tarde, with his ontology of differences, constitutes a notable exception in this

respect, but his influence was so firmly checked by the followers of Durkheim that his impact on French twentieth-century sociology may be considered marginal: see Tarde 1999.

6. Animism Restored

1. Viveiros de Castro 1996, 129; 1998, 479.

2. Durkheim 1995, 273.

3. Surrallés 2003, 66.

4. Mauzé 1998, 240.

5. Brunois 2001, 115, 199.

6. Leenhardt 1979, 164. That is the interpretation proposed by Jean-Pierre Vernant (1986).

7. Leenhardt 1979, 20.

8. Taylor 1998, 323-24.

9. Århem 1996, 188.

10. Gray 1997, 120.

11. Hallowell 1976, 368. It is true that he does explicitly say "outward appearance is only an incidental attribute of being" (373). All the same, Hallowell also, with many examples, stresses the permanence of customs, particularly dietary ones, that are linked with the form of a species. "Thunder Birds," for example, which are also the "Masters" of sparrow hawks, feed, as the latter do, on frogs and snakes, but in their human form, they will present these prey to an Ojibwa guest as a beaver stew (371).

12. Howell 1996, 131.

13. On the Makuna, see Århem 1990, 108-15; on the Wari', see Vilaça 1992, 55-63.

14. Iteanu 1998, 119.

15. Ingold 1998, 194.

16. Århem 1996, 194.

17. See the series of Matsiguenga myths published by F.-M. Renard-Casevitz (1991).

18. Contrary to what Ingold (1998, 184), who seems to follow Hallowell on this point (see n. 11, above), says: "The generation of animate form in any one region [of the cosmos] necessarily entails its dissolution in another. . . . For this reason, no form is ever permanent." This assuredly applies at the level of individuals, not at that of species.

19. Hallowell 1976, 377, 365, 372.

20. Ibid., 380.

21. On the metamorphosis of animals into humans, see the examples of the Makuna (Århem 1996, 188), circumpolar societies (Ingold 1998, 185), the Ojibwa (Hallowell 1976, 377), the Tsimshian (Guédon 1994, 142), and the Chewong (Howell 1996, 135). On the metamorphosis of humans into animals, see the examples of the Chewong (Howell 1996, 135), circumpolar societies (Ingold 1998, 185), the Ojibwa (Hallowell 1976, 374), the Tsimshian (Guédon 1994, 142), and the Makuna (Århem 1996, 188).

22. The metamorphosis of humans into plants is mentioned among the Chewong, as is the appearance of a plant in human form (Howell 1996, 135); similar cases of the latter are also reported among the Achuar and the Yagua of Peruvian Amazonia (J.-P. Chaumeil 1983, 74-79). Metamorphosis of one animal species into another is accepted among the Makuna (Århem 1996, 188).

23. On the contrasts between shamanism and possession, see Luc de Heusch's classic study (1981, 151-64).

24. Howell 1996, 133; Hamayon 1990, 296; Ingold 1998, 185; Tanner 1979, 136; J. Brown 1997, 13; Århem 1996, 190.

25. Howell 1996, 134.

26. Viveiros de Castro 1996, 1998.

27. Viveiros de Castro 1996, 117; 1998, 470.

28. Viveiros de Castro 1996, 125; 1998, 476.

29. Viveiros de Castro 1996, 126; 1998, 476.

30. Viveiros de Castro 1996, 126; 1998, 476–77.

31. Durkheim 1995, 273.

32. See the itemized list produced by Viveiros de Castro (1996, nn. 3–4; 1998, nn. 3–4).

33. Our sources are not totally silent on this question, although they do usually refer to it in a roundabout manner. The inference is that animals see humans as such thanks to the fact, attested in many examples, that animals, or their representatives, establish with humans or accept from them the ordinary relations that exist between humans themselves; and to do so they generally take on a human form that is, as it were, a token of recognition. Thus, the Yagua of Peruvian Amazonia tell the story of a hunter who pays a visit to the mistress of the animals that inhabit an *aguajal* (a flooded palm grove) in order to negotiate the hunting of game there (J.-P. Chaumeil 1983, 182–83); G. Reichel-Dolmatoff refers to animals that visit Desana hunters (in Colombian Amazonia) in their dreams in the form of young girls decked out in seductive apparel (1971, 225); an Achuar tells of his friendship with an otter in human form, one of the incarnations of the Tsunki spirit of the waters (Descola 1996b, 143); finally, among the Cree, it is customary for hunters to explain to a bear that they are about to kill the reason why they are hunting it, and they maintain that the bear understands what they say (Tanner 1979, 146). It seems unlikely that such interactions would be considered possible if the animals regarded humans simply as either predatory animals or prey.

34. Viveiros de Castro 1996, 122.

7. Totemism as an Ontology

1. Lévi-Strauss 1969b, 10–11.

2. Ibid.

3. Ibid., 114.

4. Ibid., 114–15 (my italics).

5. Some years ago I read an incisive article by Luc Racine (1989) that began to undermine my belief concerning the universality of Lévi-Strauss's explanation of totemism, although at that time it did not overcome my dogmatic laziness and persuade me to undertake the necessary task of bringing my ideas up to date. Upon rereading it ten years after it first appeared, I was convinced that I should revise my opinions. The remarks that follow owe much to that article's stimulating effect.

6. Spencer and Gillen 1899, 112.

7. The hypothesis of evolution by diversification from a common kernel was suggested by Spencer and Gillen as early as 1899 (ibid.). For a recent version of this hypothesis, founded on linguistic criteria, see Brandenstein 1982, chap. 10. The hypothesis that the number of classes varies as a result of an adaptation to water resources has been developed by A. A. Yengoyan (1968).

8. The literature on Dreaming is immense, for most specialists on Australia have tackled this

subject. For a good synthesis in French, see Glowczewski 1991, chap. 2; on Dreaming among the Aranda, see Moisseeff 1995, chap. 1.

9. Radcliffe-Brown 1956, 246.

10. Spencer and Gillen 1899, 119.

11. Elkin 1933.

12. Lévi-Strauss 1969b, 44–47.

13. Elkin 1933, 115, 116.

14. Ibid., 119.

15. Ibid., 121.

16. Ibid., 129.

17. Ibid.

18. Brandenstein 1982.

19. Ibid., 6–7, 170–72.

20. Worsley 1967.

21. J. Mathew, *Two Representative Tribes of Queensland* (London, 1910), 160, cited in Brandenstein 1982, 14.

22. Brandenstein 1982, 82.

23. Ibid., 54.

24. Brandenstein 1977.

25. Kirton and Timothy 1977.

26. Merlan 1980.

27. Ibid., 88–89 (my italics).

28. Spencer and Gillen 1899, 202.

29. Ibid.

30. Moisseeff 1995, 30.

31. Ibid., 43–44.

32. Lévi-Strauss 1966, 117.

33. Swanton 1928.

34. Long 1904.

35. Hallowell 1976, 369.

36. Fogelson and Brightman 2002.

37. Long 1904, 10.

38. Cited in Fogelson and Brightman 2002, 307.

39. William Jones, "Algonquian (Fox)," rev. Truman Michelson, in *Handbook of American Indian Languages*, vol. 1, ed. Franz Boas, Bulletin of the Bureau of American Ethnology 40 (Washington, DC: Smithsonian Institution, 1911), 735–873, cited in Fogelson and Brightman 2002, 308.

40. Désveaux 1988, 282.

41. Speck 1917.

8. The Certainties of Naturalism

1. Descola 1996a, 88.

2. Viveiros de Castro 1996, 116; 1998, 470.

3. Montaigne 1987, 25; Pierre Bayle's remark, formulated in his *Dictionnaire historique et critique*, is noted by Gossiaux (1995, 191).

4. Montaigne 1987, 29.

5. Ibid., 20.

6. Ibid., 24.

7. Pierre de la Primaudaye, *Suite de l'Académie francaise en laquelle il est traité de l'homme . . .* , 3rd ed. reviewed and expanded by the author (Paris: G. Chaudière, 1588), rediscovered by P.-P. Gossiaux, who has published extracts from it (1995, 112–17); I found my references in this work.

8. Gossiaux 1995, 114.

9. Ibid.

10. Ibid., 117.

11. Condillac 1947, 347.

12. Ibid., 365.

13. Ibid., 371.

14. Ingold 1994, 19. There are, of course, some brilliant exceptions, such as the philosopher Joëlle Proust (1997), who investigates the minimal conditions that a structure must satisfy in order to constitute a mind regardless of the nature of its physical embodiment.

15. Mentioned in Ingold 1994, 27. This attitude is hard to shift: I am told that first-year students of biology, when asked to draw a taxonomic tree including *Homo sapiens*, link this taxon to the tree by means of a dotted line!

16. Griffin 1991.

17. Griffin 1976.

18. E.g., Cosmides and Tooby 1994; and also works that claim to stem from the "optimal foraging theory," such as Kaplan and Hill 1985.

19. McGrew and Tutin 1978.

20. McGrew 1992.

21. Whiten et al., 1999.

22. Itani and Nishimura 1973.

23. Byrne and Whiten 1998, 1988.

24. Tomasello and Call 1997.

25. For an ambitious synthesis on this question, see Hauser 1996.

26. Cheney and Seyfarth 1980; Marler and Evans 1996.

27. Gyger and Marler 1988; Hauser and Marler 1993.

28. Marler 1984, 1991.

29. Varela, Rosch, and Thompson 1991.

30. Ibid., 176.

31. J. Gibson 1979.

32. Ibid., 255.

33. Ingold 2000, 166–68; Berque 1990, 101–3.

34. Ingold 2000, 165.

35. Changeux 1985, 275.

36. Ibid., 275.

37. Davidson 1980, esp. 207–27.

38. Descombes 2001, 232.

39. Unlike Joëlle Proust (1997, 72–79), who criticizes Davidson on this point.

40. This was not the case in the Middle Ages and the Renaissance, when lawsuits against animals were common, a fact that shows that they were sometimes recognized to possess the quality of a moral and legal person. For particularly striking examples, see Agnel 1858.

41. Ferry 1995 provides a good illustration, but notable exceptions do exist, e.g., Berque 1996 and, from a different point of view, Latour 2004.

42. See, e.g., Larrère 1997, which provides a succinct and excellent synthesis on this question.

43. Singer 1979.

44. Singer 1989.

45. Regan 1983.

46. Leopold 1987.

47. Ibid., 137–40, for "thinking like a mountain," and 111–15, for the odyssey of an atom.

48. Ibid., 188.

49. Callicott 1989.

50. Marguénaud 1998.

51. Darwin 1871.

52. Tort 1992, 26.

53. Both Latour (1999, 77; this passage omitted from Latour 2004) and Ingold (2000, 40–42), each in his own way, have highlighted this regressive paradox.

9. The Dizzying Prospects of Analogy

1. Lovejoy 1961.

2. Ibid., 59.

3. Plotinus, *Enneads* 3.2.16 (1967, 99).

4. See, e.g., Augustine 1982, 74.

5. Aquinas, *Summa contra Gentiles*, bk. 2, chap. 45, § 9 (1956, 138–39).

6. Leibniz, *De Rerum Originatione Radicali* (1908, 107).

7. In a letter from Leibniz cited in Lovejoy 1961, 145, from the Buchenau and Cassirer edition entitled *Leibniz: Hauptschriften zur Grundlegung der Philosophie* (1903), 2:556–59.

8. Foucault 1970, 17.

9. Granet 1968. This classic work shows clearly that, contrary to the claims of Durkheim and Mauss, the "sympathetic" actions and astrological influences that characterize Chinese divination do not in any sense testify to "a more or less complete absence of defined concepts" (Durkheim and Mauss 1963, 5–6). On the contrary, they suggest a tenacious determination to do away with all the discontinuities of reality, the better to reconstitute it in a tight web of analogies.

10. Cited in Granet 1968, to whom I am also indebted for the *Xici* commentary.

11. López Austin 1988; the original edition was published in Mexico in 1980.

12. López Austin 1988, 204.

13. On the Otomi, see Galinier 2004, 229; on *sombra*, see Aguirre Beltrán 1963, 109–10.

14. Guiteras Holmes 1961, 307, 296–98; Holland 1963, 99.

15. Fray Alonso de Molina, *Vocabulario*, pt. 1, fol. 119r; cited in López Austin 1988, 199.

16. López Austin 1988, 201.

17. Charles Wisdom, *Los Chortís de Guatemala* (Guatemala: Editorial del Ministerio de Educación Pública, 1944), 375, cited in López Austin 1988, 233.

18. López Austin 1988, 347.

19. Granet 1968.

20. López Austin 1988, 346.

21. Ibid., 354–55.

22. Ibid., 356.

23. Foster 1944.

24. Guiteras Holmes 1961, 300.

25. Ariel de Vidas 2002, 253–59.

26. Galinier 2004, 209–10.

27. López Austin 1988, 374.

28. Ibid., 373.

29. Redfield and Villa Rojas 1964, 130.

30. E. Berlin and B. Berlin 1996, 62–63.

31. Ichon 1969, 41–42.

32. Foster 1953.

33. For a detailed examination of the arguments and refutations put forward by both camps in this controversy, see López Austin 1988, 270–82.

34. In China, *yin* and *yang* are often characterized above all by the complementary opposition between hot and cold; on Ayurvedic medicine, see Zimmermann 1989; on West Africa, see the exemplary case of the Samo (Héritier 1996).

35. That is also the interpretation favored by Ryesky (1976, 33).

36. Cited in López Austin 1988, 349, on the basis of the Spanish edition of the *Comentarios al Códice Borgia*, ed. E. Seler, 1:207.

37. An example is the use of cold baths or exposure to intense heat in order to restore the thermal equilibrium of the organism, an idea that Francisco Hernandez mocks in his *Historia natural de Nueva España* (see the commentary in López Austin 1988, 274).

38. Jean Chiappino notes that there are hints of the use of the hot and the cold in the shamanistic treatments practiced by certain populations in Venezuelan Amazonia and in the Guianas (the breath of a shaman "cools" potentially contaminatory foodstuffs, and cold baths or exposure to the heat of a fire restore the equilibrium of the body), but such practices, which anyway receive little comment, are confined solely to the domain of health and affect not at all any generalized thermal classifications of the kind that are to be found in Mexico, in China, in certain parts of West Africa, and in Ayurvedic medicine, to cite but a few examples (Chiappino 1997).

39. Bachelard 2002, 176.

40. Hampaté Ba 1973, 182.

41. Ibid.

42. Ibid., 187–88.

43. Héritier 1977.

44. Ibid., 65.

45. Dieterlen 1973.

46. Griaule 1938, 160.

47. Dieterlen 1973, 215.

48. W. Van Beek and Banga 1992, 68–69.

49. Le Moal 1973, 198–99.

50. Griaule 1966, 121.

51. Hampaté Ba 1973, 187; Héritier 1977, 65.

52. Dumont 1980.

53. See the chapter "The Right and the Left in China" in Granet 1963 (English translation in Needham 1973, 43–58).

54. It is true that slightly to the south of the subarctic region, the Iroquois, the Fox, and the

Winnebago did practice a ritual killing of a dog that closely resembled a sacrifice; see Schwartz 1997, 83–85.

55. On the Cashibo, see Frank 1987; on the Ghiliak, see Sternberg 1905, esp. 260–74.

56. Lévi-Strauss 1966, 225.

57. Ibid.

58. Evans-Pritchard 1956, 183–85.

10. Terms, Relations, Categories

1. Merlan 1980, 88; Elkin 1933, 121; Glowczewski 1991, 44; Lévi-Strauss 1966, 114–15.

2. Jakobson and Halle 1975, 69–96.

3. For an example of a componential analysis, see Lounsbury 1956; for prototypical classification, see Rosch 1973; B. Berlin 1992.

4. Granet 1968, 308.

11. The Institution of Collectives

1. The term "collective" is here used in the sense popularized by Bruno Latour (1993), that is, as a procedure of grouping, or "collecting," humans and nonhumans into a network of specific interrelations. It is distinguished from the classic term "society" in that it does not apply solely to a group of human subjects who are thereby detached from the web of relations that link them to the nonhuman world.

2. Bogoras 1904–9, 281.

3. Conklin 2001, 120–21.

4. Rival 2002, 79.

5. Ingold 1996, 125–26 (italics in original).

6. Bird-David 1990.

7. Ingold 1996, 134.

8. As in the case, for example, of the contrast evoked in chapter 1 between the parrot and the oropendola, which the Mai Huna use to refer to the difference between the sexes among humans.

9. Fausto 2001, 413–18.

10. This is precisely the mechanism that I sought to emphasize when, in the past, I defined "animism" as the use of the elementary categories of social practice in order to think through the relations between humans and plants or animals. I did not, of course, have in mind the idea sanctioned by anthropological tradition ever since Durkheim according to which relations with natural objects are metaphorical projections of the relations between humans. I think it necessary to make this clear since it is on the basis of that formulation that T. Ingold (2000, 107) reckons that I have regressed into the rut of "projective" interpretations. In truth, I have never claimed that intentionality is a specifically human aptitude projected on to nonhumans, as Ingold accuses me of doing, for that would be a position all the more absurd given that even the most entrenched advocates of cognitive realism are now inclined to recognize as universally intuitive the belief that animals should be attributed an intentionality and a representational capacity that have a causal effect upon their behavior.

11. Viveiros de Castro 1986, 623–700; my interpretation simplifies a complex argument of dazzling subtlety.

12. Erikson 1996, 79.

13. *Leviathan*, 1.14 (Hobbes 1991, 97).

14. E. Viveiros de Castro (2002, 375–76), for his part, describes animism as anthropomorphic, in contrast to the narcissistic anthropocentrism of Western evolutionism.

15. Spencer and Gillen 1927, 154–57, 148–53.

16. Glowczewski 1991, 32–33.

17. Ashley Montagu 1974, 7.

18. Merlan 1986, 475.

19. Povinelli 1993, 141, 142.

20. Moisseeff 1995, 100.

21. Povinelli 1993, 141–42.

22. Ibid., 148. For analogous formulations concerning the Warlpiri and the Pintupi, see Munn 1970; Myers 1986, 50.

23. See Lévi-Strauss's discussion of the relation between totem and caste in chapter 4 of Lévi-Strauss 1966.

24. Breton 1999.

25. Wachtel 1990.

26. Ibid., 36.

27. Zuidema 1964.

28. Wachtel 1990, 187.

29. Ibid., 192.

30. Izard 1992.

31. See, e.g., Favre 1971, chap. 2.

32. See Françoise Héritier-Augé's preface to Zuidema 1986. Maurice Duval even uses the term in the title of his monograph (1986).

12. Metaphysics of Morals

1. Marx 2010, 12.

2. Lévi-Strauss 1976, 76. E. Viveiros de Castro drew my attention to this passage.

3. Viveiros de Castro 1996, 128; 1998, 478 (italics in original). My own ideas about animist epistemology owe much to the lines of inquiry opened up by this article.

4. Descola 1996b, 374–75.

5. Viveiros de Castro 1996, 126; 1998, 476.

6. S. Hugh-Jones 1996, 129; Overing Kaplan 1975, 39.

7. Reichel-Dolmatoff 1971, 82.

8. Karim 1981b, 8.

9. For a critique of the interpretation of Amazonian hunting rituals as expressions of a "guilty conscience," see Descola 1999.

10. On the nature of transformation in Australian totemism, see Munn 1970.

11. Brightman 1993, 2; see also, on the Yu'pik Eskimos, A. Fienup-Riordan's (1990, 9) comment: "Just as gender may provide the 'master code' for Melanesia . . . the relationship between humans and animals may provide a comparable master code in some parts of the Arctic."

12. Turner 1995, 168.

13. That is what is definitely implied by E. Viveiros de Castro's analyses of Tupi cannibalism (1986, 646–78) and A. C. Taylor's analyses of Jivaro head-hunting (1993).

14. This is a contrast that Alain Testart saw clearly (1987).

15. Munn 1970.

16. Ibid., n. 6.

17. Ibid., 146.

18. Ibid., 157.

19. Spencer and Gillen 1899, 202.

20. For this analysis of *churinga* as tools of individualization, I have drawn heavily upon the fine study by Moisseeff (2002).

21. Lévi-Strauss 1966, 11 (italics in original).

22. The late Francisco Varela, an eminent neurobiologist and a convinced Buddhist, provides an exemplary illustration.

23. Malamoud 1987.

24. Ibid., 175.

25. Latour 1993, 105.

13. Forms of Attachment

1. Lévi-Strauss 1969a, 84.

2. Aristotle, *Nicomachean Ethics* 5.5, 6: "But in the interchange of services Justice, in the form of Reciprocity, is the bond that maintains the association" (1926, 281). Seneca, *De beneficiis* 1.4: "What we need is a discussion of benefits and the rules for a practice that constitutes the chief bond of human society" (1935, 19).

3. *Année sociologique*, republished in Mauss 1950, 145–279.

4. Claude Lévi-Strauss, "Introduction à l'œuvre de Marcel Mauss," in ibid., xxxix.

5. Ibid., xlvi.

6. Seneca, *De beneficiis* 1.3 (1935, 13).

7. Vidal 1991. Maurice Godelier addresses another criticism to Mauss (and to Lévi-Strauss). He claims that they did not draw the consequences from the fact that a thing given is not alienated by reason of having been given, since the giver continues to be present in that thing and through it exercises pressure on the receiver, not to give it back but, himself, to give it away. According to Godelier, such an enigma becomes comprehensible only if the things that one gives are defined by those that one does not give, chief among the latter being sacred objects that represent collective identities and their temporal continuity; it is because such objects exist that exchange is possible: "The formula for social behaviour is thus . . . to keep in order [to be able] to give and to give in order [to be able] to keep" (Godelier 1999, 36, modified).

8. Testart 1997.

9. Ibid., 43.

10. Ibid., 51.

11. Bird-David 1990.

12. Bird-David 1999, 72.

13. Ingold 2000, 70 (italics in original).

14. See, e.g., Overing and Passes 2000, esp. the preface and the introduction.

15. Thom 1990, 222–31, 526–30.

16. Descola 1990, 1992, 1993.

17. Viveiros de Castro 1993.

18. See Taylor 1993, 1996; Fausto 2001; Surrallés 2003.

19. Sahlins 1968, 82–86. Sahlins adopts this typology from Service 1966.

20. Marx 2010, 277.

21. Ibid.

22. Ibid., 278.

23. Ibid., 282.

24. As Chris Gregory (1982, 31–32) saw clearly in his study of the circulation of goods in Melanesia.

25. Bird-David 1992, 40; Ingold 2000, 58–59.

26. Jullien 1989.

27. Ibid., 85.

28. Plato, *Timaeus* 33a–34c (1929, 61–65).

29. Descola 1994a, chaps. 5–9.

30. Van Velthem 2000, 2001.

31. Van Velthem 2001, 206.

32. Evans-Pritchard 1940, 36.

33. Ibid., 19.

34. Lienhardt 1961, 16.

35. Virgil, *Georgics* 2.514–15.

36. Hamayon 1990, chap. 12.

37. For a fuller analysis of the case of the Exirit-Bulagat, see chap. 15, below.

38. Fortes 1959.

39. Ibid., 50.

40. Legendre 1985, 80.

41. Sophocles, *Oedipus at Colonus*, line 1224 (1994, 547).

42. Although published over thirty years ago, the critique of the application of the African model of transmission to the Amerindian context proposed by A. Seeger, R. Da Matta, and E. Viveiros de Castro (1979) remains totally up to date.

43. Ingold 2000, 140–46.

44. Ibid., 140: "I believe that a relational model, with the rhizome rather than the tree as its core image, better conveys the sense that so-called indigenous people have of themselves and of their place in the world."

14. The Traffic of Souls

1. Mauss 1950, 391.

2. Lévi-Strauss 1943.

3. Viveiros de Castro 2002, 164.

4. That is why it is pointless to oppose, as some do, two approaches to Amazonian sociability that are irreconcilable: on the one hand, that of the "hawk" camp, the partisans of ontological predation, supposedly led by Viveiros de Castro and myself; on the other, the "dove" camp, which defends the aesthetic of conviviality, led by Overing (Santos Granero 2000). For my part, I have never suggested that predation is the only way of treating "others" in Amazonia.

5. This presentation of Jivaro head-hunting is inspired by Taylor 1985 and 1993. For a more detailed analysis of Jivaro forms of warfare, see Descola 1993.

6. The mechanisms most commonly employed to this end are the assimilation of cross-sibling relationships and relationships of conjugality, the affinization of masculine consanguines by men, the consanguinization of affines of both sexes by women, the obliteration of affinity

between coresidents of opposite sexes in the same generation and its accentuation in alternate generations. On this subject, see Taylor 1983.

7. On the Juruna, see Lima 1996; on the Araweté, see Viveiros de Castro 1986; on the Parakanã, see Fausto 2001; on the Mundurucú, see Menget 1993; on the Pirahã, see Gonçalves 2001; on the Wari', see Vilaça 1992; on the Yanomami, see Albert 1985; on the Nivacle, see Sterpin 1993.

8. On the Sioux, see J. Brown 1997; Désveaux 1997. On the Chippewa, see Ritzenthaler 1978.

9. On the Kasua, see Brunois 2001; on the Iban, see Freeman 1979.

10. I am referring to the eastern Tukanos (Desana, Makuna, Tatuyo, Barasana, etc.), who, together with the western Tukanos (Coreguaje, Siona, Secoya, Mai Huna, etc.), make up the Tukano linguistic family. I will use the term "Tukano" to refer to the entire group of eastern Tukanos.

11. In particular, Reichel-Dolmatoff 1971, 1996a.

12. Reichel-Dolmatoff 1971, 220.

13. Cayón 2002.

14. Århem 1996; Cayón 2002, 206.

15. Cayón 2002.

16. J. Jackson 1983, esp. chap. 5.

17. Reichel-Dolmatoff 1971, 17-18.

18. S. Hugh-Jones 1979.

19. On the Wayãpi, see Grenand 1980; on the Akuriyó, see Jara 1991; on the upper Xingu River, see Franchetto and Heckenberger 2001.

20. Hamayon 1990, 374.

21. Kemlin 1999, 165-283.

22. My sources on the Ashaninka are Weiss 1975; Rojas Zolezzi 1994; Varese 2002. On the Matsiguenga, my sources are Renard-Casevitz 1985, 1991; Baer 1994; Rosengren 1987.

23. According to Weiss (1975, 264), this figure is feminine, but it is presented as masculine by Rojas (and J. Elick), as is the master of the Cervidae (Rojas Zolezzi 1994, 180n24).

24. Rojas Zolezzi 1994, 205.

25. Renard-Casevitz 1985, 88; Rosengren 1987, 63-64, 161.

26. Renard-Casevitz 1985.

27. Santos Granero 1991, 201-5, 295-96.

28. Ordinaire 1892, 144-45.

29. Santos Granero 2002, 44-47; except for the Guajiros, however, who engage in permanent vendettas.

30. Admittedly, the obsession with predation is not totally absent among the northern Algonquin groups. Here it is represented by Windigo (or Wiitiko), a cannibalistic monster in human form that terrorizes the Indians. However, unlike the evil Ashaninka spirits, who are said to be responsible for very concrete evils, in the anecdotes that tell of encounters with the Windigo, the latter is always overcome by the humans (Désveaux 1988, 261-65).

31. According to A. I. Hallowell (1976, 385), the sharing of one's possessions is one of the "supreme values" of the Ojibwa culture.

32. Désveaux 1988, 264.

33. Rasmussen 1929; Howell 1989; T. Gibson 1986.

34. C. Hugh-Jones 1979, 223; Århem 1981, 160.

35. C. Hugh-Jones 1979, 64.

36. Århem 1996. When he emphasizes the predatory aspect of the Makuna cosmology,

Århem implicitly distances himself from the "exchange" interpretation of the Tukano model that I had produced in an earlier publication and that he cites but does not openly criticize (Descola 1992). The point did not pass unnoticed by Peter Rivière (2001), who declared himself in agreement with Århem on the fact that, contrary to what I had suggested when I opposed the Jivaros to the Tukanos from the point of view of their relational schemas with others, Amazonian cosmologies are transformations of one fundamental model in which predation and exchange are closely combined. Neither Århem nor Rivière seems to have noticed that in my view the predominance of predation or of exchange in a collective by no means excludes expression of the other schema, which, however, is subordinate to the dominant one.

37. Århem 1996, 191–92. To dissipate any ambiguity, he adds, "Men supply the Spirit-owners of the animals with 'spirit-foods' (coca, snuff and burning bees wax). In return, the Spirits allocate game animals and fish to human beings" (ibid.).

38. Surrallés 2003.

39. See Whitten 1976.

40. This notion of a collective is closer, in its extension if not in its meaning, to what L. Boltanski and L. Thévenot (2006) have called "cities," that is to say, social models founded on conventions that are shared by subgroups of individuals within industrial societies and that allow these to set up differentiated common worlds. "Cities" resemble collectives that are identifiable from their combination of dominant schemas of identification and relations; in the very midst of the categorial entities of classic sociology (classes, sexes, income levels, professions, political opinions), "cities" carve out contrasting forms of coexistence and social links (the "ideal city," "the domestic city," "the city of opinions," etc.), which blur the conventional frontiers between groups and redistribute the criteria for drawing distinctions.

15. Histories of Structures

1. Speck 1935, 82–86. On the connection with migrations, see Clément 1995, 280–81; on the contrast between the Caribou-Man and other masters of game, see Bouchard and Maillot 1972, 61.

2. Tanner 1979, 136–38.

3. Bogoras 1904–9, 268–87.

4. Hamayon 1990, 294, 323.

5. Anisimov 1963, 108.

6. Bogoras 1904–9, 287–88.

7. Ibid., 380–81.

8. T. Ingold (1986, chap. 10) saw this clearly in a study in which he also compared the treatment of wild animals by the hunters of northern North America and by Siberian peoples. However, his perspective differs from mine in the present work in that he considers that the killing of game in subarctic America prefigured the sacrifice of reindeer in Siberia, whereas, as will be seen below, the two phenomena seem to me to stem from different logics.

9. Bogoras 1904–9, 368–70.

10. Ibid., 348–61.

11. Ibid., 281.

12. Pedersen 2001; see also Hamayon 1990, where Hamayon draws a distinction between the "hunting shamanism" of the people of the taiga and the "livestock-raising shamanism" of the southern Buryats. See also Levin and Potapov 1964.

13. Pedersen 2001, 418–19, following Humphrey and Onon 1996.

14. Hamayon 1990, chap. 12.

15. Ibid., 629–30.

16. Ibid., 608.

17. Ibid., 671–78.

18. Van Stone 2000.

19. Some of the reflections that follow are reproduced from an earlier study (Descola 1994b).

20. For a complete inventory of taming practices in Amazonia, see Erikson 1984.

21. Geoffroy Saint-Hilaire 1861, 155, cited in Digard 1988, 34.

22. Feer 1993.

23. Grzimek 1975, 13.29.

24. Alvard and Kuznar 2001.

25. According to Digard 1990, 96–97.

26. Sowls 1974, 160.

27. See, in particular, Morton 1984, on South America, and Hunn 1982, on Central America, where the collared peccary is also present.

28. Lévi-Strauss 1970, 87.

29. This is confirmed by the example of the "Indian horsemen" of the southern part of the continent (Tehuelches, Guaycurus, etc.) and above all the Guajiros, who, having adopted the raising of cattle, horses, sheep, and goats as early as the sixteenth century, rapidly became veritable nomadic herdsmen without, however, abandoning either hunting or the system of representation associated with it (see Perrin 1987; Picon 1983).

30. Alvard 1998.

31. This was suggested by Sigaut (1980).

32. I certainly respect the reasoning of Jean-Pierre Digard (1988), who, faced with the extreme diversity of the possible relations between humans and the animals living in contact with them (captivity, familiarization, taming, domestication, etc.), prefers to consider them as variants of one and the same domesticating process rather than to distinguish stages and particular forms; these would lead to a typology that may be contradicted by exceptions. Nevertheless, it seems to me that from, not the genetic or the ethological point of view, but rather from that of representations of the actions of humans upon nonhuman living creatures, there is — as the American example suggests — a difference in nature, not in degree, between an animal that is tamed and one that is domesticated (in the restrictive sense defined above).

33. Understanding why the Indians of Amazonia tame animals with such enthusiasm is an altogether different problem, which I have examined in the above-mentioned study (1994b) and in Descola 1999.

34. E.g., among the Parakanã; see Fausto 2001, 396.

35. On the Amuesha forges, see Santos Granero 1987.

36. See Descola 1994a, 85–86, for the example of dogs among the Jivaros.

37. For an example of such a combination in New Guinea, see Brunois 2001, chap. 10.

38. Digard 1990, 108–9.

39. See Testart 1982.

Epilogue: The Spectrum of Possibilities

1. Weber 2003, 28.

Bibliography

Agnel, Émile. 1858. *Curiosités judiciaires et historiques du Moyen Âge: Procès contre les animaux.* Paris: J. B. Dumoulin. Facsimile reprint, Nîmes: Lacour, 2003.

Aguirre Beltrán, Gonzalo. 1963. *Medicina y magia: El proceso de aculturación y la estructura colonial.* Mexico City: Instituto nacional indigenista.

Albert, Bruce. 1985. "Temps du sang, temps des cendres: Représentation de la maladie, système rituel et espace politique chez les Yanomami du Sud-Est (Amazonie brésilienne)." Doctoral thesis, Paris-X.

Alvard, Michael S. 1998. "The Evolutionary Ecology of Resource Conservation." *Evolutionary Anthropology* 7:62–74.

Alvard, Michael S., and Lawrence Kuznar. 2001. "Deferred Harvests: The Transition from Hunting to Animal Husbandry." *American Anthropologist* 103 (2): 295–311.

Anisimov, Arkady Fedorovich. 1963. "The Shaman's Tent of the Evenks and the Origin of the Shamanistic Rite." In *Studies in Siberian Shamanism,* edited by Henry N. Michael, 84–112. Toronto: University of Toronto Press.

Aquinas, Saint Thomas. 1956. *Summa contra Gentiles.* Translated by James F. Anderson. Notre Dame, IN: University of Notre Dame.

———. 1989. *Summa theologiae.* Translated by Timothy McDermott. London: Eyre and Spottiswoode.

Århem, Kaj. 1981. *Makuna Social Organization: A Study in Descent, Alliance, and the Formation of Corporate Groups in the Northwest Amazon.* Uppsala: Acta Universitatis Upsaliensis.

———. 1990. "Ecosofía Makuna." In *La selva humanizada: Ecología alternativa en el Trópico húmedo colombiano,* edited by François Correa, 105–22. Bogotá: Instituto Colombiano de Antropología.

———. 1996. "The Cosmic Food Web: Human-Nature Relatedness in the Northwest Amazon." In *Nature and Society: Anthropological Perspectives,* edited by Philippe Descola and Gísli Pálsson, 185–204. London: Routledge.

Ariel de Vidas, Anath. 2002. *Le tonnerre n'habite plus ici: Culture de la marginalité chez les Indiens teenek (Mexique).* Paris: Éditions de l'École des hautes études en sciences sociales.

Aristotle. 1926. *Nicomachean Ethics.* Translated by H. Rackham. Loeb Classical Library. Cambridge, MA: Harvard University Press.

——. 1929. *Physics*. Vol. 1. Translated by Philip H. Wickstead and Francis M. Cornford. Loeb Classical Library. Cambridge, MA: Harvard University Press.

Arnould, Jacques. 1997. "Christianisme et environnement: À l'école de François d'Assise." In *Ethique et environnement*, 33–40. Paris: La Documentation Française.

Ashley Montagu, M. F. 1974. *Coming into Being among the Australian Aborigines*. 2nd ed. London, Routledge. Originally published 1937.

Atran, Scott. 1985. "Pre-theoretical Aspects of the Aristotelian Definition and Classification of Animals: The Case for Common Sense." *Studies in History and Philosophy of Science* 16:116–63.

Augustine, Saint. 1956. *Enarrationes in Psalmos*. Corpus Christianorum Series Latina, edited by D. Eligius Dekkers and Johannes Fraipont, vol. 38. Turnholt: Brepols.

——. 1982. *Eighty-Three Different Questions*. Translated by D. L. Mosher. Washington, DC: University of America Press.

Bachelard, Gaston. 2002. *The Formation of the Scientific Mind*. Translated by Mary McAllester Jones. Paris: Manchester: Clinamen. Originally published as *La formation de l'esprit scientifique: Contribution à une psychanalyse de la connaissance objective* (Paris: Librairie Vrin, 1938).

Baer, Gerhard. 1994. *Cosmología y shamanismo de los Matsiguenga (Perú Oriental)*. Quito: Ediciones Abya-Yala.

Balée, William. 1989. "The Culture of Amazonian Forests." In *Resource Management in Amazonia: Indigenous and Folk Strategies*, edited by D. A. Posey and W. Balée, 1–21. The Bronx: New York Botanical Garden.

——. 1993. "Indigenous Transformations of Amazonian Forests: An Example from Maranhão, Brazil." *L'homme* 126–28: 231–54.

——. 1994. *Footprints of the Forest: Ka'apor Ethnobotany*. New York: Columbia University Press.

Balikci, Asen. 1968. "The Netsilik Eskimois: Adaptive Processes." In *Man the Hunter*, edited by Richard B. Lee and Irven de Vore, 78–82. Chicago: Aldine.

Barth, Fredrik. 1961. *Nomads of South Persia: The Basseri Tribe of the Khamseh Confederacy*. Boston: Little, Brown.

Bechtel, William, and Adele Abrahamsen. 1991. *Connectionism and the Mind: An Introduction to Parallel Processing in Networks*. Cambridge: Blackwell.

Belaunde, Luisa E. 1994. "Parrots and Oropendolas: The Aesthetics of Gender Relations among the Airo-Pai of the Peruvian Amazon." *Journal de la Société des Américanistes* 80:95–111.

Benedict, Ruth. 1934. *Patterns of Culture*. Boston: Houghton Mifflin.

Benveniste, Émile. 1971. *Problems in General Linguistics*. Translated by Mary Elizabeth Meek. Coral Gables, FL: University of Miami Press. Originally published as *Problèmes de linguistique générale*, vol. 1 (Paris: Gallimard, 1966).

Berlin, Brent. 1977. *Bases empíricas del la cosmología aguaruna jibaro, Amazonas, Peru*. Berkeley: University of California.

——. 1992. *Ethnobiological Classification: Principles of Categorization of Plants and Animals in Traditional Societies*. Princeton, NJ: Princeton University Press.

Berlin, Elois Ann, and Brent Berlin. 1996. *Medical Ethnobiology of the Highland Maya of Chiapas, Mexico: The Gastrointestinal Diseases*. Princeton, NJ: Princeton University Press.

Berque, Augustin. 1986. *Le sauvage et l'artifice: Les Japonais devant la nature*. Paris: Gallimard.

——. 1990. *Médiance: De milieux en paysages*. Montpellier: RECLUS.

——. 1995. *Les raisons du paysage: De la Chine antique aux environnements de synthèse*. Paris: Hazan.

———. 1996. *Etres humains sur la terre: Principes d'éthique de l'écoumène*. Paris: Gallimard, coll. "Le Débat."

Bird-David, Nurit. 1990. "The Giving Environment: Another Perspective on the Economic System of Hunter-Gatherers." *Current Anthropology* 31:189–96.

———. 1992. "Beyond the Hunting and Gathering Mode of Subsistence: Culture-Sensitive Observations on the Nayaka and Other Modern Hunter-Gatherers." *Man*, n.s., 27:19–44.

———. 1999. "'Animism' Revisited: Personhood, Environment, and Relational Epistemology." *Current Anthropology* 40 (Supplement): 67–91.

Blaisel, Xavier. 1993. "Espace cérémoniel et temps universel chez les Inuit du Nunavut (Canada): Les valeurs coutumières et les rapports rituels entre humains, gibiers, esprits et forces de l'univers." Doctoral thesis, École des hautes études en sciences sociales, Paris.

Bloch, Marc. 1978. *French Rural History: An Essay on Its Basic Characteristics*. Translated by Janet Sondheimer. London, Routledge and Kegan Paul. Originally published as *Les caractères originaux de l'histoire rurale française* (Paris: Armand Colin, 1931).

Bloch, Maurice. 1992. "What Goes without Saying: The Conceptualization of Zafimaniry Society." In *Conceptualizing Society*, edited by Adam Kuper, 127–46. London: Routledge.

———. 1998. *How We Think They Think: Anthropological Approaches to Cognition, Memory, and Literacy*. Boulder, CO: Westview Press.

Bloom, Paul. 2004. *Descartes' Baby: How the Science of Child Development Explains What Makes Us Human*. New York: Basic Books.

Boas, Franz. 1887. "The Study of Geography." *Science* 9:137–41.

Bodson, Liliane. 1995. "Points de vue sur l'animal domestique et la domestication." In *Homme et animal dans l'Antiquité romaine: Actes du colloque de Nantes*, edited by R. Chevalier, 7–49. Tours: Centre A. Piganiol.

Bogoras, Waldemar. 1904–9. *The Chukchee*. 3 pts. in 2 vols. Memoirs of the American Museum of Natural History 11. Leiden: E. J. Brill; New York: G. E. Stechert.

Boltanski, Luc, and Laurent Thévenot. 2006. *On Justification: Economies of Worth*. Translated by Catherine Porter. Paris:Princeton, NJ: Princeton University Press. Originally published as *De la justification: Les économies de la grandeur* (Paris: Gallimard, 1991).

Boster, James. 1980. "How Exceptions Prove the Rule: An Analysis of Informant Disagreement in Aguaruna Manioc Identification." PhD diss., University of California, Berkeley.

Bouchard, Sege, and José Maillot. 1972. "Structure du lexique: Les animaux indiens." *Recherches amérindiennes au Québec* 3 (1–2): 39–66.

Bourdieu, Pierre. 1979. *Outline of a Theory of Practice*. Translated by Richard Nice. Cambridge: Cambridge University Press. Originally published as *Esquisse d'une théorie de la pratique, précédée de trois études d'ethnologie kabyle* (Geneva: Librairic Droz, 1972).

———. 1984. *Distinction: A Social Critique of the Judgement of Taste*. Translated by Richard Nice. London: Routledge and Kegan Paul. Originally published as *La distinction: Critique sociale du jugement* (Paris: Éditions de Minuit, 1979).

———. 2000. *Pascalian Meditations*. Translated by Richard Nice. Cambridge: Polity. Originally published as *Méditations pascaliennes* (Paris: Éditions du Seuil, 1997).

Brandenstein, Carl Georg von. 1977. "Aboriginal Ecological Order in the South-West of Australia—Meanings and Examples." *Oceania* 47 (3): 170–86.

———. 1982. *Names and Substance of the Australian Subsection System*. Chicago: University of Chicago Press.

Breton, Stéphane. 1999. "De l'illusion totémique à la fiction sociale." *L'homme* 151:123–50.

Bridges, Lucas, 1988. *Uttermost Part of the Earth: Indians of Tierra del Fuego.* Mineola, NY: Dover. Originally published 1949.

Brightman, Robert. 1993. *Grateful Prey: Rock Cree Human-Animal Relationships.* Berkeley and Los Angeles: University of California Press.

Brown, Joseph E. 1997. *Animals of the Soul: Sacred Animals of the Oglala Sioux.* Rockport, MA: Element Books.

Brown, Michael F. 1986. *Tsewa's Gift: Magic and Meaning in an Amazonian Society.* Washington, DC: Smithsonian Institution Press.

Brunois, Florence. 2001. "Le Jardin du Casoar: La forêt des Kasua." Doctoral thesis, Éditions de l'École des hautes études en sciences sociales, Paris.

Byrne, Robert W., and Andrew Whiten. 1988. "The Manipulation of Attention in Primate Tactical Deception." In *Machiavellian Intelligence: Social Expertise and the Evolution of Intellect in Monkeys, Apes and Humans,* edited by R. Byrne and A. Whiten, 211–23. Oxford: Clarendon Press.

———. 1998. "Imitation of the Sequential Structure of Actions by Chimpanzees (*Pan troglodytes*)." *Journal of Comparative Psychology* 112:270–81.

Callicott, John Baird. 1989. *In Defense of the Land Ethic: Essays in Environmental Philosophy.* Albany: State University of New York Press.

Carey, Susan. 1985. *Conceptual Change in Childhood.* Cambridge, MA: Bradford Books for MIT Press.

Carey, Susan, and Elizabeth Spelke. 1994. "Domain-Specific Knowledge and Conceptual Change." In *Mapping the Mind: Domain Specificity in Cognition and Culture,* edited by Lawrence Hirschfeld and Susan A. Gelman, 169–200. Cambridge: Cambridge University Press.

Cauvin, Jacques. 2000. *The Birth of the Gods and the Origins of Agriculture.* Translated by Trevor Watkins. Cambridge: Cambridge University Press. Originally published as *Naissance des divinités, naissance de l'agriculture: La révolution des symboles au néolithique* (Paris: Éditions du Centre national de la recherche scientifique, 1994).

Cayón, Luis. 2002. *En las aguas de Yuruparí: Cosmología y chamanismo Makuna.* Bogotá: Ediciones Uniandes.

Changeux, Jean-Pierre. 1985. *Neuronal Man.* Translated by Laurence Garey. New York: Pantheon. Originally published as *L'homme neuronal* (Paris: Fayard, 1983).

Chateaubriand, François René. 1902. *The Memoirs of Chateaubriand.* Vol. 5. Translated by Alexander Teixeira de Mattos. London: Freemantle.

Châtelet, Gilles. 2000. *Figuring Space.* Translated by Robert Shore and Muriel Zagha. Paris: Dordrecht: Kluwer. Originally published as *Les Enjeux du mobile: Mathématique, physique, philosophie* (Paris: Éditions du Seuil, 1993).

Chaumeil, Bonnie, and Jean-Pierre Chaumeil. 1992. "L'oncle et le neveu: La parenté du vivant chez les Yagua (Amazonie péruvienne)." *Journal de la Société des Américanistes* 78 (2): 25–37.

Chaumeil, Jean-Pierre. 1983. *Voir, savoir, pouvoir: Le chamanisme chez les Yagua du Nord-Est péruvien.* Paris: Éditions de l'École des hautes études en sciences sociales.

Cheney, Dorothy L., and Robert M. Seyfarth. 1980. "Vocal Recognition in Free-Ranging Vervet Monkeys." *Animal Behavior* 28:362–67.

Chiappino, Jean. 1997. "Las piedras celestes: Para una nueva forma de intercambio en el ámbito de la salud." In *Del microscopio a la Maraca,* edited by Jean Chiappino and Catherine Alès, 253–90. Caracas: Editorial Ex Libris.

Clément, Daniel. 1995. *La zoologie des Montagnais.* Paris: Éditions Peeters.

Collingwood, Robin G. 1945. *The Idea of Nature.* Oxford: Clarendon Press.

Condillac. 1947. *Traité des animaux.* 1755. In *Oeuvres philosophiques,* vol. 1. Paris: Presses universitaires de France.

Conklin, Beth A. 2001. *Consuming Grief: Compassionate Cannibalism in an Amazonian Society.* Austin: University of Texas Press.

Coppet, Daniel de. 1995. "Are'are Society: A Melanesian Socio-cosmic Point of View; How Are Bigmen the Servants of Society and Cosmos?" In *Cosmos and Society,* edited by Daniel de Coppet and André Iteanu, 235–74. Oxford: Berg.

Cosmides, Leda, and John Tooby. 1994. "Origins of Domain Specificity: The Evolution of Functional Organization." In *Mapping the Mind: Domain Specificity in Cognition and Culture,* edited by Lawrence A. Hirschfeld and Susan A. Gelman, 85–116. Cambridge: Cambridge University Press.

Damasio, Antonio R. 1999. *The Feeling of What Happens: Body and Emotion in the Making of Consciousness.* New York: Harcourt, Brace.

D'Andrade, Roy. 1995. *The Development of Cognitive Anthropology.* Cambridge: Cambridge University Press.

Darwin, Charles. 1871. *The Descent of Man.* London: John Murray. Reprint, Princeton, NJ: Princeton University Press, 1981.

Davidson, Donald. 1980. *Essays on Actions and Events.* Oxford: Clarendon Press.

Denevan, William M. 1966. *The Aboriginal Cultural Geography of the Llanos de Mojos of Bolivia.* Berkeley and Los Angeles: University of California Press.

Dennett, Daniel. 1991. *Consciousness Explained.* Boston: Little, Brown.

Derathé, Robert. 1974. *Jean-Jacques Rousseau et la science politique de son temps.* Paris: Vrin.

Descartes, René. 1912. *A Discourse on Method.* Translated by John Veitch. London: Dent. Originally published as *Discours de la méthode* (Leiden: Jan Maire, 1637).

Descola, Philippe. 1990. "Cosmologies du chasseur amazonien." In *Pour Jean Malaurie: 102 témoignages en hommage à quarante ans d'études arctiques,* edited by Sylvie Devers, 59–64. Paris: Plon.

———. 1992. "Societies of Nature and the Nature of Society." In *Conceptualizing Society,* edited by Adam Kuper, 107–26. London: Routledge.

———. 1993. "Les affinités sélectives: Alliance, guerre et prédation dans l'ensemble jivaro." *L'homme* 126–28:171–90.

———. 1994a. *In the Society of Nature: A Native Ecology in Amazonia.* Translated by Nora Scott. Cambridge: Cambridge University Press. Originally published as *La nature domestique: Symbolisme et praxis dans l'écologie des Achuar* (Paris: Éditions de la Maison des sciences de l'homme, 1986).

———. 1994b. "Pourquoi les Indiens d'Amazonie n'ont-ils pas domestiqué le pécari? Généalogie des objets et l'anthropologie de l'objectivation." In *De la préhistoire aux missiles balistiques: L'intelligence sociale des techniques,* edited by Bruno Latour and Pierre Lemonnier, 329–44. Paris: La Découverte.

———. 1996a. "Constructing Natures: Symbolic Ecology and Social Practice." In *Nature and Society: Anthropological Perspectives,* edited by Philippe Descola and Gísli Pálsson, 82–102. London: Routledge.

———. 1996b. *The Spears of Twilight.* Translated by Janet Lloyd. New York: New Press. Originally published as *Les lances du crepuscule: Relations jivaros, Haute Amazonie* (Paris: Plon, 1993).

————. 1999. "Des proies bienveillantes: Le traitement du gibier dans la chasse amazonienne." In
    De la violence, edited by Françoise Héritier, 2:19–44. Paris: Odile Jacob.

————. 2004. "Le sauvage et le domestique." *Communications* (Paris) 76 (October): 17–40.

Descombes, Vincent. 2001. *The Mind's Provisions*. Translated by Stephan Adam Schwarz.
    Princeton, NJ: Princeton University Press. Originally published as *La Denrée mentale* (Paris:
    Éditions de Minuit, 1995).

Désveaux, Emmanuel. 1988. *Sous le signe de l'ours: Mythes et temporalité chez les Ojibwa septen-
    trionaux*. Paris: Éditions de la Maison des sciences de l'homme.

————. 1995. "Les Indiens sont-ils par nature respectueux de la nature?" *Anthropos* 90:435–44.

————. 1997. "Parenté, rituel, organisation sociale: Le cas des Sioux." *Journal de la Société des
    Américanistes* 83:111–40.

Detienne, M. 1979. *Dionysos Slain*. Translated by M. Muellner and L. Muellner. Baltimore, MD:
    Johns Hopkins University Press. Originally published as *Dionysos mis à mort* (Paris: Galli-
    mard, 1977).

Dieterlen, Germaine. 1973. "L'image du corps et les composantes de la personne chez les Dogon."
    In *La notion de la personne en Afrique noire*, 205–29. Paris: Éditions du Centre national de
    la recherche scientifique.

Digard, Jean-Pierre. 1988. "Jalons pour une anthropologie de la domestication animale." *L'homme*
    108:27–58.

————. 1990. *L'homme et les animaux domestiques: Anthropologie d'une passion*. Paris: Fayard.

Dilthey, Wilhelm. 1989. *Selected Works*. Vol. 1, *Introduction to the Human Sciences*. Translated
    by Rudolf A. Makkreel and Frithjof Rodi. Princeton, NJ: Princeton University Press. Origi-
    nally published as *Einleitung in die Geisteswissenschaften: Versuch einer Grundlegung für das
    Studium des Gesellschaft und Geschichte* (Leipzig: Duncker and Humblot, 1883).

Dove, Michael R. 1992. "The Dialectical History of "Jungle" in Pakistan: An Examination of
    the Relationship between Nature and Culture." *Journal of Anthropological Research* 48 (3):
    231–53.

Duby, Georges. 1974. *The Early Growth of the European Economy*. Translated by Howard B.
    Clarke. London: Weidenfeld and Nicolson. Originally published as *Guerriers et paysans:
    VIIe–XIIe siècle, premier essor de l'économie européenne* (Paris: Gallimard, 1973).

Dumont, Louis. 1980. *Homo hierarchicus: The Caste System and Its Implications*. Translated by
    Mark Sainsbury, Louis Sumont, and Basia Gulati. Chicago: University of Chicago Press.
    Originally published as *Homo hierarchicus: Le système des castes et ses implications* (Paris:
    Gallimard, 1966).

Dupire, Marguerite. 1962. *Peuls nomades: Étude déscriptive des Wodaabe du Sahel Nigérien*. Paris:
    Institut d'ethnologie.

Durkheim, Émile. 1995. *The Elementary Forms of Religious Life*. Translated by Karen E. Fields.
    New York: New Press. Originally published in 1912 and then as *Les formes élémentaires de
    la vie religieuse: Le système totémique en Australie* (Paris: Presses universitaires de France,
    1960).

Durkheim, Émile, and Marcel Mauss. 1963. *Primitive Classification*. Translated by Rodney Need-
    ham. London: Cohen and West. Originally published as "De quelques formes primitives de
    classification: Contribution à l'étude des représentations collectives." *Année sociologique* 6
    (1903): 1–72.

Duval, Maurice. 1986. *Un totalitarisme sans État: Essai d'anthropologie politique à partir d'un
    village burkinabé*. Paris: L'Harmattan.

Duvernay-Bolens, Jacqueline. 1995. *Les géants patagons: Voyage aux origines de l'homme.* Paris: Michalon.

Dwyer, Peter D. 1996. "The Invention of Nature." In *Redefining Nature: Ecology, Culture and Domestication,* edited by Roy Ellen and Katsuyoshi Fukui, 157–86. Oxford: Berg.

Edelman, Gerald M. 1987. *Neural Darwinism: The Theory of Neural Group Selection.* New York: Basic Books.

Eliade, Mircea. 1964. *Shamanism: Archaic Techniques of Ecstasy.* Translated by Willard R. Trask. New York: Bollinger. Originally published as *Le chamanisme et les techniques archaïques de l'extase* (Paris: Payot, 1951).

Elias, Norbert. 1994. *The Civilizing Process: Sociogenetic and Psychogenetic Investigations.* Translated by Edmund Jephcott. Oxford: Blackwell. Originally published as *Über den Prozess der Zivilisation* (Bern: Francke Verlag, 1969).

Elkin, Adolphus. 1933. "Studies in Australian Totemism: The Nature of Australian Totemism." *Oceania* 4 (2): 113–31.

Ellen, Roy F. 1993. *The Cultural Relations of Classification: An Analysis of Nuaulu Animal Categories from Central Seram.* Cambridge: Cambridge University Press.

Endicott, Karen M. 1979. *Batek Negrito Religion.* Oxford: Clarendon Press.

Erikson, Philippe. 1984. "De l'apprivoisement à l'approvisionnement: Chasse, alliance et familiarisation en Amazonie amérindienne." *Techniques et Cultures* 9:105–40.

———. 1996. *La griffe des aïeux: Marquage du corps et démarquages ethniques chez les Matis d'Amazonie.* Paris: Peters.

Evans-Pritchard, Edward E. 1940. *The Nuer: A Description of the Modes of Livelihood and Political Institutions of a Nilotic People.* Oxford: Clarendon Press.

———. 1956. *Nuer Religion.* Oxford: Clarendon Press.

Fausto, Carlos. 2001. *Inimigos Fiéis: Historia, guerra, xamanismo na Amazônia.* São Paolo: Editora da Universidade de São Paolo.

Favre, Henri. 1971. *Changement et continuité chez les Mayas du Mexique: Contribution à l'étude de la situation coloniale en Amérique latine.* Paris: Éditions Anthropos.

Feer, François. 1993. "The Potential for Sustainable Hunting and Rearing of Game in Tropical Forests." In *Tropical Forests: People and Food; Biocultural Interactions and Applications to Development,* edited by Claude Marcel Hladik, Annette Hladik, Olga F. Linares, Hélène Pagezy, Alison Semple, and Malcolm Hadley, 691–708. Man and the Biosphere Series, vol. 13. Paris: Unesco and Parthenon.

Feit, Harvey. 1973. "The Ethnoecology of the Waswanipi Cree; or, How Hunters Can Manage Their Resources." In *Cultural Ecology: Readings on the Canadian Indians and Eskimos,* edited by B. Cox, 115–25. Toronto: McClelland and Stewart.

Ferry, Luc. 1995. *The New Ecological Order.* Translated by Carol Volk. Chicago: University of Chicago Press. Originally published as *Le nouvel ordre écologique: L'arbre, l'animal et l'homme* (Paris: Grasset, 1992).

Fienup-Riordan, Ann. 1990. "Eskimo Iconography and Symbolism: An Introduction." ."" In "Chasse, sexes et symbolisme/Hunting, Sexes, and Symbolism," edited by A. Fienup-Riordan, special issue, *Études/Inuit/Studies* 14 (1–2): 7–12.

Fogelson, Raymond D., and Robert A. Brightman. 2002. "Totemism Reconsidered." In *Anthropology, History, and American Indians: Essays in Honor of William Curtis Sturtevant,* edited by William L. Merrill and Ives G. Goddard, 305–13. Washington, DC: Smithsonian Institution Press.

Fortes, Meyer. 1959. *Oedipus and Job in West African Religion.* Cambridge: Cambridge University Press.

Foster, George M. 1944. "Nagualism in Mexico and Guatemala." *Acta Americana* 2 (1–2): 85–103.

———. 1953. "Relationship between Spanish and Spanish-American Folk Medicine." *Journal of American Folklore* 66 (261): 201–17.

Foucault, Michel. 1970. *The Order of Things: An Archaeology of the Human Sciences.* London: Tavistock Publications. Originally published as *Les mots et les choses: Une archéologie des sciences humaines* (Paris: Gallimard, 1966).

Franchetto, Bruna, and Michael Heckenberger, eds. 2001. *Os povos do Alto Xingu: História e cultura.* Rio de Janeiro: Editora UFRJ.

Frank, Erwin. 1987. "Das Tapirfest der Uni: Eine funktionale Analyse." *Anthropos* 82:151–81.

Freeman, Derek. 1979. "Severed Heads That Germinate." In *Fantasy and Symbol: Studies in Anthropological Interpretation,* edited by R. H. Hook, 233–46. London: Academic Press.

Galey, Jean-Claude. 1993. "L'homme en nature: Hindouisme et pensée sauvage." In *Les sentiments de la nature,* edited by Dominique Bourg, 47–71. Paris: La Découverte.

Galinier, Jacques. 2004. *The World Below.* Translated by Phyllis Aronoff and Howard Scott of *La Moitié du monde.* Boulder: University Press of Colorado. Originally published as *Le corps et le cosmos dans le rituel des Indiens otomi* (Paris: Presses universitaires de France, 1997).

Geertz, Clifford. 1963. *Agricultural Involution: The Process of Ecological Change in Indonesia.* Berkeley and Los Angeles: University of California Press.

Geoffroy Saint-Hilaire, Isidore. 1861. *Acclimatation et domestication des animaux utiles.* 4th ed. Paris: Librairie agricole de la Maison rustique.

Gibson, James J. 1979. *The Ecological Approach to Visual Perception.* Boston: Houghton Mifflin.

Gibson, Kathleen R., and Tim Ingold, eds. 1993. *Tools, Language and Cognition in Human Evolution.* Cambridge: Cambridge University Press.

Gibson, Thomas. 1986. *Sacrifice and Sharing in the Philippine Highlands: Religion and Society among the Buid of Mindoro.* London: Athlone Press.

Gick, Mary L., and Keith J. Holyoak. 1983. "Schema Induction and Analogical Transfer." *Cognitive Psychology* 15:1–38.

Glacken, Clarence J. 1967. *Traces on the Rhodian Shore: Nature and Culture in Western Thought from Ancient Times to the End of the Eighteenth Century.* Berkeley and Los Angeles: University of California Press.

Glowczewski, Barbara. 1991. *Du rêve à la loi chez les Aborigènes: Mythes, rites et organisation sociale en Australie.* Paris: Presses universitaires de France.

Godelier, Maurice. 1970. *Sur les sociétés précapitalistes: Texts choisis de Marx, Engels, Lénine.* Paris: Éditions Sociales.

———. 1996. *The Mental and the Material: Thought, Economy and Society.* Translated by Martin Thom. New York: Verso. Originally published as *L'idéel et le matériel: Pensée, économies, sociétés* (Paris: Fayard, 1984).

———. 1999. *The Enigma of the Gift.* Translated by Nora Scott. Cambridge: Polity. Originally published as *L'enigme du don* (Paris: Fayard, 1996).

Godelier, Maurice, and Michel Panoff, eds. 1998. *La production du corps: Approches anthropologiques et historiques.* Amsterdam: Éditions des Archives contemporaines.

Gombrich, Ernst H. 1966. "The Renaissance Theory of Art and the Rise of Landscape." In E.H. Gombrich, *Norm and Form: Studies in the Art of the Renaissance.* London: Phaidon, 107–21.

Gonçalves, Marco Antonio. 2001. *O mundo inacabado: Ação e criação em uma cosmologia amazónica; Etnografia pirahã*. Rio de Janeiro: Editora UFRJ.

Gossiaux, Pol-P. 1995. *L'homme et la nature: Genèse de l'anthropologie à l'âge classique, 1580–1750*. Brussels: De Boeck University.

Granet, Marcel. 1963. *Études sociologiques sur la Chine*. Paris: Presses universitaires de France.

———. 1968. *La pensée chinoise*. Paris: Albin Michel. Originally published 1934.

———. 1998. *The Chinese Civilization*. Translated by Kathleen Innes and Mabel Brailsford. London: Routledge. Originally published as *La civilisation chinoise: La vie publique et la vie privée* (1929; Paris: Albin Michel, 1968).

Gray, Andrew. 1997. *The Arakmbut of Amazonian Peru*. Vol. 2, *The Last Shaman (Change in an Amazonian Community)*. Oxford: Berghan.

Gregory, Chris A. 1982. *Gifts and Commodities*. London: Academic Press.

Grenand, Pierre. 1980. *Introduction à l'étude de l'univers wayãpi: Ethno-écologie des Indiens du Haut-Oyapock (Guyane française)*. Paris: Société d' Études linguistiques et anthropologiques de France / Centre national de la recherche scientifique.

Griaule, Marcel. 1938. *Masques dogons*. Paris: Institut d'ethnologie.

———. 1966. *Dieu d'eau: Entretien avec Ogotemmêli*. Paris: Fayard. Originally published 1948.

Griffin, Donald. 1976. *The Question of Animal Awareness: Evolutionary Continuity of Mental Experience*. New York: Rockefeller University Press.

———. 1991. "Progress towards a Cognitive Ethology." In *Cognitive Ethology: The Minds of Other Animals*, edited by Caroline A. Ristau, 3–17. Hillsdale, NJ: Lawrence Erlbaum.

Grzimek, Bernhard. 1975. *Grzimek's Animal Life Encyclopedia*. New York: Van Nostrand Reinhold.

Guédon, Marie-Françoise. 1994. "An Introduction to the Tsimshian World View and Its Practitioners." In *The Tsimshian: Images of the Past, Views of the Present*, edited by M. Seguin, 137–59. Vancouver: University of British Columbia Press.

Guiteras Holmes, C. 1961. *Perils of the Soul: The world-view of a Tzotzil Indian*. New York: Free Press of Glencoe.

Gyger, M., and P. Marler. 1988. "Food Calling in the Domestic Fowl (*Gallus gallus*): The Role of External Referents and Deception." *Animal Behaviour* 36:358–65.

Hacking, Ian. 1995. *Rewriting the Soul: Multiple Personality and the Science of Memory*. Princeton, NJ: Princeton University Press.

Hallowell, Alfred I. 1976. "Ojibwa Ontology, Behavior and World View." In *Contributions to Anthropology: Selected Papers of A. Irving Hallowell*, 357–90. Chicago: University of Chicago Press. Originally published in *Culture in History: Essays in Honour of Paul Radin*, edited by Stanley Diamond, 19–52 (New York: Columbia University Press, 1960).

Hamayon, Roberte. 1982. "Des chamanes au chamanisme: Introduction." In "Voyages chamaniques 2," special issue, *L'ethnographie* 87–88:13–48.

———. 1990. *La chasse á l'âme: Esquisse d'une théorie du chamanisme sibérien*. Nanterre: Société d'ethnologie.

Hampaté Ba, Amadou. 1973. "La notion de personne en Afrique noire." In *La notion de personne en Afrique noire*, 181–92. Paris: Éditions du Centre national de la recherche scientifique.

Haudricourt, André-Georges. 1962. "Domestication des animaux, culture des plantes et traitement d'autrui." *L'homme* 2:40–50.

Hauser, Marc. 1996. *The Evolution of Communication*. Cambridge, MA: MIT Press.

Hauser, Marc, and Peter Marler. 1993. "Food Associated Calls in Rhesus Macaques (*Macaca mulatta*), I & II." *Behavioral Ecology* 4 (3): 194–212.

Hell, Bertrand. 1994. *Le sang noir: Chasse et mythes du Sauvage en Europe.* Paris: Flammarion.

Héritier, Françoise. 1977. "L'identité samo." In *L'identité: Séminaire dirigé par Claude Lévi-Strauss,* 51–71. Paris: Bernard Graasset.

———. 1996. *Masculin/féminin: La pensée de la différence.* Paris: Odile Jacob.

Hesiod. 2006. *Works and Days.* Translated by Glenn Most. Loeb Classical Library. Cambridge, MA: Harvard University Press.

Heusch, Luc de. 1981. *Why Marry Her? Society and Symbolic Structures.* Translated by Janet Lloyd. Cambridge Studies in Social Anthropology. Cambridge: Cambridge University Press. Originally published as *Pouquoi l'épouser? Et autres essais,* Bibliothèque des sciences humaines (Paris: Gallimard, 1971).

Hobbes, Thomas. 1991. *Leviathan.* Edited by Richard Tuck. Cambridge: Cambridge University Press.

Hodder, Ian. 1990. *The Domestication of Europe.* London: Basil Blackwell.

Holland, William. 1963. *Medicina maya en los Altos de Chiapas.* Mexico City: Instituto nacional indigenista.

Homer. 1919. *Odyssey.* Vol. 1. Translated by A. T. Murray. Loeb Classical Library. Cambridge, MA: Harvard University Press.

Howell, Signe. 1989. *Society and Cosmos: Chewong of Peninsular Malaysia.* 2nd ed. Chicago: University of Chicago Press. Originally published 1984.

———. 1996. "Nature in Culture or Culture in Nature? Chewong Ideas of 'Humans' and Other Species." In *Nature and Society: Anthropological Perspectives,* edited by Philippe Descola and Gísli Pálsson, 127–44. London: Routledge.

Hugh-Jones, Christine. 1979. *From the Milk River: Spatial and Temporal Processes in Northwest Amazonia.* Cambridge: Cambridge University Press.

Hugh-Jones, Stephen. 1979. *The Palm and the Pleiades: Initiation and Cosmology in Northwest Amazonia.* Cambridge: Cambridge University Press.

———. 1996. "Bonnes raisons ou mauvaise conscience? De l'ambivalence de certains Amazoniens envers la consommation de viande." *Terrain* 26:123–48.

Humphrey, Caroline, and U. Onon. 1996. *Shamans and Elders: Experience, Knowledge and Power among the Daur Mongols.* Oxford: Clarendon Press.

Hunn, Eugene. 1982. "Did the Aztecs Lack Potential Animal Domesticates?" *American Ethnologist* 9:578–79.

Hviding, Edvard. 1996. "Nature, Culture, Magic, Science: On Meta-languages for Comparison in Cultural Ecology." In *Nature and Society: Anthropological Perspectives,* edited by Philippe Descola and Gísli Pálsson, 165–84. London: Routledge.

Ichon, Alain. 1969. *La religion des Totonaques de la Sierra.* Paris: Éditions de la C.N.R.S.

Ingold, Tim. 1986. *The Appropriation of Nature: Essays on Human Ecology and Social Relations.* Manchester: Manchester University Press.

———. 1994. "Humanity and Animality." In *Companion Encyclopedia of Anthropology: Humanity, Culture and Social Life,* edited by Tim Ingold, 14–32. London: Routledge.

———. 1996. "Hunting and Gathering as Ways of Perceiving the Environment." In *Redefining Nature: Ecology, Culture and Domestication,* edited by R. Ellen and K. Fukui, 117–55. Oxford: Berg.

———. 1998. "Totemism, Animism, and the Depiction of Animals." In *Animal, Anima, Animus,* edited by M. Seppälä, J.-P. Vanhala, and L. Weintraub, 181–207. Pori: FRAME/Pori Art Museum.

———. 2000. *The Perception of the Environment: Essays in Livelihood, Dwelling and Skill*. London: Routledge.

Isacsson, Sven-Erik. 1993. "Transformations of Eternity: On Man and Cosmos in Emberá Thought." PhD thesis, University of Göteborg.

Itani, Junichiro, and A. Nishimura. 1973. "The Study of Infrahuman Culture in Japan: A Review." In *Precultural Primate Behavior*, edited by Emil W. Menzel, 26–50. Basel: S. Kerger.

Iteanu, André. 1998. "Corps et décor chez les Orokaiva." In *La production du corps: Approches anthropologiques et historiques*, edited by Maurice Godelier and Michel Panoff, 115–39. Amsterdam: Éditions des archives contemporaines.

Izard, Michel. 1992. *L'odysée du pouvoir: Un royaume africain; État, société, destin individuel*. Paris: Éditions de l' École des hautes études en sciences sociales.

Jackson, Jean. 1983. *The Fish People: Linguistic Exogamy and Tukanoan Identity in the Northwest Amazon*. Cambridge: Cambridge University Press.

Jackson, Michael. 1990. "The Man Who Could Turn into an Elephant: Shape-Shifting among the Kuranko of Sierra Leone." In *Personhood and Agency: The Experience of Self and Other in African Cultures*, edited by Michael Jackson and Ivan Karp, 59–78. Uppsala: Acta Universitatis Upsaliensis.

Jakobson, Roman, and M. Halle. 1975. *Fundamentals of Language*. 2nd ed. The Hague: Mouton. Originally published 1963.

Jara, Fabiola. 1991. *El camino del Kumu: Ecologia y ritual entre los Akuriyó de Surinam*. Utrecht: ISOR.

Jullien, François. 1989. *Procès ou création: Une introduction à la pensée des lettrés chinois*. Paris: Éditions du Seuil.

Kant, Immanuel. 1997. *Critique of Pure Reason*. Translated by Paul Guyer and Allen W. Wood. Cambridge: Cambridge University Press. Originally published as *Kritik der reinen Vernunft* (Riga: Johann Friedrich Hartknoch, 1781).

Kaplan, H., and K. Hill. 1985. "Food Sharing among Ache Foragers: Tests of Explanatory Hypotheses." *Current Anthropology* 26:223–39.

Karim, Wazir-Jahan. 1981a. "Ma' Betisék Concepts of Humans, Plants and Animals." *Bijdragen tot de Taal-, Land- en Volkenkunde* 137:135–60.

———. 1981b. *Ma' Betisék Concepts of Living Things*. London: Athlone.

Keil, Frank C. 1989. *Concepts, Kinds, and Cognitive Development*. Cambridge, MA: Bradford Books for MIT Press.

———. 1994. "The Birth and Nurturance of Concepts by Domains: The Origins of Concepts of Living Things." In *Mapping the Mind: Domain Specificity and Cognition in Culture*, edited by Lawrence A. Hirschfeld and Susan A. Gelman, 234–54. Cambridge: Cambridge University Press.

Kemlin, Émile. 1999. *Les Reungao: Rites agraires, songes et alliances; Une société proto-indochinoise du Viêt Nam au début du XXe siècle; textes réunis et présentés par Pierre Le Roux*. Réimpressions de l' École Française d' Extrême-Orient, no. 11. Paris: École française d' Extrême-Orient.

Kirton, Jean F., and Nero Timothy. 1977. "Yanyula Concepts Relating to 'Skin.'" *Oceania* 47: 320–22.

Knight, John. 1996. "When Timber Grows Wild: The Desocialisation of Japanese Mountain Forests." In *Nature and Society: Anthropological Perspectives*, edited by Philippe Descola and Gísli Pálsson, 221–39. London: Routledge.

Kroeber, Alfred. 1952. *The Nature of Culture*. Chicago: University of Chicago Press.

Kroeber, Alfred, and Clyde Kluckhohn. 1952. *Culture: A Critical Review of Concepts and Definitions*. Cambridge, MA: Harvard University Press.

Kuper, Adam. 1999. *Culture: the Anthropologists' Account*. Cambridge, MA: Harvard University Press.

Lambek, Michael, and Andrew Strathern, eds. 1998. *Bodies and Persons: Comparative Perspectives from Africa and Melanesia*. Cambridge: Cambridge University Press.

Langton, Marcia. 1998. *Burning Questions: Emerging Environmental Issues for Indigenous Peoples in Northern Australia*. Darwin: Centre for Indigenous Natural and Cultural Reserve Management, Northern Territory University.

Larrère, Catherine. 1997. *Les philosophies de l'environnement*. Paris: Presses universitaires de France.

Latour, Bruno. 1993. *We Have Never Been Modern*. Translated by Catherine Porter. New York: Harvester. Originally published as *Nous n'avons jamais été modernes: Essai d'anthropologie symétrique* (Paris: La Découverte, 1991).

———. 1996. *Petite réflexion sur le culte moderne des dieux faitiches*. Paris: Les Empêcheurs de penser en rond.

———. 1999. *Politiques de la nature: Comment faire entrer les sciences en démocratie*. Paris: La Découverte.

———. 2004. *Politics of Nature*. Translated by Catherine Porter. Cambridge, MA: Harvard University Press.

Lave, Jean, and Etienne Wenger, eds. 1991. *Situated Cognition: Legitimate Peripheral Participation*. Cambridge: Cambridge University Press.

Leacock, Eleanor. 1954. *The Montagnais Hunting Territory and the Fur Trade*. American Anthropological Association, Memoir 78. Menasha, WI: American Anthropological Association.

Lee, Richard B. 1979. *The !KungSan: Men, Women and Work in a Foraging Society*. Cambridge: Cambridge University Press.

Lee, Richard B., and Irven De Vore, eds. 1968. *Man the Hunter*. Chicago: Aldine.

Leenhardt, Maurice. 1979. *Do Kamo: Person and Myth in the Melanesian World*. Translated by Basia Milla Gulati. Chicago: University of Chicago Press. Originally published as *Do kamo: La personne et le mythe dans le monde mélanésien* (Paris: Gallimard, 1947).

Legendre, Pierre. 1985. *L'inestimable objet de la transmission: Étude sur le principe généalogique en Occident (Leçon IV)*. Paris: Fayard.

Le Goff, Jacques. 1990. *Medieval Civilization, 400–1500*. Translated by Julia Barrow. Oxford: Blackwell. Originally published as *La civilisation de l'Occident médiéval* (Paris: Flammarion, 1982).

Legrand, Catherine, J.-F. Méjanés, and E. Starcky. 1990. *Le paysage en Europe du XVIe au XVIIIe siècle*. Paris: Éditions de la Réunion des musées nationaux.

Leibniz, Gottfried Wilhelm. 1908. *The Philosophical Works of Leibnitz*. Translated by G. M. Duncan. New Haven, CT: Tuttle, Morehouse and Taylor. Originally published as *De Rerum Originatione Radicali* (1697).

Le Moal, Guy. 1973. "Quelques aperçus sur la notion de personne chez les Bobo." In *La Notion de personne en Afrique noire*, 193–203. Paris: Éditions du Centre national de la recherche scientifique.

Lenoble, Robert. 1969. *Esquisse d'une histoire de l'idée de Nature*. Paris: Albin Michel.

Leopold, Aldo. 1987. *A Sand County Almanach*. Oxford: Oxford University Press. Originally published 1949.

Leroi-Gourhan, André. 1946. *Archéologie du Pacifique-Nord: Matériaux pour l'étude des relations entre les peuples riverains d'Asie et d'Amérique.* Paris: Institut d'ethnologie.

Levin, M. G., and L. Potapov, eds. 1964. *The Peoples of Siberia.* Chicago: University of Chicago Press.

Lévi-Strauss, Claude. 1943. "Guerre et commerce chez les Indiens d'"Amérique du Sud." *Renaissance* 1:122–39.

———. 1966. *The Savage Mind.* London: Weidenfeld and Nicolson. Originally published as *La pensée sauvage* (Paris: Plon, 1962).

———. 1969a. *Elementary Structures of Kinship.* Translated by James Harle Bell, John Richard von Sturmer, and Rodney Needham. London: Eyre and Spottiswoode. Originally published as *Les structures élémentaires de la parenté* (1949; Paris: Mouton, 1967).

———. 1969b. *Totemism.* Translated by Rodney Needham. London: Merlin Press. Originally published as *Le totémisme aujourd'hui* (Paris: Presses universitaires de France, 1962).

———. 1970. *Introduction to a Science of Mythology.* Vol. 1, *The Raw and the Cooked.* Translated by John Weightman and Doreen Weightman. London: Penguin. Originally published as *Mythologiques*, vol. 1, *Le cru et le cuit* (Paris: Plon, 1964).

———. 1972. *Structural Anthropology.* Translated by Claire Jacobson and Brooke Grundfest Schoeff. Harmondsworth: Penguin. Originally published as *Anthropologie structurale* (Paris: Plon, 1958).

———. 1976. *Tristes tropiques.* Translated by John Weightman and Doreen Weightman. Harmondsworth: Penguin. Originally published as *Tristes tropiques* (Paris: Plon, 1955).

———. 1978. *Structural Anthropology II.* Translated by Monique Layton. Harmondsworth: Penguin. Originally published as *Anthropologie structurale deux* (Paris: Plon, 1973).

Lienhardt, Godfrey. 1961. *Divinity and Experience: The Religion of the Dinka.* Oxford: Clarendon Press.

Lima, Tânia Stolze. 1996. "O dois e seu múltiplo: Reflexões sobre o perspectivismo em uma cosmologie tupi." *Mana* 2 (2): 21–47.

Lips, Julius. 1947. "Naskapi Law (Lake St. John and Lake Mistassini Bands): Law and Order in a Hunting Society." *Transactions of the American Philosophical Society* 37 (4): 379–492.

LiPuma, Edward. 1998. "Modernity and Forms of Personhood in Melanesia." In *Bodies and Persons: Comparative Perspectives from Africa and Melanesia*, edited by Michael Lambek and Andrew Strathern, 3–79. Cambridge: Cambridge University Press.

Lloyd, Geoffrey. 2000. "Images of the World." In *Greek Thought: A Guide to Classical Knowledge*, edited by Jacques Brunschwig and Geoffrey Lloyd, 20–38. Cambridge, MA: Belknap Press of Harvard University Press. Originally published in *Savoir grec: Dictionnaire critique*, 57–76 (Paris: Flammarion, 1966).

Long, John. 1904. *Voyages and Travels of an Indian Interpreter and Trader.* Cleveland, OH: Arthur Clark. Originally published 1791.

López Austin, Alfredo. 1988. *The Human Body and Ideology: Concepts of the Ancient Nahuas.* Salt Lake City: University of Utah Press. Originally published 1980.

Losonczy, Anne Marie. 1997. *Les saints et la forêt: Rituel, société et figures de l'échange entre Noirs et Indiens Emberá (Chocó, Colombie).* Paris: L'Harmattan.

Lot-Falck, Eveline. 1953. *Les rites de chasse chez les peuples sibériens.* Paris: Gallimard.

Lounsbury, Floyd G. 1956. "A Semantic Analysis of the Pawnee Kinship Usage." *Language* 32:158–94.

Lovejoy, Arthur. 1961. *The Great Chain of Being: A Study of the History of an Idea.* Cambridge, MA: Harvard University Press. Originally published 1936.

Malamoud, Charles. 1987. "Le malencontre de La Boétie et les théories de l' Inde ancienne sur la société." In *L'esprit des lois sauvages: Pierre Clastres ou une nouvelle anthropologie politique*, edited by Miguel Abensour, 173–82. Paris: Éditions du Seuil.

———. 1996. *Cooking the World: Ritual and Thought in Ancient India.* Translated by David White. Oxford: Oxford University Press. Originally published as *Cuire le monde: Rite et pensée dans l'Inde ancienne* (Paris: La Découverte, 1989).

Mandler, Jean M. 1984. *Stories, Scripts, and Scenes: Aspects of Schema Theory.* Hillsdale, NJ: Lawrence Erlbaum.

Marguénaud, Jean-Pierre. 1998. "La personnalité juridique des animaux." *Recueil Dalloz*, 20th notebook, 205–11.

Marler, Peter. 1984. "Song Learning: Innate Species Differences in the Learning Process." In *The Biology of Learning*, edited by Peter Marler and H. S. Terrace, 47–74. Berlin: Springer Verlag.

———. 1991. "The Instinct to Learn." In *The Epigenesis of Mind: Essays in Biology and Cognition*, edited by Susan Carey and R. Gelman, 37–66. Hillsdale, NJ: Lawrence Erlbaum.

Marler, Peter, and Christopher S. Evans. 1996. "Bird Calls: Just Emotional Display or Something More?" *IBIS* 138:326–31.

Marx, Karl. 2010. *A Contribution to the Critique of Political Economy.* Translated by N. J. Stone. Charleston, SC: Forgotten Books. Originally published as *Zur Kritik der politischen Ökonomie*, 2nd ed. (Berlin: F. Duncker, 1897).

Mauss, Marcel. 1904–5. "Essai sur les variations saisonnières des sociétés eskimos: Étude de morphologie sociale." *Année sociologique* 9:39–132.

———. 1935. "Les techniques du corps." *Journal de psychologie* 32 (3–4): 271–93.

———. 1950. *Sociologie et anthropologie: Précédé d'une introduction à l'œuvre de Marcel Mauss par Claude Lévi-Strauss.* Paris: Presses universitaires de France.

———. 1974. *Œuvres.* Vol. 2. Paris: Éditions de Minuit.

Mauzé, Marie. 1998. "Northwest Coast Trees: From Metaphors in Culture to Symbols for Culture." In *The Social Life of Trees: Anthropological Perspectives on Tree Symbolism*, edited by Laura Rival, 233–51. Oxford: Berg.

McGrew, William C. 1992. *Chimpanzee Material Culture: Implications for Human Evolution.* Cambridge: Cambridge University Press.

McGrew, William C., and C. Tutin. 1978. "Evidence for a Social Custom in Wild Chimpanzees?" *Man* 13:234–52.

Menget, Patrick. 1993. "Notas sobre as cabeças mundurucu." In *Amazônia: Etnologia e história indígena*, edited by Eduardo Viveiros de Castro and Manuela Carneiro da Cunha, 311–21. São Paolo: NHII-USP/FAPESP.

Merlan, Francésca. 1980. "Mangarrayi Semi Moiety Totemism." *Oceania* 51 (2): 81–97.

———. 1986. "Australian Aboriginal Conception Beliefs Revisited." *Man*, n.s., 21:474–93.

Merleau-Ponty, Maurice. 1964. *L'œil et l'esprit.* Paris: Gallimard.

———. 1994. *La nature: Notes et cours du Collège de France.* Paris: Éditions du Seuil.

Métraux, Alfred. 1967. *Religions et magies indiennes d'Amérique du Sud.* Paris: Gallimard.

Michaux, Henri. 1970. *Ecuador: A Travel Journal.* Translated by R. Magowan. London: Peter Owen. Originally published as *Ecuador: Journal de voyage* (1929; Paris: Gallimard, 1968).

Moisseeff, Marika. 1995. *Un long chemin semé d'objets cultuels: Le cycle initiatique aranda.* Paris: Éditions de l' École des hautes études en sciences sociales.

———. 2002. "Australian Aboriginal Objects, or How to Represent the Unrepresentable." In

People and Things: Social Mediations in Oceania, edited by Monique Jeudy-Ballini and Bernard Juillerat, 239–63. Durham, NC: Carolina Academic Press.

Montaigne, Michel de. 1987. *An Apology for Raymond Sebond*. Translated by M. A. Screech. Harmondsworth: Penguin.

Morton, John. 1984. "The Domestication of the Savage Pig: The Role of Peccaries in Tropical South and Central America and Their Relevance for the Understanding of Pig Domestication in Melanesia." *Canberra Anthropology* 7 (1–2): 20–70.

Moscovici, Serge. 1977. *Essai sur l'histoire humaine de la nature*. Paris: Flammarion.

Munn, Nancy D. 1970. "The Transformation of Subjects into Objects in Walbiri and Pitjantjatjara Myth." In *Australian Aboriginal Anthropology*, edited by Ronald M. Berndt, 141–63. Nedlands: University of Western Australia Press.

Myers, Fred R. 1986. *Pintupi Country, Pintupi Self*. Washington, DC: Smithsonian Institution Press.

Needham, Rodney, ed. 1973. *Right and Left*. Chicago: University of Chicago Press.

Nelson, Richard K. 1983. *Make Prayers to the Raven: A Koyukon View of the Northern Forest*. Chicago: University of Chicago Press.

Oelschlaeger, Max. 1991. *The Idea of Wilderness: From Prehistory to the Age of Ecology*. New Haven, CT: Yale University Press.

Ordinaire, Olivier. 1892. *Du Pacifique à l'Atlantique par les Andes péruviennes et l'Amazone*. Paris: Plon, Nourrit.

Osgood, Cornelius. 1936. *Contributions to the Ethnography of the Kutchin*. Yale University Publications in Anthropology, no. 14. New Haven, CT: Yale University Press.

Overing, Joanna, and Alan Passes, eds. 2000. *The Anthropology of Love and Anger: The Aesthetics of Conviviality in Native Amazonia*. London: Routledge.

Overing Kaplan, Joanna. 1975. *The Piaroa, a People of the Orinoco Basin: A Study in Kinship and Marriage*. Oxford: Clarendon Press.

Panofsky, Erwin. 1991. *Perspective as Symbolic Form*. Translated by Christopher S. Wood. New York: Zone Books. Originally published as *Die Perspektive als "symbolische Form."* Bibliothek Warburg Vorträge 4, 1924–25 (Leipzig: Teubner, 1927).

Paul, Hermann. 1890. *Principles of the History of Language*. Translated by H. A. Strong. London: Longmans. Originally published as *Prinzipien der Sprachgeschichte* (Halle: Max Niemeyer, 1880).

Paulson, Ivar, Åke Hultkrantz, and Karl Jettmar. 1965. *Les religions arctiques et finnoises*. Paris: Payot.

Pedersen, Morten A. 2001. "Totemism, Animism and North Asian Indigenous Ontologies." *Journal of the Royal Anthropological Institute*, n.s., 7 (3): 411–27.

Perrin, Michel. 1987. "L'animal à bonne distance." In *Des animaux et des hommes*, edited by Jacques Hainard and R. Kaerh, 53–62. Neuchâtel: Musée d'ethnographie.

———. 1995. *Le chamanisme*. Paris: Presses universitaires de France.

Picon, François-René. 1983. *Pasteurs du Nouveau Monde*. Paris: Éditions de la Maison des sciences de l'homme.

Piperno, Dolores R. 1990. "Aboriginal Agriculture and Land Usage in the Amazon Basin, Ecuador." *Journal of Archaeological Science* 17:665–77.

Pitarch, Pedro. 1996. *Ch'ulel: Una etnografía de las almas tzeltales*. Mexico City: Fondo de cultura económica.

Plato. 1929. *Timaeus*. Translated by R. G. Bury. Loeb Classical Library. Cambridge, MA: Harvard University Press.

Plotinus. 1967. *Enneads*. Vol. 3. Translated by A. H. Armstrong. Loeb Classical Library. Cambridge, MA: Harvard University Press.

Povinelli, Elizabeth A. 1993. *Labor's Lot: The Power, History and Culture of Aboriginal Action*. Chicago: University of Chicago Press.

Proust, Joëlle. 1997. *Comment l'esprit vient aux bêtes: Essai sur la représentation*. Paris: Gallimard.

Quinlan, Philip T. 1991. *Connectionism and Psychology*. Chicago: University of Chicago Press.

Racine, Luc. 1989. "Du modèle analogique dans l'analyse des représentations magico-religieuses." *L'homme* 109:5–25.

Radcliffe-Brown, Alfred R. 1956. *Structure and Function in Primitive Society*. London: Cohen and West.

Rasmussen, Karl. 1929. *Intellectual Culture of the Iglulik Eskimos*. Copenhagen: Glyldendaske Boghandel, Nordisk Forlag.

Redfield, Robert, and Alfonso Villa Rojas. 1964. *Chan Kom, a Maya Village*. 2nd ed. Chicago: University of Chicago Press. Originally published 1934.

Regan, Tom. 1983. *The Case for Animal Rights*. Berkeley and Los Angeles: University of California Press.

Reichel-Dolmatoff, Gerardo. 1971. *Amazonian Cosmos: The Sexual and Religious Symbolism of the Tukano Indians*. Chicago: University of Chicago Press.

———. 1976. "Cosmology as Ecological Analysis: A View from the Forest." *Man* 11:307–18.

———. 1996a. *The Forest Within: The World-View of the Tukano Amazonian Indians*. Dartington, UK: Themis Books.

———. 1996b. *Yurupari: Studies of an Amazonian Foundation Myth*. Cambridge, MA: Harvard University Press for the Harvard University Center for the Study of World Religions.

Renard-Casevitz, France-Marie. 1985. "Guerre, violence et identité à partir des sociétés du piémont amazonien des Andes centrales." *Cahiers Orstom (série Sciences humaines)* 21 (1): 81–98.

———. 1991. *Le banquet masqué: Une mythologie de l'étranger chez les Indiens Matziguenga*. Paris: Lierre and Coudrier.

Rickert, Heinrich. 1962. *Science and History: A Critique of Positivist Epistemology*. Translated by G. Reisman. Princeton, NJ: Van Nostrand. Originally published as *Kulturwissenschaft und Naturwissenschaft*, 7th ed. (1899; Tübingen: Mohr, 1926).

Ritzenthaler, Robert E. 1978. "Southwestern Chippewa." In *Handbook of North American Indians*, vol. 15, *Northeast*, edited by B. G. Trigger, 743–59. Washington, DC: Smithsonian Institution.

Rival, Laura. 2002. *Trekking through History: The Huaorani of Amazonian Ecuador*. New York: Columbia University Press.

Rivière, Peter. 1994. "WYSINWYG in Amazonia." *Journal of the Anthropological Society of Oxford* 25 (3), Michaelmas: 255–62.

———. 2001. "A predação, a reciprocidade e o caso das Guianas." *Mana* 7 (1): 31–54.

Roger, Alain. 1997. *Court traité du paysage*. Paris: Gallimard.

Rojas Zolezzi, Enrique. 1994. *Los Ashaninka, un pueblo tras el bosque: Contribucíon a la etnología de los Campa de la Selva Central Peruana*. Lima: Pontificia Universidad Católica del Perú.

Roosevelt, Anna C. 1991. *Moundbuilders of the Amazon: Geophysical Archaeology on Marajo Island, Brazil*. San Diego, CA: Academic Press.

Rosch, Eleanor. 1973. "Natural Categories." *Cognitive Psychology* 4 (3): 328–50.

———. 1978. "Principles of Categorization." In *Cognition and Categorization*, edited by E. Rosch and B. B. Lloyd, 28–49. Hillsdale, NJ: Lawrence Erlbaum.

Rosengren, Dan. 1987. *In the Eyes of the Beholder: Leadership and the Social Construction of Power and Dominance among the Matsigenka of the Peruvian Amazon*. Göteborg: Göteborgs Etnografiska Museum.

Rosset, Clément. 1973. *L'anti-nature: Eléments pour une philosophie tragique*. Paris: Presses universitaires de France.

Rostain, Stéphen. 1997. "Nuevas perspectivas sobre la cultura Upano del Amazonas." Paper presented at the 49th International Congress of Americanists, Quito.

Ryesky, Diana. 1976. *Conceptos tradicionales de la medicina en un pueblo mexicano: Un análisis antropológico*. Mexico City: Secretaría de educación pública.

Sahlins, Marshall. 1968. *Tribesmen*. Englewood Cliffs, NJ: Prentice-Hall.

———. 1976. *Culture and Practical Reason*. Chicago: University of Chicago Press.

Saladin d'Anglure, Bernard. 1988. "Penser le 'féminin' chamanique, ou le 'tiers-sexe' des chamanes inuit." *Recherches amérindiennes au Québec* 18 (2–3): 19–50.

———. 1990. "Nanook, Super-Male: The Polar Bear in the Imaginary Space and Social Time of the Inuit of the Canadian Arctic." In *Signifying Animals: Human Meanings in the Natural World*, edited by Roy Willis, 178–95. London: Unwin Hyman.

Salazar, Ernesto. 1997. "Uso del espacio en la cultura Upano." Paper presented at the 49th International Congress of Americanists, Quito.

Santos Granero, Fernando. 1987. "Templos y herrerías: utopía y recreación cultural en la Amazonía Peruana." *Bulletin de l'Institut français d'études andines* 17 (2): 1–22.

———. 1991. *The Power of Love: The Moral Use of Knowledge among the Amuesha of Central Peru*. London: Athlone Press.

———. 2000. "The Sisyphus Syndrome, or the Struggle for Conviviality in Native Amazonia." In *The Anthropology of Love and Anger: The Aesthetics of Conviviality in Native Amazonia*, edited by Joanna Overing and Alan Passes, 268–87. London: Routledge.

———. 2002. "The Arawakan Matrix: Ethos, Language and History in Native South America." In *Comparative Arawakan Histories: Rethinking Language, Family, and Culture Area in Amazonia*, edited by Jonathan D. Hill and Fernando Santos Granero, 25–50. Urbana: University of Illinois Press.

Schama, Simon. 1995. *Landscape and Memory*. London: HarperCollins.

Schank, Roger, and Robert Abelson. 1977. *Scripts, Plans, Goals, and Understanding: An Inquiry into Human Knowledge Structures*. Hillsdale, NJ: Lawrence Erlbaum.

Schieffelin, Edward L. 1987. *The Sorrow of the Lonely and the Burning of the Dancers*. New York: St. Martin's Press.

Schwartz, Marion. 1997. *A History of Dogs in the Early Americas*. New Haven, CT: Yale University Press.

Scott, Colin. 1989. "Knowledge Construction among Cree Hunters: Metaphors and Literal Understanding." *Journal de la Société des Américanistes* 75:193–208.

Seeger, Anthony, Roberto Da Matta, and Eduardo Viveiros de Castro. 1979. "A construção da pessoa nas sociedades indigenas brasileiras." *Boletim do Museu nacional (Rio de Janeiro)* 32:2–19.

Seneca. 1935. *De beneficiis*. Translated by John W. Basore. *Moral Essays*, vol. 3. Loeb Classical Library. Cambridge, MA: Harvard University Press.

Service, Elman. 1966. *The Hunters*. Englewood Cliffs, NJ: Prentice-Hall.

Shore, Bradd. 1996. *Culture in Mind: Cognition, Culture and the Problem of Meaning*. New York: Oxford University Press.

Sigaut, François. 1980. "Un tableau des produits animaux et deux hypothèses qui en découlent." *Production pastorale et société* 7:20–36.

Singer, Peter. 1979. *Practical Ethics.* Cambridge: Cambridge University Press.

———. 1989. *Animal Liberation.* New York: Random House.

Sophocles. 1994. *Oedipus at Colonus.* Translated by Hugh Lloyd-Jones. *Sophocles,* vol. 2. Loeb Classical Library. Cambridge, MA: Harvard University Press.

Sowls, Lyle K. 1974. "Social Behaviour of the Collared Peccary *Dycotiles tajacu* (L.)." In *The Behaviour of Ungulates and Its Relation to Management,* edited by Valerius Geist and Fritz Walther, 144–65. Morges: Union internationale pour la conservation de la nature et des ressources naturelles.

Speck, Frank G. 1917. "Game Totems among the Northeastern Algonquians." *American Anthropologist* 19 (1): 9–18.

———. 1935. *Naskapi: The Savage Hunters of the Labrador Peninsula.* Norman: University of Oklahoma Press.

Spencer, William B., and Franck J. Gillen. 1899. *The Native Tribes of Central Australia.* London: Macmillan.

———. 1927. *The Arunta: A Study of a Stone-Age People.* London: Macmillan.

Sperber, Dan. 1975. *Rethinking Symbolism.* Translated by Alice L. Morton. Cambridge: Cambridge University Press. Originally published as *Le symbolisme en général* (Paris: Hermann, 1974).

———. 1985. *On Anthropological Knowledge.* Cambridge: Cambridge University Press. Revised English edition of *Le savoir des anthropologues* (Paris: Hermann, 1982).

Spinoza, B. 1910. *Ethics.* Translated by A. Boyle. London: Dent. Translation of *Ethica ordine geometrico demonstrata* (The Hague: M. Nijhoff, 1895).

Squire, Larry R. 1987. *Memory and Brain.* New York: Oxford University Press.

Sternberg, Leo. 1905. "Die Religion der Giljaken." *Archiv für Religionswissenschaft (Leipzig)* 8:244–74.

Sterpin, Adriana. 1993. "La chasse aux scalps chez les Nivacle du Gran Chaco." *Journal de la Société des Américanistes* 79:33–66.

Stocking, George W., Jr. 1968. *Race, Culture and Evolution: Essays in the History of Anthropology.* Chicago: University of Chicago Press.

———, ed. 1996. *Volksgeist as Method and Ethic: Essays on Boasian Ethnography and the German Anthropological Tradition.* Madison: University of Wisconsin Press.

Strathern, Andrew. 1971. *The Rope of Moka: Big Men and Ceremonial Exchange in Mount Hagen, New Guinea.* Cambridge: Cambridge University Press.

Strathern, Marilyn. 1980. "No Nature, No Culture: The Hagen Case." In *Nature, Culture and Gender,* edited by Carol MacCormack and Marilyn Strathern, 174–222. Cambridge: Cambridge University Press.

——— 1988. *The Gender of the Gift: Problems with Women and Problems with Society in Melanesia.* Berkeley and Los Angeles: University of California Press.

Strauss, Claudia, and Naomi Quinn. 1997. *A Cognitive Theory of Cultural Meaning.* Cambridge: Cambridge University Press.

Surrallés, Alexandre. 2003. *Au cœur du sens: Perception, affectivité, action chez les Candoshi.* Paris: Éditions du Centre national de la recherche scientifique; Fondation de la Maison des sciences de l'homme.

Swanton, John R. 1928. "Social and Religious Beliefs and Usages of the Chickasaw Indians." In

44th Annual Report (1926–1927), *Bureau of American Ethnology*, 190–213. Washington, DC: Government Printing Office.

Tanner, Adrian. 1979. *Bringing Home Animals: Religious Ideology and Mode of Production of the Mistassini Cree Hunters*. London: C. Hurst.

Tarde, Gabriel. 1999. *Monodologie et sociologie*. 1893. Paris: Les Empêcheurs de penser en rond.

Taylor, Anne Christine. 1983. "The Marriage Alliance and Its Structural Variations in Jivaroan Societies." *Social Science Information* 22 (3): 331–53.

———. 1985. "L'art de la réduction." *Journal de la Société des Américanistes* 71:159–73.

———. 1993. "Les bons ennemis et les mauvais parents: Le traitement de l'alliance dans les rituels de chasse aux têtes des Shuar (Jivaro) de l'Equateur." In *Les complexités de l'alliance*, vol. 4, *Economie, politiques et fondements symboliques*, edited by Elisabeth Copet-Rougier and Françoise Héritier-Augé, 73–105. Paris: Éditions des Archives contemporaines.

———. 1996. "The Soul's Body and Its States: An Amazonian Perspective on the Nature of Being Human." *Journal of the Royal Anthropological Institute* 2 (2):201–15.

———. 1998. "Corps immortels, devoir d'oubli: Formes humaines et trajectoires de vie chez les Achuar." In *La Production du corps: Approches anthropologiques et historiques*, edited by Maurice Godelier and Michel Panoff, 317–38. Amsterdam: Éditions des Archives contemporaines.

Testart, Alain. 1982. *Les chasseurs-cueilleurs ou l'origine des inégalités*. Paris: Sociétié d'ethnologie.

———. 1987. "Deux modèles du rapport entre l'homme et l'animal dans les systèmes de représentation." *Études rurales* 107–8:171–93.

———. 1997. "Les trois modes de transfert." *Gradhiva* 21:39–58.

Thom, René. 1990. *Apologie du logos*. Paris: Hachette.

Tomasello, Michael, and J. Call 1997. *Primate Cognition*. New York: Oxford University Press.

Tort, Patrick. 1992. "L'effet réversif de l'évolution: Fondements de l'anthropologie darwinienne." In *Darwinisme et société*, edited by Patrick Tort, 13–46. Paris: Presses universitaires de France.

Turnbull, Colin. 1965. *Wayward Servants: The Two Worlds of the African Pygmies*. Garden City, NY: Natural History Press.

Turner, Terence. 1995. "Social Body and Embodied Subject: Bodiliness, Subjectivity, and Sociality among the Kayapo." *Cultural Anthropology* 10 (2): 143–70.

Tylor, Edward B. 1871. *Primitive Culture: Researches into the Development of Mythology, Philosophy, Religion, Language, Art and Custom*. 2 vols. London: Murray.

Van Beek, Albert G. 1987. "The Way of All Flesh: Hunting and Ideology of the Bedamuni of the Great Papuan Plateau." PhD diss., University of Leiden.

Van Beek, Walter E. A., and Pieteke M. Banga. 1992. "The Dogon and Their Trees." In *Bush Base: Forest Farm, Culture, Environment and Development*, edited by Elisabeth Croll and David Parkin, 57–75. London: Routledge.

Van der Hammen, Maria Clara. 1992. *El manejo del mundo: Naturaleza y sociedad entre les Yukuna de la Amazonia colombiana*. Bogotá: TROPENBOS.

Van Stone, James W. 2000. "Reindeer as Draft Animals in Alaska." *Études/Inuit/Studies* 24 (2): 115–38.

van Velthem, Lúcia. 2000. "Fazer, fazeres e o mais belo 'feito.'" In *Os Indíos, Nós*, 174–80. Lisbon: Museu nacional de etnologia.

———. 2001. "The Woven Universe: Carib Basketry." In *Unknown Amazon: Culture in Nature in Ancient Brazil*, edited by Colin McEwan, Cristina Barreto, and Eduardo Neves, 198–213. London: British Museum Press.

Varela, Francisco, Eleanor Rosch, and Evan Thompson. 1991. *The Embodied Mind*. Cambridge, MA: MIT Press.

Varese, Stefano. 2002. *Salt of the Mountain*. Translated by Susan Giersbach Rascon. Norman: University of Oklahoma Press. Originally published as *La sal de los cerros: Una approximación al mundo Campa* (Lima: Retablo de papel, 1973).

Vernant, Jean-Pierre. 1986. "Présentation du 'Corps des dieux.'" *Le temps de la réflexion* 7:10–11.

Vidal, Denis. 1991. "Les trois Grâces ou l'allégorie du Don: Contribution à l'histoire d'une idée en anthropologie." *Gradhiva* 9:30–48.

Vidal-Naquet, Pierre. 1975. "Bêtes, hommes et dieux chez les Grecs." In *Hommes et bêtes: Entretiens sur le racisme*, edited by Léon Poliakov, 129–42. Paris: Mouton.

———. 1988. "Hunting and Sacrifice in Aeschylus' *Oresteia*." In *Myth and Tragedy in Ancient Greece*, by Jean-Pierre Vernant and Pierre Vidal-Naquet, translated by Janet Lloyd, 1:141–59. New York: Zone Books. Originally published as "Chasse et sacrifice dans l'*Orestie* d'Eschyle," in *Mythe et tragédie en Grèce ancienne*, by Jean-Pierre Vernant and Pierre Vidal-Naquet, 133–58 (Paris: François Maspero, 1972).

Vigne, Jean-Denis. 1993. "Domestication ou appropriation pour la chasse: Histoire d'un choix socio-culturel depuis le Néolithique; L'exemple des cerfs." In *Exploitation des animaux sauvages à travers le temps*, 201–20. Juan-les-Pins: Éditions de la Association pour la promotion et la diffusion des connaissances archéologiques—Centre national de la recherche scientifique.

Vilaça, Aparecida. 1992. *Comendo como gente: Formas do canibalismo wari'*. Rio de Janeiro: Editora UFRJ.

Viveiros de Castro, Eduardo. 1986. *Araweté: Os deuses canibais*. Rio de Janeiro: Jorge Zahar/ ANPOCS.

———. 1992. *From the Enemy's Point of View: Humanity and Divinity in an Amazonian Society*. Chicago: University of Chicago Press.

———. 1993. "Alguns aspectos da afinidade no Dravidianato Amazônico." In *Amazônia: Etnologia e historia indigena*, edited by Manuela Carneiro da Cunha and Eduardo Viveiros de Castro, 149–210. São Paolo: NHII–Universidade de São Paolo.

———. 1996. "Os pronomes cosmológicos e o perspectivismo ameríndio." *Mana* 2 (2): 115–44.

———. 1998. "Cosmological Deixis and Amerindian Perspectivism." *Journal of the Royal Anthropological Institute*, n.s., 4 (3): 469–88.

———. 2002. *A inconstância da alma selvagem, e outros ensaios de antropología*. São Paolo: Cosac and Naify.

Wachtel, Nathan. 1990. *Le retour des ancêtres: Les Indiens Urus de Bolivie, XXe–XVIe siècle; Essai d'histoire régressive*. Paris: Gallimard.

Wagner, Roy. 1977. "Scientific and Indigenous Papuan Conceptualizations of the Innate: A Semiotic Critique of the Ecological Perspective." In *Subsistence and Survival: Rural Ecology in the Pacific*, edited by Timothy Bayliss-Smith and Richard G. Feachem, 385–410. London: Academic Press.

———. 1981. *The Invention of Culture*. Chicago: University of Chicago Press. Originally published 1975.

Weber, Max. 2003. *The Protestant Ethic and the Spirit of Capitalism*. Translated by Talcott Parsons. Mineola, NY: Dover, 2003. Originally published as *Gesammelte Aufsätze zur Religionssoziologie*, vol. 1 (1920; Tübingen: Mohr, 1988).

Weiss, Gerald. 1975. *Campa Cosmology: The World of a Forest Tribe in South America*. New York: American Museum of Natural History.

Whitehead, Alfred North. 1955. *The Concept of Nature.* Cambridge: Cambridge University Press. Originally published 1920.

Whiten, Andrew, Jane Goodall, William C. McGrew, et al. 1999. "Cultures in Chimpanzees." *Nature* 399:682–85.

Whitten, Norman E. 1976. *Sacha Runa: Ethnicity and Adaptation of Ecuadorian Jungle Quichua.* Urbana: University of Illinois Press.

Windelband, Wilhelm. 1980. "History and Natural Science, Windelband's Rectorial Address at Strasbourg (1894)." Translated by Guy Oakes. *History and Theory* 19 (2): 169–85. Originally published as "Geschichte und Naturwissenschaft," Rectorial Address, Strasbourg, 1894, in *Präludien: Aufsätze und Reden zur Einleitung in die Philosophie,* 355–79 (Tübingen: Mohr, 1907).

Worsley, Peter. 1967. "Groote Eylandt Totemism and *Le totémisme aujourd'hui.*" In *The Structural Study of Myth and Totemism,* edited by Edmund R. Leach, 141–60. London: Tavistock Publications.

Yengoyan, Aram A. 1968. "Demographic and Ecological Influences on Aboriginal Australian Marriage Sections." In *Man the Hunter,* edited by Richard B. Lee and Irven de Vore, 185–99. Chicago: Aldine.

Zelenin, Dimitri. 1952. *Le culte des idoles en Sibérie.* Translated into French by G. Wetter. Paris: Payot.

Zimmermann, Francis. 1987. *The Jungle and the Savour of Meats: An Ecological Theme in Hindu Medicine.* Translated by Janet Lloyd. Berkeley and Los Angeles: University of California Press. Originally published as *La jungle et le fumet des viandes: Un thème écologique dans la médicine hindoue* (Paris: Gallimard–Éditions du Seuil, 1982).

———. 1989. *Le discours des remèdes au pays des épices: Enquête sur la médicine hindoue.* Paris: Payot.

Zuidema, Tom. 1964. *The Ceque System of Cuzco: The Social Organization of the Capital of the Inca.* Leiden: E. J. Brill.

———. 1986. *La civilisation inca au Cuzco.* Paris: Presses universitaires de France.

Index

Made in United States
Orlando, FL
12 December 2023

40698110R10290